D0370334

★★Parc Nacional
d'Aigüestortes

Vielha

TOULOUSE   MONTPELLIER

PAU   F R A N C E

PERPIGNAN

★★★ PIRINEOS CATALANES

ANDORRA★★
Puigcerdà

★ Figueres

El Port de Llança
SANT PERE DE RODES ★★★

★★ Besalú

Cadaqués ★★

★★ Girona /
Gerona

Empúries ★★

COSTA BRAVA

Lleida /
Lérida ★

★★★ POBLET ★
★★Montblanc

BARCELONA ★★★

Sitges★★

★★★ Port Aventura Tarragona ★★

Costa Daurada★★

MEDITERRANEAN
SPAIN

Peñíscola

M A R   M E D I T E R R A N E O

MENORCA

MALLORCA

MEDITERRANEAN
COAST

VALENCIA★★★

P. Natural
de la Albufera

Cullera

IBIZA   I S L A S   B A L E A R E S

Gandia

Alcoi /
Alcoy

Xàbia / Jávea ★

Guadalest ★

Calp

Altea

Xxona

Benidorm

ALACANT /
ALICANTE ★★

Costa Blanca ★

Gardens and Galería del Grutesco, Real Alcázar, Sevilla
© Quim Roser / age fotostock

THEGREENGUIDE

Spain

 **MICHELIN**

How to...

Plan Your Trip

Understand Spain

Discover Spain

Labels within image: Planning Your Trip, Introducing Spain, Discovering Spain

Green Guides - Discover the Destination

Main sections

PLANNING YOUR TRIP
The blue-tabbed section gives you **ideas for your trip** and **practical information**.

INTRODUCTION
The orange-tabbed section explores **Nature, History, Art and Culture** and the **Region Today**.

DISCOVERING
The green-tabbed section features Principal Sights by region, **Sights, Walking Tours, Excursions,** and **Driving Tours**.

Region intros

At the start of each region in the Discovering section is a brief introduction. Accompanied by the region maps, these provide an overview of the main tourism areas and their background.

Region maps

Star ratings

Michelin has given star ratings for more than 100 years. If you're pressed for time, we recommend you visit the three or two star sights first:

★★★ **Highly recommended**

★★ **Recommended**

★ **Interesting**

Tours

We've selected driving and walking tours that show you the best of each town or region. Step by step directions are accompanied by detailed maps with marked routes. If you are short on time, you can follow the star ratings to decide where to stop. Selected addresses give you options for accommodation and dining en route.

Addresses

We've selected the best hotels, restaurants, cafés, shops, nightlife and entertainment to fit all budgets. See the Legend on the cover flap for an explanation of the price categories. See the back of the guide for an index of where to find hotels and restaurants.

Other reading

- Green Guide Portugal
- Must Sees Andalucia
- Must Sees Barcelona
- Road Atlas
  Spain & Portugal

Welcome
to Spain

If this is your first trip to Spain, welcome to a land that boasts many different cultures and languages, virtually every kind of landscape, a wealth of heritage and history, world-renowned cuisine and quality wines. Whether you opt for beach or mountains, city or countryside, the choices are enormous.

If you are a returning visitor, you'll probably note with delight how rapidly Spain's towns and cities are reinventing themselves for modern times and how much easier travel around the country is today, whether by train, road or plane. Resorts offer new cultural attractions and levels of comfort, too. Meanwhile, reassuringly, large swathes of wild Spain – mountains, marshland and rolling olive groves – remain unchanged.

Of course in recent years Spain has faced great economic hardships, and visitors to the Costa del Sol (for example) may notice the massive oversupply of empty holiday housing and speculative building.

This cloud does have a silver lining however with the real cost of many Spanish holidays low compared to other European destinations. The good news is that Spain remains the classic travel destination that it always has been.

Casa Batlló, Barcelona © Pietro Canali/Sime/Photononstop

Planning Your Trip

Introducing Spain

Discovering Spain

9

Teatro Romano, Mérida, Extremadura,
Central Spain
© pedrosala/iStockphoto.com

Regions of Spain

Central Spain (pp114-227)

The central tableland's rare grandeur and sense of history is best felt in its
Medieval court and cathedral cities, such as **Segovia**, **Ávila**, **Salamanca**, **Burgos**,
Valladolid and **Toledo**. Journeys between them take you across light-soaked
plains where castles, often dramatically rearing up above them, are a reminder
of Castille's embattled past. Yet the landscapes here can also be unexpected. **La
Mancha**'s flatlands – home to Don Quixote – contrast with **Soria**'s soft green river
valleys, **Extremadura**'s boulder-strewn hills and the high, rocky sierras north and
west of Madrid. City sights allow you to travel back in time. **Mérida**, for example,
preserves classical Roman monuments. But elsewhere, above all in **Madrid**, the
country's political and business capital, there is a taste for vibrant modernity. Its
hectic nightlife and shopping culture are as much part of any visit to the city as
the time spent lingering in its splendid art galleries and museums.

Atlantic Spain (pp228-319)

Atlantic Spain's shoreline stretches from France west to the deeply indented Galician coastline, then south to the Portuguese border. Rough seas break onto rocks, beaches and the coastal promenades of fishing villages, resorts and cities such as **Donostia-San Sebastián**, **Bilbao**, **Santander**, **A Coruña** and **Vigo**. Behind the coast lie verdant mountains and valleys in the **País Vasco**, **Cantabria**, **Asturias** and **Galicia** where traditional farming life survives along with local languages and dialects. Further inland in **Navarra** and **La Rioja** are historic vineyards, many now boasting state-of-the-art wineries such as Bodegas Ysios and museums in Briones and Elciego. The Medieval **Camino de Santiago** pilgrimage route, still walked today, provides a popular way for exploring all these northern regions. Monasteries, hermitages and hostels lie on its path. So too, do cities such as **Santiago de Compostela**, its end point, and **Pamplona**, world-famous for its bull-running. Bilbao, with its spectacular Guggenheim Museum, and the gourmet mecca of Donostia-San Sebastián catch the eye of more visitors than ever before.

Praia das Catedrais, Rías Altas, Galicia, Atlantic Spain
© Christian Guy/hemis.fr

Cala Macarella, Menorca, Mediterranean Spain
© Alvaro Leiva/age fotostock

Mediterranean Spain (pp320-469)

Spain's eastern Mediterranean coast and the Balearics are famed for their beaches. **Benidorm**'s are the most crowded, but there is variety to satisfy all tastes: the **Costa Brava** offers coves; **Murcia** has fine scuba-diving waters; and **Menorca** boasts spectacular long sands. Inland, **Aragón**'s empty mountains and flatlands, bisected by the giant River Ebro, and the hill country of **Catalunya** and **Valencia** are vast areas of unspoiled beauty. Their historic cities are made graceful by regional architectural styles. Highlights include **Zaragoza**'s Mudéjar architecture, **Tarragona**'s Roman monuments, **Gerona**'s Gothic cathedral, Murcia's Baroque splendour, **Palma de Mallorca**'s old town and Valencia's medieval quarter and striking **Ciudad de las Artes y las Ciencias**, Europe's largest cultural centre. Yet it is the port city of **Barcelona** that reigns supreme as a destination, offering world-class museums, a cosmopolitan arts scene, football, nightlife and restaurants. Rural escapes are easily made from these cities into areas of outstanding beauty protected as natural parkland.

Parque Nacional de Timanfaya, Lanzarote, The Canary Islands
© M. Bilbao/age fotostock

Andalucía and the Canary Islands (pp470-579)

Andalucía's coastline is the most heavily developed in the Iberian peninsula.
Often the resorts and golf-courses of the **Costa del Sol** stretch miles inland.
But away from the coast sit three great cities – **Granada**, **Sevilla** and **Córdoba** –
with architectural wonders dating from the centuries of al-Andalus.
The *pueblos blancos* (white villages) set among rolling olive groves, and ports
of **Almería**, **Cádiz** and **Huelva** keep their character, too. Meanwhile **Málaga**,
capital of the Costa del Sol, is rediscovering its rich cultural history. Far out in
the mid-Atlantic, the volcanic-born **Canary Islands** are often picked as winter
destinations for their balmy year-round climate.
Each island is a world apart. **El Hierro** and **La Gomera** offer rural simplicity and
La Palma preserves old-fashioned colonial elegance while **Gran Canaria**,
Tenerife and **Lanzarote** have grown around their tourism and unique landscapes
into buzzing cosmopolitan communities.

Planning
Your Trip

Tossa de Mar, Costa Brava
© José Fuste Raga/age fotostock

Planning
Your Trip

Inspiration

WHAT'S HOT

– Not just the birthplace of Pablo Picasso, **Málaga** (p488) is now home to some of Spain's finest art museums thanks to the opening of branches of the Centre Pompidou and Collection of the Russian Museum.

– The Decorative Arts have had a major makeover in **Barcelona** (p324) courtesy of the new Disseny Hub, which houses the Museu de les Arts Decoratives, Museu de Ceràmica and Museu Tèxtil i d'Indumentària in a new building at Plaça de les Glòries. A beautifully restored Gaudí house, Casa Vicens (p335), opened to the public for the first time in 2017. Catalunya is celebrating its Year of Culture in 2018 - watch out for events around the region.

– Spain may not spring to mind as a top **ski destination** but there are now over 30 excellent resorts in the country, with Granada's **Sierra Nevada** (p483) hosting to the Snowboard Cross World Cup.

– Forget running with the bulls, **Pamplona** (p233) has a new contemporary art and photography space in the form of the Museo Universidad de Navarra.

Centre Pompidou Málaga, designed by Javier Pérez de la Fuente y Juan Antonio Marín Malavé
© Málaga City Council/Turespaña

Spain's Cities

I t's a tough choice: the museums of Madrid, or the bars and beaches of Barcelona? Sizzling Seville, or vibrant Valencia? It's easily resolved – spend a long weekend in each!

MADRID See p119

Madrid's city centre may lack the old-world charm of many of Spain's major cities but its sheer energy, best seen during the paseo when Madrileños cram the promenades and tapas bars around the back streets of Plaza Mayor and Plaza Santa Ana, amazes most visitors. Of course art is the city's biggest cultural treasure and the Golden Triangle – the Prado, Thyssen-Bornemisza, and Centro Reina Sofia – is a leading art destination.

BARCELONA See p325

Historic cobbled streets oozing medieval atmosphere; a superb sandy beach just yards away from the famous Las Ramblas; vibrant nightlife; world-class museums and galleries; shops, bars and markets where local character rises above international fashion – Barcelona really does have it all. The jewel in the crown however (unless you're a football fan) is the legacy of Gaudí; don't leave the city without seeing his Casa Pedrera or, of course, la Sagrada Familia.

Plaza del Angél by Plaza Santa Ana, Madrid

© Tibor Bognar/age fotostock

Centre Pompidou Málaga

Silk Hall, La Lonja, Valencia

© Emma Durnford/age fotostock

SEVILLA
♿See p520
Beyond the Alcázar, a stunning Moorish fortress, and the cathedral with its iconic Giralda bell tower, Sevilla's Barrio de Santa Cruz is filled with romantic corners and irresistible bars and taverns. Triana, the old gypsy and fishermen's quarter across the Guadalquivir river, has flamenco secrets and restaurants along the river, while the Barrio de la Macarena and its produce market, the Museo de Bellas Artes, and the Convento de Santa Paula complete the list of must-see sites.

VALENCIA
♿See p424
The Ciutat de les Arts i les Ciències with its Caltrava-designed space-age structures have become the symbols of the new Valencia. However, the city's Gothic architecture – exemplified in buildings such as La Lonja – and the lively Modernist Mercado Central, still dazzle. The latter rivals Barcelona's Boqueria in size and aesthetics, while the Palau de la Generalitat, the Palacio del Marquès de Dos Aguas and the Estación del Norte railway station are key visits.

TOURIST OFFICES
www.spain.info

London
6th Floor, 64 North Row
W1K 7DE
☏020 731 72011

New York
60 East 42nd Street - Suite 5300 (53rd Floor)
New York, NY 10165-0039

Chicago
Water Tower Place, Suite 915 East 845 North Michigan Avenue
Chicago, IL 60611
☏312 642 1992

Los Angeles
8383 Wilshire Blvd, Suite 960
Beverly Hills, CA 90211
☏323 658 7195

Miami
2655 Le Jeune Rd (Gables Intl. Plaza), Suite 605. Coral Gables
☏305 476 1966

Toronto
2 Bloor St West, Suite 3402
Toronto, Ontario M4W 3E2
☏416 961 3131

BILBAO
♿See p256
Frank Gehry's Bilbao Guggenheim transformed the city's economy from heavy industry to tourism, art and design, but don't overlook the Museo de Bellas Artes a few streets away. One of Spain's best museums, its permanent collection can rival the temporary exhibits at its headline-grabbing neighbour. The Casco Viejo, the oldest part of town, is filled with interesting architecture and the Museo Vasco, while the 19C Ensanche holds contemporary gems such as the culture and leisure Alhóndiga Bilbao centre.

The Coast

When you visit Spain's multifarious choice of coastlines is almost as important as where you visit. Check the weather, the crowds and the prices first.

MEDITERRANEAN COAST
See p322

Spain has thousands of miles of beautiful coastline, with the Mediterranean continuing to attract millions of Spanish and foreign visitors every year to its delightful waters and magnificent beaches.

Costa Brava – The rugged and indented **Costa Brava**, or Wild Coast, with its charming coves and lively resorts, extends from north of Barcelona as far as the French border.

Levante – The **Levante** coast, characterised by long sandy beaches and built-up resorts such as Benidorm, Cullera and Gandía, is as popular as ever. This area is also favoured by Spanish families, with lots of second homes here.

Costa del Sol – The **Costa del Sol**, in particular the stretch between Málaga and Estepona, is a succession of luxury developments and golf courses. Marbella is the leading resort here, reinforced by its international jet-set reputation. The remainder of the Andalucían coast is generally quieter, attracting Spanish visitors.

Balearic Islands – The **Balearic Islands** are one of the country's most popular tourist destinations. Of the three main islands, Mallorca and Ibiza attract large numbers of Spanish and foreign visitors, who come here to enjoy their magnificent landscapes and beaches and lively nightlife. Menorca's resorts tends to be quieter, and offer a more relaxed style of holiday.

ATLANTIC COAST
See p230

Spain's North Atlantic coast stretches from the Basque Country in the east to Galicia in the west. In general, its resorts, the main ones being San Sebastián and Santander, are

© RossHeler/iStockphoto.com

Garachico, Tenerife

frequented by domestic visitors. They come for the temperate climate, beaches, excellent fish and seafood, and the impressive landscapes. With the exception of a few places, the coast of northern Spain has escaped the frenetic development of the Mediterranean, and as such has managed to preserve its natural beauty. Although less popular with foreign visitors, the **Costa de la Luz** (Coast of Light), stretching between the southernmost tip of Spain and the Portuguese border, has some of the country's finest beaches, dotted with charming family resorts and historic cities such as Cádiz, the oldest in Spain.

CANARY ISLANDS
See p552

The archipelago comes into its own in winter, when thousands of visitors flock here to escape northern European winter. The main tourist centres on the archipelago can be found in the south of the two major islands, Gran Canaria and Tenerife resectively. Inland, and on the smaller islands, natural beauty still survives.

National Parks

S pain acts as a bridge between Europe and Africa, and as such has a wealth of different landscapes including salt marshes, conifer forests, high mountains, desert areas and Mediterranean woodland. The country's national parks protect those areas of major ecological interest to ensure their continuing survival. The main aim of these parks is to preserve their unique flora and fauna and to control public access. In total, Spain has fifteen national parks – ten on the mainland and five spread across the islands. For many animal and plant species, Spain's mountain parks provide the most southerly habitat in Europe.

MOUNTAIN PARKS

Parque Nacional de los Picos de Europa ⚭p277

The country's first national park was the Parque de Montaña de Covadonga, established in 1918. In 1995, this protected area was significantly extended (from 16 925ha/41 822 acres to 64 600ha/159 626 acres) and became known as the **Parque Nacional de los Picos de Europa**. This magnificent area is characterised by breathtaking landscapes with glacial lakes and extensive forests of beech (between 800m/2 624ft and 1 500m/4 920ft) as well as chestnut and oak, where water, in the shape of rivers, streams, lagoons and lakes, is an ecological factor of great importance.

In terms of fauna, the main species found here are chamois, mountain cats, polecats, foxes, otters, squirrels, imperial eagles and partridges, with the occasional sighting of the brown bear. The main types of fish found in the park's rivers are trout and salmon.

Parque Nacional de Ordesa y Monte Perdido ⚭p417

The **Parque Nacional de Ordesa y Monte Perdido**, at the heart of the Pyrenees in the province of Huesca, covers an area of 15 608ha/38 567 acres, and was also established in 1918. The park is spread across four valleys, in which the landscape is dominated by rushing mountain rivers and streams, waterfalls, impressive precipices and forests of mountain pine, beech and fir, inhabited by mountain goats, wild boar and more.

Parc Nacional d'Aigüestortes i Estany de Sant Maurici ⚭p386

The present-day appearance of the **Parc Nacional d'Aigüestortes i Estany de Sant Maurici**, covering 9 851ha/24 342 acres in the province of Lleida, in the Catalan Pyrenees, was created by the glaciers that invaded this area during the Quaternary era. The park's varied landscape includes lakes, forests of mountain pine and fir, and Alpine meadows, populated by mountain goats, wild boar, ermine, pine martens, dormice, imperial eagles, capercaillie and partridge.

Sierra Nevada ⚭p483

The **Sierra Nevada** (90 000ha/222 390 acres) is a mountain park with several summits over 3 000m/9 840ft,

Parque Nacional de Garajonay, La Gomera

©Turespaña

including Mulhacén, the highest peak on mainland Spain at 3 478m/11 413ft. This range is also renowned for the variety of its flora and fauna, the result of its unique climatic conditions and topographical features.

Parque Nacional de Sierra de Guadarrama ♿p145
The **Parque Nacional de Sierra de Guadarrama** (33 960 ha/83 917 acres), located to the north of Madrid in Castilla y Léon, was established in 2013 and is the country's newest national park. Its landscape is dominated by rocky summits and pine forests, which are home to 133 bird species and 58 mammal species.

Parque Nacional Monfragüe ♿p218
The **Parque Nacional Monfragüe** (18 118ha/44 770 acres) runs westward along the River Tagus in Extremadura. The landscape varies from scrubland to mountainous ridges populated by deer, eagles and foxes.

FLATLANDS & WETLANDS
Parque Nacional de Cabañero ♿p203
The **Parque Nacional de Cabañeros** is spread across a flatland area between two rocky formations in the Montes de Toledo. This protected national park covering some 40 000ha/98 840 acres and is characterised by a Mediterranean-style wooded landscape abundant with deer, wild boar and birds of prey.

Tablas de Daimiel and the Parque Nacional de Doñana ♿p206, 535
The Tablas de Daimiel and the Parque Nacional de Doñana are of vital ecological importance due to the protection they offer flora and fauna in danger of extinction, and their role as a breeding, migration and wintering area for numerous species of birds. The **Tablas de Daimiel**, in the province of Ciudad Real is the smallest of Spain's national parks, with an area of just 1 928ha/4 764 acres. The flooding of

© José Ramiro/age fotostock

Parque Nacional de Sierra de Guadarrama

the Cigüela and Guadiana rivers has resulted in the formation of areas of shallow bodies of water ideal for the creation of typical marshland vegetation that has been colonised by various species of birds, some of which migrate here for the winter or to nest (grey herons, lesser egrets, red-crested pochard, for example).

The extraordinary wealth of species in the **Parque Nacional de Doñana** (50 720ha/125 329 acres) is the result of its three distinct habitats: coastal dunes, salt marshes, and former hunting grounds or *cotos*. Its strategic location on the southern tip of Europe, almost within sight of the coast of Africa, has resulted in its development as an important wetland for migratory birds. Various fauna in danger of extinction can still be found here, such as the Iberian lynx and the imperial eagle.

Parks On The Spanish Islands
♿p297, 450, 552, 570, 574, 578
The **Parque Nacional Marítimo-Terrestre de Las Islas Atlánticas de Galicia** comprises the four archipelagos of Cíes, Ons, Sálvora and Cortegada, which lie off the coast of Pontevedra. The **Cabrera archipelago**, in the Balearics, stretches across an area of some 10 000ha/ 24 700 acres. In the Canary Islands are the **Parque Nacional del Teide**, on Tenerife; the **Caldera de Taburiente**, on the island of La Palma; **Timanfaya**, on Lanzarote; and **Garajonay**, on the island of La Gomera.

The Great Outdoors

Spain has a huge choice of climates and landscapes, and a strong tradition in many sports and outdoor pursuits. Whatever you seek, you'll find experts to help.

CYCLING

Spain offers a plethora of **famous cycling routes** in the mountains and on flatter terrain. From the Pyrenees to the Picos de Europa to the Alpujarras of Granada there is no shortage of scenic highland riding for the fit and ambitious. The **three-nation loop** through Spain, Andorra and France – beginning and ending in La Seu d'Urgell – is a physical challenge with stunning Pyrenean scenery.

For flatland cycling, the Delta del Ebro south of Tarragona (see p390) and the Cerdanya Valley (see p376) in the Pyrenees north of Barcelona have a remarkably level network of roads for easy riding. Cycling the Basque coast along the old corniche road that follows the edge of the Bay of Biscay (see p253) is a perfect way to see fishing villages and rural farmhouses that motorists miss. The **Via de la Plata** route from Sevilla to Santiago de Compostela (see p290) is a favourite cycling journey, while the Baix Empordà region (see p364) in northern Catalunya has 19 bike routes through some of the Costa Brava's most picturesque and often overlooked inland villages. Spain also has 2 200km/1 367mi of abandoned railway lines that have been converted to **Vías Verdes** (green paths). Check www.viasverdes.com for itineraries.

FISHING

Spain's 76 000km/47 235mi of river courses provide a wealth of options for freshwater fishing enthusiasts, although seasons can vary from one region to another. Fishing permits are issued by the Environment Agency (**Ministerio de Agricultura, Alimentación y Medio Ambiente;** www.magrama.gob.es) in the relevant autonomous community. For further information on sea and freshwater fishing, contact the **Federación Española de Pesca y Casting (Calle Navas de Tolosa 3, 1°, 28013 Madrid; 915 32 83 53; www.fepyc.es).**

GOLF

There are over 400 golf courses across the country, a number that is steadily growing, particularly in coastal areas. For further information, contact the **Real Federación Española de Golf (Calle Arroyo del Monte 5, 28035 Madrid; 915 55 26 82; www. rfegolf.es).** A map of golf courses is also available from tourist offices. Golf courses and their telephone numbers are also listed in the **Michelin Guide Portugal Madeira.**

HIKING AND MOUNTAINEERING

Hiking is becoming increasingly popular across Spain. For information on hiking routes and paths, as well as mountaineering, contact the **Spanish Mountaineering Federation (Federación Española de Deportes de Montaña y Escalada, Carrer de Floridablanca 84, 08015 Barcelona; 934 26 42 67; www.fedme.es). Long-distance hiking trails** (designated GR for **Gran Recorrido**) can take you all over peninsular Spain as well as through the most scenic parts of the Balearic (see p450) and Canary Islands (see p552). The GR11 is the six-to-seven-week trans-Pyrenean trail that begins at Cabo Higuer west of Hondarribia (see p254) and ends at Cap de Creus (see p362), the Iberian Peninsula's easternmost point just north of Cadaqués. The GR11 intersects with the HRP (Haute Randonnée Pyrénéenne) which follows the Pyrenean crest (see p374, 419)

Hiking in the Vall de Núria, Pirineos Catalanes

on either side of the France-Spain border. Other famous hikes include the **Alberes Mountains** (see p374) walk from Puig Neulós above the Le Perthus French border crossing to Banyuls-sur-Mer (one day) or Cap de Creus (two days). The climb from Núria (see p376) to the Coll de Núria followed by the traverse east over the Sierra de Catllar to the refuge at Ulldeter is an unforgettable challenge with panoramic views north and south from the crest of the Pyrenees. The **Parc Nacional d'Aigüestortes i Estany de Sant Maurici** (see p386) offers excellent trekking between late May and September. **Parque Nacional de Ordesa y Monte Perdido** (see p417) has a good day trip up to the Cola de Caballo waterfall and back or with an overnight up at the Refugio de Góriz overlooking Spain's Grand Canyon.

HORSE RIDING

A wide choice of options is available to horse-riding enthusiasts, ranging from short excursions to treks lasting several days. Every autonomous community has a large number of companies and organisations offering equestrian activities. For further information, contact the **Spanish Horse Riding Federation (Federación Hípica Española; calle Monte Esquinza 28, 3º, 28010 Madrid; ☏914 36 42 00; www. rfhe.com)**.

USEFUL WEBSITES

www.spain.info – The official site of the Spanish Tourist Board, providing comprehensive information on all aspects of the country, including transport, accommodation, sport and leisure activities.

www.tourspain.co.uk – The Spanish Tourist Board's site for visitors from the UK.

www.spain.info/en_US – The Spanish Tourist Board's site for visitors from the US.

www.spain.info/en_CA – The Spanish Tourist Board's site for Canadian visitors.

www.fco.gov.uk – The British Government's Foreign and Commonwealth Office website.

www.state.gov – American visitors may check the US State Department website for travel advice.

www.international.gc.ca – Website of Foreign Affairs Canada with relevant travel updates.

www.tourspain.es – The business-to-business site of the Spanish Tourist Board is useful for travel professionals.

Scuba-diving in Tamariu, Costa Brava

© Dirscherl Reinhard/age fotostock

HUNTING

Spain boasts the largest hunting area of any European country, populated by big game including wild boar, red stag, roe deer, moufflon, and smaller prey such as partridge, pheasant, woodcock, rabbits, hare and duck. The hunting season generally runs from September to February, although this varies from species to species.

SAILING

The waters of the Mediterranean (♿see p320) and Atlantic (♿see p228) are one of Spain's major attractions. As a result, hundreds of sailing clubs and pleasure marinas have been established along the coastlines. For further information, apply to the **Royal Sailing Federation (Real Federación de Vela, Calle Luis de Salazar 9, 28002 Madrid; ✆915 19 50 08; www.rfev.es).**

SCUBA-DIVING

The Spanish coast, in particular the waters of the Mediterranean (♿see p320), is becoming increasingly popular with scuba-divers, with the development of diving sites such as the Cabo de Gata, the Islas Medes, on the Costa Brava, and resorts in the Balearic and Canary islands.

For further information, contact the **Spanish Scuba-Diving Federation (Federación Española de Actividades Subacuáticas; Carrer Aragó 517, 08013 Barcelona; www.fedas.es).**

WINTER SPORTS

There are 33 ski resorts in Spain including 18 in the Pyrenees (♿see p374, 419), six in the Cordillera Cantábrica (♿see p109), four in the Sistema Central (♿see p162), three in the Sistema Ibérica (♿see p277), two in the Sistema Penibético (♿near Granada, see p483) and an indoor ski slope in Madrid.

Information on these is available from the **Federación Española de Deportes de Invierno (Avenida de los Madroños 36, 28043 Madrid; ✆913 76 99 30; www.rfedi.es),** or from ATUDEM **(Asociación Turística de Estaciones de Esquí y Montaña, Avda. Diagona 652 Edificio A Bajos, Barcelona; ✆932 05 82 95; www. atudem.es).**

UNESCO World Heritage Sites

Spain has 4 World Heritage Sites. In 1972 UNESCO adopted a Convention for the preservation of cultural and natural sites. The protected cultural heritage may be monuments with unique historical, artistic or scientific features; groups of buildings; or sites which are the combined works of man and nature of exceptional beauty. Spanish customs and activities featured in this guide that are inscribed on the Representative List of Intangible Cultural Heritage include the Mystery Plays of Elche, Catalan human towers (Castells), and flamenco.

CENTRAL SPAIN

Madrid and Around p118
Alcalá de Henares: University and historic quarter.
Aranjuez: Cultural landscape.
El Escorial: Monastery.

Castilla-León: Ávila, Salamanca & Zamora p158
Ávila: Old town and extra-muros churches.
Salamanca: Old town.

Castilla-León: Segovia, Valladolid & Soria p176
Segovia: Old town; aqueduct.
Sevilla: Cathedral; Alcázar; Archivo de Indias.

Castilla-La Mancha p192
Cuenca: Historic fortified town.
Toledo: Historic city.

Extremadura p216
Cáceres: Old town.
Guadalupe: Monasterio Real de Santa María.
Mérida: Archaeological site.

ATLANTIC SPAIN

El País Vasco and La Rioja p250
San Millán de la Cogolla: Monasterio de Yuso; Monasterio de Suso.

Cantabria and Asturias p270
Oviedo: Monuments in the city; kingdom of Asturias.

Galicia p289
Lugo: Roman walls.
Santiago de Compostela: Old town; Camino de Santiago; Cathedral.

Castilla-León: Burgos, León and Palencia p307
Atapuerca (Burgos): Prehistoric remains.
Burgos: Cathedral.

MEDITERANEAN SPAIN

Barcelona and Around p324
Barcelona: Parc Güell; Palau Güell; Casa Milà; Casa Vicens; Casa Batlló; Palau de la Música Catalana; Hospital de Sant Pau; Colònia Güell Crypt.

Northern Catalunya and Principat d'Andorra p353
Vall de Boí (Lleida): Romanesque churches.

Tarragona and Southern Catalunya p390
Poblet: Monastery.
Tarragona: Roman town (Tarraco).

Aragón p403
Teruel: Mudéjar architecture.

La Comunitat Valenciana & La Región de murcia p423
Elx/Elche: El Palmeral palm grove.
Valencia: La Lonja de la Seda.

The Balearic Islands p450
Ibiza: Biodiversity and culture.

ANDALUCÍA AND THE CANARY ISLANDS

Southern Andalucía p474
Granada: Alhambra; Generalife; Albaicín.
Antequera: ancient dolmens.

Northern Andalucía p503
Córdoba: Historic centre; Mosque-Cathedral.
Úbeda & Baeza: Renaissance monumental ensembles.

Western Andalucia p519
Doñana: National Park.

The Canary Islands p552
La Gomera: Garajonay National Park.
Tenerife: San Cristóbal de la Laguna; Parque Nacional del Teide.

Michelin Driving Tours

See the driving tours map on the inside front cover. Purchase Michelin maps 571, 572, 574, 577 and 578 to make the most of these tours.

Hórreo (drying shed), Combarro, Galicia
© Jesus Nicolás Sánchez/age fotostock

1 GALICIA

Round trip of 1 031km/644mi from A Coruña/La Coruña – This region has magnificent towns and cities, verdant landscapes, an indented coastline and villages full of character and charm; Galicia is also renowned for its delicious seafood. After visiting **A Coruña/La Coruña**, with its old quarter and attractive seafront promenade, head south to **Santiago de Compostela**, one of Spain's finest cities, to marvel at the spectacular cathedral. The tour continues along the **Rías Baixas/Rías Bajas** via **Pontevedra** to the mouth of the Miño, forming a natural border with Portugal. Along this stretch of coastline, with the scenic fishing village of **Combarro** and the summer resort of **Baiona**, the sea has created a series of beautiful inlets. Follow the Miño as far as historic **Tui**, take the motorway to **Ourense**. Continue along the spectacular **Gargantas de Sil**, before following the same road into the province of León, and the town of Ponferrada, the gateway to the magical **Las Médulas**. Heading back into Galicia, make your way to **Lugo**, with its Roman walls. Continue north to the coast, driving along the **Rías Altas** before returning to A Coruña/La Coruña.

2 AROUND THE MONTES DE CANTABRIA

Round trip of 764km/477mi from Santander – Depart west from **Santander** to charming medieval **Santillana del Mar**, and visit the replica of the **Cuevas de Altamira**. Continue to the picturesque pueblo of **Comillas**, then the seaside resort of **San Vicente de la Barquera**. From here, head into the mountains, and the **Parque Nacional de los Picos de Europa;** enjoy the exquisite panorama from the **Mirador del Fito**. Drive along the **Costa Verde** to Gijón and its extensive beach, then south to **Oviedo**, its historical centre is full of outstanding architecture. Continue inland to visit historic **León**, then east across the Meseta towards Burgos along the Camino de Santiago. Visit Villalcázar de Sirga, Carrión de los Condes and **Frómista** en route. Explore the magnificent religious heritage of **Burgos** then continue towards Aguilar de Campoo. Continue to Reinosa, at the foot of the Montes

Gargantas del Cares, Picos de Europa
© Turespaña

Cantábricos. From here, make an excursion to the **Pico de Tres Mares**, or simply return to Santander, stopping at **Puente Viesgo** to admire the wall paintings in the Cueva del Castillo.

3 THE BASQUE COUNTRY, RIOJA AND NAVARRA

Round trip of 696km/435mi from Bilbao – This tour combines stunning coastline dotted with picturesque villages, the delightful inland landscapes of northern Spain and the Camino de Santiago pilgrimage route, as well as charming towns and cities renowned for their gastronomy. Start at the Guggenheim Museum before following the **Costa Vasca** eastwards through quaint fishing villages to **Donostia-San Sebastián**, with its setting on one of Spain's finest bays. From here, continue to **Hondarribia/Fuenterrabía**, a pleasant resort and fishing port with an attractive old quarter. The **Valle del Bidasoa** provides the backdrop as you head inland to **Pamplona**; its medieval old town is built around its imposing cathedral and is famous for the annual running of the bulls. The route heads deeper into Navarra, past monasteries and important staging-posts on the **Camino de Santiago (Leyre, La Oliva, Sangüesa/Zangoza** and **Puente la Reina)** and historic towns such as Sos del Rey Católico and Olite/Erriberri, before reaching **Estella**, one of the most important stops along the famous pilgrimage route. After visiting the nearby Monasterio de Irache, the Camino continues to Logroño, capital of La Rioja, and then through the extensive vineyards for which this region is renowned.' The most famous stops on this section of the path are **Nájera** and **Santo Domingo de la Calzada**. Before returning to the País Vasco via its capital city, **Vitoria-Gasteiz**, with its atmospheric old quarter and several museums of interest, visit Haro and the Museo del Vino de La Rioja. Return to Bilbao via the motorway.

Hondarribia/Fuenterrabía, Costa Vasca

4 CATALUNYA

Round trip of 1 020km/637mi from Barcelona – This Catalunya road trip is characterised by high Pyrenean peaks, rugged coasts, charming coves, long sandy beaches, picturesque villages, exquisite Romanesque churches, impressive monasteries, and towns and cities overflowing with history. Once you've spent time in **Barcelona**, begin your tour along the beautiful **Costa Brava**. After visiting the old Roman colony of **Empúries**, picture-postcard **Cadaqués**, the **Monestir de Sant Pere de Rodes** and El Port de Llançà, head inland to **Figueres**, home of the Dalí Theatre and Museum, then **Girona**, a city that still retains the vestiges of its Roman, Jewish, Moorish and Christian past. From here, the tour climbs up into the **Pirineos Catalanes**, a land of spectacular mountain roads, beautiful valleys and the charming villages of **Besalú**, Camprodón, Ripoll and Puigcerdà. From Puigcerdà head west through the **Cerdanya Valley** and **La Seu d'Urgell** with its lovely cathedral before setting off into the Noguera Ribagorçana valley and the **Parc Nacional d'Aigüestortes**. Continue north through the Val d'Aran to reach **Lleida/Lérida**. The journey back to the sea passes **Poblet**, the most famous Cistercian monastery in Spain, and the walled town of **Montblanc**. At the old Roman capital of **Tarragona** have a fun day out at **Port Aventura** theme park before heading back to Barcelona. The final leg of the tour runs past **Sitges**.

Castillo de Coca

5 CASTILLA Y LEÓN

Round trip of 756km/472mi from Salamanca – Historic towns and lofty castles dominate this tour through the lands of old Castile. After spending time exploring **Salamanca**, head north to **Zamora** to admire the cathedral. The road east towards Valladolid passes through **Toro**, and Tordesillas. In **Valladolid**, renowned for fine examples of Isabelline art, visit the National Sculpture Museum. Continue your journey through an extensive landscape of cereal crops, passing through Medina de Rioseco en route to **Palencia**, with its magnificent cathedral. Heading east into the province of Burgos, the itinerary takes in charming small towns and villages such as Lerma and **Covarrubias**. One of the highlights of this tour is the **Monasterio de Santo Domingo de Silos**; its cloisters are a masterpiece

of Romanesque art. From here, the itinerary heads south, skirting along the banks of the Duero, to visit a series of castles – the ruined fortress at **Peñaranda de Duero**, the impressive castle at **Peñafiel**, **Cuéllar** and the more unusual Mudéjar castillo at **Coca**. Continue on to **Segovia**, famous for its aqueduct and fairytale castle, then **Ávila**, a city of convents and churches, encircled by its imposing walls. Before completing your circuit, stop in the small town of Alba de Tormes.

6 ZARAGOZA, SORIA, GUADALAJARA AND TERUEL

Round trip of 869km/543mi from Zaragoza – This tour passes through impressive mountain landscapes, villages crowned by old castles and towns full of character and charm. Begin from **Zaragoza,** with a foray into Navarra to visit **Tudela**, with its interesting Mudéjar architecture and its fine cathedral. Head for Tarazona, famous for its old quarter and cathedral, and the **Monasterio de Veruela**. Continue to quiet provincial **Soria**, with its impressive churches. Head southwest, via Calatañazor – a picturesque village overlooked by a medieval castle – to **Burgo de Osma**, another charming town, renowned for its magnificent cathedral. Head across country to Berlanga de Duero, and on to San Baudelio de Berlanga, a hermitage with an 11C Mozarabic chapel. Once past Atienza, continue to historic, with its fortified cathedral and castle (now a Parador). Take the fast highway east, along the attractive banks of the Jalón, crossing the river briefly to visit the magnificent Cistercian/Renaissance **Monasterio de Santa María de Huerta**. After passing Ateca, head south to the **Monasterio de Piedra** for a stroll through its delightful park. The tour continues via Molina de Aragón, with another castle, before entering the **Sierra de Albarracín** and the charming medieval village of the same name. Next stop is **Teruel**, a town which enjoys a superb location, and

Monasterio de Santa María de Huerta

is adorned with jewels of Mudéjar architecture. Head north to the walled town of **Daroca** before joining the motorway back to Zaragoza.

7 AROUND MADRID

Round trip of 689km/431mi from Madrid – The area around the Spanish capital is home to several towns of major interest, a number of royal palaces and the scenic Sierra de Gredos and Sierra de Guadarrama. From **Madrid** drive to **Alcalá de Henares**, where the major attractions are the university buildings. From here, the route passes through **Chinchón**, with one of the country's prettiest main squares, and on to **Aranjuez**, in a verdant setting on the banks of the Tagus. After visiting the royal palace, pavilions and famous gardens here, continue to **Toledo** and the sumptuous vestiges of its rich past. Go west to Talavera de la Reina, famous for its ceramics, and then north via the **Sierra de Gredos**, where the **Cuevas del Águila** is an awesome cavern. Ávila, a city of churches and convents, boasts magnificent intact 11C walls. Head east to **El Escorial**, Philip II's immense monastery. En-route to Segovia, branch off to the **Valle de los Caídos,** where Franco is buried amid the stunning Sierra de Guadarrama foothills. In **Segovia**, admire the graceful 2 000-year-old Roman aqueduct, Romanesque churches and the exotic Alcázar. Close by are the palace and magnificent gardens of **La Granja de San Ildefonso**. Return to the mountains, cross the Navacerrada Pass and take the valley road to the **Monasterio de El Paular**. The twisting road traverses the Navafría Pass, before descending to **Pedraza de la Sierra**, a seigniorial town full of charm. Before returning by motorway to Madrid, see the small town of Sepúlveda, overlooking a deep gorge of the River Duratón.

8 EXTREMADURA AND THE PEÑA DE FRANCIA

Round trip of 780km/487mi from Plasencia – this tour focuses on

© José Ramiro/age fotostock
Laguna Grande, Sierra de los Gredos

Extremadura's strong links with the Romans, the Conquistadores and Emperor Charles V.

After visiting the cathedral and old quarter of **Plasencia**, the tour starts in the verdant Valle de La Vera, setting for the **Monasterio de Yuste** and the 15C castle in Jarandilla de la Vera (now a Parador). Leave the valley along a country road that crosses the Valdecañas Reservoir, and you come to the village of **Guadalupe**, huddled around its magnificent monastery. Visit the shrine, then continue west to the monumental town of **Trujillo**, the birthplace of several famous conquistadors, including Pizarro. From Trujillo, the tour then heads southwest by fast highway to **Mérida** to admire the city's Roman remains and the Museo Nacional de Arte Romano, which bears witness to Mérida's importance during this period. The next stops on the itinerary are **Cáceres**, a monumental town with a stunning and superbly preserved old town where time seems to have stopped in the 16C and 17C, and **Alcántara**, whose main sights of interest are a monastery, the seat of the military order of the same name, and an exceptional Roman bridge spanning the Tagus. Head northeast to Coria to visit its cathedral, and then into the province of Salamanca, to **Ciudad Rodrigo**, a pleasant small town with several buildings of interest hidden behind its walls. The tour ends with a visit to the **Peña de Francia**, a crag rising to 1 723m/5 655ft, and the Sierra de Béjar, with its typical mountain village of the same name.

Castle and windmill, Consuegra

© imagebroker/hemis.fr

9 LANDS OF LA MANCHA

Round trip of 849km/531mi from Cuenca – La Mancha is not just endless fields of cereal crops and vines, interspersed with the occasional village or town and the evocative silhouette of a windmill or castle; it is also an area of impressive mountains and dramatic landscapes.

Cuenca, spectacularly positioned between the ravines of the Júcar and Huécar, is the start-point. Begin by driving through the **Sierra** Cuenca, famous for the **Ciudad Encantada**, with its unusual stone formations. Returning to Cuenca, the itinerary heads out along the flat landscapes to the southwest to **Belmonte**, with its castle and collegiate church, and Campo de Criptana, a typical La Mancha village, After passing through Alcázar de San Juan, continue on to **Consuegra**; its castle and windmills on a hill offers perhaps the region's most enduring sight. Head south to the Parque Nacional de las Tablas de Daimiel wetland area. Next stop is **Almagro**, a delightful historic town. Southeast stands Valdepeñas, the capital of La Mancha's wine industry. Continue east, to **Villanueva de los Infantes**, then **Alcaraz**, with its outstanding main square. Albacete is home to a fine provincial museum. Head north to hilltop **Alarcón**, situated on a hill encircled by the River Júcar and crowned by an imposing medieval castle (now a Parador), before returning to Cuenca.

10 THE LEVANTE REGION

Round trip of 715km/447mi from Valencia – This tour runs along the coast and inland through the provinces of Valencia, Alicante and Murcia. Expect long sandy beaches, charming villages and towns and fascinating art and architecture. Having done **Valencia**, head along the coast to El Saler, with its long beaches. The nearby Parque Natural de la Albufera, is famous for its rice dishes. Pass through the resorts of Cullera, and Gandía, (home to the Dukes of Borja), and Denia, watched over by its castle. **Xàbia/Jávea**, with its picturesque old quarter, is a few miles north of Cabo de la Nao with spectacular coast views. Calpe and the mighty Penyal d'Ifac rock also offer tremendous views. **Altea**, to the south, is one of the area's most attractive coastal towns with its steep narrow streets. Skirt high-rise Benidorm, perhaps halting at **Terra Mítica** theme park. The tour heads inland through the mountains to **Guadalest**, in a spectacular location on a rocky ridge. Alcoy nestles in a fertile river valley, and south, Xixona, is famous for its nougat. Back on the coast, **Alicante is** a pleasant bustling provincial capital overlooked by the imposing Castillo de Santa Bárbara. Continue south, skirting Guardamar del Segura and Torrevieja, before arriving at the shallow lagoon of Mar Menor. After a visit to Cartagena, leave the coast for the town of **Murcia**, whose main sights are its fine cathedral and Museo Salzillo, dedicated to the great 18C sculptor. Continue northeast to **Orihuela**, a tranquil town with numerous churches of interest, and then to **Elx/Elche**, famous for its palm grove. From here the itinerary heads further inland, by dual carriageway, to Villena, protected by its imposing castle. The final stop on this driving tour is **Xàtiva**, "the town of a thousand fountains" and birthplace of two popes. Situated on a fertile plain, the town has preserved a good number of buildings of considerable architectural interest.

1 1 CÓRDOBA, SEVILLA, CÁDIZ AND MÁLAGA

Round trip of 890km/556mi from Córdoba – This tour takes in some of the finest cities of inland Andalucía, delightful whitewashed villages (**pueblos blancos**) in the provinces of Cádiz and Málaga, and the famous Costa del Sol resorts.

Córdoba is one of Spain's most beautiful cities, with great monuments, typically Andalucian whitewashed streets and a history influenced by Christians, Muslims and Jews. Head west to **Écija**, the "frying pan of Andalucía", a town of churches, convents, palaces and bell towers. West is glorious **Sevilla**; take several days to enjoy her to the full.

Next, head towards the Atlantic, pausing in elegant **Jerez de la Frontera**, famous for its sherry and horses, before arriving in **Cádiz**, via an impressive causeway. This provincial capital and port is one of Spain's best-kept secrets, with its 18C architecture, historic squares, impressive monuments and superb beaches. South, Chiclana de la Frontera, is the closest town to the magnificent beach of Playa de la Barrosa. From here, drive inland to **Medina Sidonia**, one of the oldest towns in Europe, its medieval quarter is perched on a hill with expansive views of the surrounding plains. The white-washed town of **Arcos de la Frontera**, has an even more outstanding location, on a ridge above a gorge.

Next is **Ronda**, also renowned for its dramatic location, stunning architecture and tradition of bullfighting. From Ronda, the tour winds through stunning mountain scenery down to the coast, dominated by the **Rock of Gibraltar**. Head east via the **Costa del Sol**'s most famous resorts (**Estepona**, **Marbella**, Fuengirola, Benalmádena…) and on to Picasso's **Málaga**, which certainly rewards exploration. Take the fast highway to **Antequera**, and from here to **Estepa**. The hilltop town of **Osuna**, last stage on the journey, has preserved a fine architectural heritage

Parque Natural de Cabo de Gata-Níjar

with numerous palaces and noble mansions. From Osuna, return directly to Córdoba.

1 2 GRANADA, ALMERÍA AND JAÉN

Round trip of 835km/522mi from Granada – This tour of eastern Andalucía visits historic towns and cities with outstanding artistic heritage, deserted beaches, breathtaking mountain scenery and an olive-carpeted landscape.

After exploring the world-famous Alhambra, and city of **Granada**, cross the **Alpujarras** mountains, via verdant valleys and picturesque pueblos blancos, to **Almería**, overlooked by a Moorish fortress. Continue through the **Parque Natural de Cabo de Gata-Níjar**, along the Almerian coast, an area of luminous skies, sand dunes, wild beaches and Africa-like desert landscapes. Stop at hill-top **Mojácar**, then follow the highway north to Vélez Blanco. A cross-country route leads to Pontones at the heart of the **Parque Natural de las Sierras de Cazorla, Segura y las Villas**, with its impressive mountain landscapes cut by deep ravines, rivers and streams. Continue to **Úbeda** and **Baeza**, two monumental Renaissance towns. Drive through extensive olive groves before reaching **Jaén**, at the foot of the Cerro de Santa Catalina, where an imposing Arab fortress, a sumptuous cathedral and historic Arab baths await.

Ciudad del Vino, Marqués de Riscal, Elciego, La Rioja

© Marqués de Riscal

Wine Tours

La Rioja, El Penedès, El Priorat and the Rías Baixas **wineries** in Galicia all offer interesting wine tours through historic wineries, many of them endowed with contemporary architecture.

Wine tour, A Taste of Spain

© A Taste of Spain

CASTILLA LEÓN
In the Ribera de Duero district, northwest of Madrid, mythical wineries such as Vega Sicilia, Pingus and Abadia Retuerta offer tastings and vineyard tours.

BASQUE COUNTRY AND LA RIOJA
Frank Gehry's wine spa at the **Marqués de Riscal** winery in Elciego in the Rioja Alavesa is the most spectacular encounter of hospitality, architecture and oenology, but there are other fantastic visits to be made, such as the **Bodegas Ysios** winery in Laguardia, designed by Pritzker prizewinner Santiago Calatrava. Agustín Santolaya's Bodegas Roda, in Haro, not only makes one of Spain's top wines, Cirsión, but also showcases modern winemaking techniques.

TARRAGONA AND SOUTHERN CATALUNYA
The **Alvaro Palacios** winery in Gratallops in the El Priorat region south of Barcelona is one of the best to visit in the region.

ANDALUCÍA
Jerez de la Frontera and Sanlúcar de Barrameda offer tours and tastings of sherry and cognac wineries.

TOUR OPERATORS
Cellar Tours (www.cellartours.com/ spain) organises wine tourism in Spain, while **Epicurean Ways (www. epicureanways.com)** and **A Taste of Spain (www.atasteofspain.com)** are expert at contracting top British and American wine experts to accompany groups through the finest wineries and cultural destinations in any of Spain's ever-more-numerous wine growing areas.

Spas

The hectic pace of modern life has resulted in an increasing number of people visiting the country's spa resorts for a few days in which to relax, recharge their batteries and help ease certain illnesses and ailments through treatments that are based on the medicinal qualities of the resorts' mineral-rich waters.

Generally speaking, spa complexes are found in areas of outstanding beauty where visitors and patients are also able to enjoy the surrounding nature and leisure facilities available. In Spain, there are a number of spa resorts dotted around the country, inheriting a tradition that has been passed down from the Greeks, Romans and Moors. For information on the treatments and facilities available at individual spas, contact the **National Spa Resort Association (Asociación Nacional de Balnearios, Calle Rodríguez San Pedro 56, 3º, 28015 Madrid; ℘902 11 76 22; www.balnearios.org)**.

Activities for Kids

Many attractions offer discounted fees for children. The following are just a few examples of places that will guarantee a fun day out for both children and their parents. In this guide, **sights of particular interest to children** are indicated with a KIDS symbol (👫).

THEME PARKS

The country's best-known theme parks are **Port Aventura** (👍see p401, **near Salou; www.portaventura.co.uk**), **Terra Mítica** (👍see p445, **Benidorm; www.terramiticapark.com**), **Isla Mágica** (👍see p527, **Sevilla; www.islamagica.es**) and **Warner Bros. Park** (👍see p144, **on the outskirts of Madrid; www.parquewarner.com**).

WILDLIFE PARKS

Wildlife parks, such as the **Parque de la Naturaleza de Cabárceno** (👍see p273, **near Santander; www.parquedecabarceno.com**); zoos and aquariums (Barcelona (👍see p324), Madrid (👍see p119), Benidorm (👍see p444), Donostia-San Sebastián (👍see p251), and O Grove (👍see p296), in Galicia), continue to be popular with youngsters of all ages, as do the bird and animal parks in the Canary Islands, including **Loro Parque (www.loroparque.com)** on Tenerife (👍see p558) and Oasis Park (www.fuerteventuraoasispark.com) on Fuerteventura (👍see p573).

WATER PARKS

The Spanish coastline, particularly the Mediterranean, boasts numerous **water parks**, which are invariably full throughout the summer. **Interactive science museums,** such as those in Valencia (👍see p432), Granada (👍see p482) and A Coruña (👍see p304), offer an interesting and educational alternative to the leisure options above, as does a visit to the **Parque Minero de Riotinto** (👍see p529, **near Huelva; www.parquemineroderiotinto.com**), where visitors are transported by miners' train to discover this fascinating site. Near Almería (👍see p487), **Oasys**/Mini Hollywood; www.oasysparquetematico.com, is where many of the early Spaghetti Westerns were part filmed.

What to Buy & Where to Shop

S pain has a rich tradition of **arts and crafts** reflecting the character of each region as well as the influence of the civilisations – Iberian, Roman, Visigothic and Muslim – that have marked the country's history. Traditional wares such as pottery, ceramics, basketwork and woven goods are produced countrywide.

POTTERY AND CERAMICS

Castilla (p158, 176, 307)

In Castilla, pottery is mainly made by women who use a simple technique. Among their specialities are kitchen utensils, jars and water pitchers. The basic items of crockery used in farmhouses – dishes, soup tureens and glazed earthenware bowls (*barro cocido*) – appear in villages and on stalls in every market. Many of the techniques (metal lustre, *cuerda seca*, decorative motifs, and colour) are influenced by Islamic traditions.

Toledo (p193)

There are two large pottery centres in the Toledo region. The first, **Talavera de la Reina**, is famous for its blue, green, yellow, orange and black ceramics, while **El Puente del Arzobispo** mainly uses green.

Catalunya (p324, 353, 390)

Pottery from **La Bisbal d'Empordà** in Catalunya has a yellow background with green decorative motifs. The Mudéjar tradition is evident in Aragón and the Levante region where blue and white pottery is made in **Muel**, green and purple ceramics in **Teruel** and lustreware in **Manises** (in the province of Valencia). Most of the figurines used as decoration for cribs at Christmas are produced in **Murcia**.

Andalucía (p474, 503, 519)

Spain's richest pottery region is Andalucía, with workshops in **Granada** (glazed ceramics with thick green and blue strokes), **Guadix** (red crockery), **Triana** in Sevilla (polychrome animal figures, glazed and decorated), **Úbeda** in Jaén, **Andújar** (jars with cobalt blue patterns) and in **Vera** (white pottery with undulating shapes).

Galicia (p289)

In Galicia, porcelain and earthenware goods with contemporary shapes and designs have been factory-made since 1806 at the **Sargadelos** centre in the province of A Coruña, but there is also a craft industry at **Niñodaguia** in Ourense (where the yellow glaze only partially covers the pottery) and at **Bruño** (where yellow motifs set off a dark brown background).

Talavera ceramics © Turespaña

Balearic Islands (p450)

Mention should be made of the famous *xiurels*, whistles decorated in red and green from the Balearic Islands.

LACE, WOVEN AND EMBROIDERED GOODS

Blankets and carpets

The textile industry prospered under the Muslims and several workshops still thrive today. Brightly coloured blankets and carpets are woven in the Alpujarras region (p484), La Rioja (p265), the area around Cádiz (p541) (Grazalema) and at Níjar near Almería (p487, where *tela de trapo* carpets are made from strips of cloth). Blankets from Zamora (p173), Palencia (p315) and Salamanca (p163) are well known.

Silk and lace

The village of **El Paso**, on the island of La Palma (p576) in the Canary Islands, is the only place in Spain that still produces silk fabrics. In some villages in the province of Ciudad Real (p206, particularly in **Almagro**) female lacemakers may still be seen at work in their doorways with bobbins and needles. Lacework from **Camariñas** in Galicia (p304) is also widely known. The most popular craft, however, is embroidery, often done in the family. The most typical, geometrically patterned embroideries, come from the Toledo region (p193, particularly **Lagartera** and **Oropesa**). Embroidery has been raised to the level of an art form in two thoroughly Spanish domains: firstly, in the ornaments used for *pasos* during Holy Week and secondly, in the bullfighters' costume, **traje de luces**.

METALWORK

Iron and copper

Iron forging, a very old practice in Spain, has produced outstanding works of art such as the wrought-iron grilles and screens that adorn many churches. Blacksmiths continue to make the grilles for doors and windows so popular in architecture in the south of Spain (see La Mancha p192, Extremadura p216, Andalucía p474, 503, 519). **Guadalupe**, in Extremadura (p223), is an important centre for copper production (boilers, braziers, etc.).

Weapons

Damascene weapons (steel inlaid with gold, silver and copper) are still produced, in **Eibar** (País Vasco, p250) and in **Toledo** (p193) particularly, according to pure Islamic tradition. The best switchblades and knives in Spain are produced in **Albacete** (p208), Las Palmas de Gran Canaria (p561) and Taramundi (p270, Asturias).

Gold and silver

Gold- and silver-smithing were developed in antiquity and throughout the Visigothic period

and have retained some traditional methods. One example is filigree ornamentation (soldered, intertwined gold and silver threads) crafted in **Córdoba** (p504) and **Toledo** (p193). Salamanca (p163), Cáceres (p219) and Ciudad Rodrigo (p169) specialise in gold jewellery. **Santiago de Compostela** (p290) is the world's leading centre for black amber ornaments.

BASKETWORK

Basket-making remains one of the most representative of Spanish crafts. Although carried out countrywide, it is particularly rich on the Mediterranean coast (p320) and in the Balearic Islands (p450).

The type of product and the material used vary from region to region. Baskets, hats and mats are made of reeds, willow, **esparto** grass, strips of olive-wood and birch and chestnut bark, while furniture may be rush or wickerwork. Willow is used in Andalucía (p474, 503, 519) and in the Levante (p32), hazel and chestnut in Galicia and Asturias (p289, 270), and straw and **esparto** grass on the island of Ibiza (p466).

LEATHERWORK

Tradition

Leather-making has always been an important trade, especially in Andalucía (p474, 503, 519), and has become industrialised in some areas. The town of **Ubrique** (in the province of Cádiz) is the leading producer of leatherwork in Spain, followed by the Alicante area (p440) and the Balearic Islands (p450). The production of famous **Córdoba** (p504) leather, including embossed polychrome leatherwork, continues.

Horses and Hunting

Workshops specialising in horses and hunting can be found in Andalucía (p470), Jerez de la Frontera, Alcalá de los Gazules, Villamartín, Almodóvar del Río and Zalamea la Real).

Wine

Typically Spanish gourds and wineskin containers are made in the provinces of Bilbao (p256), Pamplona (p233) and Burgos (p308) and in other wine-growing areas. The wineskins produced in Valverde del Camino (p533, Huelva) are known throughout Spain.

Baskets and tapestries, Pampaneira, Las Alpujarras

© C. Sanchez Pereyra/Photographer's Choice RF/Getty Images

Grande Plage, Biarritz, France

Over the Border

If you're staying close to Spain's national borders, you may wish to consider a day trip into **southwest France** or **Portugal** to visit a number of sights of interest within easy distance. The Green Guide collection covers these areas (Atlantic Coast; Languedoc Roussillon Tarn Gorges; and Portugal), in addition to the Michelin Guide France, the Michelin Guide España & Portugal, and a comprehensive range of maps and plans to enhance your touring itineraries.

FRANCE

Michelin Green Guide France.
Across the border from the province of **Guipúzcoa**, the Basque Country of France boasts some of the country's most beautiful and most famous resorts such as St Jean de Luz, Biarritz and Bayonne.

Less than 30km/18.6mi from **Roncesvalles** (Navarra) is the town of St-Jean-Pied-de-Port, a famous staging-post on the Camino de Santiago. From various passes in the **Pirineos Aragoneses** such as Somport and Portalet, it is possible to drive into the Parc National des Pyrénées, a protected area within the French Pyrenees. From the **Pirineos Catalanes**, you can cross the border to admire the impressive landscapes on the French side of the range north of the Garonne headwaters in the Vall d'Aran and, further east, the Cerdanya Valley, which is half in France, half in Spain. From **Cerbère** (Girona), the coast road winds its way north to the delightful village of Collioure, cradle of the Fauvistes and where poet Antonio Machado died, and then inland to Perpignan, capital of French Catalunya.

PORTUGAL

Michelin Green Guide Portugal.
Opposite the Galician town of **Tui/Tuy** and linked by a bridge designed by Gustave Eiffel over the River Miño, stands Valença do Minho, where you can ascend Monte do Faro to enjoy a magnificent view.

To the south lies **Puebla de Sanabria**, in the province of Zamora. It is well worth visiting the historic Portuguese city of Braganza, while from **Ciudad Rodrigo** you may wish to explore the fortified town of Almeida.

From **Cáceres**, the N 521 runs directly west into Portugal and the attractive mountain landscapes of the Serra de São Mamede, including the fortified town of Marvão and Castelo de Vide. The walled town of Elvas is located just across the border from **Badajoz**, with Estremoz and its attractive old quarter some 50km/31mi further west.

Ayamonte, the closest town to Portugal in southern Spain, is the starting-point from which to explore the summer playground of the Eastern Algarve, with its long beaches, lively resorts and quaint fishing villages.

Festivals & Events

S pain's major festivals are mentioned in the list below. In order to confirm exact dates and times, which may vary slightly, contact the relevant local tourist office, which will be able to provide an up-to-date calendar of events. During the summer months, practically every small town and village in the country hosts a fiesta in honour of its patron saint.

JANUARY

5 JANUARY
Three Kings Day
Sitges (**www.visitsitges.com**)

20 JANUARY
San Sebastián Day:
La Tamborrada San Sebastián
(**www.sansebastianturismo.com**)

MARCH

WEEK BEFORE ASH WEDNESDAY
Carnival festivities Cádiz (**www.carnavaldecadiz.com**). Santa Cruz de Tenerife (**www.santacruzmas.com**)

3RD SATURDAY OF LENT
Feast of the Magdalen
Castellón de la Plana (**www.comunitatvalenciana.com**)

15–19 MARCH
Las Fallas Festival Valencia (**www.fallasfromvalencia.com**)

3RD WEEKEND IN MARCH
Barcelona-Sitges Vintage Car Rally
(**www.rallybarcelonasitges.com**)

HOLY WEEK
Processions Cartagena, Cuenca, Málaga, Murcia, Sevilla, Valladolid, Zamora

FIRST WEEK AFTER EASTER
Spring Festival Murcia
(**www.turismodemurcia.es**)

APRIL

TWO WEEKS AFTER HOLY WEEK
April Fair Sevilla (**http://feriadesevilla.andalunet.com**)

24–27 APRIL
St George's Festival:
"Moors and Christians" Alcoy
(**www.alcoyturismo.com**)

LAST SUNDAY IN APRIL
Romería (pilgrimage) to the Virgen de la Cabeza Andújar
(**www.ayto-andujar.es**)

LATE APRIL–EARLY MAY
Horse Fair Jerez de la Frontera
(**www.turismojerez.com**)
Las Cruces Festival Córdoba
(**www.turismodecordoba.org**)

MAY

AROUND 15 MAY
San Isidro Festival Madrid
(**www.las-ventas.com**)

WHITSUN
Pilgrimage to the Nuestra Señora del Rocío shrine El Rocío (**www.andalucia.com/festival/rocio.htm**).
La Caballada Festival Atienza
(**www.atienza.biz**)

JUNE

2ND SUNDAY AFTER WHITSUN
Corpus Christi Celebration. Streets carpeted with flowers, competitions, processions Puenteareas (**www.riasbaixas.depo.es**). Sitges (**www.visitsitges.com**). Toledo (**www.toledo-turismo.com**)

20–24 JUNE
"Hogueras" St John's Festival Alicante (**www.hogueras.org**)
Festas de Sant Joan/Midsummer's Day Festival Ciutadella (**http://santjoan.ajciutadella.org**)

JULY

1st SATURDAY IN JULY
"A Rapa das Bestas" Festival A Estrada (**www.riasbaixas.depo.es**)

6–14 JULY
San Fermín Festival, the running of the bulls in Pamplona
(**www.turismodepamplona.es**)

APRIL: Moros y Cristianos festival, Alcoy/Alcoi

AUGUST

1st SATURDAY IN AUGUST
Kayak races on the River Sella
Arriondas y Ribadesella (www.
descensodelsella.es)

14–15 AUGUST
Elche Mystery Play Elche
(www.misteridelx.com)

I AST WEDNESDAY IN AUGUST
La Tomatina Buñol
(http://latomatina.info)

SEPTEMBER

7–17 SEPTEMBER
Fair (Feria) Albacete (www.
feriadealbacete.net)

21 SEPTEMBER
St Matthew's Festival Oviedo
(www.ayto-oviedo.es)

20–26 SEPTEMBER
La Rioja Wine Harvest Festival
Logroño (www.logro-o.org)

24 SEPTEMBER
**Festival of Our Lady of Mercy
(Virgen de la Merced)** Barcelona
(www.barcelonaturisme.com)

OCTOBER

8 OCTOBER
Procession of the Virgin Guadalupe
(www.monasterioguadalupe.com)
WEEK OF 12 OCTOBER Pilar Festival
Zaragoza (www.zaragoza.es)

CULTURAL FESTIVALS

HOLY WEEK
Sacred Music Festival Cuenca
(www.smrcuenca.es)

LATE JUNE–MID-JULY
**International Music and Dance
Festival Granada** (www.granada
festival.org)

JULY
**International Classical Theatre
Festival Almagro** (www.
festivaldealmagro.com)

MID-JULY
Jazz Festival Vitoria (www.jazz
vitoria.com)

LAST WEEK OF JULY
Jazz Festival Donostia-San Sebastián
(www.heinekenjazzaldia.com)

JULY–LATE AUGUST
Classical Theatre Festival Mérida
(www.festivaldemerida.es).
Castell de Perelada Festival Peralada
(www.festivalperalada.com)

LATE SEPTEMBER
**San Sebastián International Film
Festival** Donostia-San Sebastián
(www.sansebastianfestival.com)

MID-OCTOBER Sitges **Fantasy &
Horror International Film Festival**
(www.sitgesfilmfestival.com)

LAST WEEK IN OCTOBER
Seminci (International Film Week)
Valladolid (www.seminci.es)

MID-NOVEMBER
Ibero-American Film Festival Huelva
(www.festicinehuelva.com)

Practical Info

TOP TIPS

Best time to go: Late spring and late summer; avoid school hols if you can
Best way around: High-speed train (AVE) in the country; on foot in town
Best for sightseeing: Avoid Mondays and the middle of the day
Most authentic accommodation: Paradores, Casas Rurales, Palacios
Need to know: A few words of Spanish is welcome everywhere and indispensable in the countryside (see Useful Words and Phrases p604)
Need to taste: Tapas, pincos/pintxos, local wine and cava

TEMPERATURE CHART (°C)

Maximum temperatures in black. Minimum temperatures in red.

Month	Jan	Feb	Mar	Apr	May	Jun	Jul	Aug	Sep	Oct	Nov	Dec
Barcelona	6	7	9	11	14	18	21	21	19	15	11	7
	9	11	15	18	21	27	31	30	26	19	13	9
Madrid	1	2	5	7	10	14	17	17	14	9	5	2
	12	12	15	15	17	20	22	22	21	18	15	12
Santander	7	6	8	9	11	14	16	16	15	12	9	7
	15	17	20	23	26	32	36	36	32	26	20	16
Sevilla	6	6	9	11	13	17	20	20	18	14	10	7
	15	16	8	20	23	26	29	29	27	23	19	16
Valencia	5	6	8	10	13	16	19	20	17	13	9	6

Before You Go

WHEN TO GO
SEASONS

As a guideline, the best two seasons to visit Spain are spring and autumn, when temperatures across the country are generally pleasant.

Spring is the best time to explore Extremadura, Castilla-La Mancha and Andalucía, which in summer are the hottest regions in Spain. Late spring is also a good time to visit the Mediterranean and Balearic Islands, as the sea temperature starts to warm up.

In **summer**, the country's north coast comes into its own, offering a pleasant climate for sightseeing and relaxing on the beach without the oppressive heat of other areas. This time of year is also ideal for discovering the magnificent mountains of the Pyrenees, Picos de Europa, and the Sierra de Gredos, Sierra de Guadarrama and Sierra Nevada ranges.

Autumn is a generally pleasant season across most of Spain.

In **winter**, skiing enthusiasts can head for the Pyrenees or the Sierra Nevada, while those preferring to escape the cold wet winter in northern Europe and America can travel south to the Canaries for some winter sunshine.

For up-to-date weather information on **weather**, visit the Meteorological Office website at www.aemet.es.

WHAT TO PACK

Since Spain has so many days of sunshine and its temperatures are generally warmer than many other European countries, pack as few clothes as possible. Unless you choose to visit in winter, lightweight clothing is usually an ideal choice. It's a good idea to pack a sturdy pair of walking shoes, or even hiking boots. An umbrella, rainwear, a lightweight jacket and suntan lotion are good to have with you. Try to pack everything in one suitcase and a carry-on bag. Take an extra tote bag for bringing new purchases back home.

PUBLIC HOLIDAYS	
1 January	New Year's Day
6 January	Three Kings' Day
2nd day before Easter	Good Friday
1 May	Labour Day
15 August	Assumption Day
12 October	Hispanic Day
1 November	All Saints Day
6 December	Constitution Day
8 December	Immaculate Conception
25 December	Christmas Day

GETTING THERE
BY PLANE

A number of Spanish and international airlines operate direct scheduled services to airports across Spain. These include:

Iberia Airlines: ℰ0203 684 3774; within the US and Canada ℰ800 772 4642. www.iberia.com.

British Airways: ℰ0344 493 0787; within the US and Canada ℰ800 247 9297. www.ba.com.

Aer Lingus: ℰ3531 886 8505. www.aerlingus.com.

A number of low-cost airlines also offer inexpensive flights to several Spanish cities from the UK and mainland Europe.

Online booking only:

EasyJet www.easyjet.com
Flybe www.flybe.com
Ryanair www.ryanair.com
Vueling www.vueling.com

Hundreds of weekly charter flights also operate from the UK to

Spanish cities, particularly along the Mediterranean coast and in the Balearic and Canary islands.

BY SHIP

Brittany Ferries and P&O Ferries both operate services to northern Spain from the UK. **Brittany Ferries** runs a ferry service from Plymouth (20hr journey time) and from Portsmouth to Santander (24hr journey). There is also a service from Portsmouth to Bilbao; for reservations, contact: **Brittany Ferries:** ℘0330 159 7000 (UK); ℘902 108 147 (Bilbao and Santander). www.brittany-ferries.com.

BY TRAIN

Eurostar (℘03432 186 186; **www.eurostar.com**) operates high-speed passenger trains from the UK to Paris, from where you can catch a direct train to Barcelona (this part of the journey takes just over six hours) and then a connection on to Madrid as well as other parts of Spain. There are also direct trains to Barcelona (and also Madrid) from quite a few other French cities including Lyons, Marseilles and Toulouse, which stop at Figueres and Girona on the way. Services from Paris, as well as train tickets within Spain, can be booked through the Spanish State Railway Network's (RENFE) UK agent, the Spanish Rail Service: ℘0203 137 4464; www. spanish-rail.co.uk. Alternatively, log-on to the official **RENFE** website at www.renfe.com.
From Portugal, a daily overnight service connects Lisbon with Madrid. The Sud Express train hotel between Paris and Lisbon calls at Irún on the French-Spanish border, Burgos, Valladolid, Salamanca and Coimbra.
A useful website for planning is www.seat61.com.

DISCOUNTS

Consult the **Instituto de la Juventud** (Calle del Marqués de Riscal 16, 28010 Madrid; ℘91 782 76 00; www.injuve. es) for links to youth-orientated travel services. The organisation arranges hostel reservations, discounted transportation and language study, and sells certain student cards. There are offices in other major cities. The European Youth Card (www.eyca.org), issued by student organisations in 36 countries, entitles everyone under the age of 30 to a whole series of discounts on travel, cultural events, accommodation, etc. In Spain, some 50 000 outlets participate in the scheme.

The **Student Card**, available to those aged 12 and over, provides numerous discounts on a variety of services. **Senior citizens** aged 65 and over qualify for significant discounts on transport, entrance fees to monuments, and events and shows (ID required). Many museums offer half-price entry, with free entrance to many national monuments.

Most major cities offer "passport" cards giving discounts on attractions, transport, eating etc…

BY COACH/BUS

Regular long-distance bus services operate from London to all major towns and cities in Spain. For information, contact: **Eurolines UK:** ℘08717 818 181. www.eurolines.co.uk.
Busabout (℘08082 811 114; **www.busabout.com)** offers a seven-day tour including Madrid, Toledo,

Granada, Seville then onto Portugal. They also cover popular fiestas. **Avanza** (☎912 722 832; www.avanzabus.com) sells bus tickets for journeys within Spain.

DOCUMENTS

Visitors must be in possession of a valid **passport**. Holders of British, Irish and US passports do not need a visa for a visit of up to 90 days. Visitors from some Commonwealth countries or those planning to stay longer than 90 days should enquire about visa requirements at their local Spanish consulate.
US citizens should view the International Travel Information for Spain online (http://travel.state.gov/) for general information on visa requirements, customs regulations, medical care, etc.

CUSTOMS REGULATIONS

In the UK, **HM Revenue and Customs** (www.hmrc.gov.uk/customs) state customs regulations and duty-free allowances.
US Customs and Border Protection (www.cbp.gov/travel, ☎877 CBP-5511) offers a free publication **Know Before You Go** for download.

HEALTH

British and Irish citizens should apply for the European Health Insurance Card (UK: ☎0300 3301350; www.ehic.org.uk or at a post office; Ireland: www.ehic.ie or at a local health office) to obtain free or reduced-cost treatment in the EU. All visitors should consider **insurance** for medical expenses, lost luggage, theft, etc.
Pets (cats and dogs) – A general health certificate and proof of rabies vaccination should be obtained from your local vet before departure.

♿ ACCESSIBILITY

Information on facilities for disabled travellers within Spain is available from Polibea, Ronda de la Avutarda 3, 28043 Madrid. ☎917 59 53 72. www.polibea.com. You can also visit the "Culture accessible to everybody in Spain" pages on the tourist board's website, www.spain.info (type disabled into Search).

On Arrival

GETTING AROUND
BY PLANE

Spain has over 45 commercial airports, including 12 on the islands. Information on any of these is available from **AENA** (Aeropuertos Españoles y Navegación Aérea): ☎902 40 47 04. www.aena.es. The largest airports in the country are as follows: Madrid-Barajas, Barcelona, Palma de Mallorca, Málaga, Gran Canaria, Alicante, Tenerife Sur-Reina Sofia, Valencia, Girona-Costa Brava.

Major Airline companies
Iberia: ☎901 111 500 (information and bookings). www.iberia.com.
Air Europa: ☎08714 230 717. www.aireuropa.com.

BY SHIP

Several ferry companies operate services between the Spanish mainland and the Balearics, Canaries, Italy and North Africa. **Trasmediterránea** ☎902 45 46 45. www.trasmediterranea.es.

Routes: Valencia to the Balearics; Barcelona to the Balearics; inter-Balearic Island services; Cádiz to the Canary Islands; inter-Canary Island services; Algeciras to Tanger and Ceuta; Almería to Orán, Melilla, Nador & Ghazaouet; Málaga to Melilla.

Baleària – Baleària (☎902 160 180. www.balearia.com) operates the following routes: Barcelona to the Balearics; Algeciras to Ceuta and Tangier; Dénia to the Balearics; Valencia to the Balearics; inter-Balearic Island services.

BY TRAIN
RENFE ☎912 320 320; www.renfe.com.
AVE (Alta Velocidad Española; www.renfe.es) high-speed trains run from Madrid to: Sevilla (2hr 20min) Valladolid (1hr), Barcelona (2hr 45min), Valencia (1hr 38 min), Albacete (1hr 20min), Huesca (2hr 5 min), Alicante (2hr 12min), Málaga (2hr 20min); from Barcelona to: Sevilla (5hr 30min) and Málaga (5hr 50min) and from Valencia to: Sevilla (3hr 50min).

"Green" railway stations – Nine stations are designated **estaciones verdes** due to their location near nature reserves, or because of their suitability for hikers, mountain-bikers or for nature lovers wishing to discover the beauty of rural Spain. Information about attractions near designated stations is available online at www.adif.es (then search estaciones verdes).

Tourist Trains
For information on all tourist train services visit www.renfe.com/trenesturisticos or call ☎912 55 59 12.
El Transcantábrico Gran Lujo – This luxury narrow-gauge *(feve)* train journeys from Donostia-San Sebastián to Santiago de Compostela via the shores of the Bay of Biscay. The trip lasts eight days and combines rail and bus travel. The service operates from April to October. From €4980.

El Tren Al-Andalus – Despite its name, this luxury palace on wheels is not confined to southern Spain, as it also runs a six-day tour between Seville and Madrid and a seven-day tour between Madrid and Santiago de Compostela. Its famous seven-day Al-Andalus tour from Seville takes in Cordóba, Granada and Ronda. From €2980

El Expreso de la Robla – Originally a coal carrier line from Bilbao to León, this now makes the journey there and back in four days and three nights, offering spectacular scenery and old-world railroad luxury. There is also a four-day tour from Bilbao to Oviedo via Santander. From €850.

El Tren de la Fresa – The Strawberry Train operates vintage carriages between Madrid and Aranjuez (50min), on Saturdays and Sundays from May to October from the Museo del Ferrocarril near Atocha station (From €23; ☎915 068 342; www.museodelferrocarril.org/trendelafresa).

BY METRO/TRAM
Several cities in Spain host their own metro, light rail or tram network and more are being constructed every day. The mainland cities with active networks include Alicante, Barcelona, Bilbao, Granada, Madrid, Murcia, Seville, Valencia, Vitoria-Gasteiz and Zaragoza. On the islands: Palma de Mallorca and Santa Cruz de Tenerife have trams.

BY COACH/BUS
The Spanish bus network is a comfortable, modern and relatively inexpensive way of travelling across the country.

Numerous companies offer local and long-distance services. Information on routes, timetables and prices can be obtained from local bus stations.

Alsa – Extensive routes across the country, particularly in the northwest, centre, and along the Mediterranean. www.alsa.es.

Avanzabus – Madrid-based company providing nationwide services. www.avanzabus.com.

BY CAR
Road Network

Spain has over 343 000km/213 130mi of roads, including 9 000km/5 592mi of divided highways and expressways. Speed limits in Spain for cars and motorbikes are as follows: 120kph/74mph on expressways and divided highways. 100kph/62mph on the open road (with a hard shoulder of at least 1.5m/5ft). 90kph/56mph on the open road (without a hard shoulder); 50kph/31mph in built-up areas (all vehicles).

Tolls

Tolls are payable on some sections of the Spanish highway network. On Michelin maps, these sections are indicated by kilometre markers in red; toll-free sections are marked in blue. Tolls are universally payable by credit card.

Documents

In general, motorists need only have a current driving licence from their country of origin and valid papers (vehicle documentation and valid insurance) to drive in Spain, although in certain situations an International Driving Permit may be required. If in doubt, visitors should check with the AA (www.theaa.com) or RAC (www.rac.co.uk) in the United Kingdom or with the AAA (www.aaa.com) in the US.

Driving Regulations

The minimum driving age is 18. Traffic drives on the right. It is compulsory for passengers in both front and rear seats to wear **seat belts**. Motorcyclists (on all sizes of machine) must wear safety helmets. It is now a legal requirement for motorists to carry two red warning triangles and reflective vests in addition to a spare tyre, first-aid kit and headlamp beam deflectors.

Motorists should note that it is illegal to use a hand-held **cell/mobile phone** when driving. Heavy on-the-spot fines are frequent for those caught using hand-held phones.

Insurance

Those motorists entering Spain in their own vehicles should ensure that their insurance policy includes overseas cover. Visitors are advised to check with their respective insurance company prior to travel. Motorists are also advised to take out adequate **accident** and **breakdown** cover for their period of travel overseas. Various motoring organisations (AA, RAC, etc.) will be able to provide further details on options available. Bail bonds are no longer necessary, although travellers may wish to take this precaution (consult your insurance company). Members of the AA or AAA should obtain the free brochure **Offices to Serve You Abroad**, which gives details of affiliated organisations in Spain.

If the driver of the vehicle is not accompanied by the owner, he or she must have written permission from the owner to drive in Spain.

Road Information

The **National Traffic Agency** (Dirección General de Tráfico) is able to provide information (Spanish only) on road conditions, driving itineraries, regulations, etc. ☏011 for traffic conditions. www.dgt.es.

Maps And Plans
Michelin's España & Portugal spiral **road atlas** and general **road maps** will assist you in the planning of your journey. These are listed in the **Maps and plans** section at the back of this guide.

Motoring Organisations
RACE (Royal Automobile Club of Spain) ☏900 100 992; 91 594 93 94 (roadside assistance). www.race.es.
RACC (Royal Automobile Club of Catalunya) ☏902 357 357) and 902 242 242. (roadside assistance). www.racc.es.

Car Hire
Vehicles in Spain can be hired through the offices of all major international car hire companies around the world. Alternatively, cars can be hired at major airports, train stations, large hotels and in all major towns and cities around the country:
Avis ☏902 18 08 54. www.avis.es
Europcar ☏902 50 30 10. www.europcar.es.
Hertz ☏91 749 90 69. www.hertz.es.

Visitors should bear in mind that although the legal driving age in Spain is 18, most companies will only rent out vehicles to drivers over the age of 21.

PLACES TO STAY AND EAT
Hotel and Restaurant recommendations are located in the Addresses sections of individual principal sights in the Discovering Spain section of this guide. For coin ranges and for a description of the symbols used in the Addresses, see the Legend on the cover flap.

Hotel and Restaurant listings fall within the description of each principal sight in order to make the most of your stay. These have been recommended for their location, comfort, value for money and, in some cases, for their charm. We have also made a conscious effort to cover all budgets, although some regions (for example the Costa Brava, Costa del Sol and the Balearic Islands) are more expensive than others in peak season, and prices in Madrid and Barcelona can be as high as in other major cities in Europe. As a general rule, restaurants serve lunch from 1.30pm to 3.30pm and dinner from 9pm to 11pm.

STAY
This guide lists a selection of hotels, **hostales** and **pensiones** based on the price of a double room in high season and generally excluding breakfast and VAT, unless otherwise indicated. The difference in rates between high and low season can be significant, particularly on the coast and islands, so it is always advisable to receive confirmation of prices in writing at the time of booking.

Paradores
Almost all of the state-run network of luxury hotels are in restored historic monuments (castles, palaces, monasteries, etc.) in magnificent locations. For more information, contact **Paradores de Turismo de España (**Calle José Abascal 2-4, 28003 Madrid; ☏902 54 79 79; www.parador.es). The official UK representative is **Keytel International** (The Foundry, 156 Blackfriars Road, London SE1 8EN; ☏0800 160 1013; www.keytel.co.uk). Special weekend offers are often available, in addition to a five-night "go as you please"

accommodation card. In the US, contact **PTB Hotels** (☎1 800 634 1188; www.petrabax.com).

Rural accommodation

The number of visitors to Spain who wish to stay in rural accommodation is steadily increasing. Most autonomous communities publish a practical guide listing details of every type of accommodation available, including rooms in private houses, hostels for groups, entire houses for rent, and farm campsites. Contact local tourist offices listed within the Principal Sights for further details, or www.ecoturismorural.com.

Campsites

The Secretaría General de Turismo publishes an annual campsite guide. Further details on camping and caravanning are supplied by the Federación Española de Empresarios de Camping y Parques de Vacaciones (Calle Orense 32, entreplanta, 28020 Madrid; ☎618 54 89 43; www.fedcamping.com). Book in advance for popular resorts during summer.

Youth hostels

Spain's 238 youth hostels are open to travellers with an **international card**, available from international youth hostelling offices and youth hostels themselves. For further information, contact the **Spanish Youth Hostel Network** (Red Española de Albergues Juveniles, C/ Marqués de Riscal 16, 28010 Madrid; ☎91 30 84 675; www.reaj.com).

Special offers

Many chains and hotels catering to business travellers often offer reduced rates at weekends. It is also possible to purchase vouchers for one or several nights at advantageous prices.

For further information on these special offers, contact the following:
NH Hoteles ☎916 008 146. www.nh-hoteles.es. Discounts are available via NH Rewards scheme.
Halcón Viajes ☎900 802 020. (information and reservations) www.halconviajes.com.
Hoteles Meliá ☎912 764 747. www.melia.com. Discounts and special weekend offers available via the Meliá Rewards card.

Don't forget the Michelin Guide
The red-cover MICHELIN GUIDE ESPAÑA & PORTUGAL is revised annually and is an indispensable complement to this guide with additional information on hotels and restaurants including category, price, degree of comfort and setting.

EAT

The restaurants listed in the Addresses in this guide have been chosen for their surroundings, ambience, typical dishes or unusual character. Coin symbols (☙see the Legend on the cover flap) correspond to average cost of a meal and are given as a guideline only.

Tapas

Given the country's reputation for tapas (**pintxos** in northern Spain), we have also included a list of tapas bars where visitors can enjoy an aperitif or meal throughout the day and late into the evening. Prices of tapas are often not listed; do beware that although the unit price is relatively small, they soon add up!

Practical A–Z

BUSINESS HOURS

Shops are open 10am–2pm, 5–8.30pm, although large stores and malls are often open through lunch. Most shops close Sundays, and some on Saturday afternoons.

ELECTRICITY

220V AC (some establishments may still be 110V). Plugs are 2-pin.

EMBASSIES AND CONSULATES

US Embassy
Calle de Serrano 75, 28006 **Madrid**
✆91 587 22 00. http://es. usembassy.gov.
US Consulate
Paseo Reina Elisenda de Montcada 23, 08034 **Barcelona**
✆93 280 22 27
Australian Embassy
Torre Espacio, Paseo de la Castellana, 259D, Planta 24, 28046 Madrid
✆913 53 66 00
www.spain.embassy.gov.au
British Embassy & Consulate-General
Torre Espacio, Paseo de la Castellana, 259D, 28046 Madrid
✆917 146 300
www.gov.uk/world/spain
British Consular Offices
Alicante, Barcelona, Ibiza, Las Palmas, Málaga, Palma de Mallorca and Santa Cruz de Tenerife.
www.gov.uk/world/spain
Canadian Embassy
Torre Espacio, Paseo de la Castellana, 259D, 28046 Madrid
✆913 82 84 00
www.espana.gc.ca
Canadian Consulate
Barcelona ✆932 70 36 14
Málaga ✆952 22 33 46
Embassy of Ireland
Ireland House, Paseo de la Castellana 46, 4ª
28046 Madrid
✆914 36 40 93
www.dfa.ie/irish-embassy/spain
Honorary Irish Consulates
www.dfa.ie
Alicante ✆965 10 74 85
Barcelona ✆934 91 50 21
Bilbao ✆944 23 04 14
El Ferrol (La Coruña)
✆981 351 480
Lanzarote ✆928 81 52 62
Las Palmas, Gran Canaria
✆928 29 77 28
Fuengirola (Málaga)
✆952 47 51 08
Palma de Mallorca ✆971 71 92 44
Sevilla ✆954 69 06 89
Santa Cruz de Tenerife
✆922 24 56 71

EMERGENCIES

✆112 connects with all emergency services in Spain.
◆ **Police:** ✆091 (nat.), 092 (loc.)
◆ **Medical emergencies:** ✆061
◆ **Fire:** ✆080
◆ **Civil Guard:** ✆062
◆ **Mossos d'Esquadra (Catalan police):** ✆088
◆ **Directory Enquiries:** ✆11818
◆ **International Directory Enquiries:** ✆11825

MAIL/POST

Post offices (**correos**; www.correos. es) are usually open Mon–Fri from 8.30am (closing times vary) and Sat 9.30am–1pm. Stamps (**sellos**) can also be purchased at tobacconists (**estancos**).

NEWSPAPERS

El País is Spain's "newspaper of record", though certain readers find it excessively pro-socialist. Barcelona's **La Vanguardia** is a respected daily distributed nationwide. **El Mundo**

has sensationalist tabloid tendencies, but provides good information and entertainment. **El Periódico de Catalunya** is a Barcelona daily published in Spanish and Catalan. **ABC** is a monarchist and retro Madrid daily. Smaller regional newspapers around Spain have better information about local events. Free newspapers such as **20 Minutos** and **Que!** distributed in the metro are informative and time-saving. English, French and German media are available at many newspaper kiosks in cities and beach resorts.

PHARMACIES

Open Spanish pharmacies are marked by large illuminated green crosses on the street. Every neighourhood has a farmacia de guardia open around the clock. Lists of all-night and weekend pharmacies are published in the windows of all pharmacies.

SIGHTSEEING

Opening times and entrance fees for monuments, museums, churches, etc. are included in the **Discovering Spain** section of this guide. This information is given as a guideline only, as times and prices are liable to change without prior warning.

Prices shown are for individual visitors and do not take into account discounts for groups, who may also benefit from private visits. As many monuments require frequent maintenance and restoration, it is advisable to phone ahead to avoid disappointment. Information for churches is only given if the interior contains a sight of particular interest with specific opening times or if an entrance fee is payable. In general, religious buildings should not be visited during services, although some only open for Mass, in which case visitors should show appropriate respect.

SMOKING

The new Spanish anti-smoking law came into effect on 1 January 2011: smoking is prohibited in all indoor spaces including on public transport, and at airports.

TELEPHONES

Spanish public pay phones cost 50 cents for a local call. Mobile phones usually require 00-34 before the nine-digit number. For **international calls** from Spain, dial 00, then dial the country code (44 for the UK, 353 for Ireland, 1 for the US and Canada), followed by the area code (minus the first 0 of the STD code when dialling the UK), and then the number.

For calls **within Spain**, dial the full 9-digit number of the person you are calling. When calling Spain **from abroad**, dial the international access code, followed by 34, then the full 9-digit number. For more information, call ☏1004 (in Spain) or visit www.telefonica.com.

TIME

Spain is 1hr ahead of GMT. The Spanish keep different hours from the British or North Americans: as a general rule, restaurants serve lunch from 1.30pm to 3.30pm and dinner from 9pm to 11pm.

TIPPING

Restaurants and other establishments in Spain usually include both taxes and service in prices. It is customary to leave an additional cash tip of 5–10 per cent. Tip porters 1€ per bag for assistance, and chambermaids 1€ per day. Guides may be tipped 3 to 5€ per day at your discretion.

Introducing
Spain

Monasterio de Irache near Estella, Navarra, along the Camino de Santiago
© Spiegelhalter/Sime/Photononstop

Features

Spain Today

Spain is living testimony that countries can change profoundly in modern times: from a closed society where views were rarely expressed in public to one where people speak their minds; from economically isolated to a dynamic economy that attracts immigrants; from a centralised government to a land that thrives on regional debate; from a repressive state to one whose prosecutors have won international prestige for their pursuit of human rights abuses.

And yet all this transformation has come about while maintaining essential values and the Spanish family way of life. Elsewhere, the enthusiasm to be part of global culture will make the visitor feel at times as if he or she has never left home. But when you are in Spain, it is clear that you are nowhere else.

» A Way of Life p57
» Fiestas, Folklore and Culture p60
» Spanish Cuisine p64

A Way of Life

Whenever foreigners conjure up an image of Spain, their thoughts inevitably turn to a leisurely lifestyle, plentiful sunshine, noisy and lively towns and cities, and an extroverted, friendly people whose daily timetable is impossible to comprehend. Yet, irrespective of the crazy rhythms imposed by the demands of modern life, the Spaniards always attempt to extract the very maximum from life; one maxim that often applies to them is that of having to work to live rather than living for work. Despite the differences that exist between the north and south, the coast and inland areas, and towns and cities, it can be said that this is a common theme among all Spaniards in the manner in which they approach life.

STREET LIFE

There's no doubt that the excellent climate enjoyed by most parts of the country is one of the main reasons for the Spaniards' "passion" for living outdoors; there are of course others, of lesser or equal importance. Spain is a country of informal get-togethers and social gatherings, in bars, cafés, restaurants, at work, and of chance meetings of a couple of friends – any excuse is good enough to indulge in a friendly chat or animated discussion. This affection for going out as a group, meeting friends for dinner, or enjoying tapas or a drink together, is to the Spanish a sign of identity, irrespective of their age or social standing. Nor is it uncommon for Spaniards to have a relaxed drink with friends or colleagues after work before heading home.

DAILY SCHEDULE

The daily schedule of the Spanish, shaped by the extreme summer heat, differs from the rest of Europe. Spaniards don't usually have lunch before 2pm or 2.30pm, or 3pm in summer, and they rarely have dinner before 9pm, a custom that results in long mornings and afternoons and provides ample time for them to indulge in a siesta or leisurely stroll, shopping or meeting up for a snack with friends and work acquaintances. The pressures of modern life have however squeezed siesta time; in the big cities lengthy lunch breaks are no longer the norm.

TAPAS AND APERITIF TIME

This gastronomic pastime is one of Spain's most popular modern traditions with youngsters, couples and entire families, who head for bars to *tapear*, either standing at the counter or, if time allows, visiting various bars to enjoy a tapa in each. An apéritif can be drunk with just a few olives, although by ordering a number of tapas you can quite easily create an alternative to lunch or dinner.

These small platefuls come in many guises and at many price levels, ranging from the small tapa itself to larger portions known as a *media ración* or *ración*. Choose a *media ración* of Manchego cheese or Serrano cured ham, a *ración* of chorizo sausage, or a selection of vegetarian, fish, seafood or meat dishes – washed down perhaps with a glass of draught beer *(una caña)*, wine or, in southern Spain, a glass of fino sherry *(una copa de fino)*. Every region has its own specialities and its own way of presenting tapas, though they often come with a basket of bread to round them out. In the north of Spain they often come skewered with cocktail sticks and are called *pinchos/pintxos*. Yet whether you're in the Basque Country, Andalucía (in Granada tapas are still traditionally free, though as a tourist, you may be excluded!) or in the middle of the Meseta, you will always find a restaurant or bar where tempting tapas are coming out of the kitchen.

Platja de Sant Sebastià, Barcelona

BARS

There are literally tens of thousands of bars in Spain, including in the smallest and most remote hamlets. They act as a focal point for locals, who congregate here with friends or family in the evening and at weekends, especially during football matches. During the afternoon and early evening in smaller towns and villages you may come across locals playing cards or indulging in a game of dominoes over a coffee or something stronger.

The mornings are busy in bars as well, with regulars stopping by for a pastry and coffee for breakfast. Smoking is now banned in bars though seats are often supplied just outside the door for smokers.

TERRACES

With the onset of fine weather, terraces spring up across Spain – outside restaurants, cafés, bars and ice-cream parlours, on pavements and patios and in gardens and narrow alleyways. During the warmer months, it is pleasant at any time of day to take the weight off your feet for a short while and watch the world go by in front of your table. Be aware, though, that you pay a small extra price for terrace service.

Many of the most crowded bars and clubs provide outdoor terraces for their customers till the early hours of the morning in summer. In winter they often open only at midday in good weather.

BEACH BARS

These typical features of resorts along the Spanish coast come in various guises, ranging from the cheap and cheerful to the expensive and luxurious. These *chiringuitos*, as they are known, have grown in popularity, particularly given that customers can enjoy a drink or have a meal wearing only their swim suits or meet here at night for a drink or dinner on the beach. In order to meet new legal requirements some are losing their charmingly old-fashioned air.

NIGHTLIFE

The lively character of Spanish towns and cities at night is often a cause of great surprise to visitors. Nowadays, the choice of venues is often overwhelming, with something to suit every budget and taste: quiet cafés for a drink and a chat with friends; lively bars packed to the rafters, with dance floors and music played at full volume; clubs offering a variety of shows; and nightclubs ranging from holes-in-the-wall to mega-venues where the pace doesn't stop until late the next morning. On Thursday and Friday nights and on weekends, as well as in summer and during holidays, the action is almost constant, with nightclubbers migrating from one club or bar to the next – don't be surprised if you get stuck in a traffic jam at three or four in the morning! An example of this is on the Paseo de la Castellana, in Madrid, in summer when its numerous outdoor bars open until the small hours.

THE SIESTA

Although the demands of modern life prevent most people from perpetuating this healthy custom, most Spaniards like to have an afternoon nap and will make sure that they take a restorative siesta on weekends and when they're on holiday. Although less common nowadays, those Spaniards whose work schedule allows them three hours off from 2–5pm, or a workday ending at 3pm in summer, will try to make it home for lunch and a short sleep.

THE FAMILY

In line with other Latin countries, the family remains the bedrock of Spanish life, and is a determining factor in the behaviour and many of the habits of Spanish society at large.

Without a solid family base, it would be hard to understand how a country with a high rate of unemployment and one in which children continue to live with their parents until their late-20s and even early-30s could prosper without too many problems. It should also be added that numerous Spanish celebrations and fiestas are based upon these close family ties.

THE WORK ETHIC

Those foreigners who have chosen to live in Spain soon realise that the old image of Spain as a country where very little work is done – a view perpetuated by the country's way of life and daily schedule, and the Spaniards' well-documented liking for enjoying themselves to the full – is far removed from modern reality.

Nowadays, Spaniards often work as intensively as in any other European country. Visitors may wonder how this is possible, given the unusual lifestyle. The answer is that they often start work very early or continue till very late in an improvised style. Equally, from an early age the Spanish are brought up used to sleeping less during the week and trying to catch up on lost sleep at the weekend.

© Philippe Roy/hemis.fr

Pintxos at a bar, Donostia-San Sebastián, País Vasco

Fiestas, Folklore and Culture

Spain has kept alive many old traditions, most visible in the fervently celebrated fiestas held around the country throughout the year. These unique and varied outpourings of local pride, religious feeling or simply a love of streetlife reflect Spain's rich cultural heritage and diversity.

FIESTAS AND TRADITIONS

Fiestas across Spain share huge crowds, ceremony and a sense of theatre. Beyond that, though, they are extraordinarily diverse. A detailed list of major festivals in Spain can be found in the Planning Your Trip section of this guide.

Major festivals

To a greater or lesser degree, every Spanish town and city celebrates one main festival every year, normally in honour of its patron saint. These celebrations, many of which take place over the summer months, attract the entire local population, as well as inhabitants from outlying villages and rural areas. Typical events vary from one region to the next: they may include religious celebrations and processions, floral offerings, fireworks or bullfights and bullrunning. Many people, though, attend just to indulge in animated discussions with friends until the early hours, or to enjoy rides on the fairground attractions, or to eat and drink together, often on the street. The most important festivals in Spain include:

Los Sanfermines de Pamplona, in honour of San Fermín (7 July), which starts on 6 July with the setting-off of a huge firework rocket or *chupinazo*.

The city is the backdrop for a non-stop week-long party that climaxes with the morning running of the bulls *(encierros)* and early-evening bullfights. This ends at midnight on 14 July, with the candlelit singing of *Pobre de Mí* (Poor Me).

Las Fallas de Valencia, held in March in honour of San José, are renowned for bonfire sculptures and gunpowder bangs. *La despertà* (the wake-up call) begins at 8am with a heady mix of brass bands and firecrackers. It culminates in the *Nit del foc* (Night of Fire) when the impressive *ninots* (bonfire sculptures) dotted around the city are set alight.

Andalucían fairs

Sevilla's *Feria de Abril* (April Fair) is the most famous of these spring and early summer festivals held in Andalucían cities. They are renowned for their exciting atmosphere, colourful costumes and spontaneous dancing of local sevillanas, with mountains of tapas consumed, accompanied by chilled dry sherry *(fino)* such as *manzanilla*. The streets of the fairground area are a mass of colour as Andalucíans parade on foot and horseback dressed in long flounced flamenco dresses or horseriding suits.

Romerías

Romerías (pilgrimages) are an important aspect of religious life in Spain.

Although each has its own specific characteristics, the basic principle is the same: an annual pilgrimage on foot, and occasionally on horseback, to a hermitage or shrine to venerate a statue. Usually, this peregrination will also include a procession, music, dancing and a festive open-air meal.

The pilgrimage to El Rocío (Almonte, Huelva) is the largest and most deeply felt *romería* in the whole of Spain, attracting around one million pilgrims every year. Another pilgrimage of note is the St. John of the Mountain Festival in Miranda de Ebro dating from the 14C.

Semana Santa

Holy Week processions are another vivid expression of Spaniards' depth of religious sentiment. Villages, towns and

FLAMENCO

Casa Patas, Madrid

© Ingolf Pompe/hemis.fr

Flamenco – a form of song, music and dance, but also a way of life – is one of Spain's most vibrant cultural expressions. The song, or *cante*, at its heart, took shape by the end of the 18thC in the Gypsy quarters of southern cities such as Cádiz and Jérez. At that time its dance, or *baile*, often remained behind closed doors. Flamenco guitar, or *toque*, then strikingly simple, has evolved in modern times to acquire great technical complexity. All three are closely intertwined in live performance around flamenco's poetic sense of tragedy.

When in Spain, you may come upon flamenco as a stage show, as a recital in a classical auditorium, or as an acoustic session in a small club.

For aficionados it is worth timing a visit to coincide with one of the major events on the flamenco calendar. Seville's Bienal gives a sampling of pure and fusion flamenco; Jerez's annual spring festival is the main dance event; Murcia's midsummer Festival Nacional de Cante de las Minas, which grew around miners' flamenco, includes a song contest for young talent and gala performances by stars.

Performers may wear traditional flounced dresses, click castanets and play with fans, but do not be surprised if a show is contemporary in its aesthetics. Today's artists, keen to shrug off stereotypes, especially since flamenco won UNESCO World Heritage status, are often experimental. Symbolically, the national flamenco centre in Jerez's old town is housed in a radically modern building, a good expression of the flamenco community's intent on renewing their art while remaining loyal to their roots.

© JTB Photo/UIG/age fotostock

Venta El Gallo, Sacromonte, Granada

cities around the country participate in these expressions of tragic feeling, which see thousands of people taking to the streets to accompany the passion of Christ and the pain of his mother. Semana Santa tends to be a more sober affair in Castilla, and more festive in Andalucía, although across Spain the beauty of the statues (often works of art in their own right), the solemnity of the processions, some of which take place against a magnificent backdrop, and the fervour of those involved, create an atmosphere that will involve and move believers and non-believers alike. Although Holy Week in Sevilla is the most famous, the processions in Valladolid, Málaga, Zamora, Cuenca and Lorca are also worthy of particular note.

Carnival

Carnival celebrations are generally extravagant and irreverent affairs. They often involve many months of hard work rehearsing and making costumes. They remain liveliest on the periphery of Spain where Franco's 40-year ban on Carnival was avoided. In the Canaries, particularly on Tenerife, Carnival is an important aspect of island tradition, involving a procession of floats and the election of the Carnival queen. Carnival in Cádiz is full of humour and music, while Galician Carnival is famous for its folk costumes.

Christmas

The Christmas period in Spain is traditionally a time for family celebration. The Christmas tree and crib are essential decorative features; families congregate for dinner on Christmas Eve or on Christmas Day, depending on the local custom. An equally traditional aspect of Christmas is the procession of the Kings on the eve of Epiphany: the Three Wise Men and their pages ride through the streets of towns and cities on the night of 5 January, handing out sweets to excited children lining their path.

Bullfighting festivals

It is impossible to broach the subject of fiestas without mentioning bullfighting, a subject that raises passions and criticism in equal measure. Bullfighting festivals remain, despite modern protests, as much a part of Spanish culture as Holy Week processions, and their existence is often defended by those who do not wish to attend. Two regions, the Canary Islands and Catalunya, however, have banned bullfights.

Few cultural events are as ritualised as a bullfight; consequently, a basic understanding of the various moves and stages of the contest between man and bull is required to make any attempt to appreciate the spectacle.

The bullfighting season runs from the spring to the autumn, and the most important festivals are those in Sevilla, held during the April Fair, and the San Isidro festival in Madrid.

REGIONAL DANCES AND TRADITIONS

Aragón

Festivals and parties are often celebrated by a **jota**, a bounding, leaping dance in which couples hop and whirl to the tunes of a *rondalla* (group of stringed instruments), stopping only for the occasional brief singing of a *copla*.

Castilla and Extremadura

Few regions in Spain are as mystical or have such sober customs as Castilla. Traditional dances include the *seguidilla*, originating from La Mancha region, and the *paloteo*, also known as the *danza de palos*, which is accompanied by flute, tambourine, and sometimes by a bass drum or the most typical of Castilian instruments, the reed-pipe (*dulzaina*). Costumes may be richly embroidered with precious stones and silk thread.

Catalunya and the Comunidad Valenciana

The **sardana** dance is still very popular in Catalunya where it is performed in a circle in main squares on Sundays. Inscribed on UNESCO's List of the Intangible Cultural Heritage of Humanity, **Castells**, are human towers which may be seen in festivals at El Vendrell and Valls. In the Levante, the baroque local costume notable for its colour and intricate embroidery is worn during colourful festivals. Valencia's **Fallas** in March bring city life to a halt; Alicante's **Fogueres** in June rival them on a smaller scale.

La Tomatina, which takes place in the Valencian town of Buñol every August, is a brief and very messy food fight involving tonnes of over-ripe tomatoes. Lastly, the **Moros y Cristianos** festivals – those of Alcoy (April) are the best known but there are many others around Alicante province – give a colourful costumed replay of the confrontations between Moors and Christians during the Reconquest.

Galicia, Asturias and Cantabria

Romerías in Asturias and Galicia are often accompanied by the shrill tones of the **gaita**, a type of bagpipe, and sometimes by drums and castanets. The *gaita* is played during events in honour of cowherds, shepherds, sailors and other traditional occupations in these rural coastal regions. It is also part of all celebrations of Celtic music, which are held here during the summer. The most typical festivals are those held in summer for *vaqueiros*, or cowherds, in Aristébano and others for shepherds near the Lago de Enol. Common dances in Galicia include the *muñeira* or dance of the miller's wife, the sword dance performed only by men, and the *redondela*. Bowls *(bolos)* is a very popular game, supposedly brought to the region by pilgrims on the Camino de Santiago.

Murcia

Flamenco flourishes in Murcia as does improvised rhyming poetry, or *trovos*. Cuban-influenced songs, called *habaneras*, are celebrated in an annual festival in Torrevieja. Murcia city hosts the International Festival of Mediterranean Folklore.

País Vasco and Navarra

The **Basque Country** and Navarra have preserved many of their distinct traditions. Men dressed in white with red sashes and the famous red berets dance in a ring accompanied by **zortzikos** (songs), a **txistu** (flute) and a *tamboril*. The most solemn dance, the *aurresku*, is a chain dance performed by men after Mass on Sundays. The **espata-dantza**, or sword dance, recalls warrior times while others, like the spinners' dance or another in which brooms are used, represent daily tasks. Basque men love contests, such as tug-of-war, trunk cutting, stone lifting and pole throwing. But by far the most popular sport is *pelota*, played in different ways: with a **chistera**, or wickerwork scoop, or with the very similar **cesta punta** in an enclosed three-walled court *(jai alai)*, or with a wooden bat or *pala* or, finally, simply with the hand, **a mano**. If you are lucky you may see *rebote*, considered the finest form, played on a large open court. The main competitive event of the year for enthusiasts is the Manomanista championship (April–May).

Balearic Islands

Mallorca's traditional dances include the *copeo*, the *jota*, the *mateixes* and the *bolero*. Dances and festivals are accompanied by a *xeremía* (local bagpipes) and a tambourine. In Menorca a festival that dates back to medieval times and calls for about 100 horsemen in elegant costumes is held at Ciutadella (The Feast of St John or *Sant Joan*, on 23–24 June). Popular dances in Ibiza have a poetical accompaniment.

Canary Islands

The folklore of the Canaries shows influences from the Spanish mainland, Portugal and South America (the last as a consequence of the strong links created by emigration); these in turn have become intertwined with local traditions. The **isa**, the **malagueña**, the *folía* and the *tajaraste* are the four best-known types of dance from the islands. The *salto del pastor* (shepherd's leap) is a traditional folk sport throughout the islands involving long pole vaults. On La Gomera there is a revival of the traditional *siblo*, or whistling, across valleys .

Spanish Cuisine

Spanish food varies enormously from region to region. A few dishes are served throughout the country: garlic soup, *cocido* (a type of stew accompanied by beans or chickpeas), tortilla, a thick potato omelette, cured pork products like lean *serrano* hams and chorizo (a sausage), and savoury rice dishes like paella. Fish and seafood are outstanding everywhere. No description of Spanish food would be complete without a mention of tapas (see p57). A selection of tapas makes for a very pleasant lunch or supper accompanied by a glass (*caña*) of draught beer. Spain is also renowned for its magnificent wines, which include historic appellations such as La Rioja and Jerez.

REGIONAL CUISINE

Galicia

Galicia's cuisine owes its delicacy to the quality of its **seafood**: hake, scallops (*vieiras*), mussels (*mejillones*), goose-barnacles (*percebes*), king prawns (*langostinos*) and mantis shrimps (*cigalas*). There is also **caldo gallego**, a local soup, **lacón con grelos** (hand of pork with turnip tops) and **pulpo gallego** (Galician-style octopus), cooked up in big copper pots at fiestas.

The bakers' delicious flat empanada pies make good picnic food. All these may be accompanied by red or white Ribeiro or white Albariño wines. Desserts include *tarta de Santiago*, a frangipane tart, and *filloa* pancakes

Asturias and Cantabria

In both regions, fish and seafood are important but gourmets make the trip here just for the mountain cheeses, such as blue-veined Cabrales and plain Quesucos. A casserole called **fabada** made with white beans, pork, bacon and sausages has many variations. Among sweet things Cantabrian cheesecake and Asturian rice pudding reign supreme. In Asturias it is fun to eat in the ciderhouses close to the apple orchards.

País Vasco

Cooking in the **Basque Country** has been raised to the level of a fine art. Traditional and avant garde styles are found at starred restaurants and in bars for pinxtos, or tapas.

Superb aged beef is woodgrilled while saltcod or hake is good in a green parsley sauce (*salsa verde*). *Chipirones en su tinta*, a dish of baby squid in their own ink and *marmitako*, a fish soup, are good served with local *txacolí*, a tart white wine.

Navarra and La Rioja

Navarra and La Rioja are famed for their game, market-garden produce and wines, especially reds. The food is varied and refined, with partridge, saltcod and grilled red peppers competing with trout for pride of place on local menus. In Navarra, delicious Roncal cheese is made in the valleys from ewe's milk.

Aragón

Aragón is the land of **chilindrón**, a stew made with meat or poultry and peppers, and of **ternasco** (baby roast kid or lamb). These may be followed by delicious preserved peaches or pears in wine and washed down with wine from one of three vineyard areas: Cariñena, Somontano and Borja.

Catalunya

Catalunya's cuisine is Mediterranean. Look out for *pa amb tomaquet* (bread rubbed with a cut tomato and occasionally garlic and sprinkled with olive oil) and wonderful fish dishes with a variety of sauces such as *all i oli* (crushed garlic and olive oil) and *samfaina* (tomatoes, peppers and aubergines). Among pork meats are **butifarra** sausages and the *fuet* sausage from Vic. Dried fruit is used in a great many dishes or may be served at the end of a meal. The most widespread dessert is **crema catalana**, a kind of crème brûlée. Catalunya's wines include sparkling *Cava*, like champagne, fruity whites made in Penedès and superb big reds in Priorato and Montsant.

Castilla and Extremadura

Castilian specialities using local produce include roast lamb (**cordero asado**), suckling-pig (**cochinillo tostón** or **tostado**) and **cocido**, all of which may be accompanied by a light, fresh Valdepeñas red. Other wines include Rueda's fresh fruity whites, Ribera del Duero's fruity reds and Toro's very big reds. Both regions are also famed for their ewe's milk cheeses, including Manchego, which is good eaten with *membrillo*, a sweet quince paste. Among the region's sweets is Toledo marzipan *(mazapán)*. Extremadura has the largest area of grazing pasture for black-footed pigs and enjoys an excellent reputation for its cured hams from Guijuelo (Salamanca) and Montánchez (Cáceres).

Levante

The freshwater lake of l'Albufera just outside Valencia is said to be the birthplace of **paella**. A land of rice dishes, Levantine paella is prepared with seafood near the coast and with rabbit and green beans as you head inland. Further south at Jijona, **turrón**, a soft

or hard almond and honey nougat, is made. Ice creams and iced drinks, such as *horchata de chufas*, made from tiger-nuts, water and sugar, are another speciality worth sampling.

Balearic Islands

Soups are specialities in the Balearics; Mallorca's classic *sopa* has bread, leeks and garlic, while other soups are made with fish. **Tumbet** is a Mediterranean vegetable casserole and **sobrasada**, a soft lean spreading sausage. **Cocas**, a little like pizzas, and **ensaimadas**, light spiral rolls, make delicious desserts or breakfasts.

The Canary islands

Canarian specialities include **papas arrugadas**, small wrinkly potatoes with a dry, salty coating, served with green or red *mojo* or dipping sauce. Stoneground flour made from roasted maize, called *gofio*, is added to many foods. The Canary Islands are also known for Shakespearian sack wine, made from malvasia grapes.

Andalucía

The best-known dish is **gazpacho**, a cold tomato soup made with oil and vinegar, but Andalucíans also love olive-oil fried food, especially seafood. Pigs are reared in the Sierra Nevada and Sierra de Aracena for making exquisite hams. Among local desserts, *tocino de cielo* custards and convent sweets are worth searching out. The region is well known for its **Jerez** or sherry wines, traditionally drunk with tapas.

NEW SPANISH WINES

While Spain's chefs rework regional flavours in their avant-garde dishes, the country's winemakers are turning old grapes into fine wines. Natural growing methods in the vineyards and state-of-the-art bodega techniques have revealed the potential of many overlooked grape varieties. To taste such wines as you travel, look for regional appellations – *denominaciones de origen* (DO) in Spanish – on wine lists. Examples include Bierzo (Castilla León), Bullas (Murcia), Montsant (Catalunya), Ribeira Sacra (Galicia) and Utiel Requena (Valencia), all offering outstanding quality and value. In all, Spain has over 80 DO wines to sample. It is quite possible to plan a holiday around the growing number of wine museums, architect-designed bodegas, vineyard hotels and driving routes.

Spanish History

Modern Spain represents the culmination of centuries of history at the border between Europe and Africa; of political union, exclusion and division. The country's history is a complex one, enlivened by myths and legends, and punctuated by significant historical and cultural landmarks. Today's imprints left by Carthaginian, Roman, Visigothic, Muslim and Christian cultures form a heritage that has made a profound impact on world history. From the flourishing of sciences during seven centuries of Muslim rule; the arts and literature in the Spanish Golden Age; the colonisation and identity of much of Latin America; to the Movida of the 1980s after the dictatorship, Spanish culture and history have combined to create a unique and proud people upon the world stage.

» Key Events p67

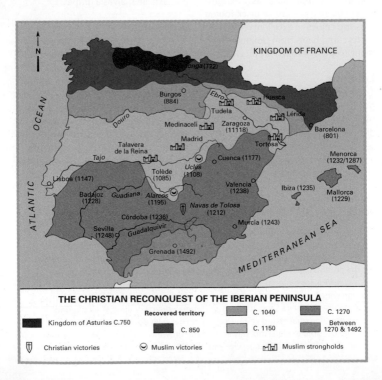

THE CHRISTIAN RECONQUEST OF THE IBERIAN PENINSULA

Recovered territory

Kingdom of Asturias C.750

C. 850

C. 1040

C. 1150

C. 1270

Between 1270 & 1492

Christian victories

Muslim victories

Muslim strongholds

Key Events

Key dates, events, characters, politics, society and cultural shifts in Spain's history: from Antiquity through to the Conquistadors, the Armada, the Civil War, Benidorm's beaches, 20C boom and 21C gloom.

ANTIQUITY TO THE VISIGOTHIC KINGDOM

11–5C	**Phoenician** and **Greek** trading posts founded on the eastern and southern coasts of Spain, inhabited by **Iberians** and **Tartessians** respectively. In the 9C BC, the central-European **Celts** settle in west Spain and on the Meseta, intermingling with the Iberians (forming **Celtiberians**).
3–2C	The **Carthaginians** take over the southeast after conquering the Greeks and Tartessians. The capture of Sagunto by Hannibal leads to the Second Punic War (218–201 BC). Rome expels the Carthaginians and begins the conquest of peninsular Spain (with resistance at **Numancia**).
1C	Cantabria and Asturias are finally pacified in AD 19. Spain is now known as Iberia or Hispania.
	Christianity reaches the Iberian Peninsula and begins to spread.
5C–6C	Early Suevi (**Swabian**) and **Vandal** invasions are followed by those of the **Visigoths** (456), who establish a powerful monarchy with Toledo as capital. The peninsula unites under King Leovigild (569–86).

MUSLIM SPAIN AND THE RECONQUEST

8C	**Moors** invade the Visigothic Kingdom after the **Battle of Guadalete** (711–18). Pelayo's victory at **Covadonga** in 718 heralds an 800-year-long Christian War of Reconquest. The first Muslim invaders are subjects of the Umayyad Caliphate in Damascus.
	Abd al-Rahman I breaks with Damascus by founding an independent emirate at Córdoba in 756.
9C	Settlement of uninhabited lands in north by Christians.
10C	Golden age of the emirate of Córdoba, which is raised to the status of a caliphate (1031) by **Abd ar-Rahman III**. A period of great prosperity ensues during which the expansion of Christian kingdoms is checked. Fortresses are built in the north along the Duero river.
11C	Christian Spain by 1100 includes the Kingdoms of León, Castilla and Navarra and the County of

Barcelona and Valencia. The Caliphate of Córdoba disintegrates into about 20 **taifa city-kingdoms** (1031). Alfonso VI of Castilla conquers Toledo (1085), and the area around the Tajo river is resettled by Christians. The *taifa* kings call upon the **Almoravids** (Saharan Muslims) for assistance and in a short time the tribe overruns a large part of Spain. Pilgrims begin to tread the Camino de Santiago. **El Cid** conquers Valencia (1094).

EL CID

Rodrigo Díaz de Vivar was born to a noble family around 1040 in Vivar, near Burgos. He served under two kings in the Reconquista, during which time he earned the honorific title of "El Campeador" for his forward thinking and leadership which prompted jealousy amongst his peers. He was exiled by King Alfonso VI in 1079 for insubordination. The bloody Christian defeat at the Battle of Sagrajas (1086) prompted King Alfonso to repeal his decision, and El Cid was welcomed back. El Cid then raised an army and beseiged Valencia, finally conquering the city in May 1094. Though officially ruling in the name of King Alfonso, Valencia became his own independent Christian fiefdom. His legend has led him to be considered as Spain's national hero.El Cid has inspired everything from epic poems ("The Song of the Cid") to Hollywood films (*El Cid*, 1961, starring Charlton Heston). His grave now lies as the centrepiece of Burgos Cathedral. Tizona, his legendary sword, can be found at the Museo de Burgos (see p310).

12C	Dissension stemming from a second age of *taifa* kingdoms assists the Reconquest, especially in the Ebro Valley (Zaragoza is taken in 1118, Tortosa in 1148 and Lleida in 1149), but after Yakub al-Mansur's victory in Alarcos (1195), the **Almohads** (who routed the Almoravids) recover Extremadura and check Christian expansion towards the Guadiana and Guadalquivir rivers. Sevilla, with Córdoba under its control, enjoys great prosperity.
	Great military orders are founded (Calatrava, Alcántara and Santiago).
	Dynastic union of kingdom of Aragón and county of Barcelona (1137).
13C	The *taifa* kingdoms enter their third age. The decline of the Muslims begins with the **Battle of Las Navas de Tolosa** (1212). Muslim influence is reduced to the Nasrid Kingdom of Granada (modern provinces of Málaga, Granada and Almería), which holds out until its capture in 1492.
	Castilla and León unified under St Ferdinand III (1230).
	The crown of Aragón under James I the Conqueror (1213–76) gains control over considerable territory in the Mediterranean.

THE CATHOLIC MONARCHS (1474–1516) AND UNIFICATION

1474	Isabella, wife of Ferdinand, succeeds her brother Henry IV to the throne of Castilla. She has to contend with opposition from the supporters of her niece Juana la Beltraneja until 1479.
1478–79	The court of the **Inquisition** is instituted by a special Papal Bull and **Tómas de Torquemada** is later appointed Inquisitor-General. The court, a political and religious institution directed against Jews, Moors and later Protestants, survives until the 19C. Ferdinand becomes King of Aragón in 1479 and Christian Spain is united under Isabella and Ferdinand.
1492	Fall of Granada marks the end of the Reconquest. Expulsion of Jews.
12 Oct 1492	Christopher Columbus lands in the Americas.

1492

If there were only one important date to remember in Spanish history, it would be 1492. That year, after 781 years of Muslim occupation, the Reconquest ended with the fall of Granada on 2 January. This was also the year that the Jews were expelled, the Spaniard Roderic de Borja (Borgia) became Pope Alexander VI and, on 12 October, Christopher Columbus landed in the Americas.

Christopher Columbus (Cristóbal Colón) (1451–1506) and the discovery of America – Born in Genoa, the son of a weaver, Columbus began his seafaring career at an early age. He travelled to Lisbon in 1476 where he developed a passion for map-making on discovering Ptolemy's Geography and Pierre d'Ailly's Imago Mundi. Convinced that the Indies could be reached by sailing west, he submitted a navigation plan to João II of Portugal and to the Kings of France and England. He ultimately managed to gain the support of the Duke of Medinaceli and that of the Prior of the Monasterio de La Rábida, Ximenes de Cisneros, who was Isabel the Catholic's confessor. The Catholic Monarchs agreed to finance his expedition and, if he succeeded, to bestow upon him the hereditary title of Admiral of the Ocean Sea and the viceroyship of any lands discovered.

On 3 August 1492, heading a fleet of three caravels (the *Santa María*, under his command, and the *Pinta* and the *Niña* captained by the Pinzón brothers), he put out from Palos de la Frontera. On 12 October, after a difficult crossing, San Salvador (Bahamas) came into sight and a short time later Hispaniola (Haiti) and Cuba were discovered by the Europeans. On his return to Spain on 15 March 1493, Christopher Columbus was given a triumphant welcome and the means with which to organise new expeditions. This marked the beginning of the Spanish and European colonisation of the New World.

1494	The **Treaty of Tordesillas** divides the New World between Spain and Portugal.
1496	Joanna (Juana), daughter of the Catholic Monarchs, marries Philip the Handsome (Felipe el Hermoso), son of Holy Roman Emperor Maximilian I of the Habsburgs.

| 1504 | Death of Isabella. The kingdom is inherited by her daughter, Joanna (Juana la Loca), but Ferdinand governs as regent until Joanna's son Charles (1500–1558), future Emperor Charles V, comes of age to rule as Charles I. |
| 1512 | The Duke of Alba conquers Navarra, thus bringing territorial unity to Spain. |

THE HABSBURGS (1516–1700) AND AMERICA

1516	**The apogee: Charles I** (1516–56) and **Philip II** (1556–98). On the death of Ferdinand, his grandson becomes Charles I (Carlos I) of Spain. Through his mother, Charles inherits Spain, Naples, Sicily, Sardinia and American territories. Cardinal Cisneros governs until the new king arrives for the first time in Spain in 1517.
1519	On the death of Maximilian of Austria, Charles I is elected Holy Roman Emperor under the name of **Charles V** (Carlos V). He inherits Germany, Austria, the Franche-Comté and the Low Countries.
1520–22	The Spanish, incensed by Charles V's largely Flemish court advisers and the increasing number of taxes, rise up in arms. The emperor quells **Comuneros** and **Germanías** revolts.
1521–56	Charles V wages five wars against France in order to secure complete control of Europe. In the first four he conquers Francis I (imprisoned at Pavia in 1525) and in the fifth he routs the new French king, Henri II, and captures Milan.
	The Conquistadores move across America. **Vasco Núñez de Balboa** discovers the Pacific; **Hernan Cortés** seizes Mexico in 1521; **Francisco Pizarro** and **Diego de Almagro** subdue Peru in 1533; **Francisco Coronado** explores the Colorado river in 1535; **Hernando de Soto** takes possession of Florida in 1539; and **Pedro de Valdivia** founds Santiago de Chile in 1541.
1555	Charles V signs the Peace of Augsburg with the Protestants in Germany after failing to suppress the Reformation.
1556	Charles V abdicates in favour of his son and retires to a monastery in Yuste. **Philip II** becomes king, inheriting Spain and its colonies, the kingdom of Naples, Milan, the Low Countries and the Franche-Comté, but not Germany and Austria, which are left by Charles to his brother Ferdinand I of Austria. Philip II turns his attention to Spain and the defence of Catholicism. He chooses Madrid as his de facto capital in 1561. Spain goes through a serious economic crisis.

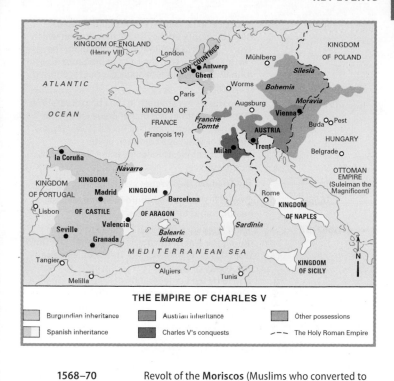

THE EMPIRE OF CHARLES V

- Burgundian inheritance
- Spanish inheritance
- Austrian inheritance
- Charles V's conquests
- Other possessions
- – – – The Holy Roman Empire

1568–70	Revolt of the **Moriscos** (Muslims who converted to Christianity) in Granada.
1571	The Turks are defeated in the **Battle of Lepanto** by a fleet of ships sent by the Pope, the Venetians and the Spanish, under the command of **Don John of Austria**, the king's natural brother. The victory seals Spain's mastery of the Mediterranean.
1580	The King of Portugal dies without an heir. Philip II asserts his rights, invades Portugal and is proclaimed king in 1581.
1588	Philip II sends the **Invincible Armada** against Protestant England, which supports the Low Countries. The destruction of the fleet marks the end of Spain as a sea power.
1598	Philip II dies, leaving a vast kingdom which, in spite of huge wealth from the Americas, is crippled by debt after 70 years of almost incessant war and monumental building projects like El Escorial.
1598–1621	**The decline** – The last Habsburgs, **Philip III** (Felipe III, 1598–1621), **Philip IV** (Felipe IV, 1621–65) and **Charles II** (Carlos II, 1665–1700), struggle to maintain the kingdom. Paradoxically, Spain enjoys its **Golden Age** of art and culture. Philip III entrusts the affairs of state to the **Duke of Lerma**, who advises him to expel the Moriscos in 1609. By 1614, 300,000 Moriscos leave Spain with disastrous consequences for agriculture.

1640	Under Philip IV (Felipe IV), the Count-Duke of Olivares adopts a policy of decentralisation which spurs Catalunya and Portugal to rebellion. The Portuguese proclaim the Duke of Braganza King John IV, but their independence is not recognised until 1668.
1618–48	Spain wastes her strength in the **Thirty Years' War**. In spite of victories like that of Breda (1624), the defeat in the Netherlands at Rocroi (1643) signals the end of Spain as a European power. The **Treaty of Westphalia** gives the Netherlands independence.
1659	The **Treaty of the Pyrenees** ends war with France.
1665	Charles II, the final Habsburg monarch, of poor health, comes to the throne.
1667–97	Spain loses strongholds in Flanders to France during the **War of Devolution** (1667–68). The Dutch Wars (1672–78) end with the **Treaty of Nijmegen**. The **Treaty of Ryswick** (1697) concludes the war waged by the Confederation of Augsburg (Spain is a member) against France (1688–97).

THE BOURBONS, NAPOLEON AND WAR OF INDEPENDENCE (1808–14)

1700	Charles II dies without issue. He wills the crown to Philip, Duke of Anjou, grandson of his sister María Teresa and Louis XIV. Emperor Leopold, who had renounced his rights to the Spanish throne in favour of his son, the Archduke Charles of Austria, is displeased.
1702–14	**War of the Spanish Succession** – England, the Netherlands, Denmark and Germany support the Archduke of Austria against France and Philip of Anjou. Catalan, Valencian and Aragonese cities side with the Archduke and war spreads throughout Spain (1705). By the **Treaty of Utrecht (1713) ending the War**, Spain cedes Gibraltar and Menorca (taken by the English) and many of her Italian possessions to Austria. **Philip V** (Felipe V) is proclaimed King of Spain (1683–1746).
1759–88	The reign of **Charles III** (Carlos III), an enlightened despot, is the most brilliant of the Bourbon dynasty. He is assisted by competent ministers (Floridablanca and Aranda) who draw up important economic reforms. Expulsion of the Jesuits from Spain and its empire in 1767.
1788	**Charles IV** (Carlos IV) succeeds to the throne. The country is largely governed by his wife María Luisa and her favourite, Manuel de Godoy.
1793	On the death of Louis XVI, Spain declares war on France (then in the throes of the Revolution).

1796–1805	Spain signs an alliance with the French Directorate against England (Second **Treaty of San Ildefonso**, 1796). **Napoleon** enters Spain with his troops on the pretext that he is going to attack Portugal. The renewed offensive against England in 1804 ends disastrously with the **Battle of Trafalgar** the following year.
1805–08	Napoleon takes advantage of the disagreement between Charles IV and his son Ferdinand to engineer Charles IV's abdication.
2 May 1808	The Madrid uprising against French troops marks the beginning of the **War of Independence** (The **Peninsular War**), which lasts until Napoleon is exiled by Wellington in 1814. During the war Napoleon's brother, Joseph, rules Spain while provincial Juntas defend Ferdinand VII's rights, supported by British and Portuguese forces. Battles at Bailén (1808), Madrid, Zaragoza and Girona.
1812	The French are routed by Wellington in the Arapiles Valley; King Joseph flees from Madrid. Valencia is taken by the French General Suchet. Spanish patriots convene the **Cortes** (parliament) and draw up the liberal **Constitution of Cádiz.**
1813–14	Anglo-Spanish forces expel Napoleon after successive victories. **Ferdinand VII** (Fernando VII) returns to Spain, repeals the Constitution of Cádiz and so reigns as an absolute monarch until 1820. Meanwhile, the Latin American colonies struggle for independence.

THE DISTURBANCES OF THE 19C

1820–23	The liberals oppose the king's absolute rule but their uprisings are all severely quelled. The 1812 constitution is reinstated after a liberal revolt led by **General Riego** in Cádiz in 1820, but only for three years. In 1823 Ferdinand VII appeals to Europe for assistance and 100 000 Frenchmen are sent in the name of St Louis to re-establish absolute rule (which lasts until 1833).
1833–39	On the death of his brother Ferdinand VII, Don Carlos disputes the right to the throne of his niece Isabel II, daughter of the late king and **Queen María Cristina**. She comes to the throne. The traditionalist **Carlists** fight Isabel's supporters, who win the **First Carlist War** (Convention of Vergara 1839). In 1835, the new prime minister **Mendizábel** has a series of decrees passed which approve sale of church and religious orders' lands (*desamortización*).

1840	A revolutionary junta forces the regent María Cristina into exile. She is replaced by General Espartero.
1843–68	Queen Isabel II comes of age. The **Narváez** moderate uprising forces Espartero to flee. A new constitution is drawn up in 1845. The **Second Carlist War** (1847–49) ends in victory for Isabel II but her reign is troubled by uprisings on behalf of progressives and moderates, one of which, the 1868 revolt led by General Prim, puts an end to her reign. Isabel leaves for France and General Serrano is appointed leader of the provisional government.
1869	The Cortes passes a progressive constitution with universal male suffrage and a monarchy. Amadeo of Savoy is elected king.
1873	**The Third Carlist War** (1872–76). The king abdicates on finding himself unable to keep the peace. The National Assembly proclaims the **First Spanish Republic**.
1874	Brigadier Martínez Campos leads a revolt. The head of the government, Cánovas de Castillo, proclaims Isabel's son **Alfonso XII** King of Spain. The Bourbon Restoration and 1876 constitution open a long period of peace.
1885	Death of Alfonso XII (at 28). His widow María Cristina (who is expecting a baby) becomes regent.
1898	Cuba and the Philippines rise up with disastrous losses for Spain.
	The United States, which supports the rebel colonies, occupies Puerto Rico and the Philippines, marking the **end of the Spanish Empire**.
1902	**Alfonso XIII** (born after the death of his father Alfonso XII) assumes the throne at 16.

THE FALL OF THE MONARCHY AND THE SECOND REPUBLIC (1931–36)

1914–18	Spain remains neutral throughout the **First World War**. A general strike in 1919 is severely put down.
1921	Insurrection in Morocco; General Sanjurjo occupies the north (1927).
1923	General **Miguel Primo de Rivera** abolishes the 1876 constitution and establishes a military dictatorship with the king's approval. Order and economic growth are restored, but opposition increases among the working classes.
1930	In the face of hostility from the masses, Primo de Rivera is forced into exile.
1931	April municipal elections bring victory to the Republicans in Catalunya, the País Vasco, La Rioja and the Aragonese province of Huesca. The king

	abdicates. The Second Republic is proclaimed and Generalitat of Catalunya created.
Jun 1931	A constituent Cortes is elected with a socialist Republican majority; a Constitution is promulgated in December. Agrarian reforms, such as compulsory purchase of large properties, meet strong right-wing opposition.
1933	The **Falange Party**, which opposes regional separation, is founded by **José Antonio Primo de Rivera**, son of the dictator. The right wins general elections.
Oct 1934	**Catalunya proclaims its autonomy**. Miners in Asturias spark a revolt against the government and are brutally repressed.
Feb 1936	The **Popular Front** wins general elections and in May Azaña becomes President of the Republic.

THE CIVIL WAR (1936–39)

17 Jul 1936	The **Melilla uprising** triggers the **Civil War**. The army takes control and puts an end to the Second Republic.
	Nationalist troops based in Morocco and led by General **Franco** cross the Straits of Gibraltar and make their way to Toledo, which is taken at the end of September. Franco is proclaimed Generalísimo of the armed forces and Head of State in Burgos. Nationalists lead an unsuccessful attack against Madrid.
	While Madrid, Catalunya and Valencia remain faithful to the Republicans, the Conservative agricultural regions – Andalucía, Castilla and Galicia – are rapidly controlled by the Nationalists. These regions out-supply the Republicans and the Republicans themselves are torn by dissension between the Anarchist CNT party, the Communist PCE and the Marxist POUM. They do, however, receive assistance from International Brigades.
1937	Industrial towns in the north are taken by Nationalist supporters in the summer (on 26 April, Gernika is bombed by German planes). The Republican Government is moved to Barcelona in November. In the battle of Teruel in December, the Republicans try to breach the Nationalist front in Aragón and thereby relieve surrounded Catalunya. Teruel is taken by the Republicans and recaptured by the Nationalists soon after.
1938	The Nationalist army reaches the Mediterranean, dividing Republican territory into two parts. The **Battle of the Ebro** lasts from July to November: Franco launches an offensive against Catalunya, which is occupied by the Nationalists in February 1939.
1 Apr 1939	The Spanish Civil War ends with the capture of Madrid.

THE FRANCO ERA

1939–49	Spain is declared a monarchy with Franco as regent and Head of State, and declares itself neutral in the Second World War. UN diplomatic boycott of Spain (1946).
1952	Spain joins UNESCO.
1955	Spain readmitted to the United Nations.
1959	Spanish entry visas abolished
1960	500 % increase in visitor arrivals in Spain. The *boom turistico* begins and helps to bring a degree of prosperity to what is still, thanks to Franco, a pariah state within Europe.
1964	The Spanish national football team win the European Championship.
1969	Prince Juan Carlos is named as Franco's successor.
20 Dec 1973	Prime Minister Carrero Blanco is assassinated.
20 Nov 1975	Death of Franco. **Juan Carlos I** becomes King.

DEMOCRACY

1977	General elections – **Adolfo Suárez** is elected prime minister.
1978	A new constitution is passed by referendum. Statutes of autonomy are approved for Catalunya, the País Vasco (Euskadi) and Galicia.
1981–82	Suárez resigns. An attempted military coup takes place on 23 February 1981. **Felipe González** becomes prime minister after the Socialist Party wins election.
1 Jan 1986	Spain joins the **European Economic Community**.
1992	Barcelona hosts the **Olympics**. The event is used to gentrify parts of the city, reclaim the port area, and to improve the infrastructure to attract visitors. Sevilla hosts Expo, and also boosts its visitor credentials. Madrid becomes a Cultural Capital of Europe.
1996	**José María Aznar** of the Popular Party becomes prime minister.
1997	The Guggenheim Museum Bilbao opens.
2000	Santiago de Compostela is European Capital of Culture.
2002	Spain adopts the **Euro**.
11 Mar 2004	The **Madrid train bombings** by terrorists leave 191 dead and 1 500 injured.
14 Mar 2004	**José Luis Rodríguez Zapatero** of the Socialist Party becomes prime minister.

22 May 2004	The Prince of Asturias, Felipe, heir to the Spanish crown, marries Letizia Ortiz Rocasolano, a journalist and divorcée.
2007	Spain becomes the second most visited country in the world (after France), receiving almost 60 million foreign tourists.
2008	Prime Minister Zapatero is re-elected. The property bubble bursts and the economy begins heading into recession (confirmed Feb 2009). The Spanish national football team claim their first major title for 44 years by winning the European Championship.
Jul 2010	Spain confirm their football preeminence by winning the World Cup. Rafael Nadal makes it a glorious summer sporting Spanish double in the same month by winning Wimbledon, and ends the year ranked as the world's number one tennis player.
2010	Unemployment in Spain is now the highest in the EU at over 20%.
Dec 2011	A new government headed by Mariano Rajoy takes office and announces a new round of austerity measures to slash public spending by 16.5bn euros in order to nearly halve the public deficit.
Jun 2012	Spain formally requests assistance from Eurozone Financial Stability funds in order to bail out its struggling bank sector.
Jul 2012	The Spanish football team provides some respite from the daily news of the beleaguered economy by becoming the first team to ever retain the European Championship.
Apr 2013	Against a backdrop of the declining popularity of the Spanish royal family, King Juan Carlos's youngest daughter, Princess Cristina, is summoned to appear in court to answer questions on the financial affairs of her husband, the Duke of Palma (suspended in Dec 2012 from all official royal engagements following allegations of involvement in a corruption scandal).
Apr 2014	Unemployment climbs to 26 per cent, with youth (under-25s) unemployment approaching a staggering 56.1 per cent. Both statistics are the highest in the Eurozone.
Jun 2014	King Juan Carlos abdicates and his son, Felipe, becomes the new monarch, King Felipe VI.
Sept 2015	Separatist parties win the majority of seats in the Catalonian parliament elections.
Dec 2015	The general election results in a hung parliament.
2016	Donostia-San Sebastián is European Capital of Culture.
Oct-Dec 2017	The Catalan regional government's declaration of independence is quashed. In a hastily called regional election seperatist parties obtain a majority.

Spanish Art and Culture

Over the centuries, Spain has amassed a horde of artistic and architectural treasures. They range from diminutive Romanesque chapels, lofty Gothic cathedrals and exuberant Baroque churches to awe-inspiring Hispano-Arab monuments, imposing castles, magnificent paintings and outstanding modern architecture.

Trascoro by Bartolomé Ordóñez,
Barcelona Cathedral
© Yann Guichaoua/Travel Pictures

Prehistory to the Muslim Conquest

The earliest inhabitants of Spain probably walked here from Africa, then linked by land to Iberia across the modern-day Straits of Gibraltar. Deer, bison and wild horses arrived with them; their images remain today.

PREHISTORIC ART

Prehistoric inhabitants of the Iberian Peninsula have left some outstanding examples of their art. The oldest European hominid settlements are at Atapuerca, in Burgos (850 780,000 BC) but the earliest cave paintings are Upper Palaeolithic (40 000–10 000 BC) in Cantabria (Altamira and Puente Viesgo), Asturias (El Pindal, Ribadesella and San Román) and the Levante region (Cogull and Alpera). Megalithic monuments like the famous Antequera dolmens were erected during the Neolithic Era (7500–2500 BC), or New Stone Age, while in the Balearic Islands stone monuments known as **talaiots** and *navetas* were built by a Bronze Age people (2500–1000 BC).

FIRST MILLENNIUM BC

Iberian civilisations produced gold and silverware treasures (Villena in its town museum and Carambolo in Sevilla's Museo Arqueológico), and fine sculpture. Some of their work, such as the Córdoba lions, the Guisando bulls and, in the Museo Arqueológico in Madrid, the *Dama de Baza* and the *Dama de Elche*, influenced 20th-century art. Meanwhile, Phoenician, Carthaginian and Greek colonisers introduced their native art: Phoenician sarcophagi in Cádiz, Punic art in Ibiza and Cartagena, Greek art in Empúries.

ROMAN SPAIN (1C BC–5C AD)

Besides roads, bridges, aqueducts, towns and monuments, Roman legacies include the Mérida theatre, the ancient towns of Italica and Empúries, the Segovia aqueduct, Tarragona's magnificent Circus and Alcalá de Henares's Forum.

THE VISIGOTHS (6C–8C)

Christian **Visigoths** built small stone churches (Quintanilla de las Viñas, San Pedro de la Nave) adorned with friezes carved in geometric patterns with plant motifs. The apsidal plan was square and the arches were often horseshoe-shaped. The Visigoths were outstanding gold and silversmiths who made sumptuous jewellery in the Byzantine and Germanic traditions. Gold votive crowns (Guarrazar treasure in Toledo), fibulae and belt buckles adorned with precious stones, or *cloisonné* enamel, were presented to churches or placed in the tombs of the great.

Dama de Elche

©Photooliassor/Dreamstime.com

79

Hispano-Arabic style (8–15C)

The three major periods of Hispano-Arabic architecture correspond to the reigns of successive Arab dynasties over the Muslim-held territories in the peninsula. Each has left a spectacular and exotic legacy.

CALIPHATE OR CÓRDOBA ARCHITECTURE (8C–11C)

This period is characterised by three types of building: **mosques**, built to a simple plan consisting of a minaret, a courtyard with a pool for ritual ablutions and finally a square prayer room with a mihrab (prayer-niche marking the direction of Mecca); **alcázares** (palaces), built around attractive patios and surrounded by gardens and fountains; and **alcazabas** (castle fortresses), built on high ground and surrounded by several walls crowned with pointed merlons – one of the best examples of these can be found in Málaga. The most famous monuments from this period are in Córdoba (the Mezquita and the Medina Azahara palace) and in Toledo (Cristo de la Luz) where, besides the ubiquitous horseshoe arch which virtually became the hallmark of Moorish architecture, other characteristics developed including ornamental brickwork

in relief, cupolas supported on ribs, turned modillions, arches with alternating white stone and red-brick voussoirs, **multifoil arches** (*see illustration*) and doors surmounted with blind arcades. These features became popular in Mudéjar and Romanesque churches. The Umayyads brought a taste for profuse decoration from Syria. As the Koran forbids the representation of human or animal forms, Muslim decoration is based on calligraphy (Cufic inscriptions running along walls), geometric patterns (polygons and stars made of ornamental brickwork and marble), and lastly plant motifs (flowerets and interlacing palm leaves).

ALMOHAD OR SEVILLA ARCHITECTURE (12C–13C)

The religious puritanism of the **Almohad dynasty**, of which **Sevilla** was the capital, was expressed in architecture by a refined, though sometimes rather austere, simplicity. One of the characteristics of the style consisted of brickwork highlighted by wide bands of decoration in relief, without excessive ornamentation (the Giralda tower in Sevilla is a good example).

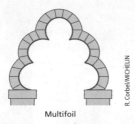

Multifoil

R. Corbel/MICHELIN

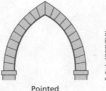

Pointed

R. Corbel/MICHELIN

THE DECORATIVE ARTS

Extremely rich and varied decorative artefacts from the Almohad period include geometric wood strapwork, brocades, weapons, ceramics with *esgrafiado* decoration and small ivory chests.

GRANADA – La Alhambra (14C)

Mocárabes:
decorative motifs of Muslim architecture formed by assembled prisms ending in concave surfaces. Used to adorn vaults, arches and cornices

A panel of **azulejos** with epigraphic and geometric decoration

H. Choimet/MICHELIN

The style was later used in the Mudéjar architecture of Aragón. Other features that emerged at this time include *artesonado* ceilings and *azulejos*. Arches of alternate brick and stonework disappeared, the horseshoe arch became **pointed** and the multifoil arch was bordered by a curvilinear festoon (ornament like a garland) as in the Aljafería in Zaragoza. Calligraphic decoration included cursive (flowing) as well as Cufic script to which floral motifs were added to fill the spaces between vertical lines.

NASRID OR GRANADA ARCHITECTURE (14C–15C)

This period of high sophistication, of which the **Alhambra** in Granada (🔍*see illustration*) is the masterpiece, produced less innovation in actual architectural design than in the decoration, whether stucco or ceramic, that covered the walls. Surrounds to doors and windows became focal points for every room's design and the spaces between them were filled by perfectly proportioned panels. Arch outlines were simplified – the stilted round arch became widespread – while detailed lacework ornamentation was used as a border.

MUDÉJAR ARCHITECTURE

This is the name given to work carried out in the Muslim style, usually by Muslim artesans, for Christian clients. It was fashionable from the 11C to the 15C in different regions depending on the area recovered by the Reconquest, although some features, like *artesonado* ceilings, continued as decorative themes for centuries.

Court Mudéjar, developed by Muslim artists (in buildings ordered by Peter the Cruel in Tordesillas and Sevilla, and in synagogues in Toledo), was an extension of the Almohad or contemporary Nasrid style. Popular Mudéjar, on the other hand, was produced by local Muslim workshops and reflects marked regional taste: walls were decorated with blind arcades in Castilla (Arévalo, Sahagún and Toledo) and belfries were faced with *azulejos* (🔍*see illustration*) and geometric strapwork in Aragón.

Pre-Romanesque and Romanesque (8–13C)

Thanks to a number of influences, not least the Reconquest and the establishment of the Camino de Santiago, Spain is blessed with some of Europe's finest surviving Romanesque religious art and architecture.

ASTURIAN ARCHITECTURE

A highly sophisticated style of court architecture, characterised by sweeps of ascending lines, developed in the small kingdom of Asturias between the 8C and the 10C.

Asturian churches (Naranco, Santa Cristina de Lena) followed the precepts of the Latin basilica in their rectangular plan with a narthex, a nave and two aisles separated by **semicircular arches** (◔see illustration), a vast transept and an east end divided into three.

Decoration inside consisted of frescoes and borrowings from the East, including motifs carved on **capitals** (strapwork, rosettes and monsters, ◔see illustration) and ornamental openwork around windows. Gold and silversmiths in the 9C and 10C produced rich treasures, many of which may be seen in the Cámara Santa in Oviedo Cathedral.

MOZARABIC STYLE

This term is given to work carried out by Christians living under Arab rule after the Moorish invasion of 711. Churches built in this style, especially in Castilla (San Miguel de Escalada, San Millán de la Cogolla), brought back Visigothic traditions (horseshoe arches) enriched by Moorish features such as ribbed cupolas and turned modillions.

Illuminated manuscripts provide the earliest known examples of Spanish medieval painting (10C). They were executed in the 10C and 11C by Mozarabic monks and have Moorish features such as horseshoe arches and Arab costumes. They portray St John's Commentary on the Apocalypse written in the 8C by the monk **Beatus de Liébana**.

CATALUNYA, HOME OF THE ROMANESQUE

Catalunya had intimate links with Italy and France and consequently developed an architectural style strongly influenced by Lombardy from the 11C to the 13C. This evolved in the Pyrenean valleys, isolated from the more travelled pilgrim and trade routes. Sober little churches were often completed by a separate bell tower decorated with Lombard bands. Interior walls in the 11C and 12C were only embellished with frescoes which, in spite of their borrowings from Byzantine mosaics (heavy black outlines, rigid postures, and themes like Christ in Glory portrayed within a mandorla), proved by their realistic and expressive details to be typically Spanish. Wooden altar fronts, painted in bright colours, followed the same themes and layout.

THE PILGRIM ROUTES

Northwest Spain opened its gates to foreign influence during the reign of Sancho the Great early in the 11C. Cistercian abbeys were founded and French merchants allowed to settle rate free in towns (Estella, Sangüesa, Pamplona…). Meanwhile, the surge of pilgrims to Compostela and the fever to build along

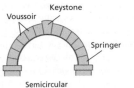

Keystone

Voussoir

Springer

Semicircular

R. Corbel/MICHELIN

Romanesque

SANTIAGO DE COMPOSTELA – Cathedral: Interior (11C-13C)

Santiago cathedral is a typical example of a Spanish pilgrimage church and shows clear French influence.

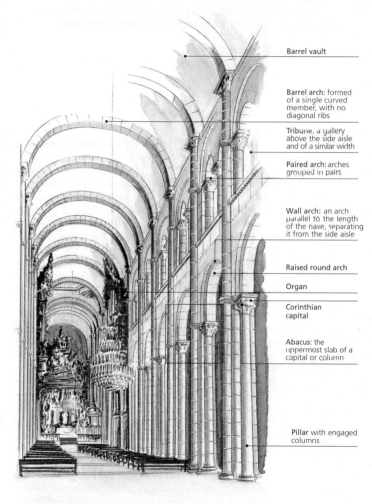

Barrel vault

Barrel arch: formed of a single curved member, with no diagonal ribs

Tribune: a gallery above the side aisle and of a similar width

Paired arch: arches grouped in pairs

Wall arch: an arch parallel to the length of the nave, separating it from the side aisle

Raised round arch

Organ

Corinthian capital

Abacus: the uppermost slab of a capital or column

Pillar with engaged columns

H. Choimet/MICHELIN

the routes brought about the construction of a great many religious buildings in which French influence was clearly marked, most notably the Cathedral of Santiago de Compostela.

In Aragón, Romanesque art was particularly evident in sculpture. In the early 12C, reform of the **Cistercian Order** with emphasis on austerity brought an important change to architecture. The transitional style which heralded the Gothic (intersecting ribbed vaulting, squared apses) was introduced and the profusion of Romanesque decoration disappeared, as may be seen in the monasteries of Poblet, Santes Creus, La Oliva and Santa María de Huerta.

Gothic Period (from the 13C)

Many of Spain's most impressive buildings – its mighty cathedrals, churches, monasteries, trade exchanges – date from this period and remain atmospheric reminders of the country's great medieval past.

THE EARLY STAGES

French Gothic architecture made little headway into Spain except in Navarra where a French dynasty had been in power since 1234.

The first truly Gothic buildings (Roncesvalles church, Cuenca and Sigüenza cathedrals) were constructed in the 13C. Bishops in some of the main towns in Castilla (**León** (*see illustration*), Burgos, Toledo) sent abroad for cathedral plans, artists and masons. An original style of church, with no transept, a single nave (aisles, if there were any, would be as high as the nave), and pointed stone arches or a wooden roof resting on diaphragm arches, developed in **Valencia**, **Catalunya** and the **Balearic Islands**. The unadorned walls enclosed a large, homogeneous space in which there was little carved decoration, and purity of line supplied a dignified elegance.

Civil architecture followed the same pattern and had the same geometrical sense of space, used with rare skill particularly in the *lonjas* or commodity exchanges of Barcelona, Palma, Valencia and Zaragoza.

THE GOTHIC STYLE DEVELOPS

During the 14C and 15C in Castilla, the influence of artists from the north, such as **Johan of Cologne** and **Hanequin of Brussels**, brought about the flowering of a style approaching Flamboyant Gothic. As it adapted to Spain, the style developed simultaneously in two different ways: in one, decoration proliferated to produce the Isabelline style; in the other, structures were simplified into a national church and cathedral style, which remained in favour until the mid-16C (Segovia and **Salamanca**, *see illustration*).

THE LAST OF THE GOTHIC CATHEDRALS

Following the example of Sevilla, the dimensions of Gothic cathedrals became ever more vast. Aisles almost as large as the nave increased the volume of the building, while pillars, though massive, retained the impression of thrusting upward lines. A new plan emerged in which the old crescendo of radiating chapels, ambulatory, chancel and transept was superseded by a plain rectangle. Gothic decoration accumulated around doors, on pinnacles and in elaborate star vaulting; a style echoed in some Andalucían cathedrals.

PAINTING

Artists in the Gothic era worked on polyptyches and altarpieces which sometimes reached a height of more than 15m/49ft. The Primitives, who customarily painted on gold backgrounds, were influenced by the Italians (soft contours), the French and the Flemish (rich fabrics with broken folds and painstaking detail). Nonetheless, as they strove for expressive naturalism and lively anecdotal detail, their work came across as distinctively Spanish.

There was intense artistic activity in the states attached to the Crown of Aragón, especially in Catalunya. The Vic, Barcelona and Valencia museums contain works by **Jaume Ferrer Bassá** (1285–1348) who was influenced by the Sienese **Duccio**, paintings by his successor **Ramón Destorrents** (1346–91), and by the **Serra** brothers, Destorrents' pupils. Among other artists were **Luis Borrassá** (c. 1360–c. 1425), who had a very Span-

Gothic

LEÓN – Cathedral: side façade (13C-14C)

In Gothic architecture, light was considered the essence of beauty and the symbol of truth. León cathedral is the brightest and most delicate of all the major Spanish cathedrals and is viewed as the best example of this concept. The beauty and magnificence of its stained glass attracts the admiration of its many thousands of visitors every year. French influence is clearly evident in its ground plan (Reims) and sculptures (Chartres).

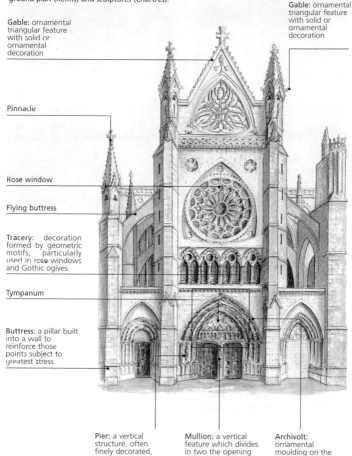

Gable: ornamental triangular feature with solid or ornamental decoration

Gable: ornamental triangular feature with solid or ornamental decoration

Pinnacle

Rose window

Flying buttress

Tracery: decoration formed by geometric motifs, particularly used in rose windows and Gothic ogives

Tympanum

Buttress: a pillar built into a wall to reinforce those points subject to greatest stress

Pier: a vertical structure, often finely decorated, supporting a door or a wall

Mullion: a vertical feature which divides in two the opening or span of a portal or window

Archivolt: ornamental moulding on the outer edge of an arch

F. Choimet/MICHELIN

ish sense of the picturesque, **Bernat Martorell**, who gave special importance to landscape, **Jaime Huguet** (1412–92), who stands out for his extreme sensitivity and is considered to be the undisputed leader of the Catalan School, and finally **Luis Dalmau** and **Bartolomé Bermejo** (c. 1440–c. 1498), both influenced by Van Eyck (who accompanied a mission sent to Spain by the Duke of Burgundy).

In Castilla, French influence predominated in the 14C and Italian in the 15C until about 1450 when Flemish artists like **Roger van der Weyden** arrived. By the end of the 15C, **Fernando Gallego** (c.1440-1507) had become the main figure in the Hispano-Flemish movement in which **Juan de Flandes** was noted for his delicate touch.

Detail, Nativity and Saint John the Evangelist *(1407-1411)* by *Guerau Gener and Lluís Borrassà, Museu Nacional d'Art de Catalunya, Barcelona*

© Museu Nacional d'Art de Catalunya (MNAC)

Sculpture

Gothic sculpture, like architecture, became more refined. Relief was more accentuated than in Romanesque carving, postures more natural and details more meticulous. Decoration grew increasingly abundant as the 15C progressed and faces became individualised to the point where recumbent funerary statues clearly resembled the deceased. Statues were surmounted by an openwork canopy, while door surrounds, cornices and capitals were decorated with friezes of intricate plant motifs. After being enriched by French influence in the 13C and 14C and Flemish in the 15C, sculpture ultimately developed a purely Spanish style, the **Isabelline**. Portals showed a French influence. Tombs were at first sarcophagi decorated with coats of arms, sometimes surmounted by a recumbent statue in a conventional posture with a peaceful expression and hands joined. Later, more attention was paid to the costume of the deceased; with an increasingly honed technique marble craftsmen were able to render the richness of brocades and the supple quality of leather. In the 15C, sculptors produced lifelike figures in natural positions, kneeling for instance, or even in nonchalant attitudes like that of the remarkable Doncel in Sigüenza Cathedral.

Altarpieces comprised a predella or plinth, surmounted by several levels of panels and finally by a carved openwork canopy. Choir stalls were adorned with biblical and historical scenes or carved to resemble delicate stone tracery.

The Isabelline style

At the end of the 15C, the prestige surrounding the royal couple and the grandees in the reign of Isabel the Catholic (1474–1504) provided a favourable context for the emergence of a new style in which exuberant decoration covered entire façades of civil and religious buildings.

Ornamentation took the form of supple free arcs, lace-like carving, heraldic motifs and every fantasy that imagination could devise. The diversity of inspiration was largely due to foreign artists: **Simon of Cologne** (son of Johan) – San Pablo in Valladolid, Capilla del Condestable in Burgos; **Juan Guas** (son of the Frenchman Pierre) – San Juan de los Reyes in Toledo; and **Enrique Egas** (nephew of Hanequin of Brussels) – Capilla Real in Granada.

Renaissance (16C)

I n the 16C, at the dawn of its Golden Age, Spain was swept by a deep sense of its own national character and so created a style in which Italian influence became acceptable only when Hispanicised.

ARCHITECTURE

Plateresque was the name given to the early Renaissance style because of its fine and lavish decoration reminiscent of silverwork (*platero*: silversmith).

Although close to the Isabelline style in its profusion of carved forms extending over entire façades, the rounded arches and ornamental themes (grotesques, foliage, pilasters, medallions and cornices) were Italian. The Plateresque style was brought to a climax in **Salamanca** in the **façade of the Universidad** (👉 *see illustration)* and that of the Convento de San Esteban. Among architects of the time were **Rodrigo Gil de Hontañón**, who worked at Salamanca (Palacios de Monterrey and Fonseca) and at Alcalá de Henares (university façade), and **Diego de Siloé**, the main architect in Burgos (Escalera de la Coronería). Together with **Alonso de Covarrubias** (1488–1570), who worked mainly in Toledo (Alcázar and Capilla de los Reyes Nuevos in the cathedral), Diego de Siloé marked the transition from the Plateresque style to the Classical Renaissance. **Andrés de Vandelvira** (1509–75) was the leading architect of the Andalucían Renaissance (Jaén Cathedral). His work introduces the

Renaissance

TOLEDO - Hospital Tavera: patio (16C)

The sense of proportion, visible on both the ground and first floors surrounding the double patio of this hospital, is a typical feature of pure Renaissance style.

Triglyph: three vertical bands separated by V-shaped grooves (characteristic of Doric frieze)

Spandrel or pendentive decorated with a rosette

Arris vault

Ionic column

Balustrade

Shaft

Base

Doric column

Superimposing of orders according to a classical plan (Doric on the lower gallery, Ionic on the upper gallery)

Metope: the triglyphs alternate with plain or sculpted panels

H. Choimet/MICHELIN

austerity which was to characterise the works of the last quarter of the century. The Renaissance style drew upon Italian models and adopted features from classical architecture such as rounded arches, columns, entablatures and pediments. Decoration became of secondary importance after architectonic perfection. **Pedro Machuca** (c. 1490–1550), who studied under Michelangelo, designed the palace of Charles V in Granada, the most classical example of the Italian tradition. Another important figure, **Bartolomé Bustamante** (1500–70), built the **Hospital de Tavera** in **Toledo** (*see illustration*).

The greatest figure of Spanish Classicism was **Juan de Herrera** (1530–93), who gave his name to an architectural style characterised by grandeur and austerity. He was the favourite architect of Philip II. The king saw in his work the sobriety that suited the Counter-Reformation and in 1567 entrusted him with the task of continuing work on El Escorial, his greatest achievement.

SCULPTURE

Sculpture in Spain reached its climax during the Renaissance. In the 16C, a great many choir stalls, mausoleums and **altarpieces** (also known as **retables**) were still being made of alabaster and wood. These latter were then painted by the *estofado* technique in which gold leaf is first applied, then the object is coloured and finally delicately scored to produce gold highlights. Carved altarpiece (*retablo*) panels were framed by Corinthian architraves (epistyles) and pilasters.

The sculptures of **Damián Forment** (c. 1480–1540), who worked mainly in Aragón, belong to the transition period between Gothic and Renaissance styles. The Burgundian **Felipe Vigarny** (c. 1475–1542) and the architect **Diego de Siloé**, who was apprenticed in Naples, both worked on Burgos Cathedral. **Bartolomé Ordóñez** (c. 1480–1520) studied in Naples and carved the *trascoro* (choir screen) in **Barcelona Cathedral** and the mausoleums of Joanna the Mad,

Plateresque

SALAMANCA – University: façade (16C)

Although the exuberant decoration used to cover the entire façade is somewhat Gothic in style, the motifs used are Classical.

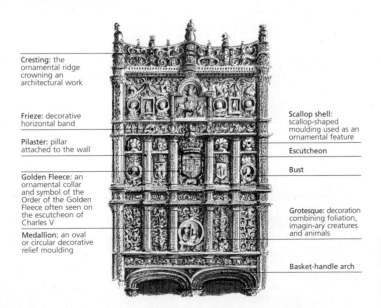

Cresting: the ornamental ridge crowning an architectural work

Frieze: decorative horizontal band

Pilaster: pillar attached to the wall

Golden Fleece: an ornamental collar and symbol of the Order of the Golden Fleece often seen on the escutcheon of Charles V

Medallion: an oval or circular decorative relief moulding

Scallop shell: scallop-shaped moulding used as an ornamental feature

Escutcheon

Bust

Grotesque: decoration combining foliation, imaginary creatures and animals

Basket-handle arch

H. Choimet/MICHELIN

Philip the Handsome (Capilla Real in Granada) and Cardinal Cisneros (Alcalá de Henares).

The home of the Renaissance School moved from Burgos to Valladolid in the mid-16C, by which time the Spanish style had absorbed foreign influences and Spain's two great Renaissance sculptors had emerged. The first, **Alonso Berruguete** (c. 1488–1561), who studied in Italy under Michelangelo, had a style which drew closely on the Florentine Renaissance and reflected a strong personality. He sought strength of expression rather than formal beauty and his tormented, fiery human forms are as powerful as those of his master (statue of San Sebastián in the Museo de Valladolid). The second, **Juan de Juni** (c. 1507–77), a Frenchman who settled in Valladolid, was also influenced by Michelangelo and founded the Catalan School of sculpture. His statues, recognisable by their beauty and the fullness of their forms, anticipated the Baroque style through the dramatic postures they adopted to express sorrow. Many of his works, such as the famous Virgen de los Siete Cuchillos (Virgin of the Seven Knives) in the Iglesia de las Angustias in Valladolid and the Entombments in the Museo de Valladolid and Segovia Cathedral, were subsequently copied.

Most of the finely worked wrought iron grilles closing off chapels and *coros* (chancels) were carved in the 15C and 16C. Members of the **Arfe** family, Enrique, Antonio and Juan, stand out in the field of gold and silversmithing. They made the monstrances of Toledo, Santiago de Compostela and Sevilla Cathedrals respectively.

PAINTING

Under Italian Renaissance influence, Spanish painting in the 16C showed a mastery of perspective, a taste for clarity of composition and glorification of the human body. These features found their way into Spanish painting mainly through the Valencian School, which had close links with Italian artists and patrons. **Fernando Yáñez de**

la Almedina and **Hernando Llanos** introduced the style of Leonardo da Vinci, while **Vicente Macip** added that of Raphael and his son **Juan de Juanes** produced Mannerist works.

In Sevilla, **Alejo Fernández** painted the famous *Virgin of the Navigators* in the Alcázar. In Castilla, the great master of the late 15C was **Pedro Berruguete** (c. 1450–1503), whose markedly personal style drew upon all the artistic influences in the country. His successor, **Juan de Borgoña**, specialised particularly in landscape, architecture and decorative motifs. Another artist, **Pedro de Campaña** from Brussels, used *chiaroscuro* to dramatic effect while **Luis de Morales** (c. 1520–86), a Mannerist, gave his work a human, emotional dimension. Ordinary people with religious sentiments responded favourably to the spiritual emotion expressed in his paintings.

At the end of the 16C, Philip II sent for a great many Italian or Italian-trained artists to paint for El Escorial. During his reign he introduced portrait painting under the Dutchman **Antonio Moro** (c. 1519–c. 1576), his cohort **Alonso Sánchez Coello** (1531–88) and **Juan Pantoja de la Cruz** (1553–1608). El Greco (1541–1614), on the other hand, was scorned and settled in Toledo.

© DEA/G DAGLI ORTI/age fotostock

Detail, Virgin of the Navigators *(1531-36) by Alejo Fernández, Real Alcázar, Sevilla*

Baroque Period (17–18C)

Spanish art reached its apogee in the mid-17C. Baroque met with outstanding success in its role as an essentially religious art in the service of the Counter-Reformation and was particularly evident in Andalucía, then enriched by trade with America.

ARCHITECTURE

Architects in the early 17C were still under the influence of 16C Classicism and the Herreran style to which they added decorative details. Public buildings proliferated and many continued to be built throughout the Baroque period. Public buildings of the time in Madrid include the Plaza Mayor by **Juan Gómez de Mora**, built shortly before the *ayuntamiento* (town hall), and the most significant building of all, the present Ministerio de Asuntos Exteriores (Ministry of Foreign Affairs) by **Juan Bautista Crescenzi**, the architect of the Panteón de Reyes at El Escorial.

Church architecture of the period showed greater freedom from Classicism. A style of Jesuit church, with a cruciform plan and a large transept that served to light up altarpieces, began to emerge. Madrid has several examples including the Iglesia de San Isidro by the Jesuits **Pedro Sánchez** and **Francisco Bautista**, and the Real Convento de la Encarnación by **Juan Gómez de Mora**. In the middle of the century, architects were less rigid, changing plans and façades, breaking up entablatures and elaborating pediments. A good example of this Italian Baroque style is Madrid's Iglesia Pontificia de San Miguel (18C).

Baroque

MADRID – Museo Municipal (Antiguo Hospicio): portal (18C)

The Baroque retable or altarpiece, which reached new architectural heights in Spain, was occasionally created on the façade of a building, rather than inside it.

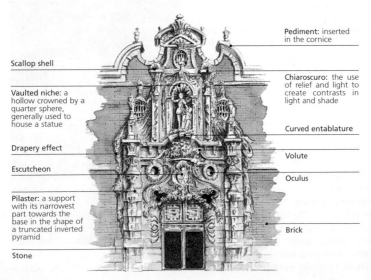

Pediment: inserted in the cornice

Scallop shell

Vaulted niche: a hollow crowned by a quarter sphere, generally used to house a statue

Chiaroscuro: the use of relief and light to create contrasts in light and shade

Drapery effect

Curved entablature

Escutcheon

Volute

Pilaster: a support with its narrowest part towards the base in the shape of a truncated inverted pyramid

Oculus

Brick

Stone

H. Choimet/MICHELIN

A new feature, the **camarín**, was introduced: at first simply a passage behind the high altar, it developed into a highly ornate chapel.

Decoration of this kind may be seen in Zaragoza's Basílica de Nuestra Señora del Pilar designed by **Francisco Herrera el Mozo** (1622–85). The Clerecía in Salamanca is a magnificent Baroque creation with a patio that anticipates the audacity and abundant decoration of the Churrigueresque style.

CHURRIGUERESQUE STYLE

In this style, named after the Churriguera family of architects (late 17C), architecture became no more than a support for dense concentrations of ornament covering entire façades.

The style is typified by the use of *salomónicas*, or barley sugar columns entwined with vines, and *estípites*, or pilasters arranged in an inverse pyramid.

Early examples of this extravagance, the altarpiece of the Convento de San Esteban in Salamanca and the palace in Nuevo Baztán near Madrid, were by **José de Churriguera** (1665–1725), who was the instigator of the style but did not make any architectural changes. His brothers **Joaquín** (1674–1724) and especially **Alberto** (1676–1750), who designed the Plaza Mayor in Salamanca, took greater liberties in their work.

Pedro de Ribera (1681–1742), a Castilian architect who worked mainly in Madrid, surpassed the Churriguera brothers in decorative delirium.

The other great Castilian, **Narciso Tomé**, is remembered for the façade of the Universidad de Valladolid (1715) and particularly for the *Transparente* in Toledo Cathedral (1721–32).

REGIONAL VARIATIONS

The popularity of the Baroque spread countrywide, differing from province to province. In **Galicia**, where the hardness of the granite precluded delicate carving, Baroque took the form of softer lines and decorative mouldings. The best example of the style was by **Fernando de Casas Novoa**, who designed the Obradoiro façade of Santiago de Compostela Cathedral (1750) at the end of his life.

In **Andalucía**, Baroque attained its utmost splendour, especially in decoration. Undulating surfaces characterised the façades of palaces (Écija), cathedrals (Guadix) and the doorways of countless churches and mansions (Jerez) in the 18C. As well as sculptor and painter, **Alonso Cano** was the instigator of Andalucían Baroque and designed the façade of Granada Cathedral. The major exponent of the style was, however, **Vicente Acero**, who worked on the façade of Guadix Cathedral (1714–20), designed Cádiz Cathedral and built the tobacco factory in Sevilla. Mention should also be made of **Leonardo de Figueroa** (1650–1730) for the Palacio de San Telmo in Sevilla and **Francisco Hurtado** (1669–1725) and **Luis de Arévalo** for La Cartuja in Granada; Hurtado worked on the monastery's tabernacle and Arévalo on the sacristy, the most exuberant Baroque works in Andalucía. In the **Levante**, Baroque artists used polychrome tiles to decorate church cupolas and spires like that of Santa Catalina in Valencia. In the same town, the Palacio del Marqués de Dos Aguas by **Luis Domingo** and **Ignacio Vergara** is reminiscent of façades by Ribera. The cathedral in Murcia has an impressive façade by **Jaime Bort y Meliá**.

THE GOLDEN AGE OF SPANISH PAINTING

This was characterised by the rejection of the previous century's Mannerism and the adoption of Naturalism. The starting point was Caravaggio's tenebrism, powerful contrasts of light and shade, and his stern realism. Painters took up portraiture and still life *(bodegón)*, while allegories on the theme of *vanitas* (still-life paintings showing the ephemerality of life) reflected a philosophical purpose by juxtaposing everyday objects with symbols of decay to illustrate the transience of wealth and the things of this world and the inevitability of death. Among 17C artists were two from the Valencian School

Detail, Las Meninas *(1656) by Diego Velázquez, Museo Nacional del Prado*

– **Francisco Ribalta** (1565–1628), who introduced tenebrism into Spain, and **José de Ribera** (1591–1652), known for his forceful realism.

Some of the greatest Baroque artists worked in Andalucía. One was **Francisco de Zurbarán** (1598–1664), master of the Sevilla School; light in his paintings springs from within the subjects themselves. Other artists included **Bartolomé Esteban Murillo** (1617–82), who painted intimate, mystical scenes, and **Valdés de Valdés Leal** whose realism challenged earthly vanities. **Alonso Cano** (1601–67), architect, painter and sculptor, settled in Granada and painted delicate figures of the Virgin.

The Castilian painters, **Vicente Carducho** (c. 1576–1638) and portraitists **Juan Carreño de Miranda** (1614–85) and **Claudio Coello** (1642–93), all excellent artists, nonetheless pale beside **Diego Velázquez** (1599–1660), whose perspective, masterly sense of composition, sense of depth, technique and psychology are recognised as those of a universal master who influenced Spain's painters over the centuries to come.

Sculpture

Spanish Baroque sculpture was naturalistic and intensely emotive. Wood was the most common medium, and while altarpieces continued to be carved, *pasos* or statues made for Semana Santa processions proved a great novelty.

The two major schools of Baroque sculpture were in Castilla and Andalucía. **Gregorio Hernández**, Juni's successor, worked in Valladolid, the Castilian centre. His style was more natural than that of his master, and his *Christ Recumbent* for the Convento de Capuchinos in El Pardo was widely copied. Sevilla and Granada were the main centres for the Andalucían School.

Juan Martínez Montañés (1568–1649) settled in Sevilla and worked exclusively in wood, carving a great many pasos and various altarpieces. **Alonso Cano** became famous for the grace and femininity of his Immaculate Conceptions while his best-known disciple, **Pedro de Mena (1628–88)**, produced sculptures of great dramatic tension which contrasted with his master's understated style. The statue of Mary Magdalene (Museo Nacional de Escultura Policromada, Valladolid), St Francis (Toledo Cathedral) and the Dolorosa (Monasterio de las Descalzas Reales, Madrid) are telling examples of his work.

The 18C saw the rise to prominence of the great Murcian, **Francisco Salzillo** (1707–83), whose dramatic sculptures were inspired by Italian Baroque.

Churrigueresque excess in sculpture took the form of immense altarpieces, often so large that they were designed by architects. Statues were smothered in decoration and lost in gilding and stucco.

Bourbons (18–19C)

S pain's Catholic imperialism was succeeded by enlightened Bourbon despotism and a change in the arts. Henceforth the rules of art were governed by officials like the Academia de Bellas Artes de San Fernando.

ARCHITECTURE

During the first half of the century archi-tecture still bore the stamp of Spanish Baroque, itself influenced at the time by French Rococo. The king and queen had palaces built in a moderate Baroque style (El Pardo, Riofrío, La Granja and Aranjuez) and began work on Madrid's Palacio Real modelled on Versailles. These buildings sought to ally French Classical harmony with Italian grace, and to this end most of the work was entrusted to Italian architects who gen-erally respected the traditional Spanish quadrangular plan of *alcázares*. The vast gardens generally had a French design. Excavations of Pompeii and Hercula-neum contributed to the emergence of a new, **Neoclassical** style which flourished between the second half of the 18C and 19C. It repudiated Baroque excess and aspired to Hellen-istic beauty and classical orders and design. The Kings of Spain, Charles III in particular, embellished the capital by building fountains (Cibeles, Neptune), gates (Alcalá and Toledo), and planting botanic gardens.

The first Spanish Neoclassical architect, **Ventura Rodríguez** (1717–85), who was actually apprenticed in Italian Baroque, quickly developed an academic Neo-classical style. His works include the façade of Pamplona Cathedral, the Paseo del Prado in Madrid and the Basílica de Nuestra Señora del Pilar in Zaragoza. **Francesco Sabatini** (1722–97), whose style developed along simi-lar lines, designed the Puerta de Alcalá. The leading architect was without doubt **Juan de Villanueva** (1739–1811), schooled in Classical principles during a stay in Rome. He designed the façade of the *ayuntamiento* in Madrid and, most importantly, the **Museo del Prado**. Two notable town planners emerged during the 19C: **Ildefonso Cerdá** (1815–76) in Barcelona and **Arturo Soria** (1844–1920) in Madrid.

PAINTING

Bourbon monarchs took pains to attract the greatest painters to court and grant them official positions. In 1752 Ferdi-nand VI founded the Academia de Bellas Artes de San Fernando where it was intended that students should learn official painting techniques and study the Italian masters. Leading artists of the time were **Anton Raphael Mengs** (1728–79) from Bohemia and the Ital-ian **Giambattista Tiepolo** (1696–1770), both of whom decorated the Palacio Real. There was also **Francisco Bayeu** (1734–95) from Aragón, who painted a great many tapestry cartoons, as did his brother-in-law **Francisco de Goya** (1746–1828). Goya's work, much of which may be seen in the Prado, Madrid, was to dominate the entire century. Painters working in the post-Goya period did not follow in the master's

Detail, The Third of May *(1814) by Francisco de Goya, Museo Nacional del Prado*

© Imagestate/Tips Images

Neo-Classical

MADRID - Observatorio Astronómico (18C)

This small building designed by Juan de Villanueva is a model of simplicity and purity which shows clear Palladian influence in its proportions and design.

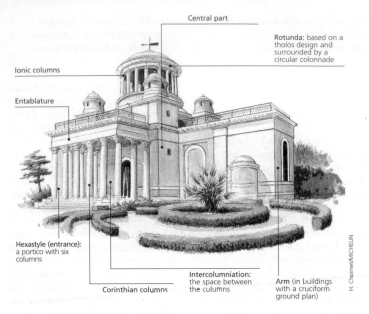

Central part

Rotunda: based on a tholos design and surrounded by a circular colonnade

Ionic columns

Entablature

Hexastyle (entrance): a portico with six columns

Corinthian columns

Intercolumniation: the space between the columns

Arm (in buildings with a cruciform ground plan)

H. Choimet/MICHELIN

footsteps as academic Neoclassical influences and Romanticism took over; Goya's legacy was not taken up until the end of the 19C. The following stand out among artists of the academic Romantic trend: **Federico de Madrazo**, representative of official taste in royal portraits and historical scenes, **Vicente Esquivel**, portrait-painter, and lastly **Leonardo Alenza**, and **Eugenio Lucas Velázquez**, the spokesmen for **Costumbrismo**, which had attained full status as a genre. (This was a style of painting illustrating scenes of everyday life which gradually developed from the simply anecdotal to a higher calling, the evocation of the Spanish soul.) Historical themes became very popular in the 19C with works by **José Casado del Alisal**, **Eduardo Rosales** and **Mariano Fortuny**. Impressionist features began to appear in naturalist paintings by **Ramón Martí Alsina** and in post-Romantic landscapes by **Carlos de Haes**. The style secured a definitive hold in the works of **Narciso Oller**, **Ignacio Pinazo Camarlench**, the best Valencian Impressionist, **Darío de Regoyos** and lastly, **Joaquín Sorolla**, who specialised in light-filled folk scenes and regional subjects.

The Basque artist **Ignacio Zuloaga** (1870–1945) expressed his love for Spain in brightly coloured scenes of everyday life at a time when Impressionism was conquering Europe.

The Decorative Arts

Factories were built under the Bourbons to produce decorative material for their palaces. In 1760, Charles III founded the Buen Retiro works, where ceramics for the famous Salones de Porcelana in the royal palaces of Aranjuez and Madrid were made. The factory was destroyed during the Napoleonic invasion.

In 1720, Philip V opened the Real Fábrica de Tapices de Santa Bárbara (in Madrid), the equivalent of the French Gobelins factory in Paris. Some of the tapestries were of Don Quixote while others depicted scenes of everyday life based on preparatory cartoons by Bayeu and Goya.

20C Creativity

The works of Picasso, Dalí and Gaudí, controversial and often unloved in their day, are now famous throughout the world. They are but the tip of a great Spanish art and architectural movement, moving into the 21C.

FROM MODERNISM TO SURREALISM

The barren period that Spanish art experienced at the end of the 19C was interrupted in Catalunya by a vast cultural movement known as **Modernism**. This was particularly strong in architecture, with outstanding work by **Antoni Gaudí, Lluís Domènech i Montaner** and **Josep Maria Jujol**.

Painting was varied and prolific. The following stand out among the many artists of the time: **Ramón Casas**, the best Spanish Impressionist, whose works are suffused with an atmosphere of grey melancholy, **Santiago Rusiñol, Isidro Nonell**, instigator of **Spanish Expressionism**, and **Pablo Picasso** (1881–1973), whose innovations were to mark the entire history of 20C painting. In the 1920s a movement began to emerge that was influenced by Cubism and, more particularly, by **Surrealism**. Its sculptors were **Ángel Ferrant, Victorio Macho, Alberto Sánchez Pérez** and lastly **Julio González**. Painters included **Daniel Vázquez Díaz**, Juan Gris, Joan Miró and Salvador Dalí. **Juan Gris** (1887–1927), the most faithful analytical Cubist, worked in Paris. The works of **Joan Miró** (1893–1983), champion of Surrealism, are characterised by childlike spontaneity. **Salvador Dalí** (1904–89), a quasi-Surrealist, dreamed up his own creative method which he called the paranoic critical. Some of his best paintings were a result of his interest in the subconscious and the dream world.

Post-war art

Spanish art was crucially affected by the Civil War in two ways: firstly, the fact that artists, including Picasso, went into exile, and secondly, official taste in architecture developed a penchant for the monumental. The most striking example of this is the Valle de los Caídos. However, even among exponents of the Nationalist style, there were innovative architects like **Miguel Fisac**. In 1950 the first signs of a new style, based on rational and functional criteria, began to emerge. Examples abound in Barcelona, including the Vanguardia building by **Oriol Bohigas** and **José María Martorell**, and in Madrid the Torres Blancas (White Towers) by **Francisco Javier Sáenz de Oíza**. The Post-war paintings of **José Gutiérrez Solana**, are full of anguish; the landscape painters **Benjamín Palencia, Rafael Zabaleta**, provide lighter moments.

Avant-Garde painters also began to emerge after the war. The first post-war Surrealists were members of a group called **Dau al Set** including **Antoni Tàpies**, one of the major abstract artists.

Contemporary Art

In the 1950s two abstract groups were formed: the **El Paso** group with **Antonio Saura, Manolo Millares** and **Rafael Canogar**, and the **Equipo 57** with **Eusebio Sempere, Ángel Duarte, Agustín Ibarrola, Juan Serrano** and **José Duarte**. The movement's sculptors included Basque artists **Jorge Oteiza** and **Eduardo Chillida**. Major international figures of the last decade, such as painter Miquel Barceló, sculptor Juan Muñoz and Ángela de la Cruz, , increasingly make their careers outside Spain. The works of Lanzarote artist, César Manrique, continue to enthrall island visitors (and a much wider audience), while in Valencia, Santiago Calatrava ended the century with his distinctive blinding-white space age architecture.

Modernism

BARCELONA –Casa Batlló (Antoni Gaudí: 1905-07)

Modernism is a colourful, decorative and sensual style which recreates organic forms in a world dominated by curves and reverse curves.

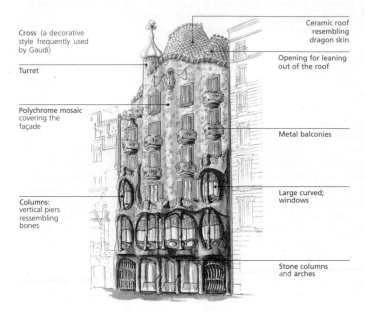

Cross (a decorative style frequently used by Gaudí)

Turret

Polychrome mosaic covering the façade

Columns: vertical piers ressembling bones

Ceramic roof resembling dragon skin

Opening for leaning out of the roof

Metal balconies

Large curved; windows

Stone columns and arches

Mediterranean Rationalist

BARCELONA – Fundació Joan Miró (JL Sert: 1972-75)

The building consists of a series of interrelated architectural features and open spaces in which natural light plays a fundamental role.

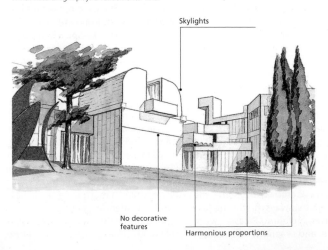

Skylights

No decorative features

Harmonious proportions

H. Choimer/MICHELIN

A–Z of Architectural Terms

Everything you always wanted to know about architectural terms, but were too afraid to ask.

Words in italics are Spanish.

Ajimez paired window or opening separated by a central column.

Alfarje wooden ceiling, usually decorated, consisting of a board resting on cross-beams (a feature of the Mudéjar style).

Alfiz rectangular surround to a horseshoe-shaped arch in Muslim architecture.

Alicatado section of wall or other surface covered with sheets of ceramic tiles *(azulejos)* cut to form geometric patterns. Frequently used to decorate dados (a Mudéjar feature).

Alhondiga (almúdin) granary or food store, often Muslim in origin, but preserved after the Reconquest.

Horseshoe (Moorish)

R. Corbel/MICHELIN

Aljibe Arab word for cistern.

Altarpiece (also retable). Decorative screen above and behind the altar.

Apse far end of a church housing the high altar; can be semicircular, polygonal or horseshoe-shaped.

Apsidal or radiating chapel small chapel opening from the apse.

Arch (☞ *see illustrations.*)

Archivolt ornamental moulding on the outer edge of an arch.

Barrel

R. Corbel/MICHELIN

Artesonado marquetry ceiling in which raised fillets outline honeycomb-like cells in the shape of stars. This decoration, which first appeared under the Almohads, was popular throughout the country, including Christian Spain, in the 15C and 16C.

Ataurique decorative plant motif on plaster or brick which was developed as a feature of the Caliphate style and was subsequently adopted by the Mudéjar.

Azulejos glazed, patterned, ceramic tiles.

Barrel vaulting vault with a semicircular cross-section. (☞ *see illustrations.*)

Cabecera the east or apsidal end of a church.

Caliphate the architectural style developed in Córdoba under the Caliphate (8C–11C) of which the finest example is the mosque in that city.

Camarín a small chapel on the first floor behind the altarpiece or retable. It is plushly decorated and very often contains a lavishly costumed statue of the Virgin Mary.

Capilla mayor the area of the high altar containing the *retablo mayor* (monumental altarpiece), which often rises to the roof.

Coro a chancel in Spanish canonical churches often built in the middle of the nave. It contains the **stalls** *(sillería)* used by members of religious orders. When placed in a tribune or gallery it is known as the *coro alto*.

Churrigueresque in the style of the Churrigueras, an 18C family of architects. Richly ornate Baroque decoration.

Crucero transept. The part of a church at right angles to the nave which gives the church a cross shape.

Estípite pilaster in the shape of a truncated inverted pyramid.

Gargoyle projecting roof gutter normally carved in the shape of a grotesque animal.

Girola (also *deambulatorio*) ambulatory. An extension to the aisles forming a gallery around the chancel and the altar.

Arches

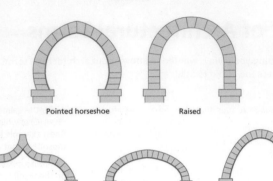

Pointed horseshoe   Raised

Ogee   Basket-handle   Rampant

Vaults

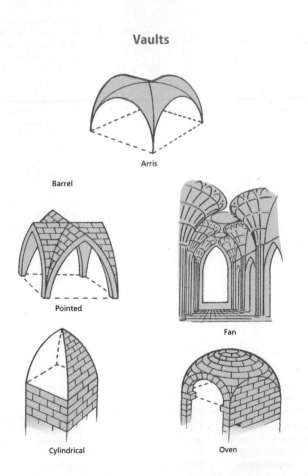

Arris

Barrel

Pointed

Fan

Cylindrical

Oven

R. Corbel/MICHELIN

Tympanum

H. Choimet/MICHELIN

Groined vaulting vault showing lines of intersection of two vaults or arches (usually pointed).

Grotesque typical Renaissance decoration combining vegetation, imaginary beings and animals.

Kiblah sacred wall of a mosque from which the mihrab is hollowed, facing towards Mecca.

Lacería geometric decoration formed by intersecting straight lines making star-shaped and polygonal figures. Characteristic of Moorish architecture.

Lombard bands decorative pilaster strips typical of Romanesque architecture in Lombardy.

Lonja commodity exchange building.

Mihrab richly decorated prayer-niche in the sacred wall (kiblah) in a mosque.

Minaret tower of the mosque (*mezquita*), from which the muezzin calls the faithful to prayer.

Minbar pulpit in a mosque.

Mocárabes decorative prismatic motifs of Muslim architecture. They resemble stalactites or pendants and adorn vaults and cornices.

Mozarabic the work of Christians living under Arab rule after the Moorish invasion of 711. On being persecuted in the 9C, they sought refuge in Christian areas bringing with them Moorish artistic traditions.

Mudéjar the work of Muslims living in Christian territory following the Reconquest (13C–14C).

Mullion slender column or pillar dividing an opening in a door or window.

Naveta megalithic monument found in the Balearic Islands, which has a pyramidal shape with a rectangular base.

Plateresque term derived from *platero* (i.e. silversmith); used to describe the early style of the Renaissance characterised by finely carved decoration.

Predella the lower part of an altarpiece.

Presbiterio the space in front of the altar (the presbytery is known as the *casa del cura*).

Púlpito pulpit.

Sagrario chapel containing the Holy Sacrament. May sometimes be a separate church.

Sebka type of brick decoration developed under the Almohads consisting of an apparently endless series of small arches forming a network.

Seo cathedral.

Sillería the stalls.

Soportales porticoes of wood or stone pillars supporting the first floor of houses. They form an open gallery around the plaza mayor of towns and villages.

Star vault vault with a square or polygonal plan formed by several intersecting arches.

Stucco type of moulding mix consisting mainly of plaster, used for coating surfaces. It plays a fundamental role in wall decoration in Hispano-Muslim architecture.

Talayot: megalithic monument found in the Balearic Islands, which takes the form of a truncated cone of stones.

Taula (*mesa* in the Mallorcan language) megalithic monument found in the Balearic Islands, which consists of a monolithic horizontal stone block placed on top of a vertical stone block.

Trasaltar back wall of the *capilla mayor* in front of which there are frequently sculptures or tombs.

Trascoro the wall, often carved and decorated, which encloses the *coro*.

Triforium arcade above the side aisles which opens onto the central nave of a church.

Tympanum inner surface of a pediment. This often ornamented space is bounded by the archivolt and the lintel of the doors of churches.

Venera scallop-shaped moulding frequently used as an ornamental feature. It is the symbol of pilgrimages to Santiago de Compostela.

Yesería plasterwork used in sculptured decoration.

Spanish Gardens

The gardens of Spain evoke the country's rich culture, and bear witness to an enviable ability to adapt to a varied climate. Although Spanish landscape gardening has inherited many of its traditions from within Europe, particularly from the Greco-Roman era, the long period of Muslim occupation added a new dimension as unique as that of its architecture.

GENERALIFE (14C), GRANADA

The Generalife is the Moorish garden par excellence. As a result of its extraordinary position it is a magnificent balcony, but above all it has been able to preserve the intimate, sensual character and evocation of paradise that was such a feature of Muslim gardens.

Despite alterations over the centuries it remains a feast for the senses and a harmonious whole which avoids grandiloquence. Nothing has been left to chance: the colour of the plants and flowers, their scent, and the omnipresence of water combine to create a serene ambience. The Generalife is laid out on several levels to ensure that the trees in one garden do not interfere with the views from another. In fact, the garden is best considered as a series of landscaped areas and enclosures, each with its own individuality, yet part of an overall design. The architectural features and vegetation, reflected in the water channels, blend together to create a perfect whole.

LA GRANJA (18C), SEGOVIA

These magnificent Baroque palace gardens bring to mind those of Versailles, where Philip V spent his childhood. He was to make **La Granja** his personal retreat. While it lacks Versailles' grandiose perspectives it gains in its backdrop of peaked mountains whose snows feed magnificent fountains. The rigidity of the French garden is lost here as there is no clear central axis; instead, La Granja consists of a succession of parts, each with a certain independence, thus adopting hints of Moorish design.

Although the French gardeners Philip V invited south brought with them a variety of species, they were able to adapt them perfectly to the local landscape in the palace's nurseries while preserving some of its wildness. Magnificent

La Granja de San Ildefonso, Segovia

© Félix González/age fotostock

sculptures scattered in small squares and along avenues add a theatrical touch. The gardens are at their very best when the fountains are switched on for selected days in spring and early summer.

PAZO DE OCA (18–19C), LA ESTRADA, LA CORUÑA

A *pazo* is a Baroque-style manor typically found in Galicia, built on a plot of land which generally comprises a recreational garden, a kitchen garden and cultivated farmland. The garden of the Pazo de Oca – or goose manor – is the oldest in Galicia and is a magnificent example of romantic garden design in green northern Spain. The damp climate has enabled vegetation to grow on rocks, creating an intimate relationship between its architectural and vegetable features. Water plays a vital role, appearing in basins or fountains or trickling through the garden. The most romantic part, with its two ponds, is hidden behind a parterre. A delightful bridge, with benches enabling visitors to enjoy this enchanting spot, separates the two sections, overcoming the difference in height between them. The lower pond contains the *pazo*'s most representative and famous feature: the stone boat, with its two petrified sailors, planted with hydrangeas.

JARDINS DE MONFORT (19C), VALENCIA

The River Turia's ribbon of green parkland running through Valencia's city centre links three older gardens: the Jardins del Reial, which date back to Muslim times, the Jardí Botànic, founded in 1567, and finally the Jardins de Montfort, the smallest but perhaps the most beautiful of the three.

When the Marqués de San Juan, an ennobled businessman, created this romantic garden in the 1860s it lay between orchards and rural palaces. Today, protected by its old brick walls, it remains an ingenious oasis with a microclimate that fosters flowering plants and aromatics around the year.

Close to a small pavilion a waist high labyrinth of trimmed hedges is decorated by Italian marble statues and a graceful fountain. From here a bougainvillea bower leads through to a larger informal area which features olive and orange trees, a fragrant rose garden and oriental bamboo pond. As in other great Spanish gardens, you are never far from the sound of splashing water.

MARIMURTRA (20C), BLANES, GIRONA

Carlos Faust, the German impresario who settled on the Costa Brava, created this botanical garden in 1921 for research purposes and to preserve plants threatened with extinction. Situated in a delightful spot between the sea and the mountains, it offers visitors magnificent views of the coast. Today Marimurtra is a fine example of a contemporary Mediterranean garden, although a number of exotic species from every continent have also adapted perfectly here. It contains an interesting cactus garden, an impressive aquatic garden, as well as a collection of medicinal, toxic and aromatic plants. The only architectural feature with a purely decorative function is the small temple built at the end of the steps running down to the sea. Like Almodóvar, contemporary filmmakers in Spain take on major social issues. Memorable examples from the last decade are **Alejandro Amenábar**'s *Mar Adentro (The Sea Inside,* 2004*)*, Fernando León's *Lunes al Sol* (*Sunny Mondays*, 2002), **Icíar Bollaín**'s *Te Doy Mis Ojos (I Give You My Eyes*, 2003) and Mexican director Guillermo del Toro's *El Laberinto del Fauno (Pan's Labyrinth*, 2006), films which deal with euthanasia, unemployment, domestic violence and the legacy of the Civil War. While new talent emerges each year Almodóvar remains a key figure, having fostered the careers of actors Antonio Banderas, Javier Bardem and Penélope Cruz, director Isabel Coixet and Oscar-winning composer Alberto Iglesias. Animation flourishes. Young stars like Javier Recio work alongside experienced hands like Javier Mariscal.

Spanish Music

A longside its folk music, Spain has developed an extraordinarily rich musical repertory since the Middle Ages, marked by a large number of influences including Visigothic, Arabic, Mozarabic and French.

CHANTS TO CHARTS

Polyphonic chants were studied in the 11C and the oldest known piece for three voices, the *Codex calixtinus*, was composed at Santiago de Compostela c.1140. During the Reconquest, the church encouraged musical creativity by liturgical chants and plays such as the *Elche Mystery,* still performed today. At the end of the 15C, the dramatist **Juan de la Encina** composed secular song. Music, like the other arts, however, reached its climax in the second half of the 16C, under the protection of the early Habsburgs. **Tomás Luis de Victoria** (1548–1611) was one of the most famous composers of polyphonic devotional pieces, while among his contemporaries, **Francisco de Salinas** and **Fernando de las Infantas** were learned musicologists and **Cristóbal de Morales** and **Francisco Guerrero** were accomplished religious composers. As for instruments, the organ became the centre of sacred music, while a favourite for profane airs was the *vihuela*, a guitar with six double strings, soon replaced with the lute and the five-string Spanish guitar. In 1629, **Lope de Vega** wrote the text for the first Spanish opera. **Pedro Calderón de la Barca** is credited with creating the **zarzuela**, a musical play with spoken passages, songs and dances, which, since the 19C, has based its plot and music on popular themes.

In the 19C, the Catalan **Felipe Pedrell** brought Spanish music onto a higher plane. He opened the way for a new generation of musicians and was the first to combine traditional tunes with classical genres. In the early 19C, while works by French composers (Ravel's *Bolero*, Bizet's *Carmen*, Lalo's *Symphonie Espagnole…*) bore a pronounced Hispanic stamp, Spanish composers turned to national folklore and traditional themes: **Isaac Albéniz** (1860–1909) wrote *Iberia*, **Enrique Granados** (1867–1916) became famous for his *Goyescas* and **Joaquín Turina** (1882–1949) for his *Sevilla Symphony*. This popular vein led to works by **Manuel de Falla** (1876–1946) including *Nights in the Gardens of Spain*, *El Amor Brujo* and *The Three-Cornered Hat*.

Among the best-known contemporary classical guitar players **Andrés Segovia** (1893–1987), **Joaquín Rodrigo** (1901–99), famous for his *Concierto de Aranjuez*, and **Narciso Yepes** (1927–97), have shown that this most Spanish of instruments can Interpret a wide variety of music. Equally, **flamenco** maestros **Paco de Lucía** and Enrique Morente have shown the potential of flamenco guitar and song to create dialogues with jazz, North African and even heavy metal music. Another Spaniard, **Pablo Casals** (1876–1973), was possibly the greatest cellist of all time. Spain holds a leading position in the world of opera with singers such as **Victoria de los Ángeles** (1923–2005), **Montserrat Caballé**, **Plácido Domingo**, **Alfredo Kraus** (1927–99) and **José Carreras**.

Today's music industry is plagued by piracy, but remains lively. Artists range from pop crooners, like Julio Iglesias and his son Enrique, to radical fusion artist Manu Chao, the "hip-hop flamenco" of Ojos de Brujo, jazzman Zenet and diva Concha Buika. Latin American stars like Shakira, Mana and Julieta Venegas have a huge following, while Spanish talent is supported by music festivals. Benicàssim is the most famous but Barcelona's Sónar, Andalucía's Dreambeach (formerly Creamfields) and Cartagena's La Mar de Músicas are also important.

Spanish Literature

Errant knights, Don Juan characters, mystics and highwaymen occupy a hallowed place in Spanish letters. Spanish literature reached its peak in the Golden Age of the 16C and 17C, but fame has returned in the early 21C.

BEGINNINGS

Roman Spain produced great Latin authors such as **Seneca the Elder** or the Rhetorician, his son **Seneca the Younger** and the poets **Martial** and **Lucan**. In the 8C, the monk **Beatus** wrote the Commentary on the Apocalypse, which gave rise to the outstanding illuminated beatus manuscripts. Arab writers, especially poets, won renown during the Muslim period.

THE MIDDLE AGES

Works written in Castilian began to emerge in the Middle Ages. The first milestone of Spanish literature appeared in the 12C in the form of *El Cantar del Mío Cid*, an anonymous Castilian poem inspired by the adventures of El Cid. In the 13C, the monk **Gonzalo de Berceo**, drawing on religious themes, won renown through his works of *Mester de Clerecía*. **Alfonso X the Wise**, an erudite king who wrote poetry in Galician, decreed that in his kingdom Latin should be replaced as the official language by Castilian, an act subsequently followed throughout Spain, except in Catalunya, where Catalan persevered. In the 14C, **Juan Ruiz, Archpriest of Hita**, wrote a brilliant satirical verse work titled *El Libro de Buen Amor*, which later influenced the picaresque novel.

THE RENAISSANCE

In the 15C, lyric poetry flourished under Italian influence with poets such as **Jorge Manrique** and the **Marquis of Santillana**. **Romanceros**, collections of ballads in an epic or popular vein, perpetuated the medieval style until the 16C when *Amadís de Gaula* (1508) set the model for a great many romances or tales of chivalry. In 1499, *La Celestina*, a novel of passion by **Fernando de Rojas**, anticipated modern drama in a subtle, well-observed tragicomic intrigue.

THE GOLDEN AGE (SIGLO DE ORO)

Spain enjoyed its greatest literary flowering under the Habsburgs (1516–1700), with lyric poets such as **Garcilaso de la Vega**, disciple of Italian verse forms, mystic verse by **Fray Luis de León** and above all **Luis de Góngora y Argote** (1561–1627) whose obscure style won fame under the name of Gongorism.

The **picaresque** novel, however, was the genre favoured by Spanish writers at the time. The first to appear in 1554 was *Lazarillo de Tormes*, an anonymous autobiographical work in which the hero, an astute rogue (*pícaro* in Castilian), casts a mischievous and impartial eye on society and its woes.

There followed **Mateo Alemán**'s *Guzmán de Alfarache* with its brisk style and colourful vocabulary, and *La Vida del Buscón*, an example of the varied talents of **Francisco de Quevedo** (1580–1645), essayist, poet and satirist. The genius of the Golden Age, however, was **Miguel de Cervantes** (1547–1616), with his masterpiece, the universal **Don Quixote** (1605 and 1615). Dramatists proliferated, among them the master **Lope de Vega** (1562–1635), who perfected drama, working on it as an art for popular audiences. This "phoenix of the mind" wrote more than 1 000 plays, including *Fuenteovejuna*, and Europe's first manifesto on modern theatre. His successor, **Pedro Calderón de la Barca** (1600–81), wrote historical and philosophical plays (*El Alcalde de Zalamea* or *The Mayor of Zalamea*) in which he brilliantly reflected the mood of Spain

A LIFE LESS ORDINARY

Miguel de Cervantes Saavedra was born in poverty at Alcalá de Henares in 1547, yet he went on to lead a life of adventure. From being a valet in Renaissance Rome, Cervantes would later fight against the Ottomans in the Battle of Lepanto (1571). He then spent five years in slavery in Algiers, before returning to Madrid as a purveyor and tax collector for the Spanish Armada. While being imprisoned for debts in La Mancha, it is said that he had the idea for his famous literary work, **Don Quixote de La Mancha,** *(vol I 1605, vol II 1615),* now considered to be one of the greatest novels of all time. He died in 1616.

in the 17C. **Tirso de Molina** (1579–1648) left his interpretation of Don Juan for posterity while **Guillén de Castro** wrote *Las Mocedades del Cid (Youthful Adventures of the Cid)*. Mention should also be made of works on the conquest of America by chroniclers **Cortés** and **Bartolomé de las Casas** among others. Finally, the moralist **Fray Luis de Granada** and the mystics **Santa Teresa de Ávila** (1515–82) and **San Juan de la Cruz** (St John of the Cross) (1542–91) wrote theological works equally inspiring for their writing.

18C AND 19C

The Enlightenment found expression in the works of essayists such as **Benito Jerónimo Feijoo**, a monk, and **Jovellanos**, while elegance dominated the plays of **Moratín**. The great romantic poet of the 19C was **Bécquer** (1836–70) from Sevilla, while **Larra** was a social satirist, **Menéndez Pelayo** a literary critic and **Ángel Ganivet** a political analyst. Realism was introduced to the Spanish novel by **Alarcón** *(The Three-Cornered Hat)* and **Pereda** *(Peñas arriba),* who concentrated on regional themes. By the end of the 19C, the best realist was **Pérez Galdós** whose prolific, lively work *(National Episodes)* is stamped with a great sense of human sympathy.

20C

A group of intellectuals known as the Generation of '98, saddened by Spain's loss of colonies like Cuba, were provoked to produce writing with a new moral spirit, as reflected in the work of essayists such as **Miguel de Unamuno** (1864–1936) who wrote *El Sentimiento trágico de la vida (The Tragic Sense of Life),* and **Azorín**, as well as the philolo-

gist **Menéndez Pidal**, the novelist **Pío Baroja** and the aesthete **Valle Inclán**, who created an elegant poetic prose style. Among their contemporaries were **Jacinto Benavente** (1922 Nobel Prize for literature winner), who developed a new dramatic style, and best-selling Valencian author **Blasco Ibañez**. Some great poets began to emerge, including **Juan Ramón Jiménez** (Nobel Prize 1956), who expressed his feelings through simple unadorned prose poems *(Platero y Yo)*, **Antonio Machado** (1875–1939), the bard of Castilla, and **Rafael Alberti. Federico García Lorca** (1898–1936), equally great as poet and dramatist *(Bodas de Sangre)*, anticipated magical realism in his rich use of symbol and metaphor. His work was, perhaps, the most fascinating reflection of a Spain whose mystery **José Ortega y Gasset** (1883–1955), essayist and philosopher, spent his life trying to fathom.

POST-WAR WRITING

Several years after the Civil War, writing rose from its ashes with works by essayists (**Américo Castro,** in exile),playwrights (**Alfonso Sastre**) and novelists such as **Miguel Delibes, Camilo José Cela** *(La Familia de Pascual Duarte)* who won the Nobel Prize for Literature in 1989, **and Ramón Sender**, all preoccupied with social issues. Contemporary writing has found international acclaim – **Javier Marías**, **Juan Goytisolo** and **Bernardo Atxaga** are examples – and produced bestselling authors like **Almudena Grandes, Carlos Ruiz Zafón** and **Arturo Pérez-Reverte**. They followed a generation of writers who found recognition late at the end of the dictatorship.

SPAIN IN WRITING

BIOGRAPHY

Juan Carlos: Steering Spain from Dictatorship to Democracy – Paul Preston (2010). A definitive study of the man who ruled Spain from 1975 until his abdication in 2014.

Reinventing Food – Colman Andrews (2010). The authorised biography of El Bulli chef Ferran Adrià.

REFERENCE

The New Spaniards – John Hooper (2006). All aspects of Spanish life are covered in this authoritative book by a foreign correspondent.

HISTORY

Ghosts of Spain – Giles Tremlett (2012). A journalist tours the country to explore the darker episodes of Spain's history.

Homage to Catalonia – George Orwell (1938; 2013). An inside look at the Spanish Civil War from the Republican side, and the Communist purges that engulfed Barcelona in 1937.

Spain – William Chislett (2013). An engaging overview of Spanish history from the Moors to the present day.

FICTION

Don Quixote de La Mancha – Miguel de Cervantes (1605; 2015). The classic novel of Castille and of Spanish character.

The Cathedral of the Sea – Ildefonso Falcones (2009). A Pillars-of-the- Earth-like historical novel about the construction of Barcelona's Santa María del Mar basilica.

The Sun Also Rises – Ernest Hemingway (1926; 2014). The Lost Generation takes on Pamplona's San Fermín festival.

For Whom the Bell Tolls – Ernest Hemingway (1938; 2005). Hemingway's story of a young American idealist fighting for the Republic in the Spanish Civil War.

Southern Seas – Manuel Vázquez Montalbán (1979; 1999). An acclaimed episode of the author's Pepe Carvalho series, involving murder, lust and nouvelle cuisine, set in Barcelona.

The Shadow of the Wind – Carlos Ruiz Zafón (2001; 2005). Contemporary allegory of post-Civil War Barcelona infused with Latin American magical realism.

TRAVEL

Death in the Afternoon – Ernest Hemingway (1932; 2007). A terse take on bullfighting, tradition, and the Spanish soul.

Driving over Lemons – Chris Stewart (1999; 2009). The first book in a trilogy about ex-pat life in rural Granada.

Duende – Jason Webster (2004). A young Anglo-American man's journey into the world of flamenco. The first of several books by this talented writer.

South from Granada – Gerald Brenan (1957; 2008). A literary and folkloric account of Spain in the last century.

Spain – Jan Morris (1970; 2008). The Morris take on Spain: history, encounters and pleasures.

The Way of St James – Alison Raju (2000; 2010). A modern guide to this famous pilgrimage route.

ART

The Shameful Life of Salvador Dalí – Ian Gibson (1998). Brilliant portrait of a tortured soul.

Picasso – Timothy Hilton (1976). An attempt to define the Spanish master's place in world art.

Spanish Cinema and Stage

Over the centuries, Spain has produced countless musicians and thespians of world renown. In more recent times, the genius of film directors such as Luis Buñuel, Luis Berlanguer and Pedro Almodóvar, composers such as Manuel de Falla, and guitarists such as Antonio Segovia and Paco de Lucía have thrilled audiences the world over.

PERFORMING ARTS

Opera, disliked by Franco, has made a comeback in Madrid's Teatro Real and Barcelona's historic Liceu. The revival of theatre is wider, with Catalunya's tradition of comedy joined by notable new work from Andalucía and Madrid.

CINEMA

Spanish cinema dates back to a short film in 1897 which shows people leaving the Basílica de Nuestra Señora del Pilar in Zaragoza after Mass. Studios for silent movies were later set up in Barcelona.

In the 1920s, several Surrealists tried their hand at the new art form. Among them were **Dalí** and above all **Luis Buñuel**, a master of Spanish cinema, who made *Un chien Andalou (An Andalusian Dog)* in 1928 and *Âge d'Or (The Golden Age)* in 1930.

When talking films appeared in the 1930s, Spain was in the throes of a political and economic crisis and so her studios lacked the means to procure the necessary equipment.

At the end of the 1930s, when films like *Sor Angélica (Sister Angelica)* by **Francisco Gargallo** tended to address religious themes, Juan Piqueras launched a magazine called *Nuestro Cinema*, which was strongly influenced by Russian ideas, and gave star billing to films such as *Las Hurdes (Land Without Bread)* by Buñuel in 1932, depicting poverty in a remote part of Spain.

During the Civil War and the ensuing Franco era, films were heavily censored and the cinema became one of the major vehicles for the ideology of the time, with historical and religious themes glorifying death and the spirit of sacrifice. One such success was *Marcelino Pan y Vino (The Miracle of Marcelino)* by Ladislao Vajda in 1955. Change came with works by Juan Antonio Bardem like *Muerte de un Ciclista (Death of a Cyclist)* and, above all, *Bienvenido Mister Marshall (Welcome Mr Marshall,* 1953) and *El Verdugo (The Executioner,* 1963) by **Luis García Berlanga**.

The 1960s enjoyed a period of renewal with directors like **Carlos Saura**, whose first film, *Los Golfos (The Delinquents),* came out in 1960. Mention should be made of Saura's *Ana y los Lobos (Anna and the Wolves,* 1973); *El Espíritu de la colmena (The Spirit of the Beehive,* 1973) and *El Sur (The South,* 1983) both by **Víctor Erice**; *La Colmena (The Beehive,* 1982) by **Mario Camus**, and films by **Manuel Gutiérrez Aragón** such as *La Mitad del cielo (Half of Heaven,* 1986) which illustrate the changes democracy brought to Franco's Spain.

Pedro Almodóvar broke with this serious, nostalgic type of cinema. His films show a completely different, modern Spain, often with a strong comic streak or powerfully dark melodrama behind the realism, and have won the hearts of critics and audiences around the world. *Mujeres al Borde de un Ataque de Nervios (Women on the Verge of a Nervous Breakdown,* 1988), *Volver* (2006) and *La Piel Que Habito (The Skin I Live In,* 2011) are three of a string of award-winning films.

SPAIN ON FILM

Un Chien Andalou
(An Andalusian Dog; 1929). A hard-to-watch surrealist masterpiece by Luis Buñuel and Salvador Dalí.

Las Hurdes (Land Without Bread, 1933). Buñuel charts the hard lives of peasants of an Extremaduran comarca.

Surcos (Furrows; 1951). A neo-realist drama by José Antonio Nieves Conde about the disintegration of a family unit in Franco's Madrid.

La Caza (The Hunt; 1966). A thriller by Carlos Saura about war veterans whose reunion turns to violence.

Cría Cuervos (Raise Ravens; 1976). A symbolic criticism of the Franco regime by Saura, with a haunting soundtrack by Jeanette.

Mujeres al Borde de un Ataque de Nervios (Women on the Verge of a Nervous Breakdown; 1988). Pedro Almodóvar's feminist comedy, marking his international breakthrough.

Jamón, Jamón (Ham, Ham; 1992). Bigas Luna's satire on Iberian machismo starring Penélope Cruz and Javier Bardem.

Los Amantes del Círculo Polar (The Lovers of the Arctic Circle; 1998). An homage to love and fate by Julio Medem.

Land and Freedom (1995). A Liverpudlian's experience of fighting for the Republic in the Civil War, with a narrative comparable to Orwell's Homage to Catalonia.

Hable con Ella (Talk to Her; 2002). An Oscar winner by Almodóvar about two men and their devotion to the comatose women who they love.

Mar Adentro (The Sea Inside; 2004). Amenábar's Oscar-winning biopic about Ramón Sampedro and his struggle with disability.

El Laberinto del Fauno (Pan's Labyrinth; 2006). The horrors of post-Civil War Spain, and a young girl embracing her fantasy world, sumptuously brought to life by Guillermo del Toro.

Vicky Cristina Barcelona (2008). A Woody Allen comedy about two friends on a holiday in Spain and their entanglement with Javier Bardem's painter.

Biutiful (2010). Directed by México's Alejandro González Iñárritu, starring Javier Bardem, and set in Barcelona, this chronicle of a man in free-fall is a portrait of the city's seamy and steamy underbelly, the flip side of Vicky Cristina Barcelona.

Agnosia (2010). Eugenio Mira's psychological and romantic thriller about a woman suffering from agnosia (the inability to recognize faces) is set in an opulent late 19C Barcelona.

Pa Negre (Pan Negro or Black Bread; 2010). Beautifully filmed post-Spanish Civil War drama by Agustí Villaronga about a young boy drawn into the lives and lies of the adults around him, and the ideological purges of post-Civil War Spain.

Balada Triste de Trompeta (Sad Trumpet Ballad; 2010). Alex de la Iglesia's drama about two 1973 circus clowns fighting for the love of a dancer is borderline surreal but riveting.

La piel que habito (The Skin I Live In; 2011). This dark multi-award winning thriller by Pedro Almodóvar casts Antonio Banderas as a troubled plastic surgeon who creates an indestructible synthetic skin for a mysterious woman.

Loreak (Flowers; 2014). The first Basque-language film to be entered by Spain for Best Foreign Language Film in the 2016 Academy Awards.

Nature

Because of its geographical location, Spain acts as a bridge between two continents – Europe and Africa. The country has myriad natural attractions, ranging from long sandy beaches, sheltered coves and steep cliffs to breathtaking mountain landscapes characterised by high peaks and enclosed valleys. By contrast, the centre of Spain, known as the Meseta, is marked by seemingly endless expanses of flat terrain.

» Spain's Landscapes p109
» Spain's Climate p110

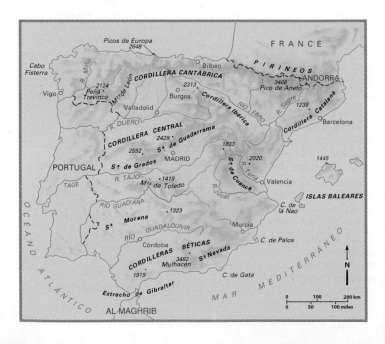

Spain's Landscapes

S uch is Spain's varied topography that in Granada you can drive in the morning to ski on the snowy slopes of the Sierra Nevada, then drive down to the baked Mediterranean coast to waterski in the afternoon.

Summit of Mulhacén, Sierra Nevada

© Jean Heintz/hemis.fr

RELIEF

The dominant feature of the peninsula is the immense plateau at its centre. This is the **Meseta**: a Hercynian platform between 600m/1 968ft and 1 000m/3 281ft high, which tilts slightly westwards. The Meseta is surrounded by long mountain ranges which form barriers between the central plateau and the coastal regions. All these ranges, the **Cordillera Cantábrica** in the northwest (an extension of the Pyrenees), the **Cordillera Ibérica** in the northeast and the **Sierra Morena** in the south, were caused by Alpine folding.

Other mountains rising here and there from the Meseta are folds of the original, ancient massif. They include the **Sierras de Somosierra**, **Guadarrama** and **Gredos**, the **Peña de Francia** and the **Montes de Toledo**.

The highest massifs in Spain, the **Pyrenees** (Pirineos) in the north and the **Sierras Béticas**, including the

Sierra Nevada, in the south, are on the country's periphery, as are Spain's greatest depressions, those of the Ebro and Guadalquivir rivers.

The average altitude in Spain is 650m/2 100ft above sea level and one sixth of the terrain rises to more than 1 000m/3 300ft. The highest peak on the Spanish mainland is Mulhacén (3 422m/11 427ft) in the Sierra Nevada. The highest point in all Spanish territory, however, is Mount Teide on the Canary Islands, rising to a height of 3 718m/12 195ft.

BEACHES

Spain's most treasured landscapes however, golden in every sense, are its beaches. With a coastline of around 5,000mi/8,000km there really is something for everyone: from built-up Benidorm to the wild strands of the Costa de la Luz; the rocky sheltered coves of Galicia and the Costa Brava, to the Robinson Crusoe sands of Fuerteventura.

Spain's Climate

Although most of Spain enjoys 300 days of sunshine a year, the great diversity of its landscapes is partly due to the country's wide variety of climates.

UNDER THE SUN

The **Meseta** accounts for 40 per cent of the surface area of Iberia and includes Castilla y León, Castilla-La Mancha, Madrid and Extremadura. It has a continental climate with extremes of temperature ranging from scorching hot in summer to freezing cold in winter. These excesses are combined with modest and irregular rainfall to form an arid landscape that complements the seemingly infinite horizons in this part of Spain. The massif of the adjoining Pyrenees has a colder alpine climate; the lowest temperatures ever recorded in Spain, -32°C/-26°F, were recorded here. This climate is also prevalent in the Sierra Nevada ("Snowy Mountains") in Andalucía.

The northern coast, which runs from **Galicia** to the **País Vasco**, is nicknamed **España verde** (Green Spain) due to its mild and very humid climate, with rainfall being much higher than in the heartlands of northern Europe. This is in stark contrast to the perceived image of Spain as an entirely dry country.

The Levante has a Mediterranean climate with rainfall being restricted mainly to autumn and spring, and warm temperatures in the winter giving way to high temperatures between June and August. This heat is tempered by the Levante, the cool wind by which this eastern coast, from Almería in the south to Catalunya in the north, is named.

A semi-arid or desert climate affects **Almería**, in southeastern Andalucía, with low rainfall to an extent that the Cabo de Gata near Almería is known as the driest region in Europe. The remaining coastline of **Andalucía** shares traits of a Mediterranean and subtropical region lending it a mild and sunny climate. Atypical of the region, inland Seville is known for its high summer temperatures and holds (with Murcia) the Spanish record high of 47 °C (117 °F). The climate of the **Balearic Islands** (Mallorca, Menorca, Ibiza, Formentera) in the Mediterranean Sea is characterised by mild and tempestuous winters, in between hot and bright summers.

The **Canary Islands** (Tenerife, Gran Canaria, Lanzarote, Fuerteventura, La Palma, La Gomera, El Hierro, ⓒsee Discovering the Canary Islands) are characterised by a subtropical climate, due to their latitude in the Atlantic Ocean. They are well known for their year-round pleasant temperatures and low rainfall, making them a haven for winter sun-seekers. Even here however there are significant climate differences between the coast and inland.

CLIMATE CHANGE

Experts' warnings that large areas of Spain may be desertified by 2050 have stimulated tree-planting: the total of 18 million hectares of woodland is the fastest growing in Europe. Drought has been exacerbated by the demands of intensive farming and coastal tourism. While the fields dry and crack in the baking Andalucian or Murcian sunshine, golf courses greedily drink thousands of gallons to remain lush year-round, while hotel laundries further deplete valuable water resources.

Desalination plants are likely to multiply to meet demand, like wind-farms, which produced over 21 per cent of the country's energy in 2014, but water supplies now limit construction right along the Mediterranean coast.

Discovering
Spain

Procession of the pilgrims of El Rocío during the Whitsun weekend, Andalucía.
© Kaos/Sime/Photononstop

Central Spain

Cáceres Viejo
© Jean-Pierre Degas/themis.fr

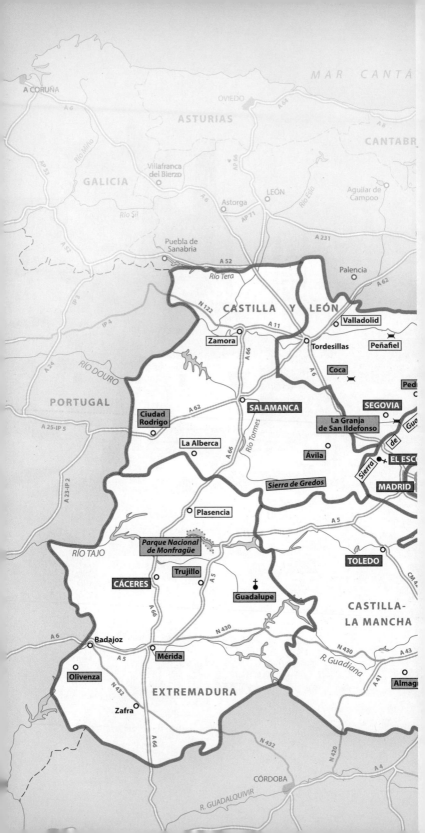

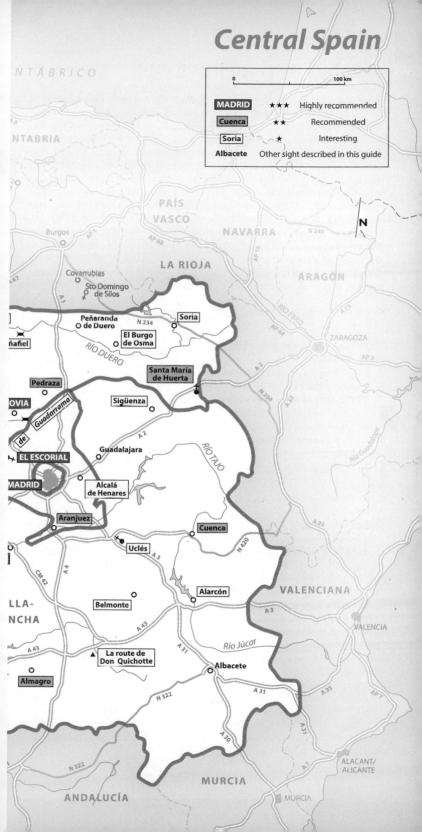

Central Spain

MADRID	★★★	Highly recommended
Cuenca	★★	Recommended
Soria	★	Interesting
Albacete		Other sight described in this guide

0   100 km

N

NTÁBRICO

NTABRIA

PAÍS VASCO

NAVARRA

ARAGÓN

Burgos

LA RIOJA

ZARAGOZA

Covarrubias

Sto Domingo de Silos

Peñaranda de Duero

Soria

El Burgo de Osma

ñafiel

RÍO DUERO

Santa María de Huerta

Pedraza

Sigüenza

OVIA

Sierra de Guadarrama

Guadalajara

RÍO TAJO

EL ESCORIAL

MADRID

Alcalá de Henares

Aranjuez

Cuenca

Uclés

Alarcón

VALENCIANA

Belmonte

VALENCIA

LLA-NCHA

Río Júcar

La route de Don Quichotte

Almagro

Albacete

MURCIA

ANDALUCÍA

ALACANT/ALICANTE

MURCIA

Madrid and around

Set on on the arid central tableland known as the *meseta*, Madrid stands at the geographical heart of Spain. Its central location contributed to Philip II's decision to settle his court here, but so, too, did its healthy climate and stunning mountain backdrop. It is one of the noisiest cities in Europe; it is also famed as a buzzing late-night metropolis, with traffic jams well into the small hours; it is the continent's richest city, alongside London, for art galleries; and, despite the fact that it is the highest European capital, at over 640m/2 100ft above sea level (and enjoys cooling breezes), Madrid is also the hottest capital with temperatures rising above 40°C (10°F) in August, when around one third of all Madrileños flee the city. As a tourist destination Madrid has not yet reached the popularity of the Catalan capital, Barcelona, lacking its proximity to the sea and old-world charm. But it is an open-hearted dynamic city that is keenly recovering its historical past while refusing to let go of old-fashioned bars, restaurants and customs. City slickers, gourmets and clubbers appreciate Madrid as much as the culture vultures who relish its stunning art collections.

Highlights

1 Taking a walk and tapas in the **Plaza Mayor** (p123)

2 Enjoying dinner and a night out around **Plaza Santa Ana** (p136)

3 Gazing in wonder at the **Prado's** Spanish **art collection** (p139)

4 Seeing Picasso's Guernica in the **Museo de Arte Reina Sofía** (p143)

5 Strolling in the palace river gardens of **Aranjuez** (p152)

Paseo del Prado

This unique avenue, lined by lofty trees, is home to the Prado museum, which houses the Spanish royal collection of classical paintings including Velázquez's *Las Meninas*. Since the Paseo was laid out in the 18C it has attracted a host of other museums, galleries and art centres, including the famous Museo Thyssen-Bornemisza and the Reina Sofía contemporary art museum where Picasso's *Guernica* hangs. Such is the richness of these and other art collections that many visitors choose to spend most of their days here, taking breaks in the green Retiro Park or Royal Botanical Garden nearby. At the Paseo's southern end, Atocha station is a central junction for the highspeed AVE train network.

Habsburg Madrid

Centring on the Plaza Mayor, the heart of the old town, also called the Barrio de los Austrias, combines narrow alleyways with squares, churches, convents and monasteries, traditional and modern shops, and a host of places to eat and drink. The grandiose 2 800-room Royal Palace, built over earlier Habsburg palaces and a Muslim Álcazar, will occupy half a day of your time alone. An evening stroll around the old Muslim town's winding streets is the easiest way to evoke the city's past.

Centro

The popular quarters around the wide arterial avenues of Alcalà and Gran Vía are a mosaic of bustling pedestrianised shopping streets and characterful old residential areas. Many of the city's hotels, theatres and cinemas are here and this is also the epicentre of its famed nightlife.

Day trips and excursions

A short trip out of Madrid allows you to visit El Escorial, the 16C royal palatial complex built by Philip II – a palace, church, monastery, mausoleum and museum all under one massive roof – or Alcalá de Henares, Cervantes' birthplace. Romantics and music lovers will want to make the trip to the palace of Aranjuez to see the gardens that inspired Rodrigo's haunting guitar concerto.

Madrid★★★

Madrid is one of Europe's liveliest cities, with wide avenues, attractive parks and a general *alegría* or joie de vivre. It became capital of Spain in the 16C when Spain ruled a vast empire, and its many monuments span the 17C, 18C and 19C. The city is world-famous for its exceptional wealth of paintings.

THE CITY TODAY

Madrid Today – Madrid is not only the judicial and political capital but also the country's main business centre.
The city's most noteworthy modern architecture includes the **Banco de Bilbao-Vizcaya** in the **AZCA centre**, the 250 m/820 ft highrise **Cuatro Torres** complex north of Plaza de Castilla, and the **Ciudad de Justicia** (City of Justice) complex on the city's eastern edge.

A BIT OF HISTORY

Madrid owes its name to the 9C fortress *(alcázar)* of Majerit. In 1085 it was captured by Alfonso VI, who discovered a statue of the Virgin by a granary *(almudín)*. He converted the mosque into a church dedicated to the Virgin of the Almudena who was declared the city's patron. Emperor Charles V rebuilt the Muslim *alcázar* and in 1561 his son Philip II moved the court from Toledo to Madrid.
The town grew dramatically quickly in Spain's Golden Age (16C). King Philip IV gave court patronage to many artists including **Velázquez** and **Murillo**, as well as men of letters such as Lope de Vega, Quevedo and Calderón.
From a town to a city – Madrid, as we know it today, underwent its greatest transformations in the 18C under the Bourbons. Philip V built a royal palace; Charles III provided Madrid with a splendour hitherto unknown in the Paseo del Prado and the Puerta de Alcalá, magnificent examples of Neoclassical town planning. The 19C began with occupation by the French and the

▶ **Population:** 3 141 991.

⚺ **Michelin Map:** 575 or 576 K 18–19 (town plan).

▣ **Info:** Plaza Mayor 27; Plaza de Neptuno; Plaza de Cibeles 1; Ronda de Atocha; Plaza de Callao; Faro de Moncloa Tourist Info Point: Avendia Arco de la Victoria 2; Aeropuerto de Barajas (T2, lounges 5 and 6; T4, lounges 10 and 11). Tourist information: ℗91 578 78 10. www.esmadrid.com; www.turismomadrid.es.

◉ **Location:** Europe's highest capital (646m/ 2 119ft), at the centre of the Iberian Peninsula, with a dry climate: hot summers and cold, sunny winters.

▣ **Parking:** It's best to park for the duration and use the excellent Metro.

☞ **Don't Miss:** The Prado, Plaza Mayor, bars in Plaza Santa Ana, Museo Colecciones Reales.

⏱ **Timing:** Start with the art museums, and take a siesta in order to enjoy Madrid's late-hours dining and bars.

👫 **Kids:** Faunia, Parque de Atracciones de Madrid, Parque Warner Madrid, Zoo-aquarium, and Aquópolis.

Madrid rebellion of May 1808 and its brutal repression. In 1857 the remaining ramparts were demolished and a vast expansion plan *(ensanche)* gave rise to the districts of Chamberí, Salamanca and Argüelles. At the beginning of the 20C, architecture was French-inspired, as in the Ritz and Palace hotels; the neo-Mudéjar style was also popular, as at the bullring. The **Gran Vía** linked Madrid's new districts in 1910. Since then its outer quarters have grown and spread in all directions around the metro underground and train system.

GETTING AROUND

Airport – Madrid-Barajas airport is located northeast of the city, 13km/8mi from downtown. The EMT Línea Exprés operates between the airport's four terminals and city centre, ending at Atocha Station (€5). www.emtmadrid.es. Departures every 15–20 mins (35 mins at night; night buses terminate in Plaza de Cibeles).

Metro line no. 8 connects the airport with the city. It's a 12 to 15-minute journey from Nuevos Ministerios to all terminals. A modern suburban train line connects Terminal 4 with several key locations in Madrid: Chamartin, Nuevos Ministerios, Atocha and Principe Pío.
Airport information: 902 40 47 04; www.aeropuertomadrid-barajas.com. Info-Iberia and bookings: 901 111 500.

RENFE (Spanish State Railways) – The city's main railway stations are Atocha (Pl. del Emperador Carlos V and Glorieta Carlos V) and Chamartín (Agustín de Foxa). For information and reservations call into a station or log on to *www.renfe.com*.
AVE high-speed trains depart from Atocha, taking just 2hr30min to reach Sevilla via Córdoba (1hr42min); to Barcelona (2hr30min) via Zaragoza (1hr15min); to Toledo (30min); to Albacete (1hr20min), to Málaga (2hr25min), to Valencia (1hr38min), to Alicante (2hr5min) and to Valladolid (1hr).
Madrid has a good suburban train network (**Cercanías**) with routes to El Escorial, the Sierra de Guadarrama, Alcalá de Henares and Aranjuez.

Inter-city buses – Most inter-city buses depart from the Estación Sur (Méndez Álvaro 83; 902 996 666; www.estacionautobusesmadrid.com).

Car hire – All the familiar names are located at Barajas airport and Atocha and Chamartín railway stations. Pepecar (807 414 243, www.pepecar.com) offers good-value car hire with a wide range of models and pick-up points, including the airport.

Taxis – Madrid has a huge number of registered taxis with distinctive white paintwork with a red diagonal stripe on the rear doors. The green light indicates that the taxi is for hire.

Local buses – For information, call 914 068 810 A good way of getting to know the city, although traffic jams may be a problem. Passengers should beware of pickpockets. Generally buses operate between 6am and 11.30pm. Night buses operate from 11.30pm onwards, with most departing from Plaza de Cibeles. In addition to single tickets (€1.50), passengers can purchase a ten-trip **metro-bus** ticket (*un bono de 10 viajes*; €18.30) valid on both the bus and metro network, as well as a zone-based 1–7 day tourist season ticket *(abono turístico)* which is valid for an unlimited number of bus and metro journeys. Bicycles may be taken on the metro all day Saturday and Sunday and public holidays and for limited hours on other days.

Metro – Metro stations are shown on the maps in this guide (902 44 44 03, www.metromadrid.es/en). The metro system is the fastest way to get around the city. It operates from 6am to 1.30am. Passengers should beware of pickpockets.

SIGHTSEEING

The **Guía del Ocio** (www.guiadelocio.com/madrid) is a weekly guide containing a list of every cultural event and show in the city. It can be purchased at newspaper stands.

Madrid City Tour Bus – This open-topped tourist bus offers two circular routes around the city (historic Madrid, modern Madrid). Tickets, which can be purchased on board, in hotels via a travel agent, or at newspaper kiosks, are valid for one or two days during which passengers can hop on and off both routes as much as they like. Services operate

10am–6pm in low season, 9am–10pm in high season. The 37 stops include the Paseo del Prado, Plaza Colón, Gran Vía, Palacio Real and Puerta del Sol. For information and prices, see www.madridcitytour.es.

Bike tours – Bravo Bike (Juan Alvarez Mendízábal, 19; ☎917 582 945, www.bravobike.com) run cycle tours in and out of Madrid, from €35. You can also rent bikes.

DISTRICTS

Madrid is a city full of charm, with its magnificent parks and impressive buildings. It is a city best explored by strolling through its streets and squares, discovering the delights of its many districts or *barrios* and getting to know its friendly inhabitants.

Centro – This district is made up of several areas, each with their own character. It has a reputation for being noisy and chaotic, although visitors are often surprised by its quieter narrow alleyways and small squares. It includes **Sol-Callao**, the shopping area par excellence, packed with locals and visitors out for a stroll, heading for the main pedestrianised precinct (Preciados district), although today younger shoppers head for fashionable **Fuencarral**. A number of cinemas are also located in this area. Visitors should take particular care in the evening, especially in streets such as Valverde and Barco.

Barrio de los Austrias – Madrid's oldest district is wedged between Calles Mayor, Bailén, Toledo, Las Cavas and the Plaza de la Cebada. Its origins are Muslim and it still retains its evocatively named streets and Mudéjar towers. An excellent area for tapas, dinner or a drink. On Sundays, the famous **Rastro** flea market (☉see Rastro) starts near here, on Ribera de Curtidores.

Lavapiés – This district runs north from the square of the same name to Calle Atocha with many houses dating from the 17C. It is considered to be Madrid's most colourful district with a mix of locals, artists and a large immigrant population.

Huertas – Huertas was home to the literary community in the 17C. Nowadays, it is largely pedestrianised and packed with bars and restaurants. It is particularly lively at night, attracting an interesting mixture of late-night revellers.

Malasaña – This part of Madrid, which used to be known as Maravillas, is situated between Las Glorietas de Bilbao y Ruiz Jiménez and around Plaza del Dos de Mayo. In the mornings, this 19C *barrio* is quiet and full of local character, but it is transformed at night by the legions of young people who head for its bars, many of them classics from the 1980s Movida years. The district also has some tranquil cafés and restaurants.

Alonso Martínez – The average age and financial standing of this district's inhabitants is somewhat higher than in neighbouring Bilbao and Chueca, as shown by the myriad upmarket bars, restaurants and food shops frequented by the city's rich and famous.

Chueca – This district's approximate outer limits are the Paseo de Recoletos, Calle Hortaleza, Gran Vía and Calle Fernando VI. At the end of the last century it was one of Madrid's most elegant districts. Today it is the city's gay area, focussed on the bohemian Plaza de Chueca, with a multitude of small and sophisticated boutiques, design shops and art galleries.

Salamanca – In the 19C the Marquis of Salamanca designed this smart residential area in the shape of a draughts board with wide streets at right angles. Nowadays, the district is one of the capital's most expensive areas and is home to some of Spain's leading designer boutiques (Serrano and Ortega y Gasset) and an impressive collection of stores selling luxury goods.

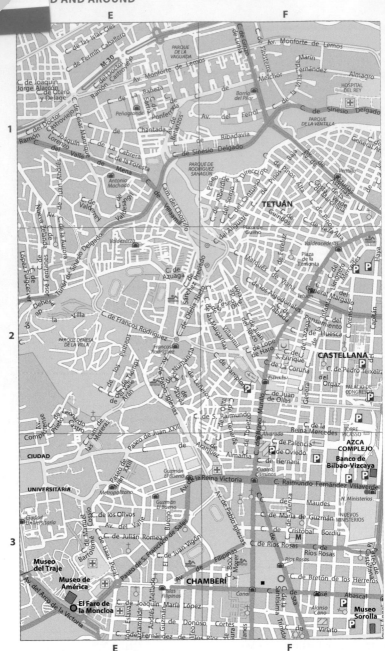

🐾 WALKING TOUR

① OLD MADRID (CENTRO)★

🔆 See map of walking tour p126–127.

🕐 Try to visit early, or late in the afternoon when the churches are open.

Steep, narrow streets, small squares, 17C palaces and mansions, houses with wrought-iron balconies dating from the 19C and early 20C characterise Old Madrid, the very heart of the city.

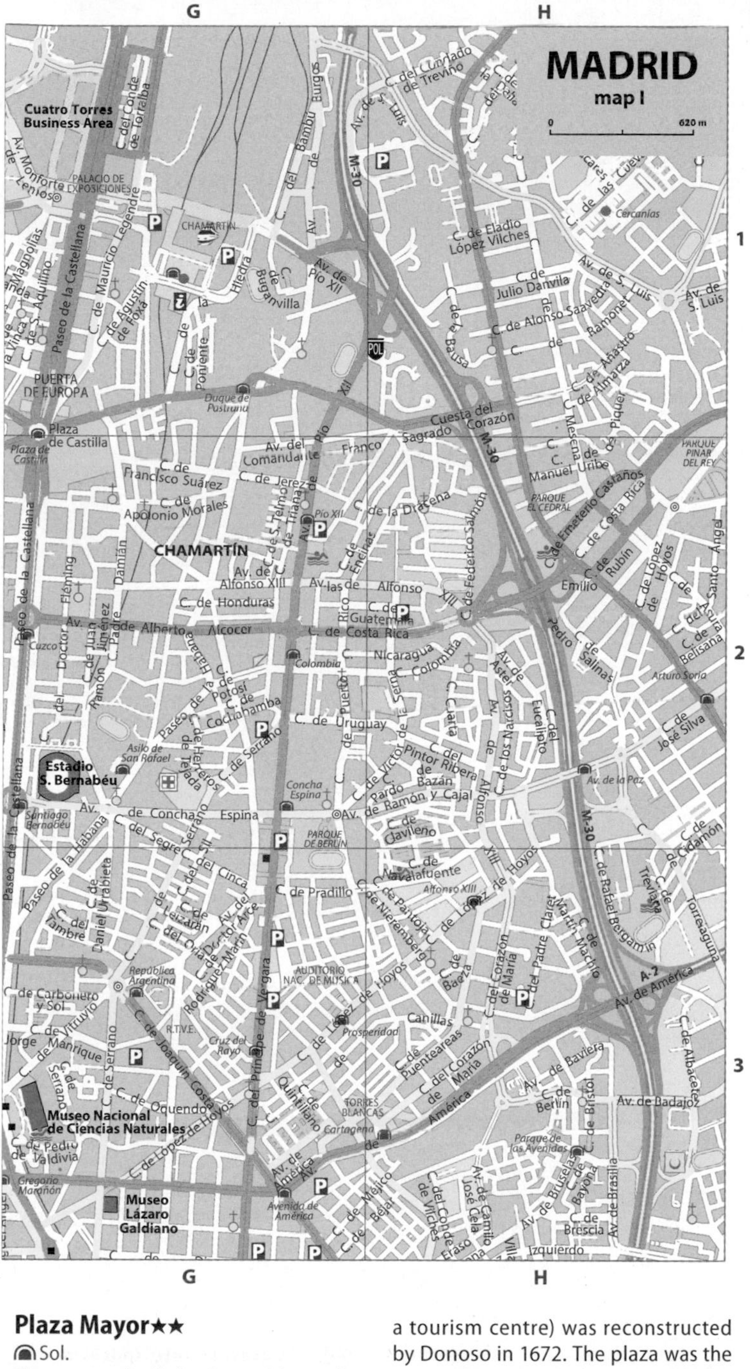

MADRID
map I

0 _____ 620 m

Map labels (grid G–H, rows 1–3):

Cuatro Torres Business Area

Av. de Monforte de Lemos

PALACIO DE EXPOSICIONES

Av. del Conde de Trevíño

Av. de Luis

Av. de S. Luis

del Condado de Treviño

C. de Eladio López Vilches

C. de Julio Danvila

C. de Alfonso Saavedra

Av. de S. Luis

PUERTA DE EUROPA

Plaza de Castilla

Plaza de Castilla

Francisco Suárez

C. de Jerez

Av. del Comandante Franco

Cuesta del Corazón

Cuesta del Sagrado Corazón

PARQUE PINAR DEL REY

C. de Manuel Uribe

PARQUE EL CEDRAL

C. de Apolonio Morales

CHAMARTÍN

Av. de Alfonso XIII

C. de Honduras

Av. las de Alfonso

C. de Guatemala

C. de Costa Rica

C. de Emeterio Castaños

Colombia

Nicaragua

C. de Uruguay

C. de Potosí

C. de Cochabamba

Pº de Serrano

Estadio S. Bernabéu

Santiago Bernabéu

Asilo de San Rafael

Concha Espina

Pardo Pintor de Ribera

Av. de Ramón y Cajal

PARQUE DE BERLÍN

de Pradillo

AUDITORIO NAC. DE MÚSICA

República Argentina

R.T.V.E.

Cruz del Rayo

Prosperidad

Canillas

TORRES BLANCAS

Av. de América

Museo Nacional de Ciencias Naturales

Gregorio Marañón

Museo Lázaro Galdiano

Parque de las Avenidas

Av. de Baviera

Av. de Badajoz

A-2

Av. de América

Izquierdo

Plaza Mayor★★

🚇 Sol.

The square built by Juan Gómez de Mora in 1619 is the centre of **Habsburg Madrid**. On the north side, the **Casa de la Panadería** (a former bakery, now a tourism centre) was reconstructed by Donoso in 1672. The plaza was the setting for **autos de fé**, mounted bullfights, and the proclamations of kings. A stamp and coin market is held on Sunday mornings and fiestas (9am–2pm)

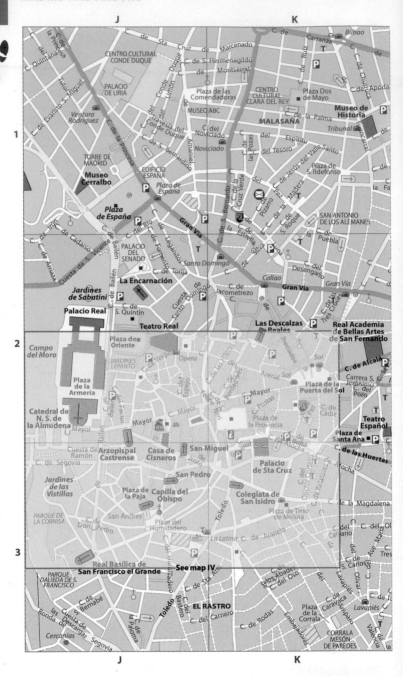

while at Christmas stalls sell decorations. Shops around the square retain a yesteryear look.

Pass through the **Arco de Cuchilleros** (pl. Mayor 9) into the street fronted by old houses with convex façades. The **Cava de San Miguel** provides a rear view of the houses on the square. This area is crowded with small restaurants *(mesones)* and bars *(tavernas)*. The

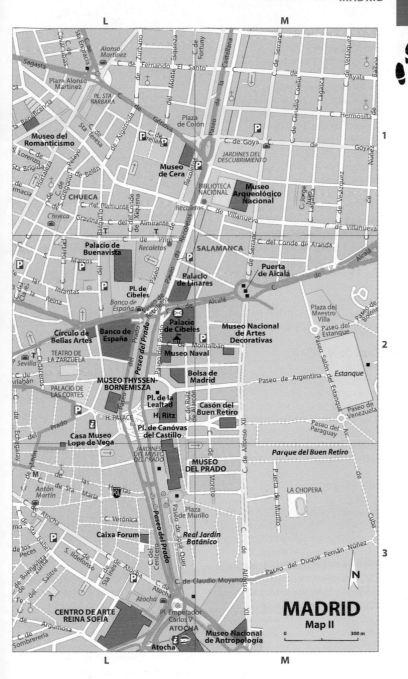

MADRID
Map II

0   300 m

N

Mercado de San Miguel, an indoor early 20C market, now a food emporium (open from 10am until 2am; www.mercado desanmiguel.es) set in an elegant iron structure.

◗ Take Conde de Miranda. Cross Plaza del Conde de Barajas and Gómez de Mora to Plaza de San Justo or Puerta Cerrada, a city gate. Continue right on San Justo.

Basílica Pontificia de San Miguel★

San Justo 4. Tirso de Molina or Ópera. Open daily 1 Jul–10 Sept 9.45am–1.15pm, 6–9.15pm, public holidays 9.45am–1.30pm, 6.30–9.15pm; 10 Sept–30 Jun 9.45am–1.30pm, 5.30–9.15pm; public holidays 9.45am–2.15pm, 6–9.15pm. 915 48 40 11. www.bsmiguel.es.

This basilica by Bonavia is a rare Spanish church inspired by 18C Italian Baroque. Its convex façade, designed as an interplay of inward and outward curves, is adorned with fine statues. The interior is graceful and elegant with an oval cupola, intersecting vaulting, flowing cornices and abundant stuccowork.

▶ Follow Puñonrostro and del Codo to Plaza de la Villa.

Plaza de la Villa★

Ópera.

Buildings around the square include the **Casa de la Villa** (town hall), built by Gómez de Mora in 1617, the **Torre de los Lujanes** (Luján Tower), a rare examples of 15C civil architecture, and the 16C **Casa de Cisneros**, connected to the Ayuntamiento by an arch.

Calle Mayor

Ópera.

The name, literally Main Street, gives an indication of its importance. At no. 61 is the narrow house of 17C playwright **Pedro Calderón de la Barca.** The Antigua Farmacia de la Reina Madre (Queen Mother's Pharmacy) at no. 59, founded in 1576, previously an alchemist, keeps a collection of chemist's jars and pots. The **Instituto Italiano de Cultura** (no. 86) occupies a 17C palace. The Palacio Uceda opposite, from the same period, is now the military headquarters of the **Capitanía General** (Captaincy General). In front of the **Iglesia Arzobispal Castrense** (17C–18C), a monument commemorates an attack on Alfonso XIII and Victoria Eugenia in 1906. In the nearby calle de San Nicolás

is the Mudéjar tower of San Nicolás de los Servita.

▶ Take del Sacramento to Plazuela del Cordón; return to del Cordón then continue to Segovia.

Across the street rises the 14C **Mudéjar tower** of the **Iglesia de San Pedro el Viejo** (Church of St Peter), a rare example of the Mudéjar style in Madrid.

▶ Go along del Príncipe Anglona.

Plaza de la Paja

This was a commercial centre in the Middle Ages. The Palacio Vargas obscures the Gothic **Capilla del Obispo**, a 16C chapel. In Plaza de los Carros, the Capilla de San Isidro (chapel) is part of the 17C Iglesia de San Andrés built in honour of Madrid's patron saint, San Isidro. The **Museo de San Isidro, Llos Orígenes de Madrid** (Pl. San Andrés 2; Latina;

MADRID
Map III

0   90 m

N

Palacio Real

Campo del Moro

Plaza de la Armería

P

Catedral de N. S. de la Almudena

Vega   C. Mayor

P. Ciudad de Plasencia

Capitanía General

Cuesta de la Vega

PARQUE DE ATENAS

PARQUE DE LA CUESTA DE LA VEGA

C. de Segovia   C. de Segovia

C. de Bailén

de

Segovia

Mazarredo

Jardines de las Vistillas

de la

C. de Moreno Nieto

Ronda

PARQUE DE LA CORNISA

Travesía de las Vistillas

C. de Yeseros

C. de Bailén

C. de Algecíras

Paseo Imperial

Real Basílica de San Francisco el Grande

Carrera

N

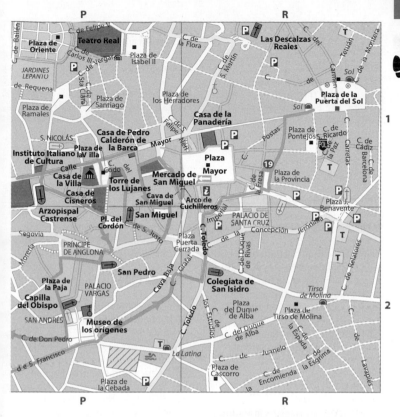

open Tue–Sun & hols 9.30am–8pm, 15 May open 9.30am-9.30pm, 15 July-15 September open Tues-Sun 10am-7pm; closed 1 Jan, 1 May, 24, 25 and 31 Dec; ℘913 66 74 15; www.madrid.es/museosanisidro), a museum containing a miraculous well and a fine Renaissance patio, is next to this complex of religious buildings. There is also an exhibit on Madrid from prehistory up until the installation of the Royal Court in the 16C.

▶ Cross Bailén and take the first street on the right.

Jardines de las Vistillas (Vistillas Gardens)

⬤ La Latina.

There are splendid **views** to the west, especially at sundown, of the Sierra de Guadarrama, Casa de Campo, the Catedral de la Almudena and the viaduct.

Basílica de San Francisco el Grande

San Buenaventura 1. ⬤ La Latina. Open Tue–Sat 10.30am–12.30pm, 4–6pm; Jul and Aug Tue–Sun 10.30am–12.30pm, 5–7pm. €3. ℘913 65 38 00.

The church's vast Neoclassical façade is by Sabatini; the circular edifice itself with six radial chapels and a large dome is by Francisco Cabezas. Walls and ceilings have 19C frescoes and paintings (18C in the chapels of St Anthony and St Bernardino). The Capilla de San Bernardino holds an early **Goya** of St Bernardino of Siena preaching before the King of Aragón (1781). Plateresque **stalls★** from the Monasterio de El Parral outside Segovia are in the chancel. 16C **stalls★** in the sacristy and chapter house are from the Cartuja de El Paular, a Carthusian monastery near Segovia.

◐ Walk along Carrera de San Francisco and Cava Alta to Toledo.

Calle de Toledo
🚇 La Latina or Tirso de Molina.
This is one of the old town's liveliest streets. The **El Rastro** flea market is held here (open Sun and public holidays 9am–3pm; 🚫 beware pickpockets).

◐ Continue up Toledo for about 200m/656ft.

Real Colegiata de San Isidro
Toledo 37. 🚇 La Latina or Tirso de Molina. Open daily 7.30am–1pm, 6–9pm. 🖉 913 69 20 37.
Formerly the church of the Imperial College of the Company of Jesus (1622), it was the cathedral of Madrid from 1885 until 1993 and contains the relics of Madrid's patron saint, San Isidro.

◐ Head north on Toledo then continue NE and along Esparteros. Turn right at Mayor then left.

Plaza de la Puerta del Sol
🚇 Gran Vía or Callao.
On the best-known square in Madrid, a small monument displays Madrid's coat of arms, next to an equestrian statue of Charles III. The clock on the former post office chimes midnight at New Year's Eve while a large crowd eats a grape

between each chime, to bring luck the next year. Nearby, traditional shops with colourful wood fronts sell fans, mantillas and delicacies.

◐ Walk east through Plaza de la Puerta del Sol, then onto Alcalá.

👣 WALKING TOUR

② BOURBON MADRID★★
👓See map of walking tour p132–133.

Charles III's Paseo del Prado remains a grand tree-shaded avenue lined by world-class museums and from them it is a short walk to the Retiro Park.

Plaza de Cibeles★
🚇 Banco de España.
In the square is the 18C fountain of Cybele, goddess of fertility, emblematic of Madrid.
Many an artist has been inspired to paint the perspectives opening from the square and the impressive buildings around, such as the **Banco de España** (1891), the 18C **Palacio de Buenavista** (Ministry of Defence), the late-19C **Palacio de Linares**, now the home of the **Casa de América** (pas. de Recoletos 2; guided tours Sept–Jul Sat–Sun 11am, noon, 1pm; €8; 🖉 915 95 48 00; www.casa

---

Paseo del Prado

With the 18C drawing to a close, Charles III wanted to develop a public area worthy of Madrid's position as capital of Spain and he called upon the court's best architects for his project. In an area outside the city at the time, Hermosilla, Ventura Rodríguez, Sabatini and Villanueva drained, embellished and built a curved avenue with two large fountains, Cybele and Neptune, at each end, and a third, Apollo, in the centre. To complete the project, the **Botanical Gardens**, **Natural History Museum** (now the Museo del Prado) and the **Observatory**, were also built. The result was a balanced combination of the functional and the ornate dedicated to science and the arts. Immediately the Paseo del Prado became a favourite place for Madrileños to meet and to relax. Today, the avenue retains its dignified air and a cluster of extraordinary museums that draw visitors from right around the world. A stroll along its tree-lined boulevard gives you a chance to appreciate the vision and imagination of King Charles.

Plaza de la Puerta del Sol

© Claudio Cassa o/Sime/Photononstop

merica.es), and the **Palacio de Cibeles** (Post and Telegraph Office, 1919), where there is a cultural centre, **Centro Centro** (open Tue–Sun 10am–8pm, closed 1 and 6 Jan, 1 May, 24, 25 and 31 Dec; ℘91 480 00 08; www.centrocentro.org) with a viewing platform (open Tue–Sun 10.30am–1.30pm and 4–7pm) as well as a restaurant, café and bar.

Paseo del Prado★

This tree-lined avenue runs from Plaza de Cibeles to Plaza del Emperador Carlos V, past the Ministerio de la Marina and Museo Naval, the **Plaza de la Lealtad** with an obelisk dedicated to the heroes of the 2 May, the Neoclassical **Bolsa** (Stock Exchange) and the emblematic **Hotel Ritz** (www.mandarinoriental.com).

▶ Take the first left, Montalbán, after the Palacio de Cibeles.

Museo Nacional de Artes Decorativas

Montalbán 12. 🚇 Retiro. Open Tue–Sat 9.30am–3pm, Thu 5–8pm (Sept–Jun only), Sun and public holidays 10am–3pm. Closed 1 and 6 Jan, 1 May, 24–25 & 31 Dec. €3; no charge Sun, Thu afternoon, Sat 2–3pm, 18 Apr, 18 May, 12 Oct, 6 Dec. ℘915 32 64 99. http://mnartesdecorativas.mcu.es.

This museum in a 19C mansion contains a splendid collection of furniture and decorative objects as well as a complete tiled 18C kitchen.

▶ Return to Paseo del Prado and continue south.

Museo Naval

Pas. del Prado 5. 🚇 Banco de España. Open year-round Tue–Sun 10am–7pm (Aug until 3pm). Closed public holidays, 1 & 6 Jan, 24–25 Dec. €3 donation requested. ℘915 23 85 16. www.armada.mde.es/museonaval. On display are ship **models★**, nautical instruments, weapons, and paintings of naval battles. The **map of Juan de la Cosa★★** (1500) is the first to show the American continent.

▶ Continue on Paseo del Prado.

Plaza de Canóvas del Castillo

🚇 Banco de España. This square, featuring the splendid Fuente de Neptuno (Neptune Fountain), is overlooked by the Neoclassical **Palacio de Villahermosa** housing the **Museo Thyssen-Bornemisza★★★** (🔍 see p141) and the luxury Westin Palace hotel.

▶ Continue walking south, on the eastern side of the Paseo del Prado.

Museo del Prado★★★
Ĝ See Museums.
The Neoclassical building of one of the world's great art museums was built in the reign of Charles III, originally intended for the Institute of Natural Sciences. Behind it is Rafael Moneo's 2007 annexe, which incorporates the Jeronimos' monastery cloister and new iron doors by Cristina Iglesias. Behind the Prado is the royal church, San Jerónimo el Real.

▶ Continue south to the Pl. de Murillo facing the Museum's southern façade.

Real Jardín Botánico
Pl. de Murillo, 2. Open Nov–Feb 10am–6pm; Mar and Oct until 7pm; Apr and Sept until 8pm; May–Aug until 9pm. €4. ℘914 20 30 17. www.rjb.csic.es.
The Botanical Garden, opened in 1781, was commissioned by Charles III and planned by Juan de Villanueva, who also built the Museo del Prado. Today one enters by just one gate facing the Museum's southern facade. Apart from its beautifully tended beds, lawns and variety of trees, the garden has a vine bower planted with grape varieties from around Spain and three greenhouses presenting ecosystems from desert to equatorial. The shop at the gate sells seeds and plants.

▶ Cross the Paseo to its western side.

Caixa Forum
Po. del Prado 36. Open daily 10am–8pm. Closed 25 Dec, 1 & 6 Jan. €4 exhibitions. ℘913 307 300. https://caixaforum.es/en/madrid
The latest addition to the Paseo del Prado, Caixa Forum is well worth a visit for its architecture alone: Jacques Herzog and Pierre de Meuron artfully converted a Modernist power station and Patrick Blanc designed its stunning vertical garden. Inside, an arts centre mixes temporary shows with concerts, talks and, on the top floor, a café-restaurant.

▶ Continue walking south, cross Calle Atocha and, 100m/110yd later, turn right into C. de Sta Isabel.

The former **Hospital de San Carlos**, an austere but imposing granite block with a towering extension and agora designed by architect **Jean Nouvel**, houses the **Museo Nacional Centro de Arte Reina Sofía**★ (Ĝ see p143).

▶ Cross the Pl del Emperador Carlos V to its southeastern side.

Estación de Atocha (Atocha Railway Station)
Pl. del Emperador Carlos V.
🚇 Atocha Renfe or Atocha.
Atocha station's vast 19C glass and wrought-iron **lobby** dominates this square. Enter to view the tropical patio garden, where turtles swim in pools, and to glimpse the AVE train platforms. The local train-station (Cercanías), nicknamed the "pillbox", was designed by Rafael Moneo. There is a memorial to those who died in the 2004 bombing: an opaque cylinder, set partly beneath the ground, engraved with messages to the dead from loved ones, rises above ground (open daily 10am–8pm). Opposite, on the north side of the Avda Ciudad de Barcelona, stands the elaborate late 19C Ministry of Agriculture.

▶ Cross the Avda Ciudad de Barcelona and turn right to the junction with C. de Alfonso XII.

Museo Nacional de Antropología
Alfonso XII, 68. Open Tue–Sat 9.30am–8pm, Sun and hols 10am–3pm. Closed 1 & 6 Jan, 1 May, 24, 25,31 Dec. €3; no charge Sat after 2pm, Sun, 18 May, 12 Oct, 16 Nov, 6 Dec. ℘915 306 418. http://mnantropologia.mcu.es.
Housed in a Neoclassical building this small museum, often overlooked, presents a fascinating ethnological collection of objects from around the world – particularly the Americas, Philippines and Africa – arranged thematically around ways of life.

Palacio de Cristal, Parque del Buen Retiro

◉ Follow Alfonso XII northeast, crossing to enter the park at the Puerta del Ángel Caído.

Parque del Buen Retiro★★ (Retiro Park)

Open daily Oct–Apr 6am–10pm; May–Sept 6am–midnight. ℘915 30 0041.

The Retiro is close to the heart of every Madrileño. Once the garden of a Hapsburg summer palace, destroyed during the War of Independence, it keeps 130ha/321 acres of greenery with dense clumps of trees, a rose garden, fountains, temples, Modernist zoo buildings, colonnades and statues.

Beside the Lake (Estanque), where boats may be hired, is the imposing *Monumento a Alfonso XII*. Art exhibitions are held in the **Palacio de Velázquez**, built for the 1883 Exposición National de la Minería, and the graceful **Palacio de Cristal★** (Crystal Palace) which overlooks a shaded pool (◉ Ibiza; open Apr–Sept daily 10am–10pm; Oct 10am-9pm, Nov–Mar daily 10am–6pm; closed 1 & 6 Jan, 1 May, 24–25, 31 Dec and may close on rainy days; ℘91 774 1000, www.museoreinasofia.es).

◉ After exploring the park, take the Avda Mejico from the Lake's northwestern corner to the Pl. de la Independencia.

Puerta de Alcalá★ (Alcalá Arch)

Pl. de la Independencia. ◉ Retiro.

The arch at the centre of Plaza de la Independencia was built by Sabatini between 1769 and 1778 to celebrate the triumphant entry of Charles III into Madrid and during the Movida years became the symbol of the city's new democracy. The perspective is particularly grand at night, taking in Plaza de Cibeles, Calle de Alcalá and the Gran Vía.

 WALKING TOUR

3 ROYAL MADRID★★

⏱ See map of walking tour p132–133.

Madrid is home to the Royal Palace, built where the Spanish Royal family lived for four centuries, and to convents and churches that sprung up around court life.

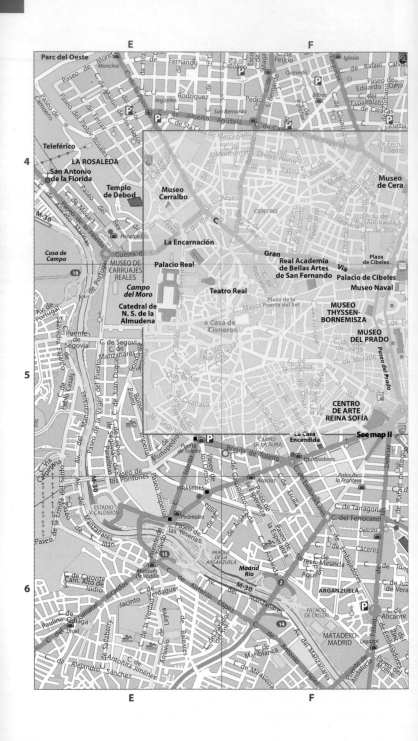

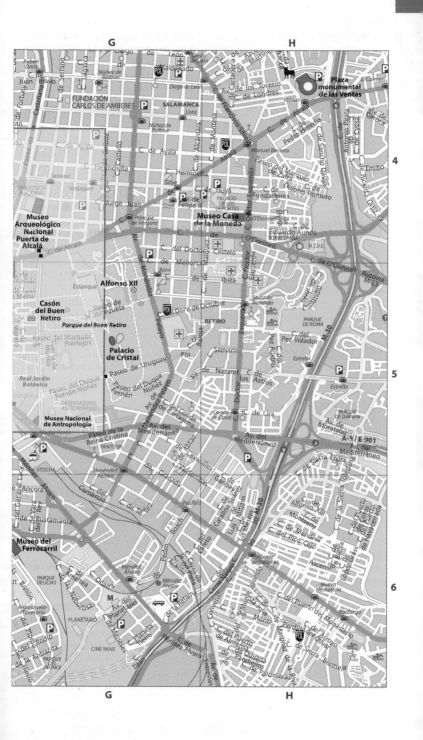

Plaza de la Armería

Along the vast arcaded square (south side) is the **Catedral de la Almudena** (⬤Ópera; Cathedral open daily 9am–8.30pm (Jul–Aug until 9pm); museum and dome Mon–Sat 10am-2.30pm; €6; ☎915 42 22 00, www.catedraldelaalmudena.es). The cathedral, begun in 1879, was finished in 1993. The neo-Baroque façade harmonises with the palace. The view towards the west extends over the Casa de Campo and the Campo del Moro gardens sloping down to the Manzanares river.

Palacio Real★★
(Royal Palace)

Bailén. ⬤Ópera. Open Oct–Mar daily 10am–6pm; Apr–Sept daily 10am–8pm; changing of the guard Wed 11am. For closing dates see website or telephone. €11 palace, art gallery and armoury; guide additional €4. Free to all visitors 18 May & 12 Oct. ☎914 54 87 00. www.patrimonionacional.es.

The best view of the palace is from Paseo de Extremadura and from the gardens of the **Campo del Moro★** (open Oct–Mar daily 10am–6pm (Apr–Sept 8pm). This imposing edifice, built by the Bourbons following a fire at the Habsburg Alcázar, was the royal residence until 1931. It is still used for major State occasions. The palace is a quadrilateral made of Guadarrama granite and white stone, 140m/459ft on the sides, on a high bossaged base. The upper register, in which Ionic columns and Doric pilasters alternate, is crowned by a white limestone balustrade. The north front gives onto the **Jardines de Sabatini**, the west the **Campo del Moro**. Plaza de la Armería stands to the south between the west and east wings of the palace. The east façade gives onto **Plaza de Oriente**.

Palacio★
(Palace)

A monumental staircase with a ceiling painted by Giaquinto leads to the Salón de Alabarderos (Halberdier Room), with a ceiling painted by Tiepolo.

This leads to the **Salón de Columnas** (Column Room) where royal celebrations and banquets are held. The **Salón del Trono★** (Throne Room) retains decoration from the period of Charles III and is resplendent with crimson velvet hangings and a magnificent ceiling by Tiepolo (1764) symbolising *The Greatness of the Spanish Monarchy*.

The consoles, mirrors and gilded bronze lions are of Italian design. The following three rooms were the king's quarters, occupied by Charles III in 1764. The Saleta Gasparini, the king's dining room, retains a ceiling painted by Mengs.

The Gasparini antechamber also has a ceiling by Mengs, and **Goya** portraits of Charles IV and María Luisa of Parma. The **Cámara Gasparini** is covered in pure Rococo decoration.

The Salón de Carlos III was the king's bedroom. The décor is from the period of Ferdinand VII. The **Sala de Porcelana** is, along with its namesake in Aranjuez Palace, the masterpiece of the Buen Retiro Porcelain Factory. Official banquets are held in the Alfonso XII **Comedor de Gala** or Banqueting Hall (for 145 guests), adorned with 16C Brussels tapestries. The two music rooms contain instruments including several made by **Stradivarius★**. In the chapel are frescoes by Corrado Giaquinto and paintings by Mengs *(Annunciation)* and Bayeu *(St Michael the Archangel)*.

Real Farmacia
(Royal Pharmacy)

Several rooms display 18C–20C jars, including a fine 18C Talavera glass jar.

Museo de Colecciones Reales ★★

This new museum, which has taken 10 years to build at a cost of €160 million, is due to open in the second half of 2016. It will display 1,000 objects from the royal collection on a rotational basis. The first floor will be dedicated to the House of Asturias, the second to the House of Bourbon and the top floor will hold temporary exhibitions.

▶ The palace faces Plaza de Oriente.

Plaza de Oriente

This attractive square between the east façade of the Palacio Real and the Teatro Real is pleasant for a stroll. The magnificent equestrian statue of Philip IV is the work of Pietro Tacca (17C).

Teatro Real

Pl. de Oriente. Ópera. Guided tours (see website for details of special technical, artistic and nocturnal tours) daily on the half hour 10.00am–1pm and audio guide tours 9.30am–3.30pm. Closed 1 Jan, 24–25, 31 Dec. Guided tour €8, audio guide €7. 915 16 06 00. www.teatro-real.com.
This hexagonal Neoclassical building was created as an opera house in 1850 for Isabel II. After reopening in 1997, it is now one of the world's great opera houses but also promotes music and dance. There is a gourmet restaurant, a café and a shop too.

▷ On the western side of the Plaza de Oriente Calle Pavia leads to the Plaza de la Encarnación.

Real Monasterio de la Encarnación★ (Royal Convent of the Incarnation)

Pl. de la Encarnación 1. Ópera. Guided tours (45min) Tue–Sat 10am–2pm, 4–6.30pm, Sun & hols 10am–3pm. See website for closing dates. €6; no charge Wed & Thu pm for EU citizens and 18 May. 914 54 87 00. www.patrimonionacional.es.
The convent, on a delightful square near the former Alcázar, was founded in 1611 by Margaret of Austria. The collection of paintings from the 17C Madrid School is particularly rich and includes the interesting *Exchange of Princesses on Pheasant Island* in 1615 by Van der Meulen. There is a polychrome sculpture of *Christ at the Column* by Gregorio Hernández on the first floor.
The Relicario★, with ceiling painted by Vicencio Carducci, holds 1 500 relics. The church with quasi-Herreran portals was reconstructed in the 18C after the Alcázar fire.

▷ Returning to the Teatro Real, turn left up Carlos III, then follow Arenal and turn left up San Martín.

Monasterio de las Descalzas Reales★★

Pl. de las Descalzas. Ópera. Guided tours (45min) Tue–Sat 10am–2pm, 4–6.30pm, Sun & hols 10am–3pm. See website for closing dates. €6; no charge Wed & Thu pm for EU citizens and 18 May. 914 54 87 00. www.patrimonionacional.es.
Joanna of Austria, daughter of Emperor Charles V, founded the convent of Poor Clares in the palace where she was born. It served as a retreat for nobles.
The magnificent grand staircase★ is totally decorated with frescoes. In a former dormitory is an extraordinary collection of tapestries★★ depicting the Triumph of the Church, woven in Brussels in the 17C to cartoons by Rubens. The 33 small chapels are sumptuously decorated; outstanding is that of the Virgin of Guadalupe.
Convent treasures include portraits of the royal family by Rubens, Sánchez Coello and others.

▷ Take Postigo de San Martín to Plaza del Callao and turn left down Gran Vía.

Plaza de España

Plaza de España.
Gran Vía, built by Alfonso XIII before his wedding, is now the city's busiest shopping street. It leads west to the Plaza de España, where a monument to Cervantes in the middle of the city's central esplanade is overwhelmed by 1950s skyscrapers.
From here Calle Princesa, popular with students, leads towards Moncloa and the Ciudad Universitaria★ (University City). From its southeastern corner Calle Bailen leads back to the Royal Palace and its splendid formal Jardines de Sabitini (open daily May–Sept 9am–10pm; Oct–Apr 9pm).

🐾 WALKING TOUR

4️⃣ LITERARY MADRID

📍 See map of walking tour p132–133.

This network of characterful old streets on the eastern side of **Plaza de Santa Ana**, is known as Huertas, or the Barrio de las Letras, as it was home to great writers and dramatists during Madrid's Golden Age. Cervantes, Quevedo and Lope de Vega lived here and were buried in the Iglesia de San Sebastián. Here you will also find one of the country's finest theatres, **Teatro Español**, on Plaza Santa Ana, as well as the **Círculo de Bellas Artes** arts centre on Marqués de Casa Riera.

There are excellent antiquarian bookshops by day while after dark, visitors and locals enjoy a hectic bohemian nightlife.

Around Plaza Santa Ana

Facing the Teatro Español the **Reina Victoria** (now the ME Madrid Reina Victoria) hotel, was once the meeting place for bullfighters.

On the square's south side the **Cervecería Alemana**, a favourite haunt of Ernest Hemingway and Ava Gardner on their visits to Madrid, remains unchanged. Elsewhere you can enjoy decorative old façades on a night-time stroll: the Villa Rosa (www.tablaoflamencovillarosa.com), an old flamenco *tablao* next door to the Hotel ME, is splendidly tiled, and the nearby Bar La Venencia on Calle Echegaray retains an old-fashioned air.

▶ Take Calle del Prado, turn right down Calle de León and left down Calle de Cervantes.

Casa Museo de Lope de Vega★

Cervantes 11. 🚇 Anton Martín. Guided tours (35min) Tue–Sun 10am–6pm. Closed national and local public holidays. Reserve in advance. 📞914 29 92 16. www.casamuseolopedevega.org. Lope de Vega bought this house at the heart of literary Madrid when he was Spain's most famous playwright. The top two floors and garden have been recreated around an inventory and his writings. Of special interest are the room where he wrote such works as *Fuentovejuna* and the chapel.

▶ Turn left out of the house, take Calle de San Agustín, first left, to come out in the Plaza de las Cortes.

When you emerge on the Plaza you face the **Congreso de los Diputados**, Spain's parliament, held at gunpoint during the attempted military coup on 23 February 1981. Walking left up San Jeronimo, and then right down Calle Sevilla to Alcalá, you pass embassies and old banks.

Real Academia de Bellas Artes de San Fernando★ (San Fernando Royal Fine Arts Academy)

Alcalá 13. 🚇 Sevilla, Sol. Open Tue–Sun & public hols 10am–3pm. Closed 1 & 6 Jan, 1 & 30 May, Aug, 9 Nov, 24–25 & 31 Dec. €8; no charge 18 May, 12 Oct, 6 Dec and every Wed. 📞915 24 08 64. www.realacademiabellasartes sanfernando.com.

Among the Royal Academy's valuable collection of 16C–20C paintings are works by Ribera, **Zurbarán**, **Murillo**, Alonso Cano *(Christ Crucified)* and **Velázquez**, but, above all, street scenes and a self-portait by **Goya**, a member of the Academy.

SALAMANCA – LA CASTELLANA
Museo Arqueológico Nacional★★ (Archaeological Museum)

Serrano 13. 🚇 Serrano. Open Tue–Sat 9.30am–8pm, Sun and public holidays 9.30am–3pm. Closed 1 &6 Jan, 1 May, 24–25 & 31 Dec. €3. No charge Sat 2–8pm, Sun morning, 18 April, 18 May, 12 Oct, 6 Dec. 📞915 77 79 12. www.man.es.

Reopened in 2014 in a splendidly remodelled building, the Museum's world-class collection runs from prehistoric art – in the garden is a reproduction of the **Cuevas de Altamira** and their paintings of bison – to treasures from churches along the pilgrimage route to Santiago. Among early pieces are the splendid bronze **Costix bulls★** of the Megalithic culture (Talayots) of the Balearic Islands. Iberian sculpture is exhibited at its peak of artistic expression: the **Dama de Elche★★★** *(Lady of Elche)* is an outstanding stone bust, with a sumptuous headdress and corsage. The **Dama de Baza★★** is a realistic goddess figure of the 4C BC. Medieval decorative arts include the magnificent **votive crowns of Guarrazar★★** dating from the Visigothic period, made of embossed gold plaques, mixing Germanic and Byzantine techniques. Romanesque portals, engravings, grilles, tombs and capitals, and Gothic sculpture in subsequent galleries, show deep Moorish influence.

The collection also includes a reconstruction of a Mudéjar interior, with a magnificent **artesonado★★** ceiling. North of the Museo Arqueológico is the Plaza de Colón (Columbus Square) with a statue of the navigator on a column. The Archaelogical Museum shares a building with the **Biblioteca Nacional** (National Library; Po. de Recoletos 20–22; ⬤Serrano; exhibition galleries open Tue–Sat 10am–8pm, Sun and public hols 10am–2pm; closed 1 and 6 Jan, 1 May, 24–25 & 31 Dec; ☎915 80 78 00; www.bne.es), whose collection of manuscripts is one of the richest in Spain.

Museo Lázaro Galdiano★★

Serrano 122. ⬤ Núñez de Balboa or Avenida América. Open Tue–Sat 10am–4.30pm (Sun until 3pm). Closed 2–3 Apr, 15 May, 15 Aug, 12 Oct, 9 Nov, 24–25 & 31 Dec. €6. guided tours 5.30–7pm (reserve in advance) €8. No charge daily during last hour. ☎915 61 60 84. www.flg.es.
This mansion houses the **collections★★** of editor and art lover José Lázaro Galdiano (1862–1947). On the **lower level**, are samples of outstanding paintings by the Master of Perea, Mengs, Zurbarán and Sánchez Coello.
The main floor – which retains ceilings painted by Villamil and some lovely

items of furniture – is entirely devoted to 15C–19C Spanish Art with magnificent Gothic and Renaissance panels. On the **second floor** are works of the **Flemish School** and Italian works. The **third floor** houses decorative arts (some 4 000 items): **ivories and enamel★★★**, among other materials.

Museo Sorolla★

General Martínez Campos 37.
⬤Gregorio Marañón or Iglesia. Open Tue–Sat 9.30am–8pm, Sun and public holidays 10am–3pm. Closed 1 Jan, 6 Jan, 1 May, 24–25 & 31 Dec, and other local hols. €3. No charge Sat 2–8pm, Sun, 18 April, 18 May, 12 Oct, 6 Dec. ☎913 10 15 84. http://mecd.gob.es/museosorolla
The Madrid home of Joaquín Sorolla (1863–1923) – the great Valencian painter of local scenes – filled with glowing Mediterranean light, is beautifully laid out, and includes his studio and a fine selection of his works. You can also relax in the garden.

🖿🖿 Museo de la Cera

Po. de Recoletos, 41. ⬤Colón. Open Mon–Fri 10am–2.30pm, 4.30–8.30pm, weekends and holidays 10am–8.30pm. €19, under 12s and over 65s €12. ☎913 199 330. www.museoceramadrid.com.
Among many wax models, often set against evocative backdrops, are historical figures such as Cleopatra and numerous actors (Penélope Cruz, Antonio Banderas). There is something here for everyone: Spain's football heroes for sports fans, Federico García Lorca and Picasso for culture-lovers, Barack Obama, Johnny Depp and George Clooney for those who would like to see "them" up close.

Museo Casa de la Moneda (Royal Mint Museum)

Doctor Esquerdo 36. ⬤ O'Donnell. Open Tue–Fri 10am–5.30pm, weekends and holidays 10am–2pm. Closed 1 & 6 Jan, 19 Mar, 1 May, 24–25 & 31 Dec. ☎915 66 65 44. www.museocasadelamoneda.es.
One of the world's largest royal mint collections, it covers not only coins,

© Hervé Hughes/hemis.fr

Fresco by Goya, Ermita de San Antonio de la Florida

stamps and medals, but also lottery tickets and gambling.

MONCLOA – CASA DE CAMPO DISTRICT
Museo Cerralbo★

Ventura Rodríguez 17. 🚇 Ventura Rodríguez. Open Tue–Sat 9.30am–3pm, Thu also 5–8pm), Sun and public holidays 10am–3pm. Closed 1 & 6 Jan, 1 May, 24–25 & 31 Dec. €3.
No charge Sat 2–3pm, Thu 5–8pm, Sun, 18 Apr, 18 May, 12 Oct, 6 Dec. ✆915 47 36 46. http://museocerralbo.mcu.es.
Housed in a late-19C mansion, recently restored, the Museo Cerralbo displays the collection of the Marquis of Cerralbo, a patron of the arts, including Spanish paintings, furniture, fans, clocks, armour and weaponry, porcelain, and archaeological finds.

Parque del Oeste★
(Park of the West)

This delightful garden, overlooking the Manzanares, was designed at the beginning of the 20C. In the southern part stands the small 4C BC Egyptian **Temple of Debod** (pas. del Pintor Rosales; 🚇Argüelles; open 10am-8pm year-round; closed 1 & 6 Jan, 1 May, 24–25 & 31 Dec; ✆913 66 74 15; www.muni-madrid.es/templodebod), rescued from

Nubia when the Aswan Dam was being built. The **Paseo del Pintor Rosales** nearby offers pavement cafés and views of Velázquez-like sunsets.

Ermita de San Antonio de la Florida★

Glorieta de la Florida 5. On the edge of the Parque del Oeste. 🚇Príncipe Pío. Open Tue–Sun & hols 9.30am–8pm. Closed 1 Jan, 1 May, 24, 25 and 31 Dec. ✆915 42 07 22. www.madrid.es/ermita
Goya was buried in this chapel, built in 1798 under Charles IV, at his own request. The chapel interior was frescoed by Goya with female angels around a central narrative scene on the cupola. One of the painter's first great realist works, these **frescoes★★** illustrate the miracle of St Anthony of Padua.

👥 Casa de Campo★

This extensive park is very popular with Madrileños. Attractions include a lake, a swimming pool and the **Parque de Atracciones de Madrid★ 👥**. Spain's biggest park of its kind, with over 40 attractions ranging from kiddy-friendly rides to white-knuckle roller coasters; it is especially popular at night on summer weekends (Ctra de Extremadura; 🚇Batán; see website for opening times and dates; €31.90 on the door, advance online tickets from €19.90, see website for child price; ℘912 00 07 95; www.parquedeatracciones.es). The **Teleférico** (cable car) connects the city (Rosales Station) to the Casa de Campo with splendid views on the way (Po. del Pintor Rosales–Cerro Garabita; Argüelles; see website for opening times and dates; €5.90 return trip; ℘912 00 07 90; www.teleferico.com).

The **Zoo-Aquarium**★★ 👫 houses one of the largest assortments of animals anywhere in Europe (Casa de Campo; Casa de Campo; see website for opening times and dates; €22.95 on the door, advance online tickets €17.90, see website for child price; ℘902 34 50 14; www.zoomadrid.com). Combined tickets for the Teléferico and Zoo are available (cheaper online).

Museo del Traje (Costume Museum)

Av. Juan Herrera 2. Moncloa. Open Tue–Sat 9.30am–7pm (Thu Jul & Aug 10.30pm), Sun and public holidays 10am–3pm. Closed 1 & 6 Jan, 1 May, 24–25, 31 Dec. €3; no charge Sat from 2.30pm, Sun, 18 April, 18 May, 12 Oct, 6 Dec. ℘915 50 47 00. http://museodeltraje.mcu.es.
A showcase of fashion from the 18C to the 20C. Couturiers Mariano Fortuny and Balenciaga are featured among everyday designs.

Museo de América★ (Museum of the Americas)

Av. Reyes Católicos 6. Moncloa. Open Tue–Sat 9.30am–3pm (Thu 7pm), Sun and public hols 10am–3pm. Closed 1 & 6 Jan, 1 May, 24–25, 31 Dec. €3; no charge Sun, 18 Apr, 18 May, 12 Oct, 6 Dec. ℘915 49 26 41. www.mecd.gob.es/museodeamerica.
Over 2 500 objects, accompanied by maps, models, reconstructions of dwellings, etc, focus on the ties between Europe and America.
Outstanding are the Stele of Madrid (Mayan), the **Treasure of Los Quimbayas**★ (Colombian), the **Tudela Manuscript** (1553) and the prized **Maya Tro Cortesiano Manuscript**★★★, one

of only four remaining. The darkened map room memorably recreates early navigators' cartography.

El Faro de Moncloa (Moncloa Beacon)

Av. de los Reyes Católicos. Moncloa. Guided tours every half hour 9.30am –1.30pm and unaccompanied visits (45 mins) 1.30–8pm. €3. ℘91 550 12 51. www.esmadrid.com/en/tourist-information/faro-de-moncloa.
From this 92m/301ft-high **observatory** ★★, built in 1992 and reopened in 2015 with a new observation deck, there is a wonderful view of Madrid and the surrounding area.

MUSEUMS
MUSEO NACIONAL DEL PRADO★★★

Allow 3–4 hours. Pas. del Prado s/n (ticket office at northern entrance by Pl. Canovas del Castillo), Banco de España or Atocha. Open Mon–Sat 10am–8pm (Sun and public holidays until 7pm; 6 Jan, 24 & 31 Dec until 2pm). Last entry 30 mins before closing. Closed 1 Jan, 1 May and 25 Dec. €15; no charge (permanent collection only) year-round Mon–Sat 6–8pm, Sun & hols 5–7pm. ℘913 30 28 00. www.museodelprado.es.
The Prado is the greatest gallery of Classical paintings in the world. The Neoclassical building was designed by Juan de Villanueva under Charles III for a science museum. After the Peninsular War, Ferdinand VII instead installed the Habsburg and Bourbon collections of Spanish painting, expanded over the years. In 2007 an extension, called the Jerónimos building, incorporating a 16C monastery cloister, led to the collection being rehung with 19C work alongside classical painting schools.

Spanish Painting★★★ (1100-1910) Rooms 50–52, 56, 60–67, 75,

Bartolomé Bermejo (Santo Domingo de Silos) and **Yáñez de la Almedina** cultivated an international style. Vicente Masip and his son **Juan de Juanes**

(The Last Supper) are associated with Raphael. Morales' favourite subject, a *Virgin and Child*, is also outstanding. In those rooms devoted to the *Golden Age*, two painters stand out: **Sánchez Coello**, and his pupil **Pantoja de la Cruz**, a portraitist at the court of Philip II. **El Greco** stands apart within the Spanish School. Works here date from his early Spanish period *(The Trinity)* to his maturity *(Adoration of the Shepherds)*. Other works are proof that he was a great portraitist, such as *The Nobleman with his Hand on his Chest*. **Ribalta** introduced Tenebrism (a dramatic illumination style of painting using very pronounced chiaroscuro) to Spain. **José (Jusepe) de Ribera** *(Lo Spagnoletto)* is represented by *Jacob's Dream* in which the vigorous use of chiaroscuro reflects Caravaggio's influence. The portraits and still lifes of **Zurbarán** are peaceful compositions in which chiaroscuro and realism triumph. **Murillo** mainly painted the Virgin *(The Immaculate Conception)* but also plain folk *(The Holy Family with a Little Bird)*. Works from Spanish historical painting include *The Last Will and Testament of Isabel the Catholic* by Rosales (Rm 61B), *Juana the Mad* by F Pradilla and *The Execution of Torrijos and his Colleagues on the Beach at Málaga* by A Gisbert.

Spanish Painting★★★ (1550-1850)
Rooms 7–18 & 32–38

The Prado possesses not only the greatest paintings of **Diego Velázquez** (1599-1660), but the world's largest collection of his work, displayed in rooms 10, 11, 12, 14 , 15, 15a & 27. He spent time in Italy (1629–31) where he painted *Vulcan's Forge*. He began to use richer, more subtle colours and developed his figure compositions as in his magnificent *Christ on the Cross*. On his return he painted *The Surrender of Breda* in which his originality emerges. The use of light in his pictures is crucial. Velàzquez strove towards naturalism in his royal hunting portraits of *Philip IV* and *Prince Baltasar Carlos as a Hunter* (1635, a wonderful rendering of a child)

and his equestrian portraits of the royal family, in particular *Prince Baltasar Carlos on Horseback* with the sierra in the background. In 1650 he returned to Italy where he painted landscapes, *The Medici Gardens in Rome*.

In his later masterpiece, *Las Meninas* (c. 1656; Rm 12), the Infanta Margarita is shown in the artist's studio in a magnificent display of light and colour. In *The Tapestry Weavers* (c. 1657), Velázquez combined myth and reality.

The paintings of **Francisco Goya** (1746-1828), varying from his portraits of the royal and famous, his war scenes, his depictions of everyday life, and his *Majas*, can be seen in rooms 32–38, in 64–67 on the first floor, and in rooms 85 and 90–94 on the second floor. They illustrate his extraordinary Realism and enthusiasm for colour. The museum contains 40 cartoons painted in oil between 1775 and 1791 for the Real Fábrica (Royal Tapestry Works). *The 3rd of May 1808 in Madrid: the Executions on Principe Pio Hill* (Rms 64-65) was inspired by the rebellion against the French occupation (⊙see ARANJUEZ, p152). His late works, the great series of so-called Black Paintings frescoed on the walls of his house, hang in Room 67.

Flemish Painting★★★ (1430–1700)
Rooms 16b, 28, 29, 55–58

The exceptional collection of Flemish painting reflects Spain's history with the Low Countries.

Among the Flemish Primitives are Robert Campen, the Mester of Flemalle *(St Barbara)*. **Van der Weyden** added great richness of colour, and a sense of composition *(Descent from the Cross*, Rm 58). Drama is interpreted through melancholy by his successor, **Memling** *(Adoration of the Magi*; Rm 58A). There follow the weird imaginings of **Hieronymus Bosch**, El Bosco *(The Garden of Earthly Delights)*, which influenced his disciple Patinir *(Crossing the Stygian Lake)* – both these in Room 56A – and a **Bruegel the Elder** *(Triumph of Death*; Rm 56A). The most Baroque of painters, **Rubens**, breathed new life into Flemish paint-

ing most notably in *The Three Graces*)
There is also a rich collection of his work
completed by that of his disciples: **Van
Dyck** and **Jordaens**.

Dutch Painting (1700–1800)
Rooms

Two interesting works by **Rembrandt**
are a *Self-Portrait* and *Artemis*.

Italian Painting★★
**(1450–1800) Rooms 4–7, 22–27,
40–44. (1300–1600) 49, 56b**

The collection is especially rich in works
by Venetian painters. The Italian Renaissance brought with it elegance and
ideal beauty as in paintings by **Raphael**
(*The Holy Family*, *The Cardinal*; Rm 49),
Roman nobility and monumental bearing in the work of **Mantegna** (*The Death
of the Virgin*; Rm 56B) and melancholic
dreaminess in **Botticelli** (*Story of Nasta-
gio degli Onesti*). The spirituality of the
Annunciation by **Fra Angelico** belongs
to the Gothic tradition.

Colour and sumptuousness triumph
with the Venetian school: **Titian** with
his exceptional mythological scenes
(*Danae and the Shower of Gold*; Rm
42, *Venus with the Organist*; Rm. 24)
and his portrait of *Charles V of Müh-
lberg*; **Veronese** with compositions
set off by silver tones; Tintoretto's
golden-fleshed figures springing
from shadow (*Christ Washing the Disciples' Feet*) and **Tiepolo**'s paintings
intended for Charles III's royal palace.

French Painting (1600–1800)
Rooms 2,3, 19, 39

The French are represented by **Poussin**
(Rm 3) and by **Lorrain**.

German Painting (1450–1800)
Room 55b

A selection includes **Dürer**'s figure
and portrait paintings (*Self-Portrait*,
Adam and Eve) and works by Cranach.
The **Casón del Buen Retiro**, part of the
Museo del Prado campus, today con-
tains the museum's shops and cafeteria.
It housed **Picasso**'s *Guernica* when it first
returned to Spain (now at the Museo
Nacional Centro de Arte Reina Sofía).

Guided visits (Sun 11am, 12.30pm) are
conducted to view the magnificent Hall
of the Ambassadors, crowned by the
ceiling fresco The *Apotheosis of the Spanish Monarchy* (1697) by Luca Giordano.

MUSEO THYSSEN-
BORNEMISZA★★★

Po. del Prado 8. ⊚ Banco de España,
Atocha. Open Mon noon–4pm, Tue–Sun
10am–7pm; 24, 31 Dec until 3pm; last
admission 1 hour before closing. Closed
1 Jan, 1 May, 25 Dec. €12 (temporary
exhibitions additional charge). No
charge Mon noon–4pm. ℰ917 911 370.
www.museothyssen.org.

The Neoclassical Palacio de Villahermosa houses an outstanding private
collection acquired by the Spanish State
from **Baron Hans Heinrich Thyssen-
Bornemisza**. The museum displays
some 800 works from the late 13C to
the present day, exhibited in chronological order on three floors. Temporary
exhibitions are shown in another wing
of the museum.

Second floor

The visit begins with the Italian Primitives (Gallery 1): **Duccio di Buoninseg-
na**'s *Christ and the Samaritan Woman*,
with its concern for scenic realism.
Gallery 3 displays splendid examples
of 15C Dutch religious painting such as
Jan van Eyck's *The Annunciation Diptych*. Next to it is the small *Our Lady of
the Dry Tree* by **Petrus Christus**; Virgin
and Child symbolise the flowering of
the dry tree. The museum possesses a
magnificent **portrait collection**. Gallery
5 contains superb examples of the Early
Renaissance and its values of identity
and autonomy. These come to the fore
in the *Portrait of Giovanna Tornuaboni* by
the Italian painter **D Ghirlandaio**.
Raphael's *Portrait of an Adolescent* can
be seen in the Villahermosa Gallery
(Gallery 6) while Gallery 7 (16C) reveals
Vittore Carpaccio's *Young Knight in a
Landscape* in which the protagonist's
elegance stands out from a background
heavy with symbolism.
The *Portrait of Doge Francesco Vernier* by
Titian shows sober, yet diverse tones.

After admiring **Dürer**'s surprising *Jesus Among the Doctors* (1506, Gallery 8), move on to Gallery 9, with portraits from the 16C German School including *The Nymph from the Fountain*, one of several paintings by **Lucas Cranach the Elder**, and the *Portrait of a Woman* by **Hans Baldung Grien**. The 16C Dutch paintings in Gallery 10 include **Patinir**'s **Landscape with the Rest on the Flight into Egypt**. Gallery 11 exhibits several works by **El Greco** as well as **Titian**'s *St Jerome in the Wilderness* (1575), with its characteristic use of flowing brushstrokes.

One of the splendid early works of **Caravaggio**, the creator of Tenebrism, *St Catherine of Alexandria*, hangs in Gallery 12. In the same gallery is a splendid sculpture (St Sebastian) by Baroque artist **Bernini**. Also here is the *Lamentation over the Body of Christ* (1633) by **Ribera**. The 18C Italian Painting section (Galleries 16–18) shows Venetian scenes by **Canaletto** and **Guardi**.

Also on this floor (Galleries 19–21) are 17C Dutch and Flemish works. **Van Dyck**'s magnificent *Portrait of Jacques le Roy*, **De Vos**' *Antonia Canis*, and two memorable **Rubens**, *The Toilet of Venus* and *Portrait of a Young Woman with a Rosary*, all hang from the walls of Gallery 19.

First floor

Galleries 22–26 represent 17C Dutch painting with scenes of daily life and landscapes. Note **Frans Hals**' *Family Group in a Landscape*, a fine collective portrait. Interesting portraits stand out from the 18C French and British schools while the 19C North American paintings, virtually unknown in Europe (Galleries 29 and 30) are exceptional. They include works by Romantic landscape artists Cole, Church, Bierstadt and the Realist Homer. The European Romanticism and Realism of the 19C is expressed by **Constable**'s *The Lock*, **Courbet**'s *The Water Stream* and **Friedrich**'s *Easter Morning*, together with the three works by **Goya** (Gallery 31).

Galleries 32 and 33 are dedicated to Impressionism and Post-Impressionism: magnificent works by Monet, Manet, Renoir, Sisley, Degas, Pissarro, Gauguin, Van Gogh, Toulouse-Lautrec and Cézanne. *At the Milliner* by **Degas** is one of his major canvases. Other works which stand out include **Van Gogh**'s *"Les Vessenots" in Auvers*, which displays the explosion of brush-strokes in some of his later works, *Mata Mua* by **Gauguin**, from his Polynesian period, and **Cézanne**'s *Portrait of a Farmer*, in which his use of colour to build volumes is a forerunner of Cubism.

Expressionism is represented in Galleries 35–40, following a small display of paintings from the Fauve movement in Gallery 34. The Expressionist movement, a highlight of this museum, supposes the supremacy of the artist's interior vision and colour over draughtsmanship. Two highly emblematic paintings by **Grosz**, *Metropolis* and *Street Scene*, hang in Gallery 40.

Ground floor

The first few galleries (41–44) contain exceptional Experimental Avant-Garde works (1907–24) from European movements: Futurism, Orphism, Suprematism, Constructivism (note the women artists' work), Cubism and Dadaism. Room 41 displays Cubist works by **Picasso** *(Man with a Clarinet)*, **Braque** (Woman with a Mandolin) and **Juan Gris** *(Woman Sitting)*, while *Proun 1C* by **Lissitzky** and *New York City, New York* by **Mondrian** are in Room 43. Gallery 45 shows post-First World War European works by **Picasso** *(Harlequin with a Mirror)* and **Joan Miró** *(Catalan Peasant with a Guitar)*, and a 1914 abstract composition by **Kandinsky** *(Picture with Three Spots)*. In the next gallery, mainly dedicated to North American painting, are *Brown and Silver I* by **Jackson Pollock** and *Green on Maroon* by **Mark Rothko**, two examples of American Abstract Expressionism. The last two galleries (47 and 48) are given over to Surrealism, Figurative Tradition and Pop Art.

Carmen Thyssen-Bornemisza Collection

The 250-plus works on exhibit build on those in the original collection. Notable are 17C Dutch painting, Impressionism and Post-Impressionism, North American painting, and early Avant-Garde.

MUSEO NACIONAL CENTRO DE ARTE REINA SOFÍA★★ (QUEEN SOFÍA ART CENTRE)

Santa Isabel 52. ⓐ Atocha. Open Mon & Wed–Sat 10am–9pm. Sun, Collection 1 10am–7pm, rest closes 2.15pm. Closed 1 & 6 Jan, 1 & 15 May, 9 Nov, 24–25, 31 Dec. €10; no charge Mon & Wed–Sat after 7pm, Sun 1.30–7pm, 18 Apr, 18 May, 12 Oct, 6 Dec. ✆917 74 10 00. www.museoreinasofia.es.

The former Hospital de San Carlos was refurbished to house the city's museum of contemporary art. A stunning modern extension, the work of Jean Nouvel, with large galleries designed for contemporary work, opened in 2005. The hanging of the permanent collection, mostly in the original Sabitini building, evolves around major themes.

Permanent collection★
First floor.

Galleries around the patio garden show modern international work, including **Juan Muñoz's** *I Saw It in Bologna* (1991). The garden sculptures include pieces by Catalan artist **Joan Miró** and Basque sculptor **Eduardo Chillida**.

Second floor (galleries 201-210).

The museum's overview of Spanish art 1900–1945 (Collection 1) is structured around "micronarratives" which give the wider context of Europe's avant-garde movements. However, the centrepiece of this floor is undoubtedly **Picasso's Guernica★★★**, which hangs in gallery 206 (⊗ strictly no photography of any kind is allowed). Considered one of the 20C's greatest paintings, commissioned for the Spanish Pavilion at the 1937 World Fair, it was inspired by the Fascist terror bombing of Gernika and is renowned for its powerful Iberian symbolism and denunciation of the atroci-

ties of war. Five other galleries give a narrative background to *Guernica*.

The Spanish masters, **Miró** and **Dalí** may also be found in this Collection, with early works by Dalí and examples from his Surrealist period *(The Great Masturbator)*. Gallery 208 is dedicated to the work of Juan Gris.

Fourth floor (Galleries 401–430).

Collection 2 galleries are dedicated to art from 1945–1968 and widen their scope to take in influences from elsewhere, especially North and Latin America, interwoven chronologically with Spanish and European work. Some galleries highlight the work of experimental Spanish pioneers such as Basque sculptor Oteiza. Photography and video are a strong suit throughout the collection, especially in this modern period. The main trends from the late 1940s are also delineated: the avant-garde in the early years of the dictatorship, abstract art in the 1950s, Neo-Realist photography and the realism of painters like Antonio López.

Collection 3 deals with 1962–1982 and includes more Experimental Art.

ADDITIONAL SIGHTS
Museo de Historia

Fuencarral 78. ⓐ Moncloa. Open Tue–Sun & hols 10am–8pm. Closed 1 & 6 Jan, 1 May, 24–25 & 31 Dec. ✆917 01 18 63. www.madrid.es/museosdehistoria.

Housed in a former city hospice, this small museum, tracing the city's history boasts a superb carved 18C decorative **portal★★** and, inside, old wells for storing ice from the sierra.

Museo Nacional de Romanticismo

San Mateo 13. ⓐ Tribunal. Open Tue–Sat 9.30am–8.30pm (Nov–Apr until 6.30pm), Sun and hols 10am–3pm. Closed 1 & 6 Jan, 1 May, 24–25 & 31 Dec. €3, no charge Sat from 2pm, Sun, 18 April, 18 May, 12 Oct, 6 Dec. ✆914 481 045. http://museoromanticismo.mcu.es.

Built in 1776 for the Marqués de Matallana, this Neoclassical palace houses a 19C decorative arts collection gathered together by Benigno Valle-Inclán, the connoisseur who opened the museum in 1924. Two dozen rooms are beautifully furnished and a ground floor garden patio – access from the tea-room – is a lush oasis.

Plaza Monumental de las Ventas★ (Bullring)

Alcalá 237. 🚇 Ventas. Guided tours daily 10am–5.30pm (with audioguide); on days of bullfight & during San Isidro, until 2pm. Closed 25 Dec,1 & 6 Jan. 🖉687 73 90 32. €12.90. www.lasventastour.com/en.

Just to the east of Salamanca is Spain's largest bullring (built 1931), with a capacity of 22 300 spectators. There are bullfights every Sunday Mar–Oct and daily during the Feria de San Isidro in May. Its **Museo Taurino** (closed at the time of writing) honours great bullfighters.

Museo del Ferrocarril (Railway Museum)

Po. de las Delicias 61. 🚇 Delicias. Open Oct-May Tue–Fri 9.30am–3pm, Sat–Sun 10am–7pm. June-Sept open 10am-7pm. Closed 25 Dec, 1 & 6 Jan €6 (Sun €3). 🖉902 22 88 22. www. museodelferrocarril.org.

The wrought-iron and glass Delicias railway station, from where trains ran 1880–1969, has a collection of steam and diesel engines, clocks, models and a delightful restaurant car for snacks. The **Strawberry Train** (🍓see page 152) leaves from here in the summer months.

👥 Museo Nacional de Ciencias Naturales

José Gutiérrez Abascal 2. 🚇 Gregorio Marañón. Open Tue–Fri, Sun & hols 10am –5pm, Sat 10am–8pm (Sat Jul–Aug closes 3pm). Closed 1 & 6 Jan, 1 May, 25 Dec. €6 🖉91 411 13 28. www.mncn.csic.es

Madrid's Natural Sciences Museum grew around an 18C royal collection, still on show as a cabinet of curiosities. But today's huge collection of fossils and dinosaurs has been reoriented to delve into the world's past and exhibit its biodiversity.

Estadio Santiago Bernabéu

Concha Espina 1 (Tour tickets sold at Ticket Office 10 next to Gate 7, Paseo de la Castellana). 🚇Santiago Bernabéu. Open non match days Mon–Sat 10am–7pm, Sun and public holidays 10.30am–6.30pm. Last tour 5 hours before kick off on match days. Closed 25 Dec, 1 Jan. €25, under 14 €18. 🖉913 98 43 70. www.realmadrid.com

Home to the mighty Real Madrid football (soccer) team, the tour takes you to the top of the stadium in a panoramic lift, into the Royal Box and changing rooms, and on to the pitch through the tunnel from which teams emerge before an 80,000-strong crowd.

Madrid Río (Madrid's Riverbanks)

River Manzanares. 🚇 Príncipe Pío, Puerta del Ángel, Pirámides, Legazpi. www.esmadrid.com/en/tourist-information/madrid-rio.

A 10-km (6mi) riverside walkway has been opened up to pedestrians and cyclists. Four new bridges link the left and right banks' sports and leisure areas, which include 10 children's play areas along the Salón de Pinas. Parks and gardens are laid out around historic monuments, including the old city bridges, the Ermita Virgen del Puerto (1718), and the Matadero Madrid, a restored Modernist contemporary arts centre (www.mataderomadrid.org) in a former slaughterhouse.

EXCURSIONS

👥 Parque Warner Madrid★

▶ San Martín de la Vega. 25km/15.5mi SE of Madrid. Open from 11am, see website for schedule. €39.90 on the door or €25.90 bought in advance online, see website for children's prices, parking €8 per day. 🖉912 00 07 92. www.parquewarner.com.

This Warner Brothers theme park is a great family-oriented getaway. Areas include Hollywood Boulevard, Movie World Studios, Super Heroes World, Old West Territory and Cartoon Village, each with rides and activities.

Movie WB World Studios will appeal to those who love special effects and car chases. In Super Heroes World you can experience spectacular combats between Batman and the forces of evil, or a 110m/360 ft freefall.

For the youngest visitors, Cartoon Village offers watergames and recreates the magical world of old-fashioned heroes like Tom and Jerry. 😊 In summer take a hat: tree-shade is not yet abundant.

👫 Faunia★

▶ Av. de las Comunidades 28. 5km/3mi E of Parque El Retiro. ⓜ Valdebernardo, Sierra de Guadalupe. Open from 10.30am, see website for schedule. €26.45, child €19.95 (online discounts), parking €4.90. ✆911 54 74 82. www.faunia.es.

A nature park which recreates the planet's ecosystems, past and present, on a 140 000sq m/167 300sq yd site. It includes some 7 000 small- and medium-sized animals and birds, and over 70 000 trees and plants plus dinosaur models. One ecosystem is Europe's largest recreation of a polar ice-cap. Hugely popular with Madrileños and their children, Faunia may be visited time and again since the area is so large that it is difficult to explore it all in one visit.

Palacio Real Sitio de El Pardo★

▶ Manuel Alonso, El Pardo. 17km/10.5mi NW of Madrid. Open daily 10am–6pm (until 8pm Apr–Sept). See website for dates of closure. €9; no charge for EU citizens Wed & Thu Oct–Mar 3–6pm, Apr–Sept 5–8pm, all visitors 18 May and 12 Oct. ✆913 76 15 00. www.patrimonionacional.es.

The palace was built by Philip III (1598–1621) on the site of Philip II's (1556–98) palace which had been destroyed in a fire in 1604. Franco lived here for 35 years and King Juan Carlos spent his teenage years here; today, it is used by Heads of State on official visits. Decorations include more than 200 tapestries★; the majority are 18C from the Real Fábrica de Tápices (Royal Tapestry Factory) in Madrid based on cartoons by Goya,

Bayeu, González Ruiz and Van Loo. The Casita del Príncipe – Prince's House – is a richly decorated pleasure pavilion in the grounds. A short walk or drive away (1km/0.6mi), at the Convento de Capuchines (Camino del Cristo de Pardo s/n), is Gregorio Fernández's Cristo del Pardo (Christ Recumbent), a highpoint of Spanish baroque sculpture (open daily 9.30am–1pm, 4.30pm–8.30pm).

👫 Aquópolis

C. de la Mirasierra s/n, Villanueva de la Cañada. Bus 627 every 10 minutes from Moncloa, or 25min drive via N6. Open mid-Jun–first week Sept from noon, see website for dates and times. €25.95, children €20.95 (online discounts). ✆912 00 07 91. www.villanueva.aquopolis.es.

Madrid's longest-established water amusement park with a wave pool, a dozen rides designed for all ages and tastes, a big swimming pool and bar-restaurants, is a blessing in the hot months.

Parque del Capricho

Avda de la Alameda de Osuna s/n. ⓜ El Capricho. Open weekends and public holidays 9am–9pm (Oct–Mar 6.30pm).

A stunning 18C landscaped garden which reveals features such as a boating lake with oriental lakeside pavilion and boathouse, a giant beekeepers' hive, a romantic cottage and classical colonnade. Paths between these run under centennial trees and between beautifully kept lawns.

Sierra de Guadarrama

Encircling the city to the north, the Guadarrama range provides splendid walking country. in 2013, it became Spain's fifteenth National Park (👟See page 120). Starting points, at the foot of the slopes, may be reached by bus (Manzanares or Miraflores) or, in the case of Cercedilla, by train (from Atocha or Chamartín, about 1 hour's journey). A 20-minute walk above Cercedilla is the town's swimming pool, set among woods and filled by river water.

ADDRESSES

🛏 STAY

Hostal Adriano – Cruz 26 (Centro). Sol. ℘915 21 13 39. www.hostal adriano.com. 22 rooms. A good central choice in this price range, notable for its recently renovated well-equipped, individually decorated rooms.

Hostal Centro Sol – San Jerónimo 5 (Centro). Sol. ℘915 22 15 82. www. hostalcentrosol.com. 33 rooms. A hotel very close to the Puerta del Sol occupying the second and fourth floors of a newly decorated building. Good-value rooms.

Hostal Gonzalo – Cervantes 34 (Centro). Antón Martín. ℘914 29 27 14. www.hostalgonzalo.com. 15 rooms. No breakfast. Located close to the Prado, Reina Sofía and Thyssen-Bornemisza museums, this excellent hostal has a good family feel and soundproofed rooms.

Hotel Carlos V – Maestro Vitoria 5 (Centro). Callao. ℘915 31 41 00. www.hotelcarlosv.com. 67 rooms. €10. A good central option in a pedestrianised street away from the noise of the city. Although small, the English-style rooms are pleasant and well appointed.

Hotel Mora – Pas. del Prado 32 (Retiro). Atocha. ℘914 20 15 69. www.hotelmora.com. 62 rooms. The Mora enjoys a superb location in an impressive building opposite the botanical gardens on paseo del Prado. Comfortable, recently renovated rooms and reasonable rates.

Hotel Oscar – Pl. Vázquez de Mella, 12 (Chueca). Banco de España or Chueca. ℘917 011 173. www.room-matehotels.com. 74 rooms. €9.95. Well-priced designer hotel in the middle of Chueca and close to the museums. There is contemporary art in the lobby, a minimalist pop café and glamorous rooftop terrace and pool.

Petit Palace Posada del Peine – Postas 18 (Centro). Sol. ℘915 23 81 51. www.hpetitpalaceposadadelpeine. com. 67 rooms. €12. Behind an elegant facade in a 17th-century building on a quiet pedestrian street just off the Plaza Mayor lies this comfortable well-decorated boutique hotel (said to be Spain's oldest hotel), which is part of a chic chain. Free use of iPads.

ME Madrid Reina Victoria – Plaza de Santa Ana 14. Sol. ℘917 016 000. www.melia.com. 192 rooms. €25. Restaurant Ana La Santa. The city's most famous hotel, an old favourite of bullfighters, has been transformed into Madrid's hippest luxury accommodation, with a rooftop bar that has been voted one of the best bars in the country. The restaurant serves posh tapas created by the founder of Tragaluz (*See BARCELONA, p346*).

Hotel Ritz – Pl. de la Lealtad 5 (Retiro). Banco de España. ℘917 01 67 67. www.mandarinoriental.com/ ritzmadrid. 137 rooms. €24. Goya Restaurant. The city's grandest hotel, a Belle Époque building, is perfectly located near the Paseo del Prado. The hotel has elegance, tradition and comfort, plus prices to match. The terrace garden is an additional delight.

🍴 EAT

Bazaar – Libertad 21 (Chueca). Chueca, Banco de España. ℘915 233 905. www.restaurantbazaar.com. Closed 24–25, 31 Dec, 1 Jan. A stylish country-modern style split-level restaurant serving good-value Mediterranean cooking with exotic modern touches. Lunchtime set menu. No reservations.

La Bola – Bola 5 (Centro). Santo Domingo. ℘915 47 69 30. www.labola.es. Closed Sun eve and 24 Dec. If you want to try a traditional cocido madrileño, look no further than this famous tavern, which has been cooking it in earthenware pots on a charcoal fire for over a century.

Casa Lucio – Cava Baja 35 (La Latina). La Latina. ℘913 65 82 17. www.casalucio.es. Closed Aug. One of Madrid's best-known addresses frequented by politicians, actors and visitors alike. Typical Castilian décor, and famous for its *huevos estrellados* (broken up fried eggs over crispy chips).

La Vaca Verónica – Moratín 38. Antón Martín. ℘914 29 78 27.

www.restaurantelavveronica.com. The outstanding décor recreates a cosy, intimate space, with ceiling mirrors, candles and soft lighting. Posters recall Pop Art and Art Nouveau. Specialities include grilled meats and the delicious pasta con carabineros (giant Atlantic shrimp).

😑🍴 **Zerain** – Quevedo 3 (Huertas). 🚇 Antón Martín. 📞 914 29 79 09. www. restaurante-vasco-zerain-sidreria.es. Closed Sun for dinner. A typical menu at this rustic Basque cider bar near plaza de Santa Ana includes *tortilla de bacalao* (saltcod omelette) and *chuletón* (meat cutlets).

😑🍴🍴 **Diverxo** – Padre Damián 23 (Nueva España). 🚇 Cuzco or Colombia. 📞 915 70 07 66. www.diverxo.com. Closed Sun, Mon. David Muñoz's Mediterranean and Japanese fusion Michelin-star cooking makes this one of Madrid's most exciting eating places. Set tasting menus. Booking is essential.

😑🍴🍴 **Santceloni** – Po de la Castellana 57 (Castellano). 🚇 Gregorio Marañón 📞 912 10 88 40. www. restaurantesantceloni.com. Closed Sat lunch, Sun and public holidays, Holy Week and Aug. Exquisite, Michelin-starred Mediterranean cookery. Its tasting menu and legendary cheese trolley change daily. Prices match its fame as one of the city's best kitchens. "Jacket and tie not compulsory, but appreciated." Booking is essential.

TAPAS

El Bocaito – Libertad 6 (Chueca). 🚇 Chueca, Banco de España. 📞 915 321 219. www.bocaito.com. Closed Sun, Aug, 24–25 Dec, 31 Dec–1 Jan. One of the city's most complete and characterful tapas bars: excellent produce, wines and waiter service while you graze standing up. The restaurant at the back is good too.

Las Bravas – Pje Matheu 5 (Centro). 🚇 Sol. 📞 915 21 51 41. www.lasbravas. com. Taste the original spicy-hot patatas bravas, invented here, and you quickly grasp why they have travelled the world. The noisy café ambience and other tapas fit the popular mood. There are also branches at Espoz y Mina 13 and Álvarez Gato 3.

Casa del Abuelo – Victoria 12 (Sol). 🚇 Sol. 📞 910 000 133, www.lacasadela buelo.es. Over a century old, this atmospheric tapas bar (think tiles and dark wood) is famous for its prawns in garlic and sweet red wine.

Casa Labra – Tetuán 12 (Centro). 🚇 Sol. 📞 915 31 00 81. www.casalabra.es. This old tavern dating back to 1860 is a Madrid institution. It was here that Pablo Iglesias founded the Spanish Socialist Party (PSOE) in 1879. Its house specialities are fried saltcod (*bacalao frito*) and saltcod croquettes; standing room or marble tables at the back. Always busy and has a restaurant menu.

Prada a Tope – Príncipe 11 (Huertas). 🚇 Sevilla. 📞 914 29 59 21. www.pradaa topemadrid.com. Closed 24–25 Dec, 31st Dec–1st Jan. A warm locale in the spirit of El Bierzo, a traditional part of León. Outstanding rustic décor of wood and slate, with long bar, large tables, and walls covered with photos. Great variety of local products on sale.

Taberna de la Daniela – General Pardiñas 21 (Salamanca). 🚇 Goya. 📞 915 75 23 29. www.tabernaladaniela.com. A bar with traditional decoration. Azulejos on the outside with vermouth on tap and a wide selection of canapés and *raciones* inside. Specialities here include cocido madrileño.

La Venencia – Echegarray 7 (Huertas). 🚇 Sevilla. 📞 914 297 313. Fabulous turn-of-the-century sherry bar that still serves Jerez's wines only from the cask with traditional tapas like *mojama* (cured tuna) and salted almonds. Worth the detour for the atmosphere and décor alone.

CAFÉS

La Pecera del Círculo de Bellas Artes – Alcalá 42. 🚇 Banco de España or Sevilla. 📞 915 31 33 02. www.lapeceradel circulo.com. Closed 24–25 Dec, 31 Dec–1 Jan. The 19C atmosphere of this great café with its enormous columns and large windows is in sharp contrast to its young, intellectual clientele. Outdoor terrace in summer. If you have time, visit the rooftop terrace for panoramic views. Highly recommended.

Café Gijón – Pas. de Recoletos 21. 🚇 Colón or Banco de España. 📞 91 521 54 25. www.cafegijon.com. This café has been famous since 1888 as a meeting point for writers and artists. Outdoor terrace with piano player in summer.

El Espejo – Pas. de Recoletos 31. 🚇 Colón. 📞913 08 23 47.
An attractive, Modernist-style café and restaurant with a charming wrought-iron and glass canopy. Open until midnight.

Café de Oriente – Pl. de Oriente 2. 🚇 Ópera. 📞915 413 974. www.cafedeoriente.es. This classic institution, located in the Plaza de Oriente opposite the Royal Palace, is a delightful place for a drink at any time of day. Pleasant terrace.

NIGHTLIFE

Clamores – Albuquerque 14. 🚇 Bilbao. 📞91 445 54 80 www.sala clamores.com. Drop by here to see what is on – live jazz, Latin, flamenco or many other sounds – the venue is a favourite with Spanish and international artists and prices are reasonable.

Berlín Cabaret – Costanilla de San Pedro 11. 📞913 66 20 34. 🚇 La Latina. www.berlincabaret.com. One of Madrid's famous venues. Live acts (magicians, drag queens, etc.) and a fun atmosphere.

Café Central – Pl. del Ángel 10. 🚇Tirso de Molina. 📞913 69 41 43. www.cafe centralmadrid.com. One of the city's main haunts for jazz lovers since the 1980s; open for coffee during the day.

Del Diego – Reina 12. 🚇 Gran Vía. 📞915 23 31 06. www.deldiego.com. Closed Aug, Sun, Holy Week. Open 7pm-3am. Elegant small cocktail bar that attracts an older crowd. If you're feeling adventurous ask for a "Barman", which contains whatever takes his fancy.

The Irish Rover – Av. del Brasil 7. 🚇 Santiago Bernabéu. 📞915 97 48 11. www.theirishrover.com. A huge pub designed like a film set of a paved old Irish street. A section which looks as though it has come straight out of one of Joyce's novels and a tiny lounge are just two features. There is live music on Thu and Fri evenings and other entertainment during the week. They also show sports matches.

Joy Madrid - Teatro Eslava – Arenal 11. 🚇Sol. 📞913 66 37 33. www.joy-eslava.com. This well-known club, occupying a former 19C theatre, has been attracting a colourful crowd of club-goers and famous faces for several decades. One-off concerts can include major international names. On your way home, you can visit the famous Chocolatería de San Ginés, in the street of the same name.

Libertad 8 – Libertad 8. 🚇 Chueca. 📞915 32 11 50. www.libertad8cafe.es. A building over a century old is the setting for this atmospheric literary café, renowned for its poetry readings, storytellers and singer-songwriter performances which draw young, bohemian audiences.

Ya'sta Club – Valverde 10. 🚇 Gran Vía. 📞651 89 42 00. www.yastaclub.net. Open 11.45pm–6am. Closed Sun–Tue. Get a real taste for the Madrid scene by sampling an eclectic mix of indie tunes at this long-established club.

FLAMENCO

Madrid remains one of live flamenco's busiest showcases. Performances by top names, often on tour from Andalucía, are given in theatres and concert halls for which advance booking is a good idea, but the city's clubs, or tablaos, famed as the heart of the flamenco scene in the 1970s, still put on accessible though pricey nightly shows. Although unpredictable in quality, they are a good chance to sample the local scene. Traditionally shows start late; earlier ones tend to attract only tourists.

Las Carboneras – Pl. del Conde de Miranda 1. 📞915 42 86 77. www.tablaolascarboneras.com. Open 7.30pm–midnight. Closed Sun. Nightly shows in a venue with pleasantly simple décor. Young up-and-coming artists perform good modern pure flamenco. The ticket comes with dinner or (the better option) a drink.

Las Tablas– Pl. de España 9. 📞915 420 520. www.lastablasmadrid.com. As much a minimalist café as a *tablao*, this is one of flamenco's newest venues, offering two live shows every night (8pm and 10pm). A good option, and one of the most economic, to sample young flamenco.

Corral de la Morería – Morería 17. ☎913 658 446. www.corraldelamoreria.com. Open 6.30pm–midnight. A long-established large venue with traditional artists giving two shows a night. Many performers here are well-known names in the local flamenco scene, making this a good spot, though pricey, for a first taste of flamenco. The food is also good traditional cooking.

Café de Chinitas – Torija 7. 🚇 Santo Domingo. ☎91 559 51 35. www.chinitas.com. Open 7pm–midnight. Closed Sun. This small central club just off Gran Vía, once a legendary name, is still very popular with tourists. The show varies: brilliant young artists have short residencies though the house group does not always sparkle.

Casa Patas – Cañizares 10. 🚇 Antón Martín. ☎913 69 04 96. www.casapatas.com. Open Mon–Fri 1–5pm, Mon-Thur 8-11pm, Fri-Sat 6.30pm-12am. Closed Sun. One of the best venues in which to enjoy a night of young flamenco, with the option of tapas or supper first in the tiled dining room. The *tablao* itself is small and tightly packed, but it is a genuine part of the city's live scene.

La Candela – Olmo 2. 🚇 Tirso de Molina. ☎914 673 382. www.flamenco candela.com. Open 10.30pm–6am. Legendary bar where flamenco artists go after shows, although you are unlikely to see the legends performing. Soak up the Andalucian atmosphere with some tapas and sangria. If you only have time for one flamenco show, this is the place to come.

ENTERTAINMENT

Madrid's thriving cinema culture supports as many as 70 subtitled screens showing *versión original* (VO) films. It also has an **Imax** cinema (www.imax.com), over 30 theatres, numerous concert halls and one casino an hour's drive outside town. The **Auditorio Nacional** (opened in 1988; www.auditorionacional.mcu.es) has a varied programme of classical music performed in two spaces, the **Teatro de la Zarzuela** (http://teatrodelazarzuela. mcu.es) hosts a wide range of dance,

operettas (zarzuelas) and ballets, while the **Teatro Real** (www.teatro-real.com) offers opera though most seats are sold as season tickets.

The **Teatro Español** (www.teatro espanol.es), a jewel of an old theatre on Plaza Santa Ana, and its spacious mixed arts extension, **El Matadero** (www.mataderomadrid.org), have interesting and challenging contemporary programming.

Veranos de la Villa (Jul–Aug; www.veranosdelavilla.com) is a varied music festival, and the **Festival de Otoño en Primavera** (mid-Oct–mid-Jun; www.madrid.org/fo) combines music, dance and opera. Both offer interesting international line-ups.

The **Festival Internacional de Jazz** (www.festivaldejazzmadrid.com) is held during Nov.

SHOPPING

El Arco Artesania - Pl. Mayor 29 (Centro) 🚇 Sol. ☎913 652 680. www.artesaniaelarco.com. Good quality handmade arts and crafts from all around Spain don't come cheap but make great souvenirs.

Camper – Gran Vía 54 (Centro). 🚇 Gran Vía. ☎915 475 223 www.camper.com. The Mallorcan family shoe firm that blazed the way with design and comfort are popular with visitors taking advantage of the lower prices on home ground.

Capas Seseña – Cruz 23 (Huertas). 🚇 Sevilla, Sol. ☎915 31 68 40. www.sesena.com. Closed Sun. A family firm that dates from 1901, where traditional and contemporary **capes** are crafted by hand from fine fabric. Photos show such clients as Hemingway, Picasso, Catherine Deneuve, Rudolph Valentino and Michael Jackson.

Custo - Fuencarral 29 (Gran Vía) 🚇 Gran Vía. ☎913 60 46 36. www.custo-barcelona.com. Catalan designer Custo's ravishing textile and clothes design is found on catwalks worldwide.

La Favorita – Pl. Mayor 25. (Centro). 🚇 Sol. ☎913 66 58 77. www.lafavoritacb.com. Closed Sun. Basque berets, panama hats and fedoras are lined up in the window of this 100-year-old city favourite.

La Violeta – Pl. de Canalejas 6. Sevilla. 915 22 55 22. www.lavioletaonline.es. Closed Aug, Sat in Jul, Sun, public holidays. This establishment has served such luminaries as King Alfonso XIII and writers Jacinto Benavente y Valle Inclán since 1915. The bonbons and caramels are popular but the *marron glacé* and violet products – glazed violets and violet jam are just two – take the biscuit.

Art Galleries – Look around the Centro de Arte Reina Sofía, in the Salamanca district (near the Puerta de Alcalá), on Paseo de la Castellana, close to calle Génova, and in and around Chueca.

FIESTAS

On 15 May the feast day of city patron, San Isidro (www.esmadrid.com/sanisidro), is celebrated with impromptu dancing, rock concerts and its famous bullfighting festival, which lasts for some six weeks.

Alcalá de Henares★

Alcalá has a **historic centre★** of 16C–17C colleges and convents and spacious squares. Medieval Calle Mayor is adorned with impressive gateways and the university and historic centre are a UNESCO World Heritage Site.

A BIT OF HISTORY

Under the Romans the city was an important centre known as **Complutum**, now being excavated, but the history of Alcalá is mainly linked to that of its university, founded by Cardinal Cisneros in 1498. It became famous for its language teaching and in 1517, Europe's first Polyglot Bible was published with parallel texts in Latin, Greek, Hebrew and Chaldean. The university was moved to Madrid in 1836.

Alcalá's most famous citizen is **Miguel de Cervantes**, Spain's greatest writer, whose memory is honoured by a week of celebrations every October. His birthplace, the **Museo Casa Natal de Cervantes**, recreated as a 16th-century house with a multi-lingual collection of editions of his novel *Don Quixote*, is open to visitors (Mayor 48; open Tue–Sun 10am–6pm; closed 1 & 6 Jan, 1 May, 24–25 & 31 Dec; 918 89 96 54; www.museo-casa-natal-cervantes.org).

▶ **Population:** 198 750
Michelin Map: Michelin maps 575 and 576 K 19 – Madrid.
Info: Plaza de Cervantes. 918 80 33 00, www.turismoalcala.es.
▶ **Location:** 33km/20mi east of Madrid.
Don't Miss: The old university.
Timing: Take a day trip from Madrid.
Kids: Tren de Cervantes.

GETTING THERE

A fun way to arrive from Madrid is to take the **Tren de Cervantes**, which runs on Sundays from Apr–mid-June and Oct–Nov. It departs Atocha at 10.35am and returns form Alcala at 7.25pm and costs €22 for adults and €16 for children aged 4–11.

During the trip, actors act out scenes from Cervantes' works and a guided tour of the main sights in the town is included in the price. See the tourist office website for details.

SIGHTS

Antigua Universidad & Colegio de San Ildefonso★

Pl. San Diego. Guided tours (40min) hourly daily Mon-Sat 10am–2pm, 4–8pm, Sun 10am-2pm). Closed 1 Jan, 25 Dec. €4.50 (includes Capilla de San Ildefonso but other combinations available). ℘918 85 64 87. www.visitasalcala.es.

The original university, on plaza de San Diego, has a beautiful **Plateresque façade★**(1543) by Rodrigo Gil de Hontañón crowned by a balustrade. The Imperial escutcheon of Charles V decorates the pediment of the central section. The majestic 17C **Patio Mayor** was designed by Juan Gómez de Mora, pupil of Herrera and architect of the Plaza Mayor and ayuntamiento (town hall) in Madrid; at the centre is a well-head with a swan motif, emblem of Cardinal Cisneros. Across the 16C Renaissance Patio de los Filósofos stands the delightful **Patio Trilingüe** (1557) where Latin, Greek and Hebrew were taught.

The **Paraninfoa** (1520), formerly used for examinations and degree ceremonies, now sees the solemn opening of the university year and the awarding of Spain's most important literary prize, the Cervantes. A gallery is in the Plateresque style, with superb **Mudéjar artesonado★★** work.

Capilla de San Ildefonso★

Next to the university.

This early 16C chapel is crowned with magnificent **Mudéjar artesonado** ceilings. The delicate **stucco** on the Epistle side of the church is Late Gothic, while the Evangelist side opposite is Plateresque. In the presbytery is the **Carrara marble mausoleum★★** of Cardinal Cisneros, by Domenico Fancelli and Bartolomé Ordóñez, one of the finest examples of 16C Spanish sculpture.

Catedral Magistral

Pl. de los Santos Niños. Open Mon–Sat 9am–1pm, 5–8.30pm, Sun and public holidays 10am–1.30pm, 6–8.30pm. €3 for cathedral, museum and cloister. ℘667 696 323. www.visitascatedraldealcala.org.

Built between 1497 and 1515, the Cathedral has been remodelled several times. The central portal mixes Gothic, Plateresque and Mudéjar features.

Outside stork-nesting season you can visit the church tower. The cloisters (calle Tercia) house a museum.

Palacio Arzobispal

In the 13C, the bishops of Toledo, lords of Alcalá, erected a palace-fortress on Plaza de Palacio. The Renaissance **façade**, by Alonso de Covarrubias, once fronted a courtyard. The Baroque coat of arms was added later. On adjoining Plaza de San Bernardo, the 17C church of the **Convento de San Bernardo** is crowned by an elliptical dome. The **Museo Arqueológico Regional de la Comunidad de Madrid** (archaeological museum), which has finds from the region - including the capital - dating from prehistoric times, is in the 17C former **Convento de la Madre de Dios** (open Tue–Sat 11am–7pm (until 3pm Sun and hols); ℘91 879 66 66).

El Corral de Comedias★★

Pl. Cervantes 15. Guided tours (30 min) hourly Tue–Sun & hols 11.30am–1.30pm, 4.30, 5.30. €3. ℘91 877 1950. www.corraldealcala.com.

The oldest working theatre in Spain (if not in Europe) was a stage for Golden Age drama performed by and for university students. Glass sections in the floor allow visitors to view the original theatre floor.

ADDRESSES

🏨 STAY AND ⌘/EAT

⊜⊜⊜⊜ **Hostal Restaurante Miguel de Cervantes** –Imagen 12. ℘918 83 12 77. www.hcervantes.es. Closed for dinner Sun and 24 Dec. This restaurant, behind Cervantes' birthplace in a restored town house, serves top-quality traditional cuisine in a Castilian setting. Set menus from €25 and tapas are also available. There are also 13 rooms (⊜⊜).

Royal Palace and the gardens

© Victor Pelaez Torres/iStockphoto.com

Aranjuez★★

Aranjuez, on the banks of the Tagus (Tajo), is an oasis in the Castilian plain, renowned for its green gardens and parkland, which are now a World Heritage landscape. The shaded walks immortalised by composers (the most famous being Joaquín Rodrigo's haunting guitar piece *"Concierto de Aranjuez"*) and painted by artists are popular at weekends but beautifully quiet during the week.

A BIT OF HISTORY

The Aranjuez Revolt (El motín de Aranjuez) – In March 1808, Charles IV, his queen and the prime minister, Godoy, were at Aranjuez. They were preparing to flee (on 18 March) first to Andalucía, then to America, in the face of popular opposition to the right-of-passage privileges granted to Napoleon's armies. On the night of 17 March, Godoy's mansion was attacked by followers of the heir apparent, Prince Ferdinand; Charles IV then abdicated in favour of his son, but Napoleon soon forced both royals to abdicate in his own favour (5 May). These intrigues and the presence of a

▶ **Population:** 58 168
⚫ **Michelin Map:** 575 and 576 L 19 – Madrid.
ℹ **Info:** Plaza de San Antonio 9. ☎918 91 04 27. www.aranjuez.es.
▶ **Location:** Off the A 4 linking Madrid with Andalucía, 47km/29.2mi from both the capital and Toledo. 🚃Aranjuez.
⊘ **Don't Miss:** The Palace and Prince's Garden.
🕐 **Timing:** Take a day trip from Madrid.
👥 **Kids:** El Tren de la Fresa is an 1851 steam train (☎902 228 822, www.museodeferrocarril.org/en/strawberry-train; mid-May–Oct, exc Jul–Aug; see website for schedule), which runs at weekends from Madrid's Museo del Ferrocarril to Aranjuez, with costumed staff serving strawberries (from €23 for adults and €9 for children aged 4–12.).

French garrison in Madrid stirred the revolt of May 1808, the beginning of the War of Independence.

SIGHTS
ROYAL PALACE AND GARDENS★★

The Catholic Monarchs enjoyed the original 14C palace, enlarged by Emperor Charles V. The present palace is mainly the result of an initiative by Philip II who called on the future architects of the Escorial to erect a new palace amid gardens. In the 18C, the town became a principal royal residence and was considerably embellished. It was, however, ravaged by fire in 1727 and again in 1748, after which the present façade was built. Ferdinand VI built the town to a grid plan; Charles III added two palace wings and Charles IV erected the delightful Labourer's Cottage.

Palacio Real Sitio ★

Pl. de Parejas. Open Tue–Sun 10am–8pm (Oct–Mar until 6pm). See website for closing dates. €9; no charge for EU citizens Wed & Thu 5–8pm summer, 3–6pm winter, no charge for all 18 May and 12 Oct. ℘91 454 87 00. www.patrimonionacional.es.

This Classical-style royal palace of brick and stone was built in the 16C and restored in the 18C. In spite of many modifications it retains considerable unity of style. The entry and façades of the wings are marked by archways and domed pavilions mark the angles. The apartments have been left as they were at the end of the 19C.

The **Salón del Trono** (Throne Room), with crimson velvet hangings and Rococo furnishings, has a ceiling painted with an allegory of monarchy – ironically it was in this room that Charles IV abdicated in 1808.

The **Salón de Porcelana**★★ (Porcelain Room) is the palace's most notable room, covered in white garlanded porcelain tiles, illustrating in relief scenes of Chinese life, exotica and children's games, all made in the Buen Retiro factory in Madrid in 1763.

In the king's apartments a music room precedes the Smoking or Arabian Room – a reproduction of the Hall of the Two Sisters in the Alhambra. A fine Mengs *Crucifixion* hangs in the bedroom, and the walls of another room are decorated with 203 small pictures on rice paper with Oriental-style motifs. A museum of palace life in the days of Alfonso XIII includes a gymnasium, and items such as a tricycle.

Parterre and Jardín de la Isla★ (Parterre and Island Garden)

Open daily Nov–Feb 8am–6.30pm, Mar 8am–7pm, Apr–15 Jun and 16 Aug– Sept 8am–8.30pm, 16 Jun–15 Aug 8am–9.30pm, Oct 8am–7.30pm.

The **Parterre** is a formal garden laid out before the palace's east front by the Frenchman Boutelou in 1746. The fountain of Hercules brings a mythological touch to the balanced display. The **Jardín de la Isla** was laid out on an island in the Tajo river in the 16C. Cross the canal to reach the park and its fountains hidden among chestnut, ash and poplar trees and boxwood hedges.

Jardín del Príncipe★★ (Prince's Garden)

Entrance in calle de la Reina.

This vast garden beside the Tajo (150 ha/371 acres) has four monumental gateways by Juan de Villanueva. In 1763, Boutelou landscaped the park for the future Charles IV according to the romantic vision then in fashion. A farm, greenhouses with tropical plants, and stables for exotic animals were added.

Casa del Labrador★★ (Labourer's Cottage) – €5. The so-called cottage at the eastern end of the Jardín del Príncipe, named after the humble cottages originally on the site, was built on the whim of Charles IV in Neoclassical style with sumptuous decoration.

Casa de Marinos (the Sailors' House)/ **Museo de Falúas Reales**– . A museum beside the former landing stage exhibits falúas reales★★ (royal vessels) that ferried the royals and guests to the Labourer's Cottage. One, a gift to Philip V from a Venetian count, is remarkable for its ornate decoration in gilded, finely carved wood.

EXCURSION
Chinchón★
▶ 21km/13mi NE along the M 305.
Chinchón is famous for its aniseed spirit and, more importantly, the Countess of Chinchón, wife of a 17C viceroy of Peru, to whom the West owes quinine, extracted from the bark of a Peruvian tree (named chinchona in the countess' honour).

Plaza Mayor★★ – The picturesque arcaded square, dominated by its church, is surrounded by houses with wooden balconies. The tourist office is at no.6 (℘918 93 53 23; www.ciudad-chinchon.com). Bullfights are held in summer and a passion play on Easter Saturday.

ADDRESSES

⫷/EAT

⊜⊜⊜⊜ **Casa Pablo** – Almíbar 42, 28300 Aranjuez. ℘918 911 451. www.casapablo.net. You can enjoy a gourmet sit-down meal in the restaurant (try one of the house specials such as the fish soup) but it's more fun to stand at the wood and zinc bar surrounded by bullfighting memorabilia and tuck into a variety of tapas.

Monasterio de
El Escorial★★★

This symbolic building on the slopes of the Sierra de Guadarrama, commissioned by Philip II and designed by Juan de Herrera, heralded a style that combined the grandeur of a palace with the austerity of a committed monastery.

A BIT OF HISTORY
In memory of San Lorenzo – On 10 August 1557, St Lawrence's Day, Philip II defeated the French at St-Quentin. The king decided to dedicate a monastery to the saint, to serve as royal palace and pantheon. The stupendous project – including 1 200 doors and 2 600 windows, involving 1 500 workmen – was completed in only 21 years (1563–84), which explains the exceptional unity of style. The general designs of Juan de Toledo were followed after his death in 1567 by **Juan de Herrera**.
In reaction to the excessive ornamentation of Charles V's reign, the architects produced a sober monument with clean, majestic lines.

- ⚑ **Michelin Map:** 575 or 576 K 17 – Madrid.
- ▤ **Info:** Grimaldi 4, San Lorenzo de El Escorial. ℘918 90 53 13. ▦San Lorenzo de El Escorial. www.sanlorenzoturismo.org.
- ▶ **Location:** El Escorial is 56km/40mi NW of Madrid, at 1 065m/3 494ft.
- ☞ **Don't Miss:** The sumptuous royal apartments. The feast day of San Lorenzo (St Lawrence), the patron saint of the village and monastery, is celebrated on 10 August every year.
- ◷ **Timing:** El Escorial is a day trip from Madrid, the full monastery visit taking an estimated 4 hours.

There is a good **view★** of the monastery and countryside from **Silla de Felipe II** (Philip II's Seat), from where the king oversaw construction (▶turn left after the monastery into the road marked Entrada Herrería-Golf).

© Turespaña

Real Monasterio de San Lorenzo de El Escorial

SIGHTS

Real Monasterio de San Lorenzo de El Escorial

Allow half a day. Juan de Borbón y Battemberg. Open Tue–Sun and public holidays Apr–Sept 10am–8pm (Oct–Mar until 6pm). Recommended last entry time 4 hours before closure.
See website for closing dates. €10 (casitas extra). No charge Wed & Thu (for EU citizens) 5–8pm summer, 3–6pm winter, free to all 18 May and 12 Oct.
𝒫914 54 87 00.
www.patrimonionacional.es.

It is said that the monastery's gridiron plan recalls St Lawrence's martyrdom. Measuring 206m x 161m (676ft x 528ft), the austerity of its grey granite emphasises the severity of the architecture. When the king commanded an increase in height, Herrera positioned windows asymmetrically to lessen monotony.

Palacios★★
(Royal Apartments)

While the Habsburgs remained on the Spanish throne, El Escorial was a place of splendour: the king resided in apartments encircling the church apse. The Bourbons preferred other palaces but when in residence, occupied suites on the north side of the church. The palace took on renewed glory in the 18C in the reigns of Charles III and IV.
A staircase built in the time of Charles IV goes up (3rd floor) to the **Palacio de los Borbones** (Bourbon Apartments), sumptuous with Pompeian ceilings and fine **tapestries★**, many from the Real Fábrica (Royal Tapestry Works) in Madrid based on cartoons by Spanish artists, notably Goya. Elsewhere are Flemish tapestries.

The large **Sala de las Batallas** (Battle Gallery) contains frescoes (1587): the Victory at Higueruela in the 15C against the Moors and, on the north wall, the Victory at St-Quentin.

The restraint of the **habitaciones de Felipe II** (Philip II's apartments, second floor) is striking in comparison with the Bourbon rooms. Those of the Infanta Isabel Clara Eugenia comprise a suite of small rooms with dados of Talavera ceramic tiles. The king's bedroom is off the church. When he was dying of gangrene in 1598, he could contemplate the high altar from his bed.

The paintings in the apartments include a *St Christopher* by Patinir and a portrait of the king in old age by Pantoja de la Cruz. Facing the gardens and the plain, the Salón del Trono (Throne Room) is hung with 16C Brussels tapestries. The Sala de los Retratos (Portrait Gallery), which follows, holds royal portraits.

Panteones★★
(Pantheons)

Access through the Patio de los Evangelistas (Evangelists' Courtyard), with frescoes by Tibaldi and his followers.

A marble and jasper staircase leads down to the **Panteón de los Reyes★★★** (Royal Pantheon) and the remains of monarchs from the time of Charles V, with the exception of Philip V, Ferdinand VI and Amadeus of Savoy.

The octagonal chapel was begun in 1617 under Philip III and completed in 1654. Facing the door is the jasper altar; on either side stand 26 marble and bronze sarcophagi in wall niches; Kings on the left and the queens whose sons succeeded to the throne, on the right. The ornate chandelier is the work of an Italian artist.

The 19C **Panteón de los Infantes★** (Infantes' Pantheon) includes princes and princesses and queens whose children did not rule. The sculptures are delicately carved. Conditions are such that the room is well preserved.

Salas Capitulares★ (Chapter Houses)

Two fine rooms, with ceilings painted by Italian artists with grotesques and frescoes, form a museum of 16C–17C Spanish and Italian religious painting. The first room contains canvases by **El Greco** and **Ribera**, a *St Jerome* by Titian, and *Joseph's Tunic* by Velázquez. The second room has works from the 16C Venetian School, including paintings by Tintoretto, Veronese and Titian (*Ecce Homo*). A room at the back contains works by Bosch and his followers: the imaginative *Haywain* and the satirical *Crown of Thorns (Los Improperios)*.

Basílica★★

Herrera based his final plan on Italian drawings. He introduced the flat vault, in the atrium. The interior owes much to St Peter's in Rome with a Greek Cross plan, a 92m/302ft high cupola above the transept crossing supported by four colossal pillars, and transept barrel vaulting. The frescoes in the nave vaulting were painted by Luca Giordano in Charles II's reign. Red marble steps lead to the sanctuary which has paintings on the vaulting of the lives of Christ and the Virgin by Cambiasso.

The massive **retable**, designed by Herrera, is 30m/98ft tall and is composed of four registers of jasper, onyx and red marble columns between which stand 15 bronze sculptures by Leone and Pompeo Leoni.

The tabernacle is also by Herrera. On either side of the chancel are the royal mausoleums with funerary figures at prayer by Pompeo Leoni. In the first chapel off the north aisle is the *Martyrdom of St Maurice* by Rómulo Cincinato, which Philip II preferred to that of El Greco (👁*See Nuevos Museos, below*). In the adjoining chapel is a magnificent sculpture of Christ by Benvenuto Cellini.

Patio de los Reyes (Kings' Courtyard)

One of the three Classical gateways opens onto this courtyard, named for the statues of the Kings of Judea on the west front of the church.

Biblioteca★★ (Library)

2nd floor.

The shelving, designed by Herrera, is of exotic woods; the ceiling, sumptuously painted by Tibaldi, represents the liberal arts with Philosophy and Theology at each end. There are also magnificent portraits of Charles V, Philip II and Philip III by Pantoja de la Cruz, and one of Charles II by Carreño. Philip II furnished the library with over 10 000 books, many of them lost in a 1671 fire. It is now a public library with over 400 00 books and historic manuscripts. The spines face inward for preservation purposes.

Nuevos Museos★★ (New Museums)

Paintings in the **Museo de Pintura** are on religious themes.

First room: 16C Venetian School canvases (Titian, Veronese and Tintoretto).

Second room: two works by Van Dyck and a small painting by Rubens.

Third room: works by Miguel de Coxcie, Philip II's Court Painter.

Fourth room: Rogier Van der Weyden's sober and expressive *Calvary*, flanked by an *Annunciation* by Veronese and a *Nativity* by Tintoretto.

Fifth room: canvases by Ribera including *St Jerome Penitent*, the *Chrysippus* and *Aesop*, with vividly portrayed faces, and Zurbarán's *St Peter of Alcántara* and the *Presentation of the Virgin*.

Last room: paintings by Alonso Cano and Luca Giordano.

On the ground floor, paintings include El Greco's **Martyrdom of St Maurice and the Theban Legionary★**, commissioned by Philip II but rejected by him. Nevertheless, it is now considered one of El Greco's greater works.

OTHER ROYAL BUILDINGS
Casita del Príncipe★
(Prince's or Lower Pavilion)

Jardín de los Moes. SE along the station road. Same opening hours as Palacios, p153.

Charles III commissioned Juan de Villanueva to build a lodge for the future Charles IV. Its exquisite decoration makes it a jewel of a palace in miniature. There are painted **Pompeian-style ceilings★** by Maella and Vicente Gómez, silk hangings, canvases by Luca Giordano, chandeliers, and a beautiful mahogany and marble dining room.

Casita del Infante
(Infante's or Upper Pavilion)

Ctra de Ávila. 3km/1.8mi SW beyond the golf course. Same opening hours as Palacio.

This lodge was designed by Villanueva for the Infante Gabriel, Charles IV's younger brother. The interior is furnished in period style; the first floor was used by Prince Juan Carlos before his accession to the throne.

EXCURSION
Valle de los Caídos★★

◗ 16km/10mi NW on the M 600 and M 527. Open Tue–Sun and public holidays Apr–Sept 10am–7pm (until 6pm Oct–Mar). Recommended last entry time 4 hours before closure. Closed 1 & 6 Jan,

1 May, 24–25, 31 Dec. €9 ticket includes basilica. No charge Wed & Thu for EU citizens. Oct–Mar 3–6pm and Apr–Sept 5–7pm, free to all 18 May. ℘918 90 54 11. www.valledeloscaidos.es.

The Valley of the Fallen is a striking and hugely controversial monument to the dead of both sides of the Spanish Civil War (1936–39), built as a "national act of atonement" by Republican prisoners on the orders of Francisco Franco, whose grave is also here. It is a rallying point for the far right, replete with National Fascist imagery.

Basílica★★

The Basilica is hollowed out of the rock face and dominated by a monumental Cross. Its west door is a bronze work crowned by a *Pietà* by Juan de Ávalos. At the entrance to the vast interior is a fine wrought-iron screen with 40 statues of Spanish saints and soldiers.

The 262m/859.5ft nave is lined with chapels between which are hung copies of 16C Brussels tapestries of the Apocalypse. Above the chapel entrances are alabaster copies of famous Spanish statues of the Virgin Mary.

A **cupola★**, 42m/137.8ft in diameter, above the crossing, shows in mosaic the heroes, martyrs and saints of Spain approaching both Christ in Majesty and the Virgin Mary. On the altar stands a painted figure of Christ Crucified, the work of Beovides. At the foot of the altar are the remains of Falangist Party founder José Antonio Primo de Rivera and Francisco Franco. Ossuaries hold remains of 40 000 soldiers and civilians.

La Cruz★

The Cross is 125m/410ft high (150m/492ft including the base), the width 46m/151ft. The immense statues of the Evangelists around the plinth and the four cardinal virtues above are by Juan de Ávalos.

Castilla-León: Ávila, Salamanca & Zamora

You will find Castilla-León in the northern part of Spain's great *meseta* – a plain around 1 000m/3 280ft above sea level. Wide terraced valleys and moors are dotted with rock pinnacles, narrow defiles and gentle hills. Vast spaces open up with a grandeur unusual in Europe. Some call it eerie and romantic, others label it harsh and monotonous. It is crossed from east to west by one of the country's great rivers, the Duero, a frontier territory during the medieval centuries that has retained its historic towns and cities. The region's history is certainly romantic; Castilla means land of castles and it was home to the legendary (and very real) El Cid, who fought both with and against the Moors. The weather is less romantic, with sub-zero winters and baking summers.

Highlights

1 Walking the **city walls** by night in **Ávila** (p159)

2 Climbing the **Roman road** at the **Puerto del Pico** (p162)

3 People-watching in **Plaza Mayor, Salamanca** (p164)

4 Relaxing in the **quiet village** of **La Alberca** (p172)

5 Exploring the **Romanesque churches** of Toro (p174)

A bit of geography

The striking Sierra de Gredos marks the southern border of Castilla y León, peaking at nearly 2 600m/8 530ft with glacial cirques and lakes. The towns at the foot of the southern slopes, which enjoy a benign climate, give access to gentle or adventurous walks up towards the peaks. Today's roads through the Sierra climb over historic passes that offer panoramic views to the south.

The cities of the north Meseta

Ávila, 107km/67mi northwest of Madrid, is a remarkable example of a town whose 11C walls and romantic towers have been neither removed nor exceeded. For a period in the 16C Ávila was the heart of Spanish religious life, thanks to its famous inhabitants, St Teresa of Ávila and St John of the Cross. The city keeps its famously chilly mountain air and an austerity of style that gives it a distinct personality.

Salamanca, northwest of that, sitting on the River Duero, is one of Spain's most beautifully preserved historic cities. Its university is as old as Oxford in England and its students make sure that the city buzzes. The double Cathedral and the central plaza – grand architectural set-pieces – alone make the visit worthwhile. To the south and west of Salamanca the Meseta's stark landscapes soften as you drive into grazing lands where bulls and pigs graze under holm-oaks. Ciudad Rodrigo, just 25km/15.5mi east of the Portuguese border, set against that landscape, is another splendidly preserved town, where nobles' mansions and palaces bristle with bold carved standards.

Close to Castila-León's southern border with Extremadura the plains turn into thickly wooded rolling hills that have kept a rural way of life and the popular architecture of past centuries. La Alberca, the best preserved of the towns and villages, makes a good base for exploring the national park of Las-Batuecas and Sierra de Francia.

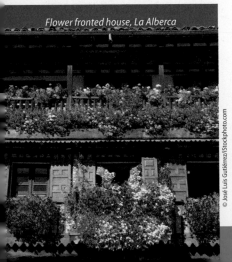

Flower fronted house, La Alberca

© José Luis Gutiérrez/iStockphoto.com

© Gannet77/iStockphoto.com

Murallas

Ávila★★

Ávila is one of the best-preserved
fortified cities in Europe; its
numerous convents and churches
shelter behind magnificent 11C walls.
The old town and churches outside
the walls are a World Heritage Site.

THE CITY TODAY

Ávila is mostly a day-tripper's city but
a night here is definitely worthwhile,
preferably in the 16C parador occupying a former palace (Calle Marqués
Canales y Chozas 2; ℘920 54 79 79;
www.parador.es). The town is hardly
hopping, but there are enough tapas
bars and drinking holes to make a night
of it – try around the Plaza del Mercado
Chico. Wherever you go in town you will
be reminded of the town's favourite
daughter, Santa Teresa, if only by the
yemas de Santa Teresa, a tooth-melting
egg-yolk-and-sugar confection produced by the local nuns.

SIGHTS
Murallas★★
(City walls)

Entry at Pta. Alcázar, Carnicerías or
Puente Adaja. Open Tue–Sun (daily 15
Jun–15 Oct) 31 Oct–31 Mar 10am–6pm,
1 Apr–30 Jun and 1 Sept–31 Oct
10am–8pm, Jul–Aug 10am–9pm.
Last ticket 30min before closing. See
website for days closed. €5. No charge

▶ **Population:** 58 358
⚅ **Michelin Map:** 575 or
576 K 15 – Map 121
Alrededores de Madrid.
🈁 **Info:** Avda. de Madrid 39.
℘920 350 000.
www.turismoavila.com.
◖ **Location:** Sitting at 1131m/
3710ft, NW of Madrid, Ávila
has a harsh and windy winter
climate. 🚆Ávila (AVE).
◉ **Don't Miss:** The city walls.
🕐 **Timing:** Start with the
walls and Cathedral.

Tue 2–4pm except hols. ℘920 35 00 00.
www.murralladeavila.com.
Europe's most striking medieval fortifications, with 90 bastions and towers and
eight gateways, enclose an area 900m/
2 953ft by 449m/1 476ft.
Most date from the 11C; and despite 14C
modifications, maintain their unity. You
can climb up on to the walls at various
points to walk the sentry path along the
top; the best **view** of the walls is from
Cuatro Postes, on the Salamanca road.

Catedral★★

Pl. de la Catedral. See website for
opening times. €5 (inc. museum). ℘608
48 68 08. www.catedralavila.vocces.com.
The fortified **east end** of the Cathedral
is set into the ramparts, crowned with

a double row of battlements. Granite and defensive design make it austere. The 14C **north doorway** with French Gothic decoration, its stone eroded, was removed in the 15C from the **west front** during a renovation by Juan Guas. Its current placement, from the 18C, is more suitable for a palace.

The surprising **interior** has a high Gothic nave, a chancel with sandstone patches of red and yellow and many **works of art**★★. The trascoro (1531) holds lovely Plateresque statues (left to right): the Presentation of Jesus in the Temple, the Adoration of the Magi and the Massacre of the Innocents. The **choir stalls** are from the same period. There are two delicate wrought-iron **pulpits** – Renaissance and Gothic.

Construction lasted from 1135 to the 14C; windows in the apse are Romanesque. The large painted **altarpiece** (c. 1500) by Pedro Berruguete and Juan de Borgoña has a gilt wood surround with Isabelline features and Italian Renaissance pilasters.

Four carved panels on the high altar show the Evangelists and the four Holy Knights. The central panel is Vasco de la Zarza's masterpiece: the **alabaster tomb**★★ of Don Alonso de Madrigal, Bishop of Ávila in the 15C, called El Tostado (Swarthy). He is shown before a beautiful Epiphany.

Museo de la Catedral

The museum contains a notable 13C **sacristy**★★ with an eight-ribbed vault, massive 16C altarpiece and sculptures of the Passion in imitation alabaster. View a head of Christ by Morales painted on a tabernacle door, a portrait by **El Greco**, a huge Isabelline grille, late 15C antiphonaries and a colossal 1571 monstrance (1.7m/5ft 8in) by Juan de Arfe. The Gothic **cloisters** are restored. In plaza de la Catedral, the **Palacio de Valderrábanos**, now a hotel, has a fine 15C doorway with family crest.

Basílica de San Vicente★★

Pl. San Vicente 1. Open May–Oct Mon–Sat 10am–6.30pm (Nov–Apr until 1.30pm then 4–6.30pm), Sun & hols 10am–2pm, 4–6pm. €2.30. ☏ 920 25 52 30. www.basilicasanvicente.es.

This vast 12C–14C Romanesque basilica, with ogive vaulting, is on the reputed site of the 4C martyrdom of St Vincent of Zaragoza and his sisters. The ensemble includes the 14C south gallery with slender columns, a cornice over the length of the nave, the tall west front porch and two incomplete towers.

The **west portal**★★ is outstanding for the statue columns below the richly decorated cornice and lifelike covings. Beneath the 14C **lantern**★ is the **martyrs' tomb**★★, a late 12C masterpiece under a rare 15C Gothic canopy with pagoda top. The martyrdom of St Vincent and his sisters is attributed to the unknown sculptor of the west portal. The scenes of their capture, flaying and torture are particularly powerful.

Monasterio de Santo Tomás★

Pl. de Granada 1. Open daily Sept–Jun 10.30am–2pm, 3.30–7.30pm and Jul–Aug 10.30am–9pm. Last ticket 1 hour before closing. €4 (church, oriental museum, cloisters and choir). ☏ 920 352 237. www.monasteriosantotomas.com.

This late 15C Dominican monastery, at times a summer residence of the Catholic Monarchs, was also the university. The **church** façade includes the common motifs of the monastery: details are emphasised with long lines of balls, and the yoke and fasces (bound bundle of wooden rods) emblem of Ferdinand and Isabel. The church has a single aisle, its arches on clusters of slender columns. Two galleries were accessible only from the cloisters by the monks. The fine **mausoleum**★ (1512) is of Prince Juan, only son of the Catholic Monarchs. Its alabaster table with delicate Renaissance sculpting is by Domenico Fancelli, who created the Catholic Monarchs' mausoleum in Granada. In a north chapel is the Renaissance tomb of Juan Dávila and his wife, the prince's tutors.

Claustro (Cloisters) – Beyond the plain 15C **Claustro de los Novicios** is the **Claustro del Silencio**★, intimate and generously carved on its upper gallery. The Catholic Monarchs' Cloister is larger

and more solemn with spectacularly bare upper arching.
From the Claustro del Silencio, stairs lead to beautiful 15C Gothic **choir stalls** with pierced canopies and arabesques; and from the upper gallery, to the high altar gallery is Berruguete's masterpiece, the **retable of St Thomas Aquinas★★** (c. 1495).

Iglesia de San Pedro

Pl. de Santa Teresa. Opening times vary, ask at the tourist office. €1.50.
This Romanesque church on the vast **plaza Santa Teresa** has early Gothic pointed arches and a delicate rose window. Elsewhere, nearby, are a number of fine urban palaces with façades to view from the street: the Gothic Reniassance **Mansión de los Verdugo** (C. Lopez Núñe, closed to the public), marked with a family crest, is flanked by two stout square towers; the **Mansión de los Polentinos** (C. Vallespín), now a barracks, has a fine Renaissance entrance and patio; the **Torreón de los Guzmanes** (Pl. Corral de las Campanas), also called the Oñates Palace, has a massive square corner tower with battlements dating from the early 16C.
Near the Cathedral the provincial Law Courts are housed in the **Palacio de Núñez Vela** (Pl. de la Catedral 10). This Renaissance palace of the Viceroy of Peru has windows framed by slender columns and coats of arms. The patio, accessible from the street, is lovely.
Two 14C Gothic buildings with coats of arms give onto Plaza Pedro Dávila and two others, belonging to the Episcopal Palace, face Plaza de Rastro.

Museo Provincial de Arte

Pl. de Nalvillos 3. Open Tue–Sun am and public holidays 10am–2pm, 5–8pm (Oct–Jun 10am–2pm, 4–7pm). €1; no charge weekends and hols.
℘920 354 000.
The fine 16C Dean's House houses Ávila province's art collection. It is comprised of traditional objects, clothes and furniture; archaeological remains ranging from prehistoric to Visigothic times; and fine art. Among the paintings, in Room VII, hangs an outstanding primitive triptych by Hans Memling.

Iglesia Santo Tomé el Viejo

Pl. de Italia. Visit included in Museum of Provincial Art ticket.
A 13C Romanesque church that serves as an annexe to the museum. On show are pieces from the archaeological collection and a fine Roman mosaic.

🚗 DRIVING TOUR

SOUTH OF ÁVILA

120km/75mi. Allow half a day.

▶ Drive northeast to Burgos, then follow the N403 south for 40km/25mi towards San Martín de Valdeiglesias.

Embalse de Burguillo

This artificial lake on the River Alberche makes a splendid landscape set against the bare or scrubby hills.

▶ Follow the N403 for another 10km/6mi before reaching San Martín de Valdeiglesias, then turn to your right where you see the signpost for the Toros de Guisando.

Toros de Guisando

The granite Bulls of Guisando are surprisingly small. They stand in a enclosure just off the road. Many interpretations have been made of their meaning.

▶ Drive through San Martín de Valdeiglesias and take the N501 towards Madrid for 5km/3mi.

Pantano de San Juan

The winding road around the edge of the reservoir offers spectacular views down over the water though often in summer its upper reaches are left bare by drought. Between the pine-covered slopes are areas for watersports and bathing, plus restaurants; busy in summer but perfect the rest of the year.

Sierra de los Gredos★★

The massif of the Sierra de Gredos includes Pico de Almanzor (2 592m/ 8 504ft), the highest peak in the Cordillera Central. The north face of the sierra is marked by glacial cirques and lakes; the south by a steep granite wall and gullies. Fertile valleys produce apples in the north and grapes, olives and tobacco on the sheltered south slope. Wildlife is protected in the Reserva Nacional de Gredos.

- **Michelin Map:** 575 or 576 K 14, L 14.
- **Info:** Avda. de Madrid 39, Avila. ℘920 350 000. www.avilaturismo.com.
- **Location:** The sierra is almost due west of Madrid (M 501 via San Martín de Valdeiglesias) and south of Ávila (N 502 to Puerto del Pico).
- **Timing:** Start early and a day should allow you to fit most sights into a lesurely drive.
- **Kids:** Cuevas del Águila.

SIGHTS

San Martín de Valdeiglesias

This old market town, with 14C castle walls built by the Lord High Constable Álvaro de Luna, is a starting point for explorations.

Toros de Guisando

⊙ 6km/3.7mi NW.

The **Bulls of Guisando** are four roughly carved granite figures in an open field. Similar ancient figures, possibly Celt-Iberian, are found elsewhere in Ávila province. They are similar to the stone **porcas** (sows) seen in the Trás-os-Montes region of Portugal.

Embalse de Burguillo★ (Burguillo Reservoir)

⊙ 20km/12.4mi NW. See p161.

Pantano de San Juan

⊙ 8km/5mi E. See p161.

⊙ From San Martín de Valdeiglesias, take the N501 (which becomes the C501), towards Arenas de San Pedro.

▲▲ Cuevas del Águila★ (The Eagle's Caves)

⊙ 9km/5.6mi S of Arenas de San Pedro. Take the C708 turn-off from the N502. Open daily 21 Sept–21 Mar 10.30am–1pm, 3–6pm; 22 Mar–20 Sept 10.30am–1pm, 3–7pm. €8. ℘920 37 71 07. www.grutasdelaguila.com.

A single vast chamber is open to the public. Among the many concretions are lovely frozen streams of calcite, ochre crystals coloured by iron oxide and massive pillars still in the process of formation. Make sure you take some warm clothes with you.

Puerto del Pico road★

⊙ 29km/18mi NE of Arenas de San Pedro.

The road through the sierra crosses the attractive small town of **Mombeltrán** (15C castle with well-preserved exterior), then winds upwards, parallel to a Roman road. From the pass (1 352m/ 4 436ft) there are stunning **views★** of the mountains, the Tiétar Valley (south) and, beyond, the Tajo. The **Parador de Gredos**, first parador in Spain (1928), stands in a **magnificent setting★★** with far-reaching views.

Laguna Grande★

⊙ 12km/7.4mi S of Hoyos del Espino. Park at the end of the road.

A marked path leads to Laguna Grande (2hr), a glacial basin fed by mountain torrents. Halfway along is a **panorama★** of the Gredos cirque.

© Jon Arnold/hemis.fr

Plaza Mayor

Salamanca★★★

Salamanca evokes its rich history through its venerable university, narrow streets, and splendid buildings of golden stone. Blessed with what is widely regarded as the most magnificent main square in Spain, Salamanca has long been a favoured destination for foreign students and visitors alike. The old town is a World Heritage site.

THE CITY TODAY

The University of Salamanca may no longer be in the same league academically as the Oxfords and Harvards of this world, but its 30 000 or so international and Spanish students bring a real joie de vivre to the city. If you are young, want to study Spanish for a couple of weeks and enjoy a lively typical Spanish social life, this is a great place to choose.

A BIT OF HISTORY

A tumultuous past – Salamanca flourished under the Romans who built the **Puente Romano** (Roman bridge). Alfonso VI took the city from the Moors in 1085. In 1218, Alfonso IX established a centre for study, later to become an important university. In 1520, Salamanca rose against the royal authority of Emperor Charles V (*See SEGOVIA, p174*) and in the 16C it reached its artistic and intellectual zenith.

▶ **Population:** 146 438
♿ **Michelin Map:** 575 and 576 J 12-13.
🚻 **Info:** Plaza Mayor 19.
&902 30 20 02.
www.salamanca.es.
▶ **Location:** Salamanca is in the western Castilla y León region, accessible from Ávila (98km/61mi SE on the N 501), Valladolid (115km/72mi NE on the A 62), and Zamora (62km/39mi N on the N 630). 🚆Salamanca.
👁 **Don't Miss:** The University and main square.
🕐 **Timing:** There's easily enough to fill two days.
👫 **Kids:** A walk on the Ciudad Rodrigo ramparts.

Los Bandos – During the 15C, rivalry between noble factions *(bandos)* saw the city's streets bathed in blood. The *bandos* remained active until 1476.
The university was founded in 1218 and grew under the patronage of kings of Castilla and high dignitaries.
Its great and famous members include the Infante Don Juan; St John of the Cross and his teacher, the humanist **Fray Luis de León** (1527–91); and **Miguel de Unamuno** (1864–1936), Professor of Greek, rector, and philosopher.

Art in Salamanca – In the late 15C and early 16C, two major painters were working in Salamanca: **Fernando Gallego**, one of the best Hispano-Flemish artists, and **Juan of Flanders** (c. 1465–1519), whose work is outstanding for the subtle delicacy of its colours.

The 15C also saw the evolution of the original Salamanca patio arch, in which the line of the Mudéjar curve is broken by counter-curves and straight lines.

The 16C brought Salamancan **Plateresque** art to an ebullient climax.

WALKING TOUR

1 OLD CENTRE★★★

Allow one day.

Plaza Mayor★★★

The Plaza Mayor is the life and soul of Salamanca. All the city's major streets converge on the square, where locals and visitors alike meet. It was built by Philip V between 1729 and 1755 and is among the finest in Spain, designed principally by the Churriguera brothers.

Four ground-level arcades with rounded arches, decorated by a series of portrait medallions of Spanish kings and famous men such as Cervantes, El Cid and Columbus, support three storeys rising in perfect formation to an elegant balustrade. On the north and east sides are pedimented fronts of the **ayuntamiento** (town hall) and the Pabellón Real (Royal Pavilion).

▶ Take Prior to Plaza de Monterrey, then Compañía.

Casa de las Muertes (House of Death)

Closed to the public.

The early 16C Plateresque façade is attributed to Diego de Siloé; it's named after the skulls carved on its upper part.

▶ Opposite is the Ursuline Convent.

Convento Museo de las Úrsulas (Ursuline Convent Museum)

Pl. de las Úrsulas 2. Open Tue–Sun 11am–1pm, 4.30–6pm. Closed last Sun in month. ☎923 21 98 77. €2.

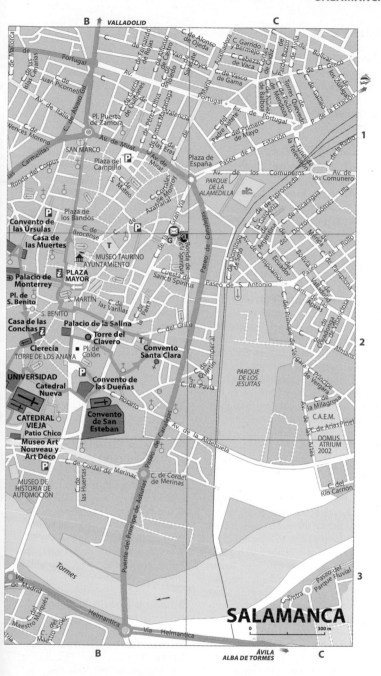

SALAMANCA

0   300 m

The 16C church contains the **tomb**★ of Alonso de Fonseca with delicate low reliefs attributed to Diego de Siloé. The **museum**, with its *artesonado* and coffered ceilings, houses panels and fragments of an altarpiece by Juan de Borgoña. There are also works by Morales.

◗ Walk back on Calle de la Compañía.

Palacio de Monterrey

Pl. Monterrey 2.
Built in 1539, this Renaissance palace has a balustrade crowning a long top-floor gallery, between corner towers.

◗ Opposite stands the Iglesia de la Purísima.

Iglesia de la Purísima (Church of the Immaculate Conception)

Pl. de Monterrey. Open for Mass (the church may be viewed before and afterwards). ℘923 21 27 38.
The **Immaculate Conception★** by **Ribera** hangs above the high altar.

◗ Take Ramón y Cajal to the end.

Colegio Arzobispo Fonseca★

Fonseca 4. Chapel and cloisters open Mon-Fri 9am-2pm €2 (inc in Universidad admission). ℘923 29 45 70.
Built in 1535 by Archbishop Fonseca, this is the last of the surviving four university colleges, and is almost perfectly preserved. Theology, liberal arts and canon law were taught here. Designed by **Diego de Siloé** it was executed by Juan de Álava and Rodrigo Gil de Hontañon. The façade is strikingly simple. The main door is flanked by Ionic columns above which stand Saints Augustine and Ildefonso.
At the top a medallion frieze shows Saint James at the Battle of Clavijo. The portico to the patio is decorated by 128 medallions mixing Biblical, mythological and historic personalities. In the chapel, immediately to the right of the entrance, a plateresque **retablo** by Alonso Berruguete, dated 1529, combines canvases with monumental statuary.

◗ Retrace your steps and turn right along Compañía to Rua Antigua, turn right and then left down Libreros.

Plaza de San Benito

On this delightful square are the **Iglesia de San Benito**, and mansions of Salamanca's old noble rival families.

Casa de las Conchas★ (House of Shells)

Compañía 2. Patio: open Mon-Fri 9am-9pm, Sat-Sun and public hols 9am-3pm, 4-7pm. ℘923 26 93 17.
This late 15C house (now a library) is carved with 400 scallop shells in its golden stone wall. It has decorative Isabelline windows and beautiful wrought-iron grilles. The **patio** has delicate mixtilinear arches and open-work balustrades, carved lions' heads and coats of arms.

◗ Opposite stands the Jesuit College.

La Clerecía

Compañía 5. Open Mon-Fri 10am-12.45pm, 5-6.30pm, Sat, Sun and public holidays 10.30am-1.30pm, 5-7.15pm. Guided tours. €3. ℘923 27 71 00.
This Jesuit College was begun in 1617; its Baroque towers were finished by Andrés García de Quiñones in 1755. You can climb the towers for views over the city (€3.75, combined tickets available).

◗ Cross the Pl. de San Isidro and take Libreros.

Patio de las Escuelas★★★ (Schools' Square)

This small square, off the old Calle Libreros, is surrounded by the best examples of Salamanca Plateresque. The former university principals' residence is the **Casa-Museo Unamuno** (open Mon-Fri 10am-2pm, last entry 1pm; €4; ℘923 29 44 00), a museum dedicated to the philosopher and former Rector of the university.

◗ Opposite the Patio, on Libreros, stands the University.

Universidad (University)

Patio de Escuelas. Open Mon-Sat 10am-6.30pm, Sun and public holidays 10am-1.30pm. Limited access during academic events. €10 ticket includes entrance to the Escuelas Mayores and Colegio Arzobispo Fonseca; no charge

Mon morning, 18 May. ℘923 29 44 00.
www.usal.es.

The University's sumptuous 1534
entrance★★★ is a brilliant composition. Above the twin doors, covered
by basket arches, the carving is in
ever greater relief, to compensate for
increasing height. A central medallion
in the first register shows the Catholic
Monarchs who presented the doorway;
in the second are portrait heads in scal-
lop-shell niches; in the third, flanking
the pope supported by cardinals, are
Venus and Hercules and the Virtues.
The most famous motif is the Death's
head surmounted by a frog (on the right
pilaster, halfway up) symbolising the
posthumous punishment of lust.

The lecture halls are around the **patio**:
the **Paraninfo** (Great Hall) is hung with
17C Brussels tapestries and a portrait
of Charles IV from Goya's studio; the
hall where Fray Luis de León lectured
in theology is as it was in the 16C.

The grand staircase rises beneath star
vaulting, its banister carved with foli-
ated scrollwork and, at the third flight,
a mounted bullfight.

A gallery on the first floor has its original, rich *artesonado* ceiling with stalactite ornaments and a delicate low
relief frieze along the walls. A Gothic
door with a fine 16C grille opens into
the 18C library, which contains books,
incunabula and manuscripts, some of
which date back to the 11th century.

Escuelas Menores
(Minor Schools)

Same opening hours as University.

Standing to the right of the hospital,
and crowned by the same openwork
Renaissance frieze, is the entrance to
the Minor (preparatory) Schools – a Plateresque portal decorated with coats of
arms, roundels and scrollwork.

The typical Salamanca **patio★★**
(1428) has lovely lines. To the right
of the entrance is a new exhibition
room with a fine Mudéjar ceiling; the
University Museum opposite exhibits
what remains of the ceiling painted by
Fernando Gallego for the former university library. This section of the **Cielo de**

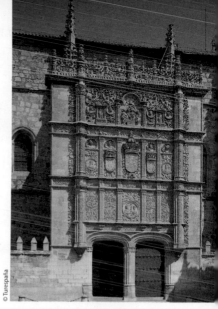

Façade of the university entrance

Salamanca★ (Salamanca Sky) illustrates
constellations and signs of the zodiac.
Several works by Juan of Flanders and
Juan of Burgundy stand out.

▷ Off the patio to the left.

Museo de Salamanca
(de Bellas Artes)

C. Patio de Escuelas 2. Open Tue-Sat
10am–2pm, 5–8pm (Oct–Jun 4–7pm),
Sun and public holidays 10am–2pm.
Closed 1, 2 & 6 Jan, 24, 25 & 31 Dec. €1;
no charge Sat and Sun and 18 May.
www.museoscastillayleon.jcyl.es

The contents of Salamanca's fine arts
museum, housed inside a small urban
palace, cover 2,000 years of history.
Many of its artistic treasures come from
convents or monasteries and others are
on loan from Madrid's Prado Museum.
Outstanding is a 14C **sarcophogus**
richly decorated with a narrative of
the stigmatisation of St Francis, and a
Mannerist *Llanto por Cristo (Mourning
at the tomb of Christ)*. Its collection of
modern paintings includes a portrait
of *Don Miguel de Unamuno*, by Basque
painter Echevarria y Zunicalday, and
Corrida en Azul★★★, a 1942 canvas by
Luis de Horna, clearly influenced by
Picasso's *Guernica*.

167

▶ Take Libreros towards the river and take the first left, Calderón de la Barca, to reach Pl. Juan XXIII to enter the Cathedrals.

Catedral Nueva★★ (New Cathedral)

Pl. Anaya. Open daily Apr–Sept 10am–8pm (last entry 7.15pm), Oct–Mar until 6pm (last entry 5.15pm). €4.75. ℘923 21 74 76. www.catedralsalamanca.com.

Construction began in 1513, although additions continued to be made until the 18C – hence the variety of architectural styles.

The **west front★★★** is divided into four wide bays outlined by pierced stonework, carved as minutely as the keystones in the arches, the friezes and the pinnacled balustrades. The Gothic decoration of the central portal, which includes scenes such as a Crucifixion between St Peter and St Paul, overflows the covings and tympanum.

The **north doorway**, facing the **Colegio de Anaya**, bears a delicate low relief of Christ's entry into Jerusalem. The restored lower section of the last archivolt contains the surprising figure of an astronaut as well as a mythological animal eating ice-cream.

The **interior** is notable for the pattern of the vaulting, the delicacy of the cornices and the sweep of the pillars. The eight windows in the lantern are given added effect by a drum with scenes from the Life of the Virgin painted in the 18C by the Churriguera brothers, who also designed the ornate Baroque stalls in the *coro*, the *trascoro* and the north organ loft.

Catedral Vieja★★★ (Old Cathedral)

Pl. Anaya. Access from the Catedral Nueva. Same conditions as Catedral Nueva.

▶ Enter by the first bay off the south aisle in the new Cathedral.

The builders of the new Cathedral respected the fabric of the old which is almost totally masked outside. It was built in the 12C and is a good example of the Romanesque, the pointed arching being a legitimate, if unusual, innovation; the *cimborrio* (lantern), or Torre del Gallo, with two tiers of windows and ribbing, is outstanding. Beneath the vaulting, capitals are carved with scenes of tournaments and imaginary animals.

The **altarpiece★★** in the central apsidal chapel was painted by Nicholas of Florence in 1445 and comprises 53 compartments decorated in surprisingly fresh colours showing the architecture and dress of the times. The Virgin of the Vega is a 12C wooden statue, plated in gilded and enamelled bronze.

Recesses in the south transept contain French-influenced 13C recumbent figures and frescoes.

Claustro – Capitals from earlier Romanesque galleries destroyed during the 1755 Lisbon earthquake remain in these cloisters. The adjoining **Capilla de Talavera**, with a Mudéjar dome on carved ribs, was where the ancient Mozarabic rite was celebrated. A museum in three rooms and the Capilla de Santa Catalina contains works by Fernando Gallego and his brother Francisco and others by Juan of Flanders (St Michael altarpiece).

The **Capilla Anaya** contains the outstanding 15C alabaster **tomb★★** of Diego de Anaya, archbishop first of Salamanca and then of Sevilla. Surrounding it is a magnificent Plateresque grille. There are also a 15C **organ★** and superb 16C recumbent statues.

From the **Patio Chico** you can see the old Cathedral apse and the scallop tiling on the **Torre del Gallo** (Cockerel Tower). From here, Calle Arcediano leads to the delightful **Huerto de Calixto y Melibea**.

▶ From Pl. Juan XXIII take Calle Tentenecio, then take the first left.

Museo de Art Nouveau y Art Déco★★

Expolio 14. Open Tue–Fri 11am–8pm (Nov-Mar 11am–2pm, 4-7pm); Sat, Sun and hols 11am–8pm. Closed 1 & 6 Jan, 25 Dec. €4, no charge Thu 11am-2pm. ℘923 12 14 25.

www.museocasalis.org.
This museum in the Modernist Casa Lis, dating from the beginning of the 20C, includes the house's own furnishings and bronzes, works by R Lalique, vases by E Gallé and sculptures by Hagenauer. Temporary shows focus on art of the period. There is a cafeteria and in summer there are live music events.

▷ From Calle Tentenecio take Po. de Rector Esperaba and C. Arroyo Sto Domingo

Convento de San Esteban★ (St Stephen's Monastery)

Pl. Concilio de Trento. Open daily 10am–2pm, 4–6pm (Mar-Nov 4-8pm). €3.50. ☎923 21 50 00. www.conventosanesteban.es.
Gothic pinnacles adorn the side buttresses of this 16C–17C Dominican monastery; the sculpture of the façade★★ is quintessentially Platervesque. A low-relief *Martyrdom of St Stephen* is by Juan Antonio Ceroni (1610). In the 17C cloisters★, note the prophets' heads in medallions and grand staircase (1553). The large church has star vaulting in the gallery and a main altarpiece by José Churriguera. Crowning it is a painting of *The Martyrdom of St Stephen*, by Coello.

▷ On the same square stands the Convento de las Dueñas.

Convento de las Dueñas

Pl. Concilio de Trento. Open Mon–Sat 10.30am–12.45pm, 4.30–7.15pm; €2. ☎923 21 54 42.
The Renaissance cloisters★★ have profusely carved capitals, extraordinarily forceful in spite of their small size.

▷ Take San Pablo towards the Plaza Mayor.

Palacio de la Salina★

C. de San Pablo, 24. Open Tue-Sun 10.30am–1.30pm 6-9pm. ☎923 29 32 33.
The city's salt was once kept in this palace; hence its name. The patio combines Salamanca mixtilinear arches at one end with a corbelled gallery – supported by distorted atlantes – on the right and an arcade on the left.

▷ Take San Pablo, then turn right on to San Justo and right again down Consuelo.

Torre del Clavero

Consuelo. Closed to the public.
The octagonal keep is all that remains of a castle built in 1450. Mudéjar trelliswork decorates its turrets.

▷ Return to San Justo, follow it to the Pl. T. Bréton, then right to Santa Clara.

Convento de Santa Clara★

C. Santa Clara 2. Open Mon–Fri 9.30am–12.45pm, 4.25–6.10pm. Sat, Sun & hols 9.30am–2.10pm. €3. ☎660 108 314.
Although the convent was founded in the 13th century, the building dates from the 15th–18th centuries. Its church contains a fine retablo and, in the choir, frescoes. One wing of the convent is now an ethnographic museum.

EXCURSIONS

Ciudad Rodrigo★

Ciudad Rodrigo appears high on a hilltop, guarded by the square tower of its 14C Alcázar (now a parador) and medieval ramparts. A Roman bridge spans the río Águeda from the Portuguese side. After the Reconquest in the 12C, the town was repopulated by Count Rodrigo González for whom it is named; later it became a border stronghold and was involved in all the conflicts between Castilla and Portugal.
Wellington's success against the French in 1812 won him the title of Duke of Ciudad Rodrigo and Grandee of Spain. The area is planted with ilex trees, under which pigs and fighting bulls graze.

 WALKING TOUR

THE OLD TOWN
Start your visit at the plaza de
las Amayuelas.

Catedral de Santa María★★
Pl. San Salvador. Open Mon am only,
Tue–Sat 11am (from 12.45pm Sun)–2pm
and 4–7pm. €3, ticket includes museum
entrance. No charge Sun after 4pm.
except Semana Santa and hols. ℘923 48
14 24. wwwcatedralciudadrodrigo.com
The Cathedral was built in two stages,
first from 1170 to 1230 and then in the
14C; in the 16C Rodrigo Gil de Hontañón added the central apse. Note
the delicate ornamentation of the blind
arcades. The 13C **Portada de la Virgen★**
(Doorway of the Virgin), masked outside by a Classical belfry, has a line of
Apostles carved between the columns
beneath the splayings and covings.
In the interior, the Isabelline choir stalls
in the *coro* were carved by Rodrigo
Alemán. The fine Renaissance **altar★**
in the north aisle is adorned with an
alabaster masterpiece by Lucas Mitata.
The **cloisters★** are made up of diverse
architectural styles. In the west gallery,
the oldest part, Romanesque capitals
illustrate man's original sin. Opening
off the east gallery is a Plateresque
door decorated with medallions. Three
flights and 140 steps lead up to the Bell
Tower, where you can see a model of the
Cathedral, an 8-min audiovisual, and
enjoy panoramic views.
The **Museo Catedralicio** is worth a
visit. Note too the 16C **Palacio de los
Miranda** on Plaza de San Salvador.

▶ The arcaded Plaza del Buen
Alcalde is to the right.
Take the street to the left to reach
Plaza del Conde.

Palacio de los Castro★
(or Palacio de los Condes
de Montarco)
Pl. del Conde.
This late 15C palace, on Plaza del Conde
(Count), has a long façade punctuated
by delicate windows.

The Plateresque doorway is surrounded
by an *alfiz* and flanked by two twisted
columns showing Portuguese influence.
It is now a restaurant; the patio may be
visited when not in use.

▶ Head to the Plaza Mayor, passing
the 16C Palacio de Moctezuma (right).

Plaza Mayor★
Two Renaissance palaces stand on
the lively main square: the first, now
the **ayuntamiento** (town hall; guided
tours Sat–Sun 12 noon; ℘923 49 84 00),
has a façade with two storeys of basket arcading forming a **gallery★** and a
loggia, while the second, the **Casa de
los Cueto**, has a decorative frieze.

▶ Continue to Juan Arias, lined by
the Casa del Príncipe or Casa de los
Águilas, a 16C Plateresque building.

Murallas (Ramparts)
The walls, built on Roman foundations
in the 12C, were converted to a full
defensive system on the north and west
flanks in 1710. There are several stairways on the 2.25km/1.4mi sentry path.

▶ The imposing keep of Henry of
Trastámara's castle stands on the SW
corner of the walls, alongside the
Roman bridge spanning the Águeda
river. The castle is the town's parador.

Alba de Tormes
▶ 23km/14mi SE on the N 501 and C 510.
Only the massive keep remains of the
Castle of the dukes of Alba (open daily
10am–2pm, 3.30–6.30pm, Sat-Sun
10am-8pm; €2.50). This is also where
the tourist office is based (℘923 30
00 24; www.villaalbadetormes.com)
The remains of St Teresa of Ávila are in
the Carmelite Convent. The Iglesia de
San Juan (open Mon–Fri 10am–2pm,
Sat–Sun and hols 10am–8pm; €2),
featuring a Romanesque-Mudéjar east
end, contains an outstanding 11C **sculpture ensemble★** in the apse, showing
a noble Christ and the Disciples. Elsewhere is a small museum of local prehistoric finds.

ADDRESSES

🏨 STAY

Hostal Concejo – Plaza de la Libertad 1. ☎923 21 47 37. www.hconcejo.com. Reservations recommended. 18 rooms. No breakfast. Cheap and very cheerful, centrally-located Concejo is a cut above your average hostel. Rooms are simple but clean and comfortable, wifi is included and room service will deliver tea or coffee delivered to your door for €1.

Hostal Plaza Mayor – Pl. del Corrillo 20. ☎923 26 20 20. www.hostalplazamayor.es. 19 rooms. No breakfast. Ideally situated just behind Pl. Mayor, opposite the Romanesque church of San Martín. The hotel's interior design highlights the main features of the house, such as its attractive wooden beams. Garage parking.

Hosteria Casa Vallejo – San Juan de la Cruz 3. ☎923 28 04 21. www.hosteriacasavallejo.com. 10 rooms. €4–13. Restaurant. Closed 2 weeks in Feb and Jul. A small hotel located off Plaza Mayor. The refurbished interior, behind a 19C façade, includes a restaurant and rustic-style tapas bar.

Hotel Rector – Po Rector Esperabé 10. ☎923 21 84 82. www.hotelrector.com. 13 rooms. €13. This charming luxury boutique hotel occupies part of a honey-colored typical Salamanca stone town house, and was formerly the private mansion of a wealthy family. It enjoys spectacular views of the Cathedral and elegant, well-appointed rooms with all mod cons.

🍴 EAT

La Cocina de Toño – Gran Vía 20. ☎923 26 39 77. www.lacocinadetoño.es. La Cocina de Toño comprises an excellent tapas bar and a main dining area with a rustic Castilian-style decor. The traditional menu encompasses modern flair and Basque influence.

Le Sablon – Calle Espoz y Mina 20, (Plaza de la Libertad). ☎923 26 29 52. www.restaurantlesablon.com. Closed Mon and Tue, all Jul. Run by a husband and wife, Le Sablon has a meticulously furnished and classically elegant dining room. The cuisine is based around an international menu with numerous game dishes in season.

Tapas 2.0 – Felipe Espino 10. ☎923 21 64 48. Closed Wed lunch, Tue all day. This simple *gastrotasca* stands out for its freshly prepared modern tapas and contemporary dishes that have great attention to detail and show a personal touch. High quality ingredients, down to the bread baked on the premises.

Victor Guttiérez – Empedrada 4. ☎923 262 973. www.restaurantevictorguttierez.com. Closed Mon and Sun eve. Michelin-star cuisine from a chef with a Spanish soul and a Peruvian heart, which translates as local ingredients with South American flavours.

TAPAS

Mesón Cervantes – Pl. Mayor 15. ☎923 217 213. www.mesoncervantes.com. A bar with typical Castilian décor and fine views of plaza Mayor serving modern, innovative cuisine. Popular with Salamanca's young crowd at night. Try the house sangría.

Momo – San Pablo 13. ☎923 28 07 98. www.momosalamanca.com. Closed Sun Jul and Aug. Contemporary style tapas and skewers come cold and hot, and in the basement dining room they serve meals of haute cuisine tapas.

CAFÉS

Café Novelty – Pl. Mayor 2. ☎923 21 99 00. www.cafenovelty.com. Famous since 1905, Miguel de Unamuno used to meet here. The wooden chairs and marble tables conjure up his times and the terrace offers a wonderful view of one of Spain's finest squares. Home-made ice creams.

La Regenta – Espoz y Mina 19–21. ☎923 12 32 30. A much-loved café with a 19C ambience. Pricey but worth it.

Café Atelier - Serranos 33. ☎625 86 83 57. Tasty and beautifully presented vegetarian and vegan tapas matched with local wines.

La Alberca★★

La Alberca is a well-preserved village in the national park of Las Batuecas-Sierra de Francia. The sierra's rolling woodland is dotted by unspoiled villages with wooden-beamed architecture.

EXCURSIONS
Peña de Francia★★
◖ 15km/9.6mi W.
The Peña, a shale crag, at 1 732m/5 682ft is the peak of the Peña de Francia range. The approach affords stunning **panoramas★★** of the Hurdes mountains and the Sierra de Gredos. A 16C Dominican monastery with an excellent **hostelry** and restaurant is at the top (℘923 16 40 00; http://hospederiapeñadefrancia.com).

Avenida de Las Batuecas★
◖ To the S.
This road climbs to the Portillo Pass (1 240m/4 068ft) then plunges into a deep, green valley where the Batuecas Monastery is situated.

🚗 DRIVING TOUR

SIERRA DE BÉJAR AND SIERRA DE CANDELARIO

76km/47mi to the SE. Allow one day. Meander through the gorges of the Alagón and Cuerpo de Hombre rivers amid walnut and oak forests.

◖ Head east. After 2km/1.2mi, turn to Cepeda, then Sotoserrano. Head towards Lagunilla to reach the N 630 at Puerto de Béjar. **Baños de Montemayor**, a pleasant spa, and **Hervás**, with its old *judería* (Jewish quarter) are in this area. Return to Puerto de Béjar. One road heads towards Candelario.

▶ **Population:** 1 121
🖖 **Michelin Map:** 575 K 11.
🅸 **Info:** Plaza Mayor 11. ℘923 41 50 36. www.laalberca.com.
◖ **Location:** La Alberca is 42km/26mi E of Ciudad Rodrigo and 77km/48mi S of Salamanca. 🚆Nearest station: Ciudad Rodrigo 49km/30mi.

Candelario★★
This picturesque village on the sierra's flanks retains traditional stone homes with elegant balconies.

Béjar
4km/2.5mi NW.
Béjar, known for its textiles, stretches along a narrow rock platform at the foot of the Sierra de Béjar.

◖ Leave Béjar along the SA 515.

Miranda del Castañar
34km/21mi W.
Pass the 15C **castle** and penetrate the old quarter through the Puerta de San Ginés; **Mogarraz** (10km/6.2mi W) and **San Martín del Castañar** (10km/6.2mi N) are charming villages worth a visit.

◖ Take the SA 202 back to La Alberca.

ADDRESSES

🍴 STAY AND 🍷 EAT

🛏🛏🛏 **Hotel Antiguas Eras** – Avda Batuecas 29, La Alberca. ℘923 415 113. www.antiguaseras.com. 34 rooms. ⌂ €4.30. Restaurant 🛏🛏🛏. A rural hotel in the heart of La Alberca which occupies wooden-beamed homes with sierra views.

Zamora★

Zamora stands in a plain on the banks of the River Duero. The 12C and 13C saw the construction of the Cathedral and numerous Romanesque churches, which stand in the well-preserved old town.

▶ **Population:** 63 831
◔ **Michelin Map:** 575 H 12.
▣ **Info:** Avenida Príncipe de Asturias 1. ☏980 53 36 94. www.zamora-turismo.es.
◖ **Location:** Zamora is NW of Madrid, 65km/40mi N of Salamanca. ▭Zamora.
▲▴ **Kids:** The Museo Etnografico's costumes and shepherds' art will amuse children.
◷ **Timing:** Allow a long morning to visit the old town, then in the afternoon take one of the excursions below.

A BIT OF HISTORY

Traces remain of the walls which made Zamora the western bastion along the Duero in the Reconquest. Zamora figured in repeated struggles for the throne of Castilla.

SIGHTS

Catedral★

Pl. de la Catedral. Open daily Apr 10am–2pm, 5–8pm; May–Sept 10am–8pm; Oct–Mar 10am–2pm, 4.30–7pm. Closed 1 & 6 Jan, 24 Dec pm, 25 Dec, 31 Dec pm. €5 (cathedral and museum), no charge Mon pm. ☏980 53 06 44. http://catedraldezamora.wordpress.com.

The Cathedral was built between 1151 and 1174 and subsequently altered. The north front is Neoclassical in keeping with the square in front; it contrasts, however, with the Romanesque bell tower and the graceful cupola covered in scallop tiling. The south front, the only original part, has blind arcades and a Romanesque portal with unusual covings featuring openwork festoons. The aisles are transitional Romanesque-Gothic, the vaulting ranging from broken barrel to pointed ogive.

Slender painted ribs support the luminous **dome★** above the transept. Late Gothic master woodcarvers worked here. Note the fine **grilles** enclosing the presbytery, the *coro* and some chapels, two 15C Mudéjar pulpits, and **choir stalls★★**, with biblical, allegorical and burlesque scenes.

The museum, off the cloisters, displays 15C Flemish and 17C **tapestries★★**. Also note the 16C Renaissance monstrance and a Virgin and Child and Little St John sculpted by Bartolomé Ordóñez. The

Jardín del Castillo (Castle Garden) to the rear commands fine views.

Baltasar Lobo Centro de Arte★

Pl. de la Catedral. Open Tue–Sun 10 –2pm, 6–9pm (Oct–Apr 10am–2pm, 5–8pm). ☏616 92 95 77. fundacionbaltasarlobo.com

This arts centre is dedicated to the work of sculptor Baltasar Lobo, whose marble and bronze works are kept here. Born in Zamora province, he lived and worked in Paris, where his work evolved towards abstraction under the influence of Jean Arp and Henry Moore.

Romanesque churches★

Open generally Tue–Sun 2 Mar–Sept 10am–1pm, 5–8pm; Oct–6 Jan 10am–2pm, 4.30–6.30pm.

The 12C saw many original Romanesque churches built in Zamora. Features included portals without tympana, surrounded by multifoil arches and often possessing heavily carved archivolts. Larger churches had domes on squinches over the transept crossing. The best examples in Zamora, open to the public with coordinated times, are the **Magdalena** (los Francos), **Santa María la Nueva** (Pl. de Santa María la Nueva), **San Juan de Puerta Nueva** (Pl. Mayor), **Santa María de la Horta** (Barrio de la Horta), **Santo Tomé** (Pl.

Zamora and the Duero

Santo Tomé) and **Santiago del Burgo**
(Santa Clara).

👥 Museo Etnográfico de Castilla y Léon★

Del Sacramento, Pl. Viriato.
Open Tue–Sun 10am–2pm, 5–8pm. €3,
no charge Sun pm and Tue–Thu 7–8pm,
6 Dec 23 Apr, 18 May, 12 Oct. ℘980 531
708. www.museo-etnografico.com.

An outstanding collection of popular
and folk art with videos and written
explanations.

Seigniorial Mansions/ Museo Provincial

Palacio del Cordón, Pl. de Santa Lucía 2.
Open Tue–Sat 10am–2pm, 5–8pm (Oct–
Jun 4–7pm), Sun and public holidays
10am–2pm. €1, free Sat, Sun.
℘980 51 61 50.
The museum features archaeology
and fine art; the **Palacio de los Momos**
(San Torcuato 7) has elegant Isabelline
windows.

EXCURSIONS
San Pedro de la Nave★

▶ 19km/11.8mi NW. Leave Zamora on
the N 122–E 82. Follow the N 122 for
12km/7.4mi then turn right to Campillo.
The Visigothic church here (open Mar–
Sept Tue–Sun 10.30am–1.30pm, 5–8pm;
Oct–6 Feb Fri–Sat 10am–1.30pm, 4.30–

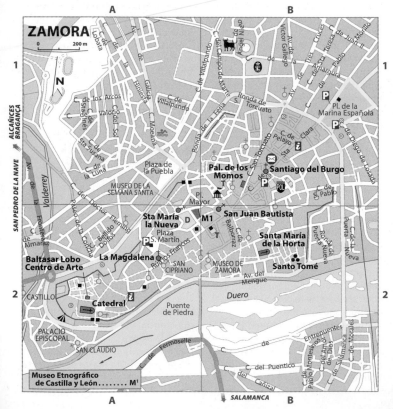

6.30pm, Sun 10am–1.30pm. &980 553 078) dates from the late 7C and was endangered by the damming of the Esla, and rebuilt at El Campillo. It is remarkable for the Biblical carving on the transept **capitals**. The frieze, half-way up, presents Christian symbols including grapes and doves.

Arcenillas

❯ 7km/4.3mi SE on the C 605.
In the village church (Nuestra Señora de la Asunción; ask for key at nearby bar), 15 **panels**★ depicting the Life, Death and Resurrection of Christ have been reassembled from the late 15C Gothic altarpiece designed for Zamora Cathedral by **Fernando Gallego**, one of the great Castilian painters of the age.

Benavente

❯ 66km/41mi N along the N 630.
The Renaissance **Castillo de los Condes de Pimentel** (&980 51 44 98; www.parador.es), now a parador, retains its 16C Torre del Caracol, with a fine carved artesanado ceiling and valley **views**. The **Hospital de la Piedad**, once a pilgrims' hospital (C. de Santa Cruz 5), keeps a magnificent carved cloister (access 9am–8pm). The transitional **Iglesia de Santa María del Azogue** (Pl. de Santa María; &980 66 42 58) has five apses and two Romanesque portals. A beautiful 13C **Annunciation** stands at the crossing. The **Iglesia de San Juan del Mercado** (Pl. de San Juan 4; &980 63 00 80) has a 12C carving on the south portal illustrating the journey of the Magi.

Toro

❯ 33km/21mi E along the N 122–E 82.
Toro, a wine-town on the River Duero, has preserved an exceptional cluster of Romanesque churches, most notably **San Salvador de los Caballeros**: the brick Mudéjar Romanesque church was originally Templar, built on circular floorplans with elongated blind arcades on the curving facades; it keeps Mudéjar frescoes and an exquisite selection of art inside (open Tue–Sun, hours as for the Colegiata). In the **Museu de Sant Espiritu** (Tue–Sun, 1 hour guided tours 10.30, 11.30, 12.30, 4.30 and 5.30) is an impressive collection of local Romanesque and other art. A number of the town's other recently restored monuments include the **Iglesia de San Lorenzo** and the bullring, one of the oldest in Spain. The town's bodegas are open certain days of the week and Toro's excellent red wines feature in the tapas bars on the market place, especially lively on a Saturday.

Colegiata de Santa María La Mayor★

Pl. de la Colegiata. Open Tue–Sun Mar–Sept 10.30am–2pm, 5–7.30pm; Oct–Feb 10am–2pm, 4.30–6.30pm. €2. &980 69 47 47. www.romanicozamora.es.
Construction began in 1160 with the elegant transept lantern and ended in 1240 with the west portal. The Romanesque **north portal** illustrates the Old Men of the Apocalypse and angels linked by a rope. Do note the Gothic **west portal**★★, repainted in the 18C. Statues on the pier and tympanum jambs have youthful faces. Start beneath the **cupola**★, one of the first of its kind in Spain, with two tiers of windows in the drum. Polychrome wood statues stand against the pillars at the end of the nave on consoles, one carved with an amusing version of the Birth of Eve (below the angel).
In the sacristy is the **Virgin and the Fly**★, a magnificent Flemish painting by either Gérard David or Hans Memling.

ADDRESSES

🏠 STAY AND 🍴/EAT

😑😑😑😑 **Parador de Zamora (Condes de Alba de Aliste)** – Plaza Viriato 5, Zamora. &902 54 79 79. www.paradores.es. 52 rooms. ⊑€17. Immaculately preserved 15C Renaissance palace, replete with armour, tapestries, canopied beds and other baronial décor. There is a swimming pool and the restaurant serves the finest traditional local dishes.

Castilla-León:
Segovia, Valladolid & Soria

The central provinces of Spain's northern tableland offer landscapes of unexpected beauty. Segovia's mountains, the wheat plains of Valladolid and Soria's river valleys and gorges make superb driving and walking country. Segovia and Valladolid, both court cities long before Madrid, have preserved contrasting architectural and artistic legacies. Soria is less regal, but keeps medieval spiritual retreats and military monuments that date back to its time as a frontier between Christian and Muslim Spain.

Highlights

1 Gazing in awe at the **Roman Aqueduct** of Segovia (p177)
2 Strolling in the gardens of **La Granja's** royal palace (p183)
3 Admiring richly coloured Baroque sculpture in **Valladolid's** museum (p185)
4 Calm in the cloisters of Santa María de Huerta, **Soria** (p190)
5 Visiting the Moorish ruins of **Gormaz castle**, the largest in Europe (p191)

Segovia
The Sierra de Guadarrama's hilltowns provide cool refuges from the summer heat: Pedraza de la Sierra, for example, a lovely village encircled by medieval walls, is popular as a weekend bolt hole. At the foot of the sierra stands the Palacio de la Granja de San Ildefonso, where a splendid formal garden runs up into woodland. Just to the north, Segovia is famous for its Roman aqueduct – a triumph of art and engineering – and Romanesque churches. Its fairytale castle (Alcázar) is actually a fanciful mid-19C recreation of the medieval original. However, most of this historic town is immaculately preserved within medieval walls.

Valladolid
By comparison Valladolid, once capital of Castille, is prosaic, although its Isabelline architecture and National Museum of Sculpture are outstanding. In Holy Week, church sculptures are processed through the streets in great solemnity. Elsewhere in the province is Tordesillas, where the famous treaty dividing the New World was signed. The castles of Medina del Campo, Montealegre Peñafiel and Simancas, rising up above the wide-horizoned vineyards and fields, are a reminder of battles fought here long ago.

Soria
One of Spain's least populated provinces, much of Soria's beauty lies in its very emptiness. Medieval monasteries, such as San Juan de Duero, and hermitages may be seen against evocative rural backdrops. Castles built on an epic scale to defend a warring medieval frontier, such as Gormaz, loom up above dramatic bare red rock. A trio of small towns – Burgo de Osma, Peñaranda and Berlanga – hold unexpected artistic wealth. Excursions to see them may be combined with walking in landscape of outstanding natural beauty.

© René Mattes/hemis.fr

Left: Roman Aqueduct, Segovia

Segovia★★★

This austere, imposing city, at 1 000m/3 280ft, rises on a triangular rock like an island in the Castilian plain. Its sturdy walls enclose a complicated maze of narrow streets dotted with Roman monuments and mansions. The old town and aqueduct are a UNESCO World Heritage Site.

A BIT OF HISTORY

Noble Segovia, residence of King Alfonso X, the Wise, and King Henry IV, played a decisive role in the history of Castilla. The 15C marked its golden age, when its population numbered 60 000.

Isabel the Catholic, Queen of Castilla

On the death of Henry IV in 1474 many grandees refused to recognise the legitimacy of his daughter, Doña Juana, known as **La Beltraneja**. In Segovia, the grandees proclaimed Henry's half-sister, Isabel, Queen of Castilla – thus preparing the way for Spain's unification (Isabel was married to Ferdinand, heir apparent of Aragón). La Beltraneja, aided by her husband, Alfonso V of Portugal, pressed her claim, but renounced it in 1479 after defeats at Toro and Albuera.

The "Comuneros"

In 1519, just three years after Charles I (Carlos I) had landed in Asturias to take possession of his Spanish dominions, he departed in order to be proclaimed Holy Roman Emperor (as Charles V).

An uprising started that was to become known as the revolt of the Comuneros. The catalysts included the absence of Charles V, his Flemish court, which overrode Castilian nobles, and his attempt to impose new taxes.

Behind the Comuneros movement lay the opposition of Castilian towns, the middle classes and merchants to the alliance between Charles V and the landed aristocracy. The Comuneros were finally crushed at Villalar in 1521.

▶ **Population:** 52 728
🚗 **Michelin Map:** 575 or 576 J 17 – map 121 Alrededores de Madrid.
🚾 **Information:** Azoguejo 1. ℘921 466 720. www.turismodesegovia.com.
◐ **Location:** Segovia is 92km/57mi NW of Madrid. The AVE high-speed train service calls at Segovia-Guiomar, 6km/3.5mi from the town centre. 🚆Segovia (AVE).
◉ **Don't Miss:** The Alcázar, and a meander along streets lined with palaces.
◕ **Timing:** Allow a full day in town, plus time for excursions.

👣 WALKING TOUR

CIUDAD VIEJA★★ (OLD TOWN)

4hr. 🚗See town plan.

Acueducto★★★

Pl. del Azoguejo.
This elegant structure was built during the reign of Trajan in the 1C to bring water from the River Acebeda to the upper part of town and remains one of the finest examples of Roman engineering still standing . It is 728m/2 388ft long, rising to 28m/92ft in Plaza del Azoguejo where the ground is lowest, and consists of two tiers of arches.

◐ Take Calle Cervantes.

Casa de los Picos

Juan Bravo 33. Open year-round (patio and exhibitions only) daily noon–2pm, 7–9pm (Oct–Mar 6–8pm). No charge. ℘921 46 26 74. www.turismodesegovia.com.
This distinctive house, faced entirely with granite blocks carved into pyramid-shaped reliefs, is the most origi-

Casa Solier................................ R
Casa de los Lozoya.................... V
Museo Esteban Vicente............. M
Palacio de los Condes de Cheste....... F
Palacio de los Marqueses de Moya.... B
Palacio del Marqués de Lozoya.......... E
Palacio del Marqués de Quintanar..... K

nal of Segovia's 15C mansions. It is now home to an art school.

⊙ Take Juan Bravo and turn off to Pl. de Platero Oquendo.

Casa del Conde de Alpuente
Pl. Conde Alpuente.
The elegant façade of this 15C Gothic house is adorned with *esgrafiado*.

⊙ Continue down Platero Oqueno.

Alhóndiga
C. de Alhóndiga. No charge.
This old 15C granary is now used as an exhibition room.

⊙ Return to Juan Bravo.

Plaza de San Martín★
This lovely square in the heart of the old aristocratic quarter is the most evocative part of historic Segovia. Around the square stand the **Casa del Siglo XV** (15C House), also known as Juan Bravo's house, with a gallery beneath the eaves, the 16C tower of the **Casa de los Lozoya**, the Plateresque façade of the **Casa Solier** (also known as Casa de Correas) and ornate entrances to other large houses.

In the middle of the square is the 12C **Iglesia de San Martín★**, a church framed on three sides by a covered gallery on pillars with carved strapwork and animal figures on the capitals.

⊙ The Pl. de las Bellas Artes opens off Pl. San Martín.

Museo de Arte Contemporáneo Esteban Vicente
Plazuela de las Bellas Artes. Open Thu–Fri 11am–2pm, 4–7pm; Sat 11am–8pm, Sun and public holidays 11am–3pm. €3; no charge Thu. ☎921 46 20 10.
www.museoestebanvicente.es.

This museum is set in the palace of Henry IV in the Hospital de Viejos (Old People's Hospital). The only trace of the original building is the fine chapel with a Mudéjar ceiling, now an auditorium. The museum exhibits the work of artist Esteban Vicente (1904–2001) and is also used for concerts.

▶ Follow Juan Bravo past the town's old prison.

Iglesia del Corpus Christi
Po. del Salón. Opening times vary so check with the tourist office. €1.
The convent church was formerly the Antigua Sinagoga Mayor, the city's largest synagogue. Close by is the **Centro Didáctico de la Judería** (Centre for interpretation of the Jewish Quarter), which once flourished here (C. Judería Vieja 12; open Mon–Tue 10am–2pm, Wed–Fri 10am–2pm, 3pm-6pm, Thu-Sat 10am 1pm, 3–6pm, Sun 10am–1pm; €2 ☏921 46 23 96, www.turismodesegovia.com).

▶ Take Isabel la Católica.

Plaza Mayor
Dominated by the impressive Cathedral, the arcaded square with its terrace cafés is a popular meeting place. Among the buildings surrounding the square are the **ayuntamiento** (town hall) and the Teatro Juan Bravo.

Catedral★★
Pl. Mayor. Open Mon–Sat 9.30am–6.30pm (Oct–Mar until 5.30pm), Sun 1.15–5.30pm. Closed 25 Dec, 1 & 6 Jan. €3; no charge Sun 9.30am–1.30pm. ☏921 46 22 05.
catedralsegovia.wordpress.com
This was built during the reign of Emperor Charles V to replace a Cathedral destroyed during the Comuneros' Revolt in 1521. It is an example of the survival of the Gothic style in the 16C when Renaissance architecture was at its height. The beautiful golden stone, the stepped east end with pinnacles and delicate balustrades, and the tall bell tower (which visitors can climb

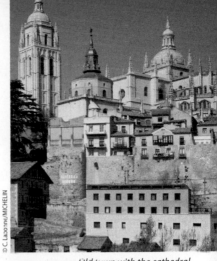
© C. Lazonne/MICHELIN

Old town with the cathedral

10.30am, 12.30pm and 4pm) bring considerable grace to the massive building. The width of the aisles combines with the decorative lines of the pillars and ribs in the vaulting to make the interior both light and elegant. The chapels are closed by fine wrought-iron screens. The first off the south aisle contains as the altarpiece an *Entombment* by Juan de Juni. The *coro* stalls, in late 15C Flamboyant Gothic style, are from the earlier Cathedral.
Claustro★ – The 15C cloisters from the former Cathedral, near the Alcázar, were rebuilt on the new site. In the Sala Capitular (chapter house) beautiful 17C Brussels **tapestries★** illustrate the story of Queen Zenobia.

▶ Follow Mqués del Arco and Daioz to Pl. de la Reina Victoria Eugenia.

Alcázar★★
Pl. de la Reina Victoria Eugenia.
Open daily Apr–Oct 10am–8pm; Nov–Mar 10am–6pm. Closed 24 Dec and 1& 6 Jan. Tower closed Nov–Jun. €8; tower €2.50; no charge 3rd Tue of month (except holidays) 2–4pm for EU citizens. ☏921 46 07 59.
www.alcazardesegovia.com.
The Alcázar, on a cliff overlooking the valley, was built above a former fortress in the early 13C and modified in the 15C and 16C by Henry IV and Philip II. In 1764, Charles III converted the building into a **Real Colegio de Artillería** (Royal

Artillery School), but in 1862 it suffered a devastating fire. Reconstruction was completed at the end of the 19C, hence its neo-Gothic look.

The furniture and richly decorated Mudéjar artesonado work, mostly from the 15C, are original and were brought from various Castilian towns. Its keep is flanked by corbelled turrets.

The main rooms of note are the Chamber Royal (Cámara Real) and the Sala de los Reyes (Monarchs' Room). The Sala del Cordón and terrace command a fine panorama of the fertile Eresma Valley, the Monasterio de El Parral, the Capilla de la Vera Cruz and the Meseta.

The artillery school houses a museum recalling the chemical laboratory located here in the 18C and the French chemist Louis Proust, who formulated his law of constant proportions in Segovia.

The views from the keep (152 steps) stretch across the city to the Sierra de Guadarrama.

▷ Take Velarde to Pl. San Esteban, passing through the medieval Porte de la Claustra.

Iglesia de San Esteban (St Stephen's Church)

Pl. de San Esteban. Closed to the public.
One of the latest (13C) and most beautiful of Segovia's Romanesque churches. The porticoes running along two of its sides have finely carved capitals. The five-storey **tower★** has elegant bays and slender columns on the corners.

▷ Take Valdeláguila to Pl. de la Trinidad.

Iglesia de la Santísima Trinidad (Holy Trinity Church)

Pl. de la Trinidad 6. Open during Mass.
This austere Romanesque church has a decorated apse with blind arcading and capitals carved with imaginary beasts and plant motifs.

▷ Take Trinidad and San Agustín, turning left down Zuloaga to Pl. de Colmenares.

Iglesia de San Juan de los Caballeros

Pl. de Colmenares. Open Wed 9am–4pm.
€1. ℘921 46 33 48.
www.turismodesegovia.com.
This is Segovia's oldest Romanesque church (11C). Its portico (taken from the church of San Nicolás) has carvings of portrait heads, plant motifs and animals. The church, which was almost in ruins at the turn of the 20C, was bought in 1905 by Daniel Zuloaga, who converted it into his home and workshop. Today it houses the **Museo Zuloaga**, exhibiting ceramics by the artist and by his nephew, Ignacio Zuloaga.

Plaza del Conde de Cheste

On the square stand the palaces of the Marqués de Moya, the Marqués de Lozoya, the Condes de Cheste and the Marqués de Quintanar.

OUTSIDE THE WALLS

Museo de Segovia★

Casa del Sol – Del Socorro, 11. Open Tue–Sat 10am–2pm, 4–7pm (Jul–Sept 5–8pm), Sun and public holidays 10am–2pm. €1; no charge weekends, hols. ℘921 460 613.
www.turismodesegovia.com.
Segovia's archaeological, ethnological and fine arts museum collection ranges from exhibits on early hydraulic systems and present-day drovers' roads to some exceptional pieces of classical art.
Galleries show prints by Rembrandt and Dürer, and fine sculpture and altarpieces from local monasteries and churches. The glass made at La Granja's Royal Factory since the 18C is also well represented.

Iglesia de San Millán★

Av. Fernández Ladreda.
Open only for Mass.
The early 12C church stands in the middle of a large square, which allows a full view of its pure, still primitive Romanesque lines and two porticoes with finely carved modillions and capitals. The three aisles have alternating pillars and columns as in Jaca Cathedral. The apse has blind arcading and a decora-

tive frieze. The transept has Moorish ribbed vaulting.

Monasterio El Parral★

Alameda del Eresma. Open Wed–Sun 11am–5pm. Donations. ℘921 43 12 98. www3.planalfa.es/msmparral/parral. The monastery was founded by Henry IV in 1445 and later entrusted to the Hieronymites. The **church**, behind its unfinished façade, has a Gothic nave with beautifully carved doors, a 16C altarpiece by Juan Rodríguez and, on either side of the chancel, the Plateresque tombs of the Marquis and Marchioness of Villena.

Iglesia de la Vera-Cruz★

Camino de Zamarramala. Open Tue–Sun 10.30am–1.30pm, 4–7pm (Oct–Mar until 6pm). Closed Tue am. €2, no charge Tue pm. ℘921 43 14 75. www.turismodesegovia.com. The unusual polygonal chapel was erected in the 13C, probably by the Templars; it now belongs to the Order of Malta. A circular corridor surrounds two small chambers, one above the other, where secret ceremonies were conducted. The Capilla del Lignum Crucis holds an ornate Flamboyant Gothic altar. There is a good view of Segovia.

EXCURSIONS
Palacio Real de Riofrío★

❯ Bosque de Riofrío, Navás de Riofrío. 11km/6.8mi S of Segovia on the N 603. Open year-round Tue–Sun & public holidays 10am–8pm (Oct–Mar until 6pm). See website for closing dates. €4; no charge for EU citizens Wed–Thu 5–8pm summer, 3–6pm winter, 18 May and 12 Oct. ℘914 54 87 00. www.patrimonionacional.es. The palace Riofrío was planned by Isabel Farnese as the equal of La Granja, which she had to vacate on the death of her husband, Philip V. Construction began in 1752 but though it was very big – it measures 84m x 84m (276ft x 276ft) – it was never more than a hunting lodge. It is built around a grand Classical-style courtyard. The green and pink façade reflects Isabel's Italian origins.

Castillo de Coca★★

❯ Camino Antigua Cauca Romana, Coca. 52km/32mi NW of Segovia along the C 605 and SG 341. Guided tours Mon–Fri 10.30am–1pm, 4.30–6pm, Sat–Sun & hols 11am–1pm, 4–6pm. Closed 1st Tue in month, Jan and 25 Dec. €2.70. ℘617 57 35 54. www.castillodecoca.com. This picturebook fortress is the most outstanding example of Mudéjar military architecture in Spain. It was built in the late 15C by Moorish craftsmen for the archbishop of Sevilla, Fonseca, and consists of three concentric perimeters, flanked by polygonal corner towers and turrets with a massive keep at its heart. The **torre del homenaje** (keep) and **capilla** (chapel), which contains Romanesque wood carvings, are open to the public.

Arévalo

❯ 60km/37mi NW along the C 605. Isabel the Catholic spent her childhood in the 14C **castle** with its massive crenellated keep which dominates the town. Of note also are Romanesque-Mudéjar brick churches, and several old mansions.

Plaza de la Villa★, the former Plaza Mayor, is one of the best-preserved town squares in Castilla with its half-timbered brick houses resting on pillared porticoes.

Pedraza★★

❯ 40km/25mi NE of Segovia on N 110. ◨Real 40. ℘921 50 86 66. www.pedraza.info. Weekend visitors flock to Pedraza, encircled by medieval walls, to wander its enchanting streets. The **Puerta de la Villa**, a fortified gateway, opens into a maze of alleys bordered by country-style houses. The first medieval building of interest is the **Cárcel de la Villa** (open daily 11.30am–2pm, 3.30–7.30pm (3.45pm weekdays); €3; ℘921 50 99 55, www.pedraza.info), the former jail. The splendid **plaza Mayor** is surrounded by ancient porticoes topped by balconies and the slender Romanesque bell tower of San Juan. The medieval

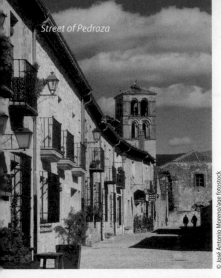
Street of Pedraza

© José Antonio Moreno/age fotostock

castle (open Wed–Sun, summer 11am–2pm, 5–8pm, winter 4–6pm ; guided tours every 30 mins; €6; 𝒫921 50 98 25; www.museoignaciozuloaga.com) houses works by artist **Ignacio Zuloaga** (🕭 see p178).

From Pedraza you can continue on the N110, once a Roman road, to Riaza and Ayllón, attractive Castilian towns. Ayllón also gives access to **Tiermes archaeological sight★★** (via Montejo and the SO-P-4120; open Tue–Sat 10am–2pm and 4–7pm, 5–8pm Jul–Sept, morning only public hols; €5; 𝒫975 35 20 52; www.tiermes.net). This Celtiberian town, built into a sandstone rock cliff, and its amphitheatre are set in an extraordinarily evocative landscape. Later Roman dwellings and a small museum stand nearby.

Sepúlveda
🅾 25km/15.5mi N of Segovia.
🅸Santos Justo y Pastor 8. 𝒫921 54 04 25. www.sepulveda.es.

As you approach this attractive village you'll get a good view of its terraced **site★** on the slopes of a deep gorge. Park at the town hall square, overlooked by castle ruins, then walk up to the **Iglesia de San Salvador** (Subida al Salvador 10; open Sat-Sun 11am-6pm; free guided tours available in summer; 𝒫921 54 04 25) for a fine view. The church is typical Segovia Romanesque with one of the oldest side doors in Spain, dating from 1093.

On Calle Conde de Sepúlveda, the **Casa del Parque Hoces del Río Duratón (Duratón Gorges)** (open Jul–Aug Mon–Thu and Sun 10am–3pm, Fri–Sat and hols until 6pm, check website for further opening hours; €1; 𝒫921 54 03 22, www.patrimonionatural.org) provides information about hiking routes and local canoeing. The park runs along the middle stretch of the river, hemmed in by spectacular 70m/230ft walls, sheltering the Romanesque hermitage of San Frutos.

🚗 DRIVING TOUR

From Segovia to Madrid via La Granja and El Paular
159km/99mi.

Allow one day including visits to the palace and monastery, two days to walk in the mountains.

The bare peaks of the **Sierra de Guadarrama★**, visible from Segovia, rise above steep granite and gneiss slopes covered in oaks and pines. Mountain-born streams feed the province's reservoirs. At the foot of the sierra's slopes on the western side stands La Granja's royal summer palace. On the eastern side you can visit the restored medieval monastery of El Paular.

🅾 Take the CL 601 from Segovia to La Granja.

Palacio Real de La Granja de San Ildefonso★★
Pl. de España 17. Open year-round Tue–Sun 10am–8pm (Oct–Mar until 6pm). €9 inc. gardens; guided tour €4; fountains €4. No admission charge Wed–Thu 5–8pm summer, 3–6pm winter for EU citizens; also 18 May and 12 Oct. 𝒫914 54 87 00. www.patrimonionacional.es.

La Granja is a little Versailles at 1 192m/3 911ft, built in 1731 by Philip V, in pure nostalgia for the palace of his childhood. Philip V and his second wife, Isabel Farnese, are buried in the collegiate church.

Palace

Galleries and chambers, faced with marble or hung with velvet, are lit by chandeliers. A **Museo de Tapices★★** (Tapestry Museum) contains principally 16C Flemish hangings, notably (**3rd gallery**) nine of the *Honours and Virtues* series and a 15C Gothic tapestry of *St Jerome* after a cartoon by Raphael.

Gardens★★

Open daily Oct and Mar 10am–6.30pm; Apr until 8pm; Nov–Feb until 6pm; May–15 Jun and Sept until 8pm; 16 Jun–Aug until 9pm. Fountains Holy Week, 30 May, 25 Jul, 25 Aug, and, water levels allowing, 5.30pm Sat–Sun and public holidays.

The ground was levelled with explosives before the French landscape gardeners (Carlier, Boutelou) and sculptors (Dumandré, Thierry) started work. The woodland vistas are more natural, however. The chestnut trees, brought from France at great expense, are magnificent. The **fountains★★** begin at the Neptune Basin, go on to the New Cascade (Nueva Cascada), a multicoloured marble staircase in front of the palace, and end at the Fuente de la Fama (Fame Fountain), which jets up a full 40m/131ft.

▷ Head south on the CL-601.

Real Fábrica de Vidrios y Cristales de La Granja (Royal Glass Factory)

Open: Museum Apr–Sept Tue–Sat 10am–6pm, Sun until 3pm; Oct–Mar Tue–Fri and Sun 10am–3pm, Sat until 6pm. Glass blowing: Tue–Fri and Sun 10am–2.45pm, Sat 11am–1.45pm, 4–5.45pm. Guided tours available. Closed 1, 6 Jan, 25 Dec. €6, no charge Wed Apr–Sept 3–6pm. ☎921 01 07 00. www.fcnv.es.

The present building, erected in 1770 under Charles III, contains magnificent exhibits of their contemporary glass and offers glass-blowing demonstrations.

▷ Leave La Granja on the CL 601; it soon starts to climb steeply, with hairpin bends.

Puerto de Navacerrada★

1 860m/6 102ft.

The pass, a ski resort on the borders of the two Castillas, commands a beautiful **view★** of the Segovian plateau. A train runs to Cercedilla.

▷ Take the M 604 at the junction on the pass.

Puerto de los Cotos

1 830m/6 004ft.

The pass is a base for ski lifts. From the upper terminus at Zabala, hike in summer to the Laguna de Peñalara (15min), a former glacial cirque, the Picos de Dos Hermanas (Summit of the Two Sisters) (30min) and Peñalara (2 429m/7 967ft), the highest point in the sierra (45min). Trails for longer walks are also marked; enquire at the information centre at Zabala.

▷ Continue on the M 604 (the descent is gentler than the ascent).

Monasterio de Santa María de El Paular★

2km/1.2mi from Rascafría.

Open: Guided tours of Monastery available daily, see website for seasonal opening hours; full sung Mass noon Sun and hols. ☎918 69 19 58. http://monasteriopaular.com.

Castilla's earliest Carthusian monastery (1390) stands in the cool Lozoya Valley. The reconstructed complex includes a hotel in a former palace. The **church** has a Flamboyant doorway by Juan Guas. There is a magnificent 15C alabaster **altarpiece★★** illustrating the Lives of the Virgin and Christ. More than 50 canvases portraying Carthusian history, painted by Vicenzo Carduccio have recently been hung in the cloister for which they were originally painted in 1635. Close to the monastery stands the old stone Puente de Perdón (Absolution Bridge), so-called as those who walked to the gallows crossed it. Today the bridge gives access to a recreational area with summer river pools and walking paths to the sierra's foothills.

Rascafría

2km/1.2mi from El Paular.
This lively small town, the capital of the Upper Lozoya valley, clustered close to an old bridge over the river, is built in traditional stone architecture. Restaurants and bars abound.

▶ From Rascafría you can continue on the M 604 along the Lozoya valley, (32 km/20 mi) through small villages to join the A1 to Madrid, or take minor roads to Puerto de la Morcuera and Manzanares el Real.

Puerto de la Morcuera

As you reach the pass (1 796m/5 892ft), an extensive view opens towards El Vellón reservoir. A descent through moorland brings you to the wooded Lozoya depression. The río Lozoya is a well-known trout stream.

Manzanares El Real

The pride of this small village is its **Castillo Viejo★** (open Mon–Fri 10am–4pm, Sat–Sun 10am–6pm; €5; ✆91 853 00 08; www.manzanareselreal. org) built in the 15C and one of the best preserved medieval fortresses in Spain.

▶ The M 608 and M 607 lead to Madrid.

ADDRESSES

🏠 STAY

🛏 **Hostal Don Jaime** – Ochoa Ondategui, 8. Segovia. ✆921 444 790. www.hostaldonjaime.com. 24 rooms.☐ €3.50. A charming simple comfortable Castilian house close to the aqueduct.

🛏🍽 **Hotel Las Sirenas** – Juan Bravo 30, Segovia. ✆921 46 26 63. www.hotel sirenas.com. 39 rooms. ☐ €7.50. A traditional hotel in the old quarter with an elegant stone façade, feature staircase and and 1950s decor.

🛏🍽🏨 **La Casa Mudéjar Hotel Spa** – Isabel la Católica 8, Segovia. ✆921 46 62 50. www.lacasamudejar.com. 40 rooms. ☐ €8.50. Beautifully renovated hotel with modern spa

facilities and delightful decoration including a coffered mudéjar-style ceiling. Enjoy Castilian and Sephardic cuisine on the patio.

🛏🍽🏨 **La Posada de Don Mariano** – Mayor, 14, Pedraza. ✆921 509 886. www.hoteldonmariano.com. 18 rooms.☐€9.50. Pretty bedrooms, helpful service and a terrace restaurant opening onto the Plaza Mayor.

🛏🍽🏨🏨 **Parador de la Granja** – Los Infantes 3, Palacio de la Granja de San Idelfonso. ✆902 54 79 79. www. parador.es. 127 rooms. ☐ €17. Built in the 18C, the princes' pavilion, once part of the royal palace, is now a luxury hotel with a spa and landscaped swimming pool.

🍴/EAT

🍽 **El Sitio** – Infanta Isabel, 9, Segovia. ✆921 46 09 96. A big favourite with locals, this easy-going tapas bars specialises in suckling pig.

🛏🍽 **Bar Taberna López** – San Cristobal, 3, Segovia. ✆921 43 36 18. A meat lover's dream - lots of roasted delicacies, plus local dishes and wines.

🛏🍽🏨 **Narizotas** – Pl. Medina del Campo 2, Segovia. ✆921 46 26 79. www.narizotas.net. Traditional restaurant serving roast suckling pig and a tasting menu; pleasant street terrace with music.

🛏🍽🏨🏨 **Casa Felipe** – Ctra. de Soria Plasencia, 40160 Torrecaballeros. ✆921 40 11 71. www.casafelipe.net. Delicious grilled meats cooked over an open fire, typically Castilian décor, and a pleasant terrace.

🛏🍽🏨🏨 **Mesón de Cándido** – Pl. del Azoguejo 5, Segovia. ✆921 42 59 11. www.mesondecandido.es. The most famous restaurant in the province, set in a 15C house beneath the aqueduct, serving rich traditional Castilian cuisine.

FESTIVALS

The Hay Festival (www.hayfestival. com), which celebrates English and Spanish literature, takes place here each September.

Valladolid★

The former capital of Castilla and of a great empire, now a largely modern city, stands amid vineyards and cereal fields.

A BIT OF HISTORY

From the 12C, Castilla's kings frequently resided at Valladolid. Peter the Cruel married there, as did Ferdinand and Isabel; it was the birthplace of Philip IV and his sister Anne of Austria, mother of Louis XIV.

THE CENTRE

The historic centre of Valladolid is a blend of carefully tended plazas, lively pedestrian ways, and a pleasant park, the Campo Grande. The Plaza Mayor, the lovely and spacious focus of the city, dates from the 16C.

SIGHTS

Colegio de San Gregorio

Cadenas de San Gregorio 1–2.
This is Valladolid's most impressive Isabelline building. On the sumptuous entrance★★★, attributed to Gil de Siloé and Simon of Cologne, fantasies from savages to interwoven thorn branches create a strongly hierarchical composition rising from the doorway. The college is the seat of the **Museo Nacional de Escultura★★★** (&see below).

Museo Nacional de Escultura★★★ (National Museum of Sculpture)

Cadenas de San Gregorio 1–2. Open Tue–Sat 10am–2pm, 4–7.30pm, Sun and public holidays 10am–2pm. Closed 1, 6 Jan, 1 May, 8 Sept, 24–25, 31 Dec. €3; no charge Sat pm, Sun am, 18 April, 18 May, 12 Oct, 6 Dec. &983 25 03 75. www.mecd.gob.es/mnescultura
From the 16C to the 17C Valladolid was a major centre for sculpture, reflected in this museum's wonderful collection of religious statues and processional figures in polychrome wood, a material well suited to the expression of the dramatic.

- ▶ **Population:** 303 905
- &ddot; **Michelin Map:** 575 H 15 (town plan).
- ☐ **Info:** Acera de Recoletos (Pabellón de Cristal). &983 21 93 10. www.info.valladolid.es.
- ◐ **Location:** The city is at the centre of the northern section of the Spanish Meseta with an AVE high-speed train service from Madrid to Valladolid Campo Grande. 🚆Valladolid (AVE).
- 👥 **Kids:** The interactive Museo de la Ciencia.

On the ground floor of the Palacio de Villena, aside from paintings (including an attractive *Pietà* by Pedro Berruguete) are the magnificent sculptures of two 16C Mannerist masters: **Alonso Berruguete** (a remarkable altarpiece designed for the San Benito church) and **Juan de Juni** (*The Crucifixion* and the portentous ensemble *Burial of Christ*). Outstanding works by **Gregorio Fernández**, leading 16C exponent of Castilian Baroque, include *Passage to the Sixth Agony* and *Christ Recumbent*. There are also works of the Andalucían School (Martínez Montañés, Pedro de Mena, Alonso Cano).
On the second floor are works from the Renaissance by **Diego de Siloé** (*The Holy Family*) and **Felipe Vigarny** (*Virgin and Child*, a model of grace and elegance). There is also an excellent painting by **Rubens** (*Democritus and Heraclitus*).
On the third floor are Late Baroque (18C) works, such as *St Francis of Assisi* by Salzillo and *Head of St Paul* by Juan Alonso de Villabrille y Ron. On the way down, admire a magnificent *Neapolitan nativity* of more than 180 figures.

Capilla del Colegio de San Gregorio★

Located within the Colegio.
Designed by Juan Guas, this lovely Gothic chapel with elevated choir

Holy Week procession in front of the entrance of Colegio de San Gregorio

contains an altarpiece by Berruguete, a tomb by Felipe Vigarny and carved choir stalls.

Iglesia de San Pablo (St Paul's Church)

Pl. de San Pablo 4. Open before and after Mass. No charge. ☎983 35 17 48.

The façade★★★ is outstanding. The lower section, by Simon of Cologne, consists of a portal with an ogee arch all framed in a segmental arch, and above, a large rose window and two coats of arms supported by angels.

Catedral★

Arribas 1 (entry from Pl. de la Universidad). Open Tue–Fri 10am–1.30pm, 4.30–7pm, Sat–Sun and public holidays until 2pm. €3 (museum). ☎983 30 43 62. www.catedral-valladolid.com.

The Cathedral, commissioned in about 1580 by Philip II from Herrera, was distorted by the architect's 17C and 19C successors – in the octagonal tower, and the Baroque upper façade by Alberto Churriguera. Never completed, the interior remains one of Herrera's triumphs. The altarpiece (1551) in the central apsidal chapel is by Juan de Juni.

Museo Diocesano y Catedralicio★

In the funerary chapels of the former Gothic Cathedral. Same entrance hours and ticket as the cathedral.

Note the Mudéjar cupolas in the Capilla de San Llorente. There is a collection★ of sculptures, paintings, silverware and ornaments.

Note two busts by Pedro de Mena (*Ecce Homo* and *Dolorosa*), two 13C tombs, two 13C Christs (one Protogothic with four nails), a dramatic *Ecce Homo* by Gregorio Fernández, the sculpture group *Lament for Christ* (c. 1500) and a 16C silver monstrance by Juan de Arfe.

Outside, note, on the Baroque University façade, sculptured and heraldic decoration by Narciso and Antonio Tomé.

Colegio Mayor de Santa Cruz

Cardenal Mendoza 1. Closed to the public.

This lovely late 15C college is one of the first Renaissance buildings in Spain; the carved decoration at the entrance is Plateresque but the rusticated stonework is Classical. The Neoclassic balconies and windows are 18C additions.

Iglesia de Nuestra Señora de las Angustias

Angustías 8. www. confradiadelasangustias.org.

The church, built by one of Herrera's disciples, contains Juan de Juni's masterpiece, the **Virgen de los Siete Cuchillos★** (Virgin of the Seven Knives).

Palacio Pimentel★

Pl. San Pablo s/n; enter via Agustinas s/n. Once a royal residence, where Charles V stayed, the building's façade has fine Plateresque details. Today it houses government offices. The meeting rooms (Salón de Plenos y Sala de Comisiones) have fine Mudéjar ceilings, which can be viewed in working hours (9am–3pm).

The entrance hall, with a tiled frieze depicting key moments in Spanish history, is also left open in the afternoons.

Museo Patio Herreriano de Arte Contemporáneo Español (Modern Spanish Art Museum)

Jorge Guillén 6. Open Tue–Fri 11am–2pm, 5–8pm, Sat 11am–8pm, Sun 11am–3pm. Closed 25 Dec, 1 Jan. ℘983 36 29 08. www.museopatioherreriano.org.

The lovely **Herreran patio**★ of the ex-monastery of San Benito and a newer annex house this collection of Spanish art dating from 1918.

Museo Oriental

Pas. Filipinos 7. Open Mon–Sat 10am–2pm, 4–7pm, Sun and public holidays 10am–2pm. €4. ℘983 30 68 00. www.museo-oriental.es.

Set in a Neoclassical college (18C) designed by Ventura Rodríguez, the city's Oriental Museum houses **Chinese art**★ (bronze, porcelain, lacquerware, coins and silk embroidery) and Philippine art with important **ivory pieces**★.

Casa-Museo de Cervantes

Rastro 2. Open Tue–Sat 9.30am–3pm, Sun 10am–3pm. Closed 1 & 6 Jan, 1 May, 24–25 and 31 Dec. €3; no charge Sun, 18 April, May, 12 Oct, 6 Dec. ℘983 30 88 10. http://museocasacervantes.mcu.es.

The author of **Don Quixote** lived in this house from 1603 to 1606; some of his simple furnishings remain.

BEYOND THE CENTRE

Museo de la Ciencia (Science Museum)

Av. Salamanca 59. Open Tue–Fri 10am-6pm, Sat and hols 10am-7pm, Sun 10am-3pm. €4. Closed 1 & 6 Jan; 24, 25, 31 Dec. ℘983 14 43 00. www.museocienciavalladolid.es.

Valladolid's interactive science museum includes a planetarium (see website for schedule) and frequently changing temporary exhibitions.

EXCURSIONS

Castillo de Simancas

❯11km/6.8mi SW. Only archive open to public; www.mecd.gob.es.

This picturesque fortress was first used by Charles V as a state archives repository; it still fulfils that function.

Peñafiel★

❯55km/34mi E along the N 122.

Peñafiel was a strongpoint along the Duero during the Reconquest and its massive 14C castle **Castillo**★ (open Oct–Mar Tue–Sun 10.30am–2pm, 4–6pm; Apr–Sept Tue–Sun 10.30am–2pm, 4–8pm; closed 1 & 6 Jan, 24–25, 31 Dec; €6.60 museum and castle, castle only €3.30; guided wine tasting (inc. museum only) €9.20; ℘983 88 11 99; www.museodelvino.es) is sited at the meeting point of three valleys. Its imposing keep, reinforced by machicolated turrets houses the **Museo Provincial del Vino**, featuring local wines. Also notable in Peñafiel is the Convento de San Pablo (ask at the tourist office about opening times; guided tours available; no charge; ℘983 881 526, www.turismopenafiel.com). Its church (1324) has a Mudéjar east end, with Renaissance vaulting in the 16C Capilla del Infante.

Tordesillas

❯ 30km/19mi SW along the A 62.

The kings of Spain and Portugal signed the famous **Treaty of Tordesillas** here in 1494, dividing up the New World.

Real Monasterio de Santa Clara★

❯ Alonso del Castillo Solorzano. Open Tue–Sat 10am–2pm, 4–6.30pm, Sun and public holidays 10.30am–3pm. €6 inc Arabic baths; free Wed pm & Thu pm for EU citizens and for all 18 May. ℘914 54 87 00. www.patrimonionacional.es.

The palace built by Alfonso XI in 1350 was converted to a convent by Peter the Cruel. He installed María de Padilla here, to whom he might have been married. For María, homesick for Sevilla, he commissioned Mudéjar decoration.

The **patio**★ has multifoil and horseshoe arches, strapwork decoration and multicoloured ceramic tiles. In the **Capilla Dorada** (Gilded Chapel) are mementoes and works of art. The choir of the **church** has a particularly intricate artesonado ceiling★★.

Medina del Campo
◐ 54km/34mi SW along the A 62 and the A 6; 24km/15mi from Tordesillas.
🚂Avenida de la Estación 27.
In the Middle Ages Medina was famous for its fairs and a large market is still held in Medina del Campo on Sundays. Isabel the Catholic died here in 1504.

Castillo de la Mota★
Av. del Castillo. Open Apr–Sept Mon–Sat Visitor Centre 11am–2pm, 3–7pm (Oct–Mar 6pm). Sun and public holidays year-round 10am–2.30pm. Castle opens at 11am. Closed 2 Sept, 1 & 6 Jan, 24–31 Dec. €4. Guided visits available (book in advance). ✆983 81 00 63.
www.castillodelamota.es.
Juana the Mad often stayed in this classic medieval castle. Cesare Borgia was imprisoned in the keep for two years.

Villa de Almenara-Puras: Museo de las Villas Romanas (Museum of Roman Villas)
◐ 51km/31.8mi S by the N 601. Turn at Almenara and continue 3km/1.9mi S. Open Tue–Sun 10.30am–2pm, 4.30–8pm; (Oct–Mar 4–6pm). Closed Jan, 24–25 and 31 Dec. €3. ✆983 62 60 36.
This museum features the remains of a sumptuous villa of the 4C and the underlying 3C structure.

Castillo de Montealegre
◐ 35km/22mi NW from Valladolid along the VA 900 and the VA 912. Visitor Centre open Apr–Sept Fri 5.30–7pm, weekends & hols 11.30am–1pm, 5–7pm. Castle open daily 7–9pm. ✆680 857 148.
www.provinciadevalladolid.com.
The imposing castle of Montealegre looms up above wide wheat fields. Twice besieged, by Peter the Cruel and later, in 1521, by Charles V, its stalwart walls, 4m/13ft thick and 24m/79ft high,

keep original Arab-medieval structures. In modern times it became a grain silo before restoration. Today it is home to the Centro de Interpretación del Medievo (Medieval Culture Centre).

Medina de Rioseco
◐ 40km/25mi NW along the N 601.
The picturesque narrow main street, or **Rúa**, of this agricultural centre is lined by porticoes on wooden pillars.
The 16C Iglesia de Santa María (Pl. de Santa María; open Tue–Sun 11am–2pm, 4–7pm; guided tours available; closed 1, 5 & 6 Jan, 24–25 & 31 Dec; €3; ✆983 72 50 26) features a central altarpiece carved by Esteban Jordán. Other churches house Holy Week processional sculptures and religious art and the **Capilla de los Benavente**★ (Benavente Chapel, 16C) contains a 16C retable by Juan de Juni.

ADDRESSES

🏨 STAY
⊜🍴**Hotel El Nogal** – Conde Ansurez 10, Valladolid. ✆983 34 03 33. www.hotelelnogal.com. 24 rooms. ⊡€6.60. This small hotel lies at the heart of the old town. Rooms are bright, airy and well equipped. Good restaurant (⊜⊜⊜).

⊜⊜**Hotel Zenit Imperial** – Pas. 4. ✆983 33 03 00. http://imperial.zenit hoteles.com. 63 rooms. ⊡€9. Restaurant ⊜⊜⊜. An authentic Valladolid institution set in an impeccably maintained 16C Gallo mansion.

🍴 EAT
⊜⊜ **Covadonga** – Zapico 1. ✆983 33 07 98. Closed 2nd fortnight in Jul. Friendly welcome, excellent service and wholesome, plentiful cuisine.

⊜⊜⊜ **El Figón de Recoletos** – Acera de Recoletos 3. ✆983 39 60 43. www.elfigonderecoletos.es. Closed 20 Jul–12 Aug; Sun pm. Popular for business lunches and family meals. Excellent local produce, roast dishes (particularly lamb) a speciality.

Soria★

This tranquil provincial capital stands on the banks of the Duero, a river that creates romantic and dramatic landscapes. The scenery and medieval atmosphere were lyricised by poet Antonio Machado.

▶ **Population:** 39 168
◉ **Michelin Map:** 575 G 22.
🛈 **Info:** Medinaceli 2.
  ℘975 21 20 52.
  www.soria.es.
◖ **Location:** Soria lies in NE Spain at an altitude of 1 050m/3 445ft on a plateau buffeted by the winds of the Meseta. 🚆Soria.

SIGHTS

Iglesia de Santo Domingo★

Pl. de los Condes de Lérida 3. Open daily 7am–9pm. No charge.

The west front of this church has two tiers of blind arcades and a richly carved **portal★★**. The church's founders were Alfonso VIII and his queen, Eleanor Plantagenet (they appear on either side of the portal), hence the French appearance. Scenes include the early chapters of Genesis (on the capitals of the jamb shafts), the 24 Elders of the Apocalypse playing stringed instruments, the Massacre of the Innocents, and Christ's childhood, Passion and Death.

Palacio de los Condes de Gómara (Palace of the Counts of Gómara)

Pl. de Aguirre 3.

The long façade, part Renaissance, part Classical, the bold tower and double patio exemplify late 16C opulence. Today the palace houses the city's law courts.

Iglesia de San Juan de Rabanera

Caballeros. Open for Mass. Ask at the tourist office about opening times.

The Romanesque portal taken from a ruined church dedicated to St Nicolas recalls the saint's life in the capitals on the slender columns on the right and on the tympanum. The decoration at the east end shows Byzantine and Gothic influences. Crucifixes inside are Romanesque over the altar and Baroque in the north transept.

Museo Numantino (Numancia Museum)

Pas. del Espolón 8. Open Tue–Sat 10am–2pm, 5-8pm (Oct–Jun 4–7pm), Sun and public holidays 10am–2pm.

Closed 1 Jan, 24–25 and 31 Dec. €1; no charge Sat–Sun. ℘975 22 13 97. www.turismocastillayleon.com.

The collections in this recently restored museum include an outstanding range of artefacts from Celt-Iberian necropolises and coloured pottery from Numancia (7 km north of Soria).

Concatedral de San Pedro

Pl. de San Pedro. Open Sat 11am–2pm, 4–7pm, Sun 11am–2pm.

This 16C Gothic Cathedral is light and spacious; the **cloisters★** are older, with three Romanesque galleries. The capitals have been delicately re-sculpted in a pure Romanesque style.

Monasterio de San Juan de Duero★★

Pas. de las Ánimas. Open Tue–Sat 10am–2pm, 4–7pm, Sun and public holidays 10am–2pm. €1; no charge Sat–Sun. ℘975 23 02 18. www.turismocastillayleon.com.

This monastery founded by the Hospitallers of St John of Jerusalem enjoys a rustic setting along the Duero. Only the graceful gallery arcading, with four different orders, remains of the 12C–13C **cloisters★**. The intersecting, overlapping arches owe much to Moorish art. The church contains a small lapidary museum. Two small chambers with beautiful historiated capitals stand at the entrance to the apse; the ciborium effect is unusual, as one might find in an Orthodox church.

Ermita de San Saturio

Pas. San Saturio. 1.3km/0.8mi S of
N 122. Open Tue–Sat 10.30am–2pm,
4.30–7.30pm (6.30pm Nov–Mar, 8.30pm
Jul–Aug), Sun 10.30am–2pm.
No charge. ℰ975 18 07 03.

A shaded path beside the Duero leads to
a cave where a hermit once sat in medi-
tation. An 18C octagonal chapel is built
spectacularly into the rock.

EXCURSIONS

Monasterio de Santa María de Huerta★★

◖ The monastery stands close to
the A 2 highway linking Madrid and
Zaragoza (131km/82mi NE). It is 85km/
53mi SE of Soria via the SC 20 A 15 and
CL 116. Allow about 1 hr for the visit.
Open Mon–Sat 10am–1pm, Sun
10am–11.15am; daily 4–6pm. €2.
ℰ975 32 70 02.
www.monasteriohuerta.org.

In 1144, a Cistercian community came
to this border region between Castilla
and Aragón. Monks settled in Huerta in
1162. The monastery is entered through
a 16C triumphal arch.

Cloisters and Claustro Herreriano (Herreran Cloisters)

16C–17C. The buildings around the
cloisters are the monks' living quarters.

Claustro de los Caballeros★ (Knights' Cloisters)

These 13–16C cloisters owe their name
to the many knights buried there. The
arches at ground level are elegant,
pointed and purely Gothic; above, the
16C gallery has all the exuberance and
imagination of the Plateresque. The
decorative medallions are of Prophets,
Apostles and Spanish kings.

Sala de los Conversos (Lay Brothers' Hall)

12C. This is divided by stout pillars,
crowned with stylised capitals. The
kitchen is famed for its monumental
central chimney. The Refectorio★★
(refectory), a masterpiece of 13C Gothic,
rises 15m/49ft above the 35m/114.8ft

long hall and has a wonderful rose window. A beautiful staircase, its arches on
slender columns, leads to the lectern.

Iglesia

The church has been restored to its
original state although the royal chapel
has kept sumptuous Churrigueresque
decoration. Between the narthex and
the aisles is an intricate 18C wrought-iron
screen. The coro alto (choir) is beautifully
decorated with Renaissance panelling
and woodwork. The Talavera azulejos on
the floor are also worthy of note.

El Burgo de Osma★

◖ 56km/35mi SW of Soria and 139km/
87mi SE of Burgos. ₽Plaza Mayor 9.
ℰ975 340 107. www.burgodeosma.com.
This attractive town with porticoed
streets and squares has long been a
bishop's seat. Its notable buildings
include the San Agustín hospital and
the imposing Cathedral★ (Pl. de la Catedral; open Tue–Sun 10.30am-1.30pm,
4–7.30pm, Oct-Jun Tue-Sat 10.30am-
1pm, 4-6pm (Sat 7pm); €2.50; ℰ975
34 03 19).

The east end, transept and chapter
house were built in the 13C; the late
Gothic cloisters and chancel received
Renaissance embellishments. The sacristy, royal chapel and 72m/236ft belfry
are from the 18C.

There is magnificent Gothic decoration on the late 13C south portal. The
interior is remarkable for the elevation
of the nave, the delicate wrought-iron
screens (16C) by Juan de Francés, the
high altar retable by Juan de Juni, and
the 16C white marble pulpit and trascoro altarpiece. The 13C polychrome
limestone tomb of San Pedro de
Osma★ is in the west transept. In the
museum are a richly illustrated 1086
Beatus and a 12C manuscript with the
signs of the zodiac.

Returning to Soria (25km/15.5mi NE
on the N 122) Calatañazor sits just off
the main road. Time has stood still in
its steep, stone-paved streets and castle ruins, from where you can view the
plains.

Peñaranda de Duero★

◯ 47km/29mi W of El Burgo de Osma along the N 122 and BU 924.

The small Castilian town is dominated by the ruins of its castle. Around the 15C pillory in the **Plaza Mayor★**(square) are half-timbered houses on stone piers. To one side is the **Palacio de los Condes de Miranda (Avellaneda)★** (open Tue–Sat 10am–2pm, 3–7pm (Oct–Mar 3–6pm) Sun 10am–2pm; last entry 1 hour before closing); no charge; ℘947 55 20 13, www.peñarandadeduero.es), a palace with a Renaissance façade. A patio with a two-tier gallery, a grand staircase and chambers with **artesonado ceilings★** make this one of the finest Renaissance residences in Spain. An 18C pharmacy, the **Botica de Ximeno**, with books and instruments, may also be visited by arrangement with the tourist office.

Cañón del Río Lobos

◯ 15km/10mi N on the SO 920 (best access from the south). Centro de Interpretación del Parque Natural. ℘975 36 35 64.

The landscape along this 25km/15.5mi stretch of the Río Lobos Is riddled with caves, depressions and chasms.

Castillo de Gormaz

These 10C Moorish castle ruins, overlooking the Duero, are the largest in Europe (446m/1 463ft in length) and boast 26 towers.

Berlanga del Duero

◯ 28km/17.4mi SE on C 116 and SO 104.

Berlanga, below its massive 15C castle, was a strongpoint on the Duero frontier. Some 8km/5mi southeast in **Casillas de Berlanga** is the **Iglesia de San Baudelio de Berlanga** (open Wed–Sat 10am– 2pm, 4–8pm (Oct–Mar until 6pm); €1; ℘975 22 13 97), an unusual 11C Mozarabic chapel, its roof supported by a massive pillar. Its 12C frescoes were removed in the 20C though hunting scenes and geometric patterns can still be made out.

🚗 DRIVING TOUR

SIERRA DE URBIÓN★★

❄ Roads may be blocked by snow Nov–May.

This hilly green part of the Sistema Ibérico mountain range rises to 2 228m/ 7 310ft. Streams rush through pine-woods and meadows; one is the source of the Duero, one of Spain's longest rivers (910km/565mi).

Laguna Negra de Urbión★★

53km/33mi NW of Soria via the N 234. Allow about 1hr.

◯ At Cidones bear right towards Vinuesa; after 18km/11mi head for Montenegro de Cameros. After 8km/5mi bear left onto the Laguna road (9km/5.6mi).

The **road★★**, after skirting the Cuerdo del Pozo reservoir (embalse), continues through pines to **Laguna Negra** (alt 1 700m/5 600ft), a small glacial lake at the foot of a semicircular cliff over which cascade two waterfalls.

Laguna Negra de Neila★★

About 86km/53mi NW of Soria via the N 234.

◯ At Abejar turn right towards Molinos de Duero; continue to Quintana de la Sierra then turn right for Neila (12km/7mi), then left for Huerta de Arriba; 2km/1mi on the left is the road to Laguna Negra.

The **road★★** through picturesque countryside commands changing views of the valley and Sierra de la Demanda. The lake lies at 2 000m/6 561ft.

Castilla-la Mancha

The southern *meseta*, which stretches south from Madrid through Castilla-La Mancha's flatlands, is a vast tableland slightly tilted towards the west, watered by two large rivers – the **Tajo** (Tagus), which cuts a deep gorge through the limestone Alcarria region, and the sluggish **Guadiana**. The word La Mancha comes from the Arab *manxa* meaning dry land, which is particularly apparent in summer. Despite this, there is considerable cultivation, with wind-ruffled cereal fields, stretches of saffron turned purple in the flowering season, and serried ranks of olives and vines. Madrid's traditional table wines come from here, and the area is also renowned for its manchego cheese. **La Mancha**'s most famous personality is **Don Quixote**, created by **Cervantes** 400 years ago. A Quixote trail leads in his (fictional) footsteps and includes (real) windmills and a glimpse of rural life here in old towns. Even today, small towns look more like large villages in which the arcaded Plaza Mayor (main square) is still the hub of activity and gossip.

Highlights

1. Gazing upon **Toledo** from the other side of the Tajo (p193)
2. The iconic "Don Quixote windmills" at **Consuegra** (p204)
3. The Museum of Abstract Art, set in a **casa colgada** in **Cuenca** (p211)
4. The spectacular natural formations of the **Serranía de Cuenca** (p212)
5. The sculptures in the cathedral and its museum at **Sigüenza** (p215)

Toledo and West

Toledo is the jewel of Castilla-La Mancha. It is surrounded, moat-like, on three sides by the Tajo, with parts of its city wall and gateways still intact, little changed in appearance over the centuries. Until 1560, when the capital moved to Madrid (70km/43.5mi north), the city was the nerve centre of not only Spain but of a burgeoning empire. In the following years it declined rapidly and slid into the political backwaters. A happy circumstance of this was that "progress" bypassed Toledo, and its old town remained largely untouched. Today it is UNESCO World Heritage-listed with many very tangible reminders of its multi-faith past. Some 80km west of Toledo, Talavera de la Reina is famous for the ceramic work which decorates its palaces, mansions and chapels, is well worth a visit. Nearby Oropesa is a charming village, home to a fine parador.

The South

The flat landscapes of the south conjure up the archetypal Don Quixote images of La Mancha. But there are surprises here too: Belmonte, with a fine 15C fortress and Almagro, once the headquarters of the Military Order of the Knights of Calatrava.

Cuenca city and province

This UNESCO World Heritage city's hanging houses, old town and superb Museum of Abstract Art place Cuenca high on most visitors' itineraries. Around the town a limestone plateau pitted with swallow-holes *(torcas)* and cut by gorges *(hoces)* makes for a spectacular and curious touring landscape.

Northeast

With fewer than 6 000 inhabitants, charming Sigüenza is remarkable for two imposing buildings set amid its medieval streets. The cathedral, which features some outstanding sculptures, would be more at home in a major metropolis. The mighty fortress was once a Moorish alcázar, then a Christian stronghold, home to most of the Castilian monarchs; today it is a parador, welcoming visitors who are happy to leave the beaten track. Workaday Guadalajara is worth a visit for the late-15C Palace of the Duke of Infantado.

Toledo★★★

Golden Toledo rises dramatically on a granite eminence encircled by a steep ravine of the Tajo (Tagus). It is as spectacular in setting as it is rich in history, buildings and art. Every corner has a tale to tell. Taken as a whole, the city reflects a brilliant intertwining of east and west, of Christian, Jewish and Moorish cultures during the Middle Ages.

▶ **Population:** 83 226
🖫 **Michelin Map:** 576 M 17 (town plan) – map 121 Alrededores de Madrid – Castilla-La Mancha (Toledo) .
🖪 **Info:** Plaza del Consistorio. ℘925 25 40 30. www.toledo-turismo.com.
▷ **Location:** Toledo is 71km/44mi SW of Madrid. 🚆Toledo (AVE).
🅿 **Parking:** Try to park below the centre of the city, and walk or take a taxi up.
◎ **Don't Miss:** El Greco's masterpiece, *The Burial of the Count of Orgaz.*
◷ **Timing:** Monumental Toledo is compact. Walk around for an overview, then return for a visit to the sites of most interest.

THE CITY TODAY

On busy days Toledo can resemble something of a medieval theme park with large groups of visitors on day trips from Madrid clogging up its narrow streets. In shop windows in the main streets are garish displays of Toledan steel, once the deadliest weaponry in the world, wielded by Spanish heroes, from El Cid to the Conquistadores. Nowadays such steel is marketed as the "official" weaponry of Holywood films such as **Lord of the Rings**. Whenever you visit, try to stay the night and do your exploration early (before the groups arrive) and late (after they have gone). Don't expect much nightlife as Toledo after dark is a fairly staid place.

A BIT OF HISTORY

Roman town to Holy Roman city – The Romans fortified the strategic settlement into a town they named Toletum. It passed into the hands of the barbarians, and in the 6C to the Visigoths, who made it a royal seat until they were defeated by the Moors at Guadelete in 711.

After the revolt of the taifas in 1012, Toledo was capital of an independent kingdom. In 1085 it was conquered by Alfonso VI, who soon moved his capital from León. Alfonso VII was crowned emperor in Toledo, hence the title of imperial city. The city of Moors, Jews and Christians began to prosper.

The Catholic Monarchs gave it the Monastery of St John but lost interest after they reconquered Granada in 1492. Emperor Charles V had the Alcázar rebuilt. In his reign the city took part in the Comuneros' Revolt led by **Juan de Padilla**, a Toledan. This was one reason why, in 1561, Philip II named Madrid as Spain's capital, relegating Toledo to the role of spiritual centre.

Toledo and the Jews – In the 12C the Jewish community numbered 12 000. **Saint Ferdinand III** (1217–1252) encouraged diversity which brought about a cultural flowering, and the city developed into a great intellectual forum. **Alfonso X the Wise** (1252–1284) gathered a court of learned Jews and established the **School of Translation**. In 1355 a pogrom was instigated by supporters of Henry IV of Trastamara. After repeated attacks, the Jews were expelled in 1492.

Mudéjar art in Toledo – The Mudéjar style established itself in Toledo after the Reconquest of the city, in palaces (Taller del Moro), synagogues (El Tránsito, Santa María la Blanca) and churches. Brick was widely used. Moorish stuccowork, *artesonado* and *azulejos* became commonplace. In the

13C and 14C, most Toledan churches were given Romanesque semicircular **east ends**, blind arcades took on variations unknown elsewhere, and **belfries** were built square and decorated until they resembled minarets. The edifices often have a nave and two aisles – a Visigothic influence – Roman tripartite apses and Moorish wood vaulting.

CATHEDRAL★★★

Pl. del Ayuntamiento. Open Mon–Sat 10am–6pm (last admission), Sun and public holidays 2–6pm. See website for Special days. Closed 1 Jan, 25 Dec. €11. ℘925 22 22 41. www.catedralprimada.es.

The Cathedral dominates the **Plaza del Ayuntamiento**. Construction began in the reign of Ferdinand III (St Ferdinand) in 1227. Unusually, the design was French Gothic, but as building continued until the end of the 15C, its architecture came to reflect Spanish Gothic. Despite late additions, the cathedral is outstanding for its decoration and works of art.

Exterior

The **Puerta del Reloj** (Clock Doorway), in the north wall, from the 13C, was modified in the 19C. The **main façade** is pierced by three tall 15C portals; the upper registers were completed in the 16C and 17C. The central **Puerta del Perdón** (Pardon Doorway) is crowded with statues and crowned with a tympanum illustrating the Virgin presenting the 7C bishop of Toledo with a chasuble. The harmonious tower is 15C; the dome was designed by El Greco's son in the 17C. In the south wall is the 15C **Puerta de los Leones** (Lion Doorway) designed by Master Hanequin of Brussels and decorated by Juan Alemán. The Neoclassical portal is from 1800.

▶ Enter through the Puerta del Mollete, left of the west front which leads you into the cloister.

Interior

The size and sturdy character of the cathedral are striking. Wonderful stained glass (1418–1561); magnificent wrought-iron grilles enclose the chancel, **coro** and chapels.

Capilla Mayor

The chancel, the most sumptuous section, was enlarged in the 16C.
The immense **polychrome retable★★**, carved in detail in Flamboyant style with the Life of Christ, is awe-inspiring. The silver statue of the Virgin at the predella dates from 1418. The Plateresque marble tomb of Cardinal Mendoza on the left is by Covarrubias.

Coro

14C high reliefs and wrought-iron enclosed chapels form the perimeter of the choir, itself closed by an elegant iron screen (1547). The lower parts of the 15C and 16C **choir stalls★★★** were carved by Rodrigo Alemán to recall the conquest of Granada; the alabaster 16C upper parts, by Berruguete (left) and Felipe Vigarny (right) portray Old Testament figures. The central low relief, the Transfiguration, is also by Berruguete. The style of his work creates the impression of movement. Two organs and a Gothic eagle lectern complete the set. The 14C marble **White Virgin** is French.

Girola

The double ambulatory, surmounted by an elegant triforium with multifoil arches, is bordered by seven apsidal chapels separated by small square chapels. The vaulting is a geometrical wonder.

There is little room to step back for a good look at the **Transparente★**, the contentious but famous work by Narciso Tomé which forms a Baroque island in the Gothic church.

Illuminated through an opening in the ambulatory roof (made to allow light to fall on the tabernacle), the **Transparente** appears as an ornamental framework of angels and swirling clouds and rays surrounding the Virgin and the Last Supper. Elsewhere, in the **Capilla de San Ildefonso** (Chapel of San Ildefonso), the central tomb of Cardinal Gil de Albornoz (14C) is the most notable.

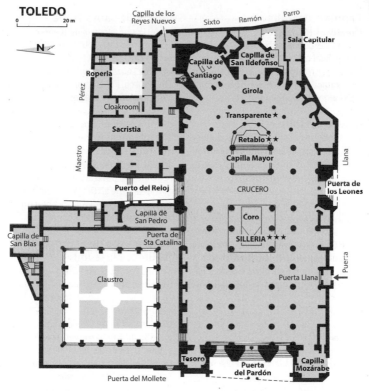

TOLEDO

0   20 m

N

Capilla de los Reyes Nuevos
Sixto
Ramón
Parro
Sala Capitular
Capilla de San Ildefonso
Capilla de Santiago
Ropería
Girola
Cloakroom
Transparente ★
Sacristia
Retablo ★★
Capilla Mayor
Pérez
Maestro
Llana
Puerto del Reloj
CRUCERO
Puerta de los Leones
Capilla de San Pedro
Coro
Puerta de Sta Catalina
SILLERIA ★★★
Capilla de San Blas
Claustro
Puerta
Puerta Llana
Tesoro
Capilla Mozárabe
Puerta del Mollete
Puerta del Pardón
Plaza del Ayuntamiento

Sala Capitular (Chapter House)

The antechamber has an impressive Mudéjar ceiling and two Plateresque carved walnut wardrobes. Remarkable Mudéjar stucco doorways and carved Plateresque panels precede the chapter house with its multicoloured **Mudéjar ceiling★**. Below frescoes by Juan de Borgoña are portraits of former archbishops including two by **Goya**.

Sacristía (Sacristy)

The first gallery, its vaulted ceiling painted by Lucas Jordán, includes **paintings by El Greco★** of which **El Expolio** (The Disrobing of Christ, c. 1577) is outstanding. It sets an exalted personality against swirling robes to establish Baroque movement.

Other works include a remarkable portrait of Pope Paul III by Titian, a Holy Family by Van Dyck, a Mater Dolorosa by Morales and the Taking of Christ by Goya,

which displays skill in composition, light and portraiture. Pedro de Mena's (17C) famous sculpture, St Francis of Assisi, is in a glass case. In the vestry are portraits by **Velázquez** (Cardinal Borja), Van Dyck (Pope Innocent XI) and **Ribera**.

The old laundry (ropería) contains liturgical objects dating back to the 15C. **The Nuevas Salas del Museo Catedralicio** (Cathedral Museum's New Galleries; c/ Cardenal Cisneros; open same hours as cathedral; closed 1 Jan, Corpus Christi, 15 Aug, 25 Dec) displays works by Caravaggio, El Greco, Bellini and Morales.

Tesoro (Treasury)

A Plateresque doorway by Covarrubias opens into the chapel under the tower. Beneath a Mudéjar ceiling note the 16C silver-gilt **monstrance★★** by Enrique de Arfe, weighing 180kg/392lb and 3m/10ft high, paraded at Corpus Christi. The pyx at its centre is fashioned from gold brought by Christopher Columbus.

Capilla Mozárabe (Mozarabic Chapel)

The chapel beneath the dome was built by Cardinal Cisneros (16C) to celebrate Mass according to the Visigothic or Mozarabic ritual which had been threatened with abolition in the 11C.

Claustro (Cloisters)

The simplicity of the 14C lower gallery contrasts with the bold murals by Bayeu of the Lives of Toledan Saints (Santa Eugenia and San Ildefonso).

Campana Gorda (Bell Tower)

Ascend the 90m/295ft high north tower (built 1380-1440), from which there are splendid panoramic views of Toledo. It takes its name, Campana Gorda ("Fat Bell") from the famous 17-ton bell, cast in 1753.

☛ WALKING TOUR

CENTRE OF OLD TOLEDO★★★

Allow 1 day. See town plan.

Surrounding the square before the Cathedral are the 18C **Palacio Arzobispal** (Archbishop's Palace), the 17C **ayuntamiento** (Town Hall), with classical façade, and the 14C **Audiencia** (Law Courts).

Iglesia de Santo Tomé

Pl. del Conde. Open daily 10am–6.45pm (5.45pm mid-Oct–Feb). Last ticket 30min before close. €2.80. Closed 1 Jan, 25 Dec. ✆925 25 60 98. www.santotome.org.

The church, like that of San Román, has a distinctive 14C Mudéjar tower. Inside is **El Greco**'s famous painting **The Burial of the Count of Orgaz★★★** (c. 1586). The interment is transformed by the miraculous appearance of St Augustine and St Stephen. Figures in the lower register are portraits of personalities of the day; the sixth from the left is said to be El Greco. Above, Christ prepares to receive the soul of the count.

Casa-Museo de El Greco★ (El Greco Museum)

Samuel Leví. Tue–Sat 9.30am–7.30pm (Nov–Feb until 6pm), Sun and hols 10am –3pm. €3, no charge Sat from 2pm, Sun, 18 Apr, 18 May, 12 Oct, 6 Dec. ✆925 99 09 82. http://museodelgreco.mcu.es.

In 1585, El Greco moved into a house similar to this one. In what would have been the artist's workroom is a signed *St Francis and Brother León*.

On the first floor are an interesting *View and Plan of Toledo* and the complete series of individual portraits of the Apostles and Christ (later and more mature than those in the cathedral). The **capilla** on the ground floor, with

Old Toledo, the Alcázar on the right

© Bertrand Gardel/hemis.fr

a multicoloured Mudéjar ceiling, has a picture in the altarpiece of *St Bernardino of Siena* by **El Greco**.

Sinagoga del Tránsito★★ (Synagogue of El Transito)

Samuel Leví. Opening hours as for Casa-Museo de El Greco. Closed 1 & 6 Jan, 1 May, 24–25, 31 Dec. €3. ☏925 22 36 65. http://museosefardi.mcu.es.

Of the ten synagogues that once stood in the Jewish quarter (Judería), only this and Santa María la Blanca remain. It was financed in the 14C by Samuel Ha-Levi, treasurer to Peter the Cruel. In 1492 it was converted into a church.

Unassuming from the outside, it is covered inside with ornate **Mudéjar decoration★★**. Above the rectangular hall is an *artesonado* ceiling of cedarwood; just below are 54 multifoil arches, some blind, others pierced with delicate stone tracery. Below again runs a frieze, decorated at the east end with *mocárabes* and on the walls with inscriptions in Hebrew to the glory of Peter the Cruel, Samuel Ha-Levi and the God of Israel. In the east wall, inscriptions describe the synagogue's foundation. The women's balcony opens from the south wall.

The adjoining rooms, once a monastery, are the **Museo Sefardí** (Sephardic Museum; opening hours and admission as above) displaying tombs, robes, costumes and books. Several are gifts from descendants of Jews expelled in 1492.

Casa Museo Victorio Macho★

Pl. de Victor Macho. Open Mon–Sat 10am–7pm, Sun 10am–3pm. Closed 1 Jan, 25 Dec. €3. ☏925 284 225. www.realfundaciontoledo.es

This impressively sited exhibition space, with views over the gorge of the River Tagus and San Martín bridge, occupies the home of avant-garde artist Victorio Macho, who went into exile in Peru on the outbreak of the Spanish Civil War. Alongside works on temporary show are numerous pieces by Macho, including an impressive portrait of his brother.

Sinagoga de Santa María La Blanca★

Reyes Católicos 4. Open daily 10am–6.45pm last admission (5.45pm Oct–Feb). €2.80. ☏925 22 72 57.

This was the principal synagogue in Toledo in the late 12C. In 1405 it was given to the Knights of Calatrava as a church. Surprisingly subsequent modifications left the Almohad-style nave untouched, with five tiered aisles separated by octagonal pillars supporting horseshoe-shaped arches. The whitewashed pillars set off intricately carved **capitals★**. The wood altarpiece is 16C.

Monasterio de San Juan de los Reyes★ (St John of the Kings Monastery)

Reyes Católicos 17. Open daily Apr–Oct 10am–6.45pm (Oct-Feb 10am-5.45pm). €2.80. ☏925 22 38 02. www.sanjuandelosreyes.org.

This Franciscan monastery commemorates the victory over the Portuguese at Toro in 1476. The overall style is Isabelline, Covarrubias designed the north portal, including in the decoration the figure of John the Baptist. The fetters depicted were taken from Christian prisoners freed from the Muslims.

Claustro

The cloisters boast Flamboyant bays and Plateresque upper galleries (1504) crowned with a pinnacled balustrade and Mudéjar *artesonado* vaulting.

Iglesia

The church, burned by the French in 1808, has a typically Isabelline single wide aisle; at the crossing are a dome and a lantern.

The **sculptured decoration★** by Flemish architect Juan Guas provides a delicate stone tracery *(crestería)* which at the transept forms twin tribunes for Ferdinand and Isabel. The transept walls are faced with a frieze of royal escutcheons, supported by an eagle, symbol of St John. Close by are a Visigothic palace and the *Puerta del Cambrón*, once part of the town perimeter, rebuilt in the 16C.

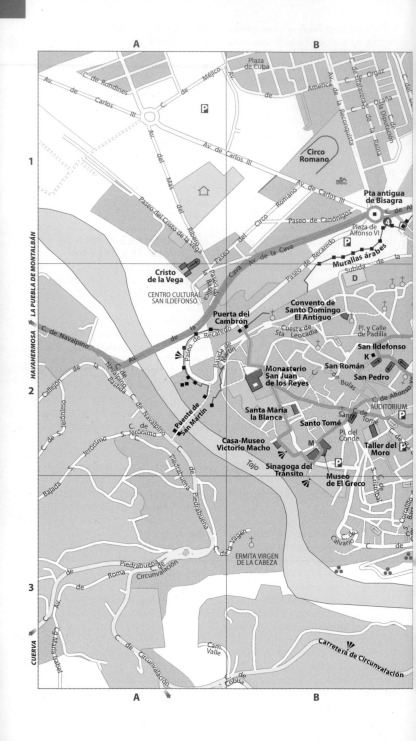

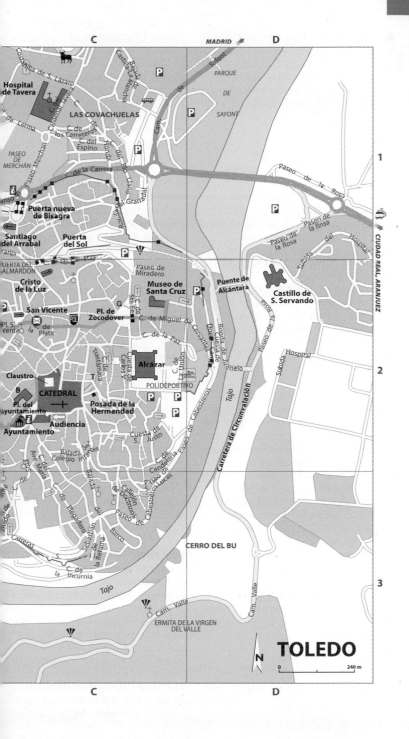

Return to San Juan and take Calle Ángel to Santo Tomé, then take the picturesque Travesía de Campana alley to the small Pl. del Padre Juan de Mariana. Cross the plaza past the monumental Baroque façade of the Iglesia de San Ildefonso and that of the Iglesia de San Pedro.

Iglesia de San Román: Museo de los Concilios y de la Cultura Visigoda★ (Museum of the Councils of Toledo and Visigothic Culture)

San Román. Open Tue–Sat 10am–2pm, 4–6.30pm (4-7pm summer), Sun and public holidays 10am–2pm. Closed 1 Jan, 1 May, 24–25 and 31 Dec. &925 22 78 72. www.turismocastillalamancha.com.

This 13C Mudéjar church, at the summit of Toledo's old town, has a tower resembling that of Santo Tomé. The walls are covered in 13C frescoes of the raising of the dead, the Evangelists and, on the far wall, one of the Councils of Toledo. The apse was modified in the 16C with a cupola by Covarrubias. The collections include fine bronze jewellery and copies of Visigothic votive crowns decorated with cabochon stones from Guarrazar (originals in the Museo Arqueológico, Madrid). On the walls are steles, fragments from capitals, balustrades from the choir and pilasters. In Plaza de San Vicente, note the Mudéjar east end of the **Iglesia de San Vicente**. Continue up Calle de la Plata with its houses with carved entrances.

Plaza de Zocodover

This bustling triangular square is the heart of Toledo. It was rebuilt after the Civil War as was the Arco de la Sangre (Arch of Blood), which opens onto calle de Cervantes.

Museo de Santa Cruz★★ (Santa Cruz Museum)

Miguel de Cervantes 3. Open Mon and Sat 10am–7pm, Sun and public holidays 10am–2.30pm. Closed 1, 6 & 23 Jan; 1 May; 24–25, 31 Dec. €5, no charge 18 & 31 May. &925 22 14 02. www.turismo castillalamancha.com.

This fine group of Plateresque hospital buildings was begun by Enrique Egas and completed by Covarrubias, who was responsible for the **façade★★**. On the gateway tympanum Cardinal Mendoza, the hospital's sponsor, kneels before the Cross supported by St Helena, St Peter, St Paul and two pages; on the arches are the cardinal virtues. Above, two windows frame a high relief of St Joachim and St Anne. The museum is known for its **16C and 17C pictures★** including 18 paintings by **El Greco★**. The large nave and transept – forming a two-tiered Greek cross – and the beautiful coffered ceilings are outstanding.

Ground floor

The first part of the nave contains 16C Flemish tapestries, **primitive paintings★**, and the *Astrolabios* or *Zodiac* tapestry, woven in Flanders in the mid-15C for Toledo cathedral, still strikingly original. Note, in the south transept, the *Ascension* and the *Presentation of Mary in the Temple* by the Maestro de Sijena. In the second part of the nave hangs the immense pennant flown by Don Juan of Austria at the Battle of Lepanto. The north transept contains a *Christ at the Column* by Morales.

First floor

A staircase leads to the upper gallery of the north transept with paintings by **El Greco★**. There are gentle portraits of the Virgin and St Veronica as well as a version of the *Expolio*, later than the original in the cathedral.

Most famous is the late **Altarpiece of the Assumption★**, from 1613, with Baroque stylings and notably elongated figures. The south transept contains a *Holy Family at Nazareth* by **Ribera**, the specialist in tenebrism who here showed himself a master of light and delicacy. In the first part of the nave are 16C Brussels tapestries showing the life of Alexander the Great; and 17C statues from the studio of Pascual de Mena.

The **Plateresque patio★** has bays with elegant lines complemented by the openwork balustrade and enhanced by Mudéjar vaulting and by the magnificent **staircase★** by Covarrubias. Adjoining rooms house a museum of archaeology and decorative arts.

WITHIN THE CITY WALLS

Alcázar (Museo del Ejército)

Cuesta de Carlos V 2. Open Thu–Tue 10am–5pm. Closed 1 & 6 Jan; 1 May; 24–25, 31 Dec. €5; no charge Sun, 29 Mar, 18 Apr, 12 Oct, 6 Dec. ℘925 238 800. www.museo.ejercito.es

The Alcázar, destroyed and rebuilt so many times, is now home to the National Army Museum. Emperor Charles V converted the 13C fortress, of which El Cid had been the first governor, into an imperial residence. The work was entrusted to Covarrubias (1538–1551) and then Herrera, who designed the austere south front. An eight-week seige in 1936 left the fortress in ruins. The Falangist commander defending it allowed his son to be shot rather than surrender.

The Alcázar is restored to its appearance at the time of Charles V. In 2010, after many years of renovation, it opened as an army museum. Now, 6,500 exhibits tell the story of Spain's complex military past, so often at the centre of the country's life and even government.

Posada de la Hermandad (House of the Brotherhood)

Hermandad 6.
This 15C building was once a prison.

Puerta del Sol

Carretas.
The Sun Gate in the second perimeter, rebuilt in the 14C, is a fine Mudéjar construction with two circumscribing horseshoe arches. At the centre a later low relief shows the Virgin presenting San Ildefonso with a chasuble. At the top, the brick decoration of blind arcading incorporates an unusual sculpture of two girls bearing the head of the chief *alguacil* (officer of justice), allegedly a rapist, on a salver.

Mezquita del Cristo de la Luz (Christ of the Light Mosque)

Cta. de Carmelitas Descalzas. Open Mar-Oct 10am-6.45pm, Nov-Feb 10am-5.45pm. €2.80. ℘925 25 41 91. www.turismocastillalamancha.com

This 12C Mudéjar church succeeded a mosque which in turn replaced a Visigothic church. It is named for the miraculous appearance in a mosque of a lamp illuminating a Crucifix when Alfonso VI first entered Toledo. Arches of different periods, intersecting blind arcades, and a line of horizontal brickwork surmounted by Cufic characters make up the façade. Inside, Visigothic pillars support superimposed arches like those in the mosque in Córdoba. Nine domes, each different, rise from square bays. The gardens lead to the Puerta del Sol. Enjoy the panorama from the top.

Iglesia de Santiago del Arrabal (St James on the Outskirts)

Real del Arrabal. Closed to the public, though discreet visits may be possible before/after evening mass. ℘925 22 06 36. www.turismocastillalamancha.com.

San Vicente Ferrer is said to have preached from the Gothic Mudéjar pulpit of this beautifully restored church.

Puerta Nueva de Bisagra (New Bisagra Gate)

Puerta de Bisagra.
The gate was rebuilt by Covarrubias in 1550 and enlarged under Philip II. Massive round crenellated towers, facing the Madrid road, flank a giant imperial crest.

Puerta Antigua de Bisagra (Old Bisagra Gate)

Pas. Recaredo.
Alfonso VI entered Toledo in triumph through this Moorish gate in 1085.

ADDITIONAL SIGHTS

Hospital de Tavera★

Cardenal de Tavera 2. Open daily 10am–2.30pm, 3–6.30pm (Sun am only). Guided tours every 45min.. €6. ℘925 22 04 51. www.fundacionmedinaceli.org/monumentos/hospital.

The Hospital de San Juan Bautista (better known as the Hopital de Tavera) was begun in 1541 and completed in the 17C. After the Civil War, the Duchess of Lerma rearranged her apartments★ in 17C style. These hold an outstanding collection of paintings. In the vast library, the hospital archives contain volumes bound in leather by Moorish craftsmen. El Greco's *Holy Family* is arresting, the portrait of the Virgin perhaps the most beautiful by the artist. Note also the *Birth of the Messiah* by Tintoretto, the *Philosopher* by Ribera and, in an adjoining room, his strange portrait of the *Bearded Woman*.

On the first floor, in the reception hall, is El Greco's sombre portrait of *Cardinal Tavera*, painted from a death mask. Beside it are *Samson and Delilah* (Caravaggio) and two portraits of the *Duke and Duchess of Navas* (Antonio Moro).

A gallery leads to the church from the twin patio.

The retable at the high altar was designed by El Greco, whose last work,

a **Baptism of Christ★**, is displayed. The artist's use of brilliant colours and elongated figures is at its most magnificent. The hospital pharmacy, facing the patio, has been restored.

Puente de Alcántara

At the ends of the 13C bridge are a Mudéjar tower and a Baroque arch. Across the Tajo, behind ramparts, is the restored 14C **Castillo de San Servando** (now a youth hostel; ℘925 22 45 54). A plaque on the town wall by the bridge recalls how *St John of the Cross* (1542–1591) escaped through a window from his monastery prison nearby.

Puente de San Martín

The medieval bridge, rebuilt in the 14C, is marked at its south end by an octagonal tower; the north end is 16C.

Iglesia de Cristo de la Vega

Travesía Cristo de la Vega.

The Church of Christ of the Vega, formerly St Leocadia, stands on the site of a 7C Visigothic temple.

VIEWPOINTS

The city's incomparable **site★★★** can be appreciated from the **Carretera de Circunvalación** (ring-road) which parallels the loop of the Tajo from the Puente de Alcántara (Alcántara Bridge) to the Puente de San Martín.

For great views, it is worth going to the **viewpoints** among olive groves on the surrounding hills. The terrace of the parador (&see Addresses), above the **carretera de circunvalación**, is a superb vantage point.

EXCURSIONS

Talavera de la Reina

◗ 80km/50mi W of Toledo. ◻ Ronda del Cañillo, 22. ℘925 82 63 22. www.talavera.org/turismo.

On the bank of the Tajo, spanned by a 15C bridge, Talavera retains part of its medieval walls and Mudéjar churches. Its name is synonymous with the *azulejos* (ceramic tiles) that brought it fame from the 15C, when they were used to decorate chapels and noble homes.

Talavera Ceramics

Since the 15C, the name Talavera has been associated with high-quality **ceramic tiles** used to decorate the palaces, mansions and chapels. Visit the town's Basilica and **Museo de Cerámica Ruiz de Luna** (Pl. de San Agustín; ℘925 80 01 49) to see ceramics dating from the 15C to modern times. Talavera now manufactures decorative crockery, and green-coloured items are made in **El Puente del Arzobispo**, a village (34km/21mi SW) specialising in pottery drinking jars.

Basílica de Nuestra Señora del Prado

Jardines del Prado 6. Open daily 7am–2pm, 5–10pm (4–9pm during summer). &925 80 14 45.
www.basilicavirgendelprado.es.
The church, virtually an *azulejos* museum, gives a good idea of the evolution of the local style. The earliest tiles, geometrically patterned and yellow in colour, may be found in the sacristy.
In the basilica later tiles (16C–18C) may be found with classic blue narrative scenes. Nearby the Museo Ruiz de la Luna (&see p202) displays more tiles.

Oropesa

◗ 32km/20mi W.
This delightful hilltop village is crowned by its **castle★** originally built in 1366 but rebuilt in 1402. Part of it is open to visitors (Pl. del Palacio 1; open Tue–Sat 10am–2pm, 4–6pm, Sun and public holidays 10am–2pm; €3; &925 26 76 66; www.parador.es/en) while most of it now serves as a parador enjoying far-reaching views across the Sierra de Gredos.

Montes de Toledo

Within the low wooded mountains lying southwest of Toledo, a central area of 1 000sq km /385sq m is protected as the Parque Nacional de Cabañeros, home to rare wildlife and shepherds' culture.

ADDRESSES

🛌 STAY

◔◔ **Hostal Santo Tomé** – Santo Tomé, 13. &925 221 712. www.hostalsanto tome.com 10 rooms. No breakfast. In the heart of the old town, with rooftop views from the top floor, this reasonably priced small hotel offers spacious rooms and car parking.

◔◔ **Hotel La Almazara** – 3.5km/2mi SW. &925 45 48 04. www.almazara devaldeverdeja.com. 28 rooms. Closed early Dec–Mar. This former olive press is reached via a lane planted with olive trees. Bedrooms are spacious and bright. Wonderful views of Toledo.

◔◔◔◔ **Hacienda del Cardenal** – Pas. Recaredo 24. &925 22 49 00. www.hostaldelcardenal.com. 27 rooms. ⊑€8.75. This charming hotel, formerly a cardinal's residence, stands at the foot of the city walls. Behind the splendid stone façade, the rooms are elegantly decorated with wood furnishings and antiques. The restaurant is superb (◔◔◔◔).

◔◔◔◔ **Parador del Toledo** – Cerro del Emperador via Ctra de Circunvalación. &902 54 79 79. www. parador.es. 79 rooms. 🅿 ⊑€17. Modern building recently given a facelift, with comfortable rooms and swimming pool. Its terraced dining room has a magnificent city view.

⑂ EAT

◔◔ **Colección Catedral** – Nuncio Viejo 1. &925 224 244. www. grupoadolfo.com. Stylish tapas bar in a 1920s building near the cathedral. Excellent-value menus including five tapas and two glasses of wine for €18.

◔◔◔ **La Abadía** – Nuñez de Arce 3 (Pl. de San Nicolás). &925 25 11 40. www.abadiatoledo.com. Complex lighting and modern furniture in the basement of a 16C palace create an atmospheric backdrop to creative cuisine.

SHOPPING

Toledo is renowned for **damascene ware** (black steel inlaid with gold, silver and copper thread).

FESTIVALS

The **Corpus Christi** procession is one of the largest of its kind in Spain (late May/early Jun, www.spain.info).

Ruta Don Quixote ★

The Quixote route, created to celebrate the 400th anniversary of the publication of Cervantes' great novel *Don Quixote* (1605), was the EU's first approved cultural route dedicated to a literary figure. It provides a good guideline for meandering through La Mancha's flatlands to explore the villages and landscapes where Cervantes set the first volume and Sancho Panza's imaginary adventures.

🚗 DRIVING TOUR

Consuegra
90km/56mi NE of Belmonte along the N 420.

A row of 12 **Molino de Vientos** (windmills) stands alongside the 13C castle on a hill overlooking the town, making up the classic picture-postcard image of Don Quixote's La Mancha.
The **Castillo de Consuegra** (open Mon-Fri 10am-2pm and 3.30-6pm, Sat, Sun and Hols 10am-6pm; Closed 1 and 6 Jan, 25 Dec. €7, inc windmills, same hours as castle, open 10 mins earlier; 𝒫925 47 57 31, www.consuegra.es) once belonged to the Knights of St John and some of the rooms have been interpreted according to this period. In the autumn, after the local saffron crocus crop is handpicked, stripped of petals and dried, it hosts a saffron festival.

Puerto Lápice
23km/14mi SE of Consuegra along the E 5/A 4.
Puerto Lapice has retained the rambling 17C inn, **Venta del Quijote**, said to be the one that Don Quixote mistook for a castle and believed the innkeeper to be a lord. The patron, taking pity on the delusional Quixote, consequently "knighted" him. The inn holds a marvellous collection of Don Quixote mra-

▶ **Population:** 2 019 (Belmonte)
🚗 **Michelin Map:** 576 N 21 – Castilla-La Mancha (Cuenca).
🈺 **Info:** Avda. Luis Pinedo Alarcón. 𝒫967 17 00 08. www.belmonte.es.
▷ **Location:** Belmonte is 157km/98mi NW) of Madrid and on the 250km/155mi Ruta Don Quixote.
👪 **Kids:** Consuegra's windmill-dotted hillsides are straight out of a fairytale.
🕐 **Timing:** You can easily spend two or three days exploring the region.

bilia, ranging from tasteful to kitsch, and you can enjoy local food there too.

▷ Take the N420 towards Cuenca for 32km/20mi.

Campo de Criptana
Barbero 1. Windmills open daily 10am–2pm and 5-7.45pm.
𝒫926 562 231. www.tierradegigantes.es
Three of the ten windmills on the hill above the town date back to the times of Don Quixote and one, which stands next to the windmill housing the tourist office, has its original working mechanism. The walk up to the windmills gives good views over the heart of La Mancha. Below the mill, a 16C miller's house, Las Cuevas de la Paz (opening times as for the windmills; €0.60) may be visited. Alongside the highest windmill is a local collector's mass of wire models, as surreal as Don Quixote's universe.

▷ Take N420 for 2km /0.8mi towards Cuenca, left on to the CM3162 for 18km/11mi (Quintanar de la Orden).

El Tobosco
Dulcinea, Don Quixote's distant love – they saw each other only three to four times and their eyes never met – came from the small village of El Toboso.

A wealthy woman of the time, Doña Morales, who may have inspired the character of Dulcinea, lived here in a 16C farmstead which is well preserved (Museo Casa de Dulcinea; open mid-Jun–mid-Sept Tue–Sat 9.45am–1.45pm, 4–7.30pm; Sun 10am-2pm; €3; 📞925 197 288; www.eltoboso.es). Nearby, the Convento de Trinitarias has a small museum of religious art. For literary lovers of the novel, the late Gothic building which houses the Centro Cervantino (open Tue–Sun 10am–2pm, 4–7pm; €2; 📞925 568 226, www.eltoboso.es). It houses a polyglot collection of 198 editions of *Don Quixote* from around the world, plus two other books.

▷ CM 3162, then N301 for Cuenca.

Belmonte★

Belmonte's whitewashed houses are overlooked by church and castle.

Iglesia Colegial de San Bartolomé★

Open Tue–Sun 11am–2pm, 4.30–7.30pm (6.30pm Oct–Mar). Sun pm only. €2. 📞967 17 02 08.

This 15C collegiate church holds 15C–17C altarpieces. **Choir stalls★** from the cathedral in Cuenca starkly illustrate scenes from Genesis and the Passion.

Castillo de Belmonte★

Open Tue–Sun 10am–2pm year-round. Also May–mid-Sept 4.30–8.30pm, Mar–Apr 4–7pm, mid-Sept–Feb 3.30–6.30pm. Closed 1 Jan and 25 Dec. €9. 📞678 64 64 86. www.castillodebelmonte.com. Now open after years of restoration, this superb 15C fortress with six circular towers was built by the Marqués de Villena, but lay long abandoned.

The rooms are now interpreted with period furnishings and feature beautiful **Mudéjar artesonado★** ceilings – the audience chamber is outstanding – and delicately carved stone window surrounds. Follow the curtain walls to the stepped merlons for views of the village and countryside.

▷ 6km/3.7mi NE along the N 420.

Villaescusa de Haro

The magnificent 1507 **Capilla de la Asunción★** (Chapel of the Assumption) of the parish church boasts a Gothic-Renaissance altarpiece and a wrought-iron screen with florid Gothic arches (open for Mass only).

▷ Take the N420 and CM 3103 S.

Argamasilla de Alba

This quiet town is thought to be where Cervantes invented Don Quixote while he languished in prison for fraud during his brief working life as a tax collector. At the time, Don Rodrigo de Pacheco, a fantasist like Cervantes's fictional character, lived here, perhaps inspiring Cervantes. You can visit the basement prison under the tourist office (Cervantes 7; open Tue–Sat 10am–2pm, 5–8 pm/4–7pm Oct–Mar; 📞926 52 32 34; www.argamasilladealba.es), and in the Iglesia de San Juan Bautista you can see Don Rodrigo's portrait, in the chapel of the Virgen de la Caridad. The church, begun in 1542, was never finished.

▷ Take the CM3109 towards La Solana, then the CM 3127 to Villanueva.

Villanueva de los Infantes

Perhaps the most charming town on the Quixote route, Villanueva claims to be the "certain village in La Mancha, which I do not wish to name" in the famous opening sentence of Cervantes' novel. Here, it is said, the knight lived before setting out on his adventures and here he returned to die. Certainly it is where the great Spanish poet **Francisco de Quevedo** (1580–1645) came to die in the **Convento de Santo Domingo**, founded in 1526. You can see the cell inside the convent, now a historic hotel. The spacious Plaza Mayor sits to one side of the old town, a network of small streets with stone houses decorated by over 200 carved shields. The **alhóndiga**, or granary, and late Renaissance Iglesia de San Andrés stand out.

Almagro★

Set in the red earth of La Mancha, Almagro's stone-paved streets and façades with coats of arms recall the Military Order of the Knights of Calatrava. The 16C Convento de San Francisco is now a parador.

▶ **Population:** 9 074
◉ **Michelin Map:** 576 P 18 – Castilla-La Mancha (Ciudad Real).
▦ **Info:** Plaza Mayor 1. ℘926 86 07 17. www.ciudad-almagro.com.
◖ **Location:** Almagro is on the plain south of Madrid. ▭Almagro.
◕ **Don't Miss:** A walk through streets frozen in time.

A BIT OF HISTORY

The impressive architecture of this charming town, the birthplace of the explorer Diego de Almagro (1475–1538), can be explained by its eventful history. From the 13C until the end of the 15C, Almagro was the stronghold of the Military Order of the Knights of Calatrava and the base from which they administered their possessions.

Between 1750 and 1761, the town became the capital of the province as a result of the favours of the Count of Valparaíso, the then Minister of Finance under Ferdinand VI. From the 16C to the 19C, a number of religious orders established convents and monasteries here.

SIGHTS

Cobbled streets lead past whitewashed houses to convents and monasteries with elegant stone doorways.

Plaza Mayor★★

This long square, one of the most beautiful in Castile, was once the scene of bullfights and tournaments. A stone colonnade frames two sides, under two rows of windows with green surrounds. The **Corral de Comedias★** (Pl. Mayor 18; open daily, see website for times; €3 self-guided tours, €4 theatrical tours; ℘926 86 15 39, www.ciudad-almagro.com) is the only intact original 17C theatre in Europe. Wooden porticoes, oil lamps, stone well and scenery wall combine in a superb example of popular architecture. Summer performances are staged here as part of the town's annual International Festival of Classical Drama (www.festivaldealmagro.com). From near the statue of Diego de Almagro, take C/de Nuestra Señora de

las Nieves (note its fine doorways) to the left, to the triangular Plaza Santo Domingo, surrounded by mansions. Turn left into Calle de Bernardas, to face the spectacular Baroque doorway of the **Palacio de los Condes de Valparaíso**. Follow C/de Don Federico Relimpio; go left on C/de Don Diego de Almagro, dominated by the 16C **Convento de la Asunción de Calatrava** (open daily, see website for opening hours, Sun 11am– 2pm year round; €2; ℘926 69 33 32, www.ciudad-almagro.com), with its fine Renaissance staircase.

At the Plaza Mayor, turn right at the end onto C/Gran Maestre, to the **Museo Nacional del Teatro** (open Tue–Fri 10am-2pm, 4-6.30pm (5-7.30pm Jul & Aug), Sat 10.30am-2pm, 4-6.30pm (5-7.30pm Jul & Aug), Sun 10.30am–2pm year round; closed 1 Jan, 5 and 24 Aug, 24–25 and 31 Dec, and some local hols; €3, no charge Sat pm, Sun am, 27 Mar, 18 Apr, 18 May, 12 Oct, 12 Nov, 6 Dec; ℘926 26 10 14; http://museoteatro.mcu.es), in an 18C palace, showing old documents, costumes, and models of theatre sets.

EXCURSIONS

Parque Nacional de las Tablas de Daimiel

◖ 31km/19mi N by the CM 4107 and N 420. From Daimiel, take a tarmac road to the right (7km/4.5mi). Centro de Información, 9am–9pm

(8.30am–6.30pm in winter). &926 850 371. www.lastablasdedaimiel.com.

These wetlands cover 1 928ha/4 764 acres in the heart of La Mancha. The *tablas* are floodplains where marshes of the Rivers Guadiana and Cigüela provide a habitat for a huge variety of birds in winter.

Parque Natural Lagunas de Ruidera

❍ 67km/42mi NE. Centro de Información, Avda Castilla La Mancha s/n. www.lagunasderuidera.net.

This park, covering 3 772ha/9 320 acres, comprises 15 lagoons linked by streams, gullies and waterfalls, linked by a country road.

San Carlos del Valle★

❍ 46km/29mi E.

The 18C **Plaza Mayor**★is charming, with a Baroque church with four lantern turrets. The house at no. 5, a former hospice, retains a stone doorway and typical patio.

Valdepeñas

❍ 34km/21mi SE along the CM 412. ▭Paseo de la Estación.

This famous wine centre is at the southern tip of the vast grape-growing area of La Mancha. Blue- and white-coloured houses rise above shady porticoes on the spacious Plaza de España.

The late Gothic **Iglesia de la Asunción** (Church of the Assumption), has a Plateresque upper gallery.

Visit the **Museo del Vino** (C/Princesa 39; open Tue–Sat 10am–2pm, 5–8pm, Sun year-round 11am–2pm; €3; &926 32 11 11, www.museodelvinovaldepenas.es), installed in one of the town's oldest bodegas, to enjoy a flavour of the local viticulture.

Sacro Castillo y Convento de Calatrava la Nueva★

❍ 32km/19.8mi SW. 7km/4.3mi SW of Calzada de Calatrava, turn right onto a paved road (2.5km/1.5mi). Open Oct–Mar Fri-Sun 10.30am-2pm, 2-6pm. April-May Thur-Sun 10am-2pm, 4-8pm,

Jun-Aug Tue-Sun 10am-2pm, 5-7.30pm (am only Tue-Thur), Sept Thu-Sun 10.30am-2pm, 4-8pm. €4. & 926 69 31 19. www.castillodecalatrava.com.

This semi-ruined citadel occupies a magnificent **hilltop site** which dominates the route to Andalucía.

The gateway leads into vaulted stables. The second perimeter, built into rock, houses religious buildings, including the impressive **church**, lit by an immense rose window, and brick swallow's nest vaulting, probably the work of Moorish prisoners. Views from the towers include the ruined **Castillo de Salvatierra**. The cracks caused by the 1755 Lisbon earthquake are clearly visible.

Viso del Marqués★★

❍ El Viso de Marqués.

The Renaissance **Palacio de Alvaro de Bazán** (open Tue-Sun 9am-1pm, 4-6pm (Jul-Aug 9am-2pm); €3; &926 33 75 18. www.visodelmarques.es/museos) – is an imposing building, unexpectedly sited in a small village. It was the home of the Marqués de Santa Cruz, admiral to Philip II.

As you approach you can see the damage left by the 1755 Lisbon earthquake, which destroyed the palace's corner towers. Behind its austere façade are magnificent frescoes in the ground floor patio, reception rooms and monumental double staircase. Upstairs in the living rooms, also frescoed, are a collection of model boats (**Museo de la Marina**). A crocodile hangs on the wall in the entrance to the chapel where the Marqués was buried on his death in 1588, just weeks before he was due to take command of the "Invincible" Armada; he brought it back from one of his expeditions.

Close by, alongside the tourist office, a small **Museo de Ciencias Naturales** (Natural Sciences Museum; open Tue–Fri 10am–2pm, 5–7pm/4–6pm winter, Sat pm 1hr later, Sun am only, no charge; &926 33 68 15, www.visodelmarques.es/museos) houses a remarkable collection of butterflies.

Albacete

Albacete (from *Al Basite*, "plain" in Arabic), capital of the province of the same name, stands on a dry plateau that juts into the fertile east. Heritage structures are grouped with modern buildings and residential districts.

SIGHTS
Museo de Albacete

Parque Abelardo Sánchez. Open Tue–Sat 10am–2pm, 4.30–7pm, (Jul Tue–Sat 10am–2pm), Sun and public holidays 9.30am–2pm. Closed 1 Jan, Maundy Thu, Good Fri, 25 Dec. €3; no charge Wed pm, Sat pm, Sun am, 18 & 31 May. ℘967 22 83 07. www.albaceteturistico.es.
This modern building is divided into two main sections. The principal one is the archaeology museum, displaying finds from sites in the province: Iberian sculptures including the *Sphinx of Haches*, the *hind of Caudete*, the lion from Bienservida, and above all **Roman dolls with movable joints★** There is also a small Fine Arts section.

Catedral de San Juan Bautista

Pl. de la Virgen de los Llanos. Open daily 10.45am–12.45pm, 5.45–8.45pm. ℘967 63 00 04.
Construction began in the late 16C. The façade and side doorway are additions. Three naves are separated by large Ionic columns. Mannerist paintings decorate the sacristy. The Capilla de la Virgen de los Llanos is a fine chapel dedicated to the Virgin of the Plains, the city's patron. The Renaissance altarpiece is by the Maestro de Albacete. Recent restoration has returned the original colours to the 19C ceiling frescoes.

Pasaje de Lodares

This narrow conservatory passageway, lined by shops and homes, links Calle Mayor with Clle del Tinte. Its Modernist architecture, dating from 1925, is emblematic of Albacete and was inspired by Milanese decoration. Allegorical figures proliferate.

▶ **Population:** 172 121
ⓖ **Michelin Map:** 576 O-P 24 – Castilla-La Mancha (Albacete).
▤ **Info:** Plaza del Altozano. ℘967 630 004. www.turismoenalbacete.com.
◗ **Location:** The A 35 and A 30 lead to Valencia (NE) and Murcia (SE); the A 32 runs SW to Andalucía. AVE high-speed trains use the central station. 🚆Albacete (AVE).
⊘ **Don't Miss:** Pasaje de Lodares to experience old Albacete.
◷ **Timing:** A morning in town, then drive out to visit caves and castles.

EXCURSIONS
Alarcón★

◗ 103km/65mi NW.

◗ Take the A 31 to Honrubia, then turn right onto the A 3.

Alarcón, named for Alaric, its Visigothic founder, rises above a loop of the Júcar river. The 13C–14C castle is now a parador. The **location★★★** made the fortress practically impregnable. It follows a triangular plan, with a double protective enclosure.
Don Juan Manuel (1282–1348) wrote many of his cautionary tales while living there. Amid the whitewashed façades of Albacete, note the **Iglesia de Santa María** (Dr Agustín Tortosa), a Renaissance church with an elegant Plateresque doorway and a fine sculpted 16C altarpiece. On **Plaza de Don Juan Manuel** are the **ayuntamiento** (town hall), with its porticoed façade, the Iglesia de San Juan Bautista, a Herreran church, and the Casa-Palacio, adorned with splendid grilles.

Alcalá del Júcar★

▶ 60km/37.3mi NE along the CM 3218.
The road winds through steep **gorges**.
The Júcar river encircles the magnificent **site★** of the village between its castle and church overlooking a fertile plain on the bottom of the gorge, unusual for arid La Mancha. A walk through Alcalá's maze of steep alleyways reveals nooks, crannies and lookout-points at every turn. Dwellings hollowed out of rock have long corridors leading to cliffside balconies; some can be visited.

Cueva de la Vieja

▶70km/43.5mi E along the A 35, via Alpera. Opening times, call Casa de Cultura. ℘967 330 555.
www.turismoenalbacete.com.
This easily accessible cave retains clearly visible prehistoric paintings, including stylised human silhouettes hunting stags with bows and arrows, females in robes and a figure with a plumed headdress.

Almansa

▶74km/46mi E along the A 35.
🚌Plaza 1º de Mayo.
Almansa's maze of streets and lanes spreads around a limestone crag crowned by a picturebook castle.

Iglesia de la Asunción – Below the castle. The church owes its mix of styles to a remodelling. The Renaissance portal is attributed to Vandelvira.

Palacio de los Condes de Cirat (Pl. de Santa María) – The fine Mannerist-style doorway of this mansion, the **Casa Grande**, bears an escutcheon flanked by crude figures.

Castillo de Almansa – Restored 15C ramparts (open daily 23 Jun–15 Sept 10am–2pm, 6–8pm; Apr, May, Oct 10am–2pm, 5–7pm; Nov–20 Mar 10am–2pm, 4–6pm; €3. ℘967 344 771), perched along the rock ridge, command a view of the plain. Keystones in the keep (torre de homenaje) bear the coat of arms of the Marqués de Villena, once the feudal lord of the town.

Alcaraz

▶ 79km/49mi SW along the A 32.
Alcaraz, the historic capital of the sierra of the same name, stands isolated on a red clay rise. The town grew rich manufacturing carpets and retains its Renaissance character in buildings influenced by the great **Andrés de Vandelvira**, born here in 1509.

Plaza Mayor – On the main square are: the 15C Pósito, once a granary; the 16C **ayuntamiento** (town hall) with emblazoned façade; the 17C **Lonja** del Corregidor, standing against the **Torre del Tardón** (clock tower); and the 15C **Iglesia de la Santísima Trinidad**. Old houses front the **Calle Mayor**. Note a façade with the two warriors and the Plateresque **Puerta de la Aduana** (Customs Doorway) of the Casa Consistorial. Stepped alleys head from the right-hand side of the square. Guided visits to the old town, including the town's revived craft carpet work-shops, need to be reserved in advance (90 mins; €2; ℘967 380 827). The path to the cemetery passes under two arches, leading to fine views over rooftops and countryside.
From Alcaraz you can make a picturesque **excursion** 46km/28.5mi south to the **source of the River Mundo** where there are wooded valleys, springs, caves and falls.

Source of the Rio Mundo

▶ 62 km/38.5mi S of Alcaraz on the CM 412.
Where the Rio Mundo, a tributary of the Segura, emerges above ground a spectacular waterfall tumbles from a sheer wall of rock into pools below at the foot of the Sierra del Calar. The source's flow varies greatly from spring to high summer, when it is best visited early in the day before coaches arrive. From the car-park, numerous signposted footpaths lead into the surrounding countryside.

Cuenca★★

Cuenca's spectacular setting★★ is a rocky gravity-defying platform, hemmed in by the Júcar and Huécar ravines *(hoces)*. The magnificently preserved old city is on the UNESCO World Heritage List. Its beauty drew artists here in the 1960s; many left superb collections to the city.

 WALKING TOUR

CIUDAD ANTIGUA★★ (OLD TOWN)
2hr 30min.

▶ From the car park, pass through the 16C Renaissance-style Arco del Bezudo, follow San Pedro to the San Pedro church, then turn left onto ronda de Julián Romero.

Ronda Julián Romero
This delightful stepped alley runs above the Huécar gorge to the cathedral.

Convento de las Carmelitas
This ex-Carmelite convent houses the **Fundación Antonio Pérez**.

Catedral de Santa María La Mayor★
Pl. Mayor. Open Sun-Fri 10am-5pm, Sat and hols 10am-7pm. Closed 1 Jan, 25 Dec. €8 (inc. Museo Diocesano). ℘969 22 46 26. www.catedralcuenca.es
The Cathedral was started in the 13C in Norman-Gothic style. One of two towers collapsed after an early 20C fire. The interior, a mix of Gothic architecture and Renaissance decoration, has superb wrought-iron **chapel grilles★**, a twin ambulatory, a triforium and an elegant **Plateresque door★** into the chapter house with carved walnut panels by Alonso Berruguete.

▶ Walk along the right-hand side of the Cathedral and take Canónigos.

▶ **Population:** 55 428
⌕ **Michelin Map:** 576 L 23 – Castilla-La Mancha (Cuenca)
🛈 **Info:** Alfonso VIII 2. ℘969 24 10 51; Avenida Cruz Roja 1. ℘969 24 10 50. www.turismo.cuenca.es.
▶ **Location:** Cuenca lies 164km/102mi E of Madrid in the Montes Universales, on the edge of the central Meseta. AVE high-speed train services from Madrid and Valencia call at Cuenca Fernando Zóbel station on the edge of town. 🚆Cuenca (AVE).
🅿 **Parking:** Follow signs for the *casco antiguo*. Cross Plaza Mayor and leave your car in the free car park.
☺ **Don't Miss:** The "hanging houses" and the vertiginous views.

.This street is lined by the Bishops Palace, housing the **Museo Tesoro de la Catedral★** (same opening times as cathedral; €8, inc cathedral; www.catedralcuenca.es) and the **Museo de Cuenca** (⌕see Sights).

Casas Colgadas★ (Hanging Houses)
These restored 14C houses contain the **Museo de Arte Abstracto** (⌕see Sights) and a restaurant. The best **view★** of these spectacular buildings can be enjoyed from across the **Puente de San Pablo**, an iron bridge that leads to the city's parador. This panorama is enchanting when illuminated.

▶ Return to the Cathedral and head along José T Mena.

Iglesia de San Miguel
Bajada de San Miguel. Open for events and performances only.
This Gothic-style former church is one of the main venues for Cuenca's Religious Music Week.

▶ Return to the Plaza Mayor. Follow calles Severo Catalina and Pilares.

Plaza de las Angustias★

An 18C Franciscan monastery and a Baroque hermitage, the Virgin in Anguish, stand in this quiet square between the town and the ravine.

▶ Return to San Pedro and continue to the San Pedro church. Bear left into an alley which ends at the edge of the Júcar ravine, for a good view.

SIGHTS

Museo de Arte Abstracto Español★★

Casas Colgadas, Canónigos s/n. Open Tue–Fri and public holidays 11am–2pm, 4–6pm (until 8pm Sat), Sun 11am–2.30pm. See website for closing dates. ℘969 21 29 83. www.march.es/arte/cuenca.

The views from the Museum of Abstract Spanish Art are worth the visit alone. The collection, hung in a series of small plain galleries within stripped-back traditional houses, some overhanging the gorge, includes works by Chillida, Tàpies, Saura, Zóbel, Cuixart, Sempere, Rivera and Millares.

The museum grew around the friendships of the Cuenca Group formed in the 1960s among abstract artists, one of whom, Gustavo Torner, was born in Cuenca. Today it is one of the best of its kind in Spain.

Museo Provincial de Cuenca★

Obispo Valero 6. Open Tue–Sat 10am–2pm, 5–7pm (mid-Jul–mid-Sept 5–7pm), Sun and public holidays 10am–2pm. ℘969 21 30 69. www.patrimoniohistoricoclm.es.

Prehistoric objects, sculpture, coins and ceramics found in Roman excavations. Note the top of a **Roman altar★** found at Ercávica illustrating ritual items.

Fundación Antonio Peréz★

Rda Julián Romero, 20. Open Tue–Sun 11am–2pm, 5–8pm. Closed 18–21 Sep. €2. No charge Wed pm. ℘969 23 06 19. www.fundacionantonioperez.com

Casas Colgadas

Within a 17C Carmelite friary, well worth a visit in its own right, works of modern Spanish art donated by local collector Antonio Pérez hang against a plain backdrop. Large canvases by Millares and Saura, among others, sit alongside small installations.

Fundación Antonio Saura – Casa Zavala

Pl. de San Nicolás 4. Open 11am–2pm, 4–7pm (5-8pm in summer). Closed Mon and Tue in summer. €2.50. www.antonio saura.es. ℘969 23 60 54.

Among the city's quartet of outstanding contemporary art spaces, this one, within a 17C palace with views over the Júcar gorge, is used for temporary shows. On the first floor is a collection of works by artist Antonio Saura (1930–1998), who lived in the town.

Museo de las Ciencias de Castilla-La Mancha

Pl. de la Merced 1. Open year-round Tue–Sat 10am–2pm, 4–7pm, Sun 10am–2pm. Closed Mon, 1 Jan, Maundy Thu, Good Fri, 18-21 Sep, 24, 25, 31 Dec. €3; no charge Sat, Sun and and 18 & 31 May. ℘969 24 03 20. http://pagina.jccm.es/museociencias.

This lively modern science museum also has a planetarium.

EXCURSIONS
Las Hoces
(Ravines)

▷ Round tour of 15km/9.6mi.

Roads parallel to the river circling Cuenca's rock spur afford amazing views of the hanging houses. The **Hoz del Júcar** is the shorter, more enclosed ravine. The **Hoz del Huécar** course swings from side to side between gentler slopes given over to market gardening.

▷ Turn left at the end of the ravine for Buenache de la Sierra and left again for the Convento de San Jerónimo.

In a right bend, there's a **view★** of grey rock columns and, in the distance, Cuenca. Enter through the gateway.

Las Torcas★

▷ Take the N 420 then bear left after 11km/6.5mi.

The road crosses a conifer wood where the *torcas*, odd and occasionally spectacular depressions, can be seen.

🚗 DRIVING TOUR

SERRANÍA DE CUENCA★
270km/168mi. Allow 1 day.

Wind and water have formed whimsical landscapes in limestone, amid pines and numerous streams. Continuing northwards, you reach a Roman settlement and Renaissance monastery lying close to the main route from Madrid to the Mediterranean coast since Classical times.

Ventano del Diablo

▷ 25.5km/15.8mi from Cuenca along the CM 2105.

The Devil's Window, an opening in rock, overlooks the depths of the **Garganta del Júcara** (Júcar Gorges).

Ciudad Encantada★

▷ Follow the road signposted to the right of the CM 2105.

🚶 A circuit directs visitors through this Enchanted Forest, to the Tobogán (Toboggan Slope) and the Mar de Piedras (Sea of Stones). To reach the **Mirador de Uña** (2km/1mi),

▷ Take the road from the car park.

Enjoy the **view** of the Júcar Valley and Uña's green lake dominated by towering cliffs.

Los Callejones
3km/1.8mi from Las Majadas.

🚳 Leave your car on the esplanade.

This isolated spot is a maze of eroded blocks, arches and the narrow alleyways which lend their name to the area: The Alleyways.

Nacimiento del Río Cuervo★
(Source of the Cuervo)
30km/18.6mi N of Las Majadas towards **Alto de la Vega.** 🚳 Leave your car after the bridge and walk up 500m/547yd.

A footpath leads to **waterfalls★** and mossy grottoes at the beginnings of the Cuervo river.

Hoz de Beteta★
(Beteta Ravine)
30km/18.6mi NW along the CM 2106 and CM 2201 towards Beteta.

This impressive ravine was cut by the River Guadiela. From Vadillos, a road to the left leads to the spa of Solán de Cabras. The road (CM 210) continues through the **River Escabas valley.** Before reaching Priego (3km/1.8mi), a branch to the right leads to the **Convento de San Miguel de las Victorias**, in an impressive **setting★**.

▷ Take the N320 E, then turn S along the CM 2006 and CM200 to the A40, which leads you to the A3. From there follow signs to Uclés.

Uclés

The monastery here was the seat of the Order of Santiago from 1174 to 1499).

Castillo Monasterio d'Uclés

Open daily Jun–Aug 10am–8 pm, Mar–May and Sept–Oct until 7pm, Nov–Feb until 6pm. Guided tours available Sat–Sun at 11am and 12.30pm. Closed 1 & 6 Jan, 25 Dec. €4.50. ℘969 13 50 58. www.monasterioucles.com.

This massive castle-like monastery was begun in 1529 in Plateresque style. Most of the work was undertaken by Herrera's disciple, **Francisco de Mora** (1553–1610), hence its nickname, the Little Escorial. The entrance is via a beautiful **Baroque portal★★**. Note too the Baroque well and the magnificent **artesonado★** ceiling in the refectory. The ramparts command a fine view.

Parque Arqueológico de Segóbriga

In Saelices, 14km/8.7mi S of Uclés.

▶ Leave the A 3 at exit 103/104 and follow signs towards Casas de Luján.

Begin your visit at the **Centro de interpretación** (Ctra. Carrascosa de Campo a Villamayor de Santiago; open Apr–Sept Tue–Sun 10am–3pm, 4–7.30pm; Oct–Mar Tue–Sun 10am–6pm; €6; allow 2–4 hours for a visit; ℘629 75 22 57) for an overview of this 5C BC Celtiberian site which became an important Roman crossroads town. By the 1C AD, it had a theatre and an imposing **amphitheatre★**, with a capacity for 5 000 spectators. Parts of its Roman baths and walls also remain.

ADDRESSES

STAY

Posada Huécar – Pas. del Huécar 3. ℘969 21 42 01. www.posadahuecar.com. 20 rooms. Excellent value hotel in the old part of Cuenca, with a delightful garden and simply furnished rooms, all with TV. Free coffee and pastries for breakfast.

Posada San José – Rúa Julián Romero, 4. ℘969 21 13 00. www.posadasanjose.com. 22 rooms. €9. A delightful hotel within one of the old-fashioned beamed hanging houses. The large comfortable rooms and bathrooms are simply decorated. The public spaces – sitting room and cafeteria for breakfast and dinner – hang over the gorge below.

Parador – Paseo del Huéscar (road up to San Pablo). ℘902 54 79 79. www.parador.es. €18. Sitting on the far bank of the River Huécar, the parador can been seen from afar. Built within a 16C convent, it offers a superb view back over the old town and its hanging houses. The tasteful decoration includes superb old tiles in the dining room.

EAT

Mesón Mangana – Pl. Mayor 3. ℘969 22 94 51. Closed 15 Oct–15 Nov, Thu. The perfect spot for a meal when visiting the old quarter. Good home cooking and local specialities, excellent sausages, mature Manchego cheese and grilled meats. Good value set menu.

Figón del Huécar – Ronda Julián Romero 6. ℘969 24 00 62. www.figondelhuecar.es. Closed Sun even and Mon. Fine modern market cooking, featuring local flavours. The dining room offers fine views over the gorges at the back of the old hanging house.

FESTIVALS

The city's Holy Week processions enjoy a spectacular setting against the steep narrow streets of the old town. Most famous is the Procesión de las Turbas (Procession of the Crowd), which sets out around dawn (5.30–6.00am) to the sound of drumbeats through silent streets as it winds its way up to the Calvary. Around this time of year there is also a festival of holy music.

Façade of Palacio del Infantado

© Javier Larrea/age fotostock

Guadalajara

In the 14C Guadalajara ("river of stones" in Arabic) became the fief of the Mendozas. This illustrious Spanish family includes the poet Íñigo López de Mendoza, the first Marquis of Santillana (1398–1458), his son, Cardinal Pedro González de Mendoza (1428–95), and the second Duke of Infantado, who built the palace at the north entrance to the town in the 15C.

SIGHTS

Palacio del Infantado★
(Palace of the Duke of Infantado)

Pl. de los Caídos. Open: Patio Tue–Sun 9am–2pm, 4–8pm. Museo: Tue–Sat 10am–2pm, 4–7pm (mid-Jun–mid-Sept closed pm), Sun and public holidays 10am–2pm. Closed 1 & 6 Jan, Good Fri, 1 May, 8 & 11 Sept, 24 & 25 Dec. €3 (museum), no charge for patio. 𝒫949 21 33 01. www.guadalajara.es

This late 15C palace, by Juan Guas, is a masterpiece of Isabelline civil architecture fusing Gothic and Mudéjar styles. The **façade★** is adorned with diamond-studded stonework and the Mendoza coat of arms. The upper gallery is a series of paired ogee windows interposed between corbelled loggias. The effect is splendid in spite of windows added in the 17C. The two-storey **patio★** is just as remarkable with multifoil arches on turned columns and extremely delicate Mudéjar ornamenta-

▷ **Population:** 83 391

🖙 **Michelin Map:** 576 K 20 – map 121 Alrededores de Madrid – Castilla-La Mancha (Guadalajara).

🖪 **Info:** Glorieta de la Aviación Militar Española. 𝒫949 88 70 99. www.guadalajara.es.

▷ **Location:** Guadalajara is NE of Madrid along the A 2 motorway. High-speed AVE trains link to Madrid and Barcelona (station 9km/5.5mi from town centre). 🚄 Guadalajara (AVE station 9km/5.5mi from town centre).

☺ **Don't Miss:** The Palacio del Infantado.

tion. The once-sumptuous interior was damaged during the Spanish Civil War. The palace houses the **Museo Provincial de Guadalajara** with ethnographical, archaeological and arts collections.

EXCURSIONS
Pastrana

▷ 42km/26mi SE on the N 320.

This picturesque town was the seat of the **Princess of Eboli**, involved in intrigues in the time of Philip II. She was imprisoned by her husband for the last five years of her life in the palace which stands on the Plaza de la Hora, so called because she was allowed to show herself at the window for an hour a day.

The 16C **Iglesia Colegiata** (Melchor Cano 1; open daily 11.30am–2pm, 4.30–7pm (Jun–Aug 5–8pm), Sun and public holidays 1–2pm, 4.30–7pm; no charge for church; €5 for entry to crypt, church and museum; 𝒫949 37 00 27, www.pastrana.org/turismo), a collegiate church, contains, in the sacristy, four **Gothic tapestries★** woven in Tournai after cartoons by Nuno Gonçalves which illustrate the capture of Arzila and Tangier by Alfonso V of Portugal in 1471. They reveal a mastery of composition, an eye for detail (armour and costume) and talent for portraiture.

Sigüenza★

⊙ 75km/46mi NE on the E 90 N 2 then the CM-1101. 🚆Sigüenza. 🚹 Serrano Sanz 9. 🖋949 34 70 07. www.siguenza.es.
Sigüenza descends in pink and ochre tiers below a cathedral fortress and castle. The old quarter is a maze of narrow streets lined by Romanesque mansions.

Catedral★★

Serrano Sanz. Open daily 9.30am–2pm, 4.30–8pm. 🖋949 23 13 70.
www.lacatedraldesiguenza.com.
The nave, begun in the 12C, was completed in 1495. In the **north aisle**, the **doorway★** into the Capilla de la Anunciación is decorated with Renaissance pilasters, Mudéjar arabesques and Gothic cusping. In the north transept is a fine **sculptured unit★★**: a 16C porphyry doorway opens onto cloisters of marble. The **sacristy ceiling★** by Covarrubias is a profusion of heads and roses between which peer thousands of cherubim.
The chancel (presbiterio) has a beautiful 17C wrought-iron grille framed by alabaster **pulpits★**. The **Doncel tomb★★**, (open only by guided tour weekends 11am–2pm) in the south transept features a realistic figure of a youth which is a major work of sepulchral art. The **outstanding** holdings of the **Museo Diocesano** (Plaza Obispo Don Bernardo; open Wed, Thu, Sun 11am–2pm, 4–7pm; Fri & Sat until 8pm; €3; 🖋949 391 023), many drawn from small churches in the countryside around Sigüenza, include a 14C alabaster Virgin, a Pietà attributed to Morales and a Salzillo statue of the prophet Eli.

Valverde de los Arroyos★

⊙ 68km/45mi N via CM 1003 & 1006.
Around Ocejón (2 048m/6 700ft) are clustered the so-called **pueblos negros** or black slate villages. Among these, Valverde is especially attractive, its houses with long wooden balconies, and its plaza retaining the old drinking fountain. A footpath leads to the splendid **Despeñal Agua** waterfall that tumbles 100m/110ft in its fall down the rock faces.

ADDRESSES

🛏 STAY

🍽🍽 **Hotel España** – Tenient Figueroa 3, Guadalajara. 🖋949 21 13 03. www.hotel-españa.es. 40 rooms. A simple two-star hotel, this long-established favourite is close to the Plaza Mayor. Its air-conditioned rooms have flat-screen TVs and balconies, and a cafeteria offers meals and coffee throughout the day. Free Wi-Fi.

🍽🍽🍽 **Tryp Guadalajara Hotel**– Autovía A 2, km 55, Guadalajara. 🖋949 209 300. www.melia.com. 159 rooms. 🛏12. Sitting on the edge of the town, the Tryp hotel, one of a large chain, is a tall modern building with good views. The decoration is clean and modern, and the cafeteria and restaurant serve decent food.

🍽🍽🍽🍽 **Parador de Sigüenza** – El Castillo. 🖋902 54 79 79. www.parador.es. 79 rooms. 🛏18. A fine example of a historic parador, this vast hilltop castle keeps an air of sobriety as well as comfort. The inner patio, with a garden where you can relax with a drink, is very atmospheric. Secure parking.

🍽 EAT

🍽🍽 **El Mesón** – Seminario 14, Sigüenza. 🖋949 39 06 49. www.hostal elmeson.com. Regional specialities, many based on the delicious local lamb, are served in an atmospheric rustic beamed dining room. The homemade puddings are delicious.

🍽🍽🍽 **Casa Palomo** – Cuesta San Miguel 5, Guadalajara. 🖋949 23 06 32. www.casapalomo.es. A small and cosy restaurant serving up plenty of locally sourced ingredients. Seasonal wild mushrooms are a delicious speciality.

🍽🍽🍽 **Calle Mayor** – Mayor 21, Sigüenza. 🖋949 39 17 48. www.restaurantelacasa.com. Traditional and creative dishes are combined on the menu of this elegant restaurant in a historic building in the centre of old Sigüenza.

Extremadura

Much of the boundary between Spain and Portugal is formed by Extremadura, which means "beyond the River Douro". In Roman times it was at one with present-day Portugal, making up the Roman territory known as Lusitania. This was the heyday of the region, when Mérida, the home of Emperor Augustus, was its capital. Some 1 500 years later Charles V also chose to retire here, far from the cares of the world. Like La Mancha, Extremadura is dominated by the harsh, unforgiving arid climate of La Meseta. Add to this its isolation from the rest of Spain (even today it is known as "the back of beyond") and an unrewarding system of absentee landlord farming, and it is no wonder that over the centuries so many Extremadurans chose to make their fortune elsewhere. The region's most famous sons were its Conquistadores: Cortés, conqueror of Mexico; Pizarro, conqueror of Peru; Hernando de Soto, first European discoverer of the Mississippi, and many more. This is one of Spain's least densely populated regions; in many areas sheep outnumber humans while storks wheel majestically overhead and nest on tall buildings and towers. Summers are punishingly hot, while spring and autumn are exceptionally beautiful times of year.

Highlights

Medieval Majesty

Upper Extremadura has the most fertile land in the region, especially in the verdant Valle de la Vera, where crops include cotton and around 80 per cent of all Spain's tobacco. The hilltop town of Plasencia, an important market town, is a highlight. Built mostly between the 12C and 14C, its old mansions and churches retain their atmosphere and the cathedral is one of Extremadura's finest. Close by is the monastery of Yuste, the retirement home of Charles V, a haven of tranquility at the foot of the mountains. In the centre of the region, the ancient walled city of Cáceres, designated a World Heritage site, offers a feast of medieval architecture, including one of Spain's finest assemblies of Gothic and Renaissance mansions.

Conquistador Towns

Guadalupe is famous for its Mudéjar monastery, the second most important Marian shrine in the country, home to the venerated effigy of the Virgin of Guadalupe. The cult of the Virgin and the village's name was exported by the Conquistadores and is widespread throughout Latin America. Trujillo is a charming small town, redolent of Conquistador wealth with mansions built from the riches accumulated by Pizarro (his four half brothers, also from Trujillo), de Orellana and other adventurers.

Small cities and towns in the south have kept extraordinary architecture and art. Mérida was the headquarters of Western Roman Iberia and retains many important monuments including the Roman Theatre, where plays are staged each summer. Olivenza, close to the Portuguese border, keeps the imprint of its Manueline architecture in quiet plazas. Its 15C castle is now a sumptuous parador. Stay the night here and you will be following in the footsteps of Hernán Cortés, who lodged in the castle before setting off for the New World. In fact Extremadura also boasts historic paradores at Plasencia, Trujillo, Guadalupe and Cáceres; stay at any of these and you will really feel part of the region's rich history.

Plasencia★

In this tranquil provincial town are interesting Renaissance buildings such as the New Cathedral. Between February and July migrating storks nest on rooftops and towers.

BARRIO VIEJO (OLD QUARTER)

Houses with wrought-iron balconies make up the neighbourhood.

Catedral★

Pl. de la Catedral. Open Apr–Sept Tue–Sun 11am–2pm, 5–8pm (Oct–Mar 4–7pm). €4 (Old Cathedral). ✆927 42 44 06. www.catedralesdeplasencia.org

Enter by the north door which has rich Plateresque decoration. A door left of the **coro** opens into the 13-14C **Old Cathedral** (parish church of Santa María). The cloisters have pointed arches and Romanesque capitals while the chapter house is covered by a fine dome. In the shortened nave is a museum of religious art.

Inside the 15C **Catedral Nueva** (New Cathedral), the tall pillars and slender ribs illustrate the mastery of architects Juan de Java, Diego de Siloé and Alonso de Covarrubias. The **altarpiece★** is decorated with statues by the 17C sculptor Gregorio Fernández; the **choir stalls★** were carved in 1520 by Rodrigo Alemán. Start from Plaza de la Catedral and leaving on your right the **Casa del Deán** (Deanery) with its unusual corner window, and the **Casa del Dr Trujillo**, now the Law Courts (Palacio de Justicia), head towards the Gothic **Iglesia de San Nicolás**, a church which faces the beautiful façade of the **Casa de las Dos Torres** (House with Two Towers). Continue to the **Palacio Mirabel** (open by appt only; ✆927410701). Flanked by a massive tower, it contains a two-tiered patio and the Museo de Caza (Hunting Museum). A passage beneath the palace (door on right-hand side) leads to **Calle Sancho Polo** and a quarter near the ramparts of stepped alleys, white-walled houses and washing hanging

from the windows. Turn right for **Plaza Mayor**, surrounded by porticoes and full of busy cafés.

EXCURSIONS

Monasterio de Yuste★

▶ 1.8km/1mi from Cuacos de Yuste. Open Tue–Sun 10am–8pm (until 6pm Oct–Mar). €7. No charge for EU citzens Wed–Thu last 3 hrs, for all 18 May and 12 Oct. ✆927 17 28 58. www.patrimonionacional.es.

In 1556, a weary Emperor **Charles V** retired to this modest Hieronymite monastery in a serene mountain setting. The monastery, devastated during the War of Independence, is partially restored. Of Charles V's small palace, the dining hall, the royal bedroom adjoining the chapel, the Gothic church and, two fine cloisters – one Gothic, the other Plateresque – remain. Leave time to wander down to Cuacos de Yuste, the picturesque village below the monastery where Charles V's illegitimate son, Don Juan of Austria, grew up.

Coria★

▶ 42km/26mi W.

▶ Take the N 630 S. After 7km/4.3mi turn right onto the EX 108.

This atmospheric town, overlooking the Alagón Valley, retains Roman walls and gateways, rebuilt in the Middle Ages. Walk through its old streets to reach the cathedral.

River Tajo running through
Parque Nacional de Monfragüe

© Juan Carlos Cantero/age fotostock

Catedral de la Asunción de Nuestra Señora★

Plaza de la Catedral. Open Mon–Sat Jun–Sept 10am–2pm, 5–7.30pm (Oct–May 4–6.30pm). €2 (museum).
℘927 50 39 60.

The Gothic cathedral, embellished with elegant Plateresque decoration in the 16C, is crowned with a Baroque tower and has a sculptured frieze.

The tall single aisle has vaulting adorned with lierne and tierceron ribs typical of the region. Note the 18C altarpiece and, in the *coro*, the wrought-iron grilles and the Gothic choir stalls. Within the cathedral is a museum of religious art, much drawn from other churches in the area, with some fine pieces.

Parque Nacional de Monfragüe

The National Park of Monfragüe, lying southeast of Plasencia, protects 500sq km/19 sq mi of rolling hill country around the dammed valleys of the River Tagus and Tiétar.

The Mediterranean scrub and woodland here, unbroken by large towns or farmland, has become a refuge for wildlife; rare birds can be seen here, albeit at a distance, from the road or lookout points, with remarkable ease. The entry point to the park, is **Villarreal de San Carlos**, where there are two information centres: one explains the park's ecosystems, and the other its fauna (Centro de Información, Villareal de San Carlos, off the EX208 from Plasencia; open 9.30am (from 9am Sat & Sun) –7.30pm, 6pm Sept–Mar; ℘927 19 91 34; www.magrama.gob.es/es/red-parques-nacionales). The little town offers simple accommodation and eating places and is the starting point of hiking and driving routes.

One road (12km/7.5mi) leads to the lake formed by the dam, which overlooks farmland outside the park; here fighting bulls and black pigs graze under holm-oaks. A second (8km/5mi) leads through the hills, past a lookout point to the Salto del Gitano (Gypsy's Leap), a peak where imperial eagles, black storks and kites breed. Shortly afterwards you can park and climb Monfragüe fortress, which gives a splendid 360° view from the top. Some of the other wildlife in the park, such as its Iberian lynx, are difficult to see, but driving slowly through its roads often surprises red deer and wild boar.

ADDRESSES

🛏 STAY

🍽 **Casa Rural Al-Mofrag** – Villareal de San Carlos, 19. ℘927 199 205. www.casaruralalmofrag.com. 6 rooms. Simple but comfortable rural accommodation, with a kitchen available, designed for ramblers. Room with jacuzzi available.

🍽🍽🍽🍽 **Parador de Jarandilla de la Vera** – Avda de García Prieto 1, Jarandilla de la Vera, Cáceres. ℘902 54 79 79. www.parador.es. 52 rooms. ⊆18. This beautiful rural parador is housed inside a modest 15C castle, entered through a long courtyard. It offers tranquil gardens, nearby mountain walks and is an ideal summer base for exploring the Plasencia area.

🍴 EAT

🍽 **La Pitarra del Gordo** – Pl Mayor, 8. Plasencia ℘927 41 45 05. A handy stopping-off point for tapas or lunch of various raciones, this popular lively traditional city-centre bar serves excellent charcuterie, including ham, and the rough red *pitarra* wine made from local grapes.

Cáceres★★★

The Almohad walls of this World Heritage Site, a provincial capital, enclose a rare ensemble of superbly preserved Gothic and Renaissance noble houses.

THE CITY TODAY

Cáceres was a thriving commercial site as far back as 25 BC under Roman rule and retains a heady mix of Roman, Moorish, Sephardic and Renaissance architecture enclosed by its medieval walls.

▰▰ WALKING TOUR

CÁCERES VIEJO★★★
(OLD CÁCERES)
1hr30min.

Within Moorish walls lies a group of Gothic and Renaissance mansions beyond compare in Spain. The shields on the unadorned, ochre façades of the 15C and 16C reflect their owners, the Ulloas, the Ovandos and the Saavedras, who in battles won prestige, not wealth. The fortified towers of Cáceres were demolished on the command of Queen Isabel in 1477. Pass beneath the **Arco de la Estrella** (Star Arch; Pl. Mayor), which was built into the wall by Manuel Churriguera in the 18C.

Plaza de Santa María★

On all sides are golden ochre façades. The front of the **Palacio Mayoralgo** (Mayoralgo Palace; closed to the public) has elegant paired windows while the **Palacio Episcopal** (Bishop's Palace; free access is available to the patio portico) has a 16C bossed doorway with medallions of the Old and New Worlds on either side.

Iglesia Concatedral de Santa María

Pl. Santa María. Open Mon–Sat 10am–2pm, 6-9pm (5-8pm Oct-Apr). €1 (€2 with belltower). ✆927 21 53 13.

▶ **Population:** 95 617
🖰 **Michelin Map:** 576 N 10 (town plan) – Extremadura (Cáceres).
🗊 **Info:** Plaza de Santa Clara. ✆927 111 222. www.turismocaceres.org.
◖ **Location:** Cáceres is strategically situated at the heart of Extremadura in west-central Spain. ▰▰▰Cáceres (AVE planned 2014).
◉ **Don't Miss:** The city walls and mansions, especially at night.
◷ **Timing:** Allow a half-day in Cáceres, then explore the region.

This 16C church has three Gothic aisles of almost equal height, with lierne and tierceron vaulting from which ribs descend into slender columns engaged in the main pillars. The fine carved high altar retable (16C) is difficult to see.

◖ Continue to the top of Calle de las Tiendas.

Palacio de Carvajal

Amargura . Open Mon–Fri 8am–8.45pm, Sat 10am–1.45pm, 5–7.45pm, Sun and public hols 10am–1.45pm. No charge. ✆927 25 55 97.
Built between the 15C and 16C, blending Gothic and Renaissance styles, this palace, flanked by a medieval tower, houses an information centre sketching out what you can see in Cáceres province. Of special interest is the architectural model of Cáceres old town.

◖ Take the narrow alley opposite, Adarve Obispo Álvarez de Castro.

Palacio Toledo Moctezuma

This 14–16C palace is now the city's history archive. Its curious name derives from the marriage of conquistador Juan

altarpiece and side chapels with tombs with decorative heraldic motifs.

In the Calle Orellana the 15C **Torre de la Plata** (Silver Tower) and **Casa del Sol** (Sun House, for the Solís family crest over the arch) have unusual parapets.

▷ Walk back to Plaza San.

Palacio de las Cigüeñas

Plaza de San Mateo. Open Sat–Sun & hols 11am–1pm.
The House of the Storks retains the town's only 15C battlemented tower.

▷ Turn left towards Plaza de las Veletas.

Casa de las Veletas

Pl. de las Veletas s/n. Open mid-Apr–Sept Tue–Sat 9am–3pm, 5–8.15pm; Oct–mid-Apr Tue–Sat 9am–3pm, 4–7.15pm. Sun and public holidays year-round 10.15am–3pm. €1.20.
☏927 01 08 77.
This 18C mansion is now home to the **Museo de Cáceres**. Collections include Bronze Age steles, Celt-Iberian statues of wild boar *(verracos)* and local dress and crafts. Its original 11C *aljibe* (cistern) is still fed from the roof and sloping square. It is covered by five rows of horseshoe-shaped arches supported by granite capitals.

▷ Take Calle Ancha opposite Iglesia San Mateo.

Casa del Comendador de Alcuéscar *Ancha 6.*

This palace, also called the **Palacio de Torreorgaz**, with a fine Gothic tower, delicate window surrounds and an unusual corner balcony, now houses the city's Parador.
Down the alley within the ramparts is the **Palacio de los Golfines de Arriba** (⊙see above). Further on, on C/Santa Ana, the **Casa de la General★** is now home to the law school.

Cano de Saavedra with the daughter of Aztec king Moctezuma II.

▷ Return to Plaza Sta María.

Palacio de los Golfines de Abajo★ (Lower Golfines Palace)

Pl. de Santa María.
⊶Closed to the public.
This splendid late 15C Gothic-Plateresque mansion is of stone. The paired window derives from the Moorish *ajimez;* the fillet, delicately framing the windows and door, recalls the *alfiz.* A Plateresque frieze with winged griffons was added in the 16C.

▷ Plaza San Jorge is adjacent to Plaza Sta María.

Plaza San Jorge

Note the austere 18C façade of the Jesuit church of **San Francisco Javier**.

▷ Take Cuesta de la Compañía to Pl. San Mateo.

Iglesia de San Mateo

Plaza de San Mateo. Open for Mass.
The church's high Gothic nave, begun in the 14C, abuts a 16C *coro alto* set on a vaulted arcade. Inside are a Baroque

▶ Go through the ramparts opposite.

The steps to Plaza Mayor del General Mola afford a fine view of the walls.

ADDITIONAL SIGHTS

Iglesia de Santiago (St James' Church)

Pl. de Santiago. No charge.

The Romanesque church is the birthplace of the Military Order of the Knights of Cáceres who in turn founded the Order of the Knights of St James. The altarpiece by Berruguete (1557) bears scenes from the Life of Christ. These surround a vigorous, finely portrayed St James the Moorslayer.

The **Palacio de Godoy** opposite has an impressive coat of arms on the corner and a fine inner patio.

EXCURSIONS

Santuario de la Virgen de la Montaña

▶ Sierra de la Mosca. 3km/1.8mi E. Open daily 8.30am–2pm, 4–8pm (9pm in summer). Closed 22 Apr 1st Sun in May. ℘927 22 00 49.

In this 17C Baroque shrine, in a lovely setting among olive trees, is a statuette of the Virgin (a *romería*, or pilgrimage, is held the first Sunday in May). The esplanade offers a **view★** of the plateau.

Museo Vostell-Malpartida

▶ 18km/11mi E. Follow the N 521 to Malpartida de Cáceres, then signposts. Open late Mar–late Sept Tue–Sun 9.30am–1.30pm, 5–8pm (late Sept–late Mar 4–6.30pm. Closed 1, 6 Jan; 17 Feb; 24,–25 & 31 Dec. €2.50, no charge Wed. ℘927 01 08 12.

http://museovostell.gobex.es.

Set in an 18C wool-washing plant this museum was created by Hispano-German artist Wolf Vostell, co-founder of the 1960s art movement Fluxus. It includes late 20C works by Canogar, the Crónica team, Saura and Brecht.

Arroyo de la Luz

▶ 20km/12.4mi W along the N 521 and C 523.

To find the **Iglesia de la Asunción**, head for the tower. The 16C altarpiece has 16 **painted tablets★** and four medallions by **Morales the Divine**, a stunning assemblage of his works in one place. The tourist office (Plaza de la Constitución, open Wed–Sat 9.30am–2pm, 4.30–8pm; Sun 10am–2pm; ℘927 270 437), directly opposite, opens the church for visitors.

Alcántara

▶ 65km/40mi NW via the N 521 and C 523. Alcántara is famed for its Roman bridge from which it took its ancient name (*Al Kantara* in Arabic).

Puente Romano★

▶ 2km/1.2mi NW on the road to Portugal. This magnificent bridge (106 AD), of massive unmortared granite blocks, has withstood formidable floodwaters. Note the small temple at one end and the central triumphal arch.

Convento de San Benito

Regimiento de Argel. Guided tours. Call for times. No charge. ℘927 39 00 81.

The old headquarters of the Military Order of Alcántara stands high above the Tajo. The 16C monastery has a Plateresque church with star vaulting, a Gothic patio and a well-restored refectory. The graceful Renaissance amphitheatre is used as the backdrop for plays.

ADDRESSES

⌂ STAY AND ¶/EAT

⌂⌂⌂⌂ **Atrio** – Av de España 30 (pasaje) ℘927 24 29 28. www.restauranteatrio.com. Closed last 2 weeks of Jul, Sun pm, Mon. A gourmet place of pilgrimage where chef-proprietor Toño Pérez has slowly created a unique repertoire updating regional flavours and produce in creative modern dishes. The wine cellars are astonishing in range and quality. Rooms are also available.

Trujillo★★

Modern Trujillo conceals the charm of its Old Town, set on a granite ledge above. It was hastily fortified by the Moors in the 13C, and embellished over centuries with mansions built by those who had made their fortunes in the Americas.

A BIT OF HISTORY

Cradle of the Conquistadores – **Francisco de Orellana** left here in 1542 to explore the country of the Amazons. Native son **Francisco Pizarro** (c. 1475–1541) plundered the riches of the Inca Emperor Atahualpa and was murdered amid untold riches in his own palace.

SIGHTS

OLD QUARTER

Trujillo's mansions, built later in the 16C and 17C, decorated with arcades, loggias and corner windows, form changing compositions along steep alleys.

One of the most beautiful squares in Spain, the **Plaza Mayor★★** is irregular, lined by mansions, its levels linked by wide flights of steps. By night, it is positively theatrical. The 16C **Iglesia de San Martín** (open daily 10am–2pm, 4–6.30pm; €1.40) encloses a vast nave chequered with funerary paving stones. The 17C **Palacio de los Duques de San Carlos★** (Palace of the Dukes of Saint Charles) is now a convent. The granite façade, decorated in Classical Baroque style, has a corner window topped by a crest with a double-headed eagle, and with chimneys on top inspired by American cultures. Calle Sillería leads away from the southeastern corner of the square. A Renaissance loggia, the **Palacio de los Marquess de Piedras Albas** (Palace of the Marquises of Piedras Albas) has been accommodated into the original Gothic wall. On the other side of the square stands the **Palacio de los Marqueses de la Conquista** (Palace of the Marquises of the Conquest), in reality the palace of Hernando Pizarro, the conquistador's brother. To the left of a Plateresque corner **window★**, added in

▶ **Population:** 9 510
🌡 **Michelin Map:** 576 N 12 – Extremadura (Cáceres).
🚹 **Info:** Plaza Mayor. ℘927 32 26 77. www.turismotrujillo.com.
◗ **Location:** Trujillo is situated on the A 5 linking Madrid and Badajoz. 🚈Nearest station: Cáceres (46km).
☺ **Don't Miss:** The Plaza Mayor and Old Town alleyways.

the 17C, are busts of Francisco Pizarro and his wife; on the right are Hernando and his niece, whom he married. Other buildings on the plaza include the Old Town Hall, now the town's law courts, fronted by Renaissance arcades and the Casa de las Cadenas (House of Chains), where Christians freed from the Moors traditionally left their chains, with a tower including a Mudéjar belfry, a favourite spot for storks.

Sometimes used as a venue for council meetings in the Middle Ages is the **Iglesia de Santiago** (open daily 9am–2pm, 5–8pm; €1.40). The church's 13C Romanesque belfry and the tower of the Palacio de los Chaves frame the Arco de Santiago (St James Arch), one of Trujillo's seven gates.

Trujillo's pantheon is the 13C **Iglesia de Santa María la Mayor★** (Pl. de Santa María; open daily 10am–2pm, 5–8pm (Nov–Mar 4.30–7.30pm); €1.40; ℘927 32 26 77). The panels of the **Gothic retable★** are by Fernando Gallego. From the top of the belfry there is a delightful **view** of brown tile roofs, the Plaza Mayor arcades and the castle. The **Castillo de Trujillo** (Cerro Cabeza de Zorro; open daily 10am–2pm, 5–8pm (Oct–May 4–7pm); €1.50; ℘927 322 677) stands out on a granite ledge, its massive crenellated wall reinforced by heavy towers. Above the keep is the patron of Trujillo, Our Lady of Victory. There are fine views from the walls.

Guadalupe★★

Guadalupe's monastery bristles with battlements and turrets above a picturesque village with brown tile roofs. Richly endowed by rulers and deeply venerated by the people, the "miraculous" Virgin of Guadalupe, in the monastery's church, made this a great place of pilgrimage during the 16C and 17C. Ferdinand and Isabelle received Christopher Columbus here and the first American Indians were brought to the church for baptism. Today the Virgin remains a symbol of Hispanidad, the community of Spanish cultures in the Old and New Worlds. The road above the old village★ commands a fine view★ onto a magical setting.

- ▶ **Population:** 2 013
- ⚲ **Michelin Map:** 576 N 14 – Extremadura (Cáceres).
- ▯ **Info:** Plaza Santa María de Guadalupe. ℘675 28 69 87. http://oficinadeturismo guadalupe.blogspot.co.uk.
- ◖ **Location:** Guadalupe is SW of Madrid, on the slopes of the Guadalupe range. 🚂Nearest station: Mérida (127km).
- ☺ **Don't Miss:** The monastery, and processions to celebrate the Día de Hispanidad (2 Oct).

SIGHTS
MONASTERIO★★

Guided tours (1hr) daily 9.30am–1pm 3.20–6pm. €5. Entrance includes museums. ℘927 36 70 00. www.monasterioguadalupe.com.
The monastery complex dates from the late 14C–early 15C, but there are numerous additions within the fortified perimeter. The monastery contains many artistic treasures, several of which reflect the Hieronymite monks' craftsmanship tradition in embroidery, gold, silversmithing and illumination.

Façade
Golden in colour, exuberant in its Flamboyant Gothic decoration, the 15C façade overlooks a picturesque square. Moorish influence can be seen in the sinuous decoration. Bronze reliefs on the 15C doors illustrate the Lives of the Virgin and Christ.

Iglesia (Church)
14C. One of the first buildings, the church received 18C additions. An intricate 16C grille by Valladolid ironsmiths closes the sanctuary, which has a large Classically ordered 17C retable by Giraldo de Merlo and Jorge Manuel Theotocopuli, son of El Greco. The Virgin of Guadalupe in the altarpiece (1) can be seen more clearly from the **camarín★**.

Camarín★
This 18C chapel-like room is where the Virgin of Guadalupe rests. Riches of every description abound: jasper, gilded stucco and marble and precious wood marquetry frames for nine canvases

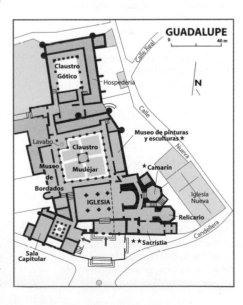

Camarín, Monasterio de Guadalupe

by Luca Giordano. The Virgin sits on an enamelwork throne (1953), a small 12C figure carved in darkened oak, obscured beneath embroidered veil and mantle.

Sala Capitular (Chapter House)
The chapter house contains a remarkable collection of 87 antiphonaries and books of hours with **miniatures★** by the monks of Guadalupe.

Claustro Mudéjar
The 14C–15C cloisters are remarkable for their size and the two storeys of horseshoe arches. Note a small Mudéjar Gothic temple and, in a corner, a lavabo faced with multicoloured tiles.

Sacristía★★ (Sacristy)
Canvases by Carreño de Miranda hang in the antechamber. The 17C sacristy combines Classical architecture and ornate Baroque decoration. The unexpected harmony and rich colouring set off **paintings by Zurbarán★★** to perfection. The 11 canvases, painted in a serene yet forceful style between 1638 and 1647, are of Hieronymite monks and scenes from the Life of St Jerome which include *The Temptation*.

Relicario (Reliquary Cabinet)
This contains the Virgin of Guadalupe's processional mantles and crown.

Claustro Gótico (Gothic Cloisters)
In the *hospedería* (hostelry). The cloisters were built in the 16C in Flamboyant Gothic style to serve as a dispensary for the monastery's four hospitals.

Museo de Bordados (Embroidery Museum)
The museum, in the former refectory, displays a fine collection of copes and **altarfronts★★**, embroidered by the monks between the 15C and the 19C. The richness of their work and artistry are exceptional.

Museo de Pinturas y Esculturas★ (Painting and Sculpture Museum)
Works include a 16C triptych of the *Adoration of the Magi* by Isembrandt, an ivory Christ attributed to Michelangelo, an *Ecce Homo* by Pedro de Mena, eight superb small canvases of the monks by **Zurbarán**, and **Goya**'s *Prison Confession*.

EXCURSION
Puerto de San Vicente (San Vicente Pass)
▶ 40km/25mi E on the C 401.
The **road★** to the pass crosses the Las Villuercas range. The climb (8km/5mi) beyond the Guadarranque Valley affords wonderful **views★** of jagged green mountain ranges above the wild moorland.

ADDRESSES

🏨 STAY
Hospedería del Real Monasterio – Pl. Juan Carlos I. ☏927 36 70 00. www.hospederiaguadalupe.com. 47 rooms. ☲ €7.50. Restaurant. Closed 15 Jan–15 Feb. The hotel's superb setting, around the monastery's Gothic cloisters, and its comfortable, quiet rooms ensure a memorable stay. Excellent value for money plus a good restaurant. Highly recommended.

Parador de Guadalupe – Marqués de la Romana, 12. ☏902 54 79 79. www.parador.es. 41 rooms. ☲ €16. An exquisite parador occupying the old monastery hospital, once famed as a school of humanities and medicine. The cloister is planted with lemon trees, there is a lovely garden and swimming pool. The charming bedrooms have been designed and furnished to retain the buildings' ancient atmosphere. The restaurant serves local traditional cuisine.

Badajoz

Once an Arab fortress, Badajoz crowns a hill along the Guadiana river and the border with Portugal. Much of the old city was destroyed during the Spanish Civil War, but original walls, a fortress and ramparts, the 16C Puente Royal bridge, Mudéjar houses and a fine gateway are reminders of the past.

▶ **Population:** 149 892

  Michelin Map: 576 P 9 (town plan) – Extremadura (Badajoz).

Info: Paseo de San Juan. ℮924 22 49 81. www.turismobadajoz.es.

▶ **Location:** The A 5 links with Mérida (62km/39mi W), the EX 100 connects the town with Cáceres (91km/57mi NE). 🚆Badajoz (AVE planned 2014).

A BIT OF HISTORY

In the 11C Badajoz became capital of a Moorish kingdom. Because of its frontier location, however, it was besieged and pillaged in the Wars of the 16C.

SIGHTS

The 13C **Gothic Catedral de San Bautista** was considerably remodelled during the Renaissance (Pl. de España; museum open Tue–Sat 11am–1pm, 6–8pm (Sep-Jun 5–7pm); €1 museum; ℮924 22 49 81, www.aytobadajoz.es). Its tower boasts delicate Plateresque friezes and window surrounds. The impressive *coro* has 16C stalls and the sacristy holds fine 17C Flemish tapestries. The cathedral museum has canvases by Luis de Morales.

The **Museo Arqueológico Provincial** is a modern museum in the 16C **Palacio de la Roca** in the alcazaba (Pl. de José Álvarez y Sáenz de Buruaga; open Tue–Sat 9am–3pm; closed 1 & 6 Jan, 24 & 31 Dec; no charge; ℮924 00 19 08, www.aytobadajoz.es). It displays prehistoric and protohistoric steles and figurines; Roman mosaics and bronze tools; Visigothic pilasters carved with plant and geometric motifs; medieval artefacts; and Islamic pieces. Unique are the finds from Cancho Ruano, the only excavated Tartessan site in Spain.

The **Museo de Bellas Artes**, in two elegant 19C mansions holds a collection of 19C and 20C paintings, sculpture and sketches, (Duque de San Germán 13; open Tue–Sun 10am–2pm, Tue–Fri 5-7pm (6–8pm Jun–Aug); closed public holidays; no charge; ℮924 21 24 69; muba.badajoz.es). The contemporary art **Museo Extremeño e Iberoamericano de Arte Contemporáneo**, set inside the town's old prison, displays cutting-edge exhibits (open Tue–Sat 9.30am–1.30pm, 4–8pm, Sun 9.30am–1.30pm; closed all hols; no charge; ℮924 01 30 60; www.meiac.es).

EXCURSIONS

Olivenza

▶ 25km/15.5mi SW.

Olivenza's Portuguese influence shows in its graceful white-walled town centre, set in olive groves, not least in its early 16C Manueline style of architecture, late Gothic, with Renaissance and Moorish elements and maritime motifs. Don't miss the **Iglesia de Santa María Magdalena★★** and the ayuntamiento (town hall).

Albuquerque★

▶ 49km/30mi N of Badajoz on EX110.

Albuquerque, close to the Portuguese frontier, boasts the well-preserved 13C Castillo de los Duques de Alburquerque (www.cuellar.es) standing on a rocky promontory. Guided visits include the terrace with its water cistern, dungeon, living quarters and tower, from the top of which you can look over to Portugal. You can also wander around the medieval quarter that lies below its walls.

Mérida★

This historic town in Extremadura, was the capital of Roman Lusitania and retains an extraordinary series of classical monuments that have earned it World Heritage status. Today it is Extremadura's regional capital.

- **Population:** 58 971
- **Michelin Map:** 576 P 10 – Extremadura (Badajoz).
- **Info:** Paseo José Álvarez Saénz de Buruaga. ℘924 33 07 22. www.turismomerida.org. A combined entrance ticket (€15), on sale at all the city's major monuments, allows entry to the theatre, amphitheatre, Roman houses, Alcazaba etc...
- **Location:** Mérida is close to the A 5 highway to Portugal. 🚆Mérida (AVE planned 2014).
- **Don't Miss:** The main Roman sites and museum.

ROMAN MÉRIDA★★

In 25 BC, the Romans founded **Emerita Augusta** on the River Guadiana and at the junction of major Roman roads. They lavished upon it temples, a theatre, an amphitheatre and even a circus.

Museo Nacional de Arte Romano★★ (National Museum of Roman Art)

José Ramón Mélida. Open Tue–Sat 9.30am–8pm (Oct–Mar 6.30pm); Sun & hols year-round 10am–3pm. Closed 1 Jan, 1 May, 24–25 & 31 Dec. €3. No charge Sat pm, Sun am, 18 Apr, 18 May, 12 Oct, 6 Dec. ℘924 31 16 90. http://museoarteromano.mcu.es.

An imposing brick **building★** by Rafael Moneo Vallés, reminiscent of a Roman amphitheatre, displays Mérida's rich archaeological collections. Sculptures include the head of Augustus (at the end of the second bay). In the last bay are statues, caryatids and giant medallions (Medusa and Jupiter) which made up the frieze of Mérida's forum. Wonderful **mosaics★** may be viewed up close. In the basement are remains of Roman villas and tombs.

Teatro Romano★★ (Roman Theatre)

Av. de los Estudiantes. Open daily Apr–Sept 9am–9pm. Oct–Mar 9am–6.30pm. €12 (combi-ticket). ℘924 31 25 30. www.turismomerida.org.

The theatre, built by Agrippa in 24 BC, seated 6 000. A high stage wall was decorated in Hadrian's reign (2C AD) with colonnade and statues. Great granite blocks over the passages are skilfully secured without mortar.

Anfiteatro★ (Amphitheatre)

Pl. José Álvarez Saenz de Buruega. Open same hours/ticket as Roman Theatre.

This 1C BC arena once held 14 000 spectators. It staged chariot races and was flooded for mock sea battles.

Original steps remain and a few tiers are reconstructed. A wall crowned by a cornice protected the noble spectators from wild beasts during gladiatorial combats.

Casa Romana del Anfiteatro (Roman Villa)

Adjacent to Amphitheatre. Closed for excavations. ℘924 31 20 24.

Water channels, pavement foundations and mosaics remain in this large villa.

Casa del Mitreo

Oviedo. Open daily 9.30am–2pm, 4–6.30pm (Apr-Sep 9am-9pm); €6.

The patios of this 1C villa served to distribute light and collect rainwater. Visible remains include the **Cosmological Mosaic★**.

Templo de Diana

Santa Catalina. No charge.

Corinthian columns and fluted shafts of this temple are visible. Its stones were used in the 16C to build the palace of the Count of Corbos. Two Roman bridges still span the Albarregas and Guadiana. Polychrome arches remain from two aqueducts.

Alcazaba

Graciano. Open same hours/ticket as Roman Theatre. ☎924 00 49 09.

The Moors built this fortress in the 9C to defend the 792m/866yd Puente Romano★ (Roman Bridge) across the Guadiana. Inside the walls is a cistern.

Zona Arqueológica de Morería★

Po. de Roma. Open daily 9.30am–2pm, 4–6.30pm (5–7.30pm Apr–Sep). €15 (combi-ticket). ☎924 00 49 08.

The riverside Morería archaeological site includes finds from Classical to modern times, ranging from sections of Roman wall to 15C–17C craftsmen's workshops.

Cripta de la Basílica de Santa Eulalia★

Av. de Extremadura 15. Open same hours/ticket as Zona Arqueológica.

The site has been occupied in turn by a palaeo-Christian necropolis, a 5C basilica and this 13C Romanesque church. (The main basilica is only open during hours of worship).

EXCURSIONS

Zafra

◖ SW of Madrid 27m/4.3mi W of the N 630.

The town's 15C alcázar (now home to a parador) guards this white-walled town, one of the oldest in Extremadura. It was built by the Dukes of Feria with nine round towers, a white marble Renaissance patio and delightful gilded salon. The large 18C Plaza Grande★ and the adjoining smaller 16C Plaza Chica★ are lined by fine arcaded houses. The 16C transitional Gothic-Renaissance Iglesia de la Candelaria (Rotonda de la Candelaria) has a massive red-brick belfry. In the south transept is an altarpiece by Zurbarán painted in 1644.

Llerena

◖ 42km/26mi from Zafra SE along the N 432.

The Plaza Mayor of this country town is one of the most harmonious in Extremadura. The composite façade of the Iglesia de Nuestra Señora de la Granada (Church of Our Lady of Granada; Pl. San Juan) built of white limestone and brick has superimposed arcades which contrast with the mass of a great Baroque belfry.

Jerez de los Caballeros

◖ 42km/26mi SW along the EX 101 and EX 112.

Jerez de los Caballeros is the birthplace of Vasco Núñez de Balboa (1475–1519), who crossed Panama and in 1513 discovered the Pacific Ocean. The town's name stems from the Knights Templar – Caballeros del Temple – to whom the town was given in 1230 by Alfonso IX of León on its recapture from the Moors. Jerez stands on a hillside and its steep lanes lined by white-walled houses are a foretaste of Andalucía. Today it is a centre of ham-making, hosting a world congress every year, and the aroma of ham hangs in the streets and surrounding hillsides where black-footed pigs snuffle.

ADDRESSES

Atlantic Spain

Las Médulas, El Camino de Santiago
© José Antonio Morenoblaye Infostock

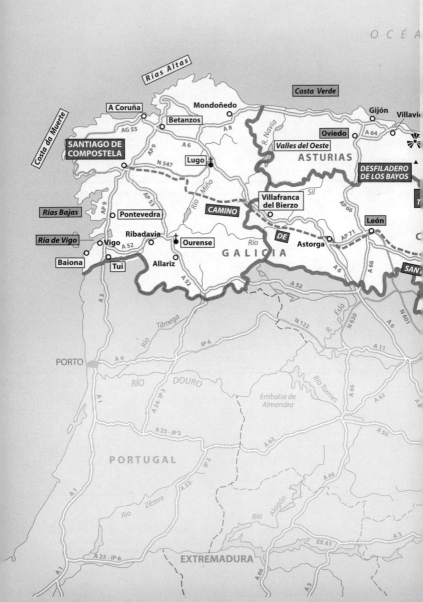

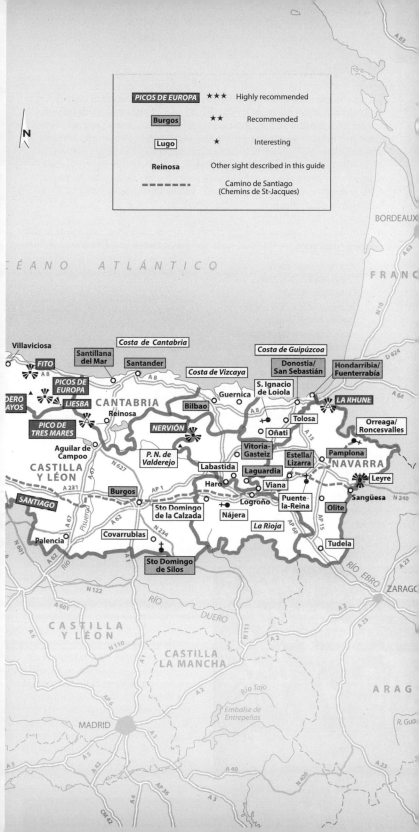

Navarra

Probably the most geographically diverse of the peninsula's northern regions, Navarra (Navarre) forms part of Spain's northeastern frontier. It sweeps from the lush and mountainous belt facing France to a semi-arid desert in the south. In the Middle Ages the towns and villages of Navarra found fame and wealth as staging points on the Camino de Santiago, leaving a rich legacy of churches, monasteries and pilgrims' hospices. Navarran gastronomy is one of Spain's finest: cheese is produced with milk from the sheep you see grazing on its green pastures, and although lesser known than neighbouring La Rioja, local wine is good, cheap and plentiful.

Highlights

1. Visiting the new Museo Universidad de Navarra in **Pamplona** (p233)
2. Spooky witches' caves near **Zugarramurdi** (p236)
3. Hiking between villages on the **Camino de Santiago** (p240)
4. Discovering the rich royal and pilgrimage legacies of **Estella/Lizarra** (p245)
5. Staying at the parador **Palacio Real de Olite**, Olite/Erriberri (p246)

Pamplona/Iruña

Pamplona/Iruña – most famous outside Spain for the hair-raising "running of the bull" San Fermín festival (held the first week of July) – has been the capital of Navarra for more than a thousand years. Its characterful medieval old town, crumbling citadel and fine Cathedral make a good base from which to explore the rest of this largely undiscovered and often-surprising region.

East of Pamplona

Estella/Lizarra was not only a medieval royal capital but also one of the main halts on the Camino de Santiago – it still is today – and it retains a rich medieval legacy. Like Estella, Sangüesa/Zangoza was once an important pilgrim's pit-stop and has all the historic religious trimmings to prove it, including some remarkable church stone carvings. Just outside the town stands the impressive Castillo de Javier, and it's worth journeying beyond to the Monasterio de Leyre, which not only occupies a magnificent position but also possesses an atmospheric church and crypt.

South of Pamplona

Olite/Erriberri and Tudela are two more charming medieval towns. Olite castle was once the fortress of the kings of Navarra; today it is a magnificent parador. Stay here, continue to Tudela to see its superb cathedral and then journey onto the spectacular Bardenas Reales, a desert landscape of rock, clay and gypsum formations, home to numerous birds and animals.

North of Pamplona

North of the capital, roads lead to the lush pre-Pyrenees, a popular day-trip destination for **Pampaloneses** fleeing the city heat for hikes in the countryside around the gorgeous Valle de Bidosa's charming "five villages". One of the finest garden estates in Spain, the Jardín de Señorio de Bertiz, is nearby at the threshold to the national park of the same name, where you might spot a Pyrenean salamander if you're lucky.

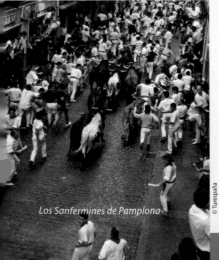

Los Sanfermines de Pamplona

© Turespaña

Pamplona/ Iruña★

The old quarter of Pamplona (Iruña in Basque) keeps its narrow medieval streets and arcaded squares. Streets around the plaza del Castillo are named after old trades: e.g. Zapatería (shoemaker) and Tejería (tilemaker).

- ▶ **Population:** 195 853
- Ⓖ **Michelin Map:** 573 D 25 (town plan).
- **Info:** Plaza Consistorial ℘948 42 01 00. www.turismodepamplona.es.
- ◐ **Location:** Modern Pamplona extends south from the riverside old town. Roads lead to Roncesvalles in the Pyrenees and to Hendaye, both in France. 🚌Pamplona.
- Ⓟ **Parking:** Don't try to park in the old city.

A BIT OF HISTORY

Pamplona is said to have been founded by Pompey, who gave his name to the town. The Moors briefly took over in the 8C but were repelled by Charlemagne, who demolished the walls. The townspeople in turn massacred Charlemagne's rearguard. In the 10C Pamplona became the capital of Navarra, though it was torn for a time between proponents of Castilla and of French rule.

SIGHTS

Catedral★★

Pl. de la Catedral. Mon–Sat 10.30am–7pm (until 5pm Oct–Mar). €5 for Museo Catedralicio. ℘948 21 25 94. www.catedraldepamplona.com.
The Gothic Cathedral was built in the 14–15C. At the end of the 18C, Ventura Rodríguez rebuilt the west front.
Interior★– The nave has wide arches and windows and great bare walls, typical of Navarra Gothic. In front of the finely wrought grille closing the sanctuary stands the alabaster **tomb★★**, commissioned in 1416 by Charles III, the Noble. The reclining figures and **mourners** were carved by Janin Lomme. Note the late 15C Hispano-Flemish altarpiece (south ambulatory chapel).
Claustro★– The 14C–15C cloisters appear delicate, with elegant Gothic arches surmounted, in some cases, by gables. Sculptured tombs and doors add interest. Off the east gallery is the Capilla Barbazán with beautiful 14C star vaulting. On the south side, the doorway of the Sala Preciosa is a masterwork of the period, its tympanum beautifully carved with scenes from the Life of the Virgin and two statues forming a fine Annunciation. In the southeast corner, a lavabo is turned into a shrine commemorating the Battle of Las Navas de Tolosa.

Epic Poems

According to legend, Roncesvalles was the site where the Basques of Navarra massacred the rearguard of Charlemagne's army in 778 as Roland was leading it back through the Pyrenees to France. The late 12C to early 13C poem of **Bernardo del Carpio** describes Bernardo as a national hero who fought alongside his Basque, Navarran and Asturian companions in arms to avenge the Frankish invasion of Spain; the 12C **Song of Roland**, the first French epic poem, on the other hand, glorifies the heroic but ultimately vain resistance of a handful of valiant Christian knights against hordes of Saracen fanatics.

Museo Catedralicio★

Dormitalería 3–5.
The Diocesan Museum is in the old refectory and kitchen, which date from 1330. The refectory, a lofty hall with six pointed arches, contains a rostrum decorated with an enchanting scene of a unicorn hunt. The square kitchen has a central lantern rising to 24m/79ft. Displays include a 13C *Reliquary of the Holy Sepulchre* donated by St Louis (Louis IX of France) and polychrome wood statues of the Virgin and Christ.
Follow the narrow, picturesque del Redín to the ramparts.

Murallas (Ramparts)

La Cuenca de Pamplona zone.
A bastion, now a garden, commands a view of the Puerta de Zumalacárregui (a gate below and to the left), and a stretch of the old walls and a bend in the rivers Arga and Monte Cristóbal. You can learn all about them at the **Centro de Interpretación** (Fortín de San Bartolomé; Tue–Sun 10am–2pm and Apr–Oct 5–7pm, Nov–Mar 4–5pm; €3; ℘948 211 554; www.murallasdepamplona.com).

Museo Universidad de Navarra★★

Campus Universitario. Open Tue–Sat 10am–8pm. Sun & hols noon–2pm. Free guided tours (reserve in advance) Mon–Fri noon and 6pm, Sat, Sun noon. Closed 1 & 6 Jan, Good Fri, 7-14 Jul, 24–25 & 31 Dec. €4.50. ℘948 42 57 00. http://museo.unav.edu/el-museo/inicio.
This museum, which was designed by Rafael Moneo and opened in 2015, contains the Colección de Maria Josefa Huarte with works by Picasso, Kandinsky and Rothko, and also the university's photography collection, which has images from the art's origins up to the present day, including works by photojournalists such as Robert Capa and Henri Cartier-Bresson. It houses a theatre, a cafe and a gourmet restaurant too.

Museo de Navarra★

Santo Domingo 47. Open Tue–Sat 9.30am–2pm, 5–7pm. Sun & hols 11am–2pm. Closed 1 Jan, 6-7 Jul, 25 Dec.
€2; no charge Sat pm, Sun, 18 May, 27 Sept, 12 Oct, 3 & 6 Dec. ℘848 426 492. www.cfnavarra.es/cultura/museo.
This museum is on the site of the 16C Hospital de Nuestra Señora de la Misericordia. Only a Renaissance gateway and the chapel remain. The Roman period (basement and first floor) is represented by funerary steles, inscriptions and **mosaic★** pavements from 2C and 4C villas. The main exhibit in the Hispano-Moorish section (Room 1.8) is an 11C ivory **casket★** from San Salvador de Leyre sculpted in Córdoba. Romanesque **capitals★** are from the former 12C cathedral of Pamplona, brilliantly carved with the Passion, the Resurrection and the Story of Job.
The museum also contains **Gothic wall paintings★** from Artaíz (13C), Artajona (14C), Pamplona (14C), and elsewhere in the province. They share an unobtrusive emphasis on faces and features reminiscent of French miniaturists. The reconstruction of the interior of the **Palacio de Oriz** is decorated with 16C monochrome panels depicting Adam and Eve and the wars of Charles V.
On the third floor are 17C–18C paintings by Luis Paret and Francisco de Goya *(portrait of the Marqués de San Adrián)*.

Iglesia de San Cernin o de San Saturnino★

Ansoleaga 21. Open Mon–Sat 9.15am–12pm, 6–7.30pm. Sun and public holidays 10am–1.30pm, 6–7.30pm. No charge. ℘948 22 11 94. www.turismo.navarra.es.
Set in a tangle of narrow streets in the old quarter, this church mingles Romanesque brick towers, 13C Gothic **portals★** and vaulting, as well as later additions.

Ayuntamiento (Town Hall)

Pl. Consistorial. Closed to the public.
This has a reconstructed **Baroque façade★** (originally late 17C) with statues, balustrades and pediments.

EXCURSIONS
Museo Oteiza

❯ Cuesta 7, Alzuza. 7 km/4.3mi E. Take the NA 150, then immediately turn left. Open Sept–Jun Thu–Fri 10am–3pm,

Sat 11am–7pm, Sun 11am–3pm. Guided visits at 11am and 1pm Tue & Wed (book in advance). Jul–Aug Tue–Sat 11am–7pm, Sun 11am–3pm. €4. No charge Fri (except hols). ☎948 33 20 74. www.museooteiza.org.

Jorge Oteiza (1908–2003) was a key figure of modern Spanish abstract sculpture. The museum is beside his house.

Santuario de San Miguel de Aralar★

45km/28mi NW. Follow the A 15, then shortly before Lecumberri, turn onto the NA 751. The NA 751 crosses the Sierra de Aralar through beech woods to this sanctuary. Open daily 10am–2pm, 4–7pm. No charge. ☎948 37 30 13. www.sanmigueldearalar.info.

The sanctuary consists of an 8C Romanesque church which encloses a totally independent chapel. The gilt and enamel altar front★★ is one of the major works of European Romanesque gold- and silverwork, attributed by some to a late 12C Limoges workshop. It consists of gilded bronze plaques adorned with enamel and mounted precious stones, arranged as an altarpiece. The outstanding multicoloured honeycomb enamelwork is adorned with arabesques and plant motifs.

Roncesvalles/Orreaga★

47km/29mi NE along the N 135. Antiguo Molino ☎948 76 03 01. www.roncesvalles.es.

This 12C ensemble of buildings served as an important hostelry for pilgrims to Santiago de Compostela. Its funerary chapel is now the Capilla del Sancti Spiritus (Chapel of the Holy Spirit), its collegiate church is rich in relics.

Iglesia de la Real Colegiata

Única. Open daily 8.30am–8pm. Closed 6–31 Jan. €5. ☎948 79 04 80. www.turismo.navarra.es/directorio.

This Gothic collegiate church, inspired by those of the Paris region, was consecrated in 1219. Beneath the high altar canopy is the silver-plated statue of Nuestra Señora de Roncesvalles, created in France in the late 13C.

The "Sanfermines"

The feria of San Fermín is celebrated with great abandon from 6 to 14 July each year. Visitors pour in, doubling the town's population, to see the evening bullfights and enjoy the carnival atmosphere (described by Hemmingway in The Sun Also Rises). The most spectacular event, and the one most prized by "Pamploneses", however, is the encierro or early morning (around 8am) running of the bulls. The beasts selected to fight in the evening are let loose with a number of steers to rush through the streets along a set route leading to the bullring. The crowd joins in the rush and injuries are common.

Sala Capitular (Chapter house)

The beautiful Gothic chamber contains the tombs of the founder, Sancho VII, the Strong (1154–1234), King of Navarra and his queen.

Museo★

Única. Same opening hours as Iglesia de la Real Colegiata. €5. ☎948 79 04 80.

The museum contains fine pieces of ancient plate: a Mudéjar casket, a Romanesque book of the Gospel, a 14C enamelled reliquary known as "Charlemagne's chessboard", a 16C Flemish triptych, an emerald, said to have been worn by Sultan Miramamolín el Verde in his turban on the day of the Battle of Las Navas de Tolosa in 1212, and a lovely Holy Family by Morales.

🚗 DRIVING TOUR

VALLE DEL BIDASOA ★

134km/83mi. Allow one whole day.

The Bidasoa Valley cuts through the lower foothills of the western Pyrenees, where villages of typical Basque houses lie amid lush meadows. The Bidasoa river is renowned for its salmon and trout.

▷ Exit Pamplona from the PA-30 ring road towards Ezcaba. Then take the the N -121A. Near the exit to Oricaín, take the N-121B and exit at Oronoz then follow the signs to the Parque Natural de Señorío Bértiz.

Señorío Bértiz Natural Park

Access beside the petrol station, on the edge of town. ✆948 592 421. www.parquedebertiz.es.

A natural park since 1984, this area covers 2040 ha/5 000 acres, about half of which is forest (mainly oak and beech). Its woods and meadows are home to diverse wildlife, from salamanders to Pyrenean desman (a type of mole). Pedro Ciga was its last lord, custodian of the land formerly given as a gift from King Charles III in the 14C. He planted exotics in the garden (situated at the entrance to the park and now open to the public) and built a new palace in the Art Nouveau style, while restoring the old. In 1949 he donated the palace and lands to the députation of Navarra, under the proviso that everything was left as it was given. The palace overlooks the Aizkolegi peak, and enjoys a wide panorama of the park and the surrounding valleys. Several marked trails leave from the park entrance (ask for the plan at the gate). The shortest (700m/765yd) and easiest bears left to follow the River Bidasoa. The others go into the forest along the path marked Aizkolegi (the only one on which you can cycle – follow the green signage).

▷ From the centre of Oronoz, take the N 121B, towards Elizondo.

Elizondo, the capital and gateway of the **Valle del Baztán**, has numerous 18–19C houses decorated with armorial bearings known as *caserios*. It's a pleasant place to wander around, soaking up the atmosphere and perhaps buying some of the village's local speciality – hazelnut chocolate.

▷ From Elizondo head to Elbete and take the N 121B (from here on the road contains many hairpin bends). At Otxondo take the NA 4402 to Leoriaz and then the NA 4401 to Zugarramurdi.

The sleepy enclave of **Zugarramurdi** is home to one of the most extraordinary places in the region – the so-called Cuevas de Brujas "witches' caves". At over 120m/130yd long and set over various levels deep in the woods, they are an eerie sight, made even more evocative by the fact that they were an alleged meeting place for medieval witches. One of the caves, La Cueva de Zugarramurdi, has been turned into a visitor attraction along with a Museo de las Brujas (museum and caves open Oct–Jun Wed–Fri 11am–6.30pm, Sat–Sun until 7pm, caves also open Tue; mid-Jul–mid-Sept Tue–Sun 11am–7.30pm, caves till 10.30am-8pm and also open Mon; closed 18 & 27 Aug; €4 cave, €4.50 museum; €7.50 combined ticket ✆948 59 90 04; www.turismozugarramurdi.com). Many who were caught here were tortured and executed by an Inquisition that targeted women and children on the fringes of society.

▷ Take the N 4401 to Urdax then follow the signs to the N 121B. Close to Oronoz follow the signs to the N121A towards Bera/Vera de Bidasoa.

The houses in Bera (Vera) de Bidasoa are adorned with coats of arms, particularly along the main street. The typically Basque façades have deep eaves over balconies with delicate balustrades.

ADDRESSES

🍽 STAY

⊖⊜🛏 **Hotel Yoldi** – Av. de San Ignacio, 11. ✆948 22 48 00. www.hotelyoldi.com. 50 rooms. 🛏 €12.10. Central, modern hotel with a tapas bar. Rooms are on the small side but nicely decorated.

⊖⊜⊜🛏 **Palacio Guendulain** – Calle de la Zapatería 53. ✆948 22 55 22. www.palacioguendulain.com. 25 rooms. 🛏 €18.70. Elegant, traditionally furnished hotel in an 18th-century palace. Gourmet restaurant with an attractive terrace.

♈/EAT

○⊜⊜⊜ **Baserri** – San Nicolás 32. ☎948 22 20 21. www.baserriberri.com. The best place for tapas in Pamplona. Try their solomillos al roquefort.

○⊜⊜⊜ **Rodero** – Emilio Arrieta 3. ☎948 22 80 35. www.restaurante rodero.com. Closed Sun and Holy Week. This luxury restaurant behind the bullring is one of the best in the whole province. Family-run with high-quality service and creative, innovative cuisine.

Monasterio de San Salvador de Leyre★

At the end of a winding road, a splendid **panorama★★** opens up: limestone crests form majestic ramparts on whose slopes appear the ochre walls of the monastery.

- **Michelin Map:** 573 E26.
- **Info:** ☎948 88 41 50. www.monasteriodeleyre.com.
- **Location:** Near the Yesa reservoir; 50km/31mi SE of Pamplona and 16km/10mi NE of Sangüesa. Nearest station: Pamplona (50km).
- **Timing:** Hear the monks' Gregorian chants inside the church daily at 7pm.

A BIT OF HISTORY

By the early 11C, the Abbey of San Salvador de Leyre was the spiritual centre of Navarra, and the final resting place of kings. In the 12C, after union with Aragón, Leyre was neglected. By the 19C it had been abandoned. In 1954, however, a Benedictine community from Silos took over. They restored the 17C and 18C conventual buildings which have now been converted into a hostelry (⊜⊜⊜).

IGLESIA★★

Open daily 10.15am–7pm. Nov-Mar 10.15am-6pm. Closed 24 & 25 Dec, 1 & 6 Jan. €3, guided visit €3.50.

East End – Built in the 11C. Three apses, the nave, turret and a square tower make a delightful group.

Crypt★★ – The robust 11C crypt, built to support the Romanesque church above, looks even older. The vaulting is relatively high but divided by arches with enormous voussoirs.

Interior★ – In the 13C the Cistercians rebuilt the central aisle with a bold Gothic vault, while retaining earlier Romanesque bays with barrel vaulting, engaged pillars, and perfectly hewn stone. In the north bay a wooden chest contains the remains of the first kings of Navarra.

West Portal★ – 12C. The portal is called the Porta Speciosa for its decorative richness. Carvings cover every available space. On the tympanum are archaic statues – Christ (centre), the Virgin Mary and St Peter (on His right) and St John (on His left); the covings are alive with monsters and fantastic beasts.

EXCURSIONS
Hoz de Lumbier★
○ 14km/8.7mi W.
The Irati gorge between Lumbier and Liédana is barely 5km/3mi long and so narrow that it appears at either end as a crack in the cliff face. There is a good **view** of the gorge from a lookout point on the road (N 240).

Hoz de Arbayún★
○ 31km/19.2mi N along the N 240 and NA 211.
The River Salazar is steeply enclosed within limestone walls. From a point north of Iso there a splendid **view★★** to the end of the canyon where the cliff walls are clad in lush vegetation.

*Detail of the south portal,
Iglesia de Santa María la Real*

© S. Sauvignier/MICHELIN

Sangüesa/ Zangoza★

Situated on the Río Aragón, Sangüesa (Zangoza in Basque) still stands guard over the bridge which in the Middle Ages brought the region and the city so much prosperity. Its monumental and artistic heritage stems from its location on the Camino de Santiago.

▶ **Population:** 5 020

◔ **Michelin Map:** 573 E 26.

🛈 **Info:** Mayor, 2. ☎948 87 14 11. www.sanguesa.es.

▷ **Location:** Sangüesa is 5km/3mi from the N 240, linking Jaca with Pamplona, 36km/22mi away. 🚈Nearest station: Pamplona (48km).

◔ **Timing:** Allow a couple of hours in town.

SIGHT

Iglesia de Santa María la Real★

Mayor. Guided tours by appt only. ☎620 110 581. www.turismo.navarra.es. The glory of the church is its late 12C–13C **Portada Sur★★** (South Portal) amazingly crowded with sculptures, executed by the Master of San Juan de la Peña. The **statue columns**, already Gothic, derive from those at Chartres and Autun. On the **tympanum**, God the Father, at the centre of a group of angel musicians, receives the chosen at His right arm, but with his down-pointing left arm reproves sinners. The **covings** swarm with motifs; the second innermost shows the humbler trades: clog-maker, lute-maker and butcher.

The older upper arches, marked by an Aragonese severity of style, show God surrounded by the symbols of the Evangelists, two angels and the disciples.

EXCURSIONS
Castillo de Javier★

▷ Javier. 7km/4.3mi NE on the NA 541. Open daily Mar–Nov 10am–6.30pm; rest of the year until 4pm. Call to confirm times. Closed 1 Jan, 24–25, 31 Dec. €2.75. ☎948 88 40 24. www.turismo.navarra.es

St Francis Xavier, the patron saint of Navarra was born in this picturesque fortress in 1506. He founded the Society of Jesus (with Ignatius Loyola), died in 1552 and was canonised in 1622. The castle was in part destroyed by Cardinal Cisneros in 1516. Its **oratorio★** (oratory) contains a 13C Christ in walnut and an unusual 15C fresco of the Dance of Death.

Sos del Rey Católico★

⊙ 13km/8mi SE along the A 127.
🏛Palacio de Sada. ✆948 88 85 24.
www.sosdelreycatolico.com.
It was in the historic town of Sos del Rey, in the **Palacio de Sada**, that Ferdinand the Catholic, was born in 1452. The town still has a medieval air. On the **Plaza Mayor** stand the imposing 16C ayuntamiento (town hall), with large carved wood overhangs, and the Lonja (Exchange) with wide arches.

Iglesia de San Esteban★

Pl. de la Iglesia. Guided tours by appt with tourist office. ✆948 88 82 03.
The Church of St Stephen is reached through a vaulted passageway. The 11C **crypt★** is dedicated to Our Lady of Forgiveness (Virgen del Perdón). Two of the three apses are decorated with fine 14C **frescoes**. The central apse contains outstanding capitals carved with women and birds. The statue columns at the **main door** have the stiff and noble bearing of those at Sangüesa. The church, in transitional style, has a beautiful Renaissance **gallery★**. A chapel contains a 12C Romanesque Christ with eyes open.

Uncastillo

⊙ 34km/21mi SE; 21km/13mi from Sos del Rey Católico.
The Romanesque Iglesia de Santa María (Pl. de la Villa) has an unusual 14C tower adorned with machicolations and pinnacle turrets. The delicate carving on the **south portal★** makes it one of the most beautiful doorways of the late Romanesque period. The church gallery with Renaissance **stalls★** and the **cloisters★** are 16C Plateresque.

Cáseda

⊙ 12km/7.5mi SW. Head from Sangüesa towards Sos del Rey Católico and turn right after 1km/.06mi onto the NA 5341.
Perched on a hillside and surrounded by fields and the Aragon River, this picturesque village is dominated by a Gothic church and a medieval stone bridge. Upstream and 10km/6mi W via the NA5321, **Gallipienzo**/Galipentzu's hilltop church perches above the remains of fortified walls, from where you can enjoy a **view★** of the surrounding fields.

ADDRESSES

🛌 STAY

⊖⊜ **Hostal Rural JP** – Avda. Padre Raimundo Lumbier 3. ✆948 87 16 93. 7 rooms. ⊠ €4.50. This friendly, modern hostal next to the River Aragón has simply-decorated rooms and a café-bar.

Sangüesa and the Camino de Santiago

Fear of the Moors compelled Sangüesans to live until the 10C on the Rocaforte hillside; by the 11C, however, the citizens had moved down to defend the bridge and clear a safe passage for pilgrims. Sangüesa reached its zenith at the end of the Middle Ages when prosperous citizens began to build elegant residential mansions. These contrasted with the austere Palacio del Príncipe de Viana (Palace of the Prince of Viana), residence of the kings of Navarra, now the ayuntamiento (town hall), with its façade (seen through the gateway) flanked by two imposing battlemented towers. The main street, the former Calle Mayor which was once part of the pilgrim road, is lined with comfortable brick houses with the Classical carved wood eaves and windows featuring rich Gothic or Plateresque surrounds. In the second street on the right coming from the bridge can be seen the Baroque front of the Palacio de Vallesantoro, a palace protected by monumental overhangs carved with imaginary animals.

El Camino de Santiago★★★

The Way of St James

The discovery of the tomb of the Apostle James, early in the 9C, transformed Santiago de Compostela into the most important medieval pilgrimage destination in Europe. From the 11C onwards, the veneration of these saintly remains gave rise to the El Camino de Santiago (the Way of St James) and today thousands of pilgrims, and interested tourists, walk the same path. The Camino Francés, the French Way, also crosses Navarra. The route and its many monuments have been granted UNESCO World Heritage status.

Michelin Map: 573.

Info: Rúa do Vilar, 63. 981 555 129. ww.santiagoturismo.com. Confraternity of St James. www.csj.org.uk.

Location: El Camino de Santiago runs from the Pyrenees to Santiago (see map opposite).

Timing: If you're fit and healthy, you can cover about 25km/15mi a day, and therefore walk between Roncesvalles and Santiago de Compostela in about a month.

A BIT OF HISTORY

The discovery of the remains of St James (Santiago) had an enormous effect on early pilgrims and by the 11C making the journey to his shrine ranked on the same level as visiting Rome or Jerusalem.

St James had a particular appeal for the French, who at the time were united with the Spanish against the Moors, but others made the long pilgrimage along routes organised by the Benedictines, Cistercians and the Knights Templars. Purpose-built hospitals and hospices received the sick and the weary and all travelled in the same pilgrim's uniform, consisting of a heavy cape, a 2.4m/8ft staff with a hollowed-out gourd attached (to carry water), sturdy sandals and a broad-brimmed felt hat marked with three or four scallop shells. A *Pilgrim Guide* of 1130, said to be the first tourist guide ever written, describes the inhabitants, climate, customs and sights on the way. Churches and towns along the route prospered, receiving between 500 000 and two million pilgrims a year.

Those from England who "took the cockleshell" often sailed from Parson's Quay in the Plymouth estuary to Soulac and followed the French Atlantic coast, or otherwise landed at La Coruña or in Portugal. Routes through France from Chartres, St-Denis and Paris joined at Tours. Villages along the main route grew into towns and some were settled by foreigners, often from France, or Jews. With time, the faith that impelled the pilgrims began to diminish; crime, particularly from bandits, increased; and infighting amongst Christians reduced the faithful. In 1589, Drake attacked La Coruña and the bishop of Compostela removed the relics from the cathedral. They were then lost and for 300 years the pilgrimage was virtually abandoned. In 1879 they were recovered, recognised by the Pope and the pilgrimage was reborn. In Holy Years, on 25 July, when the feast day of St James falls on a Sunday, elaborate religious and cultural celebrations in the major halts of St James Way attracts even more pilgrims.

THE WAY IN SPAIN

The Camino Francés is the most popular of the handful of caminos to Santiago de Compostela. Routes from France converge at either Roncesvalles or Somport and then cross the Pyrenees Mountains. The easier southerly route

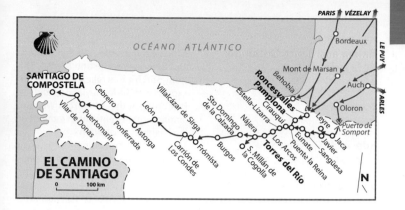

(from Somport) goes via Jaca, Santa Cruz de la Serós, San Juan de la Peña, the Monasterio de Leyre and Sangüesa and features churches and monasteries influenced by French architecture. Both routes converge at Puente la Reina.

Puente la Reina★

The town's 11C humpbacked bridge was built for the pilgrims and a bronze pilgrim marks where routes converged. The wide N 111 circles the old town outside whose walls stands the Iglesia del Crucifijo (Church of the Crucifix; open daily 9am–6pm (8pm Apr-Oct; no charge). A second nave was added to the 12C main aisle in the 14C and now contains the famous Y-shaped Cross with a profoundly Expressionist **Christ★** carved in wood, said to have been brought from Germany in the 14C. ◗ Walk along the narrow, elegant main street, calle Mayor, fronted by houses of golden brick with carved wood eaves, to the bridge. You will see the **Iglesia de Santiago** (Church of St James; open Mon-Sat 10.30am–8pm, Sun and hols 9.39am–7.30pm; no charge), its **doorway★** crowded with carvings now almost effaced. The nave, remodelled in the 16C, was adorned with altarpieces. Note two statues facing the entrance: St James the Pilgrim in gilded wood, and St Bartholomew.

Iglesia de Santa María de Eunate★★

◗ Muruzábal. 5km/3mi E of Puente la Reina. Guided visits by appt only. Closed 15 Dec–15 Jan. €1. ℘628 87 28 35. www.santamariadeeunate.es.

Human bones indicate that this isolated 12C Romanesque building might have been a funerary chapel like that of Torres del Río (◗ see below).

Cirauqui★

Steep, winding alleyways are crowded by houses with rounded doorways, their upper fronts adorned with iron balconies, coats of arms and carved cornices. At the top of the village (difficult climb) stands the Iglesia de San Román with a multifoil 13C **portal★**.

Estella★ and Monasterio de Irache★

◗ See ESTELLA/LIZARRA, p244.

Los Arcos

The **Iglesia de Santa María de los Arcos** (Church of St Mary of the Arches; Pl. de Santa María; opens 30 mins before Mass. ℘649 909 514; www.turismo.navarra.es), with its high tower, is Spanish Baroque inside, with overpowering stucco, sculpture and painting covering every available space. Above the high altar rises the 13C polychrome wood statue of the Black Virgin of Santa María de los Arcos. The cloisters are elegant 15C Gothic.

Torres del Río

The **Iglesia del Santo Sepulcro★** (Church of the Holy Sepulchre; Mayor; ℘666 988 255) is a tall, octagonal Romanesque building, which might be a funerary chapel, dating from about 1200. The Mudéjar-inspired, star-shaped **cupola** is geometrically perfect. Note also the fine 13C crucifix.

Nájera and Santo Domingo de la Calzada★
&See La RIOJA, p265.

Burgos★★★
&See BURGOS, p308.

Iglesia de Frómista★★
&See PALENCIA, p315.

Villalcázar de Sirga
The vast **Gothic Iglesia de Santa María la Blanca** (open Sat–Sun & hols 10.30am–2pm, 4–6pm; €1.50; &639 843 093) has a fine carved **portal★** and two outstanding Gothic **tombs★**. The recumbent statues of the brother of Alfonso X (who had the king murdered in 1271), and his wife Eleanor, are carved in great detail.

Carrión de los Condes
The 11C **Monasterio de San Zoilo**, rebuilt during the Renaissance, and now housing a luxury hotel and restaurant, has **cloisters★** (Obispo Souto Vizoso; open Apr–15 Oct Tue–Sun 10.30am–2pm, 4.30–8pm, 16 Oct–Mar Tue–Fri 10.30am–2pm, Sat–Sun and hols 10.30am–2pm, 4–7pm; closed Jan–Feb; €2; &979 88 09 02; www.sanzoilo.com) designed by Juan de Badajoz with distinctive vaulting. The keystones and bosses are adorned with figurines and medallions. The Iglesia de Santiago (Rúa; open Tue–Sun noon–2pm, 5–7pm; €1; &979 88 00 72) has beautiful 12C carvings on the façade.

León★★
&See LEÓN

Astorga
🚌Astorga.
Astorga is renowned for its delicious *mantecadas*, a type of rich, oily biscuit.

Catedral de Santa María★
Pl. de la Catedral. Open Mon–Sat 9am–10.30am, Sun 11am–1pm. No charge. &987 61 58 20. www.ayuntamientodeastorga.com.
Construction began in the late 15C, and was not completed until the 18C,

which explains the rich Renaissance and Baroque façade and towers. The front **porch★** low reliefs illustrate the Expulsion of the Moneylenders and the Pardoning of the Adulterous Woman, among other events. Above the door is a beautiful Deposition.

The interior is surprisingly large, with an upsweeping effect created by innumerable slender columns. Behind the high altar is a 16C **retable★**. Gaspar de Hoyos and Gaspar de Palencia were responsible for the painted, gilt decoration, and Gaspar Becerra (1520–70), an Andalucían who after study in Italy developed a style of humanist sensitivity far removed from the Expressionism of his contemporaries.

The **Museo de la Catedral** contains a 13C gold filigree Holy Cross reliquary and a 10C reliquary of Alfonso III, the Great (same hours and price as Palacio Episcopal).

Palacio Episcopal de Gaudí
Pl. de Eduardo de Castro.
Open Oct–Apr Tue–Sat 11am–2pm, 4–6pm, Sun 11am–2pm; May–Sept Tue–Sat 10am–2pm, 4–8pm, Sun 10am–2pm. €3. &987 61 68 82. www.palaciodegaudi.es.
This fantastic pastiche of a medieval palace was created by **Gaudí** in 1889. The original, brilliant interior decoration, especially in the neo-Gothic chapel on the first floor, is a profusion of mosaics, stained glass and intersecting ribbed vaults. The palace is home to the **Museo de los Caminos** where medieval art reflects the theme of pilgrimage.

Ponferrada
🚌Ponferrada.
The centre of a mining area, Ponferrada owes its name to an 11C iron bridge built across the River Sil for pilgrims. Above the town are the ruins of the **Castillo de los Templarios** (Templars' Castle; open Mon–Sun Jun-15 Oct 9am–9pm, 16 Oct–May Mon–Sun 9am–7pm; €6; &987 40 22 44).

Peñalba de Santiago★

▶ 21km/13mi SE.

Peñalba stands in the heart of the Valle del Silencio. Its houses are schist-walled with wooden balconies and slate roofs. The Mozarabic **Iglesia de Santiago** (open 10am-2pm, 4-8pm (5-9pm May–Sep), Sun 10am-2pm; no charge), is all that remains of a 10C monastery.

Las Médulas★

▶ 22km/14mi SW.

Debris from a Roman gold mine has transformed the slopes of the Aquilianos mountains into a magical landscape of rocky crags and strange shaped hillocks of pink and ochre, covered by gnarled chestnut trees. It has been declared a World Heritage Site. An information centre for the park can be found in the village of Carucedo (open Mar–Oct 10.45am–3pm, Nov–Feb 11am–2pm; ℘987 42 07 08; www.fundacionlasmedulas.info), where visitors can find out about walking routes and guided visits.

Cebreiro

Near the Puerto de Piedrafita (Piedrafita Pass, 1 109m/3 638ft), Cebreiro, is a reminder of the hardship of the pilgrims' journey. Drystone and thatched houses (pallozas) are little more than ancient Celtic huts; in one is an **Ethnographic Museum** (Museo Etnográfico; open Tue–Sat 16 Sept–14 Jun 11am–6pm, 15 Jun–15 Sept 8.30am–2.30pm; no charge). A pilgrim inn remains beside the small 9C mountain church where pilgrims venerated the relics of the miracle of the Holy Eucharist Relics in silver caskets presented by Isabel may be seen with the miraculous chalice and paten.

Portomarín

Before this ancient village was drowned by a dam, its fortified **church★** of the Knights of St John of Jerusalem (open Tue–Sun 10.30am–1pm, 4.30–7pm; no charge) was moved stone by stone. It features massive arches and Romanesque doors with delicately carved covings. The west door depicts Christ in Majesty with the 24 Elders of the Apocalypse.

Vilar de Donas

▶ 6.5km/4mi E of Palas de Rei.

Enter the village **church** (open Tue–Sun 11am–2pm, 3–6pm; no charge) via its Romanesque doorway. Lining the walls are tombs of the Knights of the Order of St James, slain in battle. 15C **frescoes★** decorate the apse, illustrating Christ in Majesty with St Paul and St Luke on his left and St Peter and St Mark on his right. On the chancel walls are the faces of the elegant young women (donas in Galician) who give the church its name.

Santiago de Compostela★★★

♿ See SANTIAGO DE COMPOSTELA

ADDRESSES

🛏 STAY

🍴🛏 **Hotel El Castillo**– Av. el Castillo 115, Ponferrada. ℘987 45 62 27. 48 rooms. Simple and centrally located near to its namesake castle, El Castillo is perfect for overnighting on the Camino.

🍴🛏 **Hostal Rural Bidean** – Mayor 20, Puente la Reina. ℘948 34 11 56. www.bidean.com. 20 rooms. 🍽 €3. This cosy little rustic hostelry has many period features and is popular with pilgrims, who get a special rate. A three-course dinner and breakfast package is available for €11.

🍴🛏🛏 **Hotel Real Monasterio San Zoilo** – Obispo Souto, Carrión de los Condes. ℘979 88 00 49. www.sanzoilo.com. 49 rooms. 🍽 €10.50. Restaurant 🍴🛏🛏. This former Benedictine monastery is now a delightful, welcoming hotel with elegant architecture. Great value.

🍴 EAT

🍴🛏🛏 **La Peseta** – Pl. San Bartolomé 3, Astorga. ℘987 61 72 75. www.restaurantelapeseta.com. This popular, family-run restaurant has an attractive dining room, serving traditional cuisine.

Estella/Lizarra★★

Estella (Lizarra in the Basque language) was the 12C capital of the kings of Navarra and the 19C base of the Carlists. It is an important stage on the Camino de Santiago.

▷ **Population:** 13 702
⎔ **Michelin Map:** 573D 23.
▯ **Info:** San Nicolás 1.
ℊ948 55 63 01. www.
estellaturismo.com, www.
turismotierraestella.com.
◖ **Location:** Estella lies in NE Spain near the Pyrenees on the slopes of the Sierra de Andía, along the N 111 linking Pamplona and Logroño (48km/30mi SW). 🚉Nearest station: Pamplona (43km).
◔ **Timing:** Allow time for simply wandering in the Old Town.

SIGHTS
Plaza de San Martín

The once-bustling small square was originally the heart of the freemen's parish. On one side is the former **ayuntamiento** (town hall) dating from the 16C. On the other side of the Río Ega on Calle de la Rúa (Pilgrim Road) stands the **Casa de Cultura Fray Diego de Estella** (ℊ948 55 17 47), built in 1565, at no. 7, with an emblazoned Plateresque façade. It now hosts regular art exhibitions.

Palacio de los Reyes de Navarra★ (Palace of the Kings of Navarre)

San Nicolás 1. Open Tue–Fri 9,30am–1.30pm. Sat Sun & pub hols 11am–2pm. Closed 1 Jan, 25 Dec. No charge. ℊ948 54 61 61. www.museogustavodemaeztu.com.
This rare 12C Romanesque civil building is punctuated by arcades and twin bays with remarkable capitals. The palace now houses the contemporary art museum, the **Museo Gustavo de Maeztu y Whitney**, featuring the works of Gustavo de Maeztu y Whitney (1887–1947).
Son of a Cuban father and French mother, he grew up in Bilbao and then moved to Paris, but travelled extensively through Spain. In 1936 he settled in Estella until his death. His œuvre, which focuses on landcapes and portraits, is marked by colour and attention to detail. The first floor of the museum holds portraits of women, and the second drawings, sketches and rural scenes.

Iglesia de San Pedro de la Rúa★

San Nicolás 2. Mon– Sat 10am-1.30pm, 6–7pm (pm only Nov-Mar), Sun & hols 10am–12.30pm. No charge.

The church stands facing the royal palace on a cliff spur formerly crowned by the city castle. It retains outstanding 12C and 13C features.
The unusual **doorway★** at the top of a steep stairway in the north wall has an equilateral scalloped arch, Caliphate influenced. Similar portals can be seen in Navarra and in the Saintonge and Poitou regions of France. Inside note the transitional Romanesque Virgin and Child, a Gothic Christ and an unusual column of intertwined serpents in the central apse, and a Romanesque Crucified Christ in the apse on the left.
The Romanesque **cloisters** lost two galleries when the nearby castle was blown up in the 16C. The skill and invention of the masons are evident in the remaining **capitals★★**; the north gallery series illustrates scenes from the lives of Christ, St Lawrence, St Andrew and St Peter, while plant and animal themes enliven the west gallery.

Iglesia de San Miguel

Mayor 46. Open 30 mins before mass. No charge. ℊ948 55 00 70.
The church dominates a quarter that retains narrow streets and a medieval atmosphere. On the tympanum of the north **portal★** is a figure of Christ surrounded by the Evangelists and mysterious personages. The covings are full

of sculptures. The capitals illustrate the childhood of Christ.

On the upper register of the walls are eight Statue columns of the Apostles; on the lower register, two **high reliefs★★**, accomplished and expressive, show St Michael slaying the dragon (left) and the three Marys coming from the Sepulchre. The noble bearing, the elegant drapery and the facial expressions make the carving a Romanesque masterpiece.

EXCURSION
Monasterio de Irache★

◯ Irache. 3km/1.8mi SW of Estella. Open Wed–Sun 10am–1.15pm, 4–7pm. Closed Nov–mid-Jan. No charge. ℘948 550 0/0. www.turismo.navarra.es.

A Benedictine abbey occupied the site in the 10C. Later, this was a major pilgrimage halt and a Cistercian community before becoming a university under the Benedictines, in the 16C.

Iglesia★ – This 12C–13C church's apse is purely Romanesque with rib-vaulted nave. The dome on squinches and the *coro alto* are Renaissance; the façade and most of the structures were rebuilt in the 17C. Brackets and capitals illustrate the lives of Christ and St Benedict in the **claustro**.

🚗 DRIVING TOUR

SIERRA DE ANDÍA AND SIERRA DE URBASA★
94km/58mi. About 3hr.

◯ Leave Estella on NA 120 north towards the Puerto (pass) de Lizarraga. The road crosses beechwoods and rises to a pass that affords extensive views.

Monasterio de Iranzu
9km/5.6mi N of Estella. Signposted from NA 120. Open daily 10am–2pm, 4–8pm (Oct–Apr 4–6pm). €2.50. ℘948 52 00 12. This 12C Cistercian monastery is now home to a college. Isolated in a wild **gorge★**, it is a fine example of the Cistercian transitional style from Romanesque to Gothic combining

Cloisters, Iglesia de San Pedro de la Rúa

robustness and elegance. The cloister bays, where they have not been given a later florid Gothic fenestration, have Romanesque blind arcades, oculi and wide relieving arches. The church, with primitive vaulting, has a flat east end decorated with three windows, symbolising the Trinity, a common Cistercian feature.

Puerto de Lizarraga Road★★
Once out of the tunnel (alt 1 090m/ 3 576ft) pause at the **viewpoint★** overlooking the Ergoyena Valley before the descent through woods and pastures.

◯ Continue to Etxarri-Aranatz; take N 240 W to Olatzi; turn left to Estella.

Puerto de Urbasa road★★
The road climbs steeply between great boulders and clumps of trees. Beyond the pass (alt 927m/3 041ft) tall limestone cliffs add character to the landscape before the road enters the gorges of the sparkling river Urenderra.

© Javi Julio Photography/Getty Images

Palacio Real de Olite

Olite/Erriberri★

Olite (Erriberri in Basque) was the favourite residence of the kings of Navarra in the 15C, and retains the seat of power, now a restored fairytale palace the size of a small village. Palace aside, Olite's many other activities and its setting attracts lots of summer visitors.

SIGHTS
👥 Palacio Real de Olite★

Pl. Carlos III El Noble. Open daily, see website for seasonal opening hours. Closed 1, 6 Jan, 25 Dec. €3.50, guided tours €4.90. ☎948 74 00 35. http://guiartenavarra.com.
The Royal Palace of Olite is divided into the Palacio Viejo (Old Palace), now a parador, and the Palacio Nuevo (New Palace), open to visitors.
The latter was built by Charles III (the Noble) in 1406. His French origins – as Count of Evreux and native of Mantes – explain the fortifications, a transition between the massive stone constructions of the 13C and the royal Gothic residences of the late 15C with galleries and courtyards. During the Peninsular War, a fire almost completely destroyed the building. Behind the 15 or so towers marking the perimeter were hanging gardens, along with inner halls and

▶ **Population:** 3 907
🚗 **Michelin Map:** 573 E 25.
ℹ **Info:** Plaza de los Teobaldos 10. ☎948 74 17 03. www.olite.es.
○ **Location:** Olite stands at the heart of the Navarran plain, 4km/2.5mi from the A 15 motorway linking Zaragoza and Pamplona/Iruña (43km/26mi S). 🚆Nearest station: Pamplona (45km).
👥 **Kids:** Palacio Real de Olite.
🕐 **Timing:** In the last week of August, Olite celebrates with a theatre festival.

chambers decorated with *azulejos*, painted stuccowork and coloured marquetry ceilings.
The most impressive rooms are the Guardarropa (Wardrobe), the Sala de la Reina (Queen's Room) and the Galería del Rey (King's Gallery).

Iglesia de Santa María la Real★

Pl. de los Teobaldos. Open half an hour before Mass; Sun 11am and 6.30pm. €1.50. http://guiartenavarra.com
The church is the former chapel royal. An atrium of slender multifoil arches precedesthe 14C façade★, a fine exam-

ple of Navarra Gothic sculpture. The only figurative carving illustrates the lives of the Virgin and Christ. A painted 16C retable frames a Gothic statue of Our Lady.

Museo del Vino de Navarra★

Plaza de los Teobaldos 4. Open Holy Week–mid-Oct Mon–Sat 10am–2pm, 4pm–7pm, Sun 10am–2pm; rest of the year Mon–Fri 10am–5pm, Sat & Sun 10am–2pm. Closed 1 & 6 Jan, 25 Dec. €3.50. ☏948 741 273. www.museodelvinodenavarra.com.

This modern museum explains the viticulture of Navarra's renowned wines. Each floor introduces a different theme: the history of wine; vineyard management; bottling and aging. Most interesting of all is the section on appreciating wine and the numerous grape varieties.

EXCURSIONS

Ujué★

◑ 19km/11.8mi NE of Olite, along NA 5 300 (Ctra de San Martin de Unx) to San Martín de Unx, then follow the NA 5310. Ujué, overlooking the Ribera region, remains, with its winding streets, much as it was in the Middle Ages.

Iglesia de Santa María

Open daily 10am–6.30pm (5.30 in winter). Guided tours of church and fortress available with prior booking. ☏618 820 414.

A Romanesque church was built at the end of the 11C. In the 14C, Charles II, the Bad, began a Gothic church, but the Romanesque chancel remains to this day. The central chapel contains the venerated Santa María la Blanca, a plated Romanesque statue honoured with a *romería* (pilgrimage) the Sunday after St Mark's Day (25 April).

Fortaleza
(Fortress)

The church towers command a view which extends to Olite, the Montejurra and the Pyrenees. Of the medieval palace there remain lofty walls and a covered watch path circling the church.

Monasterio de La Oliva★

◑ Ctra de Lerida, Carcastillo, 27km/ 16.7mi S of Ujué. Open Mon–Sat 9.30am–noon, 3.30–6pm, Sun and public holidays 9.30am–11.30am, 4–6pm. €2.50. ☏948 72 50 06. www.monasteriodelaoliva.org.

La Oliva was one of the first Cistercian monasteries built outside France. The buildings, stripped of treasure and trappings, retain a pure Cistercian beauty.

Iglesia★★ – The façade of this late 12C church is mostly unadorned, a perfect setting for the interplay of lines of the portal and two rose windows. The interior is surprisingly deep with pillars and pointed arches lined with thick polygonal ribs in austere Cistercian style.

Claustro★ – The bays in the late-15C cloisters appear exceptionally light. Ogival vaults rise from Romanesque capitals at the entry to the 13C **Sala Capitular** (chapter house).

Laguna de Pitillas★

◑ 13km/8.7mi SW of Olite on the N-121 to Pitillas. Observation area open Sat, Sun & hols, times vary with the seasons. Guided tours available. www.lagunadepitillas.org.

This marshy area covers 87ha/216 acres with an average water depth of 3m/9.8ft; a dyke regulates the level. The site was declared a nature reserve in 1987 because of its ecological importance. It also lies on the migratory routes of many species of birds, who use the marshes as a breeding ground, so the best time for birdwatching is in winter. A free bird observation area (*Observatorio de Aves*) provides telescopes.

Tudela/Tutera★

Tudela was once part of the Córdoba Caliphate, evident from its large Moorish quarter, the Morería and following the 12C Reconquest, many fascinating churches were built. Another legacy of the Moorish past, irrigation has made the surrounding Ribera region a market-gardening centre.

SIGHTS

Catedral★

Pl. Vieja. Open Tue–Sat 11.30am–1.30pm, 4–7pm; Sun 11.30am–1.30pm. €4 inc museum and cloisters. ℘948 40 21 61. www.catedraldetudela.com.

The 12C–13C cathedral exemplifies the transitional Romanesque-Gothic style. The **Last Judgement Doorway★** (Portada del Juicio Final), though difficult to see, is minutely carved with nearly 120 groups of figures. The interior is Romanesque in the elevation of the nave, Gothic in its vaulting and clerestory. Gothic works include early 16C choir stalls, the high altar retable and the Byzantine-looking 13C stone reliquary statue of the White Virgin. In the **Capilla de Nuestra Señora de la Esperanza★** (Chapel of our Lady of Hope), 15C masterpieces include the tomb of a chancellor of Navarra and the main altarpiece. The 12C–13C **cloisters★★** (claustro) are beautifully harmonious. Romanesque arches rest alternately on columns with historiated

---

St Anne's Feast Day

(26 July). Celebrated annually, as at Pamplona/Iruña, with several days of great rejoicing including *encierros* and bullfights. During Holy Week, an event known as the Descent of the Angel takes place on the picturesque **Plaza de los Fueros**, which served as a bullring in the 18C.

▶ **Population:** 35 388
◐ **Michelin Map:** 573 F 25.
▤ **Info:** Pl. de los Fueros
℘948 84 80 58.
www.tudela.es/turismo.
▷ **Location:** Tudela is on the right bank of the River Ebro in NE Spain, 50km/31mi S of Olite via N 121 and N 134.
▭Tudela/Tutera.
◷ **Timing:** During the Festival de Santa Ana at the end of July is a great time to visit.

---

capitals with scenes from the New Testament and the lives of the saints in a style inspired by the carvings of Aragón. A door of an earlier mosque remains.

Palacio Decanal y Museo de Tudela

Plaza Vieja 2. Mon–Fri 10am–1.30pm, 4–7pm. Sat & hols 10am–1.30pm. Jul & Aug guided tours of cathedral, Mon–Fri noon & 4pm, Sat & hols 10am. €4. ℘948 40 21 61. www.palaciodecanaldetudela.com.

The former bishop's palace, built in the 16C, houses the Museum of Tudela with its collection of sacred art. Before entering the museum, which also includes a visit to the cloisters, take time to admire the magnificent Plateresque portico adorning the facade.

Plaza Fueros

This richly-decorated Baroque square –originally built to stage bull fights– stands on the threshold of the old and new city and is used for large-scale community and political events.

Plaza de la Judería

Until 1498, Tudela was home to a large and learned Jewish population. On one side of the square is the 16C Renaissance Palacio del Marqués de San Adrián. Note the Aragonese style arches and eaves, which were carved by the sculptor Esteban de Obray in 1519. The interior houses a fine courtyard.

Bardena Blanca, Bardenas Reales

Plaza Vieja

Here you will find the 15C **ayuntamiento** (city hall) and the city's art museum.

Museo Muñoz Sola de Arte Moderno (Modern Art Museum)

Plaza Vieja 2. Open Wes–Sun, see website for seasonal opening hours. €1. ℘948 402 640. www.castelruiz.es.

A native of Tudela, the painter César **Muñoz Sola** (1921–2000) amassed an extensive collection of French, mid–late-19C paintings during his lifetime. Represented here are works from Girodet Roucy, Hugard Tower, Julien Tavernier and Foubert amongst others; and of course, there is also a room devoted to Muñoz Sola.

EXCURSIONS

Bardenas Reales★★

◗ Visitor Centre: Ctra. del Polígono de Tiro, km. 6, on the NA134 15km/9mi north of Tudela, just before Arguedas. Open: Park year-round daily 8am–1 hr before sunset. Visitor Centre Apr–Aug 9am–2pm, 4–7pm, Sept–Mar 9am–2pm, 3–5pm. ℘948 83 03 08. www.bardenasreales.es. ⊗ Take water and food as there are few facilities. Beware of snakes.

This awe-inspiring semi-desert consists of 42 500ha/105 000 acres of arid gypsum, clay and sandstone formations, which resemble parts of the American West, such as Monument Valley, and even lunar landscapes.

The park is divided into several areas according to the vegetation found there. The northern swathe and the southern *Bardena Negra* are characterized by pines and oaks, whilst the central *Bardena Blanca* has the most spectacular landscape.

The diversity of terrain and flora in the area allows for the coexistence of many species of birds, and by ancient decree sheep are allowed to graze here during the cooler months, an event celebrated every September 18.

Coming in via the road from Arguedas, you will first pass a military base before the surreal beauty of the Bardenas begins. From here, you can take a loop around the **Bardena Blanca**, where centuries of erosion created by wind and water have created an unforgettable, lunaresque landscape.

Enter by Nuestra Señora del Yugo, a shrine housing a 15C Madonna, to access the best known of the Bardenas, that of Blanca, where sites such as Pisquerra, Sanchicorrota and the Ralla Rallón will guarantee a change of scenery from the greenery of nearby Tudela.

El País Vasco and La Rioja

The Basque Country (País Vasco) forms part of Spain's northeastern frontier, facing the Atlantic. The region of La Rioja borders it to the south. In the Middle Ages the towns and villages of El País Vasco and La Rioja found fame and wealth as staging points on the Camino de Santiago, leaving a rich legacy of religious buildings. Today, with the exceptions of the towns of Donostia-San Sebastián and Bilbao, few people outside Spain are aware of what lies within these regions. Like the rest of northern Spain, the Basque Country and Rioja are mostly rural with none of the sun-blessed imagery or icons of the south. This is a land where isolated farms and small villages nestle in verdant valleys. While Rioja is synonymous with high-quality Spanish wine the Basque Country is renowned for its local cuisine and particularly famed for its *pinxtos*, delectable bite-size tapas.

Highlights

1 Eating and drinking your way around **San Sebastián** (p251)

2 Visiting Bilbao's **Museo Guggenheim** (p256)

3 Pottering along the scenic **Costa de Vizcaya/Bizcaya** (p259)

4 Archeological treasures in **Vitoria-Gasteiz** (p262)

5 Wine tasting in a state-of-the-art bodega in **La Rioja** (p265)

Costa Vasca

The Basque coastal region is known as Vizcaya (Biscay) and is famous for its capital, Bilbo, better known as Bilbao. Just as the 1992 Olympics led to the reinvention of Barcelona, in 1997 Frank Gehry's stunning Guggenheim Museum was the launch pad for the renaissance of a fading port city. Of course, the city's splendid fine arts museum and characterful old quarter were here long before then. Queen of the Costa Vasca is Donostia-San Sebastián, European Captial of Culture 2016. It boasts one of Spain's finest natural settings on a glorious sandy bay, attracting Spanish holidaymakers, a fashionable international set and gourmets; it is often referred to as Spain's food capital with more Michelin stars than Madrid or Barcelona, and boasts an atmospheric old quarter, chock-a-block with eating and drinking options.

País Vasco interior

The inland Basque regions of Guipúzcoa and Álava are so frequently overshadowed by the delights of the coast and overlooked by most visitors. Those who do make the effort to seek out Vitoria (Gasteiz), the sophisticated Basque capital, are rewarded with a splendid old walled town boasting fine museums and galleries. The old university town of Oñati (Oñate), and nearby Santuario de Arantzazu are worth the trip for the scenic countryside settings alone.

La Rioja

Irrigated by the Ebro river, a good proportion of Rioja's 5 034sq km/1 944sq mi is devoted to producing some of Spain's finest wines; Haro is the place to learn more. Many of its towns and villages were (and still are) on the Camino de Santiago, so there are numerous tangible reminders of a rich past. The capital, Logroño, has an atmospheric old town bursting with superb tapas bars.

La Concha, Donostia-San Sebastián

© Javier Larrea/age fotostock

Donostia-San Sebastián★★

San Sebastián (Donostia in Basque) is in a glorious setting on a scallop-shaped bay framed by two hills and the Isle of Santa Clara. Two vast sand beaches follow the curve of the bay: La Concha and fashionable Ondarreta. Gardens, promenades and statuary decorate the town, most notable of which is *El Peine del Viento XV* (Windcomb 15), by Eduardo Chillida.

▷ **Population:** 186 095

◔ **Michelin Map:** 573 (town plan or 574 C 23-24.

🗉 **Info:** Alameda Boulevard 8. ℘943 48 11 66. www.san sebastianturismo.com.

◖ **Location:** Donostia-San Sebastián is on the Gulf of Vizcaya, 25km/15.5mi W of the French border, 102km/63.3mi E of Bilbao. ▭▭Donostia-San Sebastián (only train to Bilbao airport is a local one, takes 2.5hrs).

🅿 **Parking:** Space is limited in the old quarter; walking is preferable.

◉ **Don't Miss:** A walk in the old quarter, and a fine seafood repast.

◔ **Timing:** Allow a day in town and a days for excursions.

🛎 **Kids:** The Aquarium, Eureka Science Museum.

A BIT OF HISTORY

Pioneering tourism – Queen María Cristina of Habsburg chose Donostia-San Sebastián as her summer residence in the 19C, establishing it as a leading resort; the *belle époque* atmosphere is still alive today at the beach.

Gastronomic capital – The all-male members of 30 gourmet clubs prepare outstanding meals, which they consume with cider or *txacolí* wine. Specialities include hake, cod, bream, sardines and squid *(chipirones)*.

SIGHTS
Old Town

The narrow streets of the old town (rebuilt after a fire in 1813) contrast with the wide avenues of modern Donostia. The area comes alive at the apéritif hour when locals and tourists (especially the French) crowd the bars and small restaurants in the *calles* Portu, Muñoa, 31 de Agosto and Fermín Calbetón, to enjoy tapas and the excellent seafood.

Basílica de Santa María

Mayor. Open Jun–Sept 8am–2pm, 4–8pm; Oct–May 8.30am–2pm, 5–8pm. No charge. ℘943 42 31 24.
The church has an exuberant late 18C portal and Baroque altars.

Museo de San Telmo

Pl. Zuloaga 1. Open Tue–Sun & hols 10am–8pm. Closed 1 and 20 Jan, 25 Dec. €6. No charge Tue. ℘943 48 15 81. www.santelmomuseoa.com.

This very progressive museum is set in a 16C monastery. The Renaissance cloisters display Basque stone funerary crosses from the 15C–17C, carved in traditional Iberian style. The upper gallery is the ethnographic section, with a reconstructed Basque interior. Paintings include a Ribera, an El Greco, and 19C artists. The chapel was decorated by **José María Sert** with scenes from the city's history. The museum also stages high quality, often thought-provoking, temporary exhibitions.

Paseo Nuevo (Pasealekua Berria)

This promenade almost fully circles Monte Urgull and gives fine **views**.

🛎 Aquarium San Sebastián★

Pl. Carlos Biasca de Imaz 1. Open daily Jul–Aug 10am–9pm; Holy Week–Jun and Sept Mon–Fri until 8pm, Sat–Sun until 9pm; Oct–Holy Week Mon–Fri until 7pm, Sat–Sun until 8pm. Closed 1 & 20 Jan, 25

Dec. €13; child €6.50. &943 44 00 99.
www.aquariumss.com.
One of the best aquariums in Europe,
visitors can cross its **Oceanarium**★ via
a tunnel with 360° views.

Museo Naval (Naval Museum)
Pasealekua 24. Open Tue–Sat 10am–
2pm, 4–7pm, Sun and public holidays
11am–2pm. €3; free Thu. &943 43 00 51.
www.untzimuseoa.eus.
Small Basque-oriented museum, showing a traditional way of life at sea.

Mercado de la Bretxa
Alameda del Boulevard 3.
Open: Market Mon–Sat 8am–9pm.
www.cclabretxa.com.
In order to create top-rate local cuisine, you need top-rate produce, and
many of the city's star chefs can be
seen perusing the stalls of this covered
marketplace that dates from 1870. It's
a great place to pick up ingredients for
a picnic, or to sample *pintxos* at its bars.

Kursaal
Zurriola, 1. Open hours vary depending
on programme. &943 00 30 00.
www.kursaal.com.es.
Spanish architect Rafael Moneo's cube-
shaped concert hall is a modernist landmark, home to the International Film
Festival and International Jazz Festival.

EXCURSIONS
View from Monte Ulía★
▶ 7km/4.3mi E. Follow the N 1 towards
Irún and take a right before the summit.
The twisting drive up affords excellent-
views of the town and its setting.

Astigarraga-Sagardoetxea
▶ N 10km/6mi S towards Hernani.

Basque Cider House
(Sagardoetxea)
In the centre of town on a hillside; look for
the barrel on the street. Open Tue–Sat (Jul–
Aug daily) 11am–1.30pm, 4pm–7.30pm,
Sun & hols 11am–1.30pm; €4. &943 550
575. www.sagardoetxea.com.
The Basque Country has 53 varieties of
apples. In order to make cider, you need

80% acidic varieties and 20% sweet.
Here you can discover many other
such cider-making principles, as well as
discovering the history of this popular
regional drink, strolling the orchards
where the apple trees are grafted, and
the museum itself, where all stages of
manufacturing are explained. A tasting
caps off the visit.

▲▲ Eureka! Zientzia Museoa (Science Museum)
Bus 28, from the city centre (allow
20min). Mikeletegi, 43 Open daily
year-round; generally Mon 10am–4pm,
Tue–Fri 10am–7pm, Sat, Sun 11am–8pm.
Extended hours Jul–Aug and other
hols.See website for dates. €10,
with planetarium €12; child €7, with
planetarium €9. &943 012 478.
www.eurekamuseoa.es
Each room of this large, modern exciting museum focuses on a different
scientific principle (light, energy, the
senses, mechanics, human body...)
and experiments and demonstrations
illustrate each with lots of interactive
and hands-on aspects. The building also
houses a planetarium (open Tue–Sun;
sessions in Spanish and Basque; see
website for times; €3.50, children €2.50)
and several flight and motion simulators
(extra charge €2.50–€8).

Parque de Aiete ★★
Can be accessed on foot, though it's
a long, uphill walk. Otherwise by car
or bus 19, 31.
This beautiful park – situated on a hilltop at the heart of a residential neighbourhood – is arguably the most attractive in the entire city.
Designed by the French landscape
gardener Pierre Ducasse, it surrounds
a Neoclassical palace which was built in
1878 for the Duke and Duchess of Bailen
and later in 1941 became summer residence for General Franco. Opened to
the public in 1977, it currently serves
as a cultural centre. The gardens
themselves are a haven of greenery
and peace, composed of Atlas cedars,
ginkgo biloba, plane trees, redwoods,
shrubs and flowerbeds. There are

playgrounds for children, benches for resting up with a good book and green stretches of lawn for a picnic.

Tolosa

❯ 26kms/16mi south on the N1.

A stronghold of Basque separatism, Tolosa has grown prosperous through the production of paper and has a fine historic centre replete with old houses, palaces, churches and a recently restored mill. A stroll around it will reveal colourful Basque houses, markets, shops and cafés with the bubbling River Oria never far out of view. Sites to seek out include the Plaza de Triángulo (so named because of its unusual shape), and the Plaza Zarra where the Basque flags flap high on the balconies of the 17C red-brick Ayuntamiento (City Hall). The **Plaza Berdura★** has yet more charming coloured houses and cafés. A flower market is held here every Saturday.

Tolosa's most notable church is the Baroque Santa Maria, situated on the square of the same name. From here, wander along the typically Basque Kale Nagusia, stopping at the Palacio Atodo No. 33 to admire the handsome coat of arms and eaves in the vernacular Basque style before heading to the 15C Torre Andia. Other emblematic streets and squares include the arcaded, Neo-classical Plaza Euskal Herria (which also hosts a market every Saturday morning) and the streets parallel to Kale Korreo. Tolosa is famous for its beans (*alubias*), which you can try in soups and stews while here.

Costa de Guipúzcoa★★

The Basque Coast (Costa Vasca) stretches from the Golfo de Vizcaya (Bay of Biscay) to the headland of the Cabo de Machichaco. The steep shoreline, edged by cliffs and indented by estuaries, is dotted with dozens of fishing villages nestling in sheltered inlets.

DRIVING TOUR

HONDARRIBIA TO BILBAO
70km/43mi. Allow one day.

Hondarribia/Fuenterrabía★
🚆Nearest train station: Irún (4km).
Fuenterrabía (Hondarribia in Basque) is nowadays a holiday resort, but it retains its fishermen's quarter, **La Marina,** with its characteristic wood balconies and bars and cafés. Overlooking the River Bidasoa, the **Old Town,** an old fortified town with steep streets, retains its 15C walls. These are punctuated by the Puerta de Santa María, a gateway

- 👓 **Michelin Map:** 574 B-C 21 to 24 – País Vasco (Guipúzcoa, Vizcaya).
- 🗒 **Info:** www.bizkaiacosta vasca.com.
- 📍 **Location:** The Basque Coast runs from the French border to Bilbao.
- 👪 **Kids:** Museo del Ferrocarril Vasco.
- 🕐 **Timing:** The Basque Coast can be very wet at any time of year.

surmounted by twin angels venerating the Virgen de Guadalupe. Picturesque calle Mayor is lined with houses with wrought-iron balconies.

The Iglesia de Santa María on calle Mayor, a Gothic church with massive buttresses, was remodelled in the 17C and given a Baroque tower. It was the site of a proxy wedding in 1660 between Louis XIV and the Infanta María before the real marriage in France. The Castillo de Carlos V, a fortress (pl. de Armas 14; now a parador) was constructed in the

10C by Sancho Abarca, King of Navarra, and restored by Charles V in the 16C.

▶ Leave Fuenterrabía on the harbour road.

Cabo Higuer★
4km/2.5mi N.
Turn left; as the road climbs, you can enjoy a superb **view**★ of the beach, the town and the quayside and from the end of the headland, the French coast and the town of Hendaye.

▶ Leave Fuenterrabía on the Behobia road; take the first right after the Palmera factory and bear left at the first crossroads.

Ermita de San Marcial
9km/5.6mi SE.
A narrow road leads up to the wooded hilltop (225m/738ft). The **panorama**★★ from the hermitage includes Fuenterrabía, Irún and Isla de los Faisanes (Pheasant Island) in the mouth of the River Bidasoa on the border. In the distance are Donostia-San Sebastián and Hendaye beach.

Jaizkibel Road★★
The **drive**★★ along this road (GI 3440) is at its most impressive at sunset. After 5km/3mi you reach the Capilla de Nuestra Señora de Guadalupe (Chapel of our Lady of Guadalupe) where there is a lovely **view**★ of the French coast.
Past pines and gorse is the Hostal de Jaizkibel (www.hoteljaizkibel.com) at the foot of a 584m/1 916ft peak and a lookout with a superb **view**★★. The road down affords tantalising **glimpses**★ of the indented coast, the Cordillera Cantábrica range and the mountains above Donostia-San Sebastián.

▶ Travel 17km/10.5mi W along the Jaizkibel road.

Pasaia/Pasajes
Pasaia comprises three villages around a sheltered bay. Pasai Antxo is a trading port, **Pasai Donibane**★ and Pasai San Pedro are both deep-sea fishing ports, processing cod. To get to **Pasai Donibane**★, either park at the village entrance or take a motorboat from San Pedro. The view from the water is very picturesque – tall houses with brightly painted wooden balconies, boats and docks, and a single street. A path runs to the lighthouse (🚶 45min).

Donostia-San Sebastián★★
♿See DONOSTIA-SAN SEBASTIÁN

▶ Take the N 1; 7km/4.3mi S of Donostia-San Sebastián take the N 634 towards Bilbao.

Zarautz
Queen Isabel II made this her summer residence in the 19C. Two palaces stand in the old quarter: the 16C **Palacio Narros** (Elizaurre Kalea 2; by guided tour Jul–Aug Tue–Sat at 11.30am, Apr–Jun and Sept–Nov third Sat in the month at noon; ℘943 833 641, turismo.euskadi.net), and the **Luzea tower** (open only during exhibitions; ℘943 83 09 90) on Plaza Mayor, with mullioned windows and a machicolated corner balcony.
The modern **Photomuseum** (San Ignacio11; Tue–Sun 10am–1pm, 4–8pm; ℘943 130 906; www.photomuseum.es) traces the art of photography, from its beginnings to the digital age. Beyond Zarautz, the road rises to a picturesque **corniche**★★.

Getaria-Guetaría★
Getaria is known for its *chipirones* (squid), and its rocky peak – *el ratón*, or Monte de San Antón – linked to its port area by a causeway. Native son **Juan Sebastián Elcano** set out from here with Magellan and in 1522 became one of the first sailors to circumnavigate the world. A narrow street, lined with picturesque houses, leads to the 13C–15C Iglesia de San Salvador (Church of our Saviour; Nagusia; open daily from 9.30am until afternoon mass; ℘943 14 07 51). its chancel rests on an arch above an alleyway. The gallery is Flamboyant Gothic.
The **Cristóbal Balenciaga Museo**★ (Aldamar Parkea 6; open Jun & Sept

Tue–Sun 10am–7pm; Jul & Aug daily 10am–8pm; Nov–Feb Tue–Sun 10am–3pm; €10; ☎943 00 88 40; www.cristobalbalenciagamuseoa.com) showcases key designs from the couturier's career in a purpose-built structure here in his home town.

Zumaia

Zumaia has two fine beaches: Itzurun, set between cliffs, and Santiago. Near the latter is the **Espacio Cultural Ignacio Zuloaga** (guided tours by appt Apr–Sep Fri–Sun 4–8pm; ☎677 078 445, www.espaciozuloaga.com), devoted to the artist who lived here 1870–1945. This not only displays Zuloaga's paintings – realistic and popular themes with brilliant colours and strong lines – but also works by Goya, El Greco, Rodin, Toulouse-Lautrec and Manet. The surrounding group of buildings and collections includes the remains of a Romanesque chapel and projects linked to contemporary art.

In the small town of Zumaia, the 15C **Iglesia de San Pedro** contains a 16C altarpiece by Juan de Anchieta.

▷ Past Zumaia, go left onto the GI 631.

Santuario de San Ignacio de Loyola

Zumaia. Open daily Jun–Sept 10am–1.30pm, 3.30–7.30pm (until 7pm Oct–May). Santa Casa €2; no charge for the rest. ☎943 02 50 00. www.santuariodeloyola.org.

This sanctuary was built by the Jesuits to plans by Italian architect Carlo Fontana around the Loyola family manor near Azpeitia at the end of the 17C. It is an important place of pilgrimage especially on St Ignatius' day (31 July). The basement casemates of the 15C tower are vestiges of the original Loyola manor house, the **Santa Casa**.

The rooms in which Ignatius was born, convalesced and converted have been transformed into profusely decorated chapels. The Baroque basilica is more Italian than Spanish in style, circular with a vast cupola (65m/213ft high).

Museo Vasco del Ferrocarril

Azpeitia. Open Tue–Fri 10am–1.30pm, 3pm–6.30pm, Sat 10.30am-2pm, 4-7.30pm, Sun & hols 10.30am–2pm. Steam train rides throughout the year. Museum €3, train rides €3. ☎943 150 677. www.bemfundazioa.org.

A disused railway station is the perfect setting for a railway museum, with all buildings used – including the platforms and warehouses – for the exhibits, which include lovely old locomotives dating from the late 19C. Train rides go to neighbouring Lasao.

▷ Return to the coast. The journey by road to Deba is one of the most beautiful in the Basque Country.

Deba

The Iglesia de Santa María la Real (pl. Zaharra 7; open daily 9am–1pm (Tue 9am-noon); no charge; ☎943 12 24 52) in this fishing port conceals, beneath the porch in its fortified front, a superb Gothic portal decorated with extremely lifelike statues. The cloister galleries have intricate tracery. There is a splendid **view★** of the coast from the **cliff road★** between Deba and Lekeitio. At **Mutriku** is the delightful beach of **Saturraran**.

ADDRESSES

🛏 STAY

⊜⊜⊜ **Hotel Obispo** – Pl. del Obispo, Hondarribia. ☎943 64 54 00. www.hotelobispo.com. 16 rooms. ⌷11. Charming hotel housed in a 14C–15C palace located in the upper section of the old quarter. Cosy and atmospheric.

⑂ EAT

⊜⊜⊜ **Iribar** – Nagusia 34, Getaria. ☎943 14 04 06. Closed 2 wks Apr & Oct. This highly rated traditional restaurant, in the centre of a fishing village serves grilled fish dishes at sensible prices.

Bilbao★

Bilbao has reinvigorated its infrastructure with a new metro system, with distinctive glazed station entrances by Sir Norman Foster; a new footbridge and airport terminal, both by Santiago Calatrava; and a riverside development by Cesar Pelli (designer of London's Canary Wharf tower). But the jewel in its crown is, of course, the Guggenheim, its spectacular modern art museum designed by Frank Gehry.

A BIT OF HISTORY

The city – Founded in the early 14C, old Bilbao lies on the right bank of the Nervión, under the Santuario de Begoña (Begoña Sanctuary). It was originally named **Las Siete Calles**, (the Seven Streets), for its layout. The modern **El Ensanche** ("enlargement") business district, across the river, developed in the 19C. The wealthy residential quarter spreads around Doña Casilda Iturriza park and Gran Vía de Don Diego López de Haro.

Industry – Industry developed in the middle of the 19C when iron mined nearby was shipped to England. Iron and steelworks were subsequently established.

Greater Bilbao and the ría – Since 1945 Greater Bilbao has included the towns from Bilbao itself to Getxo on the sea. Industry is concentrated along the left bank in **Baracaldo**, **Sestao**, **Portugalete** with its **transporter bridge** built in 1893, and in Somorrostro where there is an oil refinery.

Santurtzi is known for its sardines.

Algorta, a residential town on the right bank, is a contrast to heavy industry; **Deusto** is famous for its university.

MUSEO GUGGENHEIM★★★

Av. Abandoibarra 2. Open Tue-Sat 10am-8pm. Closed 1 Jan, 25 Dec. €13. Artean Pass (inc Museo Bellas Artes) €16. ℘944 35 90 00. www.guggenheim-bilbao.es.

▶ **Population:** 345 141

⚹ **Michelin Map:** 573 C 21 (town plan) – País Vasco (Vizcaya)

🛈 **Info:** Plaza Circular, 1. ℘944 79 57 60. www.bilbaoturismo.net.

▶ **Location:** Bilbao is in northeastern Spain's Basque Country. Vitoria-Gasteiz is 69km/43mi to the S, Donostia-San Sebastián 102km/63mi to the E, and Santander 103km/64mi to the W. 🚆Estacion de Abando, is the major train station in Bilbao. A fast (Basque Y) line under construction (2006-17) – will connect to Donostia-San Sebastián and Vitoria-Gasteiz (then onto Madrid via Burgos, Valladolid, Segovia). Trains do not run to the city centre from Bilbao airport.

☺ **Don't Miss:** The Guggenheim is a must-see for Spain, not just Bilbao.

🕐 **Timing:** Spend a few hours at the Guggenheim for starters, try out the metro and stroll the riverside.

👫 **Kids:** Museo Marítimo Ría del Bilbao.

This is the European showcase for the collection founded in New York by art patron Solomon R. Guggenheim (1861–1949), the youngest of the prestigious museums managed by the Guggenheim Foundation. With this stunning museum complex, inaugurated in 1997, acclaimed architect **Frank Gehry** created one of the great buildings of the late 20C, a counterpart to Frank Lloyd Wright's famous 1950 spiral housing the Guggenheim's Fifth Avenue museum.

Emblem of the City

The museum rises from the banks of the Nervión like a complex ship with billowing sails. Formal geometry and symmetry are abandoned to free

Bilbao with the Nervión and Museo Guggenheim

forms, creating harmony and lines flowing gracefully out of potential chaos. The composition, shimmering in titanium, demands to be seen from all angles and alters with every change of light. The south entrance, of golden limestone, opens to a soaring **central atrium** (50m/164ft high) which echoes Wright's great spiral, transformed here into a whirl of smoothly moulded shapes and natural light.

Access to the galleries is by glass-fronted lifts or vertiginous suspended walkways and staircases. The largest measures 130m/426.5ft long and 25m/82ft wide, running the length of the riverside site, culminating in a V-shaped metal and stone tower.

Collections

Drawing on the vast Guggenheim collections (more than 6 000 paintings, sculptures and works on paper), the Bilbao collection focuses on art from the 1950s to the present. Well represented are Modern masters (Picasso, Mondrian, Kandinsky) and major movements such as Abstract Expressionism (Rothko, De Kooning, Pollock), Pop art (Oldenburg, Rosenquist, Warhol), and Conceptual and Minimalist art (Carl André, Donald Judd). Contemporary artists likely to be on view include Anselm Kiefer, Francesco Clemente and Damien Hirst.

The museum's own acquisitions include a vast mural by Sol LeWitt and Richard Serra's Snake, three gigantic sheets of undulating steel. Notable Spanish works are by **Antoni Tàpies, Eduardo Chillida, Francesc Torres, Cristina Iglesias** and **Susana Solano**. Space is reserved for **Picasso**'s *Guernica*, now in Madrid's Reina Sofía museum.

SIGHTS
Museo de Bellas Artes★

Pl. del Museo 2. Open Wed–Mon 10am –8pm (2pm Dec 24 & 31 unless Tue). Closed 1, 6 Jan, 25 Dec. €9, no charge daily 6-8pm; Artean Pass (inc. Guggenheim) €16. ℘944 39 60 60. www.museobilbao.com.

The city's fine arts museum is in two buildings in Doña Casilda Iturriza park. The **ancient art section★★** (old building, ground floor) exhibits 12–17C Spanish paintings. Romanesque works include a 12C Crucifixion from the Catalan School. The 16–17C Spanish Classical section has works by **Morales, El Greco**, Valdés Leal, **Zurbarán, Ribera** and **Goya**. Dutch and Flemish canvases (15C–17C) include *The Usurers* by Quentin Metsys, a *Pietà* by Benson and *Holy Family* by Gossaert.

The Basque art section (first floor) holds works by the great Basque painters: Regoyos, Zuloaga, Iturrino etc. The contemporary art section (new building) displays works by artists both Spanish – Solana, Vázquez Díaz, Gargallo, Blanchard, Luis Fernández Otieza, Chillida and Tàpies – and foreign – Delaunay, Léger, Kokoschka and Bacon.

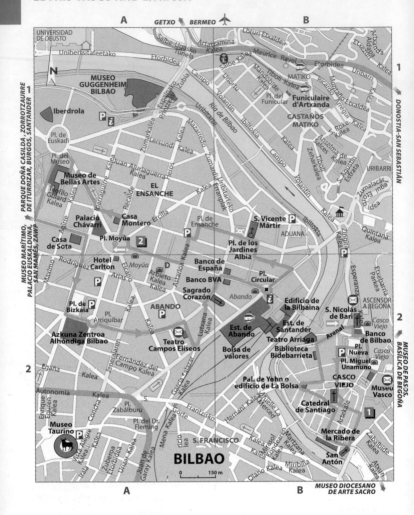

Euskal Museoa Bilbao (Basque Museum)

Pl. Miguel de Unamuno 4. Open Mon, Wed–Fri 10am–7pm, Sat 10am–1.30pm, 4–7pm Sun 10am–2pm. Closed public holidays. €3; no charge Thu. ☏944 15 54 23. www.euskal-museoa.org.
Set in the ex-**Colegio de San Andrés** in the Old Town, this collection provides an insight into traditional Basque activities (weaving, arts and crafts, fishing).

Museo Diocesano de Arte Sacro (Sacred Art Museum)

Pl. de la Encarnación 9. Open Tue–Sat 10.30am–1.30pm, 4–7pm, Sun 10.30am –1.30pm. Guided tours available. Closed 1 & 6 Jan, 24–25 & 31 Dec. €3; no charge Tue. ☏944 32 01 25. www.eleizmuseoa.com.
Basque silverware collection and 12C–15C sculptures of the Virgin and Child.

Alhóndiga Bilbao★

Arriquibar 4. Open Mon–Thu 7am–11pm, Fri until midnight, Sat 8.30am–midnight, Sun until 11pm. ☏944 01 40 14. www.azkunazentroa.com.
This Modernist wine warehouse was restored to designs by Philippe Starck, transforming the complex into a giant cultural venue encompassing the per-

forming arts, a huge leisure complex, plus library, shops, cafes and restaurants.

♁♁ Museo Marítimo Ría de Bilbao★★

Muelle Ramón de la Sota. Open Jun–Oct Tue–Sun 10am–8pm, Nov–May Tue –Fri 10am–6pm, Sat, Sun 10am–8pm. €6, child €3.50, free Tue. ✆946 08 55 00. www.museomaritimobilbao.eus.

This entertaining family-friendly museum explains Bilbao's important maritime history and culture. Located inside the outbuildings of the old shipyards (or in *astilleros* Spanish), the ground floor focuses on the development of and changes to the city's estuary, with an entire room devoted to Evaristo de Churruca (1841–1917), the engineer who constructed the city's first port. The second level focuses on Bilbao's commercial and industrial maritime prominence and the industrialisation of the city through historic maps, documents and models.

Outside in the dry docks, the tour ends with a display that includes a life boat, old wooden fishing boats and a tug from 1928, which visitors can board.

🚗 DRIVING TOUR

Costa de Vizcaya/Bizkaia

The beaches and coves that dot the Costa de Guipuzcoa are backed by rolling green hills and make for an ideal escape from busy Bilbao, with beautiful unspoiled areas, particularly around the pristine Urdaibai Biosphere Reserve. Touring the coastline will enable you to discover towns and villages brimming with Basque history and culture. For outdoor enthusiasts there are ample opportunities for sports and hiking.

▷ Exit Bilbao W along the A-8 in the direction of Vitoria-Gasteiz. At exit 14 take the N-624 towards Donostia-San Sebastián then the GI-638 towards Mutriku. Once there, take the Bi-633.

Ondárroa

10km/6.2mi W of Deba along GI 638. The village church, standing like a ship's prow, tall typical Basque houses with washing at the windows, and the encircling river, make up a picture-postcard **ensemble★**. Canning and fish salting are the main industries.

Continue around the point for a fine **view★** of the next settlement, Lekeitio, its beach and the island of San Nicolás, joined to the mainland at low tide.

▷ Leave W along BI 3438.

Lekeitio

12km/7.4mi W.

A deeply indented bay at the foot of Monte Calvario, divided by an island, makes up Lekeitio's fishing harbour. The 15C **Iglesia** (Independentzia Enparantza; open daily 8am–noon, 5–7.30pm; no charge; ✆946 84 09 54) by the harbour has three tiers of flying buttresses and a tall Baroque belfry. Nearby are **good beaches**.

Ispaster/Ispáster

This atmospheric town has retained an ensemble of old buildings, including a pretty 15C church, some Renaissance and Baroque mansions, including the Palacio Arana (1700). To get to the coast, take the road on your right just before the cemetery on the outskirts of the village. It runs though the forest before reaching Ogeyi Beach.

▷ Continue NW BI 3438.

Ea

11km/6.8mi NW of Lekeitio

This miniature harbour stands between two hills at the end of a quiet creek. Old houses follow the banks of the river, which is spanned by stone bridges and makes for a pleasant, shaded walk. To the left of the church of Nuestra Señora de Jesús, at the entrance to the village, follow the yellow-and-white markings. The walk continues through woods and meadows. Once you reach two houses overlooking the main road, take the path at the side of the second.

Back on the road, follow it left to the houses where you return to the main path. It leads to the coast and the hermitage of Talako Ama, revealing a beautiful sea **view★** (90min).

> Continue NE along BI 3438.

Elantxobe★
7km/4.3mi NW of Ea.

Fishermen have long used the bay as a natural harbour and built their houses overlooking the water, against steep-sided Cabo Ogoño (300m/1 000ft).

Beyond rose-coloured **Playa de Laga**, a beach circling Cabo Ogoño, you can see the estuary of **Gernika ría★**, Izaro island, the white outline of the town of Sukarrieta on the far bank, and Chacharramendi island. The resort of **Playa de Laida**, on the *ría*, is popular with Gernika residents.

> Go SW and bear left at Kortezubi.

Cuevas de Santimamiñe
Barrio Basondo, Kortezubi. Access only by guided tour (1hr 30mins), daily mid-Apr–mid-Oct on the hour 10am–1pm then 3.30pm, 5pm, 5.30pm. Rest of year Tue–Sun on the hour 10am–1pm. Tours must be booked at the Interpretation Centre. 5€. ℘944 65 16 57. www.santimamiñe.com.

Wall paintings and engravings from the Magdalenian period (around 17 000 to 11 000 years ago were discovered in these caves in 1917.

> Return to the main road and bear south.

Gernika
14km/8.7mi S of Elantxobe.

The town is of course famous for Picasso's painting, *Guernica* (♨ see MADRID, p143), depicting the Spanish Civil War atrocity here on 26 April 1937, when Nazi planes bombed the town, killing over 1 000 civilians.

In the Middle Ages, the Gernika oak was one of the four places where newly created lords of Biscay came to swear that they would respect the local *fueros* or privileges. The remains of this thousand-year-old tree may be seen in the small temple **behind the Casa de Juntas** (Allendesalazar; open daily 10am–2pm, 4–6pm (7pm Jun– Sept); closed 1, 6 Jan, 16 Aug, 24–25, 31 Dec; no charge; ℘946 25 11 38).

Close by is the extremely moving **Fundación Museo de la Paz** (Pl. de Foru; visits by appt. Open Mar–Sept Tue–Sat 10am–7pm, Sun 10am–2pm; Oct–Feb Tue–Sat 10am–2pm, 4–6pm, Sun 10am–2pm; ℘946 27 02 13, www.museodelapaz. org). The museum is divided into three sections: the first attempts to define the concept of peace through quotes from famous historic figures such as Martin Luther King and Gandhi, while the second discusses Guernica's tragic history. The third addresses the concept of peace today, focusing on the Basque conflict, political prisoners and torture.

> Head south on the BI 2224 and BI 3231 for 18km/11mi.

The **Balcón de Vizcaya★★** (Balcony of Biscay) viewpoint overlooks a lovely chequer board of meadows and forests.

> Return to Gernika.

Two viewpoints before Mundaka enable you to take a last look back over still waters. As the road drops downhill, you get a magnificent **view★** of Bermeo.

Bermeo
15km/9mi NW Gernika on BI 2235.

The fishermen's quarter, still crowded onto the Atalaya promontory overlooking the old harbour, was once protected by ramparts (traces remain), and the grim granite Torre de Ercilla, now the **Museo del Pescador/Arrantzaleen Museoa** (pl. Torrontero; open Tue–Sat 10am–2pm, 4–7pm, Sun 10am–2pm; €3; ℘946 88 11 71, www.bizkaikoa. bizkaia.eus), is dedicated to local fishermen.

A reconstruction of a 17C whaling boat anchored in the port, by the tourist office, is also a reminder of Bermeo's golden age of fishing and forms part of **The Whaling Interpretation Centre, Aita Guria** 👥 (reopens March 2018, call for 2018 opening hours; €2; 📞946 17 91 21; www.aitaguria.bermeo. org). An audio guide introduces the captain's cabin, galleys and the hold, and helps to understand the living conditions onboard. Call before visiting as access depends on the tides.

▶ Turn left towards Mungía.

Alto del Sollube★
(Sollube Pass)
The road up to the low pass (340m/1 115ft) affords a good view of Bermeo.

▶ Return to Bermeo, follow the coast road left for 3km/1.8mi then turn right.

Faro (Lighthouse) de Machichaco
From just left of here there is a good view west. The road winds to a **viewpoint★** over the **San Juan de Gaztelugache** headland and its hermitage (🚶 access via a pathway), the site of a *romería* (pilgrimage) each Midsummer's Day (23 Jun). There are extensive views from the **corniche road★** between Bakio and Arminza and a belvedere also commands a fine **view★** of the coast, Bakio, valley farms and wooded hinterland.

Arminza
Arminza is the only harbour along this section of wild coast.

▶ Continue SW.

Gorliz
7km/4.3mi SW of Arminza.
Gorliz is an attractive beach resort at the mouth of the River Butrón. **Plentzia** nearby (2km/1.2mi) is an oyster farming centre and resort.

Castillo de Butrón
Closed for restoration.
This fantasy castle, built on the remains of a 14C–15C construction, is a superb example of eclectic, picturesque 19C architecture, and provides insight into medieval castle life.

Getxo
13km/8mi SW of Gorliz.
The **paseo marítimo** (sea promenade) overlooks the coast. From the road up to Getxo's well-known golf course there is a view of the Bilbao inlet and on the far bank, Santurtzi and Portugalete.

Bilbao★
👆See BILBAO.

ADDRESSES

🛏 STAY

�🛏 **Bilborooms** – Victor 3, 1st Floor. 📞944 79 35 91. www.bilborooms.com. 10 rooms. Small modern rooms, all with broadband, in a modern pension in the heart of the Old Town.

�🛏🛏 **NH Collection Villa de Bilbao** – Gran Vía 87. 📞944 416 000. www. nh-hotels.com. 142 rooms. 🛏€14. Renovated in 2012, this modern four-star hotel in the centre offers comfortable, minimalist accommodation as well as a restaurant serving contemporary Basque cuisine (😛🛏🛏).

🍽 EAT

😛 **Gatz** – Sta Maria, 10. 📞944 15 48 61. www.bargatz.com. Closed Sun eve. 🍴. Old-town bar with prize-winning pintxos.

😛 **Rio-Oja** – Txakur Kalea, 4. 📞944 15 08 71. Closed Mon. In the old part of the city, this popular restaurant and tapas bar serves high quality food in a charming traditional atmosphere.

😛🛏🛏 **Mina** – Muelle Marzana. 📞944 795 938. www.restaurantemina.es. Closed Sun eve, Mon & Tue. Located in the south of the city next to the river, this rustic-chic Michelin-star restaurant serves dishes inspired by what's in the market. Three tasting menus starting at €60.

Vitoria-Gasteiz★

Vitoria-Gasteiz is the capital of the largest Basque province and the seat of the Basque government, sited in a cereal-covered plateau. It was founded in the 12C and was surrounded by walls. The old quarter is in the upper section.

CIUDAD VIEJA★★

Concentric streets – each named after a trade – ring the cathedral in the old town. The liveliest streets are to the left of the plaza de la Virgen Blanca. The **Iglesia de San Pedro** (Fundadora de las Siervas de Jesús 2), with its Gothic façade, can also be found in this part of the old town.

Plaza de la Virgen Blanca

The square, dominated by the Iglesia (church) de San Miguel, is surrounded by house fronts with glassed-in balconies, or *miradores*. The massive monument at the square's centre commemorates Wellington's decisive victory on 21 June 1813, putting to flight King Joseph Bonaparte and his army. It communicates with the nobly ordered 18C **Plaza de España** (or Plaza Nueva).

Iglesia de San Miguel

Escaleras de San Miguel 1.
Guided tours available Jul–Sept, organised by the tourist office.
In a jasper niche in the church porch is a polychrome Late Gothic statue of the Virgen Blanca, the city's patron. In the late 14C portal, the tympanum shows the Life of St Michael. In the chancel are an altarpiece by Gregorio Fernández and a Plateresque sepulchral arch.

Plaza del Machete★★

This small, long square lies behind the **Arquillos**, an arcade which links the upper and lower towns. A niche in the east end of San Miguel church contains the *"machete"* (actually a cutlass), on which the procurator general had

to swear to uphold the town's privileges *(fueros)*. The 16C **Palacio de Villa Suso** (open Mon–Fri during exhibitions 8.30am–1.30pm, 9pm in summer), on the right side, is now a congress centre.

▶ Climb the steps adjoining the palace.

A stroll along **calle Fray Zacarías Martínez**, with wood-framed houses and palaces, is pleasant. The Renaissance north doorway of the Palacio de los Escoriaza-Esquivel, built on the old town walls, is worth a look; if it is open, go inside to see its lovely covered courtyard.

Catedral de Santa María★★

Cuchillería 95–97. Open daily 10am–2pm, 4–8pm. Closed 1 Jan, 25 Dec. Guided hard-hat tours (60min) available with prior booking, direct, or via the tourist office. €8.50. ✆945 25 51 35. www.catedralvitoria.com.
The construction of this Gothic church-fortress, part of the city's first defensive ring, began at the end of the 13C. Recently however the diocese has stuggled for centuries to keep the cathedral from subsiding and tumbling. A pro-

▶ **Population:** 243 918
◉ **Michelin Map:** 573 D 21-22 (town plan) – País Vasco (Álava).
▪ **Info:** Espainia Plaza 1. ✆945 16 15 98. www.vitoria-gasteiz.org.
◖ **Location:** Vitoria-Gasteiz is about 62km/38mi south of Bilbao. ▭Vitoria-Gasteiz (fast (Basque Y) line under construction (2006–20) will connect to Madrid, Donostia-San Sebastián and Bilbao).
◕ **Timing:** Allow a day to explore the city. Vitoria hosts a jazz festival (www.jazzvitoria.com) each July attracting international stars.

gramme to realign its walls has been running for several years and an innovative hard-hat tour along walkways and passages reveals the secrets of this temple fortress.

Still on calle Cuchillería, old meets new in the exciting BIBAT complex (see below) that juxtaposes cutting-edge 21C architecture with the Renaissance **Palacio de Bendaña**. The latter is notable for its corner turret and doorway with *alfiz* surround; part of its delightful **patio** has also been preserved.

BIBAT: Museo Fournier de Naipes y Museo de Arqueología★ (Playing Cards Museum and Archaeological Museum)

Cuchillería 54. Open Tue–Fri 10am–2pm, 4–6.30pm, Sat 10am–2pm, Sun and public holidays 11am–2pm.
℘945 20 37 00. www.araba.eus.

Occupying the older building is the Naipes (playing cards) collection, founded in 1868 by Heraclio Fournier, a descendant of a Parisian family famous for printing playing cards. The collection currently comprises over 20 000 sets of cards from all around the world, dating from the 14C to the present day. They cover a wide variety of topics (such as history, geography, art, caricatures and customs) and a diversity of print media, including paper, parchment, leaves, fabric and metal.

The Archeological Museum (architect Patxi Mangado) occupies the striking modern annex and displays finds from excavations in Álava province. Note the dolmen collections and Roman monuments. At Cuchillería 24, the 16C **Casa del Cordón**, is sometimes open for exhibitions.

CIUDAD NUEVA

As Vitoria-Gasteiz grew in the 18C, neo-Classical constructions began to appear such as the **Arquillos** arcade in what is referred to as the modern town.
In the 19C, the town expanded southwards with the **Parque de la Florida** (Florida Park), the **Catedral Nueva** (New Cathedral, 1907) in neo-Gothic style and

two wide avenues, paseo de la Senda and paseo de Fray Francisco, the latter lined by mansions, such as the Palacio de Ajuria Enea, seat of the Lehendakari, or Basque government, and two museums, the Museo de Armería and the Museo de Bellas Artes.

Near Plaza de España is the modern Plaza de los Fueros, the work of architect José Luis Peña Ganchegui and sculptor Eduardo Chillida.

Museo Artium★

Francia Kalea 24. Open Tue–Fri 11am–2pm, 5pm–8pm; Sat–Sun 11am–8pm. €5, Wed and weekend after start of new exhibitions, by donation. ℘945 20 90 00. www.artium.org.

This Basque Museum of Contemporary Art and cultural centre focuses on the foundations of modern art. A significant selection from its **magnificent collection★** is shown on a rotating basis. The museum owns more than 1 800 works of Spanish artists, from the Avant Garde of the twenties and thirties (forming the majority of the collection) to recent works. Featured artists include Miró, Gargallo, Tàpies, Canogar, Palazuelo, Oteiza and Chillida.

Museo de Armería★ (Museum of Arms and Armour)

Pas. de Fray Francisco 3. Open Tue–Fri 10am–2pm, 4–6.30pm, Sat 10am–2pm, Sun & public holidays 11am–2pm. Closed 1 Jan & Good Friday. ℘945 18 19 25. www.araba.eus

The well-presented collection housed in a modern building traces the tradition and evolution of weaponry in the Basque Country from prehistoric axes to early 20C pistols. Note the 15C–17C **armour**, including suits of 17C **Japanese armour**.

Museo Diocesano de Arte Sacro (Diocesan Sacred Art Museum)

Monseñor Cadena y Eleta s/n. Open Tue–Fri 11am–2pm, 4–6.30pm Sat–Sun & public holidays, 11am–2pm. €3, no charge first Sat of the month. ℘945 15 06 31. www.museoartesacro.org.

Set in the ambulatory of the **Catedral Nueva, the Diocesan Museum** exhibits Gothic images, Flemish works (*Descent from the Cross* by Van der Goes, *The Crucifixion* by Ambrosius Benson), 16C–18C canvases (*St Francis* by El Greco, several Riberas, *The Immaculate Conception* by Alonso Cano) and various silverware.

Museo de Bellas Artes (Fine Arts Museum)

Pas. de Fray Francisco de Vitoria 8. Open Tue–Fri 10am–2pm, 4–6.30pm, Sat 10am–2pm, 5–8pm. Sun 11am–2pm. Closed 1 Jan & Good Friday. ℘945 18 19 18. www.araba.eus

This collection, housed in the early 20C **Historicist Palacio de Agustí**, displays Spanish art of the 18C and 19C, and a comprehensive selection of Basque *costumbrista* painting by such artists as Iturrino, Regoyos and Zuloaga. Highlights include *La Cuidad con Sol* by Fernando de Amárica.

EXCURSIONS

Santuario de Estíbaliz

❍ 10km/6.2mi E. Leave Vitoria-Gasteiz via the Avda de Bruselas, take the A 132 towards Argadoña. Bear left after about 4km/2.5mi. Open daily 8am–8pm. ℘639 31 07 79. http://turismo.euskadi.eus.

This Late Romanesque pilgrim shrine has an attractive wall belfry on the south front, and a 12C Romanesque statue of the Virgin.

EAST OF VITORIA-GASTEIZ: MEDIEVAL PAINTINGS

❍ 25km/15.5mi along the E5-N1 motorway as far as junction 375.

Gazeo

Superb 14C **Gothic frescoes**★★ decorate the chancel of the Iglesia de San Martín de Tours (guided tours Sept–Jun Thu and Fri; Jul–Aug and Holy Week daily; €2; ℘945 30 29 31). The south wall shows Hell as a whale's gullet, the north, the Life of the Virgin. On the roof are scenes from the Life of Christ.

Alaiza

❍ Follow the A 4111 for 3km/1.8mi, turn right, then left after a few metres.

The **paintings**★ on the walls and roof of the iglesia de la Asunción apse (guided tours, as Gazeo) probably date from the late 14C. Strange red outlines represent castles and churches, as well as soldiers and many other persons.

Oñati/Oñate

❍ At the foot of Monte Alona (1 321m/4 333ft), 45km/28mi NE of Vitoria-Gasteiz and 74km/46mi SW of Donostia-San Sebastián

Nestling amid the wild beauty of the Udana Valley, **Oñati**, with its seigniorial residences, monastery and old university, figured prominently in the First Carlist War.

The **Edificio de la Antigua Universidad (Old University Building)**★ (Universitate Etorbidea 8, open only by prebooked guided tour; ℘943 78 34 53; http://turismo.euskadi.net), now the administrative headquarters of Guipúzcoa province, was founded in 1542 and functioned as a university until the early 20C. The gateway, by Pierre Picart, is surmounted by pinnacles and crowded with statues.

The **ayuntamineto**★ is housed in a fine 18C Baroque building designed by Martín de Carrera.

The Gothic church, **Iglesia de San Miguel**, facing the university was modified in the Baroque period. In the Renaissance chapel, off the north aisle, closed by beautiful iron grilles, note the interesting gilded wood altarpiece. The golden stone cloister exterior is in **Isabelline Plateresque** style (guided tours by prior appt with tourst office; ℘943 78 34 53).

Santuario de Arantzazu★

❍ 9km/5.5mi S of Oñati/Onnate along the GI 3591. Visit by guided tour only. ℘943 71 89 11. www.arantzazu.org.

The **scenic cliff road**★ follows the River Arantzazu, which flows through a narrow gorge. The **shrine** at 800m/2 625ft in a mountain **setting**★ faces the highest peak in the province, Mount

Aitzgorri (1 549m/5 082ft). Dominating the church is an immense startlingly modern bell tower, 40m/131ft high, studded with diamond-faceted stones symbolising the hawthorn bush (*arantzazu* in Basque) in which the Virgin appeared to a local shepherd in 1469.

ADDRESSES

🛏 STAY

😊😊 **Hotel Dato** – Dato 28. ☎945 14 72 30. www.hoteldato.com. 14 rooms. Centrally located, this characterful hotel offers traditional décor with Belle Epoque flourishes. Bedrooms are impeccably maintained.

😊😊😊 **Hotel Palacio de Elorriaga** – Elorriaga 15, 1.5km/1mi E along Av. de Santiago and the N 104. ☎945 26 36 16. www.hotelpalacioelorriaga.com. 21 rooms. ☕10. Restaurant 😊😊😊. This 16C–17C mansion has been completely restored. Behind the sober walls of stone and brick, the overall effect is delightful with tasteful small touches and an abundance of wood and antique furniture. Guest rooms are cosy with en-suite bathrooms. Good value.

🍴 EAT

😊😊😊 **Gurea** – Pl. de la Constitución 10. ☎945 24 59 33. www.gurearestaurante. com. Closed Sun–Wed for dinner, 2nd fortnight Aug. Attractive trad-modern fittings in rustic dining areas where traditional foods are served.

TAPAS

El Rincón de Luis Mari – Rioja 14. ☎945 25 01 27. Closed Tue. A simple bar with a large choice of tapas and raciones, a fine selection of cured hams, and a good location near the old quarter.

La Rioja★★

The Ebro Valley in La Rioja is carpeted with vineyards and vegetable fields under the peaks of the Sierras de Cantabria and de la Demanda. La Rioja, which takes its name from the Río Oja, a tributary of the Ebro, flourished thanks to its position on the pilgrim route to Santiago de Compostela, and only later became famous for its wine.

A BIT OF GEOGRAPHY

Bustling **Rioja Alta** (Upper Rioja), to the west around Haro, is devoted to wine-growing while the lands of **Rioja Baja** (Lower Rioja) are given over to the growing of early vegetables. The main towns of the region are **Logroño** and Calahorra.

SIGHTS

Logroño

The capital of the Rioja region is on the banks of the Ebro. Pilgrims to Santiago

▶ **Population:** 317 053

⚓ **Michelin Map:** 573 E 20-23, F 20-24 – La Rioja, Navarra, País Vasco (Álava).

🔢 **Info:** Logroño: Portales 50. ☎941 29 12 60; Nájera: Plaza San Miguel 10. ☎941 36 00 41; San Millán de la Cogolla: Monasterio de Yuso. ☎941 37 32 59; Santo Domingo de la Calzada: Mayor 70 ☎941 34 12 38. www.lariojaturismo.com, http://turismo.euskadi.net/ rioja-alavesa. 🚂Logroño.

▶ **Location:** La Rioja covers approximately 5 000sq km/ 1 930sq mi in the provinces of La Rioja, Álava and Navarra.

🕐 **Timing:** Three or four days to tour the vineyards.

de Compostela would have entered this attractive town through the stone gateway, overlooking the cathedral.

TAPAS

Calle del Laurel is one of the tastiest streets in Logroño with its huge choice of bars serving delicious local specialities (sweet peppers, mushrooms, etc.) and, of course, local wines.

Concatedral Santa María la Redonda

Portales 14. Open Mon–Sat 8am–1pm, 6.30–8.45pm, Sun 9am–2pm, 6.30–8.45pm. No charge. ℘941 25 76 11. www.laredonda.org.

Dating from 1435, the church has three naves, three polygonal apses and chapels in its side aisles. The Plateresque Chapel of Our Lady of Peace (Nuestra Señora de la Paz) was founded in 1541 by Diego Ponce de León.

Museo de la Rioja

Pl. de San Agustín. Open Tue–Sat 10am–2pm, 4–9pm, Sun and public holidays 11.30am–2pm. No charge. ℘941 29 12 59. www.larioja.org

This regional museum featuring art and history reopened in 2013 after a decade of closure for major renovations. It is set in a fine 18C Baroque palace.

Laguardia/Biasteri/Guardia★

Hillside Laguardia is the most attractive town in Rioja Alavesa. The two imposing towers visible as you approach are San Juan to the south, and the 12C tower of the abbey to the north.

Iglesia de Santa María de los Reyes

Mayor. Guided tours by prior arrangement. €2. ℘945 60 08 45.

This Gothic church retains a superb late 14C **portal★★** with 17C polychrome decoration. The tympanum is divided into three scenes relating the life of the Virgin. Note the figure of Christ holding a small child in his hands representing the soul of the Virgin.

Labastida

▶ 20km/12mi W of Laguardia via A 124. The capital of Rioja Alavesa, this frontier town is perched on a rocky outcrop. Its pretty Old Town, **La Mota★**, has narrow streets lined with charming, faded, stone houses with studded doors.

Bodegas Ysios★

▶ Due north of Laguardia on the Camino de la Hoya. Guided tours (approx 2 hrs) with tasting avialable in English. Prior booking required. €12. ℘945 60 06 40. www.ysios.com.

Designed by renowned Valencian architect Santiago Calatrava, and nestled at the base of the Sierra de Cantabria Mountains, the outline of this stunning *bodega* (winery) evokes both the shape of wine barrels and the mountains' curves in its undulating form. Inside, vats and bottles are stored in soaring wall-less, arc-like spaces that allow air to circulate.

The upstairs tasting room is characterised by a high ceiling and a fabulous view onto the vineyards.

Ciudad del Vino

▶ 5km/3.1mi S of Laguardia on the A2310. Guided tours (1hr 30min) and tasting daily with prior booking. €12. ℘945 60 60 00. www.marquesderiscal.com.

In the tiny village of **El Ciego**, Frank Gehry, of Guggenheim fame, has designed an amazing luxury hotel and spa, resembling a mini-Bilbao Guggenheim, on behalf of the Marqués de Riscal winemaking company. Within the grounds, the cellars are also open to the public; the visit ends at "La Catedral", where a bottle of wine from each year of the company's long history is kept.

Centro Temático del vino Villa Lucía (Villa Lucía Wine Centre)

Ctra Logroño. Call to reserve a tour. €11 (inc tasting with tapas). ℘945 60 00 32. www.villa-lucia.com.

The museum on this lovely estate traces the history and viticulture of wines and within its tours includes a

Wines of La Rioja

In 1902, Rioja was the first Spanish appellation with the Denominación de Origen Calificada (DOC) quality label and today over 500 *bodegas* (wineries) dot the region. The wine is the result of more than seven centuries of tradition and a superb position in the Ebro Valley between the Sierra de la Demanda and the Sierra de Cantabria. The wine region is traditionally divided into three sub-zones: Rioja Alavesa, Rioja Baja and Rioja Alta. Although seven grape varieties are permitted, the

Rioja Alavesa vineyards, Laguardia

© F. J. Fdez. Bordonada/age fotostock

two most commonly used are Tempranillo and Grenache. Red wine accounts for 75 per cent of production and is produced according to two different processes: carbonic maceration and ageing. The first produces young, fresh wines which are best consumed in the year of production, whereas the ageing process, in Bordeaux oak barrels, results in three different wines, classified according to the time spent in the barrel and the time which has elapsed between the harvest and the moment the wine leaves the cellars: Crianza (12 months in the barrel, one year in the bottle), Reserva (12 months in the barrel, two years in the bottle) and Gran Reserva (24 months in the barrel, three years in the bottle).

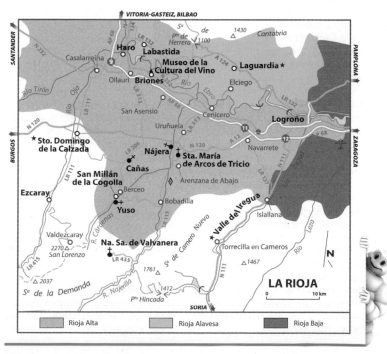

4-D presentation. The **panorama** from the **Balcón de Rioja**★★ or Rioja Balcony 12km/7.4mi northwest of Laguardia near the Puerto de Herrera (Herrera Pass, 1 100m/3 609ft), is extensive.

Haro

This small town is famous for its wines. Elegant 16C and 18C façades recall a prestigious past. In **plaza de la Paz** note the Neoclassical town hall (ayuntamiento), which was built by Juan de Villanueva in 1769; also note the Baroque tower of the **Iglesia de Santo Tomás**.

Vivanco★

○ 5km/3mi from Haro, in **Briones** (442km/275mi on the N 232).

Museo de la Cultura del Vino

See website for opening times. €18 for museum, €12 guided tours (reserve in advance), €25 combined. ☞902 32 20 13. http://vivancoculturadevino.es.
This splendid vineyard offers tours of its estate including a museum of the history and culture of wine and changing wine technology over 10 000 years.

Santo Domingo de la Calzada★

This staging post town on the Camino de Santiago was founded in the 11C and owes its name to a hermit, Dominic, who built a bridge for pilgrims. Parts of the 14C ramparts can still be seen. The **old town**★ huddles around the **Plaza del Santo**, dominated by the Cathedral and the ex-hospital, now a parador. The streets around the square, particularly the calle Mayor, retain 16C and 17C stone houses with fine doorways. The 18C ayuntamiento (town hall), in nearby plaza de España, is crowned by an impressive escutcheon.

Catedral★

Entrance via the 14C cloisters, housing the cathedral museum. Pl. del Santo. Open Jan-Feb Mon-Fri 11am-1pm, 4-6pm, Sat 11am-7.10pm, Sun 11am-12pm, 2-6pm and Apr-Oct Mon-Fri 9am-8pm, Sat 10am-7.10pm, Sun 10am-12.10pm, 1.45pm-7.10pm.

Closed public holidays. €4 donation requested. ☞941 34 00 33. www.catedralsantodomingo.com
The church is Gothic, apart from the ambulatory and apsidal chapel, which are Romanesque (second half of the 12C). The saint's tomb (13C), beneath a 1513 canopy, is in the south transept, and opposite is a sumptuous Gothic cage. This contains a live white cock and hen in memory of a miracle attributed to the saint, when a cock about to be eaten sprang to life and proclaimed the innocence of a convicted thief.
The **retable**★★ at the high altar (1538) is an unfinished work by Damián Forment. The Cathedral also contains the **Capilla de la Magdalena**★ (Evangelist's nave) with fine Plateresque decoration and magnificent screen. Visitors may also ascend the cathedral's freestanding tower (€2 donation) for a view.

Abadía de Cañas/El Monasterio de la Luz

Real, Cañas. ○ 13km/8mi SE of Santo Domingo de la Calzada. Open Tue–Sat 10.30am–1.30pm, 4–6pm, Sun 11am–1.30pm, 4–6pm (Apr–Oct opens 10am Tue–Sat, closes 7pm). €3. ☞941 37 90 83. www.monasteriodecañas.es.
This monastery has been inhabited by Cistercian monks since 1170. The 16C church and chapter house are extraordinary examples of the purity and simplicity of Cistercian art. A small shop sells delicious sweets and cakes made by the Carmelite nuns who live here.

Ezcaray

This delightful village is a summer resort and ski area. It features houses with stone and wood porticoes, noble mansions and the **Iglesia Santa María la Mayor** (guided tours available through tourist office; ☞941 35 46 79) as well as a former tapestry factory founded by Charles III in 1752.

Nájera★

This small town was Navarra's capital until 1076. The **Monasterio de Santa María la Real**★ (Pl. de Santa María; open Tue–Sat 10am–1pm, 4–6.30pm/7pm summer; Sun and public holidays 10am–12.30pm, 4–5.30pm/6pm summer; €3.50; ℘941 36 10 83; www.santamaria lareal.net) was founded by Don García III, King of Navarra, in 1032, when a statue of the Virgin was found here. The bays in the lower galleries of the **cloisters★** are filled with Plateresque stone tracery. Beneath the gallery of the **church★** is the **Panteón Real★** of 11C and 12C princes of Navarra, León and Castilla.

Basílica de Santa María de Arcos de Tricio
◐ 3km/2mi SW of Nájera. Open Sat 10.30am–1.30pm, 4.30–7.30pm, Sun 10.30am–1.30pm. €2. Call prior to visit. ℘620 92 36 44.
This ancient church, originally a 3C Roman mausoleum was transformed into a Christian basilica in the 5C.

San Millán de la Cogolla★
Turn-off from the LR 113 at Bobadilla. A World Heritage Site, this village became famous in the 5C when San Millán and his followers settled here as hermits. The first manuscripts in Castilian Spanish were also written here. Its warm honey-coloured stone buildings nestled in rolling green valleys make it a pleasant place to explore of an afternoon.

Monasterio de Yuso★
Open only by guided tour (50 mins), Holy Week–Sept Tue–Sun (Mon during Aug) 10am–1.30pm, 4–6.30pm. Oct– Holy Week Tue–Sun 10am–1pm, 3.30–5.30pm (closed Sun afternoon). €7 ℘941 37 30 49.
www.monasteriodeyuso.org.
Housed in a Mozarabic building partly hollowed out of the rock, this monastery overlooks the Cárdenas Valley. Its proudest posessions are its splendid **ivories★★** from two 11C reliquaries.

Monasterio de Nuestra Señora de Valvanera
Anguiano. Via the LR 113. Open daily 9am–7pm. No charge. ℘941 37 70 44. www.monasteriodevalvanera.es.
This monastery is in a delightful, isolated wooded mountain **setting★★**.

The church houses a 12C statue of the Virgen of Valvanera, patron of La Rioja. There is also a simple hotel here.

Valle del Iregua★
◐ 50km/31mi S of Logroño on N 111. Near Islallana appear the **rock faces★** of the Sierra de Cameros, overlooking the Iregua Valley from more than 500m/1 640ft. In the village of **Villanueva de Cameros**, half-timbered houses are roofed with circular tiles.

ADDRESSES

🏠 STAY
◔🍴🍴 **Hotel Echaurren** – Padre José García 19, Ezcaray. ℘941 35 40 47. www.echaurren.com. 27 rooms. ⌛ €15. **Restaurant** ◔🍴🍴🍴. Smart family-run boutique/gastronomic hotel.

◔🍴🍴🍴 **Parador de Santo Domingo de la Calzada** – Pl. del Santo 3, Santo Domingo de la Calzada. ℘902 54 79 79. www.parador.es. 61 rooms. ⌛ €16. Restaurant ◔🍴🍴. Housed in a former pilgrims' hospital on the Camino de Santiago, with Gothic features. Spectacular hallway.

🍴 EAT
◔ **Restuarante Arino Jatetxea** – Calle Frontin, 28, Labastida. ℘945 33 10 24. Simple yet delicious Basque cooking with a focus on fresh fish and a mix of local and visiting clientele. We recommend the pocket-friendly set menu.

◔🍴🍴 **Marixa** – Sancho Abarca 8, Laguardia. ℘945 60 01 65. www. hotelmarixa.com. Popular traditional cooking. Good views from the dining room, plus comfortable rooms (10 rooms ◔🍴🍴).

◔🍴🍴 **Héctor Oribe** – Gasteiz, 8, Páganos. ℘945 60 07 15. www. hectororibe.es. Superb quality cooking from this rising star chef.

Cantabria and Asturias

The central part of Spain's northern Atlantic coastline is made up by Asturias to the east and Cantabria to the west. The countryside, watered and made verdant by the highest rainfall in the country, rises sharply inland, and the region is frequently compared to more northern climes; perhaps a scaled-down maritime Switzerland, or a version of misty Ireland. Whichever, it is a far cry from the classic sun-baked Spanish images of the south. Roads wind along valley floors hemmed in by lush meadows with cider apple orchards and grazing dairy cows. Olive oil may be king elsewhere in Spain but here butter is the norm. Maize is an important crop, evident in the large number of distinctive *hórreos* (squat drying sheds), so typical of Asturian villages. The coast is indented by deep inlets (*rías*) and lined by low cliffs, and it boasts many beautiful beaches.

Highlights

1 Marvelling at the prehistoric paintings at **Cueva de Altamira** (p271)

2 Relaxing on the broad golden sands at **El Sardinero** (p273)

3 Exploring the old town of **Santillana del Mar** (p276)

4 The Mirador del Cable view point at **Fuente Dé** (p278)

5 The panormaic views unfolding along the **Navia Valley** (p288)

Asturias

Asturias is the only part of Spain never to have been conquered by the Moors. Aside from the bragging rights that this gives its independently minded natives – who have their own Romance language as well as many indigenous customs – it also influenced the development, or rather non-development, of the region as it became a backwater for several centuries. One of the consequences of this isolation was the development of a unique art and architectural form known as Asturian Pre-Romanesque art which can still be seen in 14 buildings, mostly churches, built between the 8C and 10C. They symbolise the birth and development of the Asturian Monarchy and of the first Christian kingdom on the Iberian Peninsula.

Other idiosyncratic Asturian features include bagpipes – keep an ear open for students practising in city squares – emphasising the region's historic Gallic influences, and cider *(sidra)* thanks to the large number of orchards. This is drunk in *sidrerías* (cider bars), where there is always a protocol: a small amount of cider is theatrically poured from a height of around 30cm/1ft in order to aerate it; this is known as "throwing the cider" to produce an *estrella*, or star.

The ideal temperature is cool but not (like lager-style beer) chilled. Asturias is also renowned for its cheeses, particularly the blue-veined *cabrales*. It goes particularly well with a glass of *sidra*.

Cantabria

Cantabria is the stretch of land sandwiched between the Bay of Biscay and the mountains of the Cantabrian Cordillera; in fact the mountains are so dominant that elsewhere in Spain Cantabria is known as La Montaña. It is too cool and wet for most northern Europeans to holiday here (it receives less than 60 per cent of the sunshine hours of the south), but for that very reason it has long been popular with the Spanish, as a respite from the summer heat.

Santillana del Mar, labelled "the prettiest village in Spain" by Jean-Paul Sartre, is the jewel of the Cantabrian coast. The medieval centre is a preserved national-historic monument, showcasing architectural styles from the 14C to the 18C. Nearby is the world-famous Altamira Cave, "the Sistine Chapel of Prehistoric Art" with its amazing ancient drawings of animals. Beautifully located on a sandy bay, Santander is the regional capital and main port of arrival for both Cantabria and Asturias.

Paintings at Cueva de Altamira

©Turespaña

The Altamira Caves

▶ 2km/1.2mi SW of Santillana del Mar.
🚃 Narrow-gauge train service from Santander (35 min). Neocueva Museum open May–Oct Tue–Sat 9.30am–8pm, Nov–Apr Tue–Sat 9.30am–6pm. Year-round Sun and pub hols 9.30am–3pm Closed 1 & 6 Jan, 1 May, 24– 25, 31 Dec. €3; child €1.50; no charge Sat afternoon, Sun, 18 Apr, 18 May, 12 Oct, 6 Dec. ℘942 81 80 05. http://museodealtamira.mcu.es.
✆ Purchase tickets in advance via Banco Santander (see website) if you plan to visit during Easter, July or August, as they often sell out on the day due to the high demand.

More than anywhere in the world, Cantabria has the richest heritage of Palaeolithic cave art. All over the region, underground caverns hold treasure troves of paintings rendered by the ancients, often dazzling in detail, colour and vivacity.

The most famous of these sites is the Cueva de Altamira. The complex consists of a series of galleries with wall paintings and engravings thought to date back to the Solutrean Age, 20 500 years ago. The most impressive paintings are in the Sala de los Polícromos (Polychrome Chamber). It has an outstanding ceiling painted mainly during the Magdalenian period (15 000–12 000 BC). Numerous poly-chrome bison are shown asleep, crouched and galloping with extraordinary realism. They were discovered in 1880 by a local amateur archaeologist Marcelino Sanz de Sautuola who was led to the entrance of the caves by his young daughter. Due to the painting's sophistication, their authen-ticity was immediately challenged and Sanz de Sautuola was even charged with forgery. The paintings forever changed our percep-tion on the "primitiveness" of the ancients. The caves were open to the public in the 1960s and 70s, but studies showed that human breath damaged their delicate state. Reopened in 1982 with a heavily restricted number of visitors, they were again closed in 2002 but at the same time a replica (called the Neocueva) near the site was installed. Using the latest in tech-nology, it simulates the forms of the cave itself and the images on its walls while an adjacent museum covers the evolution of humans and daily life in the Upper Palaeo-lithic period.

In February 2014 a handful of visitors were actually allowed inside the cave. After being chosen by ballot they donned protective clothing and spent 30 minutes there. More small groups of people are to be allowed to see the paintings in weekly visits through-out the summer after which time the situa-tion will be reassessed to see if more visitors can be allowed in the future.

Santander★

Santander enjoys a magnificent location★★ on a bay bathed by the azure waters of the Cantabrian Sea. It is best enjoyed on foot, with its long maritime front – one of the finest in Spain – lined by attractive gardens offering incomparable views. Superb beaches draw summer visitors.

THE CITY TODAY

The constant movement of passengers to and from the boat terminal of Santander in summer, and the throng of students at the international university for the rest of the year, gives the town a buzzing atmosphere. Most visitors stay at the beach resort of **El Sardinero**.

SIGHTS

The **paseo de Pereda★**, along the seafront, is lined by the imposing Banco de Santander building and the Palacete del Embarcadero, an exhibition centre. Facing the bay, the **Centro Botín** arts and culture complex, designed by Renzo Piano, is due to open in 2016 and is a flagship project for the city.

Museo de Prehistoria y Arqueología de Cantabria★

Open Oct-Apr Tue-Sun 10am-2pm, 5-7.30pm, May-Sep 10am-2pm, 5-8pm, Sat, Sun and hols 10am-2pm, 5-8pm. €5. ℘942 20 99 22. www.museosdecantabria.es/prehistoria. Finds from prehistoric caves in Cantabria and remains of extinct animals from the Quaternary era. The richest period is the Upper Palaeolithic from which there are bones engraved with animal silhouettes, and **batons★** made of horn and finely decorated. Three large circular steles, used for funerary purposes, are representative of the apogee of the Cantabrian culture (Bronze Age). Roman finds are mostly from Julióbriga and Castro Urdiales, and include coins, bronzes and pottery figurines.

▶ **Population:** 173 957
🕭 **Michelin Map:** 572 B 18.
🛈 **Info:** Jardines de Pereda ℘942 20 30 00. www.santanderspain.info.
▷ **Location:** Santander sprawls to the west of the bay. The A 8 motorway runs SE to Bilbao (116km/72mi). 🚆Santander.
👪 **Kids:** Museo Marítimo del Cantábrico. El Sardinero zoo, Parque de la Naturaleza de Cabárceno.
🕐 **Timing:** The International Music and Dance Festival (www.festivalsantander. com) in August.

Catedral de Nuestra Señora de la Asunción

Pl. del Obispo José E Eguino. Mon–Sat 10am–1pm, 4 7.30pm (Sat 8pm), Sun 8am–2pm, 5–8pm. Guided tours, Jul–Aug every 30 min. ℘942 22 60 24. This fortress-like cathedral was badly damaged in a 1941 fire, but has been rebuilt in its original Gothic style. A Baroque altarpiece dominates the presbytery; the font to the right of the ambulatory was brought here from Sevilla by soldiers of the Reconquest. **Iglesia del Cristo★** – Access to the fine 13C crypt is through the south portal. Excavations in the Evangelist nave have brought to light the remains of a Roman house with the relics of St Emeterio and St Celedonio, patron saints of the city.

Museo de Arte Moderno y Contemporáneo de Santander y Cantabria (Museum of Modern & Contemporary Art: MAS)

Rubio 6. Closed for repairs at time of writing. No charge. ℘942 20 31 20. www.museosantandermas.es. Formerly the Museum of Fine Arts, and still featuring works by **Goya** and 16C–18C Flemish and Italian artists, MAS now also displays paintings, sculptures, photographs, drawings, prints, video creations, and installations of international, Spanish and Cantabrian artists.

Biblioteca de Menéndez Pelayo

Rubio 6. Open Mon–Sat 10.30am–1pm, 5.30–8pm, Sat 10.30am–1pm only, also Tue & Thu 4.30–9pm during school term. Closed hols. ℘942 23 45 34. www.bibliotecademenendezpelayo.org. **Marcelino Menéndez y Pelayo** (1856–1912), one of Spain's greatest historians, bequeathed this fabulous library of nearly 43 000 books and manuscripts by great Castilian authors.

♣♣ Museo Marítimo del Cantábrico

San Martín de Bajamar. Open Tue–Sun 10am–7.30pm (Oct–Apr 6pm). Closed 1 & 6 Jan; 24–25, 31 Dec. €8, child €5. ℘942 27 49 62. www.museosdecantabria.es/maritimo. This thoroughly modern museum on the seafront covers all aspects of the region's maritime past and present.

Península de la Magdalena★★

With its magnificent position and sublime views, this peninsula is one of Santander's major sights. The small **zoo ♣♣** (no charge) on the El Sardinero side, and the replicas of the galleons in which Francisco de Orellana explored the Amazon are popular with children. The **Palacio de la Magdalena** was a summer residence for Alfonso XIII. Today, it is occupied by the Menéndez Pelayo International University.

Walk to Cabo Mayor★

🔼 Allow 2hr; 4.5km/3mi round trip from the junction of Calle García Lago and calle Gregorio Marañón, at the far end of El Sardinero. By car, 7km/4.3mi N. This attractive walk, adjoining the Mataleñas golf course, runs along the coast, offering magnificent views all the way.

Santander disasters

The old port and centre of Santander has been ravaged twice over the last century or so. In 1893 the *Cabo Machichaco* cargo boat blew up, killing more than 500 people and destroying much of the port area. On 15 February 1941, at a time when the city was attempting to recover from the Civil War, a tornado struck Santander: the sea swept over the quays and a fire broke out, almost completely destroying the centre. Reconstruction was undertaken to a street plan of blocks of no more than four or five storeys, and space was allocated to gardens beside the sea, promenades such as the paseo de Pereda which skirts the pleasure boat harbour known as Puerto Chico, and squares such as Plaza Porticada.

EXCURSIONS

El Sardinero★★

With its three magnificent **beaches**, the residential and resort area of El Sardinero is one of Santander's main attractions.

♣♣ Parque de la Naturaleza de Cabárceno★

Obregón.15km/9.3mi S. Opening times vary. €30, child €17; Oct–Mar €23, child €14. ℘902 210 112. www.parquedecabarceno.com. An old iron mine in the Sierra de Cabarga is part of an environmental rehabilitation project that includes a superb **wildlife park**, including jaguars, tigers, rhinos, gorillas, bears, camels, hippos, zebras, seals and many other animals. Don't miss the raptor displays or feeding the sealions.

Castañeda

🔾 24km/15mi SW via N 623 and N 634. The late 12C **Colegiata** (open for guided tours and Sun Mass at noon; no charge) a former collegiate church, stands in a pretty valley.

Cueva de El Castillo★

▶ Puente Viesgo, 26km/16mi SW along the N 623. Guided tours (45min) mid-Jun–mid-Sept Tue–Sun 9.30am–2.30pm, 3.30–7.30pm. Rest of year reduced hours /days, see website. €3. ℘942 59 84 25. http://cuevas.culturadecantabria.com. Cave dwellers began engraving and painting the walls of these caves towards the end of the Palaeolithic.

🚗 DRIVING TOUR

COSTA DE CANTABRIA★

The Cantabrian coast is a succession of gulfs, capes, peninsulas, *rías*, splendid bays (most notably at Santander and Santoña), traditional summer beach resorts and delightful towns dotted with impressive mansions. This area is also rich in caves bearing traces of human habitation since the Palaeolithic.

Castro Urdiales

The medieval heart of this attractive town, now a holiday resort is set above a vast bay. It clusters round the mighty Gothic **Iglesia de Santa María de la Asunción** (open Mon-Fri 10am–12pm, 4–6pm; no charge; ℘942 86 15 86). A ruined castle and lighthouse also add interest. Beaches lie east and west.

Laredo

25km/15.5mi W of Castro Urdiales off N 634.
The **old town** adjoins a long beach lined by modern buildings.

Limpias

8km/5mi S of Laredo.
The fishing village on the banks of the ría Asón is known for a miracle which occurred in 1919, when a venerated Baroque crucifix, attributed to Juan de Mena, shed tears of blood.

Santuario de Nuestra Señora de la Bien Aparecida

12km/7.4mi SW of Limpias.
A road winds up to the Baroque shrine offering a splendid **panorama★**.

Santoña

17km/10.5mi NW of Laredo.
This fishing port facing Laredo was a French headquarters in the Peninsular War. The **Iglesia de Nuestra Señora del Puerto** (Alfonso XII 11; open daily 10am–1pm, 4–8pm; ℘942 66 01 55), remodelled in the 18C, has, in addition to Gothic aisles, Romanesque features including carved capitals and a font.

Bareyo

14km/9mi W of Santoña off CA 141.
The tiny **Iglesia de Santa María**, overlooks the ría de Ajo. It retains original Romanesque moulded arches and historiated capitals. The **font** is probably Visigothic.

Peña Cabarga

35km/22mi SW of Bareyo off E 70.
A steep road rises to the summit (568m/1 863ft) and a monument to the Conquistadores and the Seamen Adventurers of Castilla. From the top there is a splendid **panorama★★**.

▶ Return to the E 70 and follow signs to **Santander★** (©see p274). Leave the town centre heading W on the A 67 to **Santillana del Mar★★** (©see p276), where you can visit the **Museo de Altamira★★** (©see p271).

Comillas★

54km/33.5mi W of Santander off E 70.
The small town of Comillas is a pleasant seaside resort with a lovely plaza, a good beach, and easy access to the extensive sands at Oyambre – 5km/ 3mi west. Towards the end of the 19C it received royal patronage. In its large park is the neo-Gothic **Palacio de Sobrellano and Capilla Panteón (chapel mausoleum) de los Marqueses de Comillas** (call or see website for opening times; €3; ℘942 72 03 39; http://centros.culturadecantabria.com/palacio-de-sobrellano.htm). The chapel features fittings and furnishings by Gaudí; also in the park is Gaudí's outlandish faitytale-like **El Capricho**, a summer house built in 1883 for a relative of the Marquis of Commillas, presently unoccupied and closed to the public.

San Vicente de la Barquera★

11km/6.8mi W of Comillas on N 634.
This resort attracts visitors to its vast **beach★**, across the inlet. The hilltop **Iglesia de Nuestra Señora de los Ángeles** has two Romanesque portals, Gothic aisles and tombs from the 15C and 16C. On the Unquera road is a fine **view★** of San Vicente.

Cueva el Soplao★

Near Rábago, 20km/12.4mi S of San Vicente de la Barquera. See website for opening times. Reservations advised. €12, Adventure price €32. ☏902 82 02 82. www.elsoplao.es.
You can visit these impressive caves , once lead and zinc mines, with their curiously shaped stalactites and stalagmites, either as a regular tourist, aboard an open mine-train carriage, or in "Adventure" mode, exploring remote parts with boots, helmet and lamp.

ADDRESSES

🛏 STAY

🍴🍴 **Las Brisas** – La Braña 14, El Sardinero. ☏942 27 50 11. www.hotellasbrisas.net. 13 rooms. ☐ €5. Closed Nov–Mar. This charming little place dates from 1905; its comfortable little rooms have a classic style and are filled with an interesting selection of antiques.

🍴🍴 **Hotel Escuela Las Carolinas** – Paseo General Dávila. ☏942 03 34 02. www.hotelescuelalascarolina. This hospitality school where young hoteliers and chefs come to train is set in a restored 19C mansion on a hill, with fantastic views over Santander. The city centre is a 10-minute walk away.

🍴🍴🍴 **Hotel Gerra Mayor** – Los Llaos, Gerra. 5km/3mi NE of San Vicente de la Barquera. ☏942 71 14 01. www.hgerramayor.com. 22 rooms. ☐ €4. Closed Dec 15–Mar 1. This simple hotel, formerly a farmhouse, is superbly located overlooking the sea and the mountains. It is perfect for peace and quiet and makes a pleasant base from which to explore the coastline.

🍴🍴🍴🍴 **Palacio del Mar** – Av. de Cantabria 5, El Sardinero. ☏942 39 24 00. www.hotel-palaciodelmar.com. 67 rooms. ☐ €13. **Restaurante Neptuno**🍴🍴🍴. A modern building with attractive design and comfortable rooms, including some with hydromassage baths.

🍴 EAT

🍴–🍴🍴 **Mesón Rampalay** – Daoíz y Velarde 9, Santander. ☏942 31 33 67. www.meson-rampalay-santander.com. Closed Tue. This centrally located bar-restaurant has a long bar and a number of tables where you can enjoy traditional tapas and local specialities such as red peppers with tuna, seafood salad, and mushrooms with cod.

🍴🍴 **El Bodegón** – Av. Los Soportales, San Vicente de la Barquera. ☏942 71 00 43. www.elbodegonsvb.com.
Seafood fresh from the ocean is served up as generously sized tapas. Fried squid, razor clams and fish of the day are failsafe choices.

🍴🍴🍴🍴 **El Serbal** – Andrés del Río 7, Santander. ☏942 22 25 15. www.elserbal.com. Closed Sun eve, Mon. Run with great professionalism this restaurant and bar is known for its seasonal, creative and gastronomic menus.

🍴🍴🍴🍴 **Mesón Marinero** – La Correría 23, Castro Urdiales. ☏942 86 00 05. www.mesonmarinero.com. This famous name in Cantabrian gastronomy specialises in seafood of excellent quality. Good choice of tapas.

FESTIVALS

Santander hosts the fiesta of St James (Santiago) in July, with its bullfights and range of popular concerts and performances.

BOAT TRIPS

Throughout the year, vessels known as reginas provide a shuttle service between Santander and Somo and Pedreña (two districts on the other side of the bay). In summer, excursions around the bay and along the Cubas river are also available for visitors, with departures from the **Embarcadero del Palacete dock on paseo de Pereda** (☏942 216 753; www.losreginas.com).

Santillana del Mar★★

Depsite its name, Santillana del Mar is located a few kilometres inland. The town retains its medieval appearance, with mansions embellished by family coats of arms.

A BIT OF HISTORY

Santillana developed around a monastery which sheltered the relics of St Juliana, who was martyred in Asia Minor – the name Santillana is a contraction of Santa Juliana. Throughout the Middle Ages, the monastery was famous as a place of pilgrimage and was particularly favoured by the Grandees of Castilla. In the 11C it became powerful as a collegiate church; in the 15C, the town, created the seat of a marquisate, was enriched by the fine mansions which still give it so much character.

🐾 WALKING TOUR

The **town**★★ has two main streets, both leading to the collegiate church. Start in **calle de Santo Domingo**, with the 17C Casa del Marqués de Benemejís to the left and the Casa de los Villa, with its semicircular balconies, to the right. Turn left into Juan Infante. Along the vast, pleasing triangular square of **Plaza de Ramón Pelayo** are the Parador Gil Blas and the 14C Torre de Merino (Merino Tower, right); the Torre de Don Borja, with its elegant pointed doorway; and (left) the 18C ayuntamiento (town hall), Casa del Águila and Casa de la Parra. Calle de las Lindas (end of the square on the right) runs between massive houses with austere façades to calle del Cantón and calle del Río, which lead to the collegiate church.
As you approach the church, you will see several noble residences on the right-hand side. On the left, the house of the Archduchess of Austria is decorated with coats of arms. The **Colegiata★** (collegiate church; Pl. del

▶ **Population:** 4 203
🖐 **Michelin Map:** 572 B17.
🖥 **Info:** Calle Jesús Otero.
  𝒫 942 81 82 51.
  www.santillanadel
  marturismo.com.
◖ **Location:** Santillana is surrounded by verdant hills, between Santander and Comillas (16km/10mi W). 🚃Santillana del Mar; narrow gauge station Puente San Miguel (4 km); nearest RENFE station Torrelavega (10 km).

Abad Francisco Navarro; open Tue–Sun 10am–1.30pm, 4–7.30pm; €3, inc. cloister); 𝒫942 81 88 12) dates from the 12 and 13C. The design of the 12C **cloister★** and the east end is pure Romanesque.

◖ Return to calle de Santo Domingo.

The restored 16C Convento de Clarisas (Convent of the Poor Clares) now houses the **Museo Diocesano** (open Tue–Sun 10am–1.30pm, 4–7.30pm/6.30pm Oct–May; €2; 𝒫942 84 03 17; www.santillana museodiocesano.com), featuring sacred paintings, sculptures, gold and silver, Baroque carvings and ivory.

ADDITIONAL SIGHTS
Museo de la Tortura El Solar

Escultor Jesús Otero, 1. Open Mon–Fri 10am–8.30pm, Sat–Sun until 9pm. Closed 1 Jan, 25 Dec. €4.
𝒫942 840 273.
The range of punishments used by the Inquisition, and others, from the Middle Ages onwards, is catalogued here with some 70 instruments of torture.

Museo y Fundación Jesús Otero

Plaza del Abad Francisco Navarro. Open Tue–Sat 10am–1.30pm, 4–8pm (Tue opens 11.30am). No charge.
𝒫942 84 01 98.
This collection is devoted to the town's favourite sculptor, born here in 1908.

Picos de Europa★★★

The Picos de Europa is the highest range in the Cordillera Cantábrica, yet just 30km/18.6mi from the sea, with deep gorges cut by gushing mountain rivers and snow-capped peaks jagged with erosion.
The south face is less steep than the north, where the higher peaks are concentrated, and looks out over a harsh terrain of outstanding natural beauty. The Parque Nacional de los Picos de Europa, covering 64 660ha/159 775 acres, protects the region's flora and fauna.

🚗 **DRIVING TOURS**

1 DESFILADERO DE LA HERMIDA (LA HERMIDA DEFILE)★★

From Panes to Potes
27km/16.7mi. Allow about 1hr.

A defile (**ravine**)★★, 20km/12.4mi long, extends to either side of a basin containing the hamlet of La Hermida. The narrow gorge is bare and shadowed.

Iglesia de Nuestra Señora de Lebeña★

Lebeña. Open summer Tue–Sun 10am–1.30pm, 4.30–7.30pm. Winter by appointment, €1. ℘942 840 317.
The small 10C Mozarabic church stands amid poplars at the foot of tall cliffs. The belfry and porch are later additions. The church houses a venerated 15C sculpture of the Virgin Mary.

Tama

This charming little mountain town is situated in a lush basin and surrounded by the sharp peaks of the Central Range. There are many operators offering adventure activities here plus the excellent Sotama **visitor centre** (open daily Apr–Oct 9am–8pm, Nov–Mar until 6pm; ℘942 738 109).

🔹 **Michelin Map:** 572 C 14-15-16.

ℹ **Info:** Cangas de Onís: Avenida de Covadonga. ℘985 84 80 05; Covadonga: El Repelao. ℘985 84 61 35. www.cangasdeonis.com.

▶ **Location:** The Picos de Europa rise along the northern coast, between Gijón and Santander. 🚃Picos De Europa. Narrow-gauge trains run from Santander to Arriondas (7km north of Cangas de Onís) and Unquera (40km north of Potes).

🕐 **Timing:** Roads are very busy during Jul and Aug.

Potes

9km/5.6mi S of Lebeña along N 621.
Potes is a delightful village in a pretty-**site**★ in a fertile basin, set against jagged crests. From the bridge, admire the old stone houses and the 15C **Torre del Infantado**, now the town hall.

2 THE CLIMB TO FUENTE DÉ★★

30km/19mi on the N 621.
Allow about 3hr.

Monasterio de Santo Toribio de Liébana★

Approach along a signposted road on the left. Open daily 10am–1pm, 4–7pm (until 6pm in winter). No charge. ℘942 73 05 50. www.santotoribiodeliebana.org.
The monastery was founded in the 7C and grew to considerable importance when a fragment of the True Cross was placed in its safekeeping. A chapel set above and behind the High altar contains the largest known piece of the True Cross, contained in a silver gilt wooden *lignum crucis* Crucifix reliquary. The monastery was the house of **Beatus**, the 8C monk famous for his *Commentary on the Apocalypse*, copied in the form of illuminated manuscripts.

There is a fine **view★** of Potes and the central mountain range from the lookout point at the end of the road.

Fuente Dé★★

21km/13mi W of Liébana.
A parador stands at
1 000m/3 300ft.
Nearby, a cable car (**teleférico**) rises 800m/2 625ft to the top of the sheer rock face (open weather permitting, Oct–Jun 10am–6pm; Jul–Sept 9am–8pm; €16 return; ℘942 73 66 10, www.cantur.com). During the **ascent** you may see wild chamois. The **Mirador del Cable★★** commands a splendid panorama of the upper valley of the Deva and Potes. A path leads to the Aliva refuge. Erosion of the karst limestone produces stony plateaux and huge sink-holes known as **hoyos**.

3 PUERTO DE SAN GLORIO (SAN GLORIO PASS)★

From Potes to Oseja de Sajambre

83km/52mi. Allow about 3hr.
The road crosses the Quiviesa Valley, then climbs through pastures.

Puerto de San Glorio★

Alt 1 609m/5 279ft.
A track leads north from the pass (1hr there and back) to near the Peña de Llesba and the **Mirador de Llesba**, a magnificent **viewpoint★★**.
To the right is the east range; to the left, the steep south face of the central massif. In the left foreground is Coriscao peak (2 234m/7 330ft).

▶ At Portilla de la Reina, bear right onto LE 243.

Puerto de Pandetrave★★

19km/11.8mi NW of Puerto de San Glorio.

This pass (1 562m/5 125ft) affords a **panorama** of the three ranges: in the right foreground, the Cabén de Remoña and Torre de Salinas, both in the central massif. In the distance, in a hollow, is the village of Santa Marina de Valdeón. The Santa Marina de Valdeón/Posada de Valdeón road is narrow but passable.

Puerto de Panderruedas★

21km/13 mi NW.
The road climbs to pastures at 1 450m/4 757ft. Walk up the path to the left (15min there and back) to the **Mirador de Piedrahitas★★** (viewing table) for

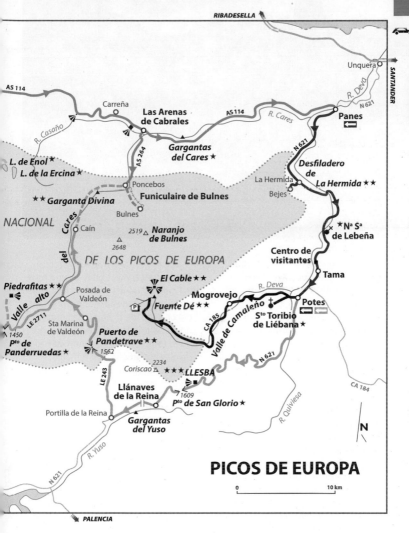

PICOS DE EUROPA

0   10 km

an impressive view of the immense cirque which closes the Valdeón Valley. To the northeast is the Torre Cerredo peak (2 648m/8 688ft), highest in the range.

Puerto del Pontón★

8km/5mi SW of Puerto de Panderruedas. Alt 1 280m/4 200ft. The pass offers a superb **view★★** of the Sajambre Valley. The descent to Oseja de Sajambre begins with hairpin bends below the western range and continues as a spectacular tunnel through the mountain.

④ DESFILADERO DE LOS BEYOS★★★ (LOS BEYOS DEFILE)

From Oseja de Sajambre to Cangas de Onís

8km/23.6mi. Allow about 1hr along N 625.

Mirador de Oseja de Sajambre★★

There is an awe-inspiring **view★★** of the Oseja de Sajambre Basin: the sharp Niaja peak at its centre rises to 1 732m/5 682ft, and of the Los Beyos defile opens between walls of broken rock strata.

279

Picos de Europa

© Slawek Staszczuk/age fotostock

Desfiladero de Los Beyos★★★
4km/2.5mi NW of the Mirador de
Oseja de Sajambre.
This is one of the most beautiful gorges
in Europe, 10km/6.2mi long, carved by
the River Sella. The limestone is thick,
marked by the occasional clinging tree.

Cangas de Onís
26km/16mi N of the Desfiladero
de Los Beyos.
A humpbacked **Roman bridge** *(puente
romano)* crosses the Sella to the west.
The Capilla de Santa Cruz (open daily
11am-2pm, 4.30-7.30pm, €2), also west,
in Contranquil, commemorates the
victory of Covadonga and houses the
region's only dolmen (megalithic tomb).
The Aula del Reino de Asturias (Iglesia
Santa María Evaristo Sanchez; open Jul–
Sept Mon–Sat 11am–2pm, 4–8pm, Sun
noon–2pm, 5–8pm; no charge; ℘985 84
80 05) is a small museum that traces the
modern history of the town.
On the outskirts, towards Arriondas is
the **Monastery of San Pedro de Villanueva**. This former 17C Benedictine
monastery from the 17C includes a
Romanesque church.

Villanueva
4km/2.5mi N of Cangas de Onís.
The 17C Benedictine **Monasterio de
San Pedro** stands in a beautiful site,
by the river, at the end of the village.

The monastery was built around a pre-
existing Romanesque church of which
there remains the apse and an elegantly
decorated side portal. The complex is
now a parador (www.parador.es), but is
open to non-residents and two rooms
display archaeological remains (especially ceramics) found during refurbish-
ment work.

⑤ THE ROAD TO COVADONGA
AND THE LAKES★★

From Cangas de Onís to Covadonga
35km/22mi. Allow about 3hr.

Cueva del Buxu
Visit by guided tour only (30min) Wed–
Sun 10.15am, 11.15am, 12.15pm, 1.15pm.
Reservation recommended as max 6
persons per tour. €3.13, no charge Wed.
℘608 17 54 67.
www.infocangasdeonis.com.
The cave in the cliff face contains charcoal drawings and rock engravings from
around 14 000 years ago, including a
stag, horse and bison.

Covadonga
16km/10mi SE of La Cueva del Buxu.
This famous shrine is nestled in a magnificent **setting**★★ at the bottom of a
narrow valley surrounded by impressive
peaks. It commemorates the victory of
Don Pelayo over the Moors at Cova-

donga in 722, marking the beginning of the Spanish Reconquest.

Santuario de Covadonga

Explanada Basílica, Cangas de Onís.
Open daily 9am–6.30pm. No charge.
℘985 84 60 35.
www.santuariodecovadonga.com.
A statue of Don Pelayo stands before this neo-Romanesque Basilica, built 1886–1901. Its museum (open daily 10.30am–2pm, 4–7.30pm; €3; ℘985 84 60 96) contains gifts to the Virgin.

La Santa Cueva

Open daily 8.30am–8pm. ℘985 84 60 35.
This holy cave, dedicated to the Virgin of the Battlefield, holds the deeply venerated 18C wooden statue of the Virgin, *La Santina*, patron of Asturias. The remains of Don Pelayo are also buried here.

Lago de Enol★ and Lago de la Ercina★ (Lake Enol and Lake Ercina)

Lake Enol and Lake Ercina (alt. 1 232m/4 042ft), are two of the most popular-places in the *sierra,* served by parking facilities, paved roads, walking trails, a restaurant and a museum.
There is a walking trail around both of the lakes (3km/1.86mi, 1h) or you can follow a longer circuit (8km/5mi) for a less crowded experience. From mid-July to early September, vehicular access to the lakes is restricted between 8.30am and 8.30pm. Shuttle buses depart regularly from Cangas de Onis.
The Pedro Pidal Visitor Centre, (Buferrera services; open mid Jun–mid Oct 10am–6pm; no charge) has several thematic exhibitions on the Picos de Europa explaining their different ecosystems. There is also a reproduction of a small shepherd's hut.

◖ Continue to the lakes along the steep CO 4; stop and look back occasionally to enjoy the extensive panoramas.

After 8km/5mi, you will reach the **Mirador de la Reina★★** with a great view of the rocky pyramids that make

up the Sierra de Covalierda. Beyond the pass, two rock cirques are the settings for lakes Enol and Ercina.

⑥ GARGANTAS DEL CARES (CARES GORGES)★★

From Covadonga to Panes
90km/56mi. Allow one day.

Just out of Portillo la Estazadas village there is a splendid **panorama★★** of the rock wall, which closes off the Río Casaño Valley. From a viewpoint on the right, shortly after Carreña de Cabrales, there is a glimpse of the fang-like crest of **Naranjo de Bulnes** (2 519m/8 264ft).

Las Arenas de Cabrales
10km/6.2mi E of Las Estazadas along the AS 114.
This is the main production centre for *cabrales*, Spain's famous pungent blue cheese made from ewes' milk.
Beyond Arenas the gorges★ are green with moss and the occasional tree. Humpbacked bridges and fragile footbridges span the emerald waters.

◖ Bear right onto AS 264, which runs through the Upper Cares Valley.

Upper Cares Valley
The Poncebos road leads south, through a **ravine★**. After the embalse (reservoir) de Poncebos, a track (3hr return on foot) leads up to the village of Bulnes. A much quicker ascent can be made by **funicular** (access at Poncebos at the intersection of the Sotres road; open Jun–Sept & hols 10am 8pm, rest of year 10am–12.30pm, 2–6pm; €17.61 one-way, €22.16 return, ℘985 84 68 00; www.alsa.es) which flies up to the Bulnes ski station (alt. 400m/1 312ft) in a mere 7 minutes. On a clear day there are great views of the summit.
⌘ From Poncebos to Caín (3hr30min one way) a path follows the Cares and plunges into the **gorge★★** to the foot of the central massif (here you can take a taxi back to Poncebos).

◖ Return to Arenas de Cabrales.

Oviedo★★

The capital of Asturias has a
long and eventful history.
Its old quarter is sprinkled with
enchanting plazas and streets
lined with sculptures. Strolling
about this World Heritage Site is
a delight.

THE CITY TODAY
Oviedo is excellent for shopping and is
particularly well known for its leather
goods. Despite its World Heritage status it is not afraid to keep its public
monuments up to date, dedicating a
prominent statue to Woody Allen (calle
de Milicias Nacionales), who won the
Prince of Asturias Arts prize in 2002.
When Allen visited the city to collect
his award he said "Oviedo is a delicious
city, exotic, beautiful: it's as if it didn't
belong to this world, as if it didn't exist
at all… Oviedo is a fairytale."

A BIT OF HISTORY
**The capital of the Kingdom of Astu-
rias (9C–10C)** – Alfonso II, the Chaste
(791–842), moved his court to Oviedo
and rebuilt the former Muslim town.
The heir to the throne of Spain is still
called the Prince of Asturias.
The Two Battles of Oviedo – In 1934,
Oviedo was heavily damaged in fighting
between miners and right-wing government forces. In 1936, it was the scene of
a three-month siege when the garrison
rose in revolt against the Republican
government during the Civil War.
The Prince of Asturias Awards – have
been presented from here since 1981,
for achievements in sciences, humanities or public affairs.

OUTSIDE THE OLD QUARTER
Antiguo Hospital del Principado
Leave Oviedo on Conde de Toreno
(marked on the plan).
The façade of the 18C former principality hospital, now the Hotel Reconquista,
bears a fine Baroque **coat of arms★**.

▶ **Population:** 221 870
⌖ **Michelin Map:** 572 B 12
▯ **Info:** Calle Marqués de
Santa Cruz 1. ℰ985 22 75
86. www.turismoviedo.es
◐ **Location:** The A 66 links
Oviedo to the north coast
at Gijón (29km/18mi) and
to León (121km/75mi S).
🚆Oviedo.
🅿 **Parking:** Avoid the Old Town.
🕐 **Timing:** Stroll the Old
Town before you do
anything else.

Iglesia de San Julián de los Prados★
Selgas 1. Open May–Jun Mon 10am
–12.30pm; Tue–Sat 10am–12.30pm,
4–6pm. Jul–Sept Mon 10am–1pm,
Tue–Fri 9.30am–1pm, 4–6pm, Sat
9.30am–12.30pm, 4–6pm. Oct–Apr
Mon–Sat 10am–noon. ℰ687 052 820.
This outstanding early 9C work has a
characteristic porch, twin aisles, wide
transept and, at the east end, three
chapels with barrel vaults. The walls are
covered in **frescoes★** of Roman influence. A fine transitional Romanesque
Christ in Glory★ is in the central apse.

Centro de Recepción e Interpretación del Prerrománico Asturiano
C. Antiguas Escuelas del Naranco.
Open Jul–Aug daily 10am–2pm,
3.30–7.30pm. Rest of year: Wed–Fri
10am–1.30pm, 3.30–6pm; Sat–Sun &
hols 10am–2pm, 3.30–6.30pm.
No charge. ℰ902 306 600
www.prerromanicoasturiano.es.
Panels explain Asturian art (in Spanish
only); a video is narrated in English,
Spanish, French and German.

Iglesia de Santa María del Naranco★★
Monte del Naranco. 4km/2.5mi along
Av. de los Monumentos to the NW.
Open Apr–Sept Tue–Sat 9.30am–1pm,

3.30–7pm, Sun–Mon 9.30am–1pm;
Oct–Mar Tue–Sat 10am–2.30pm, Sun &
Mon 10am–12.30pm. €3, no charge Mon.
℘638 260 163.

This ancient harmonious church incorporates part of the 9C summer palace of Ramiro I. It is supported by grooved buttresses and lit by vast bays. The lower floor is a vaulted crypt. On the upper floor (a former reception hall), two loggias open off the great chamber. Its decoration is delicate and unified. From outside, there is a fine view of Mount Aramo, with Oviedo in the foreground.

Iglesia de San Miguel de Lillo★

Monte del Naranco. 15min on foot.
Open same hours as Iglesia de Santa María. €3; no charge Mon.
℘902 306 600.

What remains is probably only a third of the original church, which probably collapsed in the 13C.
The aisles are narrow. Several claustral-type windows remain. The delicate carving is a delight. on the door jambs★★ are identical scenes in relief of arena contests. An Asturian cord motif is repeated on the capitals and on vaulting in the nave and gallery.

☙ WALKING TOUR

OLD TOWN
Allow 1hr30min.

▷ Enter by calle San Francisco, and proceed along the right side of the street.

Antigua Universidad

The austere 17C stone-fronted university was restored after the Civil War. Opposite the façade is *Mujer Sentada (Seated Woman)* by Manolo Hugué, one of many sculptures set in the old town.

Plaza de Porlier

View the cathedral in the next plaza. The **Palace of the Count of Toreno** (right) dates from 1673; the **Camposagrado** (opposite), an 18C edifice, houses the Law Courts (note spread eaves).

▷ Continue along C. San Francisco.

Plaza de de Alfonso II el Casto (Plaza de la Catedral)

Note the coat of arms on the façade of the 17C **Palacio de Valdecarzana**. The majestic Cathedral rises at the far end of the square. The **Palacio de la Rúa** was built at the end of the 15C.

▷ The cathedral is on the eastern side of the square.

Catedral de Oviedo★

Pl. de la Catedrál. Open year-round Mon–Fri 10am–1pm. Afternoons: 4–5pm except Mar-May, Oct (4-6pm), Jun (4-7pm). Sat year-round 10am–1pm, 4pm–5pm except Jul-Sep, 10am-5pm. €7. ℘985 22 10 33.
www.catedraldeoviedo.com.

The main work was carried out between 1412 and 1565 in Flamboyant Gothic style. The south tower tapers into a delicate openwork spire. Three 17C Gothic portals pierce the asymmetrical façade; figures of the Transfiguration are above the central portal. On the walnut-panelled doors (also 17C) are figures of Christ and St Eulalia.

Interior – The Cathedral has three aisles, the triforium surmounted by tall stained-glass windows, and an ambulatory. A splendid 16C polychrome **high altarpiece★★** shows scenes from the Life of Christ. On either end of the transepts are 18C Baroque panels, and in the south transept, next to the main chapel, the 17C polychromed stone image of The Saviour.

The **Capilla de Alfonso II "El Casto"** (The Chaste), on the site of the original church, is the pantheon of the Asturian kings. The decoration inside the gate (end of north transept) is Late Gothic. In the embrasures are figures of the Pilgrim St James, St Peter, St Paul and St Andrew, and on a mullion, a Virgin of Milk. Renaissance and Baroque elements intermingle.

The **tesoro★★** (treasury) in the apse includes outstanding ancient gold and silver plate: the *Cruz de los Ángeles* (Cross of the Angels), a gift from Alfonso

II in 808, studded with precious gems, Roman cabochons and cameos; and the *Cruz de Victoria* (908), faced with chased gold, precious stones, and enamel, supposedly carried by Pelayo at Covadonga.

The reliquary chapel of Cámara Santa (see below) is preceded by an ante-chapel, enlarged in the 12C. Its 12 **statue columns★★**, representing the Apostles, are among the most masterly sculptures of this period in Spain, and obviously influenced by the *Pórtico de la Gloria* (Doorway of Glory) in Santiago Cathedral. Capitals illustrate the marriage of Joseph and Mary, the Holy Women at the Tomb and lion and wild boar hunts.

Cámara Santa

Access by steps from the south transept. Open daily, same access as cathedral.

The Cámara Santa was built by Alfonso II early in the 9C to hold holy relics, and was reconstructed in the Romanesque period. The Arca Santa (Holy Chest), is a precious reliquary brought to Asturias after Toledo had fallen to the Moors.

Claustro

Open same hours as Cathedral.

The Gothic **cloisters** (14C–15C) have intersecting pointed arches and delicate tracery in the bays. The **Capilla de Santa Leocadia** (to the left on entering) contains an altar, tombs from the time of Alfonso II and an unusually small stone altar. The **sala capitular** (chapter house) contains fine 15C stalls.

▶ Return to Pl. de Alfonso II El Casto.

To the right of the Cathedral (leaving), low reliefs and busts compose a homage to the kings of Asturias. To the left, at calle Santa Ana, note the unexpected Moorish *alfiz* window enclosure in the remaining east wall of the 9C **Iglesia de San Tirso**.

▶ Turn left onto Tránsito de la Virgen alongside the Cathedral.

Beyond the arch that connects the Cathedral to the Palacio Arzobispal (archbishop's palace, left) is the Romanesque former cathedral. Just ahead in Plaza de la Corrada del Obispo is the rather busy façade of the Palacio Arzobispal (late 16C) and the imposing 18C Puerta de la Limosna (alms gate).

▶ Continue along San Vicente.

Museo Arqueológico

San Vicente 5. Open Wed–Fri 9.30am–8pm, Sat 9.30am–2pm, 5–8pm, Sun and public holidays 9.30am–3pm. No charge. ℰ985 20 89 77. www.museoarqueologico deasturias.com.

This archaeological museum is set in the former Convento de San Vicente (16C–18C). Two galleries off the 15C Plateresque cloisters display pre-Romanesque art. Fragments and reproductions evidence the sophistication of Asturian art. Among exhibits are the Naranco altar; low reliefs showing Byzantine influence; and column bases from San Miguel de Lillo. After the museum, go under the arch and cross the **Plaza de Feijoo**, past the Iglesia de Santa María la Real de la Corte and the palace-like façade of the 18C Monasterio de San Pelayo.

▶ Turn right onto Jovellanos and look back at the city wall. Return to Santa Ana.

Museo de Bellas Artes de Asturias (Fine Arts Museum)

Santa Ana 1–3. Open Sept–Jun Tue–Fri 10.30am–2pm, 4.30–8.30pm, Sat 11.30am–2pm, 5–8pm, Sun and public holidays 11.30am–2.30pm; Jul–Aug Tue–Sat 10.30am–2pm, 4–8pm, Sun and public holidays 10.30am–2.30pm. No charge. ℰ985 21 30 61. www.museobbaa.com.

The museum is in three buildings. The core collection of Spanish painting is enriched by Italian and Flemish works. There is also a sculpture collection. Among the works in the 18C Palacio de Velarde are a complete *Apostolado* by **El Greco** (ground floor); the Gothic panels of the *Santa Marina Retable* (on the stairway); the Triptych of *Don Alvaro de Carreño* by the master of the Legend of Mary Magdalene; a *Burial of Christ* and a magnificent *Apostle* by **Ribera**; a *Crucifixion* by **Zurbarán**; a *San Pedro* by Murillo; the portrait of *Charles II at Ten Years* by Carreño de Miranda, and two portraits by **Goya** (*Jovellanos* and *Charles IV*) on the first floor. The second floor is devoted to Asturian and Spanish art of the 19C and early 20C.

A passageway leads to the second floor of the 17C Casa Oviedo-Portal. Worth seeing are a gallery dedicated to J Sorolla; a Musketeer with Sword and Cupid by **Picasso**; and paintings by Gutiérrez-Solana, Regoyos and Nonell. As you leave, take a look at the enchanting Plaza de Trascorrales, with its brightly coloured houses and its sculpture of *The Milkmaid*.

▷ Take Cimadevilla to reach Plaza de la Constitución.

Along **Plaza de la Constitución** are the **ayuntamiento** (City Hall), with 17C and 18C porticoes, and the Iglesia de San Isidoro, from the same era.

▷ Take Fierro, where there is a covered market, to Fontán.

Fontán is a picturesque area. Porticoed houses have enchanting courtyards, reached by multiple archways.

▷ Leave by the archway that faces Plaza de Daoíz y Velarde.

The sculpture in the beautiful tree-lined **Plaza de Daoíz y Velarde** is Las Vendedoras del Fontán, honouring the women who have sold goods in the markets in these streets over the centuries. The plaza is also home to the noble Palacio de Camposagrado, currently the site of the Supreme Court of Asturias. Beside it the Biblioteca (library) de Asturias boasts an unusual façade.

EXCURSIONS
Iglesia de Santa Cristina de Lena★
▷ 34km/21mi S on the A 66 (junction 92)

At Pola de Lena, head for Vega del Rey then take the signposted road. Park before the rail viaduct and walk up the steep path (15min) to the **Iglesia de Santa Cristina de Lena** (open Tue–Sun Apr–Oct 11am–1pm, 4.30–6.30pm/Dec–Mar 11am-1pm, 4-6pm, closed Nov; €1.50; no charge Tue. ℰ984 49 35 63). This small but well-proportioned pre-Romanesque 9C golden stone church stands on a rocky crag, enjoying a fine **panorama★** of the Caudal Valley.

The building has a Greek cross plan, unusual in Asturias. It features traditional stone vaulting, with blind arcades, and columns with pyramid-shaped capitals, emphasised by a cord motif. The nave is separated from the raised choir by an iconostasis in which the superimposed arches increase the impression of balance. The low reliefs in the chancel are Visigothic sculptures including geometric figures and plant motifs.

Teverga
▷ 43km/27mi SW on the N 634 and AS 228.

The road follows the River Trubia, which, after Proaza, enters a narrow gorge. Glance back for a splendid **view★** of the Peñas Juntas cliff face. Beyond the Teverga fork the road penetrates the **desfiladero de Teverga★** (Teverga Ravine).

Just just outside La Plaza village, is the **Colegiata de San Pedro de Teverga** (guided tours Sat–Sun noon and 4.30pm; call ahead to check times; €1.50; ℰ696 816 915). This late 12C collegiate church was built in a continuation of pre-Romanesque Asturian style, it includes a narthex, a tall narrow nave and a flat east end, originally three chapels. The narthex capitals are carved with stylised animal and plant motifs.

Costa Verde★★

The Costa Verde (Green Coast) of Asturias is named for the colour of the sea, pine and eucalyptus trees along the shore, and wooded pastures inland. Towns and villages nestle in picturesque coves, where fishing is the main activity. On a clear day the Picos de Europa and Cordillera Cantábrica are a stunning backdrop.

🚗 DRIVING TOURS

Along the rocky coast, low cliffs are interrupted by sandy inlets; the estuaries are narrow and deep. West of Cudillero, the coastal plain ends in sheer cliffs overlooking small beaches.

1 LLANES TO GIJÓN
145km/90mi.

Llanes
The clifftop promenade gives a good view of the once fortified port, the rampart ruins and castle, and the squat Iglesia de Santa María. In mid-August the Fiestas de San Roque (www.san-roque.com) take place here with dancers in brilliant local costume.

▶ Take the E70 20km/12.5mi to Colombres

Fundación Archivo de Indianos - Museo de la Emigración
San Vicente de la Barquera. Open Jun–Sept daily 10am–2pm, 4–8pm; rest of the year Tue–Sat 10am–2pm, 4–7pm. Closed 1 & 6 Jan, 24–25 & 31 Dec. €5. ℘985 412 005. www.archivodeindianos.es.
Housed in the sumptuous Quinta Guadalupe palace, this museum tells the story of hundreds of thousands of Asturians who emigrated to Latin America in the 19C, an event that shaped the region and its culture.

▶ Take the E70 W back to Llanes, where it turns in to the Autovía del Cantábrico. Continue to Ribadesella.

◐ **Michelin Map:** 571 and 572 (town plan of Gijón) B8-15.

▤ **Info:** Gijón: Rodriguez Sampedro. ℘985 34 17 71; Llanes: c/Posada Herrera, 15 (La Torre building). ℘985 40 01 64; Valdés (Luarca): Plaza Alfonso X El Sabio. ℘985 64 00 83. www.infoasturias.com.

▶ **Location:** The N 634 runs along the northern coast of Asturias, affording sea and mountain views.

👪 **Kids:** The Centro de Arte Rupestre Tito Bustillo and MUJA, the Jurassic Museum, are unmissable.

Ribadesella
The town and port of Ribadesella are on the right side of the estuary opposite the holiday resort.

👪 Centro de Arte Rupestre Tito Bustillo★
Avda. de Tito Bustillo. Cave open by guided tour only (1hr), Apr–Oct Wed–Sun 10.15am–5pm (last tour). Reservations highly recommended for cave tour. Cave Art Centre open Jul–Aug Wed–Sun 10am–7pm; Sept–Dec & Feb–Jun Wed–Fri 10am–2.30pm, 3.30–6pm, Sat–Sun & hols 10–2.30pm, 4–7pm. Closed 8 & 9 Aug, 24–25 & 31 Dec. €7.27 Cave & Cave Art Centre, child €5.30, no charge Wed, 18 May. ℘902 306 600. www.centrotitobustillo.com.
These caves are well known for their Palaeolithic **paintings**★ (c. 20 000 BC) of horses, stags and a doe.

▶ 26km/16mi W of Ribadesella on the A-8. Squat drying sheds or *hórreos*, typical of Asturias, stand beside the houses in the small, attractive village of **La Isla**.

👪 MUJA (Museo del Jurásico de Asturias – Jurassic Museum)
Rasa de San Telmo, Colunga. Open Jul–Aug daily 10.30am–8pm. Feb–Jun &

Sept–Dec Wed–Fri 10am–2.30pm, 3.30–6pm, Sat–Sun & hols 10.30am–2.30pm, 4–7pm .Closed Jan, 24–25 & 31 Dec. €7.24; child €4.70, no charge Wed. ℰ902 30 66 00. www.museojurasicoasturias.com

Between Colunga and Lastres, this museum is dedicated to the giant creatures that once roamed this area.

▶ 12km SE of La Isla on AS 260.

Mirador del Fito★★★

This unusual, much-photographed, spectacular high-diving board style viewpoint gives a fabulous panorama of the Picos de Europa and the coast.

▶ 17km/10.5mi W of Fito.

Priesca

The capitals in the chancel in the **Iglesia de San Salvador** (ℰ985 97 67 12) resemble those at Valdediós (&see entry below).

▶ 11km/6.8mi W of Priesca via N 632.

Villaviciosa

Emperor Charles V arrived here in 1517 to take possession of Spain. The **Iglesia de Santa María** (open Tue–Sun 11am–1pm, 5–7pm) is decorated with a Gothic rose window.

▶ 3km/1.8mi S of Villaviciosa.

Amandi

The bell tower of the **Iglesia de San Juan** (open year-round Tue–Sat 11.30am–1.30pm, Jul-Sep also 5.30-7.30pm; ℰ985 891 759) stands on high ground. The remodelled church retains a 13C portal with sophisticated **decoration★**. Inside the **apse★**, the frieze from the façade reappears to form a winding ribbon that follows the curves of the intercolumniation.

▶ 7km/4.3mi S of Villaviciosa.

Valdediós★

The **Iglesia de San Salvador** was consecrated in 893 and is known as *El Conventín*. The adjacent **Monasterio de Santa María** consists of a 13C Cistercian church and cloisters dating from the 15C, 17C and 18C (open Tue–Sun Apr–Sept 11am–2pm, 4.30–7.30pm, Oct–Mar 11am–1.30pm; €4 both sites; ℰ670 242 372; www.monasteriovaldedios.com).

▶ Take the AS 112, A 66 and Autoveia Minera N to Gijón.

Gijón

36km/22mi NW of Valdediós.
🚄Gijón (high speed line under construction).

Gijón is a lively city with a population of 275 735. On Plaza del Marqués is the elegant late 17C **Palacio de Revillagigedo** (open depending on exhibition, but generally Tue–Sat 11.30am–1.30pm, 5–8pm/11am-1.30pm, 4–9pm summer; Sun & hols noon–2.30pm; no charge; ℰ985 34 69 21), now a cultural centre. Nearby is the fishermen's quarter, Cimadevilla. Vestiges of Gijón's Roman past include the **Termas Romanas del Campo Valdés** (Roman baths) in the old quarter (Campo Valdés; open Tue–Fri 9.30am–2pm, 5–7.30pm; Sat–Sun 10am–2pm, 5–7.30pm; closed 1, 6 Jan, 15 Aug, 24, 25, 31 Dec; €2.50, no charge Sun; ℰ985 18 51 51, http://museos.gijon.es). Nearby, the **Torre del Reloj** (Recoletas 5; open Mon–Fri 9am–2pm; no charge; ℰ985 181 120) is also well worth a visit, for its history displays and splendid views.

2 FROM GIJÓN TO CASTROPOL
179km/118mi.

Luanco

The charming port-village of Luanco mixes a workaday fishing port with tourist development, as seen in the new buildings multiplying on the watefront. Calle La Riva is the main street, with three notable Baroque monuments: the Torre del Reloj (clock tower), the Palacio de los Menéndez Pola and, overlooking the beach, Santa Maria church. Afterwards, stroll the Paseo del Muelle where restaurants overlook the charming bay.

Avilés

With 81,659 inhabitants, Avilés is the third-largest city in Asturias. Industrial and set just back from the coast, it is worth a visit for its old neighbourhood, concentrated around the town hall, and a new cultural centre designed by Brazilian architect Oscar Niemeyer.

Plaza de España is the heart of the old city, dominated by the City Hall, a former palace built in 17C and modelled on that of Oviedo. Opposite, the **Palacio Ferrera** is a beautiful example of baroque architecture. In the adjacent Calle San Francisco the 17C **Fuente de los Canos de San Francisco**, was once the city's main water source.

The striking **Centro Niemeyer** (open daily 9am–midnight; guided visits available; ℘984 835 031; www.niemeyercenter.org) is situated 500m/550yd from the Plaza de España, just over the river via a footbridge. A curious avant-garde landmark given the location, Oscar Niemeyer's clean, white rationalist forms spread out over a giant swathe of reclaimed industrial land.

Avilés' nearest beach, **Salinas**, is a rapidly expanding resort. The rock islet of La Peñona affords a **view** of the beach, one of the longest on the Costa Verde.

Ermita del Espíritu Santo

Muros de Nalón. 19km/11.8mi W of Salinas.
The hermitage commands an extensive **view**★ west along the coastal cliffs.

Cudillero★

9km/6mi W of la Ermita.
The fishing village makes an attractive **picture**★: tall hillside houses in pastel shades and white cottages with brown-tiled roofs lead down to the harbour full of fishing boats. Continue west for some of the area's best beaches: Playa Concha de Artedo (4km/2.5mi), Playa de San Pedro (10km/6.2mi) and, best of all, Playa del Silencio (15km/9.3mi).

Cabo Vidio★★

14km/8.7mi NW of Cudillero.
Catch the coastal **views**★★ from near the lighthouse on this headland.

Excursion to the Narcea River

91km/57mi to Cangas del Narcea along the N 634 and AS 216, branching S at the Cabo Busto.

Tineo

50km/31mi SW of Cabo Vidio.
Perched 673m/2 208ft up the mountainside, the town of Tineo commands an immense mountain **panorama**★★.

Monasterio de Corias

28km/17mi SW of Tineo. Open to prebooked groups. ℘983 48 40 02. www.bodegamonasterio.com.
This 11C monastery, rebuilt after a 19C fire, was occupied for 800 years by Benedictines. It is now a wine producer.

▷ Return to the coast road (N 632).

Luarca★

Luarca is in a remarkable **site**★ at the mouth of the winding río Negro, spanned by seven bridges. A lighthouse, church and cemetery stand on the headland once occupied by a fort.

Excursion along the Navia Valley

82km/51mi along the AS 12
(2hr30min each way).
The River Navia flows along a wild valley below several peaks. After Coaña, turn right at the sign "castro". Circular foundations and paving remain from a **Celtic village**. For a striking **panorama**★★ of the **Arbón dam**, pause at the viewpoint. Past Vivedro, there is another **panorama**★★, and as the road climbs, the **confluence**★★ of the Navia and the Frío is impressive from a giddy height. Beyond Boal, the valley is blocked by the high **Doiras dam**.

The **Museo Etnográfico** at Granda de Salime (av. del Ferreriro; open Tue–Sun; €1.50, no charge Tue or 18 May; ℘985 627 243; www.museodegrandas.com) traces Asturian life through re-created rooms and artefacts.

▷ Return to Navia, then continue W along the N 634. From Figueras on the ría Ribadeo you can view **Castropol**, which resembles an Austrian village.

Galicia

This remote region, around the size of Belgium, or Maryland in the US, fronts the Atlantic on Spain's northern and western borders. In appearance and culture it is akin to the Celtic regions of Ireland, Wales and Brittany; far removed from the archetypal images of southern Spain. Geologically speaking, Galicia is an ancient eroded granite massif, and the overall impression is that of a hilly and mountainous region. The climate is influenced by the sea: temperatures are mild and rainfall is abundant, providing the verdant landscapes which give the whole of Spain's northern coast its nickname, "Green Spain". The interior is primarily an agricultural region where mixed farming is the norm: maize, potatoes, grapes and rye, and cattle in Orense province. Galicia is Spain's chief fishing region and is renowned for its seafood even though most of the catch is canned. The Galician natives are a fiercely independent people – even by Spanish standards – with their own heritage, folklore and Galician language, *gallego*, not unlike Portuguese.

La Coruña and the Rías Bajas

Former capital of Galicia, the port of A Coruña is a bustling centre of industry, with a charming cobbled old town of narrow alleyways and pretty plazas. The Rías Altas, deep inlets backed by pine and eucalyptus, stretching eastwards from La Coruña, shelter some fine beaches and low-key resorts. By contrast, many a ship has been dashed against the rocks at the western Costa de la Muerte, but is worth a visit for its drama and (occasionally) calm beauty. The Rías Bajas, its inlets, creeks and coastline more spectacular than its counterpart north, is Galicia's major holiday area. There are several good resorts, chief among them A Toxa/La Toja. The best beaches are to be found on the Ilas Cíes, reached by boat from Vigo. Vigo is Spain's leading fishing port, with a picturesque harbour location. The area's other city, Pontevedra, has a charming and historic old quarter.

Camino de Santiago

There is no official starting point for the arduous Camino de Santiago (Way of St James), though the Spanish leg (measuring around 750km/465mi) begins at the French border, runs across the Pyrenees, then west through Navarra, Rioja, Castile and Galicia, waymarked by the pilgrim's symbol of a scallop shell.

Over the centuries numerous, often rudimentary, inns providing refreshments and shelter have opened along the route. It ends at Santiago de Compostela, whose narrow atmospheric streets and extraordinary cathedral rank among Spain's highlights.

Highlights

1   Standing in front of the Cathedral at **Santiago de Compostela** (p290)

2   Relaxing in a wonderful setting on the beach at **A Toxa/La Toja** (p296)

3   Touring the **Ría de Vigo** and taking in the wonderful views (p297)

4   Strolling through the delightful Old Quarter at **Pontevedra** (p299)

5   Walking atop the Roman city walls at **Lugo** (p302)

Ría de Vigo viewed from Baiona/Bayona

© Javier Larrea/age fotostock

Catedral de Santiago de Compostela

Santiago de Compostela★★★

In the Middle Ages Santiago de Compostela attracted pilgrims from all of Europe in search of eternal salvations. Today around 200 000 pilgrims make a similar trek to the city, declared a UNESCO World Heritage Site, each year. Whatever the spiritual benefits gained en route, the sightseeing highlight is fittingly, and literally, the final step of the journey: the wondrous Cathedral, which is the focal point of a city that celebrates life and piety in equal measures.

▷ **Population:** 95 612

◔ **Michelin Map:** 571 D 4 (town plan).

◈ **Info:** Rúa do Vilar 63. ☎981 55 51 29. www.santiagoturismo.com.

◖ **Location:** This pilgrimage city in NW Spain is connected by the AP 9 to Vigo (84km/52mi S) and La Coruña/A Coruña (72km/45mi N) and by the N 547 with Lugo (107km/67mi E). The AP 53 runs SE to Ourense/Orense (111km/69mi). ▰Santiago de Compostela (AVE).

◉ **Don't Miss:** The Cathedral.

THE CITY TODAY

Despite its large number of visitors, Santiago de Compostela remains one of Spain's most enchanting cities with its old quarters and maze of narrow streets containing numerous bars and restaurants. The city's 30 000 or so university students mix with the hundreds of thousands of annual visitors from all over the world and ensure a lively cosmopolitan atmosphere, which has only increased since Santiago was European City of Culture in 2000.

A BIT OF HISTORY

History, tradition and legends – The Apostle **James the Greater** crossed the seas to convert Spain to Christianity. He returned to Judaea where he fell victim to Herod Agrippa. His disciples fled to Spain with his body. A star is believed to have pointed out the grave to shepherds early in the 9C.

In 844 during an attack against the Moors at **Clavijo**, a knight on a charger, bearing a white standard with a red cross, appeared on the battlefield and brought victory. The Christians recognised St James, naming him *Matamoros* or Moorslayer. The Reconquest and Spain had found a patron saint.

In the 11C devotion spread until a journey to St James' shrine ranked with one to Rome or Jerusalem.

SIGHTS

Plaza del Obradoiro

The majesty of the square makes it a fitting setting for the Cathedral.

Catedral★★★

Pl. del Obradoiro. Open daily
7am–8.30pm. Closed 1 & 6 Jan; 25 Jul,
15 Aug, 25 Dec. Closed in evenings
Maundy Thu, Good Fri, Shrove Tue,
19 Mar, 1 Nov; 8, 24 & 31 Dec. No charge.
℘981 58 35 48.
www.catedraldesantiago.es.

The present cathedral dates mostly from the 11C to the 13C, although from the outside it appears Baroque.

Fachada do Obradoiro★★★ (Obradoiro façade) – This Baroque masterpiece by **Fernando Casas y Novoa** was completed in 1750. The central area, given true Baroque movement by the interplay of straight and curved lines, rises to what appears to be a long tongue of flame.

Pórtico de la Gloria★★★ (Doorway of Glory) – Behind the façade stands the narthex and the Pórtico de la Gloria, a late 12C wonder by **Maestro Mateo**. The statues of the triple doorway are exceptional both as a composition and in detail.

The doorway is slightly more recent than the rest of the Cathedral and shows Gothic features. Mateo, who also built bridges, had the crypt reinforced to bear the weight of the portico. The central portal is dedicated to the Christian Church, the one on the left to the Jews, that on the right to the Gentiles. The central portal tympanum shows the Saviour surrounded by the Evangelists while on the archivolt are the 24 Elders of the Apocalypse.

The engaged pillars are covered in statues of Apostles and Prophets. Note the figure of Daniel with the hint of a smile, a precursor to the famous Smiling Angel in Reims Cathedral in France. The pillar

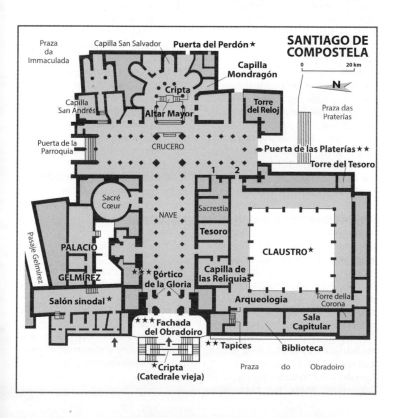

beneath the seated St James bears finger marks; traditionally, on entering the Cathedral, exhausted pilgrims placed their hands here in token of safe arrival. On the other side of the pillar, the statue of Santos Croques is known colloquially as the Saint of Bumps as it is is believed to impart memory and wisdom if you touch the brow of your head against it.

Interior – The immense Romanesque cathedral displays all the characteristics of medieval pilgrim churches: a Latin Cross plan, vast proportions, an ambulatory and a triforium. The side aisles are covered with 13C groin vaults. At major festivals a huge incense burner, the **botafumeiro** (displayed in the library), is swung from the transept dome keystone by eight men.

The **altar mayor** or high altar, surmounted by a sumptuously apparelled 13C statue of St James, is covered by a gigantic baldaquin. Beneath the altar is the **cripta★**, (crypt) built into the 9C church. It enshrines the relics of the saint and his disciples, St Theodore and St Athanasius.

The Gothic vaulting of the Capilla Mondragón (1521), and the 9C Capilla de la Corticela, formerly separate, are beautiful. The Renaissance doors to the **sacristía** (sacristy) (**1**) and *claustro* (cloisters) (**2**) on the right arm of the transept are noteworthy.

Enter the **tesoro** (treasury), in a Gothic chapel to the right of the nave, from inside of the cathedral.

The Cathedral Museum (open daily Apr–Oct 9am–8pm, Nov–Mar 10am–8pm; closed 1 & 6 Jan, 25 Jul, 25 Dec; €6 (pilgrims €4), inc Palacio Gelmírez (temporary exhibitions) is located in the westernmost part of the cloister. Exhibits include a gold and silver monstrance by Antonio de Arfe (1539–66). Use the side entry for the rooms devoted to archaeological excavations, the **biblioteca** (library), the **sala capitular** (chapter house) with its granite vault and walls hung with 16C Flemish tapestries, and the rooms with **tapestries★★** by Goya, Bayeu, Rubens and Teniers.

Claustro – Access via the museum. This Renaissance cloister was designed by Juan de Álava, who combined a Gothic structure with Plateresque decoration.

Puerta de las Platerías★★ (Silversmiths' Doorway) – This is the only intact 12C Romanesque doorway. Not all of the entrance is original. The most impressive figure is David playing the viola on the left door. Adam and Eve can be seen being driven out of the Garden of Eden; the Pardoning of the Adulterous Woman is on the right-hand corner of the left tympanum.

The **Torre del Reloj** (Clock Tower) was added at the end of the 17C. To the left stands the **Torre del Tesoro** (Treasury Tower). The 18C Baroque façade of the **Casa del Cabildo** is opposite the *fuente de los caballos,* or horse trough.

Palacio Gelmírez and Cubiertas (Cathedral rooftop tours)★

Pl. del Obradoiro. Palacio Gelmírez ticket & times as Museo. Guided tours (45min; reservations advised) Tue–Sun 10am–2pm, 4–8pm. Closed 1 & 6 Jan, 25 Jul, 15 Aug, 25 Dec. €12, pilgrims €10; €15, pilgrims €12 combined tour inc museum. ℘981 55 29 85. For tours in English or Galician ℘902 55 78 12.

This was formerly the bishops' palace; the **Salón Sinodal★** (Synod Hall) is more than 30m/98ft long and has sculptured ogive vaulting. A guided tour of the roof offers a surprising view of the Cathedral and unforgettable views of the city.

Hostal de los Reyes Católicos★

Pl. del Obradoiro. www.parador.es.
This former pilgrim inn and hospital, now a parador, has an impressive **façade★** with a splendid Plateresque doorway and four elegant patios. Even now the first ten pilgrims to arrive every day receive three free meals in the hotel, which is the most luxurious in the city.

Casco Antiguo★★ (Old Town)

The old part of the city is a maze of delightful narrow streets which open out onto lively squares.

Rúa do Franco

This street is lined by old colleges, such as the Renaissance-style Colegio de Fonseca, and shops and bars. The Porta de la Faxeiras leads to paseo de la Herradura, the hill that is the setting for fairs. The excellent **view**★ includes the cathedral and the rooftops of Santiago.

Fundación Eugenio Granell

Pl. del Toral. Open Oct–May Tue–Fri 11am–2pm, 4–8pm, Sat noon–2pm and 5–8pm. Extended hours in high season. €2. ℘981 57 63 94. www.fundacion-granell.org.
Inside the Pazo de Bendaña, a 18C noble building, the Fundación Eugenio Granell displays changing exhibitions of art, with an emphasis on Surrealism.

Rúa do Vilar

This street, leading to the cathedral, is bordered by arcaded and ancient houses, as is the parallel **rúa Nova**.

Plaza de la Quintana★★

This square at the east end of the Cathedral bustles with student life. Here are the former **Casa de la Canónica** (Canon's Residence) and the 17C Monasterio de San Peiayo de Antealtares. The latter is home to the **Museo de Arte Sacra** (Sacred Art Museum; open Apr–Dec Mon–Sat 10.30am–1.30pm & 4–7pm, Sun 4–7pm. €1.50. ℘981 56 06 23, www.santiagoturismo.com/museos/museo-de-arte-sacra). Opposite, the doorway in the Cathedral's east end, known as the **Puerta del Perdón**★ (Door of Pardon), designed by Fernández Lechuga in 161, is opened only in Holy Years (when the feast day of St James, 25 July, falls on a Sunday, next occurring in 2016. It incorporates the statues of all the Prophets and Patriarchs carved by Maestro Mateo for the original Romanesque *coro*.

Monasterio de San Martín Pinario★

Pl. de la Inmaculada 5. Call for hours. Church €3, monastery €4. ℘981 58 30 08. www.santiagoturismo.com/monumentos.

The monastery church has an ornate Plateresque front. The interior, with coffered barrel vaulting, is lit by a Byzantine-style lantern without a drum. The Churrigueresque high altar **retable**★ is by the great architect Casa y Novoa (1730). A grand staircase beneath a cupola leads to 16C–18C cloisters. The façade overlooking Plaza de la Inmaculada is colossal with massive Doric columns. Plaza de la Azabachería opposite is named for the jet ornament craftsmen *(azabacheros)* who once had workshops in this square.

Museo do Pobo Galego (Museum of the Galician People)

Open Tue–Sat 10.30am–2pm, 4–7.30pm, Sun and puholidays 11am–2pm. Closed 1 Jan, 25 Dec.€3. No charge Sun. ℘981 58 36 20. www.museodopobo.gal.
This regional museum, housed in the former Convento de Santo Domingo de Bonaval (17C–18C), provides an introduction to Galician culture. Rooms are devoted to the sea, crafts, painting and sculpture. The building has an impressive triple **spiral staircase**★.
Opposite stands the **Centro Galego de Arte Contemporáneo** (open summer Tue–Sun 11am–8pm; no charge; ℘981 54 66 19; www.cgac.org).

Museo de las Peregrinaciones (Pilgrimage Museum)

San Miguel 4. Open Tue–Fri 9.30am–8.30pm, Sat 11am–7.30pm, Sun and public holidays 10.15am–2.45pm. Closed 1, 6 Jan; 1 May; 24–25, 31 Dec. €2.40, no charge Sat pm and Sun.℘981 58 15 58. http://museoperegrinacions.xunta.gal.
A small museum devoted to the pilgrimages to Santiago.

Colegiata de Santa María la Real del Sar★

Pl. de la Colegiata de Sar. Open daily 11am-2pm, 4.30-7.30pm. €2. ℘981 56 28 91. www.colegiatadesar.com.
This 12C collegiate church is claimed to be the city's second most important Romanesque structure after the cathedral. A glance inside at the astonishing

slant of the pillars explains the 18C buttresses. Only a single elegant cloister gallery remains, its paired **arches**★ decorated with floral and leaf motifs. A museum displays gold and silverwork.

EXCURSIONS
Pazo/Palazio de Oca★

◉ 25km/15.5mi S on N 525. Gardens: open year-round daily 9am–6.30pm (Apr–Oct 8.30pm). €6. ℘986 58 74 35. www.fundacionmedinaceli.org.

This austere Galician **manor**, or *pazo*, with a crenellated tower, lines two sides of a vast square.

The romantic **park**★★ behind comes as a complete surprise (Łsee INTRODUCTION – Spanish Gardens, p100) and has been dubbed the "Generalife of the North". There are shady arbours, terraces covered with rust-coloured lichen, pools, and a lake with a stone boat.

Monasterio de Santa María de Sobrado

◉ Pl. Portal. 56km/35mi W. Open daily 10am–1pm, 4.30–7.30pm. €1. ℘981 78 75 09. www.monasteriodesobrado.org.

Sobrado is a vast weatherworn **monastery**, built between the Renaissance and Baroque periods.

Despite the severe church façade the interior displays a fertile imagination in the design of the **cupolas** in the transept, the sacristy and the Rosary Chapel. Medieval parts of the monastery include the kitchen, chapter house and Mary Magdalene Chapel.

ADDRESSES

🛏 STAY

⊜🛏 **Hostal Mapoula** – Entremuralles 10, 3º. ℘981 58 01 24. www.mapoula.com. 11 rooms. Breakfast included. A small, recently renovated family-run hostal in the old quarter. Bright simple rooms with en-suite bathrooms.

⊜🛏 **Hotel San Clemente** – San Clemente 28. ℘981 56 93 50. www.pousadasdecompostela.com. 10 rooms. ⊑ €6.50. An enviable central location a couple of minutes' walk from the Plaza del Obradoiro; rooms are decorated in brick and wood. Highly recommended.

⊜🛏🛏 **Casa Grande de Cornide** – Cornide 82, Calo-Teo. 11.5km/7mi SW of Santiago. ℘981 89 30 44. www.casagrandedecornide.es. 11 rooms. ⊑€7. This large, traditional-style Galician house offers peace and quiet. Décor and furnishings are an elegant fusion of the classic and the modern, and offer a cosy atmosphere. It's set in a lovely garden complete with a swimming pool.

⊜🛏🛏🛏 **Parador Hotel Reyes Católicos** – Pl. del Obradoiro 1. ℘902 54 79 79. www.parador.es. 137 rooms. ⊑€22. Two restaurants ⊜🛏🛏🛏. The former Royal Hospital founded by the Catholic Monarchs in 1499 has now been converted into a parador. Particularly worthy of note are its inner patios, which trace the typology of such hospitals in the 16C. Some rooms have four-poster beds.

🍴 EAT

⊜🛏🛏 **O Dezaseis** – R. de San Pedro 16. ℘981 57 76. www.dezaseis.com. Reservations recommended. Closed Sun. Impressive local gastronomy with delicious tapas and excellent wines, beneath the vines on the terrace or in a décor of wood and local stone.

⊜🛏🛏 **Don Quijote** – Galeras 20. ℘981 58 68 59. www.quijoterestaurante.com. A stronghold of traditional Galician cuisine with a popular bar.

⊜🛏🛏🛏 **Casa Marcelo Santiago** – Hortas 1. ℘981 55 85 80. www.casamarcelo.net. Closed Sun eve and Mon. A charming restaurant serving innovative Galician haute cuisine.

TAPAS

Bierzo Enxebre – Troia 10. ℘981 58 19 09. www.bierzoenxebre.es. Fine tapas bar with three rustic dining rooms including stone columns and timber rafters.

La Bodeguilla de San Roque – San Roque 13. ℘981 56 43 79. www.labodeguilla.gal. This bodega has a good reputation for its revuelta dishes, chorizos and wines. Pleasant restaurant on the first floor.

Tapas Caney – Hotel Araguaney Gran, Alfredo Brañas 5. ℘981 55 96 03. www.araguaney.com. Elegant tapas bar in a smart city-centre hotel.

Rías Bajas★★

This is Galicia's most attractive region for beach holidays and typical Spanish resorts such as A Toxa/La Toja. The coastline is famed for its deep fjord-like flooded inlets (rías), which afford safe harbour.

DRIVING TOURS

1 RÍA DE MUROS Y NOIA★★

From Muros to Ribeira
71km/44mi. About 1hr15min.

This *ría* is delightfully wild, its low coastline strewn with rocks. The northern bank is wooded. **Muros** is a seaside town with local-style houses. **Noia** is notable for its square looking out to sea, upon which stands the Gothic **Iglesia de San Martín★** (Pl. Suárez Oviedo; ℘981 82 01 31) with a magnificent carved portal and rose window.

2 RÍA DE AROUSA

From Ribeira to A Toxa/La Toja
115km/71mi. About 3hr

Ría de Arousa, at the mouth of the Ulla, is the largest and most indented inlet. **Ribeira** is a large fishing port with vast warehouses. **Mirador de la Curota★★** is 9km/5.6mi northeast of Ribeira.

▶ Take the LC 302 W towards Oleiros and after about 4km/2.5mi turn right onto a narrow road up to the viewpoint.

From a height of 498m/1 634ft there is a magnificent **panorama★★** of the four inlets of the Rías Bajas.

Padrón

41km/25.5mi NE of Ribeira.
According to legend St James landed by boat at this village. Its mooring stone (*pedrón*) can be seen beneath the altar in the parish church. The town,

- **Michelin Map:** 571 D-E-F 2-3-4.
- **Info:** Baiona: Paseo da Ribeira. ℘986 68 70 67; Vigo: Canovas del Castillo 3. ℘986 22 47 57; Tui: Colón 2. ℘986 60 17 89. www.turismoriasbaixas.com.
- **Location:** The Rías Bajas are four inlets: the Ría de Muros y Noia; the Ría de Arousa; the Ría de Pontevedra; and the Ría de Vigo, all along the northern coast.
- **Kids:** The Acuario de O Grove and Museo do Mar (Vigo) offer hands-on fishy fun.

renowned for its green peppers, was home to poet **Rosalía de Castro** (1837–85). Her house is a **museum** (Jul–Sept Tue–Sun 10am–2pm, 4–8pm, Oct-Jun 10am–1.30pm, 4–7pm; €2; ℘981 81 12 04; www.rosalia.gal).

Vilagarcía de Arousa

32km/19.8mi SW of Padrón off AP 9.
A garden-bordered promenade overlooks the sea. The **Convento de Vista Alegre**, founded in 1648, on the outskirts, is an old *pazo* (manor house) with square towers, coats of arms and pointed merlons.

Mirador de Lobeira★

4km/2.5mi S. Take a signposted forest track at Cornazo.
The view from the lookout takes in the whole *ría* and the hills inland.

Cambados★

12km/7.4mi SW of Vilagarcía de Arousa along PO 549.
The alleys of the old quarter are bordered by beautiful houses. At the northern entrance is the magnificent **Plaza de Fefiñanes★**. It is lined on two sides by the emblazoned Fefiñanes *pazo*, on the third side is a 7C church and on the fourth, is a row of arcaded

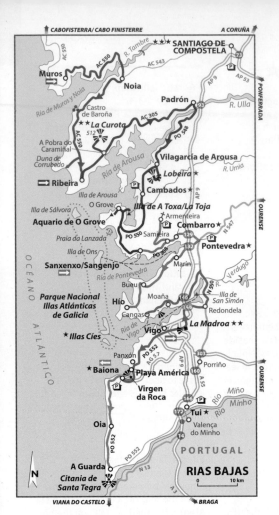

SANTIAGO DE COMPOSTELA ★★★

Muros
Noia
Padrón
Castro de Baroña
★★ La Curota
512
A Pobra do Caramiñal
Duna de Corrubedo
Ribeira
Ría de Arousa
Vilagarcía de Arousa
Lobeira ★
Cambados ★
Illa de Arousa
O Grove
Illa de Sálvora
Illa de A Toxa/La Toja
Aquario de O Grove
Armenteira
Combarro ★
Praia da Lanzada
Samieira
Pontevedra ★
Illa de Ons
Sanxenxo/Sangenjo
Ría de Pontevedra
Marín
Bueu
Parque Nacional
Illas Atlánticas de Galicia
Hío
Moaña
Illa de San Simón
Cangas
Redondela
★ Illas Cíes
Ría de Vigo
Vigo
La Madroa ★★
Panxón
Baiona ★
Playa América
Virgen da Roca
Porriño
Tui ★
Valença do Minho
Oia
PORTUGAL
A Guarda
Citania de Santa Tegra
RIAS BAJAS
0   10 km
N

houses. On the other side of the village are the romantic ruins of **Santa Mariña de Dozo**, a 12C parish church.

Isla de la Toja★

20km SW of Cambados off PO550.
According to local lore, it was a sick donkey abandoned on the island that was the first creature to discover the health-giving properties of the spring in La Toja. The stream has sadly now run dry but this pine-covered island, in a wonderful **setting★★**, remains the most elegant resort on the Galician coast, adorned with luxury villas and an early 20C palace. Its small church is covered in scallop shells. The seaside resort and fishing harbour of **O Grove** on the other side of the causeway is renowned for its seafood.

Acuario do Grove

Punta Moreiras, Reboredo. From O Grove head towards San Vicente and turn off at Reboredo. Open Holy Week and mid-Jun–mid-Oct 10.30am–8.30pm; rest of year Wed–Fri 10am–6pm, weekends 10.30am–7.30pm. €12.50; child €8. ℘986 73 23 27. www.acuariodogrove.es.
The only aquarium in Galicia, this has over 150 species, both local and exotic on display in 18 tanks. The **road★** from A Toxa/La Toja to Canelas affords views of sand dunes and rock-enclosed beaches such as **La Lanzada**.

3 RÍA DE PONTEVEDRA★

From A Toxa/La Toja to Hío
62km/39mi. About 3hr.

Sanxenxo is a lively summer resort with one of the best climates in Galicia. Further east at Samieira, a small road leads to the Monasterio de Santa María de Armenteira (open daily 9am–sunset; no charge; ℘986 71 83 00), a Cistercian monastery, where a 12C church and 17C Classical-style cloister can be visited. Some 12km/7.4mi east of Sanxenxo along PO 308 is **Combarro★**, a fishing village with winding alleyways, that has a good many Calvaries, and is famed for its **hórreos★** (drying sheds). Beyond Combarro is **Pontevedra★** (☞see PONTEVEDRA, p299).

Around 8km/5mi southwest of Pontevedra along PO 11 is **Marín**, headquarters of the Escuela Naval Militar (naval academy).

A further 19km/11.8mi southwest of Marín along AP 9 is Hío, a village at the tip of the Morrazo headland that has a famous intricately carved **Calvary★**.

4 RÍA DE VIGO★★

From Hío to Baiona
70km/43mi. About 3hr.

The deep Ría de Vigo is sheltered inland by hills and out to sea by the Islas Cíes. The scenery at Domaio, where the wooded banks draw together and the narrow channel is covered in mussel beds, is particularly beautiful.

From Cangas and Moaña you can see the white town of Vigo covering the hillside across the inlet.

Vigo
38km/23.6mi SE of Hío. www.turismodevigo.org. ☎ Vigo-Ursáiz (AVE).

Vigo is Spain's principal Transatlantic port and leading fishing port. Its **setting★** is outstanding, set in an amphitheatre on the south bank of the Ría de Vigo surrounded by parks and pinewoods. There are magnificent **views★★** from El Castro hill. Berbés is the picturesque fishermen and sailors' quarter. Adjacent is the A Pedra market where fishwives sell oysters; try them in the local bars.

MARCO (Museo de Arte Contemporáneo) (Príncipe 54; open Tue–Sat 11am–2.30pm, 5–9pm, Sun 11am–2.30pm; no charge; ☎986 11 39 00; www.marcovigo.com) displays the works of avant-garde artists, sculptors and architects.

At Punta de Muiño are splendid **views** of the *ría*. The **Museo do Mar** ♟♟(Av. Atlántida 160; open mid-Jun–mid-Sept Tue–Sun 11am–2pm, 5–8pm; mid-Sept–mid Jun Tue–Sun 10am–2pm, 5–7pm; €3,

child free; ☎986 24 77 50; www.museodomar.com) explores the history of Vigo and the sea, and includes an aquarium.

Islas Cíes★
☞By boat from Baiona, Vigo or Cangas; operates Holy Week to Oct; €18.50 return). ☎986 22 52 72.
www.mardeons.com.

This beautiful archipelago surrounded by crystalline water and white sand guards the entrance to the Ría de Vigo. Including three islands and the Playa de Rodas beach, it is part of the **Parque Nacional de las Islas Atlánticas de Galicia**.

Mirador la Madroa★★
6km/3.7mi. Leave Vigo along the airport road. After 3.5km/2mi turn left, following signposts to the "parque zoológico".

The corniche commands a fine **view★★** of Vigo and the *ría*. The beaches of Alcabre, Samil and Canido line the coast south of Vigo.

Panxón
14km/9mi SW along the C 550.
This seaside resort lies at the foot of Monte Ferro.

Playa América
2km/1.2mi S of Panxón.
A very popular, elegant resort in the curve of a bay.

Baiona/Bayona★
5km/3mi SW of Playa América.
www.baiona.org

It was here, on 10 March 1493, that Christopher Columbus's caravel *Pinta*, captained by **Martín Alonso Pinzón**, gave the first reports of the New World. Today, Baiona is a lively summer resort with a harbour fronted by a promenade of terrace cafés. In the old quarter houses may still be seen with coats of arms and glassed-in balconies. The former collegiate church (Pl. de Santa Liberata 1; open 11am–12.30pm, 4.30–6.30pm; ☎986 68 70 67) at the top of the town was built in a transitional Romanesque-Gothic style.

Monterreal

Open daily 10am–10pm. €1; €5 vehicles.
🖉986 35 50 00.
The Catholic Monarchs had a wall built
around Monterreal promontory at the
beginning of the 16C. The fort within is
now the Parador de Baiona, surrounded
by pinewood.
A walk round the battlements★ (about
30min), rising above the rocks, gives
splendid **views★★** of the bay, Monte
Ferro, Estela islands and the coast to the
Cabo Silleiro headland.

⑤ BAIONA TO TUI★

58km/36mi.

The coast between Baiona and La
Guarda is flat and semi-deserted.

Virgen de la Roca

Open Tue-Sun 11am-2pm, 4pm-7pm,
€1.50.
This huge granite statue (15m/50ft
high) of the Virgin holding a boat in her
right hand was built by architect Antonio Palacios in 1930. It can be climbed
via a spiral staircase. The view over
the bay and the ocean from the top is
impressive.

Oia

This fishing village clusters around
the Cistercian abbey of **the Real
Monasterio** (www.monasteriodeoia.
com), currently being restored.

La Guarda/A Guarda

13km/8mi S of Oia along PO 552.
This fishing village stands at the southern end of the Galician coastline. To the
south, **Monte Santa Tecla★** (341m/
1 119ft) rises above the mouth of the
Miño, offering fine **views★★**.

▶ Take Citania de Santa Trega signs.

On the slopes are the extensive remains
of a **Celtic city**, inhabited from the
Bronze Age to the 3C AD.

▶ From La Guarda, the PO 552 heads
inland parallel to the Miño river.

Tui/Tuy★

27km/17mi NE of La Guarda along PO 552.
Ancient Tui stands just across the border
from Portugal in a striking **setting★**. Its
old quarter, with its emblazoned houses
and narrow stepped alleys, climb up the
rocky hillside to the Romanesque-Gothic
catedral★ (open daily 10.45am–1pm,
4–7pm/May–Sep until 8pm; €4; 🖉986
60 05 11; www.catedraldetui.com), consecrated in 1232. The **Parque de Santo
Domingo**, including a Gothic church of
the same name, commands a good view
of Tui and the Portuguese coast.

ADDRESSES

🛏 STAY

🍽 **Canaima** – Av. de García Barbón 42,
Vigo. 🖉986 43 09 34. www.hotelcanaima
vigo.es. 50 rooms. Restaurant 🍽🍽🍽.
Centrally located, attractive modern
hotel.

🍽🍽 **Pazo de Hermida** – Trasmuro 21,
Lestrove. 1km/0.6mi SW of Padrón.
🖉981 55 42 95. http://pazosdegalicia.
com. 6 rooms. Breakfast included. A
beautifully renovated 17C Galician
manor in a tranquil setting.

🍽🍽🍽 **Tres Carabelas** – Ventura
Misa 61, Baiona. 🖉986 35 51 33. www.
hoteltrescarabelas.com. 10 rooms.
Family-run hotel in a smartly renovated
old stone house in the centre of town.

🍴 EAT

🍽🍽🍽 **Bitadorna** – Ecuador 56, Vigo.
🖉986 13 69 51. www.bitadorna.com.
Closed Sun eve. Traditional Gallegan
food, with the emphasis on seafood,
cooked by a talented young female
chef. Try the lobster with yoghurt sauce.

🍽🍽🍽 **O Fogón da Ría** – Fontecarmoa
3, Vilagarcia De Arousa. 🖉986 50 79 62.
www.ofogondaria.com. Closed Sun
and Mon for dinner, Tue. This lovely old
establishment has two dining rooms
with rustic décor with a varied menu
and good wine list.

🍽🍽🍽 **Posta do Sol** – Ribeira de
Fefiñáns 22, Cambados. 🖉986 54 22 85.
An attractive little restaurant, decorated
in regional style. The speciality is
seafood; try the empanadas and house
desserts. Good-value lunch menu.

Pontevedra★

Peaceful Pontevedra has a pleasant mix of fine buildings, plain arcades, cobbled streets and attractive parks and gardens. Terrace cafés teem in summer while bars are a cosy retreat in winter.

▶ **Population:** 82 539
◉ **Michelin Map:** 571 E 4.
🖥 **Info:** Casa da Luz, Praza da Verdura. ℘986 09 08 90. www.visit-pontevedra.com, www.turismoriasbaixas.com.
◑ **Location:** Pontevedra, near the northern coast, is linked by motorway with Vigo (27km/17mi S) and Santiago de Compostela (57km/35mi N). 🚆Pontevedra.

CASCO ANTIGUO★

The **Old Quarter** is tucked between calle Michelena, calle del Arzobispo Malvar, calle Cobián, and the river. Glass-covered passages and picturesque squares (**Plaza da la Leña; del Teucro, de la Pedreira**) are enchanting. There are endless places to stop for a drink, and there are busy shopping streets such as **Sarmiento**.

The delightful **Plaza de la Leña★** is surrounded by beautiful façades; two 18C mansions have been converted into the **Museo de Pontevedra** (Pasantería 2–12; open Tue–Sat 10am–9pm, Sun and public holidays 11am–2pm; closed 1 Jan, 25 Dec; no charge; ℘986 80 41 00; www. museo.depo.es). The ground floor holds Bronze Age **Celtic treasures★** and pre-1900 silverware. The first floor, which is dedicated to paintings, has several 15C Aragonese Primitives.

The second mansion includes a reconstruction of a stateroom from a 19C Spanish frigate, the *Numancia*. On the upper floor are an antique kitchen and 19C Sargadelos ceramics. The museum also encompasses the ruins of the Iglesia Santo Domingo and the ex-collegiate Iglesia de la Compañía de Jesús), beside the Iglesia de San Bartolomé.

Old alleyways and gardens surround the delightful 15C–16C Plateresque **Basílica de Santa María la Mayor★** (Av. de Santa María 24; museum and tower open daily 10am noon, 5-9pm; ℘986 09 08 90; http://santamarialamayor. blogspot.co.uk). The **west front★** is carved like an altarpiece, divided into separate superimposed registers on which are reliefs of the Assumption of the Virgin and the Trinity. At the summit is the Crucifixion at the centre of an openwork coping, finely carved with

oarsmen and fishermen. The interior mingles Gothic (notched arches), Isabelline (slender cabled columns) and Renaissance (ribbed vaulting) styles.

San Bartolomé is an 18C Baroque church with fine sculptures, including some by Pedro de Mena (Sarmiento 51; open Tue–Sun 9am-1pm, 6-10pm; ℘986 85 13 75).

Overlooking the gardens of Plaza da Ferrería is the simple Gothic façade of **San Francisco** church (Jardines de Castro San Pedro; open daily 7.30am-12.45pm, 4.30-6.45pm; no charge; ℘986 09 08 90). The interior features timber vaulting.

A small 18C **Pilgrim's Chapel** (Capilla de la Peregrina; Pl. de la Peregrina; open daily 9am–9pm; ℘886 15 15 55), with scallop-shaped floor plan and convex façade, contains a venerated statue of the patron saint of Pontevedra.

The **Ruinas de Santo Domingo** (Pas. de Montero Ríos; closed for renovation at the time of writing; ℘986 80 41 00) are a perfect example of medieval romanticism. The Gothic east end is overgrown with ivy. Arranged inside, from the Museo de Pontevedra, are Roman steles, Galician coats of arms and tombs of craftsmen showing the tools they used, and tombs of noblemen.

Ourense/ Orense

Orense/Ourense has been famous for its hot springs since Antiquity. Its Roman bridge was and still is a crossing for pilgrims to Santiago de Compostela. The pedestrianised old town is packed with cafés and restaurants, whose terraces spill out on to the streets, shaded by the numerous churches and the town's solid Baroque *casonas* (houses).

SIGHTS
Catedral★

Pl. del Trigo 1. Open Mon-Sat 11am-2.30pm, 4-7pm, Sun 1-3pm, 4-7pm (Oct-Feb Mon-Thu and Sun until 6pm) €5. ℘988 22 09 92. www.catedralourense.com.

The town's 12–13C cathedral has been repeatedly modified. The **Portada Sur** (South Door), in the Compostelan style, is profusely decorated with carvings. The **Portada Norte** (North Door) has two statue columns and, beneath a great ornamental arch, a 15C Deposition framed by a *Flight into Egypt* and statues of the Holy Women.

The interior is noteworthy for its pure lines. At the end of the 15C, a Gothic-Renaissance transitional-style **lantern★** was built above the transept. The ornate Gothic high altar retable is by Cornelius de Holanda. The 16C and 17C **Capilla del Santísimo Cristo** (Chapel of the Holy Sacrament), off the north transept, is decorated with exuberant sculpture in the Galician Baroque style.

The triple-arched **Pórtico del Paraíso★★** (Paradise Door), at the west end, has beautiful carvings and bright medieval colouring. The central arch shows the 24 Old Men of the Apocalypse; to the right is the Last Judgement. The pierced tympanum above, like the narthex vaulting, is 16C. A door in the south aisle opens onto the 13C chapter house, now housing the **Museo Catedralicio**, which includes church plate, statues, chasubles and a 12C travelling altar.

▶ **Population:** 106 231
& **Michelin Map:** 571 E 6, F 6 (town plan) – Galicia (Orense).
🛈 **Info:** Isabel La Católica 2. ℘988 36 60 64. www.turismo deourense.gal.
◖ **Location:** Orense is 101km/ 62.7mi E of Vigo along the A 52 motorway; 100km/62mi SE of Pontevedra via the N 541; 105km/65mi SE of Santiago de Compostela on the N 525 and the AP 53. 🚆Ourense/Orense (AVE).

Museo Arqueológico y de Bellas Artes

Pl. Mayor. Open, different buildings have own hours, see website for details. No charge. ℘988 22 38 84. www.musarqourense.xunta.es

Collections in the former bishop's palace on Plaza Mayor include prehistoric specimens, cultural objects (mainly statues of warriors) and an early 18C woodcarving of the **Camino del Calvario★** (Stations of the Cross).

EXCURSIONS
Monasterio de Oseira★

◖ 34km/21mi NW. Leave Orense on the N 525. After 23km/14mi turn right towards Cotelas. Visit only by guided tour. Mon–Sat 10am, 11am, noon, 3.30pm, 4.30pm, 5.30pm, 6.30pm; Sun 12.45pm only. €3. ℘988 28 20 04. www.mosteirodeoseira.org.

This grandiose 12C Cistercian monastery, known as the "Escorial of Galicia", was founded by Alfonso VII. It stands isolated in the Arenteiro Valley, a region that once abounded in bears (osos) as the name suggests. The **façade** (1708) is in three sections. In a niche below the statue of Hope, which crowns the doorway, is the figure of a Nursing Madonna with St Bernard at her feet. Of particular note is the **escalera de honor** (grand staircase) and the **Claustro de** los **Medallones** (Medallion Cloisters), which is decorated with 40 busts of historic figures. The **church** (12C–13C), hidden behind a Baroque façade of 1637, has retained the customary Cistercian simplicity, modified only by frescoes in the transept, painted in 1694. The **chapter house★** dates from the late 15C and early 16C and is outstanding for its beautiful rib vaulting.

Verín

◗ 69km/43mi SE along the A 52.
Verín is a lively, picturesque town with narrow paved streets, houses with glassed-in balconies, arcades and carved coats of arms. It is best known for its thermal springs, which were already famous during the Middle Ages and reputed for their treatment of rheumatic and kidney disorders.

Castillo de Monterrei

◗ 6km/3.7mi W. Open Wed–Sun 10.30am–1pm, 4–7pm. No charge. ℘988 41 80 02.
This formidable fortress compound was a frontier post throughout the Portuguese-Spanish wars. The complex included a monastery, hospital and houses, abandoned in the 19C.
The approach is up an avenue lined with lime trees, which commands a superb **panorama★** of the valley below. To enter the castle you will pass through three walls, the outermost dating from the 17C. At the centre stands the square 15C Torre del Homenaje (Keep) and the 14C Torre de las Damas (Lady's Tower). The courtyard is lined by a three-storey arcade and is less austere than the rest of the building. The 13C church has a **portal★** delicately carved with a notched design and a tympanum showing Christ in Majesty between the symbols of the Evangelists. Opposite is the Parador de Verín.

Celanova

◗ 26km/16mi S on the N 540.
This small village is dominated by its imposing **Monasterio de San Rosendo** (guided tours Mon-Sat 11am-12.30pm, 4.30-6pm, Sun 12.30pm; €2; ℘988 43

14 87) founded in 936 by San Rosendo, Bishop of San Martín de Mondoñedo. The **church** is a monumental late 17C edifice built in Baroque style. The coffered vaulting is decorated with geometrical designs, the cupola with volutes. An immense altarpiece (1697) occupies the back of the apse. Note the choir stalls, Baroque in the lower part and Gothic in the upper, as well as the fine organ.
The **cloisters★★**, among the most beautiful in the region, took from 1550 until the 18C to complete. Note too the majestic staircases.
Behind the church, the **Capilla de San Miguel** (opening hours as above; €1), is one of the monastery's earliest buildings (937) and a rare Mozarabic monument still in good condition.

Santa Comba de Bande

◗ 52km/32.5mi S along the N 540 (26km/16mi S of Celanova). 10km/6.2mi beyond Bande, head along a road to the right for 400m/440yd.
The small 7C Visigothic **church★** (call to arrange a visit; ℘988 44 31 40) overlooks the lake. The plan is that of a Greek cross, lit by a lantern turret. The apse is square and is preceded by a horseshoe-shaped triumphal arch resting on four pillars with Corinthian capitals.

Río Sil★

◗ 65km/40.3mi E. Head along the C 536; after 6km/3.7mi, turn left towards Luintra; continue for a further 18km/11mi.
The ex-Benedictine monastery is now occupied by the **Parador de Santo Estevo** in a majestic **setting★**. The former church's Romanesque east end and cloisters were built to grandiose proportions, largely in the 16C.
Return downhill on the road to the left, towards the River Sil. Two dams control the river, which flows through **deep gorges★**; their sides are dotted with vineyards.

Lugo★

Lugo was capital of Roman Gallaecia, the legacy of which includes the town walls, old bridge and thermal baths. The old quarter huddles around the cathedral.

OLD TOWN
Murallas★★
Ronda de la Muralla.
The Roman walls were built in the 3C, although they have been significantly modified. They are made of schist slabs levelled at a uniform 10m/32.8ft in a continuous 2km/1.2mi perimeter with 10 gateways and are listed as a UNESCO World Heritage site.

Catedral de Lugo★
Pl. Santa María. Open daily 8am–8.30pm; museum daily 11am–1pm. No charge; museum €2. ℘982 23 10 38.
The original Romanesque church (1129) has Gothic and Baroque additions. The Chapel of the Wide-Eyed Virgin at the east end, by Fernando Casas y Novoa (who built the Obradoiro façade of the Cathedral in Santiago de Compostela) has a Baroque rotunda and stone balustrade. The north doorway has a fine Romanesque **Christ in Majesty★**. The figure is above a capital curiously suspended, carved with the Last Supper. The nave is roofed with barrel vaulting and lined with galleries, a feature common in pilgrimage churches. There are two immense wooden Renaissance altarpieces at the ends of the transept – the south one is signed by Cornelis de Holanda (1531). A door in the west wall of the south transept leads to the small but elegant **cloisters**.

City squares
The 18C **Palacio Episcopal**, facing the north door of the cathedral on **Plaza de Santa María**, is a typical *pazo*, one storey high with smooth stone walls, advanced square wings framing the central façade and decoration confined to the Gil Taboada coat of arms on the main doorway.

▶ **Population:** 98 134
⚕ **Michelin Map:** 571 C 7 (town plan) – Galicia (Lugo).
🏛 **Info:** Rúa Miño 10–12. ℘982 231 361. www.turgalicia.es.
◗ **Location:** Lugo is 96km/ 59.6mi SE of La Coruña/ A Coruña along the A6, 94km/58.4mi NE of Ourense/ Orense on the N 540, and 135km/83.8mi SW Santiago de Compostela on the A 6 and A P9. ▭Lugo.
☻ **Don't Miss:** The sundials of the Museo Provincial.
🕐 **Timing:** See the Cathedral and walls first, then explore the surrounding area.

Plaza del Campo, behind the palace, is lined by old houses. Calle de la Cruz with its bars and restaurants, and **Plaza Mayor**, dominated by the 18C **town hall**, with its gardens and esplanade, are popular meeting places. The Alejo Madarro sweet shop (Reina 13; ℘982 22 97 14; www.madarro.net) first opened its doors in the middle of the 19C.

Museo Provincial de Lugo
Open Mon–Fri 9am–9pm, Sat 10.30am–2pm, 4.30–8pm. Sun and public holidays 11am–2pm. Closed 1, 6 Jan; 22 May; 24, 25, 31 Dec. No charge. ℘982 24 21 12. www.redemuseisticalugo.org.
This museum of regional art is housed in the former Monasterio de San Francisco. A room is devoted to ceramics from Sargadelos, and there are sundials and other objects from the Roman period. The former cloister of San Francisco contains an interesting collection of sundials, as well as several altars and sarcophagi.

La Coruña/
A Coruña★

This pleasant Galician city is set on a rocky islet, linked to the mainland by a strip of sand. At the northern end of the harbour, the charming old Ciudad quarter of small squares and Romanesque churches is a contrast to the wide streets of the business centre on the isthmus. The warehouses and industry of the Ensanche district are a reminder that La Coruña is Spain's sixth largest port and the main economic engine of the region.

▶ **Population:** 243 870
⚫ **Michelin Map:** 571 B 4 (town plan) – Galicia (La Coruña).
▪ **Info:** Pl. María Pita 6. ℘981 92 30 93. www.turismocoruna.com.
◐ **Location:** La Coruña, on the north coast, links to Santiago de Compostela by the AP 9 motorway. The A 6 heads SE past Lugo (97km/60mi SE) and on to Madrid. 🚄La Coruña/A Coruña (AVE).
▲▪ **Kids:** Aquarium Finisterrae.

A BIT OF HISTORY

Spanish Armada – Philip II's ill-fated "Invincible Armada" set out for England from La Coruña in 1588. A year later, Elizabeth I sent Drake to burn La Coruña; fortunately the town was saved by local heroine **María Pita**, who gave the alarm. **The 19C** – During the Peninsular War, Marshal Soult of France fought with the English in the Battle of Elviña/La Coruña in 1809. In the late 19C, La Coruña often supported liberal insurgents and consequently suffered severe reprisals.

SIGHTS

Colegiata de Santa María del Campo

Pl. Santa María 1. Open for tours just before and after masses. No charge. ℘981 22 03 86.

This Romanesque church has a triple barrel-vaulted nave strengthened by arches with plaster borders. Note the fine 13C–14C portal, Gothic rose window and tower. A **Museum of Sacred Art** (*Arte Sacro*) is on one side of the church. In the square stands a 15C Calvary.

Iglesia de Santiago

Parrote 1. Open Mon–Fri 11am-1.30pm, 6.30-7.30pm. No charge. ℘981 20 56 96. The building is a mix of Romanesque and Gothic, and features a beautifully carved stone pulpit.

EL CENTRO
(CENTRAL DISTRICT)
Avenida de la Marina★

This avenue facing the harbour is lined with tall houses with glassed-in balconies. Along one side is the paseo de la Dársena and on the other the **Jardines de Méndez Núñez**, gardens with a variety of flowering trees.

Plaza de María Pita

The vast café-lined square honours the lady who warned the town that Drake's fleet were arriving.

Castillo de San Antón: Museo Arqueológico e Histórico

Pas. del Parrote. Open Jul–Aug Tue–Sat 10am–9pm, Sun and public holidays 10am–3pm; Sept–Jun Tue–Sat 10am–7.30pm, Sun and public holidays 10am–2.30pm. €2. ℘981 18 98 50. www.coruna.es/cultura.

This fortress dates from the period of Philip II and now houses an archaeological museum, including exhibits of prehistoric gold and silver.

Museo de Bellas Artes

Avda. Zalaeta. Open Tue–Fri 10am–8pm, Sat 10am–2pm, 4.30–8pm, Sun 10am–2pm. Closed hols. €2.40; no charge Sat pm, Sun am and 18 May. ℘881 88 17 00. http://museo belasartescoruna.xunta.gal.

Light and spacious exhibition rooms are dedicated to art from the 16C to the 20C, including sketches by Goya.

Domus

Santa Teresa 1. Open Jan–Apr Mon–Fri 10am–6pm, Sat, Sun and public holidays 11am–7pm; May, June, Sept–Dec Mon–Fri 10am–7pm, Sat, Sun and public holidays 10am–7pm; July, Aug 10am–8pm. €2. Cinema €4. ☎981 18 98 40. www.mc2coruna.org/domus.

This landmark **building★** by **Arata Isozaki** – a double curve shaped like a sail and covered in slate – is emblematic of the city and is home to the city's museum of mankind. It claims to be the world's largest interactive museum, taking the human species as its subject. It includes a 3D cinema.

♣♣ Aquarium Finisterrae

Pas. Marítimo. Open Jan–Apr Mon–Fri 10am–6pm, Sat, Sun and public holidays 11am–8pm; May, June, Sept–Dec Mon–Fri 10am–7pm, Sat, Sun and public holidays 11am–8pm; July, Aug 10am–9pm. €10; child €4. ☎981 18 98 42. www.mc2coruna.org.

This excellent aquarium highlights local marine ecosystems.

La Casa de las Ciencias

Parque de Santa Margarita. Open, same hours as Domus (☝see above). €2. ☎981 18 98 40. www.mc2coruna.org/casa.

This entertaining hands-on museum features a planetarium and three floors of interactive exhibits. A Foucault pendulum oscillates In the central stairwell.

Torre de Hércules★

Avenida de Navarra. Open daily Oct–May 10am–6pm, Jun–Sept 10am–9pm. €3. ☎981 22 37 30. www.torredehercules acoruna.com.

This is the oldest functioning lighthouse in the world, a UNESCO World Heritage Site, dating from the 2C AD. The original outer ramp was enclosed in 1790. From the top (104m/341ft), there is a good **view** of the town and the coast.

EXCURSIONS
Costa de la Muerte (Coast of Death)

The coast between La Coruña and Cabo Finisterre is wild, harsh and majestic, whipped by storms, the graveyard of many a ship smashed against its rocks. Tucked in its more sheltered coves are fishing villages like **Malpica de Bergantiños**, protected by the Cabo de San Adrián (opposite the Islas Sisargas, with a bird sanctuary) or **Camariñas**, a lively port town famous for its bobbin-lace, which can be bought in various shops ranged around the harbour.

Cabo Finisterre or Fisterra★ (Cape Finisterre)

Legend has it that the Romans arrived here and christened it Finis Terrae ('the end of the earth'). **Cabo Finisterre** vies for the distinction of westernmost point of mainland Spain with Touriñan 29km north. The lighthouse on the headland commands a fine **panorama★** of the Atlantic and the bay.

The coast **road★** to the cape looks down over the Bahía de Cabo Finisterre, a bay enclosed by three successive mountain chains. **Corcubión★**, west of Cabo Finisterre, is an old harbour town of emblazoned houses with glassed-in balconies. South of here the coast is a succession of coves, harbours and beaches against a backdrop of hills dotted with windmills. At **Ezaro**, you can make a detour on the Rio Xallas, turning left onto the CA 2308, then right towards the **Noveira** waterfall. You will find several small waterfalls and natural pools up towards the Fervenza reservoirs.

Other nearby highlights include the long beaches 8km south of Ezaro at **Caldebarcos**. One is 6km long and 1km deep – to access it, go down the small road that runs past the church and continue straight to the car park.

Carnota

7km/4mi south of Caldebarcos, the village of Carnota is home to the longest **"hórreo"★** (typical barn on stone pillars) in Galicia. Built in 1760, it is 35m/115ft long.

Rías Altas★

The Rías Altas are characterised by deep inlets that are backed by thick forests of pine and eucalyptus, thriving despite the low level of Galicia's northern coast.
The rocky coastline and granite houses may suggest a grim climate yet holidaymakers arrive with the summer season to enjoy the scenery and sandy creeks. Galicia's *rías* are described below from east to west.

ⓖ **Michelin Map:** 571 A 5-7, B4-8, C 2-5, D 2 – Galicia (Lugo, La Coruña/A Coruña).

ⓘ **Info:** Ferrol: Praza Camilo José Cela.
℘981 33 71 31; Foz: Edificio Cenima, Avda de Ribeira. ℘982 13 24 26; Viveiró: Avenida de Ramón Canosa. ℘982 56 08 79. www.turgalicia.es.

ⓒ **Location:** In the far north-west corner of the Iberian Peninsula. 🚂 Nearest station La Coruña/A Coruña

SIGHTS

Ría de Ribadeo

ⓖ See also COSTA VERDE.
The Ría de Ribadeo is the estuary of the Eo, which slackens its pace to wind gently between wide banks. There is a beautiful **view★** up the estuary from the bridge across the mouth of the river. The old port of **Ribadeo** is an important regional centre and summer resort.

Praia das Catedrais★

The "Beach of the Cathedrals" is so-called for the curious shape of its cliffs, carved by the sea to resemble buttresses. Pass under the arches and you'll also find caves to explore, but beware high tides – check with the tourist office first.

Ría de Foz

Foz, at the mouth of its *ría*, is a small port with a fishing fleet. Its two good beaches are popular in summer.

Iglesia de San Martín de Mondoñedo★

ⓒ Barrio Caritel, Foz. 5km/3mi S of Foz. Take the Mondoñedo road, then immediately turn right. Open Jun-Sep Tue-Sat 11am-2pm, 4pm-8pm, Sun 11am-3pm, Oct-May Wed-Fri am only, Sat-Sun 11am-2pm, 4.30-7pm . No charge. ℘982 13 26 07.
Standing on a summit, this ancient church was once part of a monastery and an episcopal seat until 1112. Unusually in this region, it shows no sign of Compostelan influence. The east end, with Lombard bands, is supported by massive buttresses; the transept **capitals★** are naively carved and rich in anecdotal detail: one shows a table overflowing with food while a dog licks the feet of a suffering Lazarus.

Mondoñedo

ⓒ 23km/14mi SW along the N 634.
The small town of Mondoñedo rises out of the hollow of a lush valley. Streets are lined with balconied white houses bearing coats of arms. The cathedral square is delightful with its arcades and *solanas* (glassed-in galleries).
The immense façade of the **Cathedral★** (Pl. Catedral; open daily 10am–2pm, 4–8pm; €2 museum; ℘982 50 7 77) combines the Gothic grace of the three large portal arches and the rose window, all dating from the 13C, with the grandiose Baroque style of towers added in the 18C.
Late 14C frescoes decorate the interior, one above the other (below the extraordinary 1710 organ) illustrating the Massacre of the Innocents and the Life of St Peter. There are a Rococo retable at the high altar and a polychrome wood statue of the Virgin in the south ambulatory. It is known as the English Virgin, as the statue was brought from St Paul's, London, in the 16C. The classical **cloisters** were added in the 17C.

Ría de Viveiro

All **Viveiro** retains of its town walls is the Puerta de Carlos V (Charles V Gateway), emblazoned with the emperor's arms. In summer, the port becomes a holiday resort and on the fourth Sunday in August, visitors from all over Galicia come for the local Romeria do Naseiro festival.

Ría de Santa María de Ortigueira

The *ría* is deep and surrounded by green hills while **Ortigueira** port has quays bordered by well-kept gardens.

Santuario de San Andrés de Teixido★★

Open June–Sept 9am–10pm; Oct– May 9am–6pm. ✆981 48 24 96.
This stone hermitage has long been a site of pilgrimage and is worth a visit for the views alone.

Ría de Cedeira

A small, deeply enclosed *ría* with beautiful beaches. The road gives good **views** of **Cedeira** (summer resort).

Ría de Ferrol

The *ría* forms a magnificent harbour entered by a channel guarded by two forts. In the 18C, **Ferrol** (🚍Avenida de Compostela) became (and remains) a naval base. The symmetry of the old quarter dates from the same period.

Betanzos★

Betanzos, a one-time port which has now silted up, stands on a hill at the end of a *ría*. Its old quarter retains three richly ornamented Gothic churches and old houses with glassed-in balconies.

Iglesia de Santa María del Azogue★

Pl. de Fernán Pérez de Andrade. Open daily Jun-Sep 10am-1.30pm, 4.30-7pm, Sep-May 10am-1.30pm, 4.30-6pm. No charge. ✆981 77 04 62.
The asymmetrical façade of this 14–15C church is given character by a projecting central bay pierced by a rose window and a portal with sculptured covings. Niches on either side contain archaic statues of the Virgin and the Archangel Gabriel. Three aisles of equal height, beneath a timber roof, create an effect of spaciousness.

Iglesia de San Francisco★

Pl. de Fernán Pérez Andrade. ♿Open same hours as Iglesia Santa Maria del Azogue. No charge. Guided tours available. ✆981 770 110.
This Franciscan monastery church, in the shape of a Latin Cross, with a graceful Gothic east end, was built in 1387 by the powerful Count Fernán Pérez de Andrade, Lord of Betanzos and Puentedeume. It is remarkable for the many tombs along its walls, the carved decoration on its ogives and chancel arches and the wild boar sculpted in the most unexpected places.
Beneath the gallery to the left of the west door is the **monumental sepulchre★** of the founder, supported by a wild boar and a bear, his heraldic beasts. Scenes of the hunt adorn the sides of the tomb.

Iglesia de Santiago

Pl. de Lanzós. Open same hours as the other churches. No charge. Guided tours available. ✆981 77 66 66.
This church was built in the 15C by the tailors' guild. Above the main door is a carving of St James Matamoros (Moorslayer) on horseback. Alongside is the arcaded 16C **ayuntamiento** (town hall).

Museo das Mariñas

Emilio Romay 1. Open Mon–Fri 10am–1pm, 4–8pm; Sat 10.30–1pm. €1.20. ✆981 77 19 46.
Despite its nautical name this is a collection of general local history. Housed in a former convent, it features displays of Roman archaeology, national dress and local art.

Ría de La Coruña

♿See LA CORUÑA/A CORUÑA

Castilla-León: Burgos, León and Palencia

These three provinces of Castilla-León occupy the northern part of Spain's semi-arid *meseta*. Fortified towns such as Léon and Palencia rise above vast plains of cereal crops and remind today's visitors of this area's importance in the establishment of the kingdom of Castille and its power during the Reconquest. In addition to thriving university towns are numerous isolated and sparsely populated villages where life continues uninterrupted by many aspects of the 21C. The decline in rural population is resulting in an increase in forested land, though the importance of cereal cultivation, and the creation of pasture, means that the oaks and juniper bushes that carpeted the *meseta* before the agrarian age are now found only in the most secluded pockets.

Reclics of a glorious past

León was once the capital of a kingdom that covered nearly a quarter of present-day Iberia and its old centre retains splendid monuments from this period. In order to promote the restoration of royal authority and primacy of Catholicism Ferdinand and Isabella were keen patrons of the arts in this region; León's Cathedral, with the richest stained glass in Spain, and its Pantéon Real, are emblematic of this, patronage. The Old Town's buzzing bars entertain a sizeable student population. **Burgos** is a pleasant city. It was the ancient capital of Castilla for almost 500 years, and is famous for its magnificent Cathedral, the third largest in Spain, containing relics, and the remains of El Cid. A candiate city for European Capital of Culture, it has benefited from a recent restoration programme that has made the old town's riverfront an even more attractive place to wander. Summer festivals, such as that of San Pedro y San Pablo and the Día de las Peñas, are celebrated with processions, bullfights and traditional Castilian dishes

Highlights

1 Stunning **Burgos cathedral**, a showcase of European Gothic sculpture (p308)

2 Panorama from the **Pico de Tres Mares** (p314)

3 The 900-year-old church **San Martín de Frómista** (p315)

4 Ancient and modern artwork at **León's Museo and MUSAC** (p318)

5 Rock formations at the **Cuevas de Valporquero** (p319)

including *morcilla*, blood sausage mixed with rice.

Aguilar de Campoo marks the northeast border of the region, and from the nearby Pico de Tres Mares there is a wonderful panorama across to the Picos de Europa in Cantabria.

Burgos cathedral

Burgos★★

Burgos sits on the banks of the River Arlanzón, on a windswept plateau at the heart of the Spanish Meseta. The most famous of its monuments is the magnificent Cathedral, whose lofty Gothic spires dominate the city's skyline.

A BIT OF HISTORY

Founded by Diego Rodríguez in 884, Burgos was capital of Castilla and León from 1037 until the fall of Granada in 1492. Yet commerce and the arts flourished afterwards: the town became a wool centre for the sheep farmers of the Mesta (&see SORIA, p189); architects and sculptors from northern Europe transformed monuments.

Burgos became Spain's Gothic capital with outstanding works including the Cathedral, the Monasterio de las Huelgas Reales (Royal Convent of Las Huelgas) and the Cartuja de Miraflores (Carthusian monastery). The end of the 16C brought the decline of the Mesta and of the town's prosperity. Burgos was the seat of Franco's government from 1936 to 1938.

Land of El Cid (c. 1040–99) – The exploits of Rodrigo Díaz of Vivar (a village 9km/ 5.5mi N of Burgos) light up the late 11C history of Castilla. This brilliant captain, better known as El Cid, first supported the ambitious King of Castilla, Sancho II, then Alfonso VI, who succeeded his brother in dubious circumstances. Alfonso, jealous of his exploits against the Moors, banished the hero. As a result Díaz entered service with the Moorish King of Zaragoza and subsequently fought Christian and Muslim armies with equal fervour. Most famously, he captured Valencia at the head of 7 000 men, chiefly Muslims, after a nine-month siege in 1094. He was finally defeated in 1099 by the Moors at Cuenca and died soon afterwards. His widow held Valencia against the Muslims until 1102 when she set fire to the city, then fled to Castilla with El Cid's body. The couple were buried in

- ▶ **Population:** 177 100
- ⚷ **Michelin Map:** 575 E 18 −19 (town plan).
- ▯ **Info:** Nuño Rasura, 7 ✆947 288 874 . www.turismoburgos.org.
- ◖ **Location:** Burgos is in the north of Spain, 88km/54.6m from Palencia, 117km/73mi from Vitoria-Gasteiz and 120km/74.5mi from Valladolid; at 856m/2 808ft, it is exposed to bitter winds in winter. ▦Burgos.
- ◉ **Don't Miss:** The Cathedral, monasteries and circular main square.
- ◷ **Timing:** A least a day of exploration.

San Pedro de Cardeña (10km/6.2mi SE of Burgos), but their ashes were moved to Burgos Cathedral in 1921.

Legend has transformed the stalwart but ruthless 11C warrior, the Campeador (Champion) of Castilla, El Cid (Seid in Arabic), into a national hero. The epic poem *El Cantar del Mío Cid* appeared in 1180 and was followed by ballads. In 1618 Guillén de Castro wrote a romanticised version of El Cid, *Las Mocedades del Cid* (Youthful Adventures of El Cid), upon which Corneille, in 1636, based his drama *Le Cid*. In 1961, Charlton Heston immortalised El Cid in the eponymous Hollywood epic.

SIGHTS
Cathedral★★★

Pl. de Santa María. Open third week Mar–Oct 9.30am–7.30pm; rest of year 10am–7pm. €7 (pilgrims €4.50). ✆947 20 47 12. www.catedraldeburgos.es.

The third-largest Cathedral in Spain (after Sevilla and Toledo), Burgos illustrates the transformation of French and German Flamboyant Gothic into an exuberant Spanish style. Ferdinand III laid the first stone in 1221. At the beginning of the 13C, under Maurice the Englishman, then Bishop of Burgos, who had collected drawings during a journey through France (at that time very much influenced by the Gothic style), the nave, aisles and portals were built by local architects. The 15C saw the building of the west front spires and the Capilla del Condestable (Constable's Chapel) and the decoration of other chapels. Architects and sculptors from Flanders, the Rhineland and Burgundy were brought by another Burgos prelate, Alonso de Cartagena, on his return from the Council of Basel. These artists found new inspiration in Mudéjar arabesques and other Hispano-Moorish elements. The most outstanding, the Burgundian **Felipe Vigarny**, the Fleming **Gil de Siloé** and the Rhinelander **Johan of Cologne**, integrated rapidly and with their sons and grandsons – Diego de Siloé, Simon and Francis of Cologne – created what was essentially a Burgos school of sculpture. The cloisters were built in the 14C, while the magnificent lantern over the transept crossing – the original of which collapsed after some particularly daring design work by Simon of Cologne – was rebuilt by Juan de Vallejo in the mid-16C.

Exterior – A walk round the Cathedral reveals how the architects took ingenious advantage of the sloping ground (the upper gallery of the cloisters is level with the Cathedral pavement) to introduce delightful small precincts and closes.

West front – The ornate upper area, with its frieze of Spanish kings and two openwork spires, is the masterwork of Johan of Cologne.

Interior – The design of the interior is French inspired, while the decoration bears an exuberant Spanish stamp.

Portada de la Coronería – The statues at the jambs have the grace of their French Flamboyant Gothic originals, though their robes show more movement. The Plateresque **Portada de la Pellejería** (Skinner's Doorway) in the transept was designed by Francis of Cologne early in the 16C.

Around by the east end it becomes obvious that the Constable's Chapel, with its Isabelline decoration and lantern with pinnacles, is one of the Cathedral's later additions.

Portada del Sarmental – The covings are filled with figures from the Celestial Court. The tympanum is a remarkable showing of each Evangelist in a different position as he writes.

Crucero, Coro and Capilla Mayor★★ – The splendid star-ribbed lantern of the transept crossing rises on four massive pillars to 54m/177ft above the funerary stones of El Cid and Ximena, inlaid in the crossing pavement. The imposing unit of 103 walnut choir stalls, carved by Felipe Vigarny between 1507 and 1512, illustrates biblical stories on the upper, back rows and mythological and burlesque scenes at the front. The handsome recumbent statue of wood, plated with enamelled copper, on the tomb at the centre, from the 13C, is of Bishop Maurice. The high altar retable is a 16C Renaissance work in high relief against an intrinsically Classical background of niches and pediments.

Claustro – The 14C Gothic cloisters present a panorama of Burgos sculpture in stone, terracotta and polychrome wood.

The **Capilla de Santiago** (St James' Chapel) contains the Cathedral treasure of plate and liturgical objects.

In the **Capilla de Santa Catalina** (St Catherine's Chapel) are manuscripts and documents, including the marriage contract of El Cid. On the 15C carved and painted consoles, Moorish kings pay homage to the King of Castilla.

The **sacristía** (sacristy) houses the *Christ at the Column* by Diego de Siloé, a supreme example of Spanish Expressionism in post-16C Iberian sculpture. The **sala capitular** (chapter house) displays, besides 15C and 16C Brussels tapestries symbolising the theological and cardinal virtues, a Hispano-Flemish diptych, a *Virgin and Child* by Memling and, above, a painted wood Mudéjar *artesonado* ceiling (16C).

Capilla del Condestable★★ – A magnificent grille closes off the area. The Isabelline chapel, founded by Hernández de Velasco, Constable of Castilla, in 1482 and designed by Simon of Cologne, is lit by a lantern surmounted by an elegant cupola with star-shaped vaulting.

All the great early Renaissance sculptors of Burgos cooperated in the decoration of the walls and altarpiece. The heraldic displays in the chapel are striking.

On either side of the altar, the Constable's escutcheon, held by male figures, seems suspended over the balustrades of the tribune.

Statues of the Constable and his wife lie on their tomb, carved in Carrara marble, and beside them is an immense garnet-coloured marble funerary stone for the names of their descendants. To the right is a Plateresque door to the sacristy (1512) where there is a painting of *Mary Magdalene* by Pietro Ricci.

Girola★ – The *trasaltar* (at the back of the high altar), carved partly by **Felipe Vigarny**, includes an expressive representation of the Ascent to Calvary.

Escalera Dorada or Escalera de la Coronería – The majestically proportioned golden or coronation staircase was designed in pure Renaissance style by Diego de Siloé in the early 16C. Twin pairs of flights are outlined by an ornate, elegant gilded banister by the French master ironsmith, Hilaire.

Each of the side chapels is a museum of Gothic and Plateresque art: **Gil de Siloé** and Diego de la Cruz worked together on the huge Gothic altarpiece in the **Capilla de Santa Ana★** which illustrates the saint's life. In the centre is a Tree of Jesse with, at its heart, the first meeting of Anne and Joachim, and at the top, the Virgin and Child.

At the beginning of the Cathedral nave, near the roof, is the **Papamoscas** or **Flycatcher Clock**, with a jack which opens its mouth on the striking of the hours.

In the **Capilla del Santo Cristo** (Chapel of Holy Christ) is a Crucifixion with the particularly venerated figure complete with hair and covered with buffalo hide to resemble human flesh.

The **Capilla de la Presentación** (Chapel of the Presentation) contains the tomb of the Bishop of Lerma, carved by Felipe Vigarny, and the **Capilla de la Visitación** (Chapel of the Visitation), the tomb of Alonso de Cartagena by Gil de Siloé.

Museo de Burgos★

Miranda 13. Open Jul–Sept Tue–Sat 10am–2pm, 5–8pm, Sun and holidays 10am–2pm; Oct–Jun Tue–Sat 10am–2pm, 4–7pm, Sun and public holidays 10am–2pm. €1; no charge Sat–Sun, 18 May. ℘947 26 58 75. www.museodeburgos.com.

This excellent museum showcases the ethnography of the region.

Prehistoric and Archaeological Department – In the Casa de Miranda, a Renaissance mansion with an elegant patio, this section holds objects from the Prehistoric to Visigothic periods. Of particular interest are the rooms devoted to Iron Age sites, Roman settlement of Clunia and funerary steles.

Fine Arts Department – The Casa de Ángulo houses art from the region covering the period from the 9C to the 20C. There are several precious items from the Santo Domingo Monastery at Silas: an 11C **Hispano-Moorish casket★**, delicately carved in ivory in Cuenca and highlighted with enamel plaques, the 12C **Frontal or Urn of Santo Domingo★** in beaten and enamelled copper, and a 10C **marble diptych**. On the **tomb★** of Juan de Padilla, Gil de Siloé has beautifully rendered the face and robes of the deceased. The collection of 15C paintings includes a *Christ Weeping* by Jan Mostaert.

Museo de la Evolución Humana★

Paseo Sierra de Atapuerca. Open Tue –Fri 10am–2.30pm, 4.30–8pm; Sat, Sun and daily Jul–Aug 10am–8pm. Closed 1 & 6 Jan, 16 & 29 Jun, 25 Dec. €6. No charge Wed pm, Tue & Thu after 7pm. ℘902 024 246. www.museoevolucionhumana.com

This magnificent museum, opened in summer 2010, occupies the central part of a large modern building designed by architect, sculptor and painter Juan Navarro Baldeweg.

Exhibition themes include the archaeological site of Atapuerca; Darwin's evolutionary theories; to the differences and similarities of modern man with the hunter-gatherer 9 000 years ago;

the ecosystems fundamental to the course of evolution.

Arco de Santa María★

Pas. del Espolón. Open Tue–Sat 11am–2pm, 5–9pm, Sun 11am–2pm. Closed public holidays. No charge.
℘947 28 88 68.
The 14C gateway in the city walls was modified to form a triumphal arch for Emperor Charles V and embellished with statues of the famous including (top right) El Cid with Charles V. Inside are the **Sala de Poridad**, with magnificent Mudéjar cupola, and the pharmacy of the ex-Hospital de San Juan.

Iglesia de San Nicolás

Fernán González. Open Mon–Sat 11.30–1.30pm, 5–7pm (closed Wed in winter); Sun and public holidays only open before or after Mass. €1.50. ℘947 26 05 39.
The large, ornate **altarpiece★** of this Gothic church, carved by Simon of Cologne in 1505, has over 465 figures.

Iglesia de San Esteban: Museo del Retablo

San Esteban 1. Open Tue–Sun 11am–2pm, 5–8pm. €2. ℘947 27 37 52. www.museodeburgos.com.
This delightful 14C Gothic **church★** is a magnificent setting for 18 retables, exhibited in the church's three naves according to their religious significance. The *coro alto* contains a small collection of gold and silverwork.

Iglesia de San Gil

San Gil 12. Open mid-Jul–mid-Sept Mon–Sat 10am–2pm, 4–7pm; Oct–Jun only open before or after Mass. No charge. ℘947 26 11 49.
One of the city's most beautiful churches. Hidden behind its sober façade is a late Gothic temple. Noteworthy are the Nativity Chapel and Buena Mañana chapels, the latter containing a retable by Gil de Siloé.

Casa del Cordón

Pl. de la Libertad. Patio open Mon–Fri noon–2pm, 7–9pm. No charge.

℘947 251 791.
The 15C palace of the Constables of Castilla (now housing a bank, the Caja de Ahorros) displays a thick Franciscan cord motif, hence the name. It is where Columbus was received by the Catholic Monarchs on his return from his second voyage to America, and where Philip the Fair died suddenly of a chill.

Museo de Pintura Marceliano Santa María

Pl. de San Juan. Open Tue–Sat 11am–2pm, 5–9pm, Sun 11am–2pm. Closed public holidays. No charge.
℘947 20 56 87.
Impressionist canvases by Marceliano Santa María (1866–1952) are shown in the ruins of the former Benedictine monastery of San Juan.

Hospital del Rey

Founded by Alfonso VIII as a hospital for pilgrims, it retains its entrance, the Patio de Romeros, with its fine 16C Plateresque façade. Today, it is the seat of the University of Burgos.

Castillo de Burgos

Open daily Jun–Sept 11am–8pm and Sat–Sun and public holidays, Apr–Jun 11am–6.30pm, Oct–Mar 11am–2.30pm. €3.70. ℘947 20 38 57. www.aytoburgos.es.
This restored hilltop fortress dominates Burgos. Dating from the 9C, it was destroyed by Napoleon's troops. The views from here are magnificent.

EXCURSIONS
Monasterio Santa María Real de las Huelgas★★ (Royal Convent of las Huelgas)

Compases. ◗ 1.5km/1mi W of Burgos; take Avenida del Monasterio de las Huelgas. Open Tue–Sat 10am–2pm, 4–6.30pm, Sun 10.30am–3pm. €6, no charge for EU citizens Wed & Thu pm and for all on 18 May. ℘947 20 16 30. www.monasteriodelashuelgas.org, www.patrimonionacional.es.
Las Huelgas Reales, the summer palace of the kings of Castilla, was converted in 1180 into a convent by Alfonso VIII and

his wife Eleanor, daughter of Henry II of England. The nuns were Cistercians of high lineage, the abbess all-powerful; by the 13C the convent's influence, both spiritual and temporal, extended to more than 50 towns and it had become a place of retreat for members of the house of Castilla and even became the royal pantheon.

Rearrangement over the centuries has resulted in a somewhat divided building, featuring the Cistercian style of the 12C and 13C, alongside Romanesque and Mudéjar features (13C–15C) as well as Plateresque furnishings.

The clean lines of this **church** are pure Cistercian. The interior is divided by a screen: from the transept, open to all, you can see the revolving pulpit (1560), in gilded ironwork, which enabled the preacher to be heard on either side. Royal and princely tombs, originally coloured, rich in heraldic devices and historical legend, line the aisles, while in the middle of the nave, the nuns' *coro*, is the tomb of Alfonso VIII and Eleanor of England. The rood screen retable, delicately carved and coloured in the Renaissance style, is surmounted by a fine 13C Deposition. The altar is flanked on each side by two handsome 13C and 14C tombs.

Enough fragments of Mudéjar vaulting stucco remain in the 13–15C **Gothic cloisters** to suggest the delicacy of the strapwork inspired by Persian ivories and fabrics.

The **chapter house** holds the **pendón★**, a trophy from the Battle of Las Navas de Tolosa, decorated with silk *appliqué*. Late 12C. In these **Romanesque cloisters**, slender paired columns, topped by highly stylised capitals, combine to create an effect of elegance. Several rooms in this part of Alfonso VIII's former palace were decorated by Moors.

The **Capilla de Santiago** (Chapel of St James) retains an *artesonado* ceiling with original colour and stucco frieze. According to legend, the statue of the saint with articulated arms conferred knighthoods on princes of royal blood. The fabrics, court dress and finery displayed in the **Museo de Telas Mediev-ales★** provide a vivid view of royal wear in 13C Castilla. Some of these exhibits were found in the royal tombs; the most valuable came from the tomb of the Infante Fernando de la Cerda (who died in 1275), son of Alfonso X, the Wise. Fortunately escaping the French desecration of 1809, the tomb yielded a long tunic, *pellote* (voluminous trousers with braces) and a large mantle, all of the same material embroidered with silk and silver thread. Note too the *birrete*, a silk crown adorned with pearls and precious stones.

Cartuja de Miraflores (Miraflores Carthusian Monastery)

Ctra de la Cartuja. ⊙ 4km/2.5mi E. Open Mon–Sat 10.15am–3pm, 4–6pm, Sun and public holidays 11am–3pm, 4–6pm. No charge. ✆947 25 25 86. www.cartuja.org.

This former royal foundation, entrusted to the Carthusians in 1442, was chosen by Juan II as a pantheon for himself and his second wife, Isabel of Portugal. The church was completed in full Isabelline Gothic style in 1498.

Iglesia★ – The sobriety of the façade, relieved only by the buttress finials and the founders' escutcheons, gives no indication of the elegant interior vaulting and gilded keystones.

Sculpture ensemble in the Capilla Mayor★★★ – Designed by the Fleming Gil de Siloé at the end of the 15C, this ensemble comprises the high altarpiece, the royal mausoleum and a funerary recess. The polychrome **altarpiece**, the work of Siloé and Diego de la Cruz, is striking. The usual rectangular compartments are replaced by circles crowded with biblical figures. The white marble **mausoleo real** (royal mausoleum) is in the form of an eight-pointed star in which are recumbent statues of Juan II and Queen Isabel, parents of Isabel the Catholic. Dominating the exuberant Flamboyant Gothic decoration of scrolls, canopies, pinnacles, cherubim and armorial bearings, executed with rare virtuosity, are the four Evangelists. In an ornate **recess** in the north wall is the tomb of the Infante Alfonso, whose premature death gave the throne to his sister Isabel the Catholic. The statue of the prince at prayer is technically brilliant if informal (compared with that of Juan de Padilla in the Museo de Burgos (see Sights, p308).

Also in the church are a 15C Hispano-Flemish triptych (to the right of the altar) and Gothic **choir stalls** carved with an infinite variety of arabesques.

Sierra de Atapuerca

◯ Take the N 120 towards Logroño. In Ibeas de Juarros (13km/8mi), head to the Emiliano Aguirre hall (beside the main road). See website for times. €6 for the archaeological site and €6 for the Experimental Archaeology Centre. ℘947 42 1000. www.atapuerca.org.

These hills are the site of one of the world's most important palaeontological sites. Excavations at **La Dolina** have uncovered remains of hominids who lived around 800 000 years ago. The fossil register at the **Sima de los Huesos** (Chasm of Bones) is the largest in Europe, dating from between 400 000 and 200 000 years ago. Visitors can walk along the trench and visit a small archaeological museum.

Covarrubias★

This historic Castilian village of half-timbered houses and a Renaissance palace is partly surrounded by medieval ramparts. Covarrubias is the burial place of Fernán González, one of Castilla's great historic figures and the catalyst behind the kingdom's independence.

The Gothic collegiate church, the **Colegiata★** contains 20 medieval tombs, including those of Fernán González and the Norwegian Princess Cristina who married the Infante Philip of Castilla in 1258 (Pl. Rey Chidasvinto 3; guided visits from 10.30am Wed–Mon; no charge; ℘947 40 63 11).

Note the paintings by Pedro Berruguete and Van Eyck in the Museo Paroquial (Pl. Rey Chindasvinto 3; open Wed–Mon 10.30am–2pm, 4–7pm; €2). A 15C Flemish **triptych★**, with central relief of the Adoration of the Magi, is said to be by Gil de Siloé.

Monasterio de Santo Domingo de Silos★★

Valle de Tabladillo. ◯ 18km/11mi SE. Phone for monastery opening times. Cloisters open Tue–Sun 10am–1pm, 4.30–6pm. Closed 1 & 6 Jan, 19 Mar, 15 Aug, 12 Oct, 1 Nov; 8, 20 & 25 Dec. €3.50 ℘947 39 00 68. www.abadiadesilos.es.

This site, originally Visigothic, was occupied by Benedictine monks from France in 1880. The monastery is renowned for its concerts of Gregorian chants. The **cloisters★★★** are among the most beautiful in Spain.

Garganta de la Yecla

◯ 3km/1.8mi SW of Santo Domingo de Silos via the BU 910 – 🚶 20min. A footpath follows a narrow gorge.

Lerma

◯ 23km/14.3mi W along the C 110. Lerma owes its splendour and Classic town plan to the extravagance and corruption of the **Duke of Lerma**, Philip III's early 17C favourite.

The quarter built by the duke retains steep cobbled streets and houses with wood or stone porticoes. The ducal palace, with its austere façade, stands on the spacious **Plaza Mayor★**.

The **Colegiata** church (guided tours organised by tourist office; ℘947 17 70 02; www.citlerma.com) has a 17C gilded bronze statue by Juan de Arfe of the duke's nephew, Archbishop Cristóbal de Rojas.

Quintanilla de las Viñas

◯ 24km/15mi N. Take the C 110, the N 234 towards Burgos, then bear right onto a signposted road. The road follows the Arlanza Valley. Below and to the right, are the ruins of the **Monasterio de San Pedro de Arlanza**. Though only the apse and transcept of the **Iglesia de Quintanilla de las Viñas★** remain, it is of great archaeological importance (phone for opening hours; ℘947 28 15 00).

Aguilar de Campoo

The Castillo de Aguilar stands on a desolate outcrop typical of this part of the Meseta. Below the castle stretches the medieval old town, with its handsome main square, gateways, walls, and mansions adorned with coats of arms.

▶ **Population:** 7 033
⍟ **Michelin Map:** 575 D 17.
Info: Paseo Cascajera 10.
℮979 12 36 41.
www.aguilardecampoo.com.
► **Location:** Aguilar is 115km/ 71mi NE of Burgos.
🚄Aguila de Campoo.
◨ **Don't Miss:** A drive to the Pico de Tres Mares.
⏱ **Timing:** Take half a day.

SIGHTS

Colegiata de San Miguel

Pl. de España. Open Holy Week, Jul–15 Sept Tue–Sun 10am–1pm, 5–8pm; 16 Sept–June Mon–Sat 12-1pm, 5–8pm. €2. ℮979 12 36 41.
This Gothic church has Romanesque elements and two fine 16C tombs which bear statues of the Marquesses of Aguilar at prayer. Look for the life-like sculpted tomb of archpriest García González.

Monasterio de Santa María la Real

Ctra de Cervera. On the edge of town towards Cervera de Pisuerga. Open Sep-Jun Mon-Sat 10am-1pm, 4-6pm and Jul-Aug 10am-2pm, 5-8pm. Guided visits €5. ℮979 12 30 53. www.santamarialareal. org.
This fine, thoroughly restored transitional (12C–13C) monastery houses a Romanesque interpretation centre. There is also a hotel and restaurant here.

🚗 DRIVING TOUR

Pico de Tres Mares via Reinosa

66km/41mi N.
Cross the vast plain and ascend the south face of the Cordillera Cantábrica.

► Follow the A 67.

Cervatos

The **antigua colegiata★** (open daily 10am–2pm), a Romanesque former collegiate church, bears imaginative carved **decoration★**. The portal tym-panum bears a meticulous openwork design. There is a frieze of lions , while varied figures decorate the modillions. The carving on the capitals and con-soles supporting the arch ribs is dense and sophisticated and the 14C nave has intersecting rib vaulting.

► Continue 5km/3mi, then turn right.

Retortillo

Only an oven-vaulted apse and arch with two finely carved capitals illustrat-ing warriors remain of a small Roman-esque **church**. Adjacent are the ruins of a villa of the Roman city of **Julióbriga**.

► Return to the A 67.

Reinosa

The nearby Embalse del Ebro (a reser-voir) and the Alto Campoo ski resort (℮942 77 92 22; www.altocampoo.com) make this a growing tourist centre.

► From Reinosa, take the CA 183 to the Pico de Tres Mares (27km/17mi).

Pico de Tres Mares★★★

On the way, paths from Fontibre lead to a greenish pool, the **source of the Ebro** (Fuente del Ebro), Spain's largest river, at an altitude of 881m/2 890ft. ⏂To the Pico de Tres Mares by chairlift (Dec–Apr). Rivers flow from the peak (2 175m/7 136ft) to three seas. At the crest is a splendid **panorama★★★**.

Palencia

Palencia is a tranquil provincial capital situated in the fertile Tierra de Campos region. It was here that Alfonso VIII created the first Spanish university in 1208. Irrigation of the region has opened up an important horticultural industry.

CATHEDRAL★★

Pl. de la Inmaculada. Open May–Oct Mon–Fri 10am–1.30pm, 4–6pm, 6.35–7.30; Sat 10am–2pm, 4–5.30pm, 6.45–7.30pm; Sun 4.30–8pm (Nov–Apr Sun 4-7pm). €5. Guided tours available. ℘979 70 13 47.
www.catedraldepalencia.org.
Palencia's little-known Cathedral is a 14C–16C Gothic edifice with Renaissance features. The original 7C Visigothic chapel lay forgotten during the Moorish occupation, until Sancho III de Navarra came upon it while hunting.

Interior★★
The Cathedral contains an incredible concentration of art in all the styles of the early 16C: Flamboyant Gothic, Isabelline, Plateresque and Renaissance. The monumental high altar **retable** (early 16C) was carved by Felipe Vigarny, painted by Juan of Flanders and is surmounted by a Crucifix by Juan de Valmaseda.
The 16C tapestries on the sides were commissioned by Bishop Fonseca. The *coro* grille, with a delicately wrought upper section, is by Gaspar Rodríguez (1563); the choir stalls are Gothic, the organ gallery, above, is dated 1716.
The **Capilla del Sagrario** (Chapel of the Holy Sacrament) is exuberantly Gothic with a rich altarpiece by Valmaseda (1529), and the central **triptych★** is a masterpiece, painted in Flanders by Jan Joest de Calcar in 1505 – the donor, Bishop Fonseca, is shown at its centre.
The collection of the **Museo Catedralicio★** includes a *St Sebastian* by El Greco and four 15C Flemish **tapestries★** of the Adoration, the

▶ **Population:** 79 595
◔ **Michelin Map:** 575 F 16.
🗊 **Info:** Mayor Principal 31. ℘979 70 65 23. www.palenciaturismo.es.
◖ **Location:** Palencia is close to the A 62 heading NW to Burgos (88km/55mi) and SE to Valladolid (50km/31mi) and Salamanca (166km/104mi). 🚏Palencia.
◕ **Don't Miss:** The Cathedral.

Ascension, Original Sin and the Resurrection of Lazarus.

EXCURSIONS
Iglesia de San Martín de Frómista★★
◖29km/18mi NE along the N 611. Open Apr–Sept 9.30am–2pm, 4.30–8pm; Oct–Mar 10am–2pm, 3.30–6pm. €1.50. ℘979 81 01 28. www.fromista.com.
Pilgrims on the way to Santiago de Compostela used to stop here. However, the only vestige of the once-famous Benedictine **Monasterio de San Martín** is a church, built in 1066, with beautifully matched stone blocks of considerable size. This was a model for many others in the region.

Baños de Cerrato
◖14km/8.7mi SE.

◖ Cross the railway at Venta de Baños; turn right towards Cevico de la Torre. Bear left at the first crossroads.

Iglesia de San Juan Bautista★
Open Tue–Sun Apr–Sept 10.30am–2pm, 5–8pm; Oct–Mar 11am–2pm, 4–6pm. €2; no charge Wed, 18 May, 24 Jun, 23 Aug. ℘979 77 03 38.
This is the oldest church in Spain, built by the Visigothic king, Recceswinth, while he was taking the waters in Baños de Cerrato, in 661.

León★★

León, once the capital of a kingdom, was an important pilgrim stop on the Camino de Santiago and retains many superb Romanesque and Gothic monuments.

THE CITY TODAY

León is a lively city, thanks in no small part to its 14 000-strong student population, with lots of good places to eat drink and party. The centre of attention by night is the Plaza de San Martin in Barrio Húmedo on the edge of the historic centre. For a more old-fasioned elegant drinking stage try the Plaza Mayor. León is also good for shopping, particularly in its many small arts and crafts and antiques shops.

A BIT OF HISTORY

The medieval town – In the 10C, the kings of Asturias moved their capital from Oviedo to León, and fortified it. By the 11C and 12C León had become virtually the centre of Christian Spain. Ramparts and peeling stucco over old brick in the east of the city recall the early medieval period.

The most evocative quarter, the Barrio Húmedo (the "wet quarter", named for its proliferation of small bars), lies between the **Plaza Mayor** and the **Plaza de Santa María del Camino**, an attractive square with wooden porticoes.

The modern city – modern León is a sprawling industrial city. But its artistic tradition continues in Gaudí's neo-Gothic palace, **Casa de Botines** on plaza de San Marcelo.

PUERTA DEL CASTILLO

A good starting point for exploring León is the Puerta del Castillo, the only remaining entrance arch along the ancient city walls.

Built between the 1st and 3rd centuries and rebuilt in the 12th and 15th centuries, the walls originally formed a quadrangle, punctuated by 72 semicircular towers in addition to the eight towers that flanked the entrances. There are

▶ **Population:** 127 817
🖈 **Michelin Map:** 575 E 13.
▤ **Info:** Plaza de San Marcelo 3. ☎987 87 83 27. www.leon.es.
▶ **Location:** León is on the northern edge of the Meseta. The AP 66 motorway runs north to Oviedo (121km/75mi). Palencia (128km/79.5mi) and Valladolid (139km/86.3mi) are to the southeast. 🚆León (AVE).
☺ **Don't Miss:** The Cathedral.

now 36, from the Torre de los Ponces behind the Plaza Mayor to the tower of San Isidoro.

CATHEDRAL★★★

Pl. Regla. Open May–Sept Mon–Fri 9.30am–1.30pm, 4–8pm; Sat 9.30am–noon, 2–6pm; Sun 9.30–11am, 2–8pm (May 9.30am–2pm). See website for rest of opening times. Closed public holidays. €6. ☎987 87 57 70. www.catedraldeleon.org.

The Cathedral, built mainly between the mid-13C and late 14C, is true Gothic, right up to the very high French-inspired nave with its vast windows.

The **façade** is pierced by three deeply recessed and richly carved portals. The gently smiling Santa María Blanca (a copy: original sculpture in the apsidal chapel) stands at the pier of the central doorway; on the lintel is a Last Judgement. The left portal tympanum illustrates scenes from the Life of Christ; the right portal includes the Dormition and the Coronation of the Virgin.

The statues decorating the jambs of the central doorway on the south façade are extremely fine. Inside, the cathedral's outstanding **stained-glass★★★** – 125 windows and 57 oculi with an area of 1 200sq m/12 917sq ft– is the finest in Spain; even though due to their sheer number and areas, they weaken the walls.

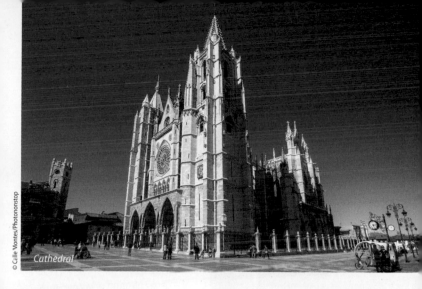

© Celie Montes/Photononstop

Cathedral

The west front rose and the three central apsidal chapels contain 13C–15C glass; the Capilla de Santiago (St James Chapel) shows Renaissance influence. The Renaissance **trascoro**★, by Juan de Badajoz, includes four magnificent alabaster high reliefs framing Esteban Jordán's triumphal arch.

The high altar **retable**, painted by Nicolás Francés, is a good example of the 15C international style. To the left is a remarkable **Entombment**★, showing Flemish influence, attributed to the Master of Palanquinos.

A silver reliquary contains the remains of San Froilán, the city patron. Several Gothic tombs can be seen in the ambulatory and transept, in particular that of Bishop Don Rodrigo – in the Virgen del Carmen Chapel to the right of the high altar – which is surmounted by a multifoil arch.

The galleries of the **claustro**★ are contemporary with the 13C–14C nave but the vaulting, with ornate keystones, was added at the beginning of the 16C. The galleries are interesting for the frescoes by Nicolás Francés and for the Romanesque and Gothic tombs.

Museo Catedralicio

Open Jun–Sept daily 9.30am–1.30pm, 4–8pm. Oct–May Mon–Sat 9.30am –1.30pm, 4–7pm; Sun 10am–2pm. Same ticket as cathedral (inc cloisters).

Among items in the museum are a French-inspired 15C statue of St Cath-erine, a Christ carved by Juan de Juni in 1576 (meant to be viewed from below), and a Mozarabic Bible.

SIGHTS
Real Colegiata de San Isidoro de León★★

Pl. de San Isidoro 4. Open Jul–Sept Mon–Sat 9am–9pm, Sun and public holidays 9am–3pm. May & Jun Mon–Thu 10am–2pm & 4–7pm, Fri–Sat 10am–2pm & 4–8pm, Sun and public holidays 10am–3pm. Rest of year Mon–Sat 10am–2pm & 4–7pm, Sun 10am–2pm Closed 1, 6 Jan, 25 Dec. €5, Thu after 4pm €1, last Thu month free. ℘987 87 61 61. www.museosanisidorodeleon.net.

The **basilica**, built into the Roman ramparts, was dedicated in 1063 to Isidore, Archbishop of Sevilla, whose ashes had been brought north for burial in Christian territory. Of the 11C church only the pantheon remains. The apse and transept of the present basilica are Gothic; the balustrade and the pediment on the south front were added during the Renaissance.

Panteón Real★★★

Colegiata Real de San Isidoro de León. This Royal Pantheon is one of the earliest examples of Romanesque architecture in Castilla. The **capitals**★ on the short, thick columns bear traces of the Visigothic tradition yet at the same time exhibit notable advances in sculpture, showing scenes for the first time.

317

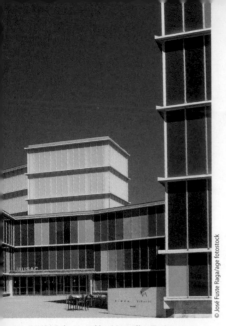

© José Fuste Raga/age fotostock

MUSAC designed by Mansilla+Tuñón

It has two storeys of windows, niches friezes and cornices, engaged columns, pilasters and medallions in high relief illustrating biblical and Spanish personages. The **church** front (on the extreme right), emblazoned with scallop shells, symbols of the pilgrimage to Santiago de Compostela, remains incomplete.

MUSAC (Museo de Arte Contemporáneo de Castilla y León)

Av. de los Reyes Leoneses 24. Open Tue–Fri 11am–2pm, 5–8pm; Sat, Sun 11am–3pm, 5–9pm. Closed 1 Jan, 25 Dec. €3, no charge Sun pm, 18 May, 12 Oct, 6 Dec. ✆987 09 00 00. www.musac.es.
This striking multi-coloured building by cutting-edge architects, Mansilla + Muñón, is covered in coloured crystals and focuses on living, working artists.

The 12C **frescoes★★★** are outstanding. They illustrate not only New Testament themes but also country life. The pantheon is the resting place of 23 kings and queens and many children.

Tesoro★★

Colegiata Real de San Isidoro de León.
The 11C reliquary containing the remains of San Isidoro is made of wood, faced with embossed silver and covered in a Mozarabic embroidery. The famous **Cáliz de Doña Urraca★** (Doña Urraca chalice) comprises two Roman agate cups mounted in the 11C in a gold setting inlaid with precious stones. The plaques of the 11C **Arqueta de los Marfiles★** (Ivory Reliquary) each represent an Apostle. The library contains over 300 incunabula and a 10C Mozarabic Bible.

Convento de San Marcos★ (Monastery of St Mark)

Pl. de San Marcos 7. ✆902 54 79 79. www.parador.es.
This former monastery, connected with the Knights of the Order of Santiago (St James) since the 12C, is now a parador. The 100m/328ft long **façade★★** has a remarkable unity of style in spite of the addition of an 18C Baroque pediment.

Museo de León★

Pl. de Santo Domingo 8. Open Oct–Jun Tue–Sat 10am–2pm, 4–7pm; Jul–Sept Tue–Sat 10am–2pm, 5–8pm, Sun and public holidays year-round 10am–2pm. €1, no charge Sat, Sun, 23 Apr, 9 & 18 May, 12 Oct, 6 Dec. ✆987 23 64 05. www.museodeleon.com.
This history museum includes the 10C Votive Cross of Santiago de Peñalba, and the **Cristo de Carrizo★★★**, an outstanding 11C Byzantine influenced small ivory crucifix. The **cloister** galleries, built between the 16C and 18C, serve as a lapidary museum. The northeast corner contains a low relief of the Nativity with an interesting architectonic perspective by Juan de Juni. The **sacristy★** is a sumptuous creation by Juan de Badajoz (1549) with decorated ribbed vaulting.

Casa de Botines★

Pl. de San Marcelo 5. ✆987 35 32 47.
Currently home to the offices of a Spanish bank (but with exhibitions sometimes open to the public), the neo-Gothic Casa de los Botines was one of Gaudí's few buildings outside Catalonia. It was commissioned by wealthy textile firm Fernández y Andrés (its official name is Casa Fernández-Andrés),

and construction began in 1891. Impressively, it was completed the following year.

Unlike most of Gaudí's fantastical buildings, it is a heavy, squared-off affair which uses iron pillars inside to give the sensation of light and space. Above the entrance there is a statue of Saint George slaying the dragon by Antonio Cantó and Vicenç Matamala.

In front of the building is a bronze statue of Gaudí, perched upon a bench.

Palacio de los Guzmanes★

Pl. de San Marcelo 6. Open Jul–Sept daily 10am–2pm, 4–8pm. Oct–Jun Mon–Fri 9am–2.30pm, 4.30–6.30pm. No charge. ℘987 29 21 00. www.turisleon.com.

Built in the late 16C by the wealthy and influential Guzmán family, this Renaissance palace is the work of two great architects, Rodrigo Gil de Hontañón (famous for the university buildings in Alcalá de Henares, among others) and Juan del Ribero. Flanked by two towers, and built on three levels, the palace bears heraldic decoration, such as the Guzmáns' shield – a cauldron with snakes crawling out of it – and warriors adorning the front façade either side of the balcony located above the main entrance. There is also a relief of St Agustín washing Christ's feet, and the façade bears various Classical allusions, with Ionic, Doric and Corinthian columns.

The Plateresque patio has a spectacular galleried upper storey, and also of note is a magnificent staircase.

EXCURSIONS

San Miguel de Escalada★

❯ 28km/17.4mi W. Leave León via N 601 to Gradefes. Open Tue–Sun May–Oct 10.30am–2.30pm, 4.30–7.30pm; Nov–Apr 10am–2pm. Guided tours available. Closed 1 & 6 Jan; 2 May; 24, 25, 31 Dec. €2. ℘618 866 790

In the 11C Alfonso III gave this abandoned **monastery** to refugee monks from Córdoba. Today the surviving church is the best-preserved Mozarabic building in Spain.

The **outside gallery★**, built in 1050, has horseshoe-shaped arches resting on carved capitals at the top of smoothly polished columns. An earlier church (**iglesia★**) from 913 has wooden vaulting, and a balustrade of panels carved with Visigothic (birds, grapes) and Moorish (stylised foliage) motifs.

Cuevas de Valporquero★★

❯ 47km/29mi N on the LE 311.
Guided tours (1hr 15min) daily mid-May–Sept 10am–6pm, rest of year 10am–5pm. €8.50. ℘987 57 64 08. www.cuevadevalporquero.es.

Ingenious lighting sets off the many extraordinary shapes in these vast caves – there is even a stalactite "star" hanging from the roof of the largest chamber. Other features include petrified "waterfalls", "church organ pipes " and a bright green lake. Choose from the 1.6km/1mi route, or the 2.5km/1.5mi route.

Puebla de Sanabria

Puebla de Sanabria is an attractive mountain village along the A 52 motorway, close to the Embalse de Cernadilla (reservoir), near the Portuguese border. The 15C castle of the Count of Benavente overlooks its white houses and late 12C church.

Valle de Sanabria

❯ 19km/11.8mi NW. Follow the lake road; turn right after 14km/8.7mi; after a further 6km/3.7mi turn left.

This valley of glacial origin, now a nature reserve, was hollowed out at the foot of the Sierras de Cabrera Baja and Segundera. It is a delightful area, well known for its hunting and fishing. **Lago de Sanabria** is the largest glacial lake in Spain, at 1 028m/3 373ft. It is used for water sports, and for salmon-trout fishing.

There are attractive **views★** of the rushing Tera and the mountain-encircled lake all the way to the Galician-looking village of **San Martín de Casteñada**, with its 11C Romanesque **church**.

Mediterranean Spain

Sagrada Família, Barcelona
© José Fuste Raga/age fotostock

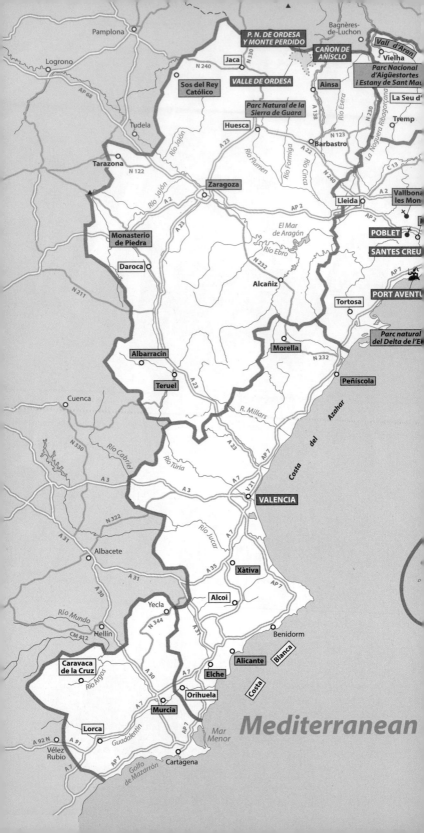

FRANCE

Foix

PERPIGNAN

d'Aran
elha
Nacional
iestortes
Sant Maurici

Principat
d'Andorra

N 116

Céret

Argelès
Collioure

AP 7

SANT PERE
DE RODES

La Seu d'Urgell

N 260

El Segre

Camprodon

Figueres

Cadaqués

Tremp

C 14

C 16

Ripoll

Empúries

Solsona

Vic

El Ter

COSTA BRAVA

13

C 25

Girona

Vallbona de
les Monges

C 25

Manresa

AP 7

Serra de
Montserrat

Terrassa

Costa de Barcelona-Maresme

Montblanc

AP 7

C 32

ES CREUS

BARCELONA

Sitges

TARRAGONA

AVENTURA

Costa Daurada

c natural
lta de l'Ebre

M A R

M E D I T E R R A N E O

MIRADOR
DES COLOMERS

COSTA ROCOSA

Ciutadella

Maó

MENORCA

Palma

ARTÀ

DRACH

Côte Est

MALLORCA

IBIZA

Eivissa

Formentera

N

0   20 km

an   Spain

BARCELONA	★★★	Highly recommended
Teruel	★★	Recommended
Alcoi	★	Interesting
Cartagena		Other sight described in this guide

Barcelona and around

Barcelona – the capital of Catalunya and the favourite Spanish city of most foreign visitors – shows no signs of flagging in the popularity stakes. It really is one of the few metropolises in the world that is all things to all people: atmospheric cobbled streets lined with cosmopolitan boutiques; medieval and Modernist masterpieces; art galleries and museums; colourful street theatre; beaches and buzzing restaurants, bars and nightlife. If it all gets a little too much, its revamped coastline and serene hinterland can provide sun-kissed downtime.

Highlights

1 Barcelona's atmospheric **Barri Gòtic and Cathedral** (p328)

2 Strolling the 19C splendour of the **Eixample** (p333)

3 The roof terrace of Gaudí's **La Pedrera/Casa Milà** (p334)

4 Admiring the wealth of artworks at the **MNAC** (p343)

5 Getting away from it on the beach at **Sitges** (p350)

Art and Architecture

Compact and easy to navigate, the best way to see the city is on foot. This is certainly true of its architectural assets. The city has long been endeared with architecture and has used the medium to make civic improvements at times of prosperity. When feisty Catalans were a force to be reckoned with on the Mediterranean trade routes, the Barri Gòtic was born. Today it is an atmospheric, moody ensemble of Medieval buildings that is a joy to wander. Similarly, the **modernisme** period, with its keynote buildings by Antoni Gaudí, was ushered in when Catalans started a brisk trade with the newly discovered Americas.

Barcelona's museums are world class. The one-time resident Pablo Picasso bequeathed an extensive collection of his early work while Joan Miró's purpose-built museum illustrates the genius of this ground-breaking abstract surrealist. A millennium's-worth of Catalan art, from ancient Romanesque frescoes to modernista decorative pieces can be seen at the MNAC. Spaces showcasing some of the world's best contemporary art include the CaixaForum and MACBA, a gleaming white edifice whose opening spearheaded the makeover of the Raval district. Yet for most, Barcelona's charms lie in its smaller pleasures: delightful squares linked by networks of winding streets, colourful neighbourhood markets and the palatable exuberance that locals have for their city.

Outside the city

More recently Cataluyna has garnered a reputation for cutting-edge gastronomy, mainly thanks to Ferran Adrià, the self-taught chef and figurehead of **cocina de vanguardia** (avant-garde cuisine). His Costa Brava restaurant El Bulli may have closed while Adrià was at his creative and professional peak, but his influence is everywhere, from creative tapas bars to haute-eateries throughout the region. One of Barcelona's greatest assets is its ease of escape. An efficient regional transport network can have you scaling the peaks of Montserrat or soaking up the sun on the beach in fashionable Sitges in less than an hour. A little further afield and you are in the Catalan heartland of Terrassa, a bustling provincial city well off the tourist trail.

Montserrat Monastery

Barcelona★★★

Combining urban sophistication with Mediterranean warmth, Barcelona is open and welcoming, traditional and avant-garde. It is a capital city in all but name.

THE CITY TODAY

Barcelona is not only southern Europe's most popular city, it is also an industrial centre and major port, a university town and seat of the Generalitat de Catalunya government. Moreover, it has a thriving cultural life with an opera house, theatres and concert halls.

The 1992 Olympic Games brought large-scale planning projects that radically changed the face of Barcelona, and since then the city regeneration and improvements have continued apace. The Forum of Cultures in 2004 led to the redevelopment of the Sant Adrià del Besòs waterfront.

A BIT OF HISTORY

The growth of the city – Founded by the Phocaeans, the city grew as Roman **Barcino**, within a 3C fortified wall. In the 12C, Barcelona became the capital of Catalunya and seat of the expanding kingdom of Aragón-Catalunya. Catalan Gothic architecture blossomed.

Catalunya sided with the Archduke of Austria in the War of the Spanish Succession (1701–14), and in defeat lost its autonomy. Montjuïc hill was fortified by the victors, and construction was prohibited except in the old city. Building outside the walls began again in the mid-19C. Industrialisation followed, along with two International Exhibitions, in 1888 and 1929. Modernist architecture flowered.

Catalan identity and cultural life – Catalan, banned under the Franco regime, is the language along with Castilian Spanish, used on all street names and in literature. Painters **Picasso**, **Miró**, **Dalí**, **Tàpies**, sculptor Subirachs and the architects **Gaudí**, Josep Lluís Sert, **Bofill** and Bohigas all lived here. Barcelona remains a hub for great artists.

▶ **Population:** 1 604 555

Michelin Map: 574 H 36 (town plan) – map 122 Costa Brava. Michelin City Plans Barcelona 40, 41 and 2040 – Catalunya (Barcelona).

Info: Main office Pl. de Catalunya 17 ✆932 853 834. Other offices (no✆): Pl. de Sant Jaume, Estació de Sants Cabina Rambla, Catedral, Aeroport (1 & 2), Terminals de creuers, Triangle, Mirador de Colom plus other tourist "cabines" in various locations. www.barcelonaturisme.com.

Location: Seaside Barcelona is the hub of northeastern Spain. The AP 7 motorway runs from Murcia to Girona and France; the C32 heads to the resorts to the north and south to Tarragona; the C 16 veers inland to Manresa (59km/37mi NE) and the C 17 to Vic. Plaça Canonge Rodó (Clot Aragó); Av. Marquès de l'Argentera (Estació de França); Pas. de Gràcia; Pl. de Catalunya Estació; Pl. Estació (Sant Andreu Comptal); Pl. dels Països Catalans (Sants).

Parking: Don't even think about driving in Barcelona. Use the excellent Bus Turistic to see the sights (www.barcelonabusturistic.cat).

Don't Miss: Sagrada Família church and the many Modernist masterpieces of architecture in the Eixample district.

Timing: Start from the Gothic Quarter, and see the Ramblas, Passeig de Gràcia and Sagrada Família before all else.

Kids: El Poble Espanyol; Parc Güell; Aquarium; Chocolate Museum; Museu Blau; beach.

GETTING THERE

Airport – 902 40 47 04. www.aena.es. 18km/11mi from the city centre. Can be reached by local train from Terminal 2 (Línea 2, Cercanías; 900 202 220) every 30min from 5.42am to 11.38pm, or by the regular no.46 TMB bus service from the Plaça de Catalunya and Plaça d'Espanya, departing every 15min from 5.30am to 12.15am (€2.15 single; 902 07 50 27). A quicker option is the Aerobus which runs, every 10 mins, makes fewer stops and takes approx 35 mins (€5.90 single, €10.20 return). By taxi, the fare from the city centre is approx €25–30.

Taxis – The city's black and yellow taxis are one way of getting around the city (but nowhere near as cheap or convenient as the Bus Turístic). Radio Taxi Barcelona: 932 25 00 00 Radio Taxi 033: 933 03 30 33 (www.tax.amb.cat).

Metro – Metro stations are shown on the maps in this guide (🚇). For further information: 932 98/ 000 or visit www.tmb.net. Information on access for disabled travellers can be obtained on the website. The network is open Mon–Thu and Sun 5am–midnight; Fri 5am–2am; Sat and days preceding public holidays 24 hours. A free metro guide is available.

Metro **tickets and cards** can also be used on buses, the "Tramvía Blau" (a tourist tram in the Diagonal section of the city) and train services operated by FGC (Ferrocarriles de la Generalitat de Catalunya). In addition to single tickets, multi-journey cards include the T-1 (valid for ten trips), T-DIA (unlimited travel for one day), T50/30 (50 trips in 30 days) and the T-MES (unlimited travel for one month).

Tram/Streetcars – There are six lines (T1, T2, T3, T4, T5 and T6).

Regional railway network – Main station Barcelona Sants (AVE). Airport to Sants 20 mins. €4.10 single. Ferrocarriles Catalanes train stations are shown on the maps in this guide (900 90 15 15; www.fgc.cat). Free connections to the metro system may be made at these stations: Avinguda Carrilet /L'Hospitalet, Espanya, Catalunya and Diagonal/Provença.

Bus Turístic – This excellent service offers visitors three bus itineraries throughout the city. Daily departures from Plaça de Catalunya starting at 9am (€29 1 day; €39 2 days; www.barcelonabusturistic.cat).

Boat trips – The Las Golondrinas company organises trips around the port (approx 35min). Departures from Portal de la Pau, opposite the Columbus monument. 934 42 31 06. www.lasgolondrinas.com.

SIGHTSEEING

Publications – The **Guía del Ocio** (www.enbarcelona.com) is a weekly online guide, also available at newspaper stands each Thursday, listing every cultural event in the city. The city's airport and tourist offices are also able to provide visitors with a full range of booklets and leaflets produced by the Generalitat de Catalunya's Department of Industry, Commerce and Tourism

DISCOUNTS

Barcelona Card – (3, 4 or 5 days; €45/€55/€60) gives unlimited transport, jumps queues and offer discounts from 20–50 per cent or free entry for dozens of museums, shows, shops, transportation and restaurants.

Articket – Valid three months, cost €30, for entry to CCCB, Fundació Antoni Tàpies, La Pedrera, Fundació Joan Miró, MNAC, MACBA and the Museu Picasso.

Arqueoticket – Valid one year, €14.50, for entry to: Museu d'Arqueologia de Catalunya, Museu Egipci de Barcelona, Museu Marítim de Barcelona and Museu d'Història de la Ciutat de Barcelona.

The above cards and passes are on sale at the city's **tourist offices**; however look online (http://bcnshop.barcelonaturisme.com) for discounted prices. For further information: ✆932 853 832; www.barcelonaturisme.com.

Ruta del Modernisme – A pack including a guidebook and discount booklet offering discounts of up to 50% on admission to the main Modernist buildings in Barcelona, exploring the works of Gaudí, Domènech i Montaner and Puig i Cadafalch. Available from the tourist office in Plaça Catalunya. ✆932 853 834. www.rutadelmodernisme.com).

DISTRICTS

Barri Gòtic – Following an intense restoration programme undertaken during the 1920s, the area containing the city's major historical buildings was renamed the Gothic Quarter.

Ciutat Vella – The old city includes districts as diverse as Santa Anna, La Mercè, Sant Pere and El Raval. The last, which used to be known as the Barri Xino (Chinatown), now contains Barcelona's leading cultural centres and is a fine example of urban renovation.

Eixample – The Eixample ("extension") developed following the destruction of the city's medieval walls. The district personifies the bourgeois, elegant Barcelona of the end of the 19C, with its prestigious boutiques, smart avenues and some of the best examples of Modernist architecture.

Gràcia – This *barrio*, situated at the end of the Passeig de Gràcia, is one of the city's most characterful areas. Gràcia developed from its early agricultural origins into an urban area as a result of the influx of shopkeepers, artisans and factory workers. It hosts a number of popular fiestas.

Ribera – With its narrow alleyways and Gothic architecture, this former mercantile quarter still retains an unquestionable charm, particularly in the EL Born district near the port. Its main attractions are the Carrer Montcada (location of the Picasso Museum) and the Església de Santa Maria del Mar.

Barceloneta – Seaside Barceloneta is famous for its outdoor stalls, fish restaurants and nautical atmosphere.

Vila Olímpica – The Olympic Village was built to accommodate sportsmen and sportswomen participating in the 1992 games. Nowadays, it is a modern district with wide avenues, landscaped areas and direct access to some of Barcelona's restored beaches.

Les Corts – This district is located at the upper end of Diagonal and includes the **Ciudad Universitaria** and the **Camp Nou**, the home of Barcelona Football Club and its much-visited **Museu FC Barcelona**.

Sarrià – Sarrià nestles at the foot of the Serra de Collserola and has managed to retain its traditional, tranquil character. The neighbouring districts of **Pedralbes** and **Sant Gervasi de Cassoles**, at the foot of Tibidabo, have become a favourite hangout for the city's well-heeled inhabitants.

Sants – One of the city's main working-class districts close to the railway station of the same name.

Horta-Guinardó – This *barrio* at the foot of Collserola was first populated by peasants and then by factory workers. It is home to the **Laberinto de Horta** (to the north), an 18C property with attractive gardens, and the **Velódromo**, a venue for sporting events and major music events.

Poble Sec – Nestled at the foot of Montjuïc – the city's garden and museum belt – Poble Sec is a cozy neighbourhood of pretty 19C apartment buildings and outdoor cafés.

Castilian vs Catalan: Common Spelling Differences

Ayuntamiento	Ajuntament
Avenida	Avinguda
Calle	Carrer
Capella	Capella
Iglesia	Església
Paseo	Passeig
Plaza	Plaça

Castell on the Plaça Sant Jaume, Festival of Our Lady of Mercy on the 24th September

🐾 WALKING TOUR

BARRI GÒTIC★★

The Gothic quarter, named for the many buildings constructed between the 13C and 15C, holds traces of Roman settlement and massive 4C walls.

Plaça Nova

This is the heart of the quarter, where the Romans built an enclosure with walls 9m/29.5ft high. Two watchtowers that flanked the West Gate (converted to a house in the Middle Ages) remain. Opposite the Cathedral, the **Col.legi d'Arquitectes** (College of Architects; Pl. Nova amb carrer del Bisbe) is a contemporary building with a facade etched with a mural designed by Picasso.

Catedral Santa Eulàlia (La Seu)★

Pl. de la Seu. Open Mon–Fri 8am–12.45pm, 1pm–5.30pm, 5.45–7.30pm. Sat 8am–12.45pm, 1–5pm, 5.15–8pm. Sun and hols 8am–1.45pm, 2–5pm, 5.15–8pm. €3 choir, €3 rooftop, or €7 suggested donation (afternoon openings). No charge before 12.45pm (1.45pm Sun) or after 5.45pm. ℘933 42 82 62. www.catedralbcn.org.

The cathedral was built on the site of a Romanesque church, from the late 13C to 1450. The façade and spire are 19C, based on old French designs.

The Catalan Gothic **interior**★ has an outstanding elevation with slender pillars. The nave is lit by a fine lantern-tower; the perspective is broken by the **coro**★★, with double rows of beautifully carved **stalls**. Note the humorous scenes adorning the misericords. In the early 16C, the backs were painted with the coats of arms of knights of the Order of the Golden Fleece by Juan de Borgoña, in one of the most impressive achievements of European heraldry.

The side chapels hold exquisite retables and marble tombs. The white marble **choir screen**★ was sculpted in the 16C after drawings by Bartolomé Ordóñez. Statues illustrate the martyrdom of St Eulàlia, patron of Barcelona. Her relics lie in the **crypt**★ in a 14C Pisan-style alabaster sarcophagus. The **Capella del Santísimo** (right of the entry) contains the 15C *Christ of Lepanto*, said to have been on the prow of the galley of Don Juan of Austria in the Battle of Lepanto (1571). In the next chapel is a Gothic retable by Bernat Martorell, also the artist of the **retable of the Transfiguration**★ in the ambulatory.

Cathedral roof visit – by lift from an ambulatory chapel. Metal walkways under the imposing silhouettes of the cathedral towers and cupola allow exceptional **views**★★ of the city.

The **cloisters★** are an oasis of quiet, and are home to a flock of geese. In the chapter house, a museum houses a *Pietà* by Bermejo (1490), altarpiece panels by the 15C artist Jaime Huguet and the missal of St Eulàlia, enhanced by delicate miniatures.

Around the corner from the cathedral is the **Museu Diocesà de Barcelona** (Av. de la Catedral 4; open daily Nov–Feb 10am–6pm Mar–Oct until 8pm; closed 1 Jan, 25–26 Dec; €6; ℘932 687 582.

◘ Facing the façade of the Cathedral, turn right into Carrer Sant Llúcia.

Casa de l'Ardiaca★

Santa Llúcia 1. See website for opening times. ℘933 181 195. http://w110.bcn. cat/portal/site/ArxiuHistoric.

Constructed in the 12C and altered in the 15C, the Archdeacon's House (now housing Arxiu Històric de la Ciutat or Historical City Archives) combines Gothic and Renaissance elements.

◘ Turn left into the Carrer del Bisbe and take the first right.

Plaça de Sant Felip Neri

The Renaissance houses on this square were moved here when via Laietana was built.

◘ Return to Carrer del Bisbe.

Carrer del Bisbe

To the left is the side wall of the Palau de la Generalitat (Provincial Council). Above a door is a fine early 15C medallion of St George by Pere Johan. On the right side is the **Casa dels Canonges** (Canons' Residence), residence of the President of the Generalitat.

A neo-Gothic covered gallery (1929), over a star-vaulted arch, links the two.

◘ Continue along Carrer del Bisbe.

Plaça Sant Jaume

This handsome square, once the main crossroads of the old Roman city, is the hub of Catalan political life; major celebrations (and protests) take place here.

Palau de la Generalitat

Pl. de Sant Jaume 4. Open to the public 23 Apr, 11 & 24 Sept. Guided tours (50min); online booking required. No charge. catalangovernment.exili.eu. This vast 15C–17C edifice is the seat of the Autonomous Government of Catalunya. It has a Renaissance-style façade on Plaça de Sant Jaume (c. 1600).

Ajuntament (Town Hall)

Pl. de Sant Jaume 1. Guided tours Sun 10am–2pm; 11 Feb, 23 Apr, 15 Jun 10am–8pm. No charge. ℘934 02 70 00. www.guia.barcelona.cat.

The town hall façade on Plaça Sant Jaume is Neoclassical; that on Carrer de la Ciutat is an outstanding 14C Gothic construction.

◘ Cross Plaça St. Jaume, turn left.

Carrer del Paradis

At no. 10 stand four Roman **columns★**, remains of the Temple of Augustus (same ticket as MUHBA, see below). Carrer Paradis leads into Carrer de la Pietat, bordered on the left by the Gothic façade of the Casa dels Canonges. The Cathedral cloister doorway opposite is adorned with a wooden 16C *Pietà*.

◘ Right on Baixada de Sant Clara.

Plaça del Rei★★

On this splendid square stand the Palau Reial Major (at the back), the **Capella de Santa Àgata** (right) and the **Palau del Lloctinent**. In the right corner, the Casa Clariana-Padellàs, housing the **Museu d'Història de Barcelona (MUHBA)★★**, is a 15C Gothic mansion moved stone by stone when the via Laietana was built in 1931.

Museu d'Història de Barcelona (MUHBA)★★

Pl. del Rei s/n. Multiple sites, Tue-Sat 10am-7pm, Sun 10am-8pm. €7. ℘932 56 21 22. ajuntament.barcelona.cat.

The ticket covers 12 various locations, including the the Temple of Augustus, Roman City, and Palau Reial Major.

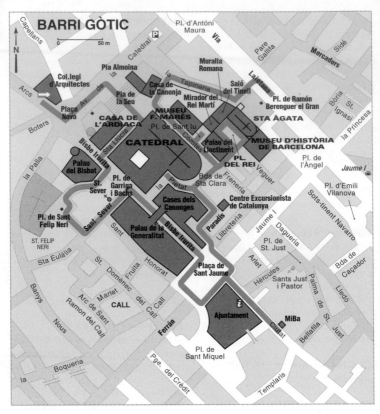

BARRI GÒTIC

The Roman city★★★

Under the museum and Plaça del Rei are Roman foundations, drainage, and reservoirs. In adjoining vaulted rooms are sculptures from the 1C–4C (busts of Agrippina, Faustina and Antoninus Pius). Two 13C Gothic frescoes were uncovered in the Sala Jaime I in 1998.

Palau Reial Major

Built in the 11C and 12C, the palace acquired its present appearance in the 14C. It was the seat of the counts of Barcelona and the kings of Aragón. Arches link huge buttresses in the façade; the original façade has rose windows. The lofty 14C **Saló del Tinell**, 17m/56ft high, is topped with a double-sloped ceiling set on six monumental arches. It is said that the Catholic Monarchs welcomed Columbus here after his first voyage.

Capella Reial de Santa Àgata★★

This 14C palatine chapel is covered by intricate polychrome woodwork panelling. The **Altarpiece of the Constable**★★ by Jaime Huguet (1465) depicts the life of Jesus and the Virgin Mary. In the centre, the *Adoration of the Three Wise Men* is a Catalan masterpiece. A staircase leads to the **Torre del Rei Martí**, a five-storey tower, which is closed to the public but can be seen duirng a visit to the MUHBA.

◗ Return to the Baixada de Sant Clara and turn right into the Carrer Comtes.

Palau del Lloctinent

This 16C late-Gothic palace was the residence of the viceroys of Catalunya.

◗ Continue on the Carrer Comtes.

Museu Frederic Marès★

Pl. de Sant Lu 5–6. Open Tue–Sat 10am
–7pm, Sun & hols 11am–8pm. Closed
1 Jan, 1 May, 24 Jun, 25 Dec. €4.20;
no charge first Sun in month, every
Sun from 3pm. ℘923 56 35 00.
www.museumares.bcn.cat.

The threshold to this wonderfully
eccentric museum is on the tiny **Plaça
de Sant Lu**, which is always full of
mime artists and street musicians.
The collections were left to the city by
sculptor Frederic Marès (1893–1991).
Sculpture Section – The works on
two floors and in the crypt are in
chronological order from the Iberian
period to the 19C. Note the **Christs and
Calvaries★** in polychrome wood (12C–
14C), Romanesque and Gothic **Virgins
with Child★**; a 16C **Holy Entombment★**
and **The Vocation of St Peter★**, an
expressive 12C relief by Cabestany.
Gabinete del Coleccionista – Everyday objects, mainly 19C, include items
from recreational rooms, the smoking
parlour and the women's boudoir (spec-
tacles, fans, clothes, etc.).

◗ Return to Plaça de la Seu; right into
Carrer Tapinera; follow it to the end.

Plaça de Ramon Berenguer el Gran

From the Plaça, Roman walls are visible,
incorporated into the Palau Reial.

👣 WALKING TOUR

LA RAMBLA★★

The most famous promenade in
Barcelona, La Rambla's five sections
follow an old riverbed bordering the
Gothic quarter. La Rambla separates
the Eixample district from the old
quarter, and is alive at all hours with
locals, tourists and down-and-outs and
vendors. The upper section, by Plaça
de Catalunya, is Rambla de Canaletes,
followed by Rambla dels Estudis or
Rambla dels Ocells (Avenue of the Birds).

◗ Walk S (towards the port) and stop
at the corner of Carrer Portaferrisa.

Palau Moja

The former home of poet Jacinto Ver-
daguer (1845–1902), is a Baroque palace dating from the late 18C. It houses
a great bookshop specialising in Catalan
history and culture on the ground floor.

◗ Continue walking southwards.

Església de Betlem

La Rambla 107. No charge.
This Baroque church – the interior was
razed by a fire in 1936 – has retained its
imposing façade, facing Carrer Carme.

◗ Walk in the same direction to the
corner of Carrer Carme and turn right.

Antic Hospital de la Santa Creu

Hospital 56.
These Gothic, Baroque and Neoclassical buildings are a haven in this district. An ex-hospital is the Library of
Catalunya. A charming planted **Gothic
patio★** (Jardines de Rubio y Lluch) can
be reached through a hall decorated
with *azulejos*.

◗ Return to La Rambla.

Rambla de les Flors

This stretch of La Ramblas is so-named
for the abundance of flower stalls here,
a scene that has been immortalised by
many local painters.

Palau de la Virreina★

La Rambla 99. Open Tue–Sun & hols
noon–8pm. No charge. ℘933 16 10 00.
www.ajuntament.barcelona.cat.
The elegant 1778 palace of the Vicereine
of Peru, with Baroque and Rococo
decorations, hosts exhibitions on
the theme of image. Alongside is the
traditional Mercat (market) de Sant
Josep (La Boqueria).
Down La Rambla on the right side
stands the city's opera house, the **Gran
Teatre del Liceu★** (La Rambla 51–59;
℘934 85 99 00; www.liceubarcelona.
com), rebuilt after a 1994 fire. Opposite
lies **Plaça de la Boqueria**, a charming

esplanade whose pavement was decorated by **Joan Miró**.

Mercat de la Boqueria★★★

La Rambla 91. Mon–Sat 8am–8.30pm.
www.boqueria.barcelona
One of the world's great food markets, this is where locals shop alongside Michelin-star chefs. Wander around admiring the incredible local produce and make sure you stop at whichever tapas counter takes your fancy, or enjoy a proper sit-down meal in one its six restaurants. An unmissable experience.

▷ Turn left into Carrer Cardenal Casañas.

Església/Basílica de Santa Maria del Pi★

Pl. del Pi 7. Open daily 10am–6pm. €4.
Guided tours available. ✆933 18 47 43.
www.basilicadelpi.com.
This lovely 14C Catalan Gothic church is striking for its simplicity and the size of its single nave. The plaza is noted for its many fine tapas bars.

Palau Güell★★

Nou de la Rambla 3. Open Tue–Sun 10am–8pm (5.30pm Nov–Mar). Closed Dec 25 & 26, Jan 1, 6. €12. No charge summer Sun (limited number of free tickets available from 4.45pm on day);

no charge first Sun of month, all day, in winter months (similar restrictions). Guided tours in English Tue 2pm (no additional charge). ✆934 725 775. www.palauguell.cat.
Gaudí designed the Güell residence (1886–90). Note the parabolic entry arches and the extravagant bars typical of the Modernist movement. The most striking interior features are the **grand hall** and the innovative use of materials and the treatment of light as a design element of each space.
La Rambla meets the sea at **La Rambla de Santa Mònica**. The former **Convent de Santa Mònica** (no. 7; open Tue–Fri 2–9pm, Sun 11am–7pm; no charge; ✆935 67 11 10; www.artssanta monica.cat) is a modern arts centre hosts changing exhibitions.
The Wax Museum **(Museu de Cera)**, complete with a new Horror Experience, opened in 2014, is also here (Pas. de la Banca 7; open Mon–Fri 10am–1.30pm, 4–7.30pm, Sat–Sun and holidays 11am–2pm, 4.30–8.30pm; summer 10am–10pm; €15; ✆933 17 26 49; www.museocerabcn.com).

Plaça Reial★★

This lively pedestrianised square shaded by palms and lined with cafés is surrounded by Neoclassical buildings. Gaudí designed the lampposts by the

Mercat de la Boqueria

© Sylvain Grandadam/age fotostock

Plaça Reial

fountain. A stamp and coin market is held here on Sunday mornings.

Mirador de Colom

Pl. Portal de la Pau. Open daily 8.30am–8.30pm (7.30pm Oct–Feb). Closed 1 Jan, 25 Dec. €6. ℘932 853 854. www.barcelonaturisme.com.

This famous 1886 landmark monument commemorates Christopher Columbus. A lift to the top gives a view over the city but it can be uncomfortably crowded in the small viewing space.

ADDITIONAL SIGHTS

Museu d'Art Contemporàni de Barcelona (MACBA)★★

Pl. dels Àngels 1. Open Mon, Wed–Fri 11am–7.30pm, Sat 10am–8pm, Sun and public holidays 10am–3pm; third week Jun–third week Sept extended hours Mon–Sat. Closed 1 Jan, 25 Dec. €10. ℘934 12 08 10. www.macba.es.

The monumental **building★★**, designed by American architect Richard Meyer, fuses the rationalist Mediterranean tradition with contemporary architecture. Two significant works can be found outside: *La Ola* by Jorge Oteiza and Eduardo Chillida's mural, *Barcelona*. The **permanent collections★**, set in dazzling white halls, cover major artistic movements of the past 50 years. Exhibits include works influenced by Constructivism and Abstract art (Klee, Oteiza, Miró, Calder, Fontana), as well as creations by experimental artists (Kiefer, Boltanski, Solano) and names of the 1980s (Hernández, Pijuán, Barceló, Tàpies, Ràfols Casamada, Sicilia).

There is also an excellent Modernist collection and the views from the roof terrace are spectacular.

Centre de Cultura Contemporània de Barcelona (CCCB)

Montalegre 5. Open (usually) Tue–Sun 11am–8pm. Closed 1 Jan, 25 Dec. €6. No charge Sun 3–8pm. ℘93 306 41 00. www.cccb.org.

This is another of the city's main cultural and creative arts centres. Its **patio★** combines original mosaics and silk-screen floral motifs with striking modern elements, including a soaring wall of mirrored glass.

WALKING TOUR★★

L'EIXAMPLE & MODERNIST ARCHITECTURE

Barcelona's Eixample (or enlargement) grew in the 19C. Ildefons Cerdà's 1859 grid plan circumscribe blocks of houses (*mançanes* in Catalan or *manzanas* in Castilian), octagonal in shape with trimmed corners.

The busy thoroughfares of avinguda Diagonal and La Meridiana cross to meet on Plaça de les Glòries Catalanes. In this ordered new section, architects transformed L'Eixample into the centre of Modernism in Barcelona.

Plaça de Catalunya

This vast square is considered the centre of the city and acts as a link between the old town and Eixample. Always buzzing, it is Barcelona's principal transport hub

La Pedrera (Casa Milà)

© Anna Serrano/hemis.fr

and is lined with well-known department stores, the city's main tourist office and the long-established Café Zurich – a popular people watching spot.

▷ N along the Passeig de Gràcia then turn left into Carrer de la Diputació then take the second right into Carrer de Balmes.

Museu del Modernisme★

Carrer de Balmes 48. Tue–Sat 10.30am–7pm, Sun and hols until 2pm. Closed 1 & 6 Jan, 1 May, 25 & 26 Dec. €10. &932 722 896. www.mmbcn.cat. Housed in a Modernista textile warehouse dating from 1902 and designed by Enric Sagnier, this museum, which opened in 2010, is the only museum in Europe which is dedicated to this style of architecture. The exhibits, from a private collection, include furniture, sculpture and decorative arts by all the main players.

▷ Continue up Carrer de Balmes and take the second right into Carrer d'Aragó.

Fundació Antoni Tàpies★★

Aragó 255. Open Tue–Sun 10am–7pm. Closed 1, 6 Jan, 25, 26 Dec. €7. &934 87 03 15. www.fundaciotapies.org.
Tàpies established his foundation in an ex-publishing house designed by Domènech i Montaner. The brick building is crowned by a sculpture by Tàpies, *Núvol i Cadira* (cloud and chair), the emblem of the museum.
The newly renovated interior, where white walls are contrasted with original wooden detailing, is lit by skylights (a cupola and a pyramid). Paintings and sculptures trace the development of Tàpies' work since 1948.

▷ Continue N along the Passeig de Gràcia to Carrer Valencia and turn left.

Museu Egipci de Barcelona – Fundació Arqueològica Clos

Valencia, 284. Open Mon–Sat 10am–8pm (early Jan–third wk Jun & mid-Sept–Nov closed 2–4pm, except Easter & hols). Sun and hols 10am–2pm. Closed 1, 6 Jan, 25-26 Dec. €11. &934 88 01 88. www.museuegipci.com.
This fascinating private museum has about 600 exhibits representing various periods of Egyptian civilization, in addition to pieces from the Roman period.

▷ Return to Passeig de Gràcia.

Passeig de Gràcia★★

Along this boulevard, with elegant wrought-iron **street lamps★** by Pere Falqués (1900), lies some of Barcelona's finest Modernist architecture, in the **Manzana de la Discordia★★** (Block of Discord): no. 35 **Casa Lleó More-ra★** (1905) by Domènech i Montaner, no. 41 **Casa Amatller★** (1900) by Puig i Cadafalch (daily guided tours (1hr) in English at 11am and in Spanish at 1pm; €17; ℘934 617 460; www.amatller.org), and no. 43 **Casa Batlló★★** (1904–06) by Gaudí, with its extraordinary mosaic façade and fairy-tale dragon-like roof (open daily 9am–9pm; €23.50; ℘932 16 03 06; www.casabatllo.es).

▷ Continue in the same direction until you reach the corner of Carrer Provença.

La Pedrera (Casa Milà)★★★

Provença 261–265. Open Mon–Sun 9am-6.30pm, 7-9pm. Closed 1, 6 Jan, 25–26 Dec. See website for variety of tours and prices. ℘902 202 138. www.lapedrera.com.

With its unmistakable shapes and undulating lines, this magnificent Gaudí building has become an icon of the city. Visit the **roof and attic★** and **a residential floor★**. The **Espai Gaudí** exhibits drawings and models by the artist. The roof, with its forest of chimneys resembling medieval knights, provides fine **views★**. **El Piso★** is a re-created apartment of an early 20C upper-class family. There is also a smart café-restaurant on the ground floor (open daily 8.30am–midnight; www.lapedrera.com).

▷ Continue along the Passeig de Gràcia to the busy Avinguda Diagonal and turn right.

Avinguda Diagonal

Palau Baró de Quadras, a Modernist building on the right (no. 373), was designed by **Puig i Cadafalch** and now houses the Institut Ramón Llull (Mon–Fri 9am–5.30pm), which promotes Catalan language and culture abroad. Along on the left (no. 416), his **Casa de les Punxes (Casa Terrades★)** bears the stamp of Flemish influence.

▷ Continue along the Diagonal to the intersection of Carrer Mallorca.

Continue along Carrer Mallorca in the same direction.

La Sagrada Família★★★ (Church of the Holy Family)

Mallorca 401. Open daily Apr–Sept 9am–8pm, Mar & Oct until 7pm, Nov–Feb until 6pm. 25–26 Dec, 1, 6 Jan 9am–2pm. €15, guided tours in English (50min) or with an audioguide (1hr 15mins) €22. ℘932 08 04 14. www.sagradafamilia.org. This unfinished project was begun in 1882 and taken over by Gaudí in 1883. He planned a Latin Cross church with five aisles and a transept with three aisles. Three façades were each to be dominated by four spires representing the Apostles with a central spire to represent Christ and the Evangelists. The nave was to be a forest of columns. In his lifetime, only the crypt, the apsidal walls, one of the towers and the **Nativity façade★★** were finished. The Nativity façade comprises three doorways, Faith, Hope and Charity. Work resumed in 1940. The Passion façade was completed in 1981. The top of the east spire affords a wonderful **view★★** of the work on the church, and of Barcelona. Domènech i Montaner's **Hospital Sant Pau★** (Sant Antoni Maria Claret 167; guided tours daily in English at noon and 1pm; €13; ℘93 553 78 01, www.santpaubarcelona.org), with its remarkable glazed roof tiles, may be seen at the end of Avinguda de Gaudí.

ADDITIONAL SIGHTS
Casa Vicens★★

Carrer de les Carolines 20. Open Mon-Sun 10am-8pm (last visit 7pm), closed 1 & 6 Jan, 25 Dec. €15. ℘93 547 59 80. www.casavicens.org

A preciously unvisitable Gaudí masterpiece, Casa Vicens was the first private house the architect designed in 1883 and his first important commission. The result was this candy-striped tiled fantasy of a dwelling. Wander through the original rooms and the charming garden, then visit the permanent exhibition on the second floor.

Modernist Architecture

Modernism developed between 1890 and 1920 alongside similar movements in other parts of Europe, such as Art Nouveau in both France and Great Britain, and Jugendstil in Germany. Modernist architecture sprang from artistic exploration that combined new industrial materials with modern techniques, using decorative motifs like curve and counter-curve and asymmetrical shapes in stained glass, ceramics and metal. The Catalan cultural movement of modernsime was an expression of the region's striving for independence at a time when large fortunes were being made as a result of industrialisation, with designs frequently containing hints and symbols of Catalan identity. The most

Casa Vicens by Antoni Gaudí

© Lucas Vallecillos/age fotostock

representative architects of the style were Antoni Gaudí, Domènech i Montaner, Puig i Cadafalch and Jujol. A parallel movement in Catalan literature known as Renaixença also flourished during this period. The mixture of regional and foreign architectural tradition in the work of **Josep Puig i Cadafalch** (1867–1956) reflects the Plateresque and Flemish styles. His main works are the Casa de les Punxes, the Casa Macaya (1901) and the Palau Baró de Quadras (1904). **Lluís Domènech i Montaner** (1850–1923) attained his highly decorative style through extensive use of mosaics, stained glass and glazed tiles. His main works include the Palau de la Música Catalana and Castell dels Tres Dragons.

Teatre Nacional de Catalunya

Plaça de les Arts 1. ✆933 06 57 00. www.tnc.cat.
Built by local architect Ricardo Bofill, Catalunya's National Theatre is a synthesis of modern and classical architecture. All shows are performed exclusively in the Catalan language.

Torre Agbar

Plaça de les Glorìes Catalans s/n.
Designed in 2005 by French architect Jean Nouvel, the Torre Agbar has become a new city landmark. A sophisticated LED system lights up the building's cigar-shaped form in hues of red, blue and green.

▲▲ Parc Güell★★

Olot 1–13. Open daily. Apr, Sept, Oct & Apr 8am–8.30pm, May–Aug 8am–9.30pm, Jan-Feb 8.30am-6.30pm, Mar 8.30am-7pm. No charge to enter Park; Monumental Zone (limited numbers) €8, €7 online. ✆902 200 302. www.parkguell.cat.
Gaudí's imagination shines with his mushroom-shaped pavilions, a mosaic dragon, the **Chamber of the Columns**, whose undulating mosaic roof covers a forest of sloping columns, and a remarkable **rolling bench★★**. All these, and more, are to be found in the " Monumental Zone".
Not included in the zone is the **Casa-Museu Gaudí** (Ctra del Carmel entrance; open daily Oct–Mar 10am–6pm; Apr–Sept 9am–8pm; closed during the afternoon of 1 & 6 Jan and 25 & 26 Dec; €5.50; ✆932 19 38 11; www.casamuseu-gaudi.org), which offers the chance to see how much of his work the architect actually took home with him.

WALKING TOUR★

LA RIBERA

Mercat de Santa Caterina

Av. Francesc Cámbo 16. Originally opened in 1848, this is Barcelona's oldest market. In 2004 it was given a stunning makeover by the late Catalan architect Enric Miralles and his wife Benedetta Tagliabue. The pair modernised the interior and added an undulating roof scattered with colourful mosaic patterns of fruit and vegetables. Inside, the Espai Santa Caterina (open Jul–Sept Mon– Sat 10am–2pm, rest of the year until 3pm, and 8pm Thur–Fri; no charge) highlights the remains of the former Dominican Convent of Santa Catarina that stood on this site.

▶ Facing the market's entrance, take the street on the right (Carrer Giralt el Pellisser) and follow it to the end.

Carrer de Montcada★★

During the 13C and 14C, the Catalan fleet exercised unquestionable supremacy over the western basin of the Mediterranean. Important merchant families acquired considerable social status and the Carrer de Montcada became a showcase for their high expectations and new standards of living. This street, named after an influential family of noble descent, is a unique ensemble of merchants' palaces and aristocratic mansions, most dating back to the late Middle Ages and many now occupied by museums and galleries.
Behind the austere façades are beautiful patios with galleries and porches typical of Catalan Gothic architecture.

Palau Berenguer d'Aiguilar★

This magnificent residence (Montcada 15, part of the Picasso Museum) which was modified in the 15C and again in the 18C has retained many architectural elements typical in the noble houses of medieval Barcelona. The sober façade features decorative windows on the lower floor, whilst a central patio (now the entrance to the museum) is enlivened by arches and mouldings.

Museu Picasso

Montcada 15–23. Open Tue–Sun and public holidays 9am–7pm (Thu until 9.30pm). Closed 1 Jan, 1 May, 24 Jun, 25 Dec. €11; exhibitions €6.50; joint ticket €12; free Thu from 6pm. ✆932 56 30 00. www.museupicasso.bcn.cat/en.
The Gothic palaces of Berenguer de Aguilar and Baron de Castellet, and the Baroque Palau Meca are the setting for the museum. The works here are dedicated, in most cases, to Picasso's friend Sabartès, shown in several portraits.
Picasso's early genius is evident in his (conventional) portraits of his family, *First Communion* and *Science and Charity* (1896). Examples of his early Paris work are *La Nana* and *La Espera; Los Desemparados* (1903) is from his Blue Period, *Señora Casals* from his Rose Period. His **Las Meninas series★** consists of variations on the famous picture by Velázquez. Picasso's skill as an engraver is seen in his outstanding etchings of bullfighting, and his talent as a ceramicist shines through in his vases, dishes and plates from the 1950s.

▶ Continue to the end of Carrer de Montcada.

Església/Basílica de Santa Maria del Mar★★

Pl. de Santa Maria 1. Open Mon–Sat 9am –1pm, 5–8.30pm; Sun 10am–2pm, 5–8pm. Guided visits available. No charge. ✆933 10 23 90. www.santamariadelmarbarcelona.org.
This is one of the most beautiful churches in the Catalan Gothic style, built in the 14C by ordinary sailors to compete with the cathedrals of the wealthy. The result is a graceful church of outstanding simplicity.
The west front is adorned only by a portal gable and the buttresses flanking the superb Flamboyant **rose window★**. The **interior★★★** gives the impression of spaciousness due to the elevation of

the nave, and side aisles divided only by slender pillars.

Fossar de les Morenes (Mulberry Graveyard)

Opposite the Santa Maria del Mar, this little square is surrounded by pink-hued façades of apartment buildings. An "eternal flame" has been burning here since 1999, in memory of the victims of the 1714 siege on the city.

▷ From the rear entrance of the Santa Maria del Mar, stroll along the Passeig del Born to the end.

Mercat del Born

This steel structure, by Josep Fontseré (1874) was once the city's principal wholesale market, and is one of the first examples of Spanish industrial architecture. It is currently being converted into a museum of the La Ribera neighborhood and a library. The first part of the conversion, the **El Born Centre Cultural** (open Mar–Sept Tue–Sun 10am–8pm; until 7pm Oct–Feb Tue–Sat; €6; http://elbornculturaimemoria. barcelona.cat) opened in late 2013. One of its main objectives is to illustrate iife in the city before and after the siege of 1713–14. The whole conversion process was made more complicated by the fact that substantial remains of the medieval city were found when work started and these are also on display.

▷ Take the Carrer del Comerç.

▲▲ Museu del Xocolata (Chocolate Museum)

Comerç, 36. Open Mon–Sat 10am–7pm, Sun & hols 10am–3pm. Closed 1 & 6 Jan, 1 May, 25 & 26 Dec. €6. ✆932 68 78 78. www.museuxocolata.cat.

This lively museum traces the history of commercial worldwide chocolate making as well as local specialities, such as *monas*, elaborate chocolate sculptures that are a Catalan Easter tradition.

▷ Turn left out of the Chocolate Museum, onto the Passeig Picasso.

Parc de la Ciutadella★

Open daily 10am–dusk.

A citadel was built here by Philip V to control the rebellious city inhabitants, but was demolished in 1868 and replaced by gardens. Gaudí collaborated on the design of the park waterfall while still a student. In 1888 the World Fair was held here and the **Castell dels Tres Dragons★★** is a surviving pavilion, built in neo-Gothic style, using unadorned brick and iron by Domènech i Montaner. It now houses the Laboratori de Natura, (currently closed for renovations).

▲▲ **Zoo Barcelona★** (check the website for daily changing opening hours; ticket office closes 1hr before zoo; closed afternoon 25 Dec; €19.90; child €11.95; ✆902 45 75 45; www.zoobarcelona.cat) covers much of the park. Animals from all over the world are kept in settings ranging from natural habitat to quite antiquated cages. The zoo has a strong primate community and a dolphin show is held in its Aquarama.

ADDITIONAL SIGHT
Palau de la Música Catalana★★

Palau de la Música 4–6. Guided tours every 30 mins (55 mins) Aug 9am–6pm, Easter & Jul 10am–6pm, rest of the year 10am–3.30pm. €18; advanced purchase recommended. ✆93 295 72 00. www.palaumusica.cat.

This concert hall (1905–08) is Domènech i Montaner's most famous work. The **exterior★** displays lavish mosaics. The interior, dominated by an **inverted cupola★★** of polychrome glass, is decorated with sculpted groups and mosaic figurines. A concert in this remarkable venue is a memorable occasion.

☙ WALKING TOUR

SEAFRONT★

Allow half a day. Bus 157, 57 follows the seafront to Vila Olímpica.

The seafront, from Montjuïc to the Besòs river, was completely redesigned for the 1992 Olympic Games, turning

Palau de la Música Catalana

Barcelona once again towards the sea. The wide promenade is a great place to people watch and escape the bustle of the city.

Drassanes (Shipyards)★★ and Museu Marítim★★

Av. de les Drassanes. Open daily 10am–8pm. €10, no charge after 3pm Sun. ℘93 342 99 20. www.mmb.cat.

The old shipyards that are home to the museum are among the best examples of civil Gothic architecture in Catalunya. Ten sections remain, under a timber roof supported by sturdy stone arches. The museum is currently in the final phases of a major restoration and not all areas may be open to visitors; see the website for details.

Among its many impressive models is a lifesize replica of the **Royal Galley of Don Juan of Austria**★★, Christian flagship at the Battle of Lepanto (1571). Also of note is The **Portulan of Gabriel de Vallseca** (1439), a nautical map which belonged to Amerigo Vespucci.

On the waterfront in Portal de la Pau is the restored 1918 schooner, **Santa Eulàlia**★ (Apr–Oct Tue–Fri & Sun 10am–8.30pm, Sat 2–8.30pm; Nov–Mar Tue–Fri & Sun 10am–5.30pm, Sat 2–5.30pm; €3 adults, €1 children), named after the city's patron saint. Pleasure boats depart from here too.

The area around the port includes the palm-lined promenade known as the Moll de Bosch i Alsina (**Moll de la Fusta**), where there is a sculptre by American Pop Artist Roy Lichtenstein.

Monument a Colom

♿See La Rambla.

Port Vell★

The old harbour is a lively leisure area featuring bars, the **Maremàgnum** shopping and leisure centre (www.maremagnum.es) and an **aquarium**.

▷ From the Passeig Isabel II, cross the "Rambla del Mar" footbridge in front of the Columbus Monument.

👥 Aquàrium★

Moll d'Espanya del Port Vell. Open Jan-Mar and Nov-Dec Mon-Fri 10am-7.30pm, Jun and Sep 10am-9pm, Jul-Aug 10am-9.30pm, Apr-May and Oct 10am-8pm; last admission one hour before closing. €20; child €15. ℘932 21 74 74. www.aquariumbcn.com.

One of Europe's most impressive aquaria, the highlight is a spectacular viewing tunnel, 80m/262ft long.

▷ Return to the Passeig del Colom and turn right, following the water's edge to the intersection of Via Laitana.

La Llotja★

Pas. Isabel II 1. ℘935 478 849. www.casallotja.com.

The building housing the Chamber of Commerce and Industry was completely rebuilt in the 18C. The **Gothic hall**★★, a lofty chamber with three naves, remains from the medieval building.

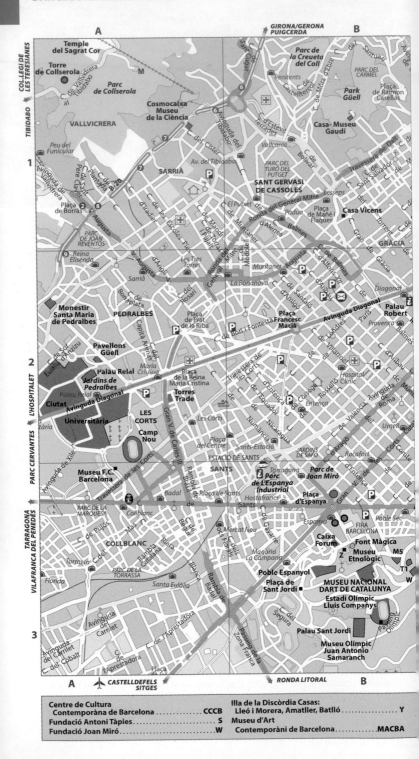

Temple
del Sagrat Cor
Torre
de Collserola
Parc de
la Creueta
del Coll
PARC DEL
CARMEL
Park
Güell
Plaça
de Raimon
Casellas

Parc
de Collserola

VALLVICRERA

Cosmocaixa
Museu
de la Ciència

Casa- Museu
Gaudí

Peu del
Funicular

PARC DEL
TURÓ DEL
PUTGET

SARRIÀ

Av. del Tibidabo

SANT GERVASI
DE CASSOLES

Casa Vicens

Plaça
de Borras

El Putxet

Plaça
de Mañé i
Flaquer

GRÀCIA

PARC
DE JOAN
REVENTÓS

Reina
Elisenda

Les Tres
Torres

La Bonanova

Muntaner

Diagonal

Monestir
Santa Maria
de Pedralbes

PEDRALBES

Sarrià

Plaça
de Prat
de la Riba

Plaça
Francesc
Macià

Avinguda Diagonal

Palau
Robert

Pavellons
Güell

María
Cristina

Hospital
Clínic

Palau Reial

Plaça
de la Reina
Maria Cristina

Torres
Trade

Jardins de
Pedralbes

Ciutat

Avinguda Diagonal

LES
CORTS

Les Corts

Universitària

Camp
Nou

Plaça
del Centre

Sants-Estació

JARDINS
DE SAFO

ESTACIÓ DE SANTS

Museu F.C.
Barcelona

SANTS

Parc
de L'Espanya
Industrial

Parc de
Joan Miró

Badal

Rambla
Brasil

Plaça de Sants

Plaça
d'Espanya

Hostafrancs

PARC DE LA
MAROUESA

Collblanc

Sants

FIRA
BARCELONA

Espanya

COLLBLANC

Mercat Nou

Poble Sec

Caixa
Forum

Magória
La Campana

Museu
Etnològic

Font Màgica

Torrassa

PARC DE LA
TORRASSA

Poble Espanyol

Plaça de
Sant Jordi

MUSEU NACIONAL
D'ART DE CATALUNYA

Florida

Santa Eulália

Estadi Olímpic
Lluís Companys

Palau Sant Jordi

Museu Olímpic
Juan Antonio
Samaranch

Plaça

Centre de Cultura Contemporàna de Barcelona .... **CCCB**	Illa de la Discòrdia Casas: Lleó i Morera, Amatller, Batlló .... **Y**
Fundació Antoni Tàpies .... **S**	Museu d'Art
Fundació Joan Miró .... **W**	Contemporàni de Barcelona .... **MACBA**

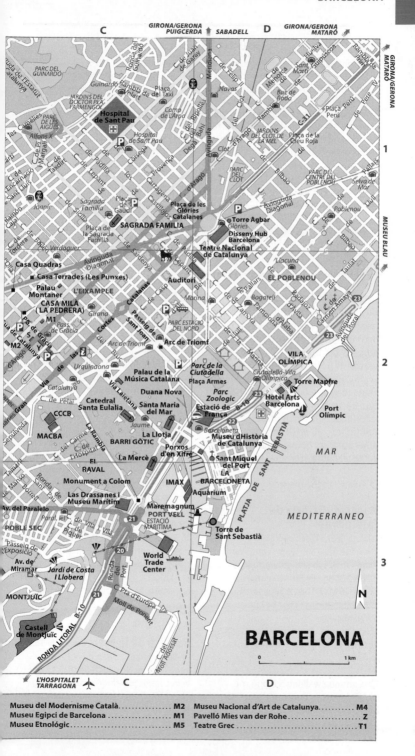

BARCELONA

0   1 km

Gaudí (1852–1926)

Antoni Gaudí, born in Reus, studied architecture in Barcelona. His style was influenced first by Catalan Gothic architecture with its emphasis on large areas of space (wide naves, the effect of airy spaciousness) and subsequently by the Islamic and Mudéjar styles. He also studied nature, observing plants and animals, which inspired his shapes, colours and textures. He gave full rein to these images – liana-like curves, the rising and breaking of waves, rugged rocks and the serrations on leaves and flowers – when designing his fabulous buildings. Part of his great originality lay in his use of parabolic arches and spirals (as can be seen in the chimneys of Casa Milà). An intensely religious man, Gaudí drew upon a great many religious symbols for his buildings, especially for the Sagrada Família (Church of the Holy Family) on which he worked for over 40 years. He spent his last years here, hidden away in a small room in the middle of the site, until his tragic death when he was run over by a tram. Gaudí worked a great deal for the banker **Eusebi Güell**, his patron and admirer, who asked him to design his private houses. Gaudí's main works are the Sagrada Família, Casa Batlló, La Pedrera, Casa Vicens, Palau Güell, Pavellons Güell and the Parc Güell.

Porxos de Xifré

After the discovery of America, many Catalans went there to seek their fortune. When they returned, these *Indianos* (as they were called) built beautiful homes to show off their wealth. Josep Xifré Cases (1777–1856) amassed such a large fortune in Cuba that he became the richest man in Barcelona. This block of Neoclassical buildings – all with arcades – now rather ironically houses a maze of cheap electrical goods stores.

▶ Head S to the marina.

Museu d'Història de Catalunya★

Palau de Mar, Pl. de Pau Vila 3.
Open Tue, Thu–Sat 10am–7pm, Wed 10am–8pm, Sun and public holidays 10am–2.30pm. €4.50; no charge 12 Feb, 23 Apr, 18 May, 11 & 24 Sept, last Tue of month Oct–Jun. ℘932 25 47 00. www.mhcat.net.
This museum, set in an ex-warehouse, details Catalunya from prehistory to now.

▶ Continue walking S along the Passeig Joan de Borbó, either following the marina or venturing into the maze of streets on the opposite side of the road.

La Barceloneta★

The "Iberian Naples" has quaint narrow streets, and restaurants and stalls offering seafood dishes.

▶ At the end of Passeig Joan de Borbó, your will hit the beach. Now take the boardwalk in the opposite direction.

Vila Olímpica★

Built for the 1992 Olympics, this is one of Barcelona's most modern areas. Gardens and avenues of the Olympic Village are dotted with sculptures.
The **marina★★**, designed by JR de Clascà has bars, restaurants and pavement cafés. Most striking are the two 153m/502ft **towers** belonging to the Hotel Arts and the Torre Mapfre respectively. The **view★★★** from the top takes in Mallorca on a clear day but neither are open to the public on a walk-in basis.

ADDITIONAL SIGHTS
Basílica de la Mercè★

Pl. de la Mercè 1. Open daily 10am–1pm, 6–8pm. No charge. ℘933 15 27 56. www.basilicadelamerce.com.
This 1760 church has an unusual curved Baroque façade. The façade on Carrer Ample is Renaissance and was moved from elsewhere. A Gothic statue in the

interior, the **Mare de Déu de la Mercè★**, is by Pere Moragues (1361).

👥 Museu Blau

Parque del Forum, Plaza Leonardo da Vinci. Mar–Sept Tue–Sat 10am–7pm, Sun until 8pm. Oct–Feb Tue–Fri 10am–6pm, Sat until 7pm, Sun until 8pm. Closed 1 Jan, 1 May, 25 Dec. €6, €5 exhibitions; no charge Sun from 3pm, first Sun of the month, 12 Feb, 18 May, 24 Sept. ℘932 566 002. www.museuciences.cat.

Continue east along the seafront and you'll come to the Natural Science Museum's journey through life on earth, from its origins to the present day and beyond. The multi-media, interactive exhibiton has plenty to interest all the famiy.

👣 WALKING TOUR

MONTJUÏC★

Alllow 1 day, including museum visits. The castle built on this 173m/568ft hill during the 1640 rebellion is undergoing major renovations, but the exterior and ramparts can still be visited (open Apr–Sept daily 10am–8pm; rest of the year 10am–6pm; €5; ℘932 56 44 40; www.bcn.cat/castelldemontjuic) and the superb city and harbour **views★** make the journey worthwhile.

The **Plaça d'Espanya** remains from the 1929 exhibition, along with the illuminated **fountain** (*Font Magica*) by Carles Buïgas, the **reception pavilion★★** by Mies van der Rohe, a structure of outstanding simplicity, and the Spanish Village (Poble Espanyol, or Pueblo Español in Castilian).

👥 El Poble Espanyol★ (Spanish Village)

▷ Av. Francesc Ferrer i Guàrdia 13. Open Mon 9am–8pm, Tue–Thu & Sun 9am–midnight. Fri 9am–3am, Sat 9am–4am. Craftshops and shops close 6–8pm. €12.60; child €6.30. ℘935 08 63 00. www.poble-espanyol.com.

This Disneyesque Spanish folk villagecum open-air architectural museum reflects life in the various parts of Spain,

and was built for the 1929 exhibition. Its re-creations are very convincing and indeed contain many original artefacts; within a few minutes you can wander from a small Castilian square to a street in an Andalucían village with white houses and geraniums, on to a Mudéjar tower from Aragón, and so on…

The scene is lively: craftsmen making traditional Spanish wares, shops, restaurants, bars and even two nightclubs.

▷ Walk down Av. Francesc Ferrer i Guàrdia.

CaixaForum

Av. Francesc Ferrer i Guàrdia 6–8. Open daily 10am–8pm (Wed Jul & Aug 11pm). Closed 1, 6 Jan, 25 Dec. Permanent exhibitions free, temporary exhibitions €4. ℘934 76 86 00. http://obrasocial.lacaixa.es.

This magnificent Modernist landmark early-20C textile factory was built by **Puig i Cadafalch**. It now houses a social and cultural centre with exhibits from a splendid modern art collection of more than 800 works, alongside exciting temporary exhibitions.

▷ Climb the stairs to the MNAC.

Museu Nacional d'Art de Catalunya (MNAC)★★★

Palau Nacional, Parc de Montjuïc. Open Tue–Sat 10am–8pm (Oct–Apr 6pm); Sun and public holidays year-round 10am–3pm. €12 (two days), roof €2; no charge 12 Feb, 18 May, 11 & 24 Sept, Sat from 3pm and first Sun of month. ℘936 22 03 60. www.museunacional.cat.

The Palau Nacional was built for the 1929 fair; its museum of Catalan art includes remarkable **Romanesque and Gothic collections★★★**.

Romanesque art – The display evokes contemporary churches. Note 12C frescoes by Sant Joan de Boí (Room 2), the late 11C lateral apses by Sant Quirze de Pedret (Room 3), the Santa Maria de Taüll ensemble (12C), dominated by a fine *Epiphany* and Sant Climent de Taüll (Room 5) with the remarkable *Christ in*

Majesty: the apse is a Renaissance masterpiece. Note the anti-naturalism and geometry.

Altar frontals are painted on a panel or carved. In the magnificent sculpture galleries is the polychrome *Majestad de Batlló* (13C). The museum also presents superb **capitals★** (Room 6), silverware and enamels. Paintings from the chapter house of **Sigena** (1200) evidence a great stylistic shift.

Gothic art – Exhibits of 13C–14C Catalan Gothic art include stone retables attributed to **Jaime Cascalls** (Rooms 15 and 16); the collection of Catalan Gothic art (Room 30), with works by **Guerau Gener, Juan Mates, Ramon de Mur, Juan Antigó, Bernardo Despuig** and **Jaime Cirera**; a room dedicated to **Bernardo Martorell** (Room 32), for whom detail and shading were paramount.

Dalmau; works by the **Master of La Seu d'Urgell** (Room 34); and, lastly, 14C–15C funerary sculpture (Room 50).

Other Collections – The **Cambó Collection** includes painters of the rank of **Zurbarán**, Tintoretto, **El Greco**, Rubens, Cranach the Elder and **Goya**. The **Thyssen-Bornemisza Collection**, selected from the Museu Thyssen, comprises works from the Middle Ages to the 18C, notably paintings of the Virgin and Child. Portraits represent several schools of the 15C–18C.

In the **Renaissance and Baroque** section are Flemish and Italian masters along with works of Ayne Bru, Pere Nunyes and Pedro Berruguete. Other **19C–20C** artworks include paintings by Fortuny, Modernist furniture, sculpture, and posters by **Gaudí, Domènech i Montaner**, Casas, Rusiñol and others.

▶ Go to the rear of the MNAC and take the escalator to the Av. l' Estadi.

Anella Olímpica★

High on the mountainside is the "Olympic Ring" complex. The **Olympic Stadium★**, with its 1929 façade now hosts athletics chamionships and major concerts. The nearby **Palau Sant Jordi★★**, designed by Arata Isozak, was one of the main venues of the 1992 Summer Olympics. It also hosts major sporting event s, concerts and shows. The **telecommunications tower** is the work of Santiago Calatrava.

▶ Continue on Av. l' Estadi, following the signs to the Fundació Joan Miró.

Fundació Joan Miró★★★

Parc de Montjuïc. Open Tue–Fri & Sat 10am–6pm (8pm Jul–Sept), Thu 10am–9pm, Sun and public holidays 10am–3pm. €12. ☏934 43 94 70. www.fmirobcn.org.

The works of Avant-Garde artist **Joan Miró** (1893–1983), are ubiquitous in Barcelona: a mural at the airport, pavement mosaics on La Rambla, the famous logo of the savings bank La Caixa…

Born in Barcelona, Miró spent 1921 and 1922 in Paris; his painting **La Masía**, signalled his departure from figurative art. Between 1939 and 1941 he executed **Constellations**, 23 panels expressing the horror of World War II.

Miró's Foundation is housed in a modern building of harmonious proportions designed by Josep Lluís Sert, a close friend.

The 10 000 items were largely executed during the last 20 years of his life. A small exhibition of contemporary art includes Alexander Calder's **Fountain of Mercury**.

ADDITIONAL SIGHTS
Museu d'Arqueologia de Catalunya (MAC)★

Pg. de Santa Madrona 39–41. Open Tue–Sat 9.30am–7pm, Sun and public holidays 10am–2.30pm. €5.50; no charge last Tue in month Oct–Jun, 12 Feb, 23 Apr, 18 May and 11 & 24 Sept. ☏934 23 21 49. www.mac.cat.

Household effects, ceramics and votive figures trace the history of Catalunya from Palaeolithic times through to the Visigothic. The collection is housed in the former Palace of Graphic Arts on Montjuïc, which was built for the 1929 International Exhibition.

©Turespaña

Fundació Joan Miró

Monestir de Santa Maria de Pedralbes★★

Bajada Monestir 9. Closed at time of writing for restoration.
℘932 56 34 34. http://monestir pedrables.bcn.cat.

Founded in the 14C by King James II of Aragón and his fourth wife, the monastery has a fine Catalan Gothic **church★** with the tomb of the foundress.

The three-storey **cloisters★** surrounded by cells and oratories are sober and elegant. The Sant Miquel Chapel is adorned with beautiful **frescoes★★★** by Ferrer Bassá (1346), whose works combine the style of the Siena School with a Tuscan sense of volume and perspective.

Disseny Hub Barcelona

Plaça de les Glóries, Av. Diagonal 686. Open Tue–Sun 10am–8pm. Closed 1 Jan, 1 May, 24 Jun, 25 Dec. €6, no charge Sun 3–8pm, first Sun of the month, 8 & 12 Feb, 24 Sept. ℘932 56 68 00. www.museudeldisseny.cat.

This stunning new building, which opened in 2014, houses three of the city's major collections (they moved here from elsewhere in the city).

The **Museu de les Arts Decoratives** (Decorative Arts) is a rich collection that spans domestic objects from the medieval to *modernista* and onto contemporary industrial design, all movements Catalans have excelled at. Exhibits ranging from chests and desks, lamps, chairs and even bottles illustrate the changing face of design and technological breakthroughs through mass production.

The **Museu Tèxtil i d'Indumentaria** (Textile & Clothing) takes the visitor on a journey from 16C fashion to today with the work of Spanish designers (such as Balenciaga and Paco Rabanne), to the haute couture of Dior and Karl Lagerfeld. Also noteworthy is the jewellery collection, comprising some 500 pieces made and produced in Spain.

The **Museu de Ceràmica** (Ceramics) has a rotating collection of Catalan and Valencian pieces, focusing on 18 and 19C and in particular Alcora, a Valencian town that excels in the medium. Do not miss the works of the famous Catalan ceramicist **Josep Llorens Artigas**, alongside those of **Picasso** and **Miró**.

A fourth collection, the **Gabinet de les Arts Gràfiques**, featuring Graphic Art and Typography, will also open here.

Camp Nou Experience Museum & Tour

Av. Aristides Maillol. Open daily, see website for times. €25 (age 6–13 €20). ℘934 963 600. www.fcbarcelona.com/camp-nou.

FC Barcelona stadium has a capacity of nearly 100 000 and its extensive facilities include the **Museu FC Barcelona**, where fans can contemplate the many trophies won by their beloved worldfamous Barça team, and take a tour of the stadium.

🚹🚺 Cosmo Caixa★

Isaac Newton s/n. Open Tue–Sun & hol Mons 10am–8pm. Closed 1 & 6 Jan, 25 Dec. €4 (under 16 free). Additional charges: Planetarium €4; Toca Toca

(Hands-on area) €4. ☎932 12 60 50. http://obrasocial.lacaixa.es.

The city's new Science Museum combines scientific fact with fun through a diverse range of exhibits such as a Foucault pendulum; the Drowned Forest; the giant Geological Wall demonstrating the main rocks of the planet; the amazing Amazon rainforest area, complete with 82 species of animals and 52 species of plants, where it really does rain. You'll also find a 3-D Planetarium, dozens of hands-on stations, including the Toca-Toca (Touch-Touch) animal area, and a great gift shop.

ADDRESSES

🏨 STAY

The Barri Gòtic has the highest concentration of cheap accommodation. Crossing La Rambla, the Raval district should be approached with caution by night. For the most chic and generally safest accommodation, the Fixample has a wide range of luxury and design hotels.

🛏🛏🛏 **Hotel Condal** – Boquería 23 (Barri Gòtic). 🚇 Liceu. ☎933 18 18 82. www.hotelcondal.es. 52 rooms, ⌑ €4–6. Situated between La Rambla and the Barri Gótic, this smart modernised hotel is a fine base for visiting the old city. Request a quieter rear room.

🛏🛏🛏 **Hotel Gaudí** – Nou de la Rambla 12 (Ciutat Vella). 🚇 Liceu. ☎933 17 90 32. www.hotelgaudibarcelona. com. 73 rooms, ⌑ €12. The location opposite the Palau Güell and Modernist décor evoke the namesake artist. Rooms with a balcony or those on an upper floor enjoy superb views of the city and the Palau Güell.

🛏🛏🛏 **Hotel Hesperia Barri Gòtic** – Ample 31 (Barri Gòtic). 🚇 Jaume I. ☎933 10 51 00. www.nh-hotels.com. 71 rooms, ⌑ €18. This pleasant hotel close to the waterfront is situated in a narrow street in the old quarter, between the post office and the Basílica de La Mercè. An attractive feature here is the lobby in a covered patio. The guest rooms are comfortable, with the usual creature comforts.

🛏🛏🛏 **Hotel Granvía** – Gran Via de les Corts Catalanes 642 (Eixample). 🚇 Cataluyna. ☎933 18 19 00. www. nnhotels.es. 53 rooms, ⌑ €12. This impressive banker's residence from the late 19C was converted into a hotel in 1936 and has recently undergone major renovations.

🍴 EAT

🍽🍽 **Senyor Parellada** – L'Argentaria 37 (Ribera). 🚇 Jaume I. ☎933 10 50 94. www.senyorparellada.com. Located in a 19C building, this restaurant has various dining rooms adorned with chandeliers and wooden furniture along with a delightful patio, topped with a glass roof. Traditional Catalan at good value prices.

🍽🍽🍽 **Los Caracoles** – Escudellers 14 (Ciutat Vella). 🚇 Liceu. ☎933 01 20 41. www.loscaracoles.es. Founded in 1835, this famous restaurant, one of the gastronomic emblems of Barcelona, is located on the corner of carrers Escudellers and Nou de Sant Franc. The décor here consists of tiled floors, wine barrels, murals and photos. Regional and traditional cuisine.

🍽🍽🍽 **L'Olivé** – Balmes 47 (Eixample). 🚇 Passeig de Gràcia. ☎934 52 19 90. www.restaurantlolive.com. Closed Sun eve. Beautiful old stone house with a kitchen in view to one side, and the elegant dining room at the back. Fish and seafood specials.

🍽🍽🍽🍽 **El Tragaluz** – Pas. de la Concepció 5 (Eixample). 🚇 Diagonal. ☎934 87 06 21. www.grupotragaluz. com/tragaluz. One of Barcelona's most charismatic and dynamic restaurants takes up three storeys, with a sliding greenhouse roof. It serves Mediterranean and avant-garde fare.

🍽🍽🍽🍽 **Casa Leopoldo** – Sant Rafael 24 (Ciutat Vella). 🚇 Liceu. ☎934 41 30 14. www.casaleopoldo.es. Closed Sun eve (all day in Jul) and Mon. This classic Barcelona restaurant is decorated with blue-and-white tiles, bullfighting mementoes, signed photos of famous customers and a superb bottle collection.

🍽🍽🍽🍽 **Casa Calvet** – Casp 48 (Eixample). 🚇 Urquinaona. ☎934 12 40 12. www.casacalvet.es. Closed Sun and public holidays. The former offices of a textile company, in a magnificent Modernist building designed by Gaudí, are dominated by iron beams and wood floors. Traditional Mediterranean dishes.

TAPAS

Euskal Etxea – Placeta Montcada 1–3 (Ribera). ⊚ Jaume I. ☏ 933 10 21 85. www.euskaletxeataberna.com. Closed fortnight in Aug. By the church of Santa Maria del Mar, a bar and cosy dining room, this is the perfect setting for a glass of txacolí (a Basque white wine) and Basque pork chops and fried fish.

Irati Taverna Basca – Cardenal Casañas 17 (Barri Gòtic). ⊚ Liceu. ☏ 933 02 30 84. www.iratitavernabasca.com. Near Plaça de la Boqueria, this is a typical buzzing city centre tapas bar with a counter full of Basque tapas skewers (pintxos) along with a grill room.

Tickets – Parallel 164 (Poble Sec). ⊚ Poble Sec. ☏ 606 225 545. Reserve in advance online at www.ticketsbar. es or call on the day for cancellations. Closed Sun and Mon. Tapas and cocktail bar from superchefs Ferran Adrià and brother Albert.

El Xampanyet – Montcada 22 (Ribera). ⊚ Jaume I. ☏ 933 19 70 03. Closed Sun, Holy Week and Aug. In an alleyway close to the Picasso Museum, this bar is famous for its anchovies and sparkling wine.

BARS / CAFÉS

Café de la Opera – Rambla dels Caputxins 74 (Ciutat Vella). ⊚ Liceu. ☏ 933 17 75 85. www.cafeoperabcn.com. Thanks to its colourful history, Modernist façade and 19C atmosphere, this café (est. 1929), is one of the most famous in the city.

Jamboree – Pl. Reial 17 (Ciutat Vella). ⊚ Liceu. ☏ 933 017 564. www.jamboree jazz.com. The meeting point in Barcelona for jazz musicians and aficionados.

Luz de Gas – Muntaner 246 (Eixample). ⊚ Barceloneta. ☏ 932 09 77 11. www. luzdegas.com. Beautiful venue hosting a whole variety of different musical acts.

Margarita Blue – Josep Anselm Clavé 6 (Ciutat Vella). ⊚ Drassanes. ☏ 934 12 54 89. margaritablue.com. Unusual

decoration, mirrors of all shapes and sizes, and antique lamps help make this one of the city's most popular bars, hosting weekly shows and concerts. Tex-Mex and Mediterranean cuisne.

Quatre Gats – Montsió 3 bis (Ciutat Vella). ⊚ Catalunya. ☏ 933 02 41 40. www.4gats.com. A byword for Modernist Bohemian Barcelona, this landmark café was a meeting place for artists such as Picasso, Casas and Utrillo. Reasonably priced lunchtime menu.

SHOPPING

ANTIQUES

Bulevard dels Antiquaris – Pas. de Gràcia 55 (Eixample). ⊚ Diagonal. ☏ 932 15 44 99. www.bulevarddelsantiquaris. cat. An area containing over 70 shops selling a range of artwork and antiques.

Plaça de la Catedra – Ciutat Vella. ⊚ Jaume I. A small market with stalls selling antiques is held here on public holidays.

Plaça Sant Josep Oriol – Ciutat Vella. ⊚ Liceu. Mirrors, furniture, and paintings are sold at this popular weekend market.

La Palla and Banys Nous – Ciutat Vella. ⊚ Liceu. These two streets are well known for their reputable antique shops.

FASHION

Custo Barcelona – Plaça de les Olles 7 (La Ribera). ☏ 933 687 893. www.custo. com. Colourful casualwear for men, women and children; several other stores throughout the city.

Mango – Passeig de Gràcia 65 (Eixample). ☏ 932 15 75 30. www.mango.com. Flagship store of the international fashion chain which started in Barcelona.

La Manual Alpargatera – Carrer Avinyó 7 (Barri Gòtic). ☏ 933 01 01 72. www. lamanualalpargatera.es. A stunning array of handmade espadrilles.

ART GALLERIES

Barcelona's most prestigious galleries can mainly be found in Carrer Consell de Cent along the Rambla de Catalunya and the Carrer Montcada in La Ribera.

Masía Freixa

© Oscar García Bayerri/age fotostock

Terrassa/Tarrasa

Located in the great industrial belt of Barcelona, Terrassa is best known for its textile production, an industry that has made the township prosperous. It is surrounded by the mountains of the Sant Llorenç del Munt i l'Obac natural park. Along its streets, various examples of industrial architecture and modernista buildings reflect the economic growth of the city in the early 20C.

- ▶ **Population:** 215 214
- ⌖ **Michelin Map:** 576 H 36.
- ℹ **Info:** Plaça Freixa i Argemí 11. ℘937 39 70 19. www.terrassa.cat.
- ◗ **Location:** 31km/19mi NW of Barcelona along the C 58. ▭Metro link with Barcelona
- ♟ **Kids:** Museu de la Ciència y la Tècnica de Catalunya.
- ◷ **Timing:** Terrassa makes a good day trip out from Barcelona.

SIGHTS
Conjunto Monumental de Esglésias de Sant Pere★★

Open Tue–Sat 10am–1.30pm, 4–7pm, Sun & hol Mons 11am–2pm. Closed 1 Jan, 1 May, 25, 26 Dec. €3. ℘937 83 37 02. www.terrassa.cat.

The **Antiguo baptisterio de Sant Miquel★** was built in the 9C using late Roman remains. The dome rests on eight pillars; four have Roman capitals, four are Visigothic. Alabaster windows in the apse filter light onto 9C–10C pre-Romanesque wall paintings. The crypt's three apses have horseshoe arches.

The magnificent Romanesque Lombard church of **Santa Maria★** has an octagonal cupola and a *cimborrio* (lantern); a 5C mosaic survives in front. A 13C wall fresco in the south transept, of the martyrdom of Thomas à Becket, retains bright colours. Note the 15C north transept altarpiece by Jaime Huguet of **St Abdon and St Sennen★★**.
Sant Pere is a rustic church begun in the 6C on a trapezoid plan with a Romanesque transept crossing. In the apse is a curious **stone altarpiece★**.

Castell Cartoixa de Vallparadís

Salmerón. Open Wed–Sat 10am–1.30pm, 4–7pm; Sun 11am–2pm. No charge. ℘937 85 71 44.

Built in the 12th century, this castle and former monastery is now home to an exhibition of the town's history.

♟♟ Museu de la Ciència y la Tècnica de Catalunya★

Rambla d'Ègara 270. Open Sept–Jun Tue–Fri 10am–6pm, Sat–Sun 10am–2.30pm, 4.30–8.30; Sun and hols 10am–2.30pm. Jul–Aug Tue–Sun 10am–2.30pm. Closed 1, 6 Jan, 25–26 Dec. €4.50 adults and €3.50 kids; no charge first Sun of month. ℘937 36 89 66. www.mnactec.cat.

This excellent modern National Museum of Science and Technology is housed in an Art Nouveau 1909 woollen mill.

Museu Textil

Salmerón 25. Open Fri-Sun 10am-2pm, Tue & Thu 10am-2pm, 4-7pm. No charge. ℘937 31 52 02. www.cdmt.es.

This museum of textile and fashion presents a comprehensive overview of the development of the industry throughout the 19C. Beautiful oriental fabrics are highlights of the collection.

Masía Freixa★

Parc de San Jordi.

This 1907 modernist building houses the tourist office. The repetition of parabolic arches is stunning.

Serra de Montserrat★★

The grand site★★★ of the Macizo de Montserrat (Montserrat Massif) was the setting for Wagner's *Parsifal*. where hard Eocene conglomerates rise above eroded formations. It is the main site of devotion to the Virgin in Catalunya. Views★★ from the road are impressive. The Montserrat cable car runs from near Monistrol de Montserrat.

- **Michelin Map:** 574 H 35.
- **Info:** Pl. de la Creu, opposite the funicular 1. ℘938 77 77 01. www.montserratvisita.com
- **Location:** 49km/31mi NW of Barcelona along the C 58, 19km/12mi E of Terrassa. Metro link with Barcelona, Plaça Espanya station.

A BIT OF GEOGRAPHY

Montserrat (the serrated mountain) is a mountain range of impressive beauty. Source of inspiration for musicians, poets, geographers and travellers, Montserrat is considered Catalunya's spiritual heart and remains an important place of devotion.

VISIT

Monastery and Basilica

Open daily 7.30am–8pm. (museum). ℘938 77 77 66. www.abadiamontserrat.net.

The Benedictines arrived in the 9C and every century since then has seen additions to the monastery. In 1812, it was ransacked by the French. The present buildings are 19C and 20C. Within the dark, ornate **basilica** (15C) is **La Moreneta ★★**, the shrine of the Black Madonna. According to legend, this 12C polychrome statue of the Black Madonna, now above the high altar, was discovered in a cave by shepherds. You can learn more about the history of the monastery in its Musuem (open daily 10am–5.45pm/summer weekends 6.45pm; €7; www.museudemont serrat.com). The Basilica is famous for its **Gregorian chant**, particularly during Mass at 11am and Vespers at 6.45pm. The **Escolanía**, (Mon–Thu 1pm and 6.45pm, Fri 1pm, Sun and festivals noon and 6.45pm; 938 77 77 67; www.escolania.cat) one of the world's oldest boys' choirs, is another fantastic aural experience.

Hermitages and viewpoints

Access via the mountain trails, cable cars or funiculars - all run regularly, but note the closing times, particularly out of season. 93 204 10 41 www.cremallerademontserrat.com. The 13 hermitages, abandoned since the arrival of Napoleon's troops, offer historical interest and fine views. To see more of the beautiful terrain without really tiring yourself out, take the cable car or funicular up , then walk back down.

Ermita de la Trinitat (45min on foot), charmingly nestled in a bucolic plain, is sheltered by three mountains: El Elefante (The Elephant), La Preñada (Pregnant Woman) and La Momia (The Mummy). On a clear day, **Sant Jeroni★** (1hr30min on foot or go by car) at 1 238m/4 062ft, offers a **panorama** from the Pyrenees to the Balearic Islands. **Ermita de Santa Cecilia** features an attractive 11C **Romanesque church★** which hosts temprary art exhibitions (€7). Its east end is circled by Lombard bands. The statue of the Virgin was found in **Santa Cova** (holy cave, 1hr walk), which has views of the Llobregat Valley. **Sant Miquel★** (30min from the monastery; 1hr from the upper terminal of the Sant Miquel funicular) has a general view of the monastery. **Sant Joan** (30min from upper terminal of the Sant Joan funicular) offers a beautiful panorama; the Ermita de San Onofre may be seen clinging to the rock face.

Sitges★★

Sitges is a resort famous for its lovely beaches, exemplary Modernist architecture and exuberant Carnival, made all the more lively by the town's large gay population. The seafront promenade, Passeig Marítim, is dotted with hotels and luxury residences.

OLD TOWN★★

1hr 30min.
The parish church dominates the breakwater of La Punta. Balconies of white houses are brilliant with flowers. Museums in neo-Gothic mansions display canvases from the late 19C, when Rusiñol and Miguel Utrillo (father of the French painter) painted here.

Museu Cau Ferrat★★

Fonollar. Open Tue–Sat Jul–Sept 10am–8pm, Mar–Jun & Oct until 7pm, Nov–Feb until 5pm. €10, combined with

- ▶ **Population:** 28 269.
- **Michelin Map:** 574 I 35 – Catalunya (Barcelona)
- **Info:** Plaza Eduard Maristany, 2. 938 94 42 51. www.sitgestur.cat.
- **Location:** Between Barcelona and Tarragona. Sitges.
- **Kids:** The Museu del Ferrocarril is the place to admire steam engines.
- **Timing:** While away a few days at the beach.

Museu Maricel. 93 894 03 64. www.museusdesitges.cat.
Santiago Rusiñol (1861–1931) added Gothic features to two 16C fishermen's houses, which he left to the town, along with ceramics, paintings and sculptures. Among the **paintings**, note two remarkable works by **El Greco**: *Penitent Mary Magdalene* and *The Repentance of St*

Sitges

Peter. The gallery also contains canvases by Picasso, Casas and Rusiñol himself *(Poetry, Music and Painting)*. The museum takes its name from its **wrought-iron** collection *(cau ferrat)*. There is also a **ceramics** section.

Museu Maricel★

Fonollar s/n. Same hours and price as Museu Cau Ferrat. www.museusdesitges.cat. Next door to Museu Cau Ferrat, this museum in a 14C hospital takes visitors on a tour of the different periods of art from the 10th to early 20th centuries. Modernisme features prominently.

Fundació Stämpfli - Art Contemporani★

Plaça de l'Ajuntament. Open Jul–Sept Wed–Fri 5 8pm, Sat–Sun 11am–2pm, 5–8pm. Mar–Jun & Oct Fri 5–7pm, Sat–Sun 11am–2pm, 5–7pm. Nov–Feb Fri 4–7pm, Sat–Sun 11am–2pm, 4–7pm. €5. ✆93 894 03 64. www.fundacio-stampfli.org.
Opened in 2010, this former fish market houses one of the finest contemporary art collections in Catalonia. There are 60 works by 90 artists from around the world.

Casa Bacardi★

Plaça Ajuntament. Wed-Sat noon-2pm, 4-8pm, Sun noon-2pm, 4-7pm. €9. ✆938 94 81 51 . www.casabacardi.es.
The founder of the Bacardi brand, Facundo Bacardí Massó (1814-1886), was born and raised in Sitges before emigrating to Cuba. Housed in a former market, this 'museum' tells the story of the company and ends with a tasting.

Museu Romàntic★

Sant Gaudenci 1. Closed for renovation. www.museusdesitges.cat.
This late-18C bourgeois house gives a good idea of middle- and upper-class life during the Romantic period with frescoes on the walls, English furniture, mechanical devices and musical boxes. Dioramas show scenes of daily life.

Festivals in Sitges

Sitges is known for its Corpus Christi flowers, for the Sitges (Fantasy & Horror) Film Festival (early October; http://sitgesfilm festival.com), vintage car rally (Mar) and international theatre festival (Jun). Its major fiesta is on 24 August, the feast day of Sant Bartomeu, celebrated with a huge firework display and a traditional parade of giant figures. The town is also renowned for its exuberant Carnival. But perhaps it's most famous for being an international gay resort. The rainbow flag is a common sight on the streets here and many bars and clubs cater specifically to a gay clientele.

The **Lola Anglada collection** is an outstanding display of 17–19C dolls from all over Europe.

EXCURSIONS

Vilanova i la Geltrú★

❍7km/4.3mi SW. ▬▬Vilanova i la Geltrú.
Set in a small bay, this is an important fishing harbour and a holiday resort.

Museu Romàntic Can Papiol★

Major 32. Open Fri-Sat 11am–2pm, 4–6pm (Jun–Sept 6–8pm), Sun 10am–2pm. Guided visits only, which begin on the hour. €4. ✆938 93 03 82. www.museucanpapiol.cat.
This mansion, built 1780–1801 by the Papiol family, evokes the life of the devout, well-to-do industrial middle class. Austerity reigns in the library, with its 5 000 or so volumes, in the chapel with its strange relic of St Constance, and in the reception rooms with their biblical scenes in grey monochrome. However, the opulence of the house is also evident in the furnishings and in the ballroom.

Biblioteca-Museu Balaguer★

Av. Víctor Balaguer. Open Mon-Fri 9.30am-2pm, Weds 9.30am-7pm. €3. ✆938 15 42 02. www.victorbalaguer.cat.
This library-museum in a curious Egyptian-Greek building was an initiative of poet-historian-politician **Víctor Balaguer** (1824–1901). The **contemporary art collection** includes Catalan works from the 1950s and 1960s (*Legado 56*). Small works outline the evolution of painting since the end of the 14C. There are also **16C and 17C paintings** (El Greco, Murillo, Carducho, Maino, Carreño, etc.) and Egyptian and Asian art.

👥 Museu del Ferrocarril★

Pl. d'Eduard Maristany. Open mid-Jul–Aug daily 10.30am–2.30pm, 5–8pm; Sept–mid-Jul Tue–Sun 10.30am–2.30pm (Sat after-noons 4–6.30pm). €6; child €4.50. ✆938 15 84 91. www.museudelferrocarril.org.
This is one of the most impressive collections of railway engines in Spain.

Vilafranca del Penedès★

❍ 29km/18mi NW by the C 158 and C 15.
▬▬Vilafranca del Penedès.
Situated in the centre of the Penedés wine-growing region, Vilafranca proudly wears the badge of "Catalunya's Wine Capital". The Penedés is famous for producing cava and the most famous wineries in the region include Cordoníu, whose cellars are a glorious Modernista affair (www.codorniu.com/es/cavas) and Freixenet (www.freixenet.es). In fact there are over 60 other *bodegas* within a short drive, including Torres and Jean León, and many can be visited (www.enoturismepenedes.cat).

Vinseum – Museu de les Cultures del Vi de Catalunya ★★

Pl. Jaume I5. Open Tue–Sat May–Sept 10am–7pm, Oct–Apr Tue–Sat 10am–2pm, 4–7pm; Sun 10am–2pm year round. Closed Mon, 1 May, 25–26 December, 1 & 6 Jan. €7, no charge first Sun of the month and 18 May. ✆938 900 582. www.vinseum.cat.
More than a museum, this lively, innovative, family friendly centre celebrates the culture of wine, the evolution of the region through wine production and and even how local music and folklore have been inspired by wine.

ADDRESSES

🏠 STAY

🛏🍽 **Hotel Medium Romàntic** – Sant Isidre 33. Sitges. ✆938 94 83 75. www.mediumhoteles.com. 69 rooms. This establishment takes up two 19C buildings, each with period décor and a certain decadent charm.

🍴 EAT

🍽 **La Oca** – Parellades 41. ✆938 94 79 36. www.laocadesitges.com. Closed mid-Oct–mid-Dec and 25 & 31 Dec. This inexpensive, modern restaurant in the centre of Sitges is known for its grilled meats.

Northern Catalunya and Principat d'Andorra

Geographically, Catalunya is a triangle of varied landscapes, from snow-topped peaks to sun-kissed beaches, set between the French border, Aragón and the Mediterranean. Culturally, Catalunya is a nation unto itself. It has its own language, its own flag, its own proud history. Barcelona has been the shop window and public face of Catalunya since the hugely successful Olympics of 1992. However, as early as the 1950s north European visitors were flocking to the deep blue water and pine-fringed coves of the Costa Brava. The Pyrenees and the Principality of Andorra welcome mostly domestic and cross-border visitors, skiers and walkers.

The Mountains

The Pyrenees, between Andorra and the Cap de Creus headland, is a green wooded area with peaks over 3 100m/ 10 170ft high. This is wonderful walking territory, dotted with delightful villages and a smattering of ski resorts and other adventure sports opportunities. Andorra is famous for its shopping but excels in its skiing and walking opportunities; the spectacular Port d'Envalira pass, the highest in the Pyrenees, is well worth the trip. The Pyrenees also contain one of Spain's richest cultural legacies. During the 10C and 12C, Romanesque art and architecture became prolific throughout the Pyrenees as Catalunya emerged as a nation. Particularly in the Vall de Boí, a UNESCO World Heritage site, stout, slate-roof Romanesque churches are dotted everywhere over the bucolic landscape. Art of the period was manifested in highly expressive religious frescoes featuring vivid colour and elongated, doe-eyed creatures. Most of the originals have been moved to Barcelona's MNAC but sensitive reproductions evoke a sense of time and place.

Costa Brava and Inland

The Costa Brava was "discovered" and made fashionable by artists such as Dalí, Picasso and Marc Chagall, and was in the vanguard of Spain's plunge into mass-market tourism. Fortunately, it has, with a few ugly exceptions (most notably Lloret de Mar), remained true to its name, meaning "wild" or "rugged coast", and is still the most beautiful of Spain's holiday costas. Beaches range from rocky coves to long soft golden sands, while the rugged coastlines softened

Highlights

1 **Girona** in early May during the flower festival (p351)

2 The archetypal and art-filled village of **Cadaqués** (p356)

3 The coastal scenery of the **Cap de Begur** on the Costa Brava (p360)

4 Lose yourself at the Teatre-Museu Dalí in Figueres (p365)

5 Romanesque art and architecture in the **Vall de Boí** (p376)

by greenery are rarely less than interesting. The international gateway to the coast is Girona, a typical Catalan city with real character and history and many of the features of a "mini-Barcelona". Figueres, the spiritual home of Salvador Dalí, is likely to delight even the most doubtful art sceptics.

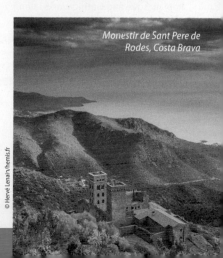

Monestir de Sant Pere de Rodes, Costa Brava

© Hervé Lenain/hemis.fr

Vic★★

This important commercial centre and thriving industrial town (leather goods, food processing and textiles) lies in the foothills of the Pyrenees. Monumental buildings testify to its history as a Roman centre. Vic makes a good base for exploring the mountains while also being within striking distance of Barcelona.

▶ **Population:** 42 498
◔ **Michelin Map:** 574 G 36 – Catalunya (Barcelona).
▤ **Info:** Pl. del Pes. ℘938 86 20 91. www.victurisme.cat.
◖ **Location:** Vic is in NE Spain, 70km/43mi N of Barcelona. 🚉Vic.
◉ **Don't Miss:** Museu Episcopal.
◷ **Timing:** A famous farmer's market is held in Vic's main square (Plaça Major) every Saturday.

THE CITY TODAY

Vic sees few overnighting north European visitors. It is known locally for its wide choice of good quality restaurants, so if you wish to escape fellow tourists and fill up on authentic Catalan cooking, before walking it off in the mountains, this is the place to come.

SIGHTS

Old Quarter★

Wide avenues (ramblas) follow the old walls, of which a few remnants remain.

Museu Episcopal★★★

Pl. Bisbe Oliba 3. Open Apr–Sept Tue–Sat 10am–7pm, Sun and public holidays 10am–2pm; Oct–Mar Tue–Fri 10am–1pm, 3–6pm, Sat 10am–7pm, Sun and public holidays 10am–2pm. Closed 1, 6 Jan, Easter Sunday, 25–26 Dec. €7. ℘938 86 93 60. www.museuepiscopalvic.com.

This magnificent museum displays Romanesque and Gothic works, along with fabrics and costumes, jewellery, ceramics and other arts.

Sala del Románico★★★ (Romanesque Gallery) – On exhibit are the Descent of Erill la Vall, a sculptural ensemble; the painting Canopy of Ribes de Freser; and outstanding altar fronts. The Lluça Altar marks the transition to the Gothic style.

Salas del Gótico★★★ (Gothic Galleries) – Among items from the early Gothic period (after 1275) are a magnificent marble altarpiece by Bernat Saulet, a Virgin of Boixadors, the altar front of Bellver de Cerdanya and parts of an altarpiece by **Pere Serra**. The impressive collection of international Gothic altarpieces (15C) includes the **Santa Clara** and Sant Antoni i Santa Margarida altars, both by Borrasà, the de Guimerà altar, the work of Ramon de Mur, and the Verdú altarpiece of Jaume Ferrer II. The paintings of Jaume Huguet mark the transition to the Renaissance.

Tejido e Indumentari★★★ (Textiles and Costumes) – A superb display of liturgical wear and 13C–18C textiles.

Catedral★

Pl. de la Catedral. Open daily 10am–1pm, 4–7pm. No charge. ℘938 86 44 49. www.victurisme.cat.

An elegant 11C Romanesque belfry and crypt remain from earlier churches. The Neoclassical Cathedral was built between 1781 and 1803. In 1930 the famous Catalan artist **Josep Maria Sert** decorated the **interior★** with wall paintings. These were burned during the Civil War, and repainted by Sert before his death in 1945.

The **paintings★★** have a power reminiscent of Michelangelo. They evoke the mystery of the Redemption (chancel) from the time of Adam's original sin (transept) to the Passion (apse), the Evangelists and the Martyrs (nave). Scenes on the back of the west door illustrate the triumph of human injustice in the Life of Christ and in the history of Catalunya: Jesus chasing the moneylenders (right); Jesus condemned (centre) and the road to Calvary (left). The monochrome golds and browns in the murals lend the effect of a relief. The former high altar **retable★★** (end of the ambulatory) is a 15C alabaster work in 12 panels. Tracery-filled 14C arches surround the small **clasustro★**. In a cloister gallery is the tomb of the painter JM Sert, surmounted by his unfinished *Crucifixion*.

Palau Episcopal

Santa Maria. ✆938 86 15 55.

The 12C episcopal palace has been modified significantly. The **Sala dels Sínodes**, decorated in 1845, and the patio are the main features.

Plaça Major★

Note façades with Modernist, Gothic and Baroque details on this busy arcaded square. A popular market is held in the square every Saturday.

EXCURSIONS
Monestir de Sant Pere de Casserres★

◗17km/11.6mi NE of Vic. Take the C 153 NE from Vic, then turn right towards Tavernoles and the Parador. At the Parador take a paved lane to the left (3.5km/2.2mi). Open Tue–Sun: Oct–May 10am–5.30pm, Jun–Sept until 7.30pm. Closed Tue if Mon a bank hol, also 1 & 6–31 Jan, 24–25 Dec. €3. ✆937 44 71 18. www.santperedecasserres.com.

Stop just before the Parador for a fine **view★★**. The small Romanesque monastery enjoys a picturesque **location★★** at the end of a long and narrow peninsula in the marsh. For many centuries, Sant Pere de Casserres was the only working Benedictine Monastery in the Osona region. Monastic life ended at the hands of King Carlos III in 1797, but the complex's medieval structures have been well preserved for posterity.

Monestir de Santa Maria de L'Estany★

◗ 24km/15mi SW of Vic. Leave Vic on the C 25 towards Manresa. Go right at exit 164, follow the BP 4313 to L'Estany.

Open 20 Jan–20 Dec Tue–Sun & pub hols 10am–2pm. €3.50. ✆938 30 30 40. www.monestirestany.cat.

The village of **L'Estany★** grew up around this medieval Augustinian monastery. The bell tower of the 12C Romanesque church was rebuilt in the 15C. The arcades of the beautiful **cloisters★** are supported by matching columns and decorated with 72 remarkable **capitals ★★**.

The north gallery is Romanesque and narrative; the west, decorative with palm fronds and gaunt griffons; the south, geometrical and interlaced; the east features wedding scenes and musicians.

🚗 DRIVING TOURS

Serra de Montseny★

The Serra de Montseny, an extension of the Pyrenees, is a granite massif covered in beeches and cork oaks. To the southeast, the **Parque Natural de Montseny** covers 17 372ha/42 925 acres; its highest peaks are Matagalls (1 695m/5 560ft) and **Turó de l'Home** (1 707m/5 601ft).

Vic to Sant Celoni via the Northern Road

60km/37.3mi. Leave Vic to the S; turn left after 6km/3.7mi.

The road goes through pine and beechwoods past delightful **Viladrau**. After **Arbùcies**, it runs beside the river then turns for **Breda**, with the Romanesque tower of the **Monestir de Sant Salvador★**, and Sant Celoni (🚌Plaça de l'Estació).

Beyond Campins, the road rises with **views**, to the lake *(embalse)* of Santa Fè (1 130m/3 707ft). The **Ermita de Sant Marçal★★** hermitage is 7km/4.3mi ahead on Matagalls ridge. There are good **views** of the serra from the road between Sant Celoni and Tona via **Montseny★**. Beyond Montseny, the road rises to a wild area, then descends to Tona past the Romanesque church in **El Brull** and the tower of **Santa Maria de Seva**.

Girona/ Gerona★★

Girona stands on a strategic site that has made it the target of repeated sieges. Its ramparts were built and rebuilt by Iberians, Romans and Catalans. Charlemagne's troops assaulted the city, and in 1809, Girona resisted Napoleon's troops for more than seven months.

THE CITY TODAY

Once seen as merely the international gateway to the region, Girona is now welcoming curious foreign visitors who have "done" Barcelona and are seeking similarly historic characterful Catalan cities to explore. With a mix of atmospheric streets and historic sights which reflect the city's rich multicultural heritage, all in a compact centre with a river running through its heart, Girona makes for a very satisfying day away from the coast.

☙☙ WALKING TOUR

BARRI VELL (OLD TOWN)

Allow 3hr

Narrow alleys lead up to the Cathedral, with its monumental stairway, the **Escaleras de la Pera**. The 14C **Pia Almoina** building (right) is a fine example of Gothic architecture.

For a fine view of the old town ascend to the **Paseo de la Muralla** (Wall Walk) where you can take a spectacular stroll along the path running around the ancient walls dating from the 9C and early medieval times. There are various entrances and exits.

Antic Hospital Santa Caterina

Plaça de l'Hospital. Pharmacy: Sat–Sun and hols 11am–1pm. ℘972 20 38 34.

Facing the Plaça Pompeu Fabra, this baroque building was modernised with a glass annex when it became the home of the Generalitat (local government) in April 2010. But you can still admire its

▶ **Population:** 97 586
🖒 **Michelin Map:** 574 G 38 (town plan) – map 122 Costa Brava – Catalunya (Girona).
🅘 **Info:** Rambla de la Llibertat 1 ℘972 22 65 75. www.girona.cat/turisme.
◖ **Location:** Girona connects with Barcelona (97km/60.2mi SW) and France via the N II and AP 7. The C 255 leads to Palafrugell (39km/24mi SW) and the C 250 to Sant Feliu de Guíxols (36km/22mi SW), both on the coast. 🚌Gerona (no train transfer from Barcelona airport).
🅿 **Parking:** Park along one of the wider streets and walk into the old city.
☺ **Don't Miss:** A walk through the old Jewish quarter is essential.
🕔 **Timing:** Walk around the old town, not only to the main sites, but simply to wander among its orange-and-ochre heritage buildings.

---

elegant Neoclassical façade and austere lines. As well as administrative offices, the building houses a large Catalan library and an auditorium, the latter in the old chapel. Its pharmacy, which houses a collection of 300 apothecary jars from the 18th century, opened to the public in 2015.

◗ After Plaça Pompeu Fabra, cross Plaça de Catalunya, over the river.

Rambla de Llibertat

Following the Onyar River and lined with cafés and shops, the lively Rambla de la Llibertat is the main route of entry into the old town. Beyond the stone bridge, medieval arcades once housed a large market. La Rambla flows onto the Carrer Argenteria, which is much narrower but just as colourful, and then leads to the bridge of Sant Agustí.

Girona by the Onyar

▷ At the bridge, turn right into Plaça Lucerne then turn right again into Carrer Bonaventura Carreras Peralta.

Fontana d'Or

Known by this name since the 18C, this Romanesque building has had various functions over the centuries. It now hosts art exhibitions.

▷ Return to Plaça Lucerne.

El Call

Parallel to the Carrer Bonaventura Carreras Peralta, the Carrer de la Força winds through the "Call", the former Jewish quarter of Girona. This ensemble of tall buildings is crisscrossed with alleyways and steep staircases winding around the site of the ancient synagogue.

This road leads directly to the cathedral, but rather than heading straight on, meander around the looped side streets. Although the current layout no longer corresponds entirely to that of medieval times, and buildings have undergone various transformations, this is still a very atmospheric quarter.

Museu d'Història dels Jueus (Museum of Jewish History)

Carrer Força, 8. Open Sept–Jun Tue–Sat 10am–6pm, Sun, Mon and hols 10am–2pm; Jul–Aug: Mon–Sat 10am–8pm, Sun & hols 10am–2pm. Closed Jan 1 and 6, 25–26 Dec. €4, no charge on the first Sun of the month. ☎972 216 761. www.girona.cat/call/cat. This museum reveals a moving history and tells the daily life of the Jewish community of 10C Girona through documents, text panels and engravings. They narrate the Jews' economic and cultural significance, which was protected by both the Church and by the Catalan-Aragonese state, then of the circumstances leading to their tragic banishment.

Further along the same street, the **Centre Ca Porta Bonastruc** is located at the site of the ancient synagogue. The centre houses the Nahmanides Institute of

Girona and Judaism

Girona's Jewish community, which settled on both sides of **Carrer de la Força** in the city's old quarter, was the second largest in Catalunya after Barcelona, and became famous in the Middle Ages for its prestigious Kabbalistic School, which existed for over 600 years from the 9C until the expulsions of 1492. This past can be felt in atmospheric narrow alleyways such as Carrer Cúndaro and Carrer Sant Llorenç, the latter home to the **Centro Bonastruc ça Porta**, dedicated to the town's Jewish history.

Jewish Studies, named after the physician, philosopher and Rabbi Moshe ben Nahman (1194–1270), a leading member of Girona's Jewish community.

Museu d'Història de Girona

Força, 27. Open Tue–Sat May–Sept 10.30am–6.30pm, Oct–Apr until 5.30pm; Sun and hols until 1.30pm year round. Closed 1 & 6 Jan, 25–26 Dec. €4, no charge on the first Sun of the month. ☎972 222 229. www.girona.cat/museuhistoria.

This fascinating museum housed in a former monastery, gives an overview of the city from its Roman origins (check out the Roman wall in the basement) until the end of Franco's reign. The 14 exhibition rooms include info about the town's industrial heritage, the local *sardana* dance and the Civil War.

▶ Continue along Carrer de la Força.

Catedral★

Pl. de la Catedral. Open daily Apr–Oct 10am–7.30pm; Nov–Mar 10am–6.30pm. €7 (including nave, cloisters and museum); no charge Sun (10am–2pm cloister and treasury). ☎972 21 58 14. www.catedraldegirona.cat.

The Baroque façade of the Catedral resembles an altarpiece with a huge single oculus. The structure, except the 11C Torre de Carlomagno (Charlemagne Tower) – from an earlier Romanesque cathedral – is Gothic and its single nave★★ is, remarkably, the largest Gothic nave in the world, though it remains largely unadorned. The chancel (1312) is surrounded by chapels. A silver-gilt embossed 14C altarpiece★ traces the Life of Christ. In the Sant Honorat chapel is the cathedral's outstanding tomb, set in a Gothic niche, of Bishop Bernard de Pau.

Museu-Tresor de la Catedral★★

The treasury houses one of the most beautiful copies of the Beatus★★, or *St John's Commentary on the Apocalypse* (8C), still in existence The 10C embossed silver Hixem Casket is a fine example

of Caliphate art, and there is Gothic silver and plate of the 14C and 15C. The end room contains the Tapís de la Creació★★★ (Tapestry of Creation), dating from about 1100, showing Christ in Majesty surrounded by creation. The 12–13C cloisters★ remain (like the 11C tower) from the Romanesque cathedral.

Museu d'Art de Girona★★

Pujada de la Catedral 12. Open May–Sept Tue–Sat 10am–6.30pm, Sun 10am–1.30pm; Oct–Apr Tue–Sat 10am–5.30pm, Sun 10am–1.30pm. Closed 1, 6 Jan, 25–26 Dec. €4.50. ☎972 20 38 34. www.museuart.com.

Set in the Palau Episcopal, the city's principal art collection dates from the Romanesque to the present. Holdings include a 10C portable altar from Sant Pere de Rodes of embossed silver, a 12C–13C beam from the village of Cruïlles★, and apse paintings from Pyrenean churches.

Among altarpieces in the Throne Room is one from Sant Miquel de Cruïlles★★ by Luis Borrassá (15C), Catalunya's greatest Gothic artist. Note the splendid Púbol altarpiece★, by Bernat Martorell (1437) and the Sant Feliu altarpiece by Juan de Borgoña.

▶ Return to Carrer de la Força and take the first stairs on the left.

Basilica de Sant Feliu★

Pujada Sant Feliu 29. Open Mon–Sat 10am–5.30pm, Sun 1–5.30pm. €7. ☎972 20 14 07. www.catedraldegirona.cat.

This church outside the walls must originally have been a martyry over the tombs of St Narcissus, Bishop of Girona, and St Felix. The later Gothic church holds eight early Christian sarcophagi★, two with outstanding carvings, including a spirited lion hunt★.

▶ Return to Carrer de la Força, cross it and veer to the left.

Banys àrabs★ (Arab Baths)

Ferran el Católic. Open Apr–Sept Mon –
Sat 10am–7pm, Sun and public holidays
10am–2pm; Oct–Mar daily 10am–2pm.
Closed 1, 6 Jan, 25–26 Dec. €2. ℰ972 19
09 69. www.banysarabs.org.
These picturesque late-12C baths were
built in Muslim tradition. Steps opposite
lead to the Passeig Arqueològic, with its
view of the Ter Valley.

Monestir de Sant Pere de Galligants/Museu d'Arqueologia★

Santa Lucía 8. Open Tue–Sat Jun–Sept
10am–7pm, Oct–May until 6pm; Sun and
public holidays 10am–2pm year round.
Closed 1 & 6 Jan, 24–26 Dec. €4.50, no
charge last Tue of month Oct–Jun. ℰ972
20 26 32. www.macgirona.cat
The fortified Romanesque church of
Sant Pere, set into the town walls, now
houses the Museu Arqueològic. Highlights include its medieval memorial
plaques and the magnificent 4C Roman
tomb of Las Estaciones★.

ADDITIONAL SIGHTS

Casa Masó

Ballesteries 29. Open daily for guided
tours by prior appointment. €5. ℰ972
413 989. www.rafaelmaso.org.
Before heading into the Jewish quarter,
you might want to check out the family
home of architect Rafael Masó (1880-
1935). This stunning house overlooking
the river is in the *noucentisme (1900s)*
style, which continued on from *modernisme*. The beautiful interior is filled with
antiques dating from the 18th century.

Museu del Cinema

Sèquia 1. Open Oct–Apr Tue–Fri
10am–6pm, Sat 10am–8pm, Sun & hol
Mons 11am–3pm. May–Jun and Sept
Tue–Sat 10am–8pm, Sun & hol Mons
11am–3pm. Jul–Aug daily 10am–8pm.
Closed Jan 1 & 6, 25–26 Dec. €5, no
charge first Sun of month. ℰ972 412
777. www.museudelcinema.cat.
This collection brings to life the early
days of cinema through screenings and
varied exhibits. From silhouette mon-
tages to delightful magic lanterns, visitors can discover the wonders of an age
where a lack of technology was offset
by an exuberant imagination.

Plaça de la Independencia

Designed by architect Martí Sureda
Deulovol in 1855 (yet only completed
in 1993 more or less according to his
original design), this beautiful square
is surrounded by Neoclassical buildings and affords some glimpses of the
colourful facades along the Onya River.

Parc de la Devesa★

This park contains the largest grove of
plane trees in Catalunya.

EXCURSION

Casa-Museu Castell Gala Dalí★

▶ In Púbol. 16km/10mi E along the C 66
towards La Bisbal d'Empordà. Open mid-
Mar–6 Jan, Tue–Sun & Mons Jun–Sept
from 10am, see website for more details.
Closed 7 Jan. €8. ℰ972 48 86 55.
www.salvador-dali.org.
In 1970, Salvador Dalí gave this 14C
castle to his wife Gala. It now displays
objects in a Surrealist setting.

🚗 DRIVING TOUR

GIRONA TO SANTA PAU

64.5km/40mi. Allow one day.

▶ Head N from Girona along the C 66.

Banyoles

20km/12.4mi NW of Girona.
This small town enjoys a beautiful
lakeside setting. The Museu Arqueològic Comarcal★ (Placeta de la Font
11; open Tue–Sat 10.30am–1.30pm,
4–6.30pm/7.30pm summer, Sun
10.30am–2pm; €3; ℰ972 57 23 61,
www.museusdebanyoles.cat) is set in
a Gothic building; the star exhibit is its
Palaeolithic Jaw of Banyoles.
An 8km/5mi road around the lake
passes the 13C Església de Santa
Maria de Porqueres★; its columns
are sculpted with odd figures (Ctra
Circumval·lació de l'Estany; open by

Medieval bridge, Besalù

© Lucas Vallecillos/age fotostock

arrangement; enquire at the Museu Arqueològic Comarcal).

Estany de Banyoles★

Lake Banyoles, over 2km long and 235m wide (1.2mi by 770ft), is flanked to the west by the Serra de Rocacorba and overlooks planes of oak trees alternating with green fields. Besides the beauty of its landscape, it is of great ecological importance because of the many protected species that dwell here. Rowing is popular and the lake served as a gorgeous setting for the 1992 Olympic regatta events.

▶ Take the C-66 7kms/4.3mi northwards.

Serinya

The church in this little village, devoted to Sant Andreu, is a remarkable example of 13C Romanesque architecture, with a gate adorned with archivolts.
Archaeological finds in the area include some splendid Middle and Upper Paleolithic remains in two caves: the Cova dels Encantats and Cova del Mollet (enquire about visiting at the Museu Arqueològic Comarcal).

▶ Continue northwards on the C-66 for 7kms/4.3mi.

Besalù★★

The first view of Besalú, across the river, with its Roman **fortified bridge★**, rebuilt in the medieval period, is extremely picturesque. This small

ancient city★★ retains ramparts and many medieval buildings, including the Romanesque **Església de Sant Pere★** with an unusual lion-flanked window. In the Jewish quarter are traditional 12C **ritual baths** (both church and baths may be visited on guided tours arranged through the Tourist Office, C/del Pont 1, ℰ972 59 12 40, www.besalu.cat/turisme).

▶ Head 14km/8.7mi W along the N 260.

Castellfollit de la Roca★

This village set in the **Parc Natural de la Garrotxa★**, includes a medieval centre around the church of Sant Salvador.

▶ Continue 8km/5mi on the N 260.

Olot★

The 18C Neoclassical and Baroque **Església de Sant Estève★**, houses an unusual painting by El Greco – **Christ Bearing the Cross★**.
The **Museu Comarcal de la Garrotxa★** displays a fine **collection of paintings and drawings★★** by 19C and 20C Catalan artists (Hospici 8; open Tue–Fri 10am–1pm, 3–6pm; Sat 11am–2pm, 4–7pm; Sun and public holidays 11am–2pm; €3; no charge first Sun of month; ℰ972 27 11 66).
Note also the splendid **Modernist façade★** of the **Casa Solà-Morales★**, by Domènech i Montaner.

▶ Take the GI 524 E 9.5km/6mi.

Zona Volcánica de la Garrotxa

Casal dels Volcans, Av. Sta Coloma de Farners. ℘972 266 012. www.gencat.cat/parcs/garrotxa.

Declared a national park in 1982, the Zona Volcanica de la Garrotxa covers 11 300ha (27 923 acres) through the upper Fluvià valley. Thirty Strombolian-type volcanic cones, craters and more than 20 basaltic lava flows have created a lunaresque landscape of extreme beauty. In the valleys and escarpments it is not uncommon to see wild cats and boars. The park has also become a sanctuary for birds: nearly 150 different species have found refuge here. On the road from Olot to Santa Pau, the Fageda D'en Jordà is an ancient beech forest standing on lava flow. Here there are easy walks to El Croscat (the youngest volcano in the park) and the Santa Margarida volcano, the largest in Garrotxa. Measuring 110m/360ft high and 1 200 m/3 930 ft wide, it is now covered in abundant vegetation.

Four signed routes start from the information point of Can Serra (open 10am–3pm; parking €4 all day).

Santa Pau★

The Castillo de Santa Pau and the 15C–16C parish church both stand on the arcaded square of this village.

ADDRESSES

🛏 STAY

⊖🛏🛏 **Pensió Bellmirall** – Bellmirall 3, Girona. ℘972 204 009. www.bellmirall.eu. 7 rooms. In the heart of the old town, this B&B is in an attractive three-storey house furnished with antiques. Free public parking nearby.

⊖🛏🛏🛏 **Llegendes de Girona Catedral** – Portal de la Barca 4, Girona. ℘972 22 09 05. www.llegendeshotel.com. 15 rooms, 🍽12. Next to Sant Feliu church, this four-star hotel offers contemporary, themed rooms, in an atmospheric old building. Cocktail bar.

🍽/EAT

⊖🛏🛏 **Café Le Bistrot** – Pujade de Sant Domènec 4, Girona. ℘972 21 88 03. www.lebistrot.cat. Traditional cuisine served in a Parisian-style dining room or in the attractive square outside.

⊖🛏🛏🛏 **Divinum** – Albereda 7, Girona. ℘972 872 08 02 18. www.divinum.cat. Closed Sun. Modern Catalan dishes served in stylish surrounds. Good-value lunchtime set menus and superb wine list. Gastronomic menu also served.

Cadaqués★★

This beautiful fishing village between mountains and sea is one of the most charming in Catalunya. It is located on the southern coast of Cape Creus, a peninsula that marks the meeting point between the Pyrenees and the Mediterranean. Its picturesque streets and bohemian atmosphere fascinated many famous artists in the first half of the 20C, including Picasso, Man Ray, Buñuel and Thomas Mann. Salvador Dalí spent much of his life in nearby Port Ligat. Cap de Creus became a recurring theme in his work.

▶ **Population:** 2 840
🚗 **Michelin Map:** 574 F 39.
🛈 **Info:** Cotxe 1. ℘972 258 315. www.visitcadaques.org.
◐ **Location:** 36km/21mi S of the French border and 39km/24mi E of Figueres. 🚉Nearest train station: Figueres (34km).
🕐 **Timing:** July/August can be very crowded.

Cadaqués

© Proformabooks/iStockphoto.com

THE TOWN TODAY

In high summer, Cadaqués has remained a fashionable retreat for Catalans and a large number of French visitors, so at times it can feel more like a resort on the French Riviera than a remote village in Northern Spain. Chic galleries and cafés line the waterfront and the local fleet of fishing boats is joined by pleasure yachts. Such is the town's cachet that a seaside development in China will reproduce the whitewashed and bougainvillea-covered houses in a project that aims to replicate this archetypal Catalan seaside resort.

SIGHTS
Museu de Cadaqués

Narcís Monturiol 15. See website for opening times and prices. ℰ972 25 88 77. www.visitcadaques.org.
The town's museum holds temporary exhibitons by local artists as well as artists associated with Cadaqués. Naturally, there are also permanent displays on Dalí.

Església de Santa Maria

Pl. Dr Callis 15. Open Mass only: Sat 7pm, Sun 11am (altarpiece can be viewed from the exterior via window).
Overlooking the **casco antiguo** and indeed the focal point of the village, white-washed houses with picturesque porticoes cluster around the Església de Santa Maria, whose sober exterior con-

trasts with its interior: note the lovely **Baroque altarpiece★★** in gilded wood by Joan Torres. The town hosts an international music festival (late Jul–early Aug; www.festivalcadaques.cat).

EXCURSIONS
Portlligat★

Less than a mile northeast of Cadaqués this little village is set in a small bay on the Cap de Creus peninsula. Blending into a charming cluster of whitewashed fishermen's houses is the **Casa-Museu Salvador Dalí★** (open mid-Jun–mid- Sept daily 9.30am–9pm; rest of the year Tue–Sun 10.30am–6pm; reservation required; closed 25 Dec, 1-2 Jan, Jan 9–second week Feb, 29 May, 2 Oct; €11; ℰ972 25 10 15; www.salvador-dali.org) where Dalí lived and worked from 1930–82. Works inspired by the local scenery include *The Sacrament of the Last Supper*, and *The Madonna of Port Lligat*. Dalí's workshop, library, rooms and garden are all open.

Parque Natural de Cap de Creus★★

Steep roads and paths wind between cliffs and hidden bays to Cap de Creus, Spain's most easterly point. Many people come to enjoy the spectacular **view at sunset, ★★★** from the terrace of the Restaurant Cap de Creus (ℰ972 19 90 05), by the lighthouse.

Costa Brava★★★

Spain's Costa Brava (literally "Wild Coast") is a twisted, rocky shoreline where the Catalan mountains fall away into the sea. Beautiful inlets, clear waters, picturesque harbours, and leisure and sporting activities draw tourists to these shores. Inland there are delightful medieval towns and villages.

🚗 DRIVING TOURS

1 BLANES TO PALAMÓS

51km/31mi. Allow one day.

The circuit through two narrow coastal roads (GI 682 from Blanes to Sant Feliu) and C 253 from Sant Feliu to Palamós) provides excellent views of the coast.

Blanes★

🚂 Blanes (airport via Barcelona Sants).

The **Passeig Marítim★** offers a lovely panorama of Blanes and its beach. The remains of the Castillo de Sant Joan are to the east, above the 14C Gothic Església de Santa Maria.

To the southeast is the **Jardí Botànic de Marimurtra★** (Pg. Karl Faust; open daily; Apr–Oct 9am–6pm/Jun–Sept 8pm; Nov–Mar 10am–5pm; €6.50; ℘972 33 08 26, www.jbotanicmarimurtra.org), a botanical park with 5 000 plant species including many rare exotic varieties. At each bend the twisting paths reveal wonderful **views★** of the bay of Cala Forcadera and the coastline.

Created in 1945, the **Jardí Botànic Pinya de Rosa★** (Platja Santa Cristina (above the Marimurtra Jardí Botànic); open year-round daily 9am–6pm; closed 1 Dec-30 Jan; €4; ℘972 350 689, www.pinya-de-rosa.es) has became the largest cactus garden in the world, with over 7 000 varieties.

Its founder, Fernando Riviere de Caralt, was an engineer who spent several decades on its development. Trails

ℹ️ **Michelin Map:** 574 E 39, F 39, G 38-39 – Catalunya (Girona).

ℹ️ **Info:** Girona: Rambla de la Llibertat 1. ℘972 22 65 75; Blanes: Pg. Catalunya 2. ℘972 33 03 48; Cadaqués: Cotxe 1. ℘972 25 83 15. en.costabrava.org.

ℹ️ **Location:** The Costa Brava is the coastline from Blanes up to Portbou on the border with France. Lloret de Mar, Tossa de Mar and Platja d'Aro are major tourist centres; towns to the north are more low key.

🧒 **Kids:** Beaches are the main attractions.

through the garden meander over the side of a steep cove, leading to a small pool surrounded by palm trees.

The foothills of the Serra de l'Albera form huge enclosed bays, like those of Portbou and El Port de la Selva. The clifftop **road section★★** from Portbou to Colera offers fine views of one of the most craggy coastlines in Catalunya.

ℹ️ Take the GI 682 NE for 7km/4.3mi.

Lloret de Mar

Lloret de Mar has become the epitome of bucket-and-spade tourism on the Costa Brava, replacing its original maritime ambiance with one of high-rise hotels, outdoor discos, water parks and overcrowded beaches.

Jardins de Santa Clothilde★★

Leave Lloret de Mar in the direction of Blanes.Open year-round daily 10am–5pm/Apr–Oct until 8pm. Closed 25 Dec & 1, 6 Jan. €5. ℘972 370 471. www.lloretdemar.org.

This rare oasis of tranquility in Lloret de Mar was created in 1919 by architect and landscape designer Nicolau Maria Rubió i Tudurí (1891–1981). It draws inspiration from the Italian Renaissance, its terraced gardens are crossed by paths and stairs lined with ivy. Pines and cypresses abound and jazz concerts are held here in summer.

▷ Take the G1 682 NE for 11km/6.8mi.

Tossa de Mar★

🚌 Tossa de Mar
(airport via Barcelona Sants).

A long beautiful sandy beach with large rock formations curves around to Punta del Faro, the promontory on which stand the lighthouse and the 13C walls of the **Vila Vella★** (old town).

The **Museu Municipal★** (Pl. Pintor Roig i Soler; open Jun–Sept daiiy 10am–8pm; Oct–May Tue–Fri 10am–1.30pm, 3–5pm; Sat 10am–2pm, 4–6pm; Sun 10am–2pm; €3; ℘972 34 07 09; www.tossademar.com/museu) contains artefacts from an ancient Roman villa nearby, and works by artists who stayed at Tossa in the 1930s, including Chagall, Masson and Benet. Between Tossa and Lloret de Mar, the road follows a spectacular **clifftop route★★**.

▷ Take the G1 682 N for 22km/13.6mi.

Sant Feliu de Guíxols★

🚌 Sant Feliu de Guíxols
(airport via Barcelona Sants).

Sheltered from the last spurs of the Serra de les Gavarres, this is one of the most popular locations of this coast. Its seaside boulevard, Passeig de la Mar, is lined with pavement cafés.

The **Església-Monastir de Sant Feliu★** (open for Mass; ℘972 82 15 75) is part of a former Benedictine monastery. Its remains tower over the small municipality. It has retained its Romanesque façade, known as the **Porta Ferrada★★**, with horseshoe arches dating to pre-Romanesque times. The interior (14C) is Gothic in style.

The lookout by the chapel of Sant Elm commands beautiful **views★★**.

Located on the edge of the town, towards Santa Cristina d'Aro, the **Roca de Pedralta★**, is one of the largest rocking or "logan" stones in Europe, set on a wonderful vantage point on the bay.

▷ Head up the coast 4km/2.5mi.

S'Agaro★

An elegant resort with chalets and luxury villas surrounded by tidy gardens and pine forests. The Camino de Ronda offers fine **views★** of the sheer cliffs.

▷ Take the C 253 5.5km/3.4mi N.

Platja d'Aro

This coastal resort was built for the sole purpose of holidays. It comes alive during the summer when the streets become cosmopolitan and noisy and its fine stretch of sand is packed with holiday makers.

Cova d'en Daina★

Access the C 31 to Calonge then Cabanyes Road.

The quiet winding road to Gavarres leads to this interesting megalithic tomb. A little further along is the medieval village of La Selva Romanyà.

▷ Take the C 253 5.5km/3.4mi N.

Palamós

This small fishing village has a vibrant marina offering range of leisure and services, making Palamós one of the busiest areas of the Costa Brava.

Museu de la Pesca

Open mid-Jun–mid-Sept daily 10am–9pm; rest of the year Tue–Sat 10am–1.30pm, 3–7pm; Sun & hols 10am–2pm, 4–7pm. €5. ℘972 600 424. www.museudelapesca.org.

This museum takes you on a voyage into the world of fishing and trawls its traditions, particularly those inherent to the Costa Brava. The traditional boats collection is a highlight.

2 PALAFRUGELL TO THE ILLES MEDES

59km/36.5mi. Allow half a day.

This northern swathe of the Costa Brava is where the scenery is at its most spectacular, particularly around the Cap de Begur.

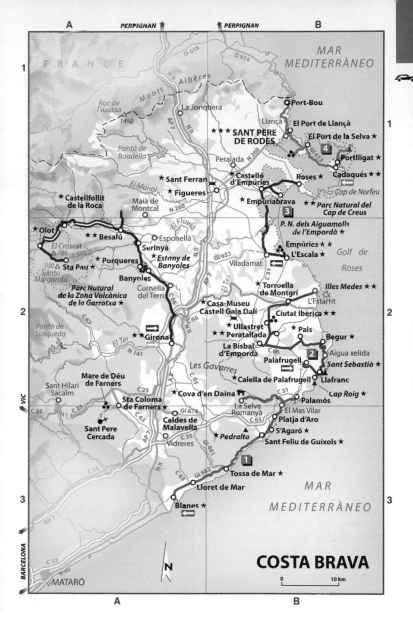

Palafrugell

Located a few miles from the coast, the town of Palafrugell has a thriving cultural scene. In the early 20C, the production of cork made it extremely prosperous.

It is also the birthplace of the prolific writer Josep Pla (1897–1981). Palafrugell is very popular with visitors, especially in summer when they come for its festive atmosphere. *Suquet* – a fish stew – is a local speciality.

Museu del Suro (Cork Museum)

Placeta del Museu. Open Jul-Aug Mon-Sat 10am-2pm, 5-8.30pm, Sun 10am-2pm, rest of year Tue-Fri 10am-1pm, 4-7pm, Sat 10am-2pm, 5-8pm, Sun 10am-2pm . €3. ℘972 307 825. www.museudelsuro.cat.

This museum explains the different processes involved in the manufacture of cork. Most interesting are the old utensils used for to wash and cut the cork.

Cala Estreta, Cap Roig near Calella de Palafrugell

▷ 4.5 km/2.7 mi S on the GIV 6546.

Calella de Palafrugell★
🚆Nearest station: Gerona (58km)
Traditional fishermen's houses are juxta-posed with modern summer residences in this picturesque fishing port. It is known for its **Festival de Habaneras** on the first Saturday in July when visitors can enjoy Afro-Cuban songs, dances and *cremat* (flambéed coffee with rum). A road southward leads to the **Jardin Botánic del Cap Roig** (open Apr–Sept daily 10am–8pm; Oct–Mar daily 10am–6pm, Jan–Feb Sat–Sun 10am–6pm; €7; ℘972 61 45 82, https://obrasocial.lacaixa.es). These terraced gardens, carved out of the rock, enjoy wonder-ful **views★★** of the coast, and include over 1 200 plant species laid out along shaded avenues.

Llafranc
2km/1.2 mi from Calella de Palafrugell by the small coastal road leading to Cap de Sant Sebastià or walk by the GR 12 that runs along the coast (15min).
Like Calella de Palafrugell, Llafranc is an attractive mix of old and new. The marina, which has 140 moorings, is the main attraction, along with a small beach offering many summer activities.

Far de Sant Sebastià★
2km/1.2mi from Llafranc.
Built in 1857, the lighthouse stands on a tiny isthmus surrounded by steep cliffs; the hermitage has a lovely **view★**.

▷ From Calella de Palafrugell, take the GIV 6591 and GIV 6542 11km/6.8mi NE.

Begur★
The town overlooks pretty creeks from an altitude of 200m/656ft above the sea. The castle ruins (16C–17C) offer a fine view of the Cap de Begur.

Pals★★
At the mouth of the Ter river, Pals has an attractive old quarter, **El Pedró**. The vestiges of fortified ramparts enclose ancient houses and winding alleyways, some with covered stairways.

▷ 12km/7.5mi N of Pals on the C 66.

La Bisbal d'Emporda
The capital of the Baix Empordá region has been famous for its ceramics and pottery for centuries and around this a vibrant crafts community has evolved. Along its main streets you will find dozens of shops selling the distinctive yellow, green and clay-coloured pots, vases and cookware of the Costa Brava.

Castell★
Pl. Castell.
www.hotelcastellemporda.com.
The former residence of the Bishops of Girona is the most remarkable building in La Bisbal, combining Romanesque and Gothic elements. It has recently been converted into a luxury hotel and restaurant.

◐ Back on the C 66, turn left on the C 252, then right on the IM 651.

Peratallada★★

🚆 Nearest station: Flaça (25km)

This fortified village is considered one of the finest medieval ensembles in the **Empordà**. Winding old streets lead to the Plaça Major (main square) where a grand castle-fortress sits, now a luxury hotel. Also seek out the Plaça de les Voltes, with charming porticoes and ancient dwellings, one of the most characteristic snapshots of the village. The church of Sant Esteve, an austere 13C building situated outside the village, has a bell perforated with a pattern common to the region.

◐ Continue on the IM 651

Ullastret★

This is one of the most picturesque villages in Empordà's hinterland. Its old medieval streets exude bags of character and it's a great place to buy regional products. The Church of Sant Pere – located in the centre of the village – is a fine example of Romanesque architecture. Notice the curious Gothic ossuary with its carvings of characters and animals.

Ciutat Ibérica

1km E of Ullastret. Open mid-Jun–Sept Tue–Sun 10am–8pm. Rest of year Tue– until 6pm. Closed 25–26 Dec and 1 & 6 Jan. €4, no charge last Tue of month Oct– Jun. ℘972 179 058. www.mac.cat.

One of Catalunya's most extensive Iberian discoveries is situated near Ullastret on the crest of Mont de Sant Andreu. Here you can see the remains of a settlement built by the Indiket tribe in the 5C, who constructed canals, a reservoir and a main square. Artefacts such as scripts can be viewed in the Archaeological Museum on the same site.

◐ Continue on the IM 644 and then turn right on the IM 643.

Torroella de Montgrí★

Despite a Baroque front, the 14C **Església de Sant Genís** (*Pas. de l'Església*) is a fine example of Gothic Catalan art. The **castle** on Montaña de Montgrì (🚶1hr on a signposted path among the rocks) is an extraordinary **belvedere★★** with a view to the sea and the Gavarres mountain range.

◐ Take the G1 641 towards the coast.

🏖 Illes Medes★★

Boat trips around the islands are offered from l'Estartit. 🚩 For information contact the tourist office; Passeig Marítim, ℘972 75 19 10. www.visitestartit.com. These seven islets and coral reefs are the extension of the calcareous massif of Montgrí. The islets are popular with lesure divers and ecologists on account of their marine life and ecosystems.

3 GULF OF ROSES

36km/22mi.

The vast majority of this stretch of coastline forms part of the Parc Natural dels Aiguamolls de l'Empordà.

L'Escala★

This resort has sandy beaches and a long fishing tradition (anchovies are salted). Two inlets protect its harbour. The Empúries ruins are located to the N.

Empúries/Ampurias★★

Puig i Cadafalch. Open from 10am: Jun–Sept daily closes 8pm; mid-Nov– mid-Feb Tue–Sun closes 5pm; rest of year daily closes 6pm. Closed 25, 26 Dec and 1 Jan. €5.50; no charge last Tue of month Oct–Jun. ℘972 77 02 08. www.mac.cat.

Greco-Roman Ampurias (*Emporion* to the Greeks, meaning market) was built on a striking seaside **site★★**. It is still possible to make out the old town, or **Paliápolis**, the new town or **Neápolis**, and the Roman town. In the mid-6C BC, the Phoenicians founded Paliápolis, on an offshore island, now joined to the mainland and occupied by the village of Sant Marti d'Empúries. A town began to develop on the shore opposite: Neápolis. As a Roman ally during the Punic Wars, it saw the arrival of an expedition led by Scipio Africanus Major in 218 BC. In 100 BC the Roman town was established to the west. The two centres coexisted until Augustus bestowed Roman citizenship upon the Greeks. The colony suffered from barbarian invasions in the 3C AD. At one time it was a bishopric, as basilica ruins show.

Neápolis – The **Templo de Asclepio** (Aesculapius – god of healing) and a sacred precinct contained altars and statues of the gods. Nearby stood a **watchtower** and drinking water cisterns. The **Templo de Zeus Serapis** (a god associated with the weather and with healing) was surrounded by a colonnade. The **Agora** was the centre of town life; three statues remain. A street from the agora to the sea was bordered on one side by the **stoa** or covered market. Behind it are the ruins of a 6C **palaeo-Christian basilica** with a rounded apse.

Museu Arqueológic d'Empúries – A section of Neápolis is displayed along with models of temples and finds from the excavations.

The Roman Town – Unlike Neápolis, this is a vast, geometrically laid out town, partially excavated, with some restored walls. **House no. 1** (entrance at the back) has an atrium (inner courtyard) with six columns. Around this are residential apartments, the peristyle, or colonnaded court, and the impluvium, or rainwater catchment. The reception rooms are paved in geometric black-and-white mosaic. **House no. 2B** has rooms paved with their original mosaic. One has been reconstituted in clay with its walls resting on stone foundations. The **forum**, a large square lined by porticoes and, to the north and south respectively, by temples and shops, was the centre of civic life.

A porticoed street led through the city gate to the oval **amphitheatre** which is still visible.

Castelló d'Empúries★

Situated a short walk from the archaeological site, the former capital of the principality of Empúries (11C–14C) is on a promontory near the coast. The 14C–15C **Basílica de Santa Maria★** is flanked by a typical Catalan belfry. The **portal★★** is a unique example of Gothic art in Catalunya: the tympanum illustrates the Adoration of the Magi while the Apostles are shown on the jambs. The large central nave is lined by fine cylindrical pillars. The alabaster **retable★** in the high altar (15C), with conical pinnacles, depicts the Passion. (open daily noon–2pm, 4–8pm; ✆972 25 05 19). The village retains buildings from its golden age: the **Ajuntament** (Maritime Commodities Exchange), combining Romanesque and Gothic elements, and the Gothic **Casa Gran**.

▶ Take the C 68 towards the coast.

Empuriabrava★

This luxury marina-residential development features one of the largest marinas in the world.

▶ 9.5km/6mi N on the C 68.

Roses

🚃Nearest station: Figueres (17km)
The modern-day resort and fishing port may take its name from sailors from Rhodes who founded a colony in the 5C with a splendid natural harbour overlooking the gulf.

Its 16C Renaissance **citadel★** (Av. de Roses; open Jun & Sep daily 10am–8pm, Jul-Aug 10am-9pm, rest of year Tue–Sun 10am–6pm; closed 25 Dec, 1, 6 Jan; €5; ✆972 15 14 66; http://visit.roses. cat/en), a pentagon with many bastions, was commissioned by Charles V. The Benedictine monastery inside was destroyed by the French during the War of Independence.

④ CADAQUÉS TO PORT-BOU

52km/32mi. Allow half a day.

This route traverses the northernmost stretch of the Catalan coast, from the beautiful peninsula of Cap de Creus (&see p362) reaching Port-Bou at the French border. Begin the drive at Cadaqués (&CADAQUÉS, p361).

El Port de la Selva★

This bay is bathed in golden sunlight at dusk. Traditional white houses stand beside numerous flats and hotels. Fishing is still one of the main activities.

◗ 7km/4.3mi inland from El Port de la Selva on the GI 612.

Monestir de Sant Pere de Rodes★★★

Leave your car in the car park and proceed on foot for 10min.
Open Jun–Sept 10am–8pm; Oct–May until 5.30pm. Closed 1 & 6 Jan, 25–26 Dec. €4.50; no charge last Tue of month Oct–Jun. ℘972 38 75 59. www.mhcat.cat.

This imposing Benedictine monastery stands in a beautiful **setting★★** that dominates the Gulf of León and the Cap de Creus peninsula. Begun in the 10C, it was pillaged, and abandoned in the 18C. The remarkable **church★★★**, showing pre-Romanesque influence, is an unusual example of architectural harmony. The central nave has barrel vaulting, the two lateral ones have surbased vaulting. They are separated by huge pillars, reinforced with columns on raised bases. Splendid **capitals★**, intricate tracery and acanthus leaves evoke the tradition of Córdoba and Byzantium. The left arm of the transept leads to an upper ambulatory offering a sweeping view of the central nave.
The 12C **bell tower★★** is a magnificent example of Lombardy Gothic.
The coast between El Port de la Selva and Cadaqués features many irregular creeks with crystal-clear waters, accessible only by sea. The road inland offers lovely views of the region.

◗ 20km/12.5mi N on the GIP 6041, then the N 260 motorway.

El Port de Llançà

Plaça de la Estación.
A pleasant tourist resort sited on a bay sheltered from winds like the *tramontana* and sudden Mediterranean storms. The shallow waters are ideal for swimming.

◗ 10km/6mi N via the N 260.

Port-Bou★

Bordering French Roussillon, this popular holiday spot is also one of Catalunya's main border crossings, especially for rail traffic. The nucleus of Port-Bou is in fact situated next to the railway station, Nevertheless, Port-Bou does offer some amazing coastal scenery. Whether you come in via the N 260 or by the magnificent M 612 coastal route, you can admire some of the steepest cliffs on the Catalan coast and countless pristine coves.

ADDRESSES

⌂ STAY

Accommodation on the **Costa Brava** can be expensive, and it is often difficult to find a room during high season without having booked well in advance. For more reasonable prices and better availability search the hinterland as well.

⊜⊜⊜ **Hotel La Goleta** – Pintor Terruella 22, El Port de Llançà. ℘972 38 01 25. www.hotellagoleta.com. 28 rooms. Restaurant ⊜⊜⊜. Close to the port, the La Goleta offers comfort and an interesting décor of paintings and other furnishings. Rooms and prices vary.

⊜⊜⊜ **Hotel Plaça** – Pl. Mercat 22, Sant Feliu de Guíxols. ℘972 32 51 55. www.hotelplaza.org. 19 rooms, ☲ €5. A practical choice for location and functional character. Pleasant, bright rooms – some overlook a square that's lively on market days. Outdoor jacuzzi and solarium on the top floor.

⊜⊜⊜ **Hotel Port Lligat** – Avenida Salvador Dalí 1, Port Lligat. ℘972 25 81 62. www.port-lligat.net/hotel. 30 rooms, ☲ €11. This attractive blue-and-white building in a cove full of fishing boats very near Dalí's house has panoramic sea views, a swimming pool solarium and jacuzzi. Every room is different.

Hotel Rosa – Pi i Rallo 19, Begur. ☎972 62 30 15. www.hotel-rosa.com. 21 rooms. Restaurant ⊜⊜⊜. This small hotel in a restored stone house by the church is popular for its modern décor and beautiful location with roof-rop terrace. The restaurant serves traditional slow cuisine.

Hotel Sant Roc – Pl. Atlántic 2 (Sant Roc district), Calella de Palafrugell. ☎972 61 42 50. www.santroc.com. 47 rooms. Restaurant ⊜⊜⊜. Closed mid-Nov–mid Feb. This charming building crowned by a small tower enjoys a peaceful, relaxing setting amid pine groves overlooking the Mediterranean. The rooms are spacious and elegant, while the restaurant terrace enjoys fine views of neighbouring coves. Half-board compulsory in summer.

Hotel Diana – Plaça de Espanya 6, Tossa de Mar. ☎972 34 18 86. www.hotelesdante.com. 21 rooms. The interior of this splendid Modernist building by the sea is exquisite, with high ceilings, cool rooms and a patio adorned with a marble fountain. The rooms are comfortable and furnished in style.

⛛/EAT

Can Bolet – Sant Mateu 6, Lloret de Mar. ☎972 371 237. Closed Sun eve and Mon. This family-run restaurant which opened in 1961 serves traditional Catalan food, with plenty to appeal to fish fans. Try the squid fried with brandy, garlic and parsley. Good-value lunch menu.

Portal de la Gallarda – Pere Estany, 14, Mollet de Peralada. Castelló d'Empúries. ☎972 250 152. Closed Tue out of season. The restaurant specialises in grilled fish and is set in a lovely 12C building with a beautiful terrace embracing part of the Natural Park.

Victoria – Passeig del Mar 23, Tossa de Mar. ☎972 34 01 66. www.hrvictoriatossa.com. Closed 15 Nov–31 Jan, Tue (Sept–Jun). A pleasant restaurant specialising in seafood and fish dishes, with a terrace overlooking the beach. There are also hotel rooms available with sea views (⊜⊜).

La Brasa – Pl. de Catalunya, 6 El Port de Llançà. ☎972 38 02 02. Closed Mon eve and Tue Sept–Jun. Low-key restaurant serving excellent grilled meat and fish on its shady terrace.

Pa i Raïm – Torres i Jonama 56, Palafrugell. ☎972 30 45 72. www.pairaim.com. Closed Sun eve, Mon and Tue. Smart, gourmet restaurant in the beautiful family home of writer Josep Pla (⛛see p365). Lovely terrace.

CAFE BARS

Music Bar Café Latino – Rbla Roma, 10, Lloret de Mar. ☎697 431 304. A lively dance bar where Latin music and cocktails are king.

Cala Banys – Cami Cala Banys, Lloret de Mar. ☎972 365 515. www.calabanys.es. Pleasant bar with a romantic shaded garden terrace overlooking the sea.

ACTIVITIES

Nautilus – Pg Marítim 23, L'Estartit. ☎972 751 489. www.nautilus.es. Various tours of the Medes Islands and surrounding coastline on-board glass-bottom boats, ranging from €20 to €28 per person.

International Diving Center – At the far end of the port, L'Escala. ☎872 20 15 20 and 698 821 834. www.international diving.com. All levels, from beginners courses to authorised dives around the Medes Islands.

Creuers Mare Nostrum – Maranges 3, L'Escala. ☎972 773 797. www.creuers-marenostrum.com. A fleet of 10 glass-bottom boats (including 2 catamarans) that tour the coastline, including the Medes Islands.

Parc Aquàtic Aqua Brava – Ctra de Cadaqués. 1km/0.5mi from Roses. Jun–mid-Sept 10am–7pm. ☎972 254 344. www.aquabrava.com. Water park known for its huge wave pool, sandy beach and tropical vegetation. €30, children up to 1.20m/3ft 6in €19.

Hípica dels Aiguamolls – Rte de Palau Savardera, Castelló d'Empúries. ☎639 787 732. www.haiguamolls.com. Horseriding, from 30min to a whole day. Courses available.

SHOPPING

Carrer de l'Aigüeta – La Bisbal d'Empordà. Ceramics are a centuries-old tradition, and you'll find all sorts of objects in the shops on this street. Try El Risser.

Figueres★

Figueres, capital of Alt Empordà, the birthplace of Surrealist artist Salvador Dalí (1904–89), is one of Catalunya's premier destinations. Dalí spent his last years here, building his extravagant museum.

A BIT OF HISTORY

The end of the Spanish Civil War – The last meeting of the Republican Cortes was held here on 1 February 1939. Three days later, Girona fell to the Nationalists. Two days after, the Republican leaders crossed into France.

TEATRE-MUSEU DALÍ★★

Pl. de Dalí i Gala. Open Mar–June and Oct Tue–Sun 9.30am–5.15pm (last admission); Jul–Sept daily 9am–7.15pm; Nov–Feb Tue–Sun 10.30am–5.15pm. Closed 11, 18 & 25 Dec, 1 Jan. €14. ℘972 67 75 05. www.salvador-dali.org.

This theatre-museum, a world of folly and caprice, may charm or exasperate but never fails to impress. The artist himself said: "The museum cannot be considered as such; it is a gigantic surrealist object, where everything is coherent, where nothing has eluded my design." To a restored 1850 theatre Dalí added an immense glass dome (beneath which he is buried) and patio, and decorated everything with fantasy objects: giant eggs, bread rolls, basins and gilt dummies.

Note the vivid colours and fantasy objects on the circular **Torre Galatea★** He gave his eccentricity full rein not only in the exhibits – some of his canvases are exhibited as well as works by Pitxot and Duchamp – but in the squares around the museum where figures perch on columns of tyres, and on the outside of the building too.

CIUTAT VELLA
(OLD TOWN)

Figueres also has a pleasant historical centre with attractive squares and alleys. The Rambla is a pleasant street full of outdoor bars and restaurants.

▶ **Population:** 45 436
⊙ **Michelin Map:** 574 F 38 – map 122 Costa Brava. See local map under Costa Brava p359.
▪ **Info:** Plaça del Sol. ℘972 50 31 55. http://en.visitfigueres.cat.
◖ **Location:** Figueres is located 20km/12.4mi inland, at the heart of the area known as the Ampurdán, at the crossroads of routes leading to the Costa Brava and the French city of Perpignan, 58km/36mi N. ▭Figueres (AVE).
⊚ **Don't Miss:** Everything Dalí and a trip down memory lane to the Toy Museum.
⊙ **Timing:** Take a day.

Museu de Joguets★

Hotel París, Sant Pere 1. Open Jun-Jul & Sept Mon–Sat 10.30am–7pm, Sun and public holidays 10.30am–2.30pm; Oct–May Tue–Fri 10am–6.30pm, Sat 10am–7.30pm, Aug Mon–Sat 10.30am–8pm, Sun and public holidays 10.30am–2.30pm. Closed 25–26 Dec, 1 Jan, mid-Jan–mid-Feb. €7. ℘972 50 45 85. www.mjc.cat.

This fascinating museum displays all manner of toys and stuffed animals from different countries. Do check out, (and play on) its wonderful website before visiting.

Museu de l'Empordà

Rambla 2. Open Tue–Sat 11am–8pm (Nov–Apr 7pm), Sun & hols 11am–2pm. Closed 1 & 6 Jan and 25–26 Dec. €4; no charge with Museu Dalí ticket. ℘972 50 23 05. www.museuemporda.org.

This lively collection is devoted to the art, history and archaeology of the region. Of note is the exhibition of works by 19C and 20C painters (Nonell, Sorolla, Dalí and **Tàpies**).

Teatre-Museu Dalí, Figueres

© Turespaña

The World of Dalí

Born in 1904, Dalí was to become the world's most famous Surrealist artist. His "paranoid-critical" method, based on an ironic vision of reality, resulted in his expulsion from the Surrealist ranks by its founder, André Breton. In his most famous paintings (*The Great Masturbator, The Persistence of Memory, Atomic Leda...*) Dalí expresses his personal world through bland forms loaded with sensuality and sexual connotations.

Just round the corner from the stunning Teatre Museu in Figueres, is the much smaller, oft overlooked **Dalí Joies** (Jewels) museum, a collection of 37 extravagant jewels plus drawings and paintings that Salvador Dalí designed in his inimitable style (see website for times and prices: www.salvador-dali.org).

A short drive away are also the **Casa-Museu Salvador Dalí**, in the charming fishing village of **Portlligat★★** (see p362), and the **Casa-Museu Castell Gala Dalí** (GIRONA, p356) housed in the castle that Dalí gave to his wife, Gala.

EXCURSION

Castell de Sant Ferran★

Guided tours (2hr) daily Jul–mid-Sept and Holy Week 10am–8pm; late Oct–late Mar 10.30am–3pm; rest of year 10.30am–6pm. Closed 25 Dec, 1 Jan. €3. 972 50 60 94. www.castillosanfernando.org.

This mid-18C fortress, with star-shaped perimeter once defended the border with France; with a parade ground alone that covered 12 000sq m/14 340sq yds, it was the second largest of its kind in Europe. The **stables★** are worthy of particular note. The **views★** from the walls take in the Empordà plain.

ADDRESSES

STAY

Hotel Duràn – Lasauca 5. 972 50 12 50. www.hotelduran.com. 65 rooms, €11. Restaurant. Town centre hotel with large, comfy rooms. Dalí used to dine here.

Hotel Empordà – Avda. Salvador Dalí i Domènech. 972 500 562. www.hotelemporda.com. 42 rooms, €13. Restaurant. While the hotel is nice enough, the reason to come here is for the restaurant, El Motel. This was the birthplace of modern Catalan cuisine.

Mas Falgarona – Avinyonet de Puigventós. 5.4km/3.3mi SW of Figueres on the N 260. 972 54 66 28. www.masfalgarona.com. 11 rooms. Restaurant. This luxury hotel is housed in an old farmhouse. Minimalist décor and works of modern art grace the walls. Lovely garden with pool.

Mas Jonquer – Can Prat. 9.6km/6mi SW of Figueres on the N 260. 972 54 72 54. www.masjonquer.com. 8 rooms. This charming hotel feels more like a country house, complete with a cosy living room full of books, a tennis court, two outdoor pools and cycling and horseriding available. Rooms are simple but comfortable.

Solsona★★

Solsona is a tranquil town with a noble air and attractive squares. Elegant medieval residences line its gently sloping streets.

SIGHTS

Museu Diocesà i Comarcal★★ (Diocesan and Regional Museum)

Pl. del Palau 1. Open mid-Dec–mid-Mar Fri–Sat 11am–5pm, Sun & public holidays 10am–2pm; mid–Mar–mid-Dec Wed–Sat 11am–6.30pm (also open Tue Jul–Aug), Sun & public holidays 10am–2pm. Closed 1 & 6 Jan, 25–26 Dec. €4. ℘973 48 21 01. www.museusolsona.cat.

Romanesque and Gothic **paintings★★** in the Palau Episcopal (Episcopal Palace, an 18C Baroque building), are excellent examples of Catalan art.

The frescoes include a painting from the **Sant Quirze de Pedret church★★**, discovered beneath an overpainting. Executed in an archaic style, it shows God, with arms outstretched, in a circle which represents Heaven, surmounted by a phoenix symbolising immortality. Totally different are the thinly outlined 13C paintings from **Sant Pau de Caserres★** – in particular, wonderful **angels★★** of the Last Judgement.

Known for its **altar fronts**, another highlight of the museum is **La Cena de Santa Constanza★**, a realistic Last Supper, by Jaime Ferrer (15C). In the **Museu de la Sal** (Salt Museum), everything is carved out of rock salt from Cardona.

Catedral★

Pl. de la Catedral. Open Mon–Sat 9am–1pm, 4–8pm, Sun 9am–1pm, 4–6pm. No charge. ℘973 48 23 10.

Only the belfry and the apse remain of the Romanesque church; the rest is Gothic with Baroque additions such as the portals and the sumptuous 18C Capella de la Virgen (Lady Chapel). This chapel houses the **Mare de Déu del Claustro★**, a beautifully carved Romanesque figure of the Virgin Mary in black stone. After visiting the Cathedral, stroll around the rest of the old city, particu-

larly the Plaça Major, which is framed by medieval houses and porches, the Carrer del Castell (home of the 16C ajuntament), and the Plaça de Sant Joan.

EXCURSION

Cardona★

◗ 20km/12.4mi SE along the C 55, at the foot of an imposing castle.

Castillo de Cardona★

This spectacular hilltop fortress, at 589m/1 933ft, dates back to the 8C. Of the 11C buildings there remain only a truncated tower, the **Torre de la Minyona**, and the collegiate church, surrounded by Vauban-style walls and bulwarks built in the 17C and 18C. The castle is now a Parador, commanding a marvellous **view★** over the Parc Cultural de **Muntanya de Sal ★★** (open Tue–Fri 10am–3pm, descent to mine 11.30am and 1.30pm; Sat–Sun open 10am–6pm descent to mine every 30min; €11; ℘938 69 24 75; www.cardonaturisme.com), at the heart of which is a salt mine working since Roman times.

Colegiata de Sant Vicenç★★

Open Tue–Sun Oct–end May 10am–1pm, 3–5pm; Jun–Sept 10am–1pm, 3–7pm. Closed 1, 6 Jan, 25–26 Dec. €3; no charge Tue. ℘938 68 41 69.

The collegiate church built in 1040 has Lombard features. The groined vaulting in the **crypt★** rests on six graceful columns. The Gothic cloisters are 15C.

▶ **Population:** 9 004
⚬ **Michelin Map:** 574 G 3 – Catalunya (Lleida).
🛈 **Info:** Carretera Bassella 1. ℘973 48 23 10. www.turismesolsones.com.
◗ **Location:** The capital of the Solsonès region is on the C 1410 road linking Manresa with the C 1313 heading into the Pyrenees. 🚆Nearest station: Manresa (48km).
🕐 **Timing:** Avoid Mondays, when musuems are shut.

Pirineos Catalanes★★★

The Catalan Pyrenees form a barrier 230km/143mi long and 100km/62mi wide, stretching from the Vall d'Aran to the Mediterranean, with altitudes above 2500m/8202ft. These mountains are deeply cut by isolated valleys, with their own personality and traditions. All offer delicious regional cuisine and opportunities for skiing, hunting, fishing, mountain climbing and adventure sports. The area is great for driving around and the following tours can be followed on the map in this section.

ART AND ARCHITECTURE

The Pyrenean villages and valleys of Catalunya denote a unique Romanesque style of art and architecture. In the 11C, as the local population was fighting against the Arabs, small village churches were built and painted with entrancing murals graphically depicting Christian doctrine for a largely illiterate population. The movement reached its climax in the Vall de Boí (&see p376), which has been listed as a World Heritage Site by UNESCO.

🚗 DRIVING TOURS

1 VALL DE CAMPRODON

30km/18.6mi. Allow half a day.

Two large valleys lie in the Ripollès area under mountains towering to 3 000m/ 10 000ft.

Camprodon★

Camprodon is at the confluence of the Ritort and Ter rivers, crossed by a 12C humpbacked bridge, **Pont Nou★**. The community developed around the **Monesteri de Sant Pere**. Only the 12C **Romanesque church★** remains. The cloisters of **Monasterio de Sant**

- 🍴 **Michelin Map:** 574 D 32, E 32–37 and F 32–37 – Catalunya (Girona, Lleida)
- 🅸 **Info:** Camprodon: Sant Roc 22; ℘972 74 00 10; www.vallde camprodon.org.Puigcerdà: Pl. Santa Maria; ℘972 88 05 42; www.puigcerda.cat. La Seu d'Urgell: Calle Mayor 8; ℘973 35 15 11. www. turismeseu.com. Tremp: Passeig del Vall; ℘973 65 34 70; www.ajuntamentdetremp.cat. Vielha: Avda. Libertat 16; ℘973 64 06 88; www.visitvaldaran.com.
- ▶ **Location:** The Pyrenees extend almost unbroken for 230km/143mi from the Mediterranean to the high Aran Valley (2 500m/8 202ft). The last range, the Montes Alberes, plunges into the Mediterranean from 700m/ 2 297ft. 🚂Nearest major station: Lleida Pirineus (AVE Barcelona-Madrid line).
- 🕐 **Timing:** Geography will oblige you to select one or two valleys to explore from the south access.

Pere de Camprodon★ (Pl. de Santa Maria; no charge) are simple and elegant, with sweeping arches and slender columns with capitals decorated with plant motifs. The **museum** houses a collection of embroidered fabric. Opposite the church on the square stands the 14C former Abbatial Palace. The **medieval bridge★** spans the Ter river on the way towards Ripoll.

▶ Leave N via the C 38 and after 3.5km/2mi take the winding Carretera Camprodón-Baget mountain road.

Beget★★

This attractive mountain village with stone houses enjoys a pleasant **setting★** deep in a peaceful valley.

The **San Cristófol church★★** (10C–12C) with Lombard arcatures and slender lantern-tower, houses the **Majestad de Beget★**, a magnificent figure of Christ carved in the 12C (open daily 9am–7pm; ask for the keys from Joan Coma, Carrer Bellaire; €1; ℘972 74 01 36).

▶ Continue on the Carretera Camprodon-Baget before taking the C 38 to Molló.

Molló

The 12C Romanesque church has a lovely Catalan belfry. Further along the C 38 and at 1 513m/5 000ft, the Col d'Ares marks the Spanish-French border.

2 VALL DE RIBES

22km/13.6mi from Ripoll to Vall de Núria. Allow a couple of hours.

The Vall de Ribes is popular with Barceloneses as an easily-reached skiing and hiking spot, particularly the Vall de Núria.

Ripoll★

℘972 71 41 42. www.ripoll.cat.
Nestled in a valley deep in the first Pyrenean cliffs, this small industrial city and commercial centre is considered the "cradle of Catalonia. " It derives its fame from the great Benedictine monastery of Santa Maria, founded in the 9C by Count Wilfred the Hairy, which, until the 12C, served as a necropolis for the Counts of Barcelona, Besalú, Girona, Ausona and Cerdanya. Ripollès's capital is also a former small core at the confluence of two rivers and a few modernist houses (Can Codina, Can Dou and Casa Bonada).

Monasterio de Santa Maria★

Pl. de l'Abat Oliba. Open daily Oct–Mar 10am–1.30pm, 3.30–6pm; Apr–Sept 10am–2pm, 4–7pm; Sun 10am–2pm year round. €5.50. ℘972 70 42 03.
www.monestirderipoll.cat.
All that remains of the original monastery are the church portal and the cloisters. In 1032, Abbot Oliba consecrated

Portada, Monasterio de Santa Maria

© Luis Castañeda/age fotostock

an enlarged **church★**, a jewel of early Romanesque art that was damaged over the years. It was rebuilt at the end of the 19C to the original plan.
The **portada★★★**, or portal design, is composed of a series of horizontal registers illustrating the glory of God victorious over His enemies (Passage of the Red Sea). The **Claustro★** (cloisters) abutting the church dates to the 12C; others were added in the 14C.

Museu Etnografic

Opposite the monastery. Open Tue–Sat 10am–1.30pm, 4–6pm (Jul–Aug & Semana Santa 7pm). Sun & hols 10am–2pm. €4, no charge last Sun of the month. ℘972 70 31 44.
www.museuderipoll.org.
The Ethnographic Museum traces the history of the area. Inaugurated in 1920, it contains more than 5 000 pieces: from clothing and ceramics to rooms devoted to the iron industry, showing ancient forges and firearms from the 16 to 19C.

▶ Take the C 26 NW.

Monasterio de Sant Joan de les Abadesses★★

Open Mon–Sat & hols: Mar–Apr and Oct 10am–2pm, 4–6pm; May–June and Sept 10am–2pm, 4–7pm; Jul–Aug 10am–7pm; Nov–Feb Mon–Fri 10am–2pm; Sat & hols 10am–2pm 4–6pm. €3. ℘972 72 23 53.
www.monestirsantjoanabadesses.cat.
The monastery was founded in the 9C under the rule of a Benedictine abbess, though it soon shut out women.

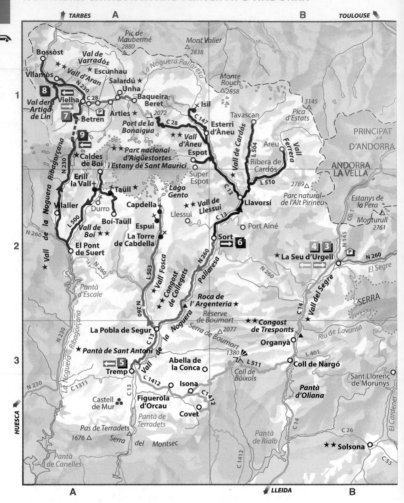

With its arches and columns with carved capitals the church recalls those of southwest France. A magnificent 1251 **Descent from the Cross**★★ in polychrome wood is in the central apse. In 1426 an unbroken host was discovered on the Christ figure's head; it is venerated to this day.

◐ Head N along the N 152 for 17km/10.5mi.

Ribes de Freser

www.vallderibes.cat.
This famous spa stands at the confluence of three rivers and is known for the healing properties of its waters. A rack railway runs to the Vall de Núria.

◐ Continue 7km/4.3mi on N 152 to the Vall de Núria, passing scenic Queralbs and its **rack railway** 🚠🚡.

Vall de Núria★

The valley is surrounded by a rocky amphitheatre stretching from Puigmal to the Sierra de Torreneules. The Virgin of Núria, the patron saint of Pyrenean shepherds, is venerated in a sanctuary in the upper part of the valley.

③ LA CERDANYA★★

145km/90mi from La Seu d'Urgell to La Molina. Allow about 5hr. 🚂Nearest station: Puigcerda (25km).

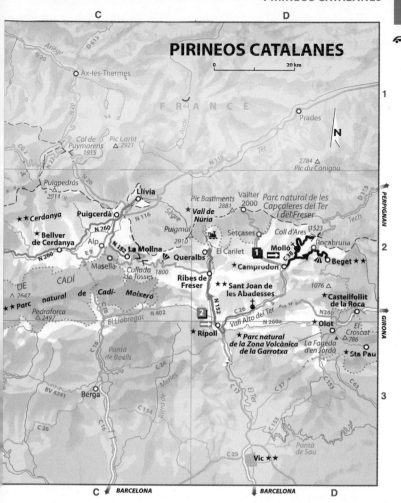

PIRINEOS CATALANES

La Seu d'Urgell – Past and Present

Relics from Bronze-age settlements have been discovered at the nearby mount of Castellciutat, but Romans preferred to settle on the plain at the confluence of the Segre and Valira rivers. In the 5C, the bishops of Urgell established their Episcopal (or Seu), making way for expansion of the city. Thus, La Seu d'Urgell became the capital of this region, which by the 10C was the most powerful in Catalunya.

Today, this lively township – gateway to Andorra, capital of the Alt Urgell region and unofficial capital of the Catalan Pyrenees – has important agriculture, livestock and tourism industries, as well as a significant industrial sector. Its dairy products, particularly cheese, are renowned and protected by their own DOC (designation of origin label).

Due to an historical twist of fate, the Bishop of Urgell (along with the President of France) is bestowed with the title of Co-Prince of Andorra.

The fertile Cerdanya Basin, watered by the River Segre, was formed by subsidence. The northern section, La Cerdagne, was ceded to France under the Treaty of the Pyrenees in 1659. The **Túnel del Cadí**, opened in 1984, facilitates access from Manresa.

From Ribes de Freser to Puigcerdà, the road cut into the cliff face up to the Collado de Toses commands impressive **views**★ of the Segre and its slopes.

▷ 66 km/41mi W on the N 116 then N 152, passing Pugicerdá.

La Seu d'Urgell/Seo de Urgell★

This city of prince-archbishops stands where the Valira, which rises in Andorra, joins the Segre river.

Catedral de Santa Maria★★

Santa Maria. Open Mon–Sat 10am–1.30pm, 4–6pm (Jul–Aug 7pm), Sun and public holidays 10am–1.30pm. €3 (inc. museum). ℘973 35 32 42.

The cathedral, started in the 12C, shows strong Lombard influence. The central section of the west face, crowned by a small campanile, is typically Italian. Inside, the nave rises on cruciform pillars, surrounded in French style by engaged columns.

The **cloisters**★ are 13C; the east gallery was rebuilt in 1603 and features granite capitals illustrating humans and animals carved by masons from the Roussillon. The Santa Maria door (southeast corner) opens into the 11C **Església de Sant Miquel**★, the only remaining building of those constructed by St Ermangol. The cathedral houses the **Museu Diocesano**★, which has works of art dating from the 10C to the 18C. The most precious is a beautifully illuminated 11C **Beatus**★★, one of the best-preserved copies of St John's Commentary on the Apocalypse written in the 8C by the priest Beatus of Liébana.

Of note also is an interesting **papyrus**★ belonging to Pope Sylvester II. The crypt contains the 18C funerary urn of St Ermangol.

▷ Follow the N 260 W for 31km/19mi.

Bellver de Cerdanya★

Poised on a rocky crag dominating the Vall del Segre, Bellver de Cerdanya has a fine main square with beautiful balconied stone houses and wooden porches.

▷ 18km/11mi NW on the N 260.

Puigcerdà

The capital of Cerdanya, which developed on a terrace overlooking the River Segre, is one of the most popular holiday resorts of the Pyrenees, with old-fashioned shops, ancient streets and balconied buildings.

▷ Follow signs to Llívia on the D 68.

Llívia

This 12sq km/5sq mi Spanish enclave is in France, 6km/3.7mi from Puigcerdà. Under the Treaty of the Pyrenees, France was granted the Roussillon area plus 33 villages from Cerdanya. Llívia was classed a town, so it remained Spanish. Llívia features Europe's oldest chemist shop, the **Farmacia de Llívia** (mid-Jun–mid-Sept Tue–Fri 10am–8pm, mid-Sept–mid-Jun until 6pm, Sat until 8pm year round, Sun until 2pm year round; €3.50; ℘972 89 63 13; www.llivia.org), which now houses the Museu Municipal.

▷ Ca. Barcelona-Puigcerdà N 152 SE.

La Molina

www.lamolina.cat.

This is one of Catalunya's most important ski resorts. The village of Alp is popular in winter and in summer.

▷ From here it is possible to continue your visit on the E 9 to the Parc Naturel del Cadí-Moixeró.

Parc Natural del Cadí-Moixeró

Information Centres in Talló near Bellver de Cerdanya, ℘973 51 08 02 and Bagà (approx. 20 km/12.5mi N of Berga), Centro del Parque ℘93 824 41 51. www.parcsnaturals.gencat.cat/es/cadi
The 41,342 ha park is located between the Cadí and Moixeró mountain ranges, which form an imposing 30km/18.6mi-

Parc Natural del Cadí-Moixeró

long barrier of altitudes of between 900m/2 952ft and 2 647m/8 684ft. Vertical cliffs enclose the deep valleys and canyons and the vegetation is exceptional; low temperatures and high humidity favour the proliferation of unusual Mediterranean flora. More than 400km/248.5mi of trails for all levels wind throughout the park.

4 VALL DEL SEGRE★

73km/45mi. Allow 3hr.

The River Segre forms a huge basin where it flows into the Valira.

Congost de Tresponts★★
The Segre winds through dark rocks (*puzolana*) and pastures. Downstream, the limestone of Ares and Montsec de Tost offers a typically Pyrenean landscape dropping to a cultivated basin, where the river disappears.

Organyà
This picturesque village has a small medieval centre, with the old streets lined with arcades, porches and Gothic mansions. Organyà is renowned for the **Homilies**, the oldest text written in Catalan, from the late 12C.

Pantà d'Oliana★
The dam is surrounded by grey rocks with lively waterfalls in spring. From the road the sight is quite spectacular.

◗ 6km/3.7mi S on the C 14.

Coll de Nargó
http://collnargo.ddl.net.
This hamlet has one of the most splendid Romanesque churches in Catalunya, dating back to the 11C: **Sant Climent★** has a single nave and a pretty apse adorned with Lombard bands. Its sober **bell tower★** is pre-Romanesque.

Collado de Bòixols Road★★
Between the Coll de Nargó and Tremp, the L 511 follows canyons on slopes clad in pine and holm oak, or barren hillsides. Further on, the road proceeds up the slope, under yellow and pink crests, offering lovely **landscapes**, especially from the Collado de Bòixols. Then the road enters a wide U-shaped valley, where terraced cultivation extends to the foot of the glacial ridge of Bòixols, to which cling the church and nearby houses. The road descends the valley until it eventually merges into the Conca de Tremp.

Abella de la Conca
This tiny, don't-blink-or-you'll miss-it-village is tucked behind the rocky Sarsús summit. Do not miss the Romanesque church of Sant Esteve (11C).

◗ Head back to the L 511 and continue to Isona.

Isona
This ancient Roman city was founded around 100 BC. Isona hosts an interesting museum, mainly devoted to Roman times and palaeontological sites in the area where the remains of dinosaurs

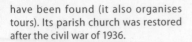

have been found (it also organises tours). Its parish church was restored after the civil war of 1936.

▷ Head out of Isona via the C 1412 in the direction of Lleida and turn right for Covet.

Covet

Covet's Esglesia de Santa Maria boasts a beautiful interior. The vaulted nave, is reinforced by supporting arches and columns topped with carved capitals yet the **doorway★★** is the most remarkable. It features a beautiful carved tympanum and skillfully sculptured arch-based columns. Notice the figurines of angels, musicians, beasts, the characters of the Holy Family and scenes from the book of Genesis.

▷ Continue on the C 1412 towards Tremp.

Figuerola d'Orcau

This small medieval town has interesting streets lined with arcaded houses.

▷ Continue to Tremp.

⑤ VALL DEL NOGUERA PALLARESA

143km/89mi. Allow 1 day, from Tremp to Llavorsí.

Pallars is in the uppermost region of the Catalan Pyrenees. The highest summit is Pica d'Estats (3 145m/10 318ft). To the north is **Pallars Sobirà**, at the heart of the Pyrenees; to the south, **Pallars Jussà** incorporates the vast pre-Pyrenean zone formed by Conca de Tremp. The road follows the bed of the Noguera Pallaresa, and after La Pobla de Segur, cuts across a limestone landscape of remarkable uniformity.

Tremp

In the centre of the Conca de Tremp – a huge basin with lush crops – the village retains its old quarter and three towers from its walls. The **Església de Santa María★** houses an astonishing 2m/6.5ft

high Gothic statue in polychrome wood: **Santa Maria de Valldeflors★** (14C). The municipality has a reservoir, the **pantano de Sant Antoni★ ♣♣**, an ideal spot to fish, canoe/kayak, windsurf, sail and water ski.

▷ 13km/8mi N on the C 13.

La Pobla de Segur

☎973 68 00 38. www.pobladesegur.cat. This popular resort is the only means of access to the Valle de Arán, Alta Ribagorça and Pallars Sobirà.

▷ The C 147 follows the course of the river and along the lake of Sant Antoni.

Vall Fosca★

Hemmed in by peaks, this valley is dotted with delightful hamlets, including **Torre de Capdella** (www.torredecapdella.org), **Espui** and **Capdella**, each with its Romanesque church. In the upper valley, in a large lake area, the main attraction is **Lago Gento**.

▷ Return to La Pobla de Segur and proceed upwards along the N 260.

Congost de Collegats★★

Eroded by torrents, the red, grey and ochre limestone rocks take on the appearance of spectacular cliffs. Note the **Roca de l'Argenteria★**, stalactite-shaped rocks near the Gerri de la Sal.

Sort

www.sortturisme.com. The resort is famous throughout Europe because of its wild waters and kayaking and rafting events held on the Noguera Pallaresa. Sort means "luck" in Catalan and is consequently a favourite place to buy lottery tickets; perhaps not surprisingly it has won big prizes many times.

▷ At Rialp, bear left towards Lessui.

Vall de Llessui★★

The road winds way up to the northwest, through a steep granite landscape featuring numerous ravines.

Take the C 13 N to Llavorsí.

6 UPPER VALLEY OF THE NOGUERA PALLARESA★

105km/65mi. Allow half a day, from Llavorsí to Port de la Bonaigua.

On this drive through three valleys, mountains dominate a wild landscape.

Llavorsí
http://llavorsi.ddl.net.
This peaceful village sits at the confluence of the Aneu, Cardós and Ferrera basins.

Take the L 504 then turn right on to the L 510 in a NF direction.

Vall Ferrera
http://vallferrera.com.
The easternmost and closest of the three valleys is wedged between high mountains including the Pica d'Estats (3 145m/10 318ft), the highest mountain in Catalunya. From here, some beautiful hikes can be taken to Andorra.

Rejoin the L 504 and continue N.

Vall de Cardós★
http://vallcardos.ddl.net.
The Noguera de Cardós River forms the axis of this valley which is studded with over 20 pretty hamlets.

Return to Llavorsí and take the C 13 towards Baqueira.

Vall d'Aneu★★
www.vallsdaneu.org.
Below the road is the valley of Espot, a picturesque village beside a mountain stream, gateway to the Pallars section of a national park★★ (*see PARC NACIONAL D'AIGÜESTORTES I ESTANY DE SANT MAURICI, p380*). Beyond Esterri d'Aneu the road crosses a breathtaking landscape, dotted with Romanesque churches such as the Església de Sant Joan d'Isil★, glimpsed between summits, and twists up to Port de la Bonaigua (2 072m/6 799ft), circled by many peaks.

Esterri d'Àneu
The Ecomuseu Àneu Valls, situated inside an 18C homestead, explains the traditional lifestyles of the region. (open daily; ℘973 626 436; www.ecomuseu.com). After Esterri Àneu, the road rises to an imposing landscape where Romanesque churches are hidden among the peaks.

7 LA VALL D'ARAN★★

45km/28mi. Allow half a day, from Vielha to Baqueira Beret.

The Aran Valley, in the northwest tip of the Catalan Pyrenees, occupies the upper valley of the Garonne river. Its isolation has helped it to preserve its local traditions and language (*aranés* is a variation of the *langue d'oc* of southern France). The Vielha Tunnel ended the valley's seclusion in 1948. In recent years the region has seen the creation of several ski resorts.

Vielha
At an altitude of 971m/3 186ft, the capital of the Arán Valley is a holiday resort. Don't miss the 16C and 17C homes in the old town as well as the Església Parroquial de Sant Miquèu★ with its 14C octagonal tower and 13C Gothic doorway. Inside lies the Cristo de Mijaran★, a fragment dating from a 12C Descent from the Cross.

Musèu dera Val d'Aran
Major, 28. Open Tue–Sat 10am–1pm, 5–8pm, Sun & hols 10am–1pm. €3. ℘973 641 815. www.cultura.conselharan.org.
Housed in an elegant 16C manor house, this museum introduces visitors to the geology, glaciology, history and the peculiar local language.

Leave Vielha to the E on the C 28.

Betren
The Església de San Esteve★, built during the transition from Romanesque to Gothic, boasts archivolts on the portal★★, decorated with human faces,

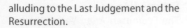

alluding to the Last Judgement and the Resurrection.

▶ Continue along the C 28 1.3km/1mi to Escunha.

Escunhau
The **Església de San Pedro★** has a fine 12C **portal★★** bearing an expressive Christ and unusual capitals decorated with human faces.

▶ Continue along the C 28 3km/2mi to Arties.

Arties★
The Romanesque church here has an apse decorated with scenes illustrating the Last Judgement, Heaven and Hell.

▶ Continue on C 28 3km/2mi.

Salardú★
℘973 64 51 97. www.visitvaldaran.com. Salardú is a charming village with granite-and-slate houses gathered around the **Església de Sant Andreu★** (12C–13C), whose interior contains some interesting 16C **Gothic paintings★★** and a fine 12C **Christ in Majesty★★**, a stylised 65cm/25in wooden statue of remarkable anatomical precision. Note the slender octagonal belfry (15C).

▶ Head north for 1.5km/1mi.

Unha
This tiny hamlet is home to the 12C Romanesque church of Santa Eulàlia. Inside there are vestiges of Romanesque paintings. In the village itself, the fortified, late 16C residence Çò de Brastet, features Renaissance windows and doors.

▶ Return to the C 28 and follow the road W for 9km/5mi.

Baqueira Beret
℘973 63 90 25. www.baqueira.es. This ski resort, rising from 1 500m/4 900ft to 2 510m/8 230ft, offers excellent lodging and services.

⑧ VIELHA TO BOSSÒST
52km/32mi. Allow half a day.

Vall de Varrados
The most famous natural site in this valley is the Sauth deth Pish waterfall, which descends through a gorge.

▶ From Vielha, take the N230 12km/7.5mi NW.

Vilamòs
This ancient village, suspended on a natural platform 400m/1 300ft above the valley, has retained its traditional architecture and affords magnificent, unobstructed views. At the far end, a home has been restored, illustrating traditional Aranese life. (Çò de Joanchiquet; open mid-Jun–mid-Sept daily 11am–2pm, 5–8pm, mid-Sept–mid-Jun Tue–Sun 11am–2pm, 4–7pm; ℘973 64 01 10; www.visitvaldaran.com).

▶ On the N 230, head for Bossòst.

Vall de la Artiga de Lin
The Joeu River crosses this valley, which is resplendent with magnificent pine and beech trees.

Bossòst
The **Església de la Purificació de Maria★★** is the area's best example of Romanesque architecture (12C). Its three naves are separated by sturdy columns. Its three apses are adorned with Lombard bands and the pretty, colourful north **doorway** features archaic relief work in its tympanum, depicting the Creator surrounded by the Sun, the Moon and symbols of the Evangelists.

⑨ LA VALL DE BOI★★ AND LA VALL DE LA NOGUERA RIBAGOCANA
58km/36mi. Allow half a day, from Caldes de Boí to Vielha.

Watered by the Noguera de Tor and the Sant Nicolau rivers, this valley is renowned for its cluster of Lombard

Romanesque churches (11C–12C); they are the finest in the Pyrenees and collectively form a UNESCO World Heritage Site. With their slate roofs and irregular masonry, they stand out for their pure, sober lines and for the fine wall frescoes (several reproductions remain) now in the **Museu d'Art de Catalunya** (&see *BARCELONA, p343*).

Note the distinctive high silhouette of the belfries, separate but resting against the nave, and ornamentation of Lombard bands.

Caldes de Boí★

&973 69 62 10.
www.caldesdeboi.com.
At an altitude of 1 550m/5 084ft, Caldes de Boí is a thermal spa with 37 springs at temperatures between 240ºC and 560ºC (750ºF to 1330ºF). Nearby is the ski resort of **Boí-Taüll**.

Taüll★

Taüll is famous for the frescoes of its two early 12C churches. Considered to be masterpieces of Romanesque art, they are exhibited in Barcelona's Museu d'Art de Catalunya.

The village of labyrinthine streets, stone houses and wooden balconies clusters around the **Església de Santa Maria★** (open daily 10am–7pm, Jul-Aug until 8pm; &973 69 40 00) a Romanesque church with three naves separated by cylindrical pillars.

Just outside the village is the **Església de Sant Climent★★** (open daily 10am–2pm, 4–7pm; €1.50; &973 69 40 00) with its slender six-storey belfry. A replica of the famous Pantocrator of Taüll is in the apse.

▶ Return to the L 500.

Erill la Vall

As well as the beautiful Romanesque church of Santa Eulália, the village has an information centre on Romanesque art, the **Centre del Romànic**.

Vall D'Erill to the Pont de Suert

Continuing on the L 500, your discovery of Romanesque heritage continues with visits to the churches of Sant Felíu de Berruera, and La Nativitat in Durro (2km/1.2mi on the left). Shortly after the pretty village of Castelló de Tor marks the entrance of the Vall de Boí.

▶ Take the N 230 on the left to El Pont de Suert.

El Pont de Suert

This area, dotted with attractive hamlets – **Castelló de Tor, Casòs, Malpàs** – retains its rusticity and charm.

▶ Take the N 230 9km/6mi N to Vilaller.

Vilaller

Perched on a rocky outcrop, the village has retained the steep and narrow streets of his ancient heart. In medieval times, the village was surrounded by walls and some remains are still visible.

▶ Continue on the N 230 and take the the tunnel to Vielha.

ADDRESSES

🏠 STAY

🍴🍴 **Casa Rural La Vall del Cadí** – Ctra Cerc-Tuixent, 1km/.06mi from La Seu d'Urgell, near the Parc Olímpic. &973 350 390. www.valldelcadi.com. ▣ 7 rooms, ⚏€7.50. This period building has beautifully renovated rustic rooms featuring wood with wrought-iron and stone elements.

🍴🍴 **Hostal del Ripollès** – Pl. Nova 11, Ripoll. &972 700 215. www.hostal delripolles.com. 8 rooms ⚏. Clean rooms with a pleasant restaurant on the ground floor with an outdoor terrace serving Italian and Catalan dishes.

🍴🍴 **Hotel Vall d'Àssua** – Altron in the Vall de la Noguera Pallaresa, 4km/2.5mi NE of Sort. &973 621 738. www.hostal valldassua.com. ▣ 9 rooms ⚏. This small good value hotel has comfortable en suite rooms. The restaurant's specialty is chargrilled meat.

⊖🍽 **Mas la Casanova** – Ctra de Ribes de Freser, 3km/1.87mi from the Queralbs in the Vall de Ribes. 📞972 198 077. www.maslacasanova.es. 6 rooms, 🛏 €6.50. Pretty little stone cottages set around a homestead in the heart of the Vall de Ribes. It provides home-cooked meals on request and a warm welcome

⊖🍽 **Hotel Estel** – Sant Fruitós 39, Berga. 📞938 213 463. www.hotelestel.com. 🅿. 37 rooms. This friendly hotel in one of the main avenues into the city is modern and comfortable.

⊖🍽 **Hotel Segle XX** – Pl. de la Creu 8, Tremp. 📞973 650 000. www.hotelseglexx.info. 🏊 48 rooms. Restaurant ⊖🍽. Founded in 1880, this hotel has comfortable rooms that have been renovated over the years. Its classic restaurant has a warm, slightly old-fashioned atmosphere.

⊖🍽 **Hotel Vall de Núria** – Vall de Núriaski resort, Queralbs. 📞972 732 020. www.valldenuria.cat/en/summer/bookings/accomodation/hotel-vall-de-nuria/. 75 rooms. This hotel has a wonderful natural setting, attentive service and a good restaurant serving local dishes. Min. stay of two nights.

⊖🍽 **Edelweiss** – Ctra de Sant Joan 28, Camprodon. 📞 972 740 614. www.hoteledelweiss.cat/en. 🅿. 21 rooms. Classic hotel with very nice common areas and comfortable rooms.

⊖🍽 **Hotel Fonda Biayna** – Sant Roc 11, Bellver de Cerdanya. 📞973 510 475. www.fondabiayna.com. Closed 25 Dec. 16 rooms 🛏. Restaurant⊖🍽. The comfortable rooms in this traditional late 19C stone house have retained their original features, including tiny bathrooms.

⊖🍽 **Hotel Calitxó** – Passatge El Serrat, Molló. 📞972 740 386. www.hotelcalitxo.com. 🅿. 25 rooms 🛏. Restaurant ⊖🍽. An elegant Swiss-chalet style building surrounded by gardens and meadows. Functional rooms with all round comfort. Ideal for mountain and sports enthusiasts.

⊖🍽 **Hotel La Coma** – Setcases, 10km/6mi N of Comprodon. 📞972 136 074. www.hotellacoma.com. 🅿 🎿 22 rooms 🛏. Restaurant ⊖🍽. This high mountain hotel, popular with skiers, is situated in an old stone building.

Facilities include a welcoming rustic-style restaurant.

⊖🍽 **Hotel del Lago** – Av. Dr. Piguillem 7, Puigcerdà, Cerdanya. 📞972 881 000. www.hotellago.com. 🅿 30 rooms, 🛏 €11. This small family hotel with garden, spa and wellness facilities, near the lake, is surrounded by a large landscaped area with a pool. Classically styled bedrooms.

⊖🍽 **Hotel Can Boix** – on the outskirts of Peramola, 17km/10.5mi SW of Coll de Nargó in the Vall del Segre. 📞973 470 266. www.canboix.cat. Closed mid-Jan–mid-Feb and 2 weeks in Nov. 🅿🏊♿ 41 rooms, 🛏 €12.40. Restaurant ⊖🍽. Nestled in the mountains, attention to detail is evident throughout this hotel. The rooms combine the warmth of wood with soft-toned furnishings and more modern touches, especially in bathrooms.

⊖🍽 Hotel **Catalunya Park** – Pg. Mauri 9, Ribes de Freser. 📞972 727 198. www.catalunyaparkhotels.com. Open Easter and Jul–Sept. 45 rooms, 🛏€6. Restaurant ⊖. This hotel in the mountains is comfortable without being luxurious, and the pool is a wonderful asset. Good base for exploring the beautiful sites nearby and the Vall de Núria.

⊖🍽 **Parador de La Seu d'Urgell** – Sant Domènec 6, La Seu d'Urgell. 📞902 54 79 79. www.parador.es. 🅿🏊 79 rooms, 🛏 €15. Restaurant ⊖🍽. Set around a former Renaissance cloister, this hotel offers modern amenities and minimalist design. The restaurant serves traditional regional dishes of varying quality.

⊖🍽 **Riberies** – Camí de Riberies, Llavorsí. 📞973 622 051. www.riberies.com. 🏊🅿. 34 rooms 🛏. Restaurant ⊖🍽. This pleasant, relaxing hotel offers both contemporary rooms and a more traditional feel in the attic rooms. The restaurant has some daring dishes on the menu.

⊖🍽 **Parador de Vielha** – 2.5km/1.5mi S of Vielfa on the N 230. 📞902 54 79 79. www.parador.es. 🅿🏊 118 rooms, 🛏 €17. Restaurant ⊖🍽. Great views over the valley, especially from the circular living area. Spacious rooms with outstanding comfort.

⚲/ EAT

🍴 **In** Puigcerdà, typical dishes include tiró amb naps (goose with turnips) and rabbit cooked with the famous pears of the region.

🍷🍽 **Boixetes de Cal Manel** – on Ctra N 230 at Pont d'Arròs. ✆973 641 168. Closed May, Nov and Mon. In a traditional homestead located just outside the village, this restaurant specialises in local cuisine.

🍷🍽 **Restaurant Dachs** – on Ctra de Ripoll at Berga (C 26), 7.5km/4.5mi SW of Ripoll. ✆972 714 425. 🍴 Thu–Sun for lunch; Fri–Sat for dinner; daily in Aug. Excellent cuisine based on regional products. Specialities include meats grilled over a wood fire.

🍷🍽 **Can Jan Restaurant** – Sant Roc 9, Camprodon. ✆972 130 107. Closed first two weeks Nov. A cheerful and friendly atmosphere reigns in this central restaurant decorated with wooden furniture painted in different colours and featuring the work of local artists. It serves typical dishes from the valley.

🍷🍽 **Cal Teo** – Av. Pau Claris 38, La Seu d'Urgell. ✆973 36 05 35. Closed Sun–Thu eve. Small, personable restaurant in the heart of La Seu, which offers rustic specialities including grilled meats. Good recent reviews.

🍷🍽 **Llacs de Cardós** – Vall de Cardós on Ctra Tavascan, Tavascan in the Vall de l'Alt. ✆973 623 178. www.hotelllacsdecardos. com. This rustic mountain hotel restaurant serves hearty local fare; trout is a specialty. Comfortable rooms. (🍷🍽).

🍷🍽 **Miscela** – Av. Pau Claris 24, La Seu d'Urgell. ✆973 354 620. www.avenhotel. com. This brightly decorated modern restaurant serves traditional dishes as well as pizzas, salads, pasta and a cheap daily lunch menu.

🍷🍽 **Mikado** – Carrer Pere III 3, Berga. ✆938 212 106. The friendly staff and relaxed atmosphere at Mikado make it an easy lunch choice. Local ingredients are given imaginative flourishes and a very reasonable daily menu (€16,50) will satisfy the heartiest appetite.

🍷🍽 **Dolcet** – Zulueta 1, Alàs i Cerc, 7km/6mi E of La Seu d'Urgell. ✆973 361 349. Closed Fri, Nov and 15 days in Jun–Jul. In the centre of the village, this family-run restaurant serves traditional Catalan cuisine based on market products. Its

strategic location on the road to Cadí-Moixeró natural park makes it a popular destination, but absolutely worth the wait.

🍷🍽 **La Taverna dels Nogueres** – El Pont de Bar, 15km/9mi E of La Seu on the N 260. ✆973 384 020. http:// tavernadelsnoguers.com. Friendly, rustic place with a fireplace, wooden-beamed ceilings and red-checkered tablecloths. Great value home cooking.

🍷🍽 **La Fonda Xesc** – Pl. Roser 1, Gombrèn, 12.5km/7.5mi NW of Ripoll via the N 152 (towards Puigcerdà) then left on the GI 401. ✆972 730 404. www. fondaxesc.com. Closed Sun eve, Mon, Tue eve, Wed eve, 15 days in Jan and 10 days in Jul. Restaurant with a spacious vaulted dining room where you can enjoy creative Michelin-starred Catalan cuisine. Comfortable rooms available (🍷🍽).

🍷🍽 **Casa Irene** – Major 4, Arties, in the Vall de l'Alt. ✆973 644 364. www. hotelcasairene.com. Gourmet restaurant in a beautiful rustic hotel (🍷🍽) in the valley serving local specialities with a smile.

🍷🍽 **Fogony** – Av. Generalitat 45, Sort. ✆973 621 225. www.fogony.com. Closed Sun eve, Mon and 2 weeks in Jan. Innovative Catalan dishes that will delight and surprise you; try their "Slow Food 0km" menu (🍷🍽). Excellent service.

SPORT AND RECREATION

Hiking and skiing are the most popular sports in the Pirineos Catalanes. The region has numerous ski resorts, some with large hotels. The best known include: **HG Molina** (✆972 89 29 75; www.hghoteles.com), in La Molina in Girona province; and the **Melia Royal Tanau Boutique** (✆973 64 44 46; www.melia.com/RoyalTanau) in the resort of **Baquelra-Beret**, in the Val d'Aran (Lleida), which is popular with the Spanish royal family. The website www.onthesnow.co.uk provides a useful overview.

Parc Nacional d'Aigüestortes i Estany de Sant tall★★

This national park in the Catalan Pyrenees abounds in falls and rushing streams. Twisting waterways – *aigües tortes* – wind between mossy meadows and wooded slopes. Glaciers created the harsh beauty of U-shaped valleys, high mountain lakes and snow-covered peaks. Vegetation includes firs and Scots pines. Birch and beech trees provide a stunning splash of colour in autumn.

⌚ **Michelin Map:** 574 E 32–33. Local map, see PIRINEOS CATALANES map, p376–377 – Catalunya (Lleida)

ℹ **Info:** Casa del Parque de Boí: Graieres 2. ✆973 69 61 89; Casa del Parque de Espot: Sant Maurici 5. ✆973 62 40 36. www.gencat.cat/parcs/aiguestortes.

▶ **Location:** The park is just west of Andorra and south of France. 🚃Nearest station La Poble de Segur (70km).

👁 **Don't Miss:** A forest walk up to grand panoramas.

🕐 **Timing:** Allow a day for the park, with hikes.

SIGHTS

The park's 14 119ha/34 888 acres, between altitudes of 1 500m/4 921ft and 3 000m/9 842.5ft, are mainly granite and slate, formed in the Paleozoic era when they emerged from the depths of the sea, drawing steep cliffs and deep valleys. Cows graze in the meadows and the grouse and partridge inhabit the woods. Wild deer inhabit the higher, less accessible peaks. Both entries, Espot, to the east, and Boí, to the west, have parking areas (driving private vehicles in the park is prohibited). Paths are well signposted.

🚌Head first for the **Casa del Parc del Boí** or the **Casa del Parc del Espot** (both open year-round daily 9am–2pm, 3.30–5.45 pm, except Sun pm; closed 1 & 6 Jan, 25–26 Dec).

Lago de Sant Maurici (reached by a tarmac road from Espot) is the most accesble and therefore most visited of the 24 lakes in the park. It is surrounded by forest and reflects the peaks of the Sierra dels Encantats.

Hikes

Portarró d'Espot – 🚶 3hr there and back on foot from the Estany de Sant Maurici. The path crosses the Sant Nicolau Valley. At Redó lake, admire the splendid **panoramas★★**.

Estany Gran d' Amitges – 🚶 3hr there and back on foot from Sant Maurici lake. Beside the lake, mountain streams form impressive waterfalls. The snow-capped Bassiero (2 887m/9 472 ft) and peak Saboredo (2 814m/9 232ft) dominate this unique area of high mountains.

Estany Negre – 🚶 5hr there and back on foot from Espot; 4hr from Sant Maurici lake. Cross the stunning Peguera Valley to Estany Negre (Black Lake), hemmed in by awesome summits.

Aigüestortes – Western section. 🚶 3hr there and back. The entry road leads to Aigüestortes where a stream winds through rich pastures. Hike to Estany Llong.

ADDRESSES

🛏STAY

Camping is prohibited but there are 14 mountain refuges. Most are open from June to September and during Holy Week.

Principat d'Andorra★★

Principality of Andorra

The seven parishes that make up the principality of Andorra occupy high plateaux and valleys cut by charming mountain roads. In recent years Andorra has seen urbanisation, hydroelectric schemes and a tourism boom. But tradition remains in the terraced slopes planted with tobacco and in religious pilgrimages (notably the famous Catalan *aplec*).

ANDORRA TODAY

Andorra is well known for the duty-free shopping opportunities it offers, primarily in the tiny capital of Andorra la Vella. In fact an astonishing 10 million visitors a year descend upon the principality, many clutching their credit card. The main skiing valleys are also very busy in season, with some €50 million recently invested in their infrastructure. By contrast the outlying villages remain largely uncommercialised.

A BIT OF HISTORY

Until 1993 Andorra was a co-principality subject to an unusual political regime dating back to the days of feudalism. The neighbouring rulers, the Bishop of Urgell and the President of the French Republic, enjoyed rights and exercised powers over this small territory, which was jointly governed by them. At present Andorra is a sovereign state – a full member of the United Nations.

🚗 DRIVING TOURS

VALL DEU VALIRA D'ORIENT

30km/18.6mi from Pas de la Casa to Andorra la Vella. Allow half a day.

This drive will lead you around Andorra's stunning countryside, slowly easing into the shopping, spa and hotel frenzy of Andorra La Vella.

▶ **Population:** 80 153
🕐 **Michelin Map:** 574 E 34-35.
🛈 **Info:** Andorra la Vella: Plaça de la Rotonda. ✆376 750 100. www.visitandorra.com.
◑ **Location:** Between Spain and France, 20km/12.4mi from La Seu d'Urgell. 🚇Nearest Spanish station is Puigcerda (80km) – or L'Hospitalet (France, 3 km).
👪 **Kids:** Museu Nacional de l'Automòbil.
🕐 **Timing:** Spend a day driving through the valleys.
🅿 **Parking:** Forget about parking in Andorra la Vella.
😊 **Customs and Formalities:** Visitors need a valid passport; drivers need a Green Card and current driving licence. There are customs checkpoints on the borders. If calling from Spain prefix numbers with 00.

Pas de la Casa★

Alt 2 091m/6 861ft. Once only a frontier post, the highest village in Andorra is the main ski resort of the region.

◑ The road snakes through the mountains before reaching Port d'Envalira, offering great views of Font Negre.

Port d'Envalira★★

😊 Roads may be snow-blocked but usually reopen within 24hr.
Alt 2 407m/7 897ft. Envalira boasts the highest altitude of major Pyrenean passes. On the Atlantic-Mediterranean divide, it commands a lovely mountain panorama.

◑ Take the CG-2 in the direction of Canillo, stopping just outside the town.

Església de Sant Joan de Caselles

Av. Sant Joan de Caselles, Canillo.
Ask at the tourist office about times.

No charge. ℮376 851 434.
Below an openwork tower and rows of ornamental windows, this church is one of the best examples of Romanesque architecture in Andorra. Behind the wrought-iron grid of the presbytery stands a painted altarpiece by the master **Canillo** (1525), representing the life and visions of the Apostle St John. The Romanesque **Crucifixion★** was restored in 1963: a Christ in stucco was placed atop a fresco illustrating the Calvary.

◗ Continue to Canillo.

Canillo
The bell tower of the church set against rocks is the highest in Andorra. At its side is an ossuary, characteristic of early Iberian occupation.

Santuari de Meritxell
Beyond Los Bons pass lies a lovely **site★** of houses gathered under a ruined castle and the Capella de Sant Romà. Nearby stands the church of Nuestra Señora de Meritxell (open mid-Jul–mid-Sept daily 10am–7pm; rest of year 9am–1pm, 3–7pm (closed Sun eve and Tue); no charge; ℮376 85 12 53, www.cultura.ad/per-visitar/monuments), national sanctuary of the principality since 1976.

◗ Continue on the same road to Encamp.

Encamp
This village has two interesting museums and two interesting churches: Santa Eulàlia has the highest steeple in Andorra (23 m/75.5ft), a 14C porch and Baroque altarpieces; Sant Romà de les Bons contains reproductions of Gothic paintings.

Casa Cristo - Museu Etnografic★
Cavallers 2. Open Jul–Aug Tue–Sat 9.30am – 1.30pm, 3–7.30pm, Sun 9.30am–1.30pm; rest of the year 9.30am–1.30pm, 3–6.30pm, Sun 10am–2pm. €3. ℮376 833 551. www.encamp.ad.
Set in a 19C homestead, this museum aims to illustrate everyday life was once like for a modest agrarian family.

Museu Nacional de l'Automòbil★
Av. de Joan Martí, 66. Open May–Oct Tue–Sat 10am–2pm, 3–6pm, Sun 10am–2pm. Dec–Apr Tue–Sat 10am–1pm, 3–8pm. €5. ℮376 83 22 66.
This collection offers over a century of automotive history, with 88 cars, 105 bicycles and 68 motorcycles from classic and vintage marques such as Bugatti, Rolls-Royce, Ferrari and Cadillac.

Estany d'Engolasters (Engolasters Lake)
The Engolasters plateau is a pastured extension of Andorra la Vella used for sports and recreation. The fine Romanesque tower of the church of Sant Miquel rises above the rolling plains.
Climb over the crest among the pine trees at the end of the road and descend on foot to an impressive hydroelectric dam, surrounded by trees, which has raised the waters of the lake (alt 1 616m/5 301ft) by a total of 10m/33ft.

◗ Continue S on the CS 200.

Andorra la Vella
Houses in the capital cluster onto a terrace overlooking the Gran Valira. Streets in the old quarter remain almost intact. The ancient stone building, **Casa de la Vall** (Parliament House; Vall; by guided tour (30min) onlyMay–Oct 10am–2pm, 3–6pm; closed Sun pm & Mon pm; €5; ℮376 82 91 29, www.casadelavall.ad). This houses the Consell General de les Valls, both Parliament and courthouse to the small nation. To the east, Andorra la Vella joins Les Escaldes, dominated by **Caldaea** (www.caldea.com), a family-friendly thermal spa with futuristic lines.

VALLS DE GRAN VALIRA AND VALIRA DEL NORD
9km/5.5mi from Sant Julia de Loria to La Cortinada to Andorra la Vella.
Allow half a day.
This drives takes you through the valleys of Andorra's ski country, but is beautiful out of season too.

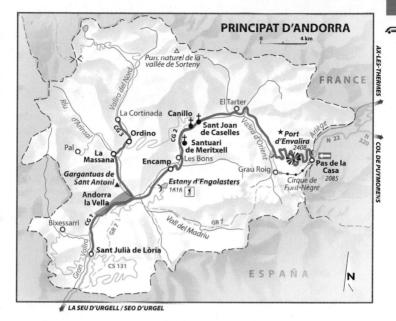

Sant Julia de Loria

Museu del tabac★ – Dr. Palau, 17; open
Jul–Aug Tue–Sat 9am–6.30pm, Sun 9am–
1pm; Sept–Jun Tue–Fri 9am–6pm, Sat
until, 6.30pm, Sun 10am–1pm. €5. ℘376
74 15 45. www.museudeltabac.com. This
museum occupies a former tobacco
factory, and takes you on a journey
through the tobacco making process,
from the way the leaves were dried,
to cigarette rolling and packaging, all
accompanied by a video narrated by
former workers.

▷ Continue N on the CS 100, then
take the CG 3 towards La Massana.

Gargantas de Sant Antoni

From the bridge over the Vall de Valira
de Nord you can see the old bridge used
by medieval shepherds on your right.
It was restored in the 19C.

▷ Go through the Túnel de Sant
Antoni on the CG 3.

La Massana

Casa Rull de Sispony★ – Carrer Major.
Open Tue–Sat 10am–2pm, 3–6pm; also
Sun 10am–2pm May–Oct. €5. ℘376
83 69 19. www.cultura.ad/per-visitar/
museus. This 17C homestead recon-
structs local everyday life. It belonged
to one of the richest families in La Massana, and there are many details to pon-
der over, particularly in the kitchen.

▷ Continue N on the CG 3.

Ordino

⊙ Park by the church in the upper town.
Ordino is a quaint village with a maze of
charming alleyways. The **Casa d'Areny-
Plandolit**★ (open same hours as Casa
Rull; €5; ℘376 83 97 60, www.cultura.
ad/per-visitar/museus) dates from 1676
and belonged to a family that included
the village's master ironworker. Highlights include the metal work on the
balconies, the Art Nouveau dining room
and the ceramic-tiled kitchen.
Nearby are the **Museu Postal d'Andorra**
(Camí de Segudet; open same hours
as Casa Rull; €5; ℘376 839 760; www.
cultura.ad/per-visitar/museus) and the
Museu de la Miniatura (Edifici Mar-
agda; ℘376 838 338; www.andorra.ad).

▷ From here continue to La
Cortinada to visit the Cal Pal Mola i
Serradora (mill and sawmill; ℘376
878173 www.ordino.ad).

389

Tarragona and Southern Catalunya

With the exception of coastal resorts like Salou, which boasts Port Aventura – Spain's largest theme park – Southern Catalunya (Tarragona and Llerida provinces), is often overlooked by visitors. This seems unfair. The capitals of both regions, particularly Tarragona, offer a wealth of cultural interest, from expansive Roman remains to soaring Gothic cathedrals, while many inland towns are every bit as atmospheric as the prettied-up medieval hamlets of the north, and restaurants and hotels are cheaper, too. The landscape is diverse, with blankets of vineyards and licorella terraces around Montsant – one of Spain's most promising new wine-growing regions – to the wide plains of orchards around Lleida and the wetlands of the Ebro Delta.

Highlights

1 Tarragona's atmospheric **Medieval Quarter** and **Cathedral** (p393)
2 The peaceful **Monastery of Poblet** (p397)
3 Soaking up the sun on the **Costa Daurada** (p401)
4 A day out out with the kids at **Port Aventura** (p401)
5 Getting away from it all in the **Ebro Delta** wetlands (p402)

Little Egret in the Ebro Delta

© Jean-Claude Carton/Biosphoto/Photoshot

Tarragona and the Coast

Easily accessible by both car and train, the Costa Daurada takes its name from the long golden beaches that begin south at the Ebro Delta and stretch north almost as far as Sitges. With the exception of Salou, the resorts here are mostly low-key and (again, aside from Salou) geared to Spanish holidaymakers. Tarragona also has good beaches but this fine old historic town is best known for its UNESCO World Heritage recognised Roman archeological ensemble and a magnificent cathedral.

When Barcelona was a mere trading post, Tarragona (or Tárraco, as it was called) was the Roman capital of Hispania. The Romans built a forum, amphitheatre, sophisticated aqueduct and many other infrastructures in this bustling port, many of which today form part of Tarragona's multilayered cityscape. By contrast just 10km/6.2mi away is Spain's best theme park, Port Aventura.

Inland and Lleida

Lleida on the other hand had its golden age during the 11 and 12C, when nobles and knights set about making a stronghold of the Catalan plains. The small town of Montblanc also boasts many surviving medieval features, while Poblet and Santes Creus are two of the finest monasteries in Spain.

The Delta Ebro and Tortosa

Spain's most voluminous river meets the sea at the Delta Ebro, scene of one of the bloodiest battles of the Spanish Civil War. Today people come to watch its abundant bird life, to fish or simply laze around alongside the marshy waters. Well beyond the cities and resorts, the town of Tortosa has a fine cathedral and makes an ideal base from which to explore the delta wetlands.

Tarragona★★

Tarragona, with its ancient and medieval heritage, is also a modern town with wide avenues and a lively commercial centre. Its gardened seafront promenade skirts the cliffside and surrounds the old city and Palace of Augustus, following the city walls in the shadow of the Cathedral. Long a major port, Tarragona also has 15km/9.3mi of beaches that attract summer visitors.

▶ **Population:** 131 255
◔ **Michelin Map:** 574 I 33 – Catalunya (Tarragona)
▤ **Info:** Major 37. ℘977 25 07 95. www.tarragona turisme.cat.
◖ **Location:** Tarragona is in Cataluña in NE Spain, SW along the coast from Barcelona. 🚃Camp de Tarragona (AVE).
👥 **Kids:** The city's beaches.

ROMAN TARRAGONA★★

Passeig Arqueològic★ (Archaeological Promenade)

Av. Catalunya. Open Holy Week & May–Sept Tue–Sat 9am–9pm. Rest of year Tue–Sat 9am–7pm. Sun & public hols 9am–3pm. Closed 1, 6 Jan, 1 May, 25–26 Dec. €3.30, €7.40 combined with other Museu d'Història sites. ℘977 24 57 96. http://museuhistoria. tarragona.cat.

Scipios built Tarragona's walls in the 3C BC on existing Cyclopean bases. They were so massive that they were long thought to have been barbarian or pre-Roman. Medieval inhabitants rebuilt the ramparts; 18C citizens remodelled them but still left us with walls bearing the marks of 2 000 years of history.

A garden walk follows the walls. Part of the walls can be inaccessible due to renovation.

Museu Nacional Arqueològic de Tarragona★★ (Archaeological Museum)

Pl. del Rey 5. Open Mon–Sat 9.30am–8.30pm (Oct–May until 6pm), Sun and public holidays 10am–2pm. €4.50 (includes entry to Necròpolis). No charge last Tue of month Oct–Jun. ℘977 23 62 09. www.mnat.cat.

The exhibits, mostly from Roman times, are from Tarragona or its environs. The **Roman architecture** (Room II, ground floor) section gathers vestiges of the most imposing buildings in Tar-

Capital of Tarraconensis

The history of Tarragona dates back many centuries. The imposing ramparts built of enormous Cyclopean blocks of stone indicate that it was founded by peoples from the eastern Mediterranean early in the first millennium BC. In due course it suffered occupation by the Iberians. The Romans, who by 218 BC had control of the larger part of the peninsula, developed Tarraconensis into a major city and overseas capital. Although it could never equal Rome, it enjoyed many of the same privileges as the imperial capital and Augustus, Galba and Hadrian did not disdain to live in it. Conversion to Christianity, often attributed to the work of St Paul, brought it appointment as a metropolitan seat, and its dignitaries the primacy of Spain. This honour was retained throughout the barbarian invasions of the 5C and the destruction of the Moors in the 8C but lost finally to the ambition of Toledo in the 11C. The city was then abandoned until the 12C, when it reverted to the Christians.

© cwrgutierrez/iStockphoto.com

raconensis. The **Roman mosaics★★** collection is the finest in Catalunya. Exhibits in Rooms III (first floor) and VIII (second floor) testify to the high craftsmanship of the Romans.
The most extraordinary piece is the **Mosaic of the Medusa★★** (late 2C), with its penetrating gaze.
Roman sculpture★ (Rooms VI to X, second floor) is exemplified by superb **funerary sculptures** (Room IX). Note (Room VI) the bust of Lucius Verusa, executed in the 2C, a perfect example of the art, and the small **votive sculpture of Venus★**.

Recinte Monumental del Pretori i del Circ Romà★ (Praetorium and Roman Circus)

Pl. del Rey 5. Open Holy Week & Apr–Sept Tue–Sat 9am–9pm. Rest of year Tue–Sat 9am–7.30pm. Sun & public hols 9am–3pm. Closed 1, 6 Jan, 1 May, 25–26 Dec. €3.30 (€7.40 combined with other Museu d'Història sites).
℘977 24 22 20.
http://museuhistoria.tarragona.cat.
Visit the **vaulted underground galleries★** of a restored 1C BC square tower, or enjoy the sweeping **view★★** from the top. **Hippolyte's sarcophagus★★**, found virtually intact on the bed of the Mediterranean, bears fine and lively sculptured ornamentation. The vast **Roman Circus** (325m x 115m/1 066ft x 378ft) was designed for chariot races. Only a few terraces, vaults and sections of the façade remain.

Amfiteatre★★

Parque del Miracle. Opening times and prices as Praetorium and Circus.
℘977 24 22 20.
http://museuhistoria.tarragona.cat.
The seaside elliptical amphitheatre is in a naturally sloped **site★**. Bishop Fructuosus and his deacons, Augurius and Eulogius, were martyred here in 259. The Església de Santa Maria del Miracle (church) replaced a Visigothic basilica in the 12C and is itself now in ruins.

Forum Romà

Opening times and prices as Passeig Arqueològic. ℘977 24 22 20.
The Forum was the core of the Roman city. A few reliefs, pieces of frieze and sections of a street remain.

Museu i Necrópolis Paleocristianas

Av. Ramon y Cajal 80. Open Jun–Sept Tue–Sat 9.30am–1.30, 4–8pm, Sun and public holidays 10am–2pm; rest of the year Tue–Sat 9.30am–1.30pm, 3–5.30/6pm; Sun and public holidays 10am–2pm. €4.50 (includes entry to Museu Arqueològic). ℘977 211 175. www.mnat.es.
A 3C–7C burial site, including over 2 000 tombs, were uncovered at this location in 1923. A section has been restored for viewing, with many of the remains now in the Archaeological Museum.

MODERNIST HERITAGE

Tarragona's *modernista* buildings, include a clutch of residential houses along the Rambla Nova, the Mercat Central (1905), southwest of the Rambla Nova and El Escorxador, the old abattoir (1902).

El Serrallo

▷ Southwest of the centre, beyond the railway tracks. Access by bus #2 or # 5 or a 20-minute walk.

This old fishermen's district, created in the mid 19C, hosts some of the best restaurants in town, and a famous fish market is held here every day. Consisting of a handful of narrow alleys around the church of Sant Pere, El Serrallo comes alive at night and is very popular with locals.

Museu del Port de Tarragona

Moll de Costa. Open Tue–Sat 10am–2pm, 5–8pm (Oct–May 4–7pm) Sun and hols year-round 11am–2pm. No charge. www.porttarragona.cat.

Housed in an outbuilding of the old ferry terminal, this museum traces the history of the Port of Tarragona from Roman times.

 WALKING TOUR

CIUDAD MEDIEVAL

In the Middle Ages, the higly visible remains of the Roman City were integrated into medieval Tarragona.

Plaça de la Font

Dominated by the façade of the **Ajuntament** (city hall) and adorned with fountains, this pedestrianised square is Tarragona's main meeting point and is a great place to relax at one of its many café terraces.

▷ Turn right on Carrer de l'Ajuntament Sant Domènec, then right again on Carrer Roser.

Plaça del Pallol

Roman remains are hidden under the Medieval buildings in this peaceful square. Next to the Antiga Audiència

building (an old courthouse) porches and large Gothic windows survive, as well as the remains of the Roman gate to the provincial forum.

▷ From the plaça, take the exit onto Carrer dels Cavallers.

Carrer dels Cavallers

As is the case of Barcelona's Carrer de Montcada (◑see p337), the Carrer dels Chevaliers, was the main artery of medieval Tarragona. It is still lined with a few mansions that belonged to the wealthiest families in the city.

Casa-Museu Castellarnau★

Cavallers 14. Closed to the public.

The Emperor Charles V is said to have stayed in this wealthy 14C–15C residence. It features a pretty Gothic patio and fine 18C furniture.

▷ Turn left into the Carrer Major.

Carrer Major

The "Main Street" of Tarragaona leades directly to the cathedral's main portal. Arcades and shops, sometimes beautifully historic, at times with a distinct retro feel, lend an attrative amabiance. **Arcades on Carrer Merceria** (on the right before you reach Plaça del Seu). These are the only remnants of the old medieval market. In summer, the arcades provide respite from the heat.

▷ Continue to the Plaça de la Seu.

Catedral★★

Pl. de la Seu. Open Mon–Sat mid-Mar–mid-Jun 10am–7pm, mid-Jun–mid-Sept until 8pm, mid-Sept–Oct until 7pm; Nov–Feb Mon–Fri until 5pm, Sat until 7pm. Closed Sun & public holidays. €5 (includes Museum, cloister and treasury). ℘977 22 69 35. www.catedraldetarragona.com.

Construction began in 1174 on the site of Jupiter's Temple, in transitional Gothic style, although the side chapels are both Plateresque and Baroque.

Façade★

A Gothic central section with rose window is flanked by Romanesque sections. The **main doorway** displays the Last Judgement, with expressive relief work. The archivolts are carved with Apostles and Prophets. On the pier, the Virgin (13C) receives the Faithful.

Interior★★

Following a Latin cross plan, there are three naves and a transept. The Romanesque apse has semicircular arches. At each end of the transept are 14C rose windows with stained glass. The three naves are mostly Gothic. The finest work of art is undoubtedly the **altarpiece of Santa Tecla★★★** (Capella Mayor, 1430), closing off the central apse, which is reached by two Gothic doorways. Santa Tecla (St Thecla) is the city's patron saint. This work by Pere Joan shows a talent for detail, ornamentation and the picturesque.

To the right of the altar lies the 14C **Tomb of the Infante Don Juan de Aragón★★**, attributed to an Italian master. The **Capella de la Virgen de Montserrat** (second chapel, left) houses a **retable★** by Luis Borrassà (15C).

Reliefs★ in the Capella de Santa Tecla (third chapel in the right-hand aisle) recount the saint's life. The **Capella de los Sastres★★** (to the left of the Capella Major) features intricate ribbed vaulting, a lovely altarpiece and paintings. Sumptuous tapestries are decorated with allegorical motifs.

Claustro★★

The 12C–13C cloisters are unusually large – each gallery is 45m/148ft long. The arches and geometric decoration are Romanesque, but the vaulting is Gothic, as are the supporting arches. Moorish influence is evident in the *claustra* of geometrically patterned and pierced panels filling the oculi below the arches, the line of multifoil arches at the base of the Cathedral roof and the belfry in one corner, rising 70m/230ft. Inlaid in the west gallery is a *mihrab*-like stone niche, dated 960. A remarkable **Romanesque doorway★**, with a

Christ in Majesty, links the cathedral to the cloisters.

Museu Diocesá★★

Pl. de la Seu. Open same hours/ticket as Cathedral.

The capitular outbuildings contain religious vestments, paintings, altarpieces and reliefs. Tapestries in Room III include the 15C Flemish **La Buena Vida★**. In the Capella del Corpus Christi are a richly ornate **monstrance★** (nº105) and a polychrome alabaster relief work depicting St Jerome (16C).

▷ Retrace your steps to the Carrer Major, then turn left into the Carrer Sant Lorenç.

Antic Hospital★

Coques.

This 12C–14C hospital, now used by the local council, is a surprising mix of styles, including the original Romanesque façade and doorway.

▷ Backtrack along Carrer de Sant Lorenç.

Museu d'Art Modern

Carrer Santa Anna 8. Open Tue–Fri 10am–8pm, Sat 10am–3pm, 5–8pm, Sun and hols 11am–2pm. Closed 1, 6 Jan, 1 May, 11 Sept, 25–26 Dec. No charge. ✆977 235 032. www.dipta.cat/mamt.

Inaugurated in 1991, this museum presents a harmonious collection of *modernisme*, the Catalan equivalent to Art Nouveau. The local sculptor Julio Antonio (1889–1919), author of the monument to the heroes of 1811 on La Rambla, is well represented.

EXCURSIONS

Acueducto de Les Ferreres★★

▷ Leave the city along rambla Nova.

4km/2.5mi from Tarragona you will see the well-preserved two-tier Roman aqueduct on your right, 217m/712ft long. You can walk (30min) through the pines to the base then ascend and walk right across the top of it, in safety, in the channel, where the water used to flow.

Vil·la Romana de Centcelles★★

◗ 4km/2.5mi NW. Exit the city along avinguda Ramon I Cajal. Take the Reus road; bear right after crossing the Francolí. Turn right in Constanti into Centcelles; continue 450m/492yd on an unsurfaced road; turn left just before the village. Open Tue–Sat 10am–1.30pm, 3–6pm (Nov–Feb closes 5.30pm, Jun–Sept 4–8pm), Sun & hols 10am–2pm. Closed 1 & 20 Jan , 1 May, 1 Aug 25–26 Dec. €2.50. ℘977 52 33 74. www.mnat.cat.

Two monumental buildings in a vine-yard are faced in pink tiles. They were built in the 4C by a wealthy Roman near his vast summer residence. The first chamber is covered by an immense cupola (diameter: 11m/36ft), decorated with **mosaics★★** on themes such as hunting, Daniel in the lion's den, etc. The adjoining chamber has an apse on either side.

Torre de los Escipiones★

◗ Leave Tarragona along via Augusta. After 5km/3mi turn left.

The upper and central parts of this square funerary tower (1C) bear reliefs portraying Atis, a Phrygian divinity associated with death rituals (not the Escipion brothers as once thought).

Vil·la Romana de Els Munts★

◗ 12km/7.4mi E along the N 340. Leave Tarragona along via Augusta. Open same hours as Villa Romana de Centcelles. Closed 1 & 6 Jan, 1 May, 11 Nov, 25–26 Dec. €2.50. ℘977 65 28 06. www.mnat.cat.

This Roman villa nestles in Altafulla, in a privileged **site★★** gently sloping towards the sea. The L-shaped arcaded passage was flanked by gardens and **baths★** with a complex plan.

Arco de Berà★

◗ Follow the via Augusta. The arch is situated in the locality of Roda de Berà, 20km/12.4mi along the N 340.

The Vía Augusta once passed under this imposing, well-proportioned arch (1C). Its eight grooved pilasters are crowned by Corinthian capitals.

ADDRESSES

🏨 STAY

⊜🍽 Hotel Plaça de la Font – Plaça de la Font 26. ℘977 246 134. www.hotelpdelafont.com. 20 rooms. ⊐€5. Restaurant⊜🍽. In an attractve square in the old town, this four-storey hotel and restaurant is an excellent budget option. Public parking nearby.

⊜🍽🍽 Hotel Sercotel Urbis Centre – Pl. Corsini 10. ℘977 24 01 16. www.hotelurbiscentre.com. 44 rooms. ⊐€9.50. Restaurant ⊜🍽🍽. Situated near the old city, this comfortable 3-star hotel hotel offers functional rooms with modernised bathrooms.

⊜🍽🍽🍽 Hotel La Boella – La Canonja, 7.9km/4,9mi SE of Tarragona on the T 11. ℘977 77 15 15. www.laboella.com. 13 rooms. ⊐€14. Restaurant ⊜🍽🍽. A charming, castle-like country hotel a short drive from the city centre, La Boella boasts huge gardens and olive groves from which the estate's own extra virgin oil is produced, a smart restaurant and an expensive wine cellar. Perfect for foodies and wine lovers.

🍽 EAT

⊜🍽 El Llagut– Carrer de Natzaret 10. ℘977 22 89 38. www.elllagut.com Mediterranean-inspired tapas and excellent fish dishes - the prawns are a favourite with regulars.

⊜🍽🍽 Racó de l'Abat – Carrer de l'Abat 2. ℘977 780 371. www.abatrestaurant.com. Call for opening times. In an attractive old house, complete with interior Gothic arches, in the old town, this restaurant is renowned as one of the best for traditional Catalan cuisine and seafood.

⊜🍽🍽🍽 AQ Restaurant – Carrer de les Coques 7. ℘977 215 954. www.aq-restaurant.com. Closed Sun and Mon. Elegant, gourmet dining in a stylish, minimalist old house with exposed brickwork. Creative menus with an emphasis on seafood such as mackerel grilled with Teriyaki and aubergine.

Montblanc★★

Montblanc lies in an impressive setting★ amid vineyards and almond orchards. Within its ancient walls lie narrow, cobbled streets, stone buildings, and legends and deep secrets from a golden age in the 14C.

▶ **Population:** 7 283
◉ **Michelin Map:** 574 H 33 – Catalunya (Tarragona)
▤ **Info:** Antigua Església de Sant Francesc. *℘*977 86 17 33. www.montblancmedieval.cat.
◗ **Location:** At the crossroads of the N 240 (Tarragona-Lleida) and the C 240 from Reus (29km/18mi S). ▭ Montblanc.

SIGHTS

The Ramparts★★

Enquire at tourist office for opening details, €3. www.montblancmedieval.cat

The ramparts were commissioned by Peter IV of Aragón in the mid-14C. Two thirds of the original walls (1 500m/5 000ft) remain, along with 32 square towers and two of four gates: that of Sant Jordi (S) and Bover (NE).

Església de Santa Maria★★

Pl. de l'Església. Open daily 11am–1pm, and Mon–Sat 4–6pm. No charge. *℘*977 86 17 33 (tourist office). www.montblancmedieval.cat

This beautiful Gothic church overlooking the city has a single nave and radiating chapel. The unfinished façade is Baroque. The interior features a sumptuous 17C organ★★, a Gothic altarpiece in polychrome stone (14C) and an elegant silver monstrance.

Museu Comarcal de la Conca de Barberà★ (CIAR i Museu d'Art Frederic Marès de Montblanc)

Pedrera, 2. Open Tue–Fri 10am–2pm, 4–7pm, Sat–Sun and hols by appointment. Closed 1 Jan, 25–26 Dec. €2.90. *℘*977 860 349. www.mccb.cat.

The ground floor of this dual-themed museum feaures an interpretation centre of local rock art (Centre d'Interpretació de l'Art Rupestre - CIAR) practiced by its first inhabitants.

On the first floor, the magnificent Marès collection (◉see Museu Frederic Marès, Barcelona, p331) was bequeathed to the city in 1975 from the sculptor and collector who between 1945 and 1952 stayed in Montblanc in order to restore the Royal Tombs of the Poblet Monastery (◉see p397). The religious paintings and sculptures from the 14C to 19C are remarkable, particularly the early Gothic wooden figurines.

There are several other attractions under the Museu Comarcal's umbrella including the Molins de la Vila, two ancient flour mills, 1km/0.6mi out of town towards Prenafeta.

Plaça Mayor

Among the arcades of shops and cafés around the main square, note the town hall (ayuntamiento) and the Gothic-style Casa dels Desclergue.

Església de Sant Miquel★

Pl. de Sant Miquel. Guided tours by arrangement. *℘*977 86 17 33.

Fronted by a Romanesque façade, this small 13C Gothic church has pure, sober lines. It hosted the Estates General of Catalunya several times in the 14C and 15C. Next to the church stands the **Palau del Castlà**, formerly the residence of the king's representative. A 15C prison is on its ground floor.

Call Judío (Jewish Quarter)

Until 1489, Montblanc was a thriving town with a prosperous Jewish community (*Jueus*). Its golden age was the 14C, when its economic supremacy was reflected in the political arena with several Estates General being held in the town at the instigation of Catalan-Aragonese monarchs. Only the Carrer dels Jueus (Street of Jews) and part of a Gothic house in Plaça dels Àngels remain of the former Jewish district. Another interesting building is the 14C **Casa Alenyà**, a slender Gothic house.

OUTSIDE THE WALLS
Convent i Santuari de la Serra★
Open 8.15am–2pm, 4–6pm (7pm May–Oct). Closed Fri morning. €4.
℘977 86 17 33 (tourist office).
This ex-convent of the Order of St Clare stands on a small hill. It houses the venerated **Mare de Déu de la Serra**, an alabaster statue made in the 14C.

Hospital de Santa Magdalena★
Open Aug–mid-Sept daily 11am–3pm; rest of the year 10m–7pm.
The remarkable though small 15C **cloisters** illustrate the transition between Gothic and Renaissance. The vertical perspective on the ground floor, featuring fluted columns and pointed arches, is broken in the upper section.

EXCURSION
Valls
The prosperous city of Valls is wedged between two tributaries. Its historic center has kept its medieval character. The city is still known for its famous *castellers* and especially for its *calçots*, tender, over-sized spring onions that are considered a Catalan delicacy.
In season in early winter, they are fire-grilled over vines and served on curved tiles, together with a *romesco* sauce that combines almonds, tomatoes, garlic, peppers and other ingredients. Traditionally they are eaten whole with your hands – messy, but delicious!

🚗 DRIVING TOUR

CISTERCIAN ROUTE
90km/56mi. Allow one day
www.larutadelcister.info.

Along this route, visit the most important Cistercian monasteries in Catalunya, founded in the 12C after the reconquest of Catalunya by Ramon Berenguer IV.

▷ Exit Montblanc on the N 240 to l'Espluga de Francolí. From here, follow the T 700 for 4km/2.5mi.

Monestir de Poblet★★★
🚃Nearest station: Valls 18km (Tarragona, on AVE line 50km). Zona del Monasterio, Vimbodí. Guided tours. Open daily 10am (Sun and hols 10.30)–12.30pm, 3–5.25pm (5.55pm mid-Mar–mid-Oct). Closed 1 Jan, 27 Jun, 25–26 Dec. €7.50, €10 guided tour.
℘977 870 089. www.poblet.cat.
The splendid **site★** of one of the largest and best-preserved Cistercian monasteries is sheltered by the Prades mountains. Founded in the 12C, it enjoyed the protection of the crown of Aragón. A 2km/1.2mi-perimeter protected the monastery and its vegetable gardens.

Capella de Sant Jordi★★
The Late Gothic interior of this tiny 15C chapel features splendid broken barrel vaulting. An inner wall with polygonal towers enclosed annexes where visitors were received. The 15C **Porta Daurada** (Golden Door), named after the gilded bronze sheets that form its covering, was commissioned by Philip II.

Plaça Major★
On this irregular main square stand the 12C **Capella de Santa Caterina**, shops, a hospital for pilgrims and a carpentry workshop. On the right are the ruins of the 16C Abbatial Palace and the **stone cross** erected by Abbey Guimerà, also 16C. A third wall (608m/1 995ft long, 11m/36ft high and 2m/6.5ft thick), built by Peter the Ceremonious, surrounds the monastery proper, fortified by 13 towers. On the right stands the **Baroque façade of the church**, built around 1670 and flanked, 50 years later, by heavily ornate windows. Pleasing in itself, it breaks with the overall austerity.

Porta Reial★
This is the gateway to the conventual buildings, appearing somewhat like the entrance to a fortress.

© José Fuste Raga/Getty Images

Palau del Rei Martí★

Beyond the door, to the right, a narrow staircase rises to this 14C Gothic palace. Its splendid rooms are wonderfully light thanks to pointed bay windows.

Locutorio

Originally a dormitory for converts, this room became a wine press. The 14C vaulting rests on the walls. Magnificent Gothic **cellar** and concert hall.

Claustro★★

The size of these cloisters (40 x 35m/ 131 x 115ft) and their sober lines indicate the monastery's importance. The south gallery (c. 1200) and huge lavabo or **templete★** with its marble fountain and 30 taps are in pure Romanesque style; the other galleries, built a century later, have floral motif tracery; beautiful scrollwork adorns the **capitals★**. The **kitchen** (cocina) and the huge **monk's refectory** (refectorio de los monjes), both built around 1200 and still in use, open onto the cloisters. The **library** (biblioteca) – the former scriptorium – is crowned by ogival vaulting on 13C columns. The 13C **chapter house★★** (sala capitular), through a Romanesque doorway, has four slender octagonal columns and palm-shaped vaulting.

Església★★

The light, spacious church is typically Cistercian. It has pure lines, broken barrel vaulting and unadorned capitals. The windows and wide arches dividing the nave join in a large eave. The church incorporated numerous altars for its growing community; the apse was ringed by an ambulatory and radiating chapels, a feature more commonly found in Benedictine churches.

The **royal pantheon★★** (panteó reial), the church's most original feature, has immense shallow arches spanning the transepts, surmounted by the royal tombs. These were constructed of alabaster in about 1350.

The **retable★★** (retablo) at the **high altar** (altar mayor) is a monumental marble Renaissance altarpiece carved by Damián Forment in 1527. Figures in four superimposed registers can be seen glorifying Christ and the Virgin.

In the narthex, an opening to the outside world added in 1275, is the Renaissance **altar of the Holy Sepulchre**.

Wide stairs leads from the transept to the dormitory. Massive central arches support the ridge roof above the vast, 87m/285ft long **Dormitorio gallery**.

▷ Leave Poblet on the T 232 towards Maldà and take the road to Vallbona.

Monestir de Vallbona de les Monges★★

🚃 Nearest station: Lleida on AVE line (55km). Mayor. Visit by guided tour only (45min), see website for guided tour times on the hour in Spanish or Catalan (usually Mon-Fri 10.30am-6pm, Sat-Sun noon-6pm). Closed 1 & 6 Jan, Good Friday, 25 Dec. €4 (€9 with Poblet and Santes Creus monasteries). ✆973 33 02 66. www.monestirvallbona.cat.

The Cistercian **Monestir de Santa Maria** was founded in 1157 by the hermit Ramon de Vallbona and became a Cistercian community for women.

Església★★

Built chiefly in the 13C and the 14C, this church is a fine example of transitional Gothic. The interior is simple and surprisingly light thanks to two octagonal lantern towers: one (13C) lies above the transept crossing while the other (14C) overlooks the centre of the nave. The church contains the beautiful tombs of Queen Violante of Hungary, wife of James I the Conqueror of Aragón, and her daughter, as well as a huge polychrome Virgin from the 15C.

Cloisters★

The east and west galleries are Romanesque (12C–13C). The 14C Gothic north wing features attractive capitals with plant motifs. In the south gallery (15C) note the 12C statue of Nuestra Señora del Claustro (of the Cloisters).

▶ Head towards Rocallaura then towards Montblanc along the C 240 to link up with the AP 2. Turn off onto the TP 2002 at exit 11.

Monestir de Santes Creus★★★

🚃Nearest station: Valls 18km (Tarragona on AVE line 33km). Pl. Jaume el Just, Aiguamurcia. 46km/29mi SE of Vallbona. Guided tours (2hr). Open Tue–Sun & hol Mons 10am–5.30pm (until 7pm Jun–Sept). €4.50; no charge last Tue of the month Oct–Jun. ℘977 63 83 29. www.mhcat.cat.

The monastery was founded in the 12C by monks from Toulouse and its plan is similar to that of Poblet, with three perimeter walls. A Baroque gateway leads to the courtyard where the monastic buildings, enhanced with fine *sgraffiti*, now serve as shops and private residences. To the right is the abbatial palace, with its attractive patio, now the town hall; at the end stands the 12C–13C church.

Gran Claustro★★★

Construction began in 1313 on the site of earlier ("great") cloisters. The ornamentation on capitals and bands illustrates Gothic motifs: plants and flowers, animals, biblical, mythological and satirical themes. The Puerta Real or Royal Gate on the south side opens onto cloisters with Gothic bays with lively carvings – note Eve shown emerging out of Adam's rib, and the fine tracery of the arches (1350–1430). In contrast, the transitional style of the **lavabo** appears almost clumsy. Carved noble tombs fill the niches.

The **chapter house★★** (sala capitular) is an elegant hall. Stairs next to the chapter house lead to the 12C **dormitory** (dormitorio), a gallery divided by diaphragm arches supporting a timber roof, now used as a concert hall.

Església★★

The church (1174) closely follows the Cistercian pattern of a flat east end and overall austerity. The lantern (14C), stained glass, and the superb apsidal **rose window** relieve the bareness. Ribbed vaults rest on pillars which extend back along the walls and end in unusual consoles. Gothic canopies at the transept openings shelter the **royal tombs★★**: on the north side (c. 1295) that of **Pere the Great** (III of Aragón, II of Barcelona) and on the south (14C), that of his son, **Jaime II**, the Just, and his queen, **Blanche d'Anjou**. The Plateresque decoration below the crowned recumbent figures in Cistercian habits, was added in the 16C.

Claustro Viejo

Although they were built during the 17C, these "old cloisters" occupy the site of former cloisters dating back to the 12C. The design is simple with a small central fountain and eight cypresses in the close. Leading off are the kitchens, refectory and the **royal palace** (note a splendid 14C **patio★**).

ADDRESSES

🛏 STAY

😊😊 **Fonda dels Àngels** – Pl. Els Àngels 1. ℘977 86 01 73. www.fonda delsangels.com. ⊠ ⊇€5. Simple rooms in a bay-windowed Gothic house. Small dining room (😊😊).

Lleida/Lérida★

Lleida, an ancient citadel, was stormed by the legions of Caesar, and occupied by the Moors from the 8C to the 12C. The Arab fortress, the Zuda, sited like an acropolis, was savaged by artillery fire in 1812 and 1936. The glacis has been converted into gardens. Lleida is an important fruit-growing centre.

SIGHTS
LA SEU VELLA★★★ (OLD CATHEDRAL)

To reach the Cathedral, take the lift from Plaça de Sant Joan. Turó la Seu Vella. Open: cathedral May–Sept Tue–Sat 10am–7.30pm. Oct–Mar Tue–Fri 10am–1.30pm, 3–5.30pm, Sat 10am–5.30pm. Sun & hols year-round 10am–3pm. Open: Suda (Castle area), slightly different times, see website. Closed 1, 6 Jan; 25–26 Dec. €7, inc Cathedral and Suda; no charge first Tue. of month ℘973 23 06 53. www.turoseuvella.cat.

The Cathedral site★ dominates the city from inside the walls. It was built between 1203 and 1278 over a mosque; the octagonal belfry was added in the 14C. Philip V converted the military fortification that surrounds the site into a garrison fortress in 1707, now known as the Castillo del Rey o Suda (Castle of the King or Suda – the latter is an Arabic word which means a closed urban area).

Església★★

The capitals★ of this transitional-style church are outstanding for their variety and detail. Moorish influences show in the exterior decoration. The extremely delicate carving, reminiscent of Moorish stuccowork, has come to be known as the Romanesque School of Lleida. It is seen throughout the region, in particular on the superb portal★★ of the Església de Agramunt (52km/32.3mi NE).

Claustro★★

The cloisters' 14C galleries are remarkable for the size of the bays and the beautiful stone tracery. The Gothic style shows Moorish influence in the

▶ **Population:** 138 542
◔ **Michelin Map:** 574 H 31 – Catalunya (Lleida)
▣ **Info:** Major 31a. ℘973 700 319. www.turismedelleida.cat.
◖ **Location:** Lleida is linked to Barcelona by the AP 2 motorway, the Pyrenees by the C 1313 and N 240, and Huesca via the N 240. 🚄Lleida/Lérida Pirineus (AVE).
🅿 **Parking:** Space is limited in the old quarter.
◉ **Don't Miss:** A walk up to the Suda for commanding views of city and plain.

plant motifs on the capitals★. There is a fine view from the south gallery. In the southwest corner stands the Gothic bell tower★★, 60m/197ft high. Along Carrer Major are three major monuments. The 13C Palau de la Paeria is now the town hall (ajuntament; open Mon–Sat 11am–2pm, 5–8pm, Sun 11am–2pm; no charge; ℘973 70 03 00), with a fine façade★. The old Hospital de Santa Maria (Jun–Sept Tue–Fri 10am–2pm, 6–9pm; Sat 11am–2pm, 7–9pm; Sun 11am–2pm; Oct–May Tue–Fri until 8.30pm; Sat noon–2pm, 5.30–8.30pm; Sun noon–2pm; no charge) is now the Institut d'Estudis Ilerdencs cultural centre, with a patio★ showing Renaissance influence. The 18C Seu Nova (New Cathedral; open daily 9am–1pm, 5–7pm; no charge; www.cataloniasacra.cat) was built 1761–81.

Museu de Lleida i Diocesà Comarcal

Jaume I el Conqueridor 1. Open Tue–Thu & Sat 10am–2pm, 5–7pm (4–6pm Oct-May), Sat, Sun & hols year-round 10am–2pm . Closed 1, 6 Jan, Good Fri, Easter Mon, and 25–26 Dec. €5; no charge first Tue in month, 2 Feb, 11 & 18 May, 11 Sept, 30 Nov. ℘973 28 30 75. www.museudelleida.cat.

An excellent chronological history display of the region, from the Bronze Age to Muslim occupation, the Christian reconquest and beyond.

La Costa Daurada★★

The Golden Coast unfolds along the shores of the province of Tarragona with beautiful beaches offering calm, shallow waters. The tourist resorts here cater more to local and north European package holidaymakers than the upmarket Costa Brava. Some high-rise hotels have caused a blip in the landscape, but there are plenty of opportunities to escape the crowds.

Michelin Map: 574 I-K31-34.
Info: Xalet Torremar, Pg. Jaume I, Salou. ℘977 350 102. www.costadaurada.info.
Location: A 150km/93mi stretch of coast in Tarragona province. Port Aventura.
Kids: Days on the beach, at a water park, or at Port Aventura.

SIGHTS
Coastal Towns

Easily reached via the train line between Barcelona and Tarragona, the towns and villages of the Costa Daurada make ideal day or overnight beach destinations. The best include **Altafulla**, with its long stretch of unspoilt sand and impressive Roman Villa, **Els Munts** and **Cambrils**. These resorts, as well as Calafell, Torrdembarra and Coma-Ruga, are popular with Spanish holidaymakers. **El Vendrell** was the birthplace of the famed cellist Pau Casals and you can visit his former home (Casa-Natal Pau Casals, (www.elvendrellturistic.com). The area's most famous son is Gaudí, born in Reus, celebrated at the **Gaudí Centre** (www.gaudicentre.cat).

Port Aventura★★

10km/6.2mi SW towards Salou. Open from 10am. Second week Apr–Oct daily, weekends only Nov–third week Dec, third week Dec– 6 Jan daily (see website for schedule). €47; child €40 (different rates available for multiple day tickets and evening visits late Jun–Sept). Parking €7. ℘902 20 22 20. www.portaventuraworld.com. Buy tickets in advance from agents or online. The huge Universal Studios Port Aventura amusement park is divided into five geographical zones, each with characteristic rides, performances, shops etc, plus its SésamoAventura area, specifically for little ones, based around the Sesame Street theme. **Mediterrània** is a coastal town; in **Polynesia★**, a path winds through tropical vegetation; **China★★** is the heart of the park, including the magic and mystery of a millenary civilisation. The newest addition, inspired by the great Temple of Angkor Wat, is **Angkor** featuring the longest theme park boat ride, in Europe. A perennial star attraction is **Dragon Khan★★★**, one of the world's most spectacular roller coasters, with eight gigantic loops, though now the park has other thrill rides to match. **Mexico★★** spans Mayan ruins, colonial Mexico, Mariachi music and traditional Mexican cuisine. In the **Far West★★** (Wild West) town of **Penitence**, visitors can play the lead role in a western or dance in the saloon. Adjacent is the excellent **Caribe Aquatic Park** (open mid-May–Sept see website for schedule; €28; child €24), with a Caribbean island theme.

Salou★

10km/6.2mi SW. Salou.
This is the principal resort on the Costa Dorada, popular with British and German tourists. Aside from Port Aventura (see above) the most popular day off the beach is at **Aquopolis** water park and dolphinarium (La Pineda; open mid-May–mid-18 Sept; water park €28.95; child €20.95; dolphinarium €7.95 (€5.95 online), child same price; see website for schedules and online discounts; ℘977 033 448; www.costa-dorada.aquopolis. es). Salou merges west into the attractive little fishing port of **Cambrils**, renowned for its restaurants.

Tortosa★

Tortosa, for centuries the last town before the sea, once guarded the region's only bridge. From the Castillo de la Suda, a castle (now a Parador), you can enjoy a fine view of the river Ebro and its valley. Tortosa's artistic endowment ranges from Gothic monuments to fine examples of Modernism.

▶ **Population:** 33 864
🚗 **Michelin Map:** 574 J 31.
🅶 **Info:** Rambla Felip Pedrell 3. ℘977 44 96 48. www.tortosaturisme.cat.
▶ **Location:** 14km/8.7mi off the coastal motor-way 90km/56mi south of Tarragona. 🚉Tortosa.

SIGHTS

Catedral★★

Croera. Open Tue–Sat 10am–2pm, 4–7pm (10am-1.30pm, 4–6.30pm mid-Oct–Mar), Sun 11–2pm. €4. ℘977 44 61 10. www.tortosaturisme.cat.

The Cathedral was built in pure Gothic style even though construction, begun in 1347, continued for 200 years. The 18C Baroque **façade★** is lavishly decorated: capitals with plant motifs, curved columns and outstanding reliefs.

In Catalan tradition the lines of the **interior★★** are plain, the high arches divided into two tiers only in the nave. The retable at the high altar has a large 14C wood **polyptych★** illustrating the Life of Christ and the Virgin Mary. Another interesting work is the 15C **altarpiece of the Transfiguration★**. Two stone 15C **pulpits★** in the nave are carved with low reliefs: on the left are the Evangelists, those on the right, Saints Gregory, Jerome, Ambrose and Augustine.

Built in Baroque style between 1642 and 1725, the **Capella de Nuestra Señora de la Cinta★** (Chapel of Our Lady of the Sash) is decorated with paintings and local jasper and marble; at its centre is the sash of Our Lady (services of special veneration: first week in September). The stone **font** is said to have stood in the garden of the antipope Benedict XIII, Pedro de Luna, and bears his arms.

Palau Episcopal★

Croera 9. Open Mon-Fri 10am-2pm. Closed public holidays & Aug. No charge. ℘977 44 96 48. www.tortosaturisme.cat.

The 14C Catalan patio of this Bishop's Palace, built in the 13C–14C, is known for its straight flight of steps which occupies one side, and the arcaded gallery. On the upper floor, the **Gothic chapel★**, has ogive vaulting in which the ribs descend to figured bosses.

Reials Col·legis de Tortosa★

Sant Doménec. 12. Open Tue–Sat 10am–1.30pm, 4.30–7.30pm (3.30–6.30pm Apr–Oct), Sun 11am–1.30pm. €3, no charge last Sun of the month. ℘977 44 46 68. www.tortosaturisme.cat.

In 1564 Emperor Charles V sponsored this lovely Renaissance ensemble. The **Colegio de Sant Lluís★** at one time educated newly converted Muslims. The fine oblong **patio★★** is curiously decorated with characters in a wide range of expressions and attitudes. The Renaissance façade of the **Colegio de Sant Jordi y de Sant Domingo** bears a Latin inscription (*Domus Sapientiae*, House of Knowledge). The adjacent **Església de Sant Domènec** was built in the 16C and once formed part of the Reales Colegios.

EXCURSION

Parque Natural del Delta del Ebro★★ (Ebro Delta Nature Reserve)

▶ 25km/15.5mi E. of Tortosa.

This vast delta (www.deltebre.net), a swampy stretch of alluvium deposits dumped by the Ebro, now acts as a bird reserve. **Boat trips** between the main settlement of Deltebre and the river mouth can be taken (℘977 480 128; www.creuersdeltaebre.com).

Aragón

One of Spain's least known and least visited regions, Aragón is over twice the size of Wales or New Jersey, but is a sparsely populated wild land with more than half its 960,000 population huddled into its only city, Zaragoza. The very name Aragón evokes images of a romantic, medieval Spain and is well known in European history as its kingdom once held sway across Barcelona, Valencia and as far afield as Sardinia. The Crown of Aragón was disbanded after its union with Castile, however, and, by the early 18C, had reverted to its sleepy provincial role. Today it is largely a destination for lovers of the great outdoors.

Zaragoza and Central Aragón

The tongue-twisting capital of Aragón – its present name supposedly derives from the name of the Roman colony of Caesar Augusta – is a vibrant city.

At first sight it is unprepossessing with traffic-laden streets and numerous unattractive modern buildings, many designed to accommodate the steady influx from the countryside over the last 50-or-so years, but at its heart is the historical old town (*casco viejo*) so typical of many Spanish cities.

Outside the capital, much of central Aragón is flat and featureless. The main source of livelihood is farming around Huesca and stock-raising in the valleys. Huesca, the quiet capital of Upper Aragón, has an appealing historic centre. Nearby Barbastro boasts fine 16C architecture and makes a good base for exploring the Central Pyrenees and picturesque historic villages such as Roda de Isábena.

Northern Aragón

The northernmost part of Aragón butts right up to the French border and is known as the Aragonese Pyrenees (Pirineos Aragoneses). The highlight of this spectacular region is the Parque Nacional de Ordesa y Monte Perdido, while the Ordesa Canyon is one of Spain's natural wonders and Europe's riposte to the Grand Canyon in the US. Near here, the Monasterio de San Juan de la Peña occupies a spectacular location beneath overhanging rock.

Southern Aragón

The clay hills bordering the Ebro Basin in Bajo Aragón (Lower Aragón) around Daroca and Alcañiz are planted with vineyards and olive groves. Brick villages and ochre-coloured houses merge with the tawny-hued and deeply scored hillsides. The jewel of

Highlights

1. The sheer size and various styles of the cathedral, La Seo, **Zaragoza** (p404)

2. Magnificent Mudéjar towers and other architecture in **Teruel** (p409)

3. The location of **Monasterio de San Juan de la Peña** (p415)

4. Trekking amid breathtaking scenery in the **Parque Nacional de Ordesa** (p417)

5. Crossing the **Valle de Pineta** in the Aragonese Pyrenees (p420)

Bajo (Lower) Aragón is Teruel, declared a UNESCO World Heritage Site on account of its rich Mudéjar (Christian-Moorish) architecture.

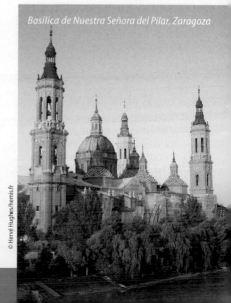

Basílica de Nuestra Señora del Pilar, Zaragoza

© Hervé Hughes/hemis.fr

Zaragoza★★

The domes of the Basílica del Pilar, the leading Marian shrine in Spain, dominate Zaragoza, on the right bank of the River Ebro. The city, rebuilt after the 19C War of Independence, combines historic monuments with bustling modern boulevards. Zaragoza is a university and religious centre, while Expo 2008 brought a much needed tourism facelift.

▶ **Population:** 664 953
⬙ **Michelin Map:** 54 H 27 (town plan).
🅱 **Info:** Ntra. Sra. del Pilar, s/n. ℘902 142 008. www.zaragoza.es/turismo.
◉ **Location:** Zaragoza is in NE Spain in a fertile pocket watered by the Aragón canal and the Ebro, Gállego, Jalón and Huerva rivers. 🚆Zaragoza (AVE).

THE CITY TODAY

Like major events in other Spanish cities, the legacy of Zaragoza's successful Expo 2008 (⬙see sidebar) is a much more visitor-friendly city. The most notable addition is the Parque del Agua, a development along the Ebro of outdoor bars and restaurants, urban beaches and bike lanes. New hotels, better infrastructure (within the city and with the rest of Spain) and improvements in tourist facilities are also evident. The only downside, of course, is an inevitable hike in prices.

A BIT OF HISTORY

Caesaraugusta-Sarakusta – Salduba, at the confluence of the Ebro and its tributaries, became Roman Caesaraugusta in 25 BC. On 2 January in AD 40, according to tradition, the Virgin appeared to St James, leaving the pillar around which the **Basílica de Nuestra Señora del Pilar** was later built. The

Uncounted Martyrs of the 3C, persecuted by Diocletian, are interred in the crypt of **Santa Engracia**.

To learn more of the Roman city, visit the four **Caesaraugusta museums**: **Museo del Teatro de Caesaraugusta** (Theatre Museum, San Jorge 12; ℘976 72 60 75); **Museo de las Termas Públicas** (Public Baths Museum, San Juan y San Pedro; ℘976 72 14 23); **Museo del Foro de Caesaraugusta** (Forum Museum, pl. la Seo 2; ℘976 72 12 21); **Museo del Puerto Fluvial de Caesaraugusta** (River Port Museum, pl. San Bruno 8; ℘976 72 12 07). All sites open Tue–Sat 10am–2pm, 5–9pm, Sun 10am–2.30pm. €3 each or €7 combined ticket, no charge first Sun of the month. www.zaragoza.es/ciudad/museos.

The Muslim occupation of the city (renamed Sarakusta) lasted four centuries. The **Aljafería** (⬙see Sights), a palace built by the first Benihud monarch of an 11C taifa kingdom, is a unique example of Hispano-Muslim art.

Capital of Aragón – The Aragón kings freed Zaragoza from the Moors and proclaimed it capital. The city retained its autonomy and prospered. It protected its Muslim masons, who embellished the apse of **La Seo** (Cathedral, ⬙see Sights, p405), and the **San Pablo** (San Pablo 42) and **Magdalena** (pl. Magdalena) churches in Mudéjar style. Houses with elegant patios and *artesonado* ceilings reflect prosperity in the 16C.

Water, Water...

The theme of **Expo 2008** was Water and Sustainable Development. The most iconic structures from the Expo are located in Avenida de Ranillas: the **Water Tower**, a 76m/249ft high skyscraper in the shape of a water droplet, and the **Bridge Pavilion**, a 270m/295yd long bridge shaped in a curving line over the River Ebro.

Two heroic sieges – Zaragoza had resisted a siege by Napoleon's army from June to 14 August 1808 and exultant Zaragozans sang "The Virgin of Pilar will never be French." Alas, General Lannes laid siege again from 21 December until 20 February, 1809. By its end, 54 000 inhabitants, around half of the city, had died. The shrapnel-pitted **Puerta del Carmen** (Carmen Gate; av. César Augusto) still bears witness.

SIGHTS
La Seo★★
Pl. de la Seo. Open summer Mon–Thu 10am 6pm, 8-8.30pm, Fri 10am–6pm, Sat 10am-noon, 1–8.30pm, Sun 10-11.30am, 1.30am–8.30pm; winter Mon–Fri 10am–2pm, 4–6.30pm, Sat 10am–12.30pm, 4–6.30pm, Sun 10–noon, 4–6.30pm. €4 (inc. museums). ℘976 29 12 31. www.zaragoza.es.
Not to be confused with the Basilica, the Cathedral of Zaragoza, La Seo, is of remarkable size and includes all styles from Mudéjar to Churrigueresque, although it is basically Gothic. The tall belfry was added in the 17C, the Baroque façade in the 18C. View the Mudéjar **east end** from calle del Sepulcro. The interior has five aisles of equal height. Above the high altar is a Gothic **retable★** with a predella carved by the Catalan Pere Johan, and three central panels of the Ascension, Epiphany and the Transfiguration sculpted by Hans of Swabia (the stance and modelling of the faces and robes strike a German note). The **surrounding wall of the chancel** (trascoro) and some of the side chapels were adorned in the 16C with carved figures, evidence of the vitality of Renaissance Spanish sculpture. Other chapels, ornamented in the 18C, show Churrigueresque exuberance. One exception is the **Parroquieta**, a Gothic chapel with a Burgundian-influenced 14C tomb and a Moorish **cupola★** in polychrome wood with stalactites and strapwork (15C).

Museo Capitular★
In the sacristy. Exhibited are paintings, an enamel triptych and church plate including silver reliquaries, chalices and an enormous processional monstrance made of 24 000 pieces.

Museo de Tapices★★
An outstanding collection of Gothic hangings, woven in Arras and Brussels.

La Lonja★
Pl. del Pilar. Open only during exhibitions, usually Tue Sat 10am–2pm, 5–9pm, Sun and public holidays 10am–2.30pm. ℘976 39 72 39. www.zaragoza.es.
Zaragoza, like many other principal Spanish trading towns, founded a commercial exchange during the 16C. These buildings, in a style between Gothic and Plateresque, include some of the finest civil architecture in Spain. The vast hall is divided in three by tall columns, their shafts ornamented with a band of grotesques. Coats of arms supported by cherubim mark the start of the ribs which open into star **vaulting**. The **ayuntamiento** (town hall; pl. del Pilar 18) has been rebuilt in traditional Aragón style with ornate eaves. Two modern bronzes stand at the entrance.

Basílica de Nuestra Señora del Pilar★
Open daily 6.45am–8.30pm (9.30pm Sun). No charge. ℘976 39 74 97. www.basilicadelpilar.es.
Successive sanctuaries on this site have enshrined the miraculous pillar (pilar) above which the Virgin appeared. The present building, Zaragoza's second cathedral, was designed by Francisco Herrera the Younger in about 1677.
A buttressed quadrilateral, it is lit by a central dome. The cupolas, with small lantern towers, whose ornamental tiles reflect in the Ebro, were added by Ventura Rodríguez in the 18C. Inside, some of the frescoes decorating the cupolas were painted by Goya as a young man. The **Capilla de la Virgen** (Lady Chapel) by Ventura Rodríguez is virtually a miniature church. It contains,

in a niche on the right, the pillar and a Gothic wood statue of the Virgin. The Virgin's mantle is changed every day except on the 2nd of the month (the Apparition was on 2 January), and the 12th of the month (for the celebration of the Hispanidad, 12 October). Pilgrims kiss the pillar through an opening at the rear. The **high altar** is surmounted by a **retable**★ by Damián Forment of which the predella is outstanding. The **coro** is closed by a high grille and adorned with Plateresque stalls.

Museo Pilarista★

Open Mon-Fri 10am-2pm, 4-8pm, Sat 10am-2pm. €2. ☎976 299 564.
On display are sketches made by Goya, González, Velázquez and Bayeu for the cupolas of Our Lady of the Pillar, a model by Ventura Rodríguez, and some of the jewels which adorn the Virgin during the Pilar festivals. Among old ivory pieces are an 11C hunting horn and a Moorish jewellery box.

Aljafería★

Av. de Madrid. Open Apr-mid-Oct daily 10am-2pm, 4.30-8pm; mid-Oct-Mar 10am-2pm, 4-6.30pm, Sun 10am-2pm. Guided tours in English Jul-Aug at 10am and 5pm. Last admission 30mins before closing. €5, no charge Sun. ☎976 28 96 83. www.turismodezaragoza.es.
It is unusual to find such magnificent Moorish architecture in this part of Spain. Built in the 11C by the Benihud family, it was modified by the Aragonese kings (14C) and Catholic Monarchs (15C) before being taken over by the Inquisition and later converted into a barracks. The Moorish palace centres on a rectangular patio bordered by porticoes with delicate tracery and carved capitals.
The **musallah**, the mosque of the emirs, is restored with *mihrab* and multifoil arches and floral decoration.
The first floor and the staircase are in the Flamboyant Gothic of the Catholic Monarchs. Only the ornate **ceiling**★, its cells divided by geometric interlacing and decorated with fir cones, remains of the throne room.

Museo Goya - Collección Ibercaja★

Calle Espoz y Mina 23. Open Mon–Sat Mar–Oct 10am–pm, Nov–Feb 10am–2pm, 4–8pm, Sun year round 10am–2pm. Closed 1 & 6 Jan, 25 Dec. €4, no charge second Sun of the month, 29 Jan, 5 Mar, 23 Apr, 18 May. ☎976 397 387, http://museogoya.ibercaja.es.
This museum, fruit of a collection gathered by the historian Jose Camón Aznar (1898–1979) and his wife, consists of a plethora of paintings from the 15–20C exhibited in the Casa Alguilar, a sumptuous Renaissance palace. An entire section is devoted to drawings and prints by Goya, from the famous *Los Caprichos* to *The Disasters of War* and the *Tauromaquia* (Bullfighting) series.
Executed at the turn of the 18–19C, these works were a creative breakaway for Goya as he embarked upon controversial social subjects in a dynamic and realistic way.

Museo Pablo Gargallo★

San Felipe Pl 3. Open Tue–Sat 10am–2pm, 5–9pm, Sun 10am–2.30pm. €4, no charge first Sun of the month, 29 Jan, 18 May, 12 Oct. ☎976 72 49 23. www.zaragoza.es.
The beautiful Condes de Argillo palace plays host to this delightful and surprising museum dedicated to the great Aragonese sculptor Pablo Gargallo (1881–1934). A good friend of Picasso and Juan Gris, Gargallo divided his time between Barcelona and Paris and worked mainly in metals (copper, iron, lead etc.), mainly focusing on the human body in a figurative style.
The museum also includes drawings, documents, his working tools and a timeline, all which help place this little known artist in context amongst his contemporaries.

Museo de Zaragoza★

Plaza de los Sitios 6. Open daily Tue–Sat 10am–2pm, 5–8pm, Sun 10am–2pm. No charge. ☎976 22 21 81. www.museodezaragoza.es.
Founded in 1848 to house artworks from defunct convents and monaster-

ies, this grand museum has gone on to extend its collection to archaeological remains from the city's Iberian origins and also fine art, including works by local lad Goya.

Centro de Historias★

Plaza San Agustín 2. Open Tue–Sat 10am–2pm, 5–9pm, Sun 10am–2.30pm. No charge. ℘976 72 18 85. www.zaragoza.es

Housed in a former convent, this interesting museum thematically traces Zaragoza's history, including the important role that trade played in the city's development. It also often holds temporary art exhibitions.

IAACC Pablo Serrano

Paseo María Agustín 20. Open Tue–Sat 10am–2, 5–9pm, Sun 10am–2pm. No charge. ℘976 28 06 60. www.iaacc.es. This institute of contemporary art and culture, named after a local sculptor, has a wide range of exhibits including those relating to architecture and design.

Caixa Forum

José Anselmo Clavé 4. Open daily 10am–8pm. No charge, €4 for exhibitions. ℘976 76 82 00. https://obrasocial.lacaixa.es/ nuestroscentros/caixaforumzaragoza. Opened in 2014, this cultural centre hosts exhibitions on the themes of art and science.

EXCURSIONS

Fuendetodos
Casa Natal de Goya

◗ 45km/28mi SW along the N 330; after 21km/13mi bear left onto the Z 100. Open Tue–Sun and public holidays 11am–2pm, 4–7pm. Closed 1 Jan, 24, 25, 31 Dec. €3. ℘976 14 38 30. www.fundacion fuendetodosgoya.org.

It was in a modest house in this village – now the Casa Natal de Goya y Museo del Grabado – that the great painter Francisco Goya y Lucientes was born in 1746. There is a display of his etchings next door.

Tarazona

◗ 21km/13mi SW on the N 121.

Tarazona was once the residence of the kings of Aragón. The royal mansion, now the Palacio Episcopal (Episcopal Palace; Rúa Alta de Bécquer; open Sat–Sun and public holidays 11.30am–2.30pm, 4.30–8.30pm; ℘976 64 28 61), is in a quarter with narrow streets overlooking the quays of the River Queiles.

Catedral de Tarazona

Juicio. Open Apr–mid-Sept Tue–Sat 11am–2pm, 4–7pm, (Sun until 6pm). See website calendar for winter schedule. €4, inc. museum. ℘976 64 02 71. www.catedraldetarazona.es.

The Cathedral was largely rebuilt in the 15C and 16C. Its mix of styles includes Aragón Mudéjar in the belfry tower and lantern, Renaissance in the portal and, in the second chapel★ as you walk left round the ambulatory, delicately carved Gothic tombs of the two Calvillos cardinals from Avignon. The Mudéjar cloisters have bays filled with 16C Moorish plasterwork tracery.

Monasterio de Veruela★★

◗ 39km/24mi S from Tudela. From Tarazona (17km/10.5mi), take the N 122 towards Zaragoza then bear right onto the Z 373. Open Apr–Sept Wed–Mon 10.30am–8pm; Oct–Mar Wed–Mon 10.30am–6pm. ℘976 64 90 25. http:// monasteriodeveruela.blogspot.co.uk. Cistercian monks from France founded a fortified monastery in the mid-12C. The 19C Sevillian poet Bécquer stayed here while writing Letters from My Cell, in which he described the Aragón countryside.

Iglesia★★

The church, built in the transitional period between Romanesque and Gothic, has a sober façade with a single oculus, a band of blind arcades lacking a baseline, and a doorway decorated with friezes, billets and capitals. Inside, vault groins are pointed over the nave, and horseshoe-shaped elsewhere.

Claustro★

The cloisters are ornate Gothic. At ground level the brackets are carved with the heads of men and beasts; above are three Plateresque galleries. In the **Sala Capitular★** (chapter house), in pure Cistercian style, are the tombs of the first 15 abbots.

Daroca★

◯ At the crossroads of the N 234 and N330, close to Calatayud (40km/25mi N); Zaragoza (85km/53mi NE); Teruel (96km/59.6mi S).

Daroca's battlemented walls★, originally with 100 towers and gateways, lie between two ridges. **Puerta Baja** (Lower Gate) is flanked by square towers.

Colegiata de Santa María

Pl. de España 8. Open Tue–Sun 8am–1pm, 5.30–6.30pm. €3. ℘976 80 07 32. www.turismodezaragoza.es.

This Romanesque collegiate church, a repository for the holy cloths, was modified in the 15C and 16C.

Beside the belfry is a Flamboyant Gothic portal.The late Gothic nave includes a Renaissance cupola above the transept crossing. The **south chapels** are partly faced with 16C *azulejos*. To the right of the entrance is a 15C **altarpiece★** in multicoloured alabaster believed to have been carved in England. The 15C **Capilla de los Corporales★** (Chapel of the Holy Relics) is on the site of the original Romanesque apse. The altar includes a shrine enclosing the holy altar cloths. Statues in delightful poses are carved of multicoloured alabaster. The painted Gothic **retable★** is dedicated to St Michael.

Museo Parroquial★

Pl. de España. Open Tue–Sun 11am–1pm, 6–8pm. €3. ℘976 80 07 61.

Holdings include two rare though damaged 13C panels and **altarpieces** to St Peter (14C) and St Martin (15C), and gold and silver plate mostly of local manufacture, as well as **chasubles**.

Monasterio de Piedra★★

Open Monastery: open daily 10am–1pm, 3–5pm. €8. Park & Waterfalls: open daily Apr–Sept 9am–7pm, Oct–Mar 9am–6pm. €15,50. ℘976 87 07 00. www.monasteriopiedra.com.

Hidden in a fold of this arid plateau is an oasis fed by the River Piedra. Approach the monastery via Ateca, across a parched landscape above the Tranquera Reservoir and past the village of Nuévalos. The site was discovered by Cistercian monks, who generally chose pleasant surroundings. Monks from the Abbey of Poblet in Tarragona established a monastery in 1194. It was rebuilt several times and recently some of the buildings have been reconstructed to incorporate a hotel, but the main part of the abbey is open to visitors. Here you can not only appreciate the beautiful Cistercian architecture but also a **Museum of Wine**, an exhibition on chocolate making and a **Carriage Museum**. There is also a hotel and spa here.

The monastery park **waterfalls and cascades★★** are everywhere along the footpath through the forest (follow red signposts to go, blue to return). The paths, steps and tunnels laid out last century by **Juan Federico Muntadas** have transformed an impenetrable forest into a popular park.

The first fall is the **Cola de Caballo** (Horse's Tail), a cascade of 53m/174ft. You come on it again at the end of your walk if you descend steep and slippery steps into the **Cueva Iris** (Iris Grotto). **Baño de Diana** (Diana's Bath) and **Lago del Espejo** (Mirror Lake), are nearby.

ADDRESSES

🏨 STAY

🛏 **Be Hostel Zaragoza** – Predicadores 70. ℘976 282 043. www.behostels.com/zaragoza/. In a 15th-century palace near the river, this hostel has double rooms as well as dorms. There is also a kitchen. They also offer free guided tours and there is often live music in the bar.

Catalonia El Pilar –
Manifestación 16. ✆976 20 58 58.
www.hotelscatalonia.com. 66 rooms.
⊑€13. Restaurant ⊜⊜⊜. Housed in a
lovely Modernista building in the heart
of the old town, this four-star hotel with
a gym is a good, comfortable choice
with modern rooms and a decent
restaurant .

Ⲩ/EAT

Bodegas Almau – Estébanes 10.
✆976 299 834. www.bodegasalmau.
es Lively tapas bar with a tiled interior

dating from 1870; there's also a
courtyard. Try the chicken stuffed with
cheese and spinach, covered in orange
sauce.

Casa Lac – Mártires 12. ✆976
396 196. www.restaurantecasalac.com.
Situated in the lively 'El Tubo' district,
this restaurant, with a tapas bar and two
dining rooms, is said to be the oldest
restaurant in Spain. Vegetables from
their own garden feature prominently.

Teruel★

Isolated amid rugged hills and
deep ravines, Teruel has retained
the charm of its narrow streets and
splendid buildings which transport
visitors back through the centuries.
The smallest provincial capital,
of Bajo (Lower) Aragón, it is a
UNESCO World Heritage Site for its
magnificent Mudéjar architecture.

▶ **Population:** 35 590
⚲ **Michelin Map:** 574 K 26.
🛈 **Info:** Plaza Amantes 6.
✆978 62 41 05.
www.turismo.teruel.net.
◐ **Location:** Teruel is at 916m/
3 005ft directly east of Madrid
on the Turia river. ▭Teruel.

SIGHTS

Plaza del Torico, the heart of the town,
is lined with Rococo-style houses. It is
named for a small statue of a bull calf.

Torre de San Martín★

Plaza del Perá Prado.
The most central of the four Mudéjar
towers in Teruel actually consists of
two; one embedded within the other.
Observe the lovely green and white
ceramic embellishment.

Casa de la Comunidad-
Museo Provincial★

Pl. Fray Anselmo Polanco 3. Open Tue–Fri
and public holidays 10am–2pm, 4–7pm,
Sat–Sun 10am–2pm. Closed 1 Jan, 1 May,
24, 25, 31 Dec. No charge. ✆978 60
01 50. http://museo.deteruel.es.
The museum, in a mansion with an
elegant Renaissance façade crowned
by a gallery, displays ethnological and

archaeological collections, including
tools and everyday objects. Note the
reconstitution of a forge and the 15C
Gothic door knocker. The first floor is
given over to ceramics, for which Teruel
has been renowned since the 13C. The
upper floors contain objects from many
time periods: prehistory (note the Iron
Age sword from Alcorisa); Iberian age;
the Roman period (a catapult); and from
Arab times (see the 11C incense burner).

Catedral de Santa María
de Mediavilla

Pl. de la Catedral. Open Jun–Oct Mon–
Sat 11am–2pm, 4–8pm, Sun 4–8pm;
Nov–May Mon–Sat 11am–2pm, 4–7pm,
Sun 4–7pm. ✆978 61 80 16.
http://turismo.teruel.net.
The cathedral, originating in the 13C
(tower), was enlarged in the 16C and 17C.
The late 13C **artesonado ceiling★**, once
hidden beneath star vaulting, is a precious

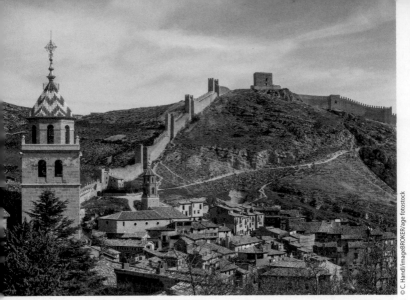

Albarracín

example of Mudéjar art. Its beams and consoles are painted with decorative motifs, people at court and hunting scenes. In the north transept is a 15C **altarpiece** of the Coronation of the Virgin.

Iglesia de San Pedro & Mausoleo de los Amantes

Matías Abad. Open daily 10am–2pm, 4–8pm, Sun 10am-8pm . €7, mausoleum €3. ℘978 618 398.
www.amantesdeteruel.es.

The church retains a Mudéjar tower and east end. The adjoining **Mausoleo de los Amantes** (The Mausoleum of the Lovers) houses the town's very own 13C star-crossed Romeo and Juliet – *Juan (Diego) Martínez de Marcilla and Isabel de Segura*. The deceased are depicted in a 20C alabaster relief by Juan de Ávalos.

EXCURSIONS
Albarracín★

◗ 38km/23.6mi W along the N 234 and A 1512.

Hidden in the Sierra de **Albarracín**, this medieval city, tinged with pinkish hues has an exceptional **site★**, on a cliff above the Guadalaviar river. The ramparts rising behind the town were built by the Moors in the 10C and restored by the Christians in the 14C. Caves in the surrounding sierra contain **rock engravings** from the Upper Palaeolithic era, such as the sites at Callejón del Plou and Cueva del Navaza (5km/3mi SE towards Bezas and Valdecuenca).

Alcañiz

◗ 49km/92mi NE of Teruel along the N 420 and N 211.

Alcañiz, set in olive groves, is the capital of Lower Aragón. The region is famous for its Holy Week ceremonies.

Two memorable façades meet on the **Plaza de España★**: the tall Catalan Gothic arcade of the **Lonja**, once a market, and the Renaissance town hall *(ayuntamiento)*. Both are crowned by an Aragón gallery with overhanging eaves. Vertical lines and a Baroque **portal★** mark the collegiate **Colegiata de Santa María la Mayor** (open daily 9am–1pm, 4–7pm; no charge), rebuilt in the 18C. Massive columns with composite capitals rise to a projecting cornice. The hilltop **Castillo de los Calatravos** (open daily 10am-7pm, ℘978 83 12 13; www.alcaniz.es) was the local seat of the Order of Calatrava in the 12C. The part used as a Parador dates from the 18C. Note the Gothic chapel, with its aisle of equilateral arches, and in the keep, 14C wall paintings.

Huesca★

The tranquillity of Huesca, capital of Alto Aragón (Upper Aragón), belies its turbulent past. The old town huddles around the top of a promontory crowned by an imposing cathedral.

A BIT OF HISTORY

Historical notes – Huesca was the capital of a Roman state, a Moorish stronghold until its reconquest by **Pedro I of Aragón** in 1096, and capital of Aragón until 1118.

The origins of a well-known Spanish saying – "Ringing like the bell of Huesca" – is a Spanish way to describe a dire event. In the 12C, King **Ramiro II** summoned his truculent nobles to watch the casting of a bell – and promptly had them beheaded.

SIGHTS
OLD QUARTER
Catedral★

Pl. de La Catedral 4. Open Mon–Fri 10am–1.30pm, 4–6pm, Sat 10am–1.30pm. €4 (inc. museum and tower). ℘974 23 10 99. www.huescaturismo.com.

The 13C Gothic façade is divided unusually by a gallery and an Aragonese carved wood overhang. A gable encloses a rose window and the portal covings with weathered statues. On the tympanum are the Magi and Christ before Mary Magdalene.

The alabaster **altarpiece★★** dates from 1533. In this masterpiece by Damián Forment, three scenes of the Crucifixion appear in high relief in the middle of Flamboyant canopy and frieze decoration. Facing the Cathedral, the town hall is a tastefully decorated town house.

Museo de Huesca★

Pl. Universidad 1. Open Tue–Sat 10am–2pm, 5–8pm, Sun and public holidays 10am–2pm. Closed 1 & 6 Jan, 24–25, 31 Dec. No charge. ℘974 22 05 86. www.museodehuesca.es

▸ **Population:** 52 239
Ⓖ **Michelin Map:** 574 F 28.
🅸 **Info:** Plaza Luis López Allué. ℘974 29 21 70. www.huescaturismo.com.
Ⓒ **Location:** Huesca is 72km/44.7mi N of Zaragoza, 91km/56.5mi S of Jaca and 123km/76.4mi NW of Lleida/Lérida, along the E 7 motorway. It is a good base for excursions into the Pyrenees. 🚆Huesca (AVE).
Ⓠ **Timing:** 2hr for the town.

This museum is set in the old university, built in 1690 around a fine octagonal patio incorporating parts of the royal palace (the site of the notorious "bell" massacre). The collection includes prehistoric artefacts and **Aragonese primitive paintings★**, several by the Maestro de Sigena (16C).

Iglesia de San Pedro el Viejo★

Pl. de San Pedro. Open Mon–Sat 10am–1.30pm, 4–6pm; Sun 11am–noon, 1–2 pm. €2.50. ℘974 22 23 87. www.huescaturismo.com.

The 11C monastery's **cloisters★**, with their historiated capitals, are a jewel of Romanesque sculpture in Aragón. The tympanum of the cloister doorway has an unusual Adoration of the Magi with all the emphasis on movement. A Romanesque chapel holds the tombs of kings Ramiro II and Alfonso I, the Battler.

CDAN – Fundación Beulas

Av. Doctor Artero, by bus from Coso Bajo and Alto, on the Zaragoza/Pamplona road. Open Thu–Fri 6–9pm, Sat 11am–2pm, 6–9pm (Nov–Mar afternoons 5–8pm); year-round Sun and hols 11am–2pm. €3. ℘974 23 98 93. www.cdan.es.

Huesca's Centro de Arte y Naturaleza, was founded by local artist José Beulas in order to create a space dedicated to contemporary art in a serene setting.

Rock formations of Los Mallos de Riglos

© santirf/iStockphoto.com

EXCURSION
Monasterio de Monte Aragón
◉ 5km/3mi E along the N 240.
This monastery was originally a fortress built by Sancho I Ramírez.

🚗 DRIVING TOUR

SIERRA DE LOARRE – LOS MALLOS DE RIGLOS
100km/62mi NW. Allow half a day.
♿See Pirineos Aragoneses map p421.

◉ Leave Huesca on the A 132 towards Pamplona. After 12.5km/7.5mi just beyond Esquedas, take the A 1206 right.

Bolea
The main church **altarpiece** is a superb example of 15C Hispano-Flemish art.

◉ Follow the road to Loarre; before the village, follow signs to the castle.

Castillo de Loarre★★
Open Nov–Feb Tue–Sun 11am–5.30pm; mid-Jun–mid-Sept daily 10am–8pm; rest of the year daily 10am–7pm. Closed 1 Jan, 25 Dec. €4.50. Guided tours €5.50. ☎974 34 21 61. www.castillodeloarre.es.
In the 11C, Sancho Ramírez, King of Aragón and Navarra, had this picture-book fortress built. At an altitude of 1 100m/3 609ft, the walls, flanked by round towers, command a vast

panorama★★ of the Ebro Basin. After the massive keep and fine covered stairway, view the 12C church. The capitals are very beautiful.

◉ Take the A 206 9.5km/6mi to Ayerbe.

Los Mallos de Riglos★★
The Río Gállego is banked by tall crumbling cliffs, red ochre in colour. **Los Mallos** are a formation of rose puddingstone, eroded into sugar loaf forms. The most dramatic group (to the right) dominates the village of **Riglos**.

◉ Return to the A 132 and after 1.5km/1mi bear left towards Agüero.

Agüero
The village is set against the spectacular background of **Los Mallos**. Before Agüero, a road leads (right) to the Romanesque **Iglesia de Santiago**.

ADDRESSES

🛏 STAY
🍽🍽 **La Posada de la Luna** – Joaquín Costa 10, Huesca. ☎974 24 17 38. www.posadadelaluna.com, 8 rooms, 🍽 €7. Adjacent to the city's ancient wall this hotel has an eclectic yet warm atmosphere with each of the rooms named after a planet. Extras include WiFi and hyrdromassage baths.

Barbastro

Barbastro's interesting architecture bears witness to its 16C importance. Today it's the capital of the Somontano wine region and a good base for Pyrenees excursions.

▶ **Population:** 17 020
⚬ **Michelin Map:** 574 F 30 – Aragón (Huesca).
🅸 **Info:** Avenida de la Merced 64. ☏974 30 83 50. www.barbastro.org.
◗ **Location:** Barbastro is at the end of two Pyrenean valleys, one leading to Parque de Ordesa, the other to the Maladeta range, via the Congosto de Ventamillo canyon. 🚃 Nearest station: Huesca (51km, AVE).

SIGHTS
Catedral★
San José de Calasanz.
Museo Diocesano – Open Tue–Sat 10am–1pm and Jun–Sept 5–8pm, Oct–Apr 4–7pm. €5, inc cathedral. ☏974 31 55 81. www.museodiocesano.es. The cathedral is a standard hall-church with three elegant aisles beneath richly ornamented vaulting with gilded decoration, borne by slender columns. The predella on the high altar **retable** is an important work by Damián Forment. Several side chapels are Churrigueresque; the first on the left-hand side holds a fine early 16C retable.

Complejo de San Julián y Santa Lucía
Av. de la Merced.
The former Hospital de San Julián houses the tourist office, a wine shop, and a **museum** dedicated to the excellent Somontano appellation. The 16C Renaissance church of San Julián opposite houses the **Centro de Interpretación del Somontano★** (open Mon–Sat 10am–2pm, 4–7.30pm, also Sun 10am–2pm Jul–Aug; €2; ☏974 30 83 50; www.rutadelvinosomanto.com), highlighting the area from the visitor's perspective.

EXCURSIONS
Alquézar★
◗ 23km/14mi NW on the A 1232, following the Río Vero.
Alquézar enjoys a magnificent isolated **setting★★** amid red earth, appearing to cling to a rocky promontory in a loop of the river.

Old Quarter
The medieval old quarter is a maze of uneven streets lined by houses adorned with rounded stone doorways and coats of arms. The arcaded main square is enchanting.

Colegiata★ A Moorish **alcázar** on the site fell to Sancho Ramírez, King of Aragón. In the late 11C and early 12C, the walls were constructed, along with a church (rebuilt in 1530). A beautiful Romanesque Christ dates from the 12C.

Cañón de Río Vero★ – 🅺 Allow a day to walk up and in some places wade or swim this spectacular canyon. Or hike only to the Roman bridge at Villacantal (2hr round trip) for an overview and to see impressive ochre and grey walls.

Alquézar
© Antoni Traver / Fotolia.com

🚗 DRIVING TOUR

THROUGH THE RIBAGORZA

85km/53mi. Allow one day.
🚗See Pirineos Aragoneses map p421.

Follows the Esera and Isábena rivers, through the historic county of Ribagorza, in the pre-Pyrenees of Aragón.

▶ Leave Barbastro on the N 123; after 16km/10mi go right onto the A 2211.

Santuario de Torreciudad

Open Jul–Aug 10am (Sun 9.30am)–2pm, 4–6.30pm, slightly reduced hours rest of the year (check website). ☎974 30 40 25. www.torreciudad.org.
In 1804, an 11C Romanesque statue of Our Lady of Torreciudad was placed in a small shrine and locally venerated. In 1975 a pilgrimage church was built under the auspices of José María Escrivá de Balaguer, founder of Opus Dei (1928). Before the brick buildings, a vast esplanade affords beautiful **views★** of the Pyrenees and the El Grado dam. The statue of Our Lady of Torreciudad is in the lower part of the altarpiece.

▶ From Torreciudad, return to the A 2211, heading towards La Puebla de Castro, then take the N 123ª.

Graus

The village huddles around the **Plaza de España**, lined by old houses decorated with frescoes, carved beams and brick galleries. The 16C **Santuario de la Virgen de la Peña★★** has a Renaissance doorway and single aisle.

▶ The A 1605 crosses the Esera river.

Roda de Isábena★

26.5km/16.5mi from Graus.
This picturesque village perches on a promontory in a beautiful mountain **setting★**. Construction of the impressive **cathedral★** (guided tours (30min); €2.50; reserve in advance; ☎974 54 45 35) began in the 11C. Most of the interior, basilical in plan with three aisles, was built in the 12C.

In the central **crypt** is the **tomb of San Ramón★★**, with interesting polychrome low reliefs. A 13C fresco adorns a chapel off the cloisters.

▶ Continue 16km/10mi N on A 1605.

Monasterio de Santa María de Obarra

Only the 10C–11C church, built by Lombard masters, remains of this monastery. A 12C hermitage stands beside it.

ADDRESSES

🛏 STAY

🍴🍴 **Hospedería de Roda de Isábena** – Pl de la Catedral, Roda de Isábena. ☎974 54 45 54. www.hospederia-rdi. com. 10 rooms. ⊂€7.50. This medieval building, which overlooks the cathedral, has clean rooms at competitive prices. The rear balconies offer magnificent views.

🍴🍴🍴 **Hotel El Mudayyan** – Nueva 18, Teruel. ☎978 62 30 42. www. elmudayyan.com ?8 rooms. ⊂€5. In the heart of the old town, this three-star hotel has individually decorated rooms (traditional and contemporary) as well as a cafe and a Moroccan-style tearoom. Underground are a series of medieval tunnels, which can be visited.

🍴 EAT

🍴🍴 **Hospedería Roda de Isábena** – Pl Pons Sorolla, Roda de Isábena. ☎974 54 45 45. www.hospederia-rdi.com. Closed Sun evening, Nov, 20–26 December. This restaurant occupies the former refectory of the monastery. It is decorated with reproductions of paintings by Velázquez and furniture from the same period as well as original 14C frescoes on one wall.

🍴🍴🍴 **Flor** – Goya 3, Barbastro. ☎974 311 056. www.restauranteflor.com. A famous restaurant in the area serving dishes based on local produce accompanied by wines from the Somontano region.

Jaca★

Jaca, the "pearl of the Pyrenees" stands strategically at their feet, under the Peña de Oroel. It was an important stop along the Camino de Santiago, and became the capital of Aragón in the 9C.

SIGHTS

Catedral★

Open Cathedral: daily noon–2pm, 4–7pm. No charge. ℘9/4 35 63 78. www.diocesisdejaca.org.

Spain's oldest Romanesque cathedral, dating from the 11C, influenced craftsmen who worked on churches along the pilgrim route to Santiago de Compostela. Note the historiated capitals★ of the south porch and great detail in the south doorway figures. Gothic vaulting covers unusually wide aisles. The apse and side chapels are decorated with sculpture but the cupola on squinches over the transept crossing has retained its simplicity.

Museo Diocesano (Diocesan Museum)

Pl. de San Pedro. Open Sept–Jun Mon–Fri 10am–1.30 pm, 4–7pm (Sat until 8pm), Sun 10am–1.30 pm. Jul–Aug Tue–Sun 10am–1.30pm, 4–8pm, €6. ℘974 35 63 78. www.diocesisdejaca.org

The cloisters and adjoining halls contain Romanesque and Gothic wall paintings★ from village churches in the area, and Romanesque paintings.

Castillo de San Pedro

Av. del Primer Viernes de Mayo. See website for opening times. €6 castle, €6 toy soldier museum, €10 both; ℘974 35 71 57. www.ciudadeladejaca.es.

Built in 1595 during the reign of Philip II as part of a network of castles and towers to guard the French border, this citadel is an outstanding example of 16C military architecture and has been declared a National Monument. Surrounded by a moat, the fortress has a perfect pentagonal plan, with defensive bulwarks at each vertex. Inside the

▶ **Population:** 13 088
Michelin Map: 574 E 28.
Info: Plaza de San Pedro nº 11–13. ℘974 36 00 98. www.jaca.es.
Location: Jaca is along the A 23, from Huesca to El Puerto de Somport, and the N 240, to Pamplona (111km/69mi NW). Jaca.

Museo de Miniaturas Militares (www. museominiaturasjaca.es), has over 32 000 military figurines.

DRIVING TOURS

1 MONASTERIO DE SAN JUAN DE LA PEÑA★★

25km/15.5mi. Allow half a day. Take the N 240 from Jaca. After 11km/6.8mi, turn off towards Santa Cruz de la Serós.

Santa Cruz de la Serós★

Pl. Mayor. Open year-round 10am–2pm. Also Nov–Feb Sat 10am–5pm, Mar–May & Sept–Oct 3.30–7pm, Jun–Aug 3–8pm. €7, see Monasterio de San Juan de la Peña for combined ticket. Closed 1 Jan, 25 Dec. ℘974 35 51 19.

This 10C convent, endowed by nobles and princesses, was abandoned in the 16C. Only the Romanesque church★, surrounded by small Aragonese houses, remains. The stout belfry, crowned by an octagonal turret, abuts the lantern. The portal recalls Jaca Cathedral.

▶ Beyond Santa Cruz de la Serós the road winds through the sierra.

Monasterio de San Juan de la Peña★★

Open same hours as Santa Cruz de Seros. €7, inc Santa Cruz de los Serós €8.50; €12, all areas (see website). ℘974 35 51 19. www.monasteriosanjuan.com.

The most spectacular feature of this monastery is its setting★★ in a hol-

Capitals of the cloisters,
Monasterio de San Juan de la Peña

© Jose Fuste Raga/age fotostock

The bucolic twin valleys of Hecho and Ansó played an important role during the Spanish Reconquest. Self-sustaining for centuries, they have retained an almost archaic economic structure based on sheep farming and agrarian activities and a lost-in-time landscape; grey stone mountain homes with distinctive, conical chimneys are clustered together in pretty hamlets in order to provide protection against the harsh winters. The inhabitants of both valleys speak a distinct dialect and their ancient culture and traditional dress is celebrated with charming festivals, that attract more locals than tourists.

low beneath overhanging rocks. The monastery was chosen as a pantheon for the kings and nobles of Aragón and Navarra, and expanded in the 12C.
The oldest features can be seen on the lower storey, where the Lower Church dates from the early Mozarabic monastery. The **Sala de Concilios** (Council Chamber) was built by King Sancho Garcés around the year 922.
The 11C–14C **Panteón de Nobles Aragoneses** are niches with coats of arms, sacred monograms and in many cases a cross with four roses, the emblem of Iñigo Arista, founder of the Kingdom of Navarra.
The late 11C **Iglesia Alta** (Upper Church) comprises a single aisle, while the three apsidal chapels with blind arcades are hollowed out of the cliff. The **Panteón de Reyes** (Royal Pantheon) opens off the north wall. The 12C **cloisters★★**, between precipice and cliff, are accessed by a Mozarabic door. Only two galleries and fragments of another remain. The **capitals★★** exhibit a personal style and use of symbolism which influenced sculpture in the region for years. There are two interpretation centres to visit; one dedicated to the monastery, the other to the Kingdom of Aragon.

2 VALLE DE HECHO AND VALLE DE ANSÓ★

114km/71mi (146km/91mi with the detour to Zuriza). Allow one day.

▷ Leave Jaca on the N 240. In Puente la Reina de Jaca, go right on the A 176.

The road follows the Aragón Subordán. The traditional houses of **Hecho★** (www.hecho.es) have stone doorways, many with coats of arms.
The **Museo de Arte Contemporáneo al aire libre**, by the tourist office, shows sculpture in the open. There is also the **Museo Etnológico Casa Mazo** (open Jul–mid-Sept 10.30am–1.30pm, 6–9pm; €1; ℘ 974 37 50 02, www.museosaspeecho.com). 2km/1.2mi to the north in Siresa is the 11C **Iglesia de San Pedro★★**, once part of a monastery. The **altarpieces★** are principally 15C (open daily 11am–1pm, 3–5pm; summer 11am–1pm, 5–8pm; €1.50).

▷ The road continues through a narrow valley towards Selva de Oza. Return to Hecho and go right on the A 17 and right again to Ansó.

Surrounded by spectacular landscape, the sleepy village of **Ansó** consists of traditional mountain homes clustered around the village church. Inside is the interesting **Museo del Traje Ansotano**, which focuses on traditional costumes of the area (call for opening times; €2; ℘ 974 370 250; www.aspejacetania.com). After taking a stroll around the village, head to Zuriza (16km/10mi away) at the bottom of the valley which opens out on to a large field dominated by

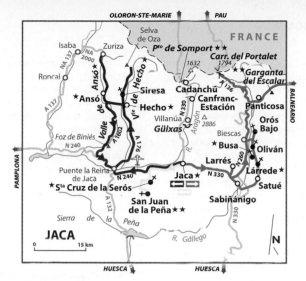

JACA

OLORON-STE-MARIE · PAU · FRANCE

Selva de Oza · Pto de Somport★★ · Carr. del Portalet · Garganta del Escalar

Isaba · Zuriza · Roncal · Ansó★ · Siresa · Cadanchú · Canfranc-Estación · Panticosa · Orós Bajo

Hecho★ · Villanúa · Güixas · Biescas · Busa★ · Oliván

Foz de Biniés · Larrés · Lárrede★

Puente la Reina de Jaca · Jaca★ · Satué

S⁺ª Cruz de la Serós · San Juan de la Peña★★ · Sabiñánigo

Sierra de la Peña · R. Gállego

JACA

0 · 15 km

HUESCA · HUESCA

---

mountains. By following the course of the Veral River via the 1602 you'll come across the 500m/1640ft-long Foz de Biniés (Biniés Gorge) enclosed by two natural stone overhanging arches.

▷ Take the N 240 back to Jaca.

3 TOUR THROUGH SERRABLO

20km/19.5mi. Allow half a day.

This excursion follows the rio Gállego and includes extraordinary 10C and 11C Mozarabic churches.

▷ Leave Jaca on the A 23 E towards Sabiñánigo.

Museo de Dibujo (Sketch Museum)

In Larrés, 18km/11mi E of Jaca along the A 23. Open Jul-Aug daily 10am-2pm, 4.30-8.30pm, Sep-Jun 10am-1.30pm, 4-7pm. €4. ☎974 48 29 81. www.serrablo.org/museodibujo. This sketch museum, set in the 14C Castillo de Larrés, displays works by Martín Chirino, Salvador Dalí and others. A section covers graphic humour.

Mozarabic churches

The churches of the Serrablo region are small and rectangular, with a semicircular apse. The most impressive are in Orós Bajo, San Martín de Oliván, **San Juan de Busa★** (with unfinished apse), **San Pedro de Lárrede★** and Satué.

Museo Ángel Oresanz y Artes de Serrablo★

San Nicolás 1, Sabiñánigo. In Puente de Sabiñánigo S of the town centre. Open Tue–Sun 10.30am–1.30pm also Sept–Jun 3–6.30pm and Jul–Aug 5–8.30pm. Closed 1 Jan, 25 Jul, 25 Dec. €2. ☎974 48 42 61. http://museo-orensanz-serrablo.blogspot.com.es. The major ethnographic collection in the Huescan Pyrenees is in a wonderful ancient traditional Serrablan house.

▷ From here you can continue to the Graganta del Escalar and Carretera del Portalet (◐see p421).

EXCURSION
Parque Nacional de Ordesa y Monte Perdido★★★

▷ This national park is 61km/38mi E of Jaca in the central Pyrenees (with its twin on the French side) and can be approached from Torla to the W or Ainsa from the SE. www.ordesa.net. 🚆Nearest station: Jaca (61km). The Ordesa canyon cuts through vast, layered limestone folds. Escarpments rise nearly 1 000m/3 280ft in grey and ochre strata, streaked in spring with cascades of snowmelt. Monte Perdido peaks at 3 355m/11 004ft. Growing up the lower slopes are pines, larches, firs

– some 25m/82ft tall – and a carpet of box, hawthorn and service trees.

Walks

A viewpoint on the entry road offers a general panorama. A second point, near the road's end, overlooks the 60m/197ft-high **cascada de Tamborrotera**.

The rest of the park may only be visited on foot. The best route for inexperienced walkers is the shaded path along the bottom of the canyon. Allow a day from the car park to the end of the canyon and back. The following walks are feasible for experienced, well-equipped hikers.

Circuito del Circo de Soaso
(Soaso Cirque Route)

Start from the Cadiera hut beyond the car park; 7hr. The walk to the valley floor is easy. The second part, via the Cola de Caballo (Horse's Tail), is only recommended to those who are well equipped and in good physical condition (steep climbs).

This walk provides the best and most complete tour of the Ordesa Valley. From the Circo de Soaso path several waterfalls can be seen including the **Gradas de Soaso**, or Soaso Steps, followed by the impressive, 70m/230ft high **Cola de Caballo**. The path continues along the **Faja de Pelay** overlooking the canyon to a depth of 2 000m/6 550ft at the foot of the Sierra de Cutas. Continue on the **Senda de los Cazadores** (Huntsman's Path) for a wonderful view of the canyon. The best panorama is from the **Mirador de Calcilarruego**. The path back to the hut drops almost 1 000m/3 281ft.

Circo de Cotatuero
(Cotatuero Cirque)

Start from the restaurant; 4hr.
On the park's northern border are the **Cotatuero** and the **Copos de Lana** waterfalls, each some 250m/820ft high.

Circo de Carriata

From the Centro de Información; 4hr. The walk is worth doing although the *clavijas* (mountaineering peg track) is

not for those who suffer from vertigo. A long hike is possible to Monte Perdido via the Goriz refuge; or to the Cirque de Gavarnie in France via the Brecha de Rolando (Roland Gap) (ask at the Centro de Información).

Cañón de Añisclo★★★

Access from Escalona village on the Bielsa-Ainsa road – a 13km/8mi drive. In the cool and lovely Añisclo Canyon; pine trees cling to the limestone walls.

Walk to Ripareta

Start from the San Urbez bridge. 5hr there and back.
A wide, well-defined path follows the enclosed Río Vellos down to its confluence with the Pardina.

ADDRESSES

STAY

A Boira – Calle Valle de Ansó 3, Jaca. ✆974 36 35 28. www.hotel aboira.com. 30 rooms. ⊒€5–8. Within walking distance of the centre of Jaca, this hotel has comfortable rooms of varying size that combine natural wood with bright colours.

Conde Aznar – Paseo de la Constitución 3, Jaca. ✆974 36 10 50. www.condeaznar.com. 34 rooms. ⊒€8. This characterful hotel is located in a shady setting and decorated with antique furniture.

Parador de Bielsa – 14km/8.5mi from Biesal in the Pineta Valley via the HU-V-6402. ✆902 54 79 79. www.parador.es. 39 rooms. Closed Feb–mid-March. ⊒€16. A haven of luxury and comfort, with a restaurant that specialises in Aragonese Pyrenean cuisine.

EAT

Bodegas Langa – Plaza San Pedro, Jaca. www.bodegaslanga.es. ✆974 36 04 94. An institution in Jaca, this tapas bar uses wine barrels as impromptu tables, and serves local cheeses, chacuterie and all manner of tapas, as well as a wide range of Spanish and local wines.

Pirineos Aragoneses★★

The central Pyrenees, in the north of Huesca province, include the highest peaks: Aneto (3 404m/11 165ft), Posets (3 371m/11 060ft) and Monte Perdido (3 355m/11 004ft). The foothills are often ravined with sparse vegetation; at the heart of the massif, accessible up the river courses, valleys lead to mountain cirques well worth exploring.

A BIT OF HISTORY

Structure and relief – Vast longitudinal bands are clear in this region. The **axis of Palaeozoic terrain** comprises the Maladeta, Posets, Vignemale and Balaïtous massifs, where there are remains of Quaternary glaciers.

In the **Pre-Pyrenees** (Monte Perdido), deep **Mesozoic limestone** is eroded into the canyons, gorges and cirques of the upper valleys. The limestone area, which extends in broken mountain chains to the Ebro Basin, is divided at Jaca by the long depression of the River Aragón. Tertiary sediment has accumulated into hills; some are bare of vegetation, in an unusual blue marl landscape like that around the **Yesa Reservoir**.

Life in the valleys – The upper valleys of the Kingdom of Aragón developed self-contained communities. Folk traditions are still followed and native costume is worn in certain valleys.

Emigration has led to the abandonment of a number of villages. Tourism is a major economic activity. Winter resorts include Candanchú, Astún, Canfranc, Panticosa, El Formigal and Benasque.

🚗 DRIVING TOURS

1 FROM AINSA TO BENASQUE

121km/75mi. Allow half a day.

◆ **Michelin Map:** 574 D 28-32, E 29-32 and F 30-31 – Aragón (Huesca)

🔢 **Info:** Avenida Ordesa 5, Ainsa. ℘974 50 07 67. www.pirineo.com.

◗ **Location:** From Pamplona/Iruña follow the N 240 to Jaca (111km/69mi SE); from Huesca the N 330 to Jaca (91km/57mi N); from Barbastro the N 123 and the A 138 to Ainsa (52km/32.5mi N).

◈ **Don't Miss:** Spectacular canyons.

Ainsa★

� Nearest station: Jaca (71km).

Ainsa, one of the prettiest towns in the Pyrenees, stands on a promontory still girded by a wall, commanding the juncture of the River Cinca and River Ara. In the 11C it was the capital of the kingdom of Sobrarbe.

Its arcaded **Plaza Mayor★★** in the upper town, under the tower of a Romanesque church, is a gem of Aragonese architecture. The contemporary-style **Museo de Oficios y Artes Tradicionales★** (pl. San Salvador 5; open Jul–Aug daily 10.30am–2pm, 5.30–9.30pm, Sept–Jun Sat–Sun 11am–2pm, 4.30–7pm; €2.40; ℘974 51 00 75, www.villadeainsa.com) is an arts and crafts museum.

◗ N 260. At Morillo de Liena, head N.

Campo

👥 **Museo de los Juegos Tradicionales** (park near the tourist office, on the N 260 and walk up; open Tue–Sat 11am–2pm, 5–8pm, Sun 11am–2pm; €1.50; ℘974 55 01 36). This museum aims to keep alive the memories of bygone games played in the region, mainly in rural areas.

◗ 11km/7mi further on is Siera.

Seira

Museo de Electricidad (in the tourist office; Tue–Fri noon–2pm; ℘974 55 31 31, www.seira.es). Known for its power plant, the municipality has opened a museum which shows the construction of the plant between 1913 and 1918, and production equipment (turbines, transformers, ammeters, etc).

Congosto de Ventamillo★★

This 3km/1.8mi defile has sheer limestone rock walls.

▶ Take the N 260 to Castejón de Sos, a paragliding centre, then the A 139. The road goes through Villanova, which has two 11C churches

Valle de Benasque★

Benasque (1 138m/3 734ft) lies in an open valley, lush and green, overshadowed by the Maladeta massif, a base for walkers, climbers (ascending the Aneto) and skiers (Cerler, 5km/3mi). Streets are lined with old mansions.

Anciles, 1.6km/1mi away, is known for its attractive houses. 15km/9.3mi further north, just before the road ends, a turn-off leads to the Hospital de Benasque (www.llanosdelhospital. com), a spa-hotel departure point for excursions into Parque Natural Posets-Maladeta.

2 NORTH OF AINSA

50km/31mi to Gistaín.

▶ From Ainsa take the A 138 towards Escalona and Bielsa. At Labuerda, take the San Vicente de Labuerda turning.

San Vincente de Labuerda

3km/1.2mi from Labuerda. Open daily in summer, rest of year, ask for the key at the local bar.
By a narrow and sometimes steep road, you arrive at this small 12C church, set apart

from the village. You enter through an *esconjuradero* (a small stone shelter). Inside, is a beautiful late 15C Gothic altarpiece. From the church, a walk of 40 mins leads to the hermitage of San Visorio, a French saint whose relics are preserved in the church. From there, the view extends over the valley of the Cinca.

▶ Take the A 138 towards Bielsa.

In **Escalona**, you can turn left into the **Cañón de Añisclo★★★** (&see p418) or continue on the A 138 through dramatic landscape up to the **Desfiladero de las Devotas★★**.

▶ Take the A 138 and bear right at Salinas de Sin.

Valle de Gistaín★

In this valley, also known as the Valle de Chistau, are some of the most picturesque villages in the Pyrenees, including **Plan**, **San Juan de Plan** and **Gistaín**.

▶ Following the A 138 N will take you to Biesla and the Vall de Pineta.

Bielsa and Valle de Pineta

19km/11.8mi NW of Plan, along A 138.

Ordesa Valley, Parque Nacional de Ordesa y Monte Perdido

From the pleasant village of Bielsa, a narrow road climbs the valley of the Cinca River, traversing the impressive landscapes of the **Valle de Pineta★★** to the Parador de Bielsa, nestled in a spectacular glacial cirque.

3 FROM AINSA TO BIESCAS

81km/51mi. Allow about 3hr.

Between **Boltaña** (16C church; www.boltana.es) and **Fiscal** (medieval tower; www.aytofiscal.es), the river course reveals underlying strata. Beyond Broto, the great mass of the Mondarruego (alt 2 848m/9 341ft), closing the Ordesa Valley, backdrops the spectacular **landscape★★** where the village of **Torla★** lies on the western slope of the Ara Valley. The church, the Iglesia de San Salvador, houses noteworthy 18C altarpieces.

The castle-abbey in Torla has an **ethnographic museum** (for information, call town hall; €1; ☏ 974 48 63 78).

Broto, Torla and Fiscal are good bases from which to explore the **Parque Nacional de Ordesa y Monte Perdido ★★★** (⌖ see p417).

4 THE PORTALET ROAD

52km/32.3mi.
Allow about 2hr.

The **Tena** Valley beyond Biescas widens out into the vast Búbal reservoir.

▶ A short distance before Escarilla, bear right onto HU 610 for Panticosa.

Garganta del Escalar★★ (Escalar Gorge)

The sun rarely penetrates this gorge. The road cuts down the west slope by ramps and hairpin bends to an austere mountain cirque, the setting

for the **Balneario de Panticosa★** (℘974 48 71 61; www.panticosa.com), a spa resort with six sulphurous and radioactive springs, and a charming 19C air.

▶ Return to Escarilla and continue to the Portalet Pass.

The mountain town Arriel of **Sallent de Gállego**, at 1 305m/4 281ft, hosts a summer music festival and is renowned for trout fishing and mountaineering. **El Formigal** (alt 1 480m/4 856ft), further on, is a ski resort.

Carretera del Portalet
Alt 1 794m/5 886ft.
The pass lies between Portalet peak and Aneu summit to the west. The view extends to the Aneu cirque and Pic du Midi d'Ossau in France (alt 2 884m/9 462ft).

5 FROM BIESCAS TO THE PUERTO DE SOMPORT

58km/36mi. Allow about 2hr.

▶ Continue S on the N 260 to Sabiñánigo – from here it is possible to follow the tour through the Serrablo (◔see JACA p4) – then take the N330 to Jaca (◔see JACA) and continues northwards.

The **Cueva de las Güixas**, (www.turismo villanua.net) a cave in Villanúa, has some 300m/330yd of galleries. Canfranc is best known for its huge, long abandoned **international railway station★★** (www.canfranc.es) that once linked Spain with France. This extraordinary example of early 20C architecture, still awaiting redevelopment, was used during the filming of Doctor Zhivago. The **Puerto de Somport★★** (alt 1 632m/5 354ft), beside the Somport tunnel, is the only pass in the Central Pyrenees that remains snow-free all year.
Candanchú (www.candanchu.com), the best-known ski resort in Aragón, is less than 1km/0.6mi away. Climb the mound to the right of the monument

for an extensive **panorama★★** of the Spanish Pyrenees.

ADDRESSES

🛌 STAY

🍴 **Hotel Dos Ríos** – Av Central 2, Aínsa. ℘974 50 09 61. www.hoteldos rios.com. 18 rooms. ☒ €7.50. Located in the lower part of the resort beside the road, this two-star hotel offers well-kept recently refurbished rooms.

🍴 **Los Arcos** – Plaza Mayor 23, Aínsa. ℘974 50 00 16. www.hotellos arcosainsa.com. 7 rooms. ☒ €7. This romantic getaway has tasteful rooms. features natural stone walls and wooden beams, modern bathrooms and comfortable furniture.

🍴 **Peña Montañesa** – 2km/0.75mi S of Labuerda on the 138 road. ℘974 51 00 51. www.hotel penamontanesa.com. 49 rooms. ☒ €6. Mountain hotel in lovely grounds, with pool, offering high levels of comfort.

🍴 **Monastario de Boltaña-Spa** – 6km/4mi NE from Aínsa on the N 260. ℘974 50 80 00. www.monasteriode boltana.es. 130 rooms. ☒ €18. This 17C monastery is a magnificent setting for a surprisingly welcoming and remarkably furnished and decorated hotel. Rooms are large, comfortable and there is a great pool.

🍽 EAT

🍴 **El Portal** – Calle Portal Bajo 5, Aínsa. ℘974 50 03 53. Opposite the Plaza Mayor, this restaurant has a pretty terrace that affords a view of the river and serves simple cocina de mercado.

🍴 **Bodegón de Mallacán** – Plaza Mayor 6, Aínsa. ℘974 500 977. www. posadareal.com. Typical Pyrenean cuisine featuring game and wild mushrooms. Good-value lunch menu. They also have a charming hotel.

🍴 **Callizo** – Plaza Mayor, Aínsa. ℘974 50 03 85. www.restaurante callizo.es. Much-loved and recently renovated, Callizo specialises in traditional, local ingredients served in a lovely, modern dining room.

La Comunitat Valenciana and La Región de Murcia

The eastern coastal strip of Valencia, Alicante and Murcia comprises the lesser-known Costa del Azahar (Orange Blossom Coast), the hugely popular Costa Blanca (White Coast) and the Costa Cálida (Warm Coast). The beaches and dunes are mostly low-lying with offshore sandbars, pools and lagoons. The climate is Mediterranean but drier than average; little rain falls except during the autumn months when the rivers sometimes flood. The natural vegetation, of olives, almond and carob trees and vines, has been gradually replaced, and the countryside transformed into *huertas* (irrigated areas), lush citrus orchards and market gardens. There are palm groves around Elche/Elx and Orihuela in the south, and rice is grown in swampy areas but in recent decades, the region's economy has based itself increasingly around the tourism industry.

Alicante and Costa Blanca

Alicante province is expat and package holiday territory, while the coastal landscape is badly scarred by huge swathes of building projects. Its most (in)famous resort is Benidorm. An evergreen with package tourists since the 1960s, its two beautiful (man-made) beaches, excellent theme parks, and cheap accommodation amid ugly high-rise hotel canyons have come to be a stereotype of tourism in Spain. Alicante/Alacant town on the other hand has remained very Spanish, while inland destinations such as Elche/Elx and the beautiful Sierra Serella provide a different perspective.

Murcia

In the hot, flat region of Murcia, visitors tend to flock around the tourist beach developments of the Costa Cálida and particularly the Mar Menor, both the largest natural lake in the country and the largest salty lagoon in Mediterranean Europe. In the midst of the tourist development, the city of Murcia remains an unspoiled oasis with a beautiful Cathedral.

Valencia and Costa del Azahar

Valencia City has always had a fascinating Old Town, fine beaches and excellent food (it is famous as the home of paella). More recently La Ciudad de las Artes y las Ciencias – a high-profile museum-arts complex – has put it on the international tourist radar. The city's image was also boosted when it played host to the America's Cup in 2007 and the port area was converted into a pleasure ground.

Highlights

1 Enjoying a plate of paella in Valencia's **Old Town** (p424)

2 Valencia's stunning **Ciudad de las Artes y las Ciencias** (p432)

3 Exploring the old quarter of picture-postcard **Peñíscola** (p435)

4 Sheltering from the heat in Elche's remarkable **Palm Grove** (p434)

5 The view from the Castillo de Santa Bárbara, **Alicante** (p441)

Much less built up than the southern costas, the Costa del Azahar is a favourite with Spanish holidaymakers who like their resorts low-key. The jewel here is Peñíscola (Spain's Mont St-Michel) while inland, the mountain region of El Maestrazgo boasts wonderful scenery and some charming villages. Xàtiva/Játiva also makes a pleasant inland excursion.

© T. Hassler/age fotostock

L'Oceanogràfic, Ciudad de las Artes y las Ciencias, Valencia

Valencia★★

Spain's third-largest city, Valencia is unprepossessing at first glance with anonymous high-rise suburbs at its outer limits. However, wide palm-lined avenues encircle the old quarter with its fortified gateways, quaint shops and Gothic houses. This is a city reborn, thanks to works by Santiago Calatrava and Sir Norman Foster and by its hosting the America's Cup in 2007. Its superb beaches are easily reached by tram from the city centre.

THE CITY TODAY

Over the last five years Valencia has become a popular city break to rank almost alongside Barcelona. Like its Catalan cousin, it too has turned its face back to the sea with its beach and particularly its port area revitalised since 2007. The eating, drinking and nightlife, here and in the Old Town are excellent.

A BIT OF HISTORY

2 000 years of history – The city founded by the Greeks in 138 BC passed into the hands of Carthaginians, Romans, Visigoths and Arabs, was briefly reconquered in 1094 by **El Cid**, and taken definitively in 1238 by James the Conqueror. Valencia prospered until the discovery of America, and again with a silk renaissance in the 17C. Valencia sided with Charles of Austria in the War of the Spanish Succession, and lost its privileges. In 1808, it rose against the French. In 1939 it was the last Republican redoubt.

Art in Valencia – Valencia flourished economically in the 15C, and artistically as well, as seen in the Gothic architecture of palaces, the Cathedral and the Lonja (Exchange). Among painters were **Luis Dalmau**, who developed a Hispano-Flemish style; **Jaime Baço (Jacomart)**, **Juan Reixach** and the **Osonas**, father and son. Notable 15C decorative arts were wrought ironwork, gold- and silversmithing, and ceramics (see the Museo Nacional de Cerámica

▶ **Population:** 786 189
◔ **Michelin Map:** 577 N 28 (town plan) or 574 N 28.
▯ **Info:** Pl. de la Reina 19. ℘963 15 39 31. www.visitvalencia.com
◐ **Location:** Valencia is the main city of the Levante region. ▭▭Valencia (AVE). Metro, 30 mins, connects airport to city centre.
▣ **Parking:** Don't try to find a space in the old quarter.
◉ **Don't Miss:** A walk in the old quarter and the Ciudad de las Artes y las Ciencias.
◕ **Timing:** Start with unmissable modern architecture (Santiago Calatrava's City of Arts and Sciences and the convention centre) and Sir Norman Foster's Turia bridge; or with the heritage section of the city.
▲▲ **Kids:** L'Oceanogràfic is one of the world's great aquariums.

in Sights, p422). **The Valencia huerta and Albufera** – The Roman irrigation system around Valencia was improved by the Moors. Orchards and market gardens produce fruit and early vegetables for Europe. South of Valencia lies a vast lagoon, the **Parque Natural de La Albufera** (see p437).

◤◣ WALKING TOUR

① CIUDAD VIEJA★ (OLD TOWN)

Allow 3hr. Follow route on town plan. Start at El Miguelete, the bell tower of the Cathedral.

El Miguelete★

Pl. de la Reina. Open daily 10am–7.30pm, Nov-Mar Mon-Fri 10am-6.30pm, Sat 10am-7pm, Sun 10am-1pm, 5.30-7pm.

The World's Largest Food Fight

The town of **Buñol** (40km/25mi W of Valencia off the A 3), numbering some 10 000 inhabitants, lies in the tranquil setting of the Sierra de Las Cabrillas. At the end of every August, the town swells beyond all proportion for the celebration of one of the most famous festivals in Spain, **La Tomatina** (www.tomatina.es). A week-long festival of parades honour the town's patron, San Luis Bertràn. This culminates on the Wednesday, when at 10am, the crowds are challenged to snatch a ham placed on a greasy pole. The feat achieved, the firing of water cannons mark the release of over a hundred metric tons of tomatoes and one hour of chaotic tomato throwing. Legend has it that this helter-skelter celebration has its roots from when a food fight among the town's youths broke out in 1945. It has now become one of the defining images of the Spanish lust for life.

€2. &963 91 81 27.
www.catedraldevalencia.es.
"Little Michael" is the main bell of this octagonal Gothic tower, dating from 1418. Climb up for a view of the cathedral and the town's roofscape.

Catedral★

Pl. de la Reina. Open Jun-Sep daily 10am (from 2pm Sun)–6.30pm. Rest of the year daily 10am–5.30pm (Sun 2-5.30pm), closed Sun Nov-Mar. €7 (including museum). &963 91 81 27.
www.catedraldevalencia.es.
Work on the cathedral began in 1262 though most of the building is 14C and 15C Gothic. The elegant and slender early 18C west face imitates Italian Baroque style. The Assumption on the pediment is by Vergara and Esteve.
The south door is Romanesque; the north, the **Portada de los Apóstoles** (Apostles' Door), is Gothic, decorated with time-worn sculptures. A statue of the Virgin and Child on the tympanum is surrounded by angel musicians.
Inside, light filters through the alabaster windows in the beautiful Flamboyant Gothic **lantern**. The **retable** in the capilla mayor (chancel), the work of Fernando de Llanos and Yáñez de la Almedina (early 16C), influenced by Leonardo, illustrates the Lives of Christ and the Virgin. In the ambulatory, a Renaissance portico protects an alabaster relief of the Resurrection (1510).

Opposite is the 15C late Gothic Virgen del Coro (Chancel Virgin) in alabaster. In a chapel is a Baroque Cristo de la Buena Muerte (Christ of Good Death).

Capilla del Santo Cáliz or Sala Capitular★ (Chapel of the Holy Grail or Chapter House)

Last chapel along the north aisle.
This chapel has elegant star vaulting and, behind the altar, 12 alabaster low reliefs. In the centre, a magnificent 1C carnelian agate cup is said to be the Holy Grail, brought to Spain in the 3C. The **museum** (same hours as cathedral) beyond contains a sizable body of work from the Valencian painter Juan de Juanes (1523–79).

▷ Leave by the main entrance, cross C. de la Correjería to Plaza de la Reina.

L'Almoina

Pl Décimo Junio Bruto. Open Mon–Sat 10am–7pm, Sun & hols 10am–2pm.
&962 08 41 73. €2, no charge Sun & hols.
Archaeological excavations have uncovered Roman and Visigothic remains. An underground tour lets you discover the substructure of ancient Valencia including remains of the Visigothic cathedral.

▷ Cross C. de la Correjería again and follow C. de la Bachilla to Plaza de la Amoina.

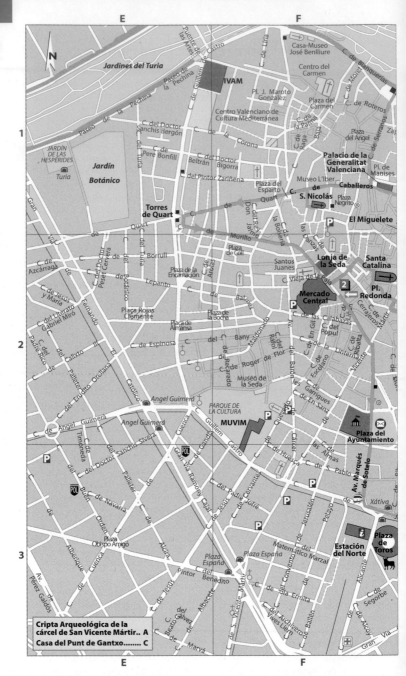

Casa del Punt de Gantxo

Plaza de la Almoina.

The façade of this building built by Manuel Peris Ferrando is distinguished by the use of original decorative elements. Against a background of coloured ceramic decorated with foliage stand pilasters whose capitals are made with plant motifs (branches and flowers). These ornaments are reminiscent

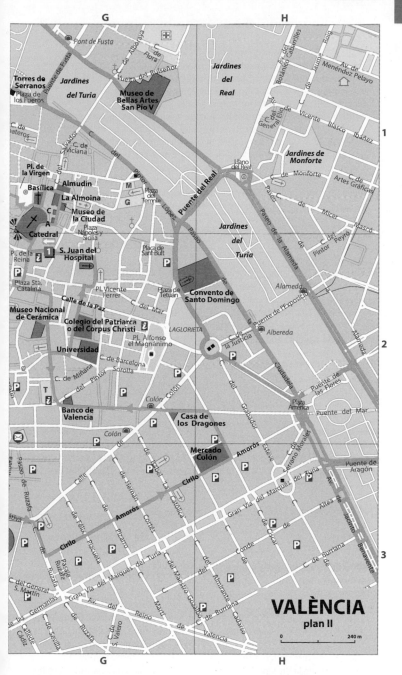

VALÈNCIA
plan II

0   240 m

of those that were used in the 15C to decorate the Lonja (see p424).

▶ Return to C. de la Bachilla and turn left.

Museo de la Ciudad

Pl del Arzobispo, 3. Open Mon–Sat 10am–7pm, Sun & hols 10am–2pm. €2; no charge Sun. ☎ 962 08 41 26. www.valencia.es.

Las Fallas

The origins of this festival date back to the Middle Ages when on St Joseph's Day, the carpenters' brotherhood burned their accumulated wood shavings in bonfires known as **Fallas** (from the Latin *fax*: torch). The name became synonymous with a festival for which, in time, objects were made solely for burning – particularly effigies of less popular members of the community. In the 17C single effigies were replaced by pasteboard groups or floats produced by neighbourhoods: rivalry is such that the figures today are fantastic in size, artistry and satirical implication. Prizes are awarded during the general festivities, which include fireworks, processions, bullfights, etc., before everything goes up in the *cremá* (fires) on the evening of 19 March. Figures *(ninots)* dating from 1934 to the present day, which have been spared from the bonfires, are on display in the **Museo Fallero** (pl. Monteolivete 4; open Mon–Sat 10am–7pm, Sun & hols 10am–2pm; closed 1 & 6 Jan, 1 May, 25 Dec; €2; no charge Sun; ☎ 963 52 54 78; www.fallas.com).

Situated inside the palace of the Marquis de Campo (18C–19C), this museum displays the municipal art collections. Exhibits are varied, from beautiful 14C and 15C ivory carvings to a large collection of old weights and measures.

Cripta Arqueológica de la Cárcel de San Vicente

Pl. del Arzobispo 1. Open Mon–Sat 9.30am–7pm, Sun & hols 10am–3pm. €2, no charge Sun & hols. ☎ 962 084 573. www.valencia.es.

The remains of a Visigothic funerary chapel with four finely worked screens and a 6C burial, and two Visigothic stone sarcophagi.

▶ Cross C. Almudín.

Almudín

Pl. San Luis Bertrán. Open Tue–Sat 10am–2pm, 4.30-8.30pm (mid-Oct–mid-Mar until 6pm), Sun & hols 10am–3pm. €2; no charge Sun & hols. ☎ 963 52 54 78. www.valencia.es.

This is a 14C–16C granary with primitive frescoes and two 19C *azulejos* altars.

▶ Head in the direction of the cathedral to P. de la Virgen.

Plaza de la Virgen★

The Basilica of the Virgen de los Desamparados and the Apostle Doorway of the Cathedral face this pleasant plaza.

Real Basílica de Nuestra Señora la Virgen de los Desamparados

Pl. de la Virgen, s/n. Open: Basilica, daily 7am–2pm, 4.30–9pm. No charge. Open: Museu Mariano, Mon & Thu 11am–2pm; Sat 10.30am–2pm, 5–8pm; Sun 10.30am–2pm. €2. ☎ 963 91 92 14. www.basilicadesamparados.org.

This late 17C church is linked to the apse of the Cathedral by a Renaissance arch. The floor plan is oval. Beneath the painted cupola is the venerated statue of the patron of Valencia, the Virgin of the Abandoned *(desamparados)*, which receives a steady flow of devotees.

▶ Go to c. Caballeros, on the west of the Plaza.

Palacio de la Generalitat★

Caballeros 2. Open Mon–Fri 9am–2pm, bookings required. No charge. ☎ 963 42 46 36. www.valencia.es.

A tower was added to this fine 15C Gothic palace in the 17C and an identical one in the 20C. Until 1707 this was the meeting place of the Valencia Cortes. In the Gothic patio is Benlliure's sculpture of Dante's Inferno (1900).

A golden salon has a wonderful gilt and multicoloured **artesonado ceiling★** and a large painting of the Tribunal de las Aguas. On the first floor are the Sala de los Reyes (Royal Hall) with portraits of the Valencian kings, and the Gran

Salón de las Cortes Valencianas (Grand Council Chamber). The *azulejos* frieze and the coffered ceiling are 16C. The rear façade and the Palau de la Batlia (provincial administration) give onto the **plaza de Manises**.

▶ From P. Manises take C. Serranos and walk to the end.

Torres de Serranos★

Pl. Fueros. Open Mon–Sat 9.30am–7pm, Sun & hols 10am–2pm. €2; no charge Sun. ℘963 91 90 70. www.valencia.es. These iconic picture-postcard towers guarding one of the city entrances are a superb example of late 14C military architecture. Great views from the top.

▶ Return to P. de Manises.

Calle Caballeros

The most important street of the old city heads from Plaza de la Virgen into the colourful Carmen district. Some of the houses have Gothic patios.

Iglesia de San Nicolás de Bari

Caballeros 35. Open Tue-Fri 10.30am-7.30pm, Sat until 6.30pm, Sun 1-7pm, Jul-Sep Tue-Fri 10.30am-9pm, Sat until 7.30pm, Sun 11.30am-9pm. €5. ℘963 91 33 17. www.sannicolasvalencia.com. This is one of Valencia's oldest churches, built Churrigueresque style, with an altarpiece by Juan de Juanes (to the left) and, by the baptismal font, *Calvary* by Osona the Elder.

▶ Continue to P. del Esparto, then follow C. de Quart to the end.

Torres de Quart

Av. Guillem de Castro. These 15C towers were damaged in the 19C by Napoleon's cannons.

▶ From P. del Esparto, take C. Bolsería.

La Lonja★★ (Silk Exchange)

Pl. del Mercado. Open Mon–Sat 10am–7pm, Sun & hols 10am–2pm. €2; no charge Sun & hols. ℘962 08 41 53. www.valencia.es.

This 15C Flamboyant Gothic building, designated a UNESCO World Heritage Centre, replaced an earlier exchange outgrown by prosperous merchants. The left wing, separated from the entrance by a tower, is crowned by a gallery with a medallion frieze. The old commercial **silk hall★★** is lofty, with ogival arches supported on slender, elegantly cabled columns; the bays are filled with delicate tracery.

Iglesia de Santa Catalina

Pl. de Santa Catalina. Open daily 10.30am–2.30pm, 5.30–7.30pm. €2 (inc tower). ℘963 91 77 13. The church is notable for its magnificent 17C **Baroque belfry★**. Climb the tower for a close up view. The church interior is sober Gothic.

Plaza Redonda

A passage on the right leads to this curious little 19C circular plaza.

▶ Out on C. Pere Compte, cross C. San Vicente Martyr then immediately turn right into C. Abadía San Martín.

Palacio del Marqués de Dos Aguas★★

Poeta Querol 2. This magnificent Baroque building houses the Museo Nacional de Cerámica y de las Artes Suntuarias González Martí The 18C marble portal was once covered by paintings.

Museo Nacional de Cerámica y de las Artes Suntuarias González Martí★★ (National Museum of Ceramics and Decorative Art)

Poeta Querol 2. Open Tue–Sat 10am–2pm, 4–8pm, Sun and public holidays 10am–2pm. Closed 1 Jan, 1 May, 24–25 & 31 Dec. €3; free Sat afternoon, Sun. ℘963 51 63 92. www.mecd.gob.es/mnceramica. This museum occupies the lovely Baroque **Palacio del Marqués de Dos Aguas★★**. On the **ground floor** is the richly decorated **carriage★** of the Marquis of Dos Aguas (1753). Rooms on the first floor include the Chinese salon, the *fumoir*, and the chapel.

The **ceramic collection** on the **second floor** includes Moorish ceramics (the basis of the craft in Spain), green and black porcelain, and later pieces from Málaga, Murcia and Manises. Christian ceramics of the 13C and 14C evidence continuity from the Moorish. Outstanding are green and manganese ceramics from **Paterna** (6km/3.7mi N of Valencia). The golden age of ceramics in **Manises** (8km/5mi N of Valencia) is represented by lovely pieces. Also on display are Chinese porcelain and European imitations, and an impressive Toledo urn. The **Real Fábrica de Alcora**, established in 1727, became the centre of innovation in Spain, spreading the Louis XIV, Classic and Baroque styles. Pieces from 19C **Manises** evidence later styles that spread through southern and eastern Spain. There is also a Valencian kitchen with 18C and 19C tiles.

▷ Go down C. Poeta Querol and turn left into C. Salva.

Colegio del Patriarca o del Corpus Christi★ (Patriarch or Corpus Christi College)

Nave 1. Guided tours (55 mins) Mon–Fri 10am–1pm, 5–6pm; Sat 10am–1pm. Open daily 11am–1.30pm. Reserve in advance. €7. ℘692 49 17 69. www.valencia.es.

This ex-seminary dates back to the 16C. The **church** (enter by left door) is one of the few Renaissance churches in Spain with frescoes; on the lower wall sections are Manises tiles. The seminary is built around a harmonious patio decorated with Talavera *azulejo* friezes.

The small **museum** of 15C–17C art includes paintings by Juan de Juanes, a **triptych of the Passion★** by Dirk Bouts, a 14C Byzantine crucifix from the Monastery of Athos, a 13C Romanesque *Christ* and a portrait of the founder, Ribera, by Ribalta, and paintings by Ribalta, Morales and El Greco. In the same plaza is the **Universidad** (University; www.uv.es).

▷ Return to C. Juan de la Ribera, cross C. de la Paz, right on C. Medines.

Iglesia de San Juan del Hospital ★ (Church of St John of the Hospital)

Trinquete de Caballeros 5 (access through courtyard). Open Mon–Sat 9.30am–1.30pm, 5–9pm; (Mon–Fri also 6.45–7.45am); Sun 11am–2pm, 5–9pm. No charge. ℘963 92 29 65. www.sanjuandelhospital.es.

This early 13C Gothic church consists of a single nave with pointed barrel vault. In the first chapel are beautiful 13C murals. There is also a museum to visit.

🐾 WALKING TOUR

2 MODERNIST VALENCIA★

Allow 1.5hr from the Mercado Central to Plaza de la Reina. 🚶Follow the route on the town plan.

Valencia's important economic development at the end of the 19C created the need for new neighbourhoods and a partial remodelling of the historic district. The bourgeoisie, the local administrative powers and financial movers and shakers, including banks, seized the opportunity to show off their wealth by building spectacular edifices. This architectural movement adopted the *modernista* style in the early years of the 20C, before returning to a more conformist approach.

Mercado Central

Pl. Ciudad de Brujas. Open Mon–Sat 7am–3pm. ℘963 82 91 00. www.mercadocentralvalencia.es.

Dating from 1928, the enormous metal and glass Central Market is fine example of *modernista* architecture. It is busiest in the mornings when the stalls are bursting with fish and local produce.

▷ Head S to the P. del Ayuntamiento.

Plaza del Ayuntamiento

This vast square Is Valencia's meeting point and a flower market makes it more colourful than most. The building that holds the town hall *(ayuntamiento)*, was built in 1915 and has a colossal façade with two corner towers topped with domes, and a grandiose entrance with a portico and campanile.

The main post office (**Correos** at the corner of Calle Correos) sits opposite. Inaugurated in 1923, its is distinguished by a dome decorated with neoclassical garlands of flowers and ribbons. North of this stand two **neo-Gothic buildings** with colourful façades.

Avenida Marqués de Sotelo

Many buildings along this avenue feature detailed façades and a wide range of decorative elements including monumental gates, towers, terraces, steeples and pediments.

▷ Walk down to C. de Xativa.

Estación del Norte★★

This landmark *modernista* railway station was built by Demetrio Ribes between 1909 and 1917. Very strongly influenced by the architecture of the Austrian Secession (note its geometric structure), it also pays homage to local culture and imagery; ceramic relief friezes depict orange trees and mosaic murals scenes of Valencian agrarian life. The lobby has a riot of decorative details: columns, lamp posts, signs of gold mosaic with phrase *buen viaje* in several languages and carved wooden windows.

Next to the station, **Plaza de Toros** (bullring), built in the mid-19C, is one of the most beautiful and important in Spain.

▷ Pass the P. de Toros, then turn right on C. Ruzafa and left into C. Cirilo Amorós.

Calle de Cirilio Amorós

This road passes through the El Pla del Remei residential neighbourhood which developed in the late 19C–20C. It now hosts chic designer and fashion boutiques, clustered around the Mercado Colón. At no. 26, notice the beautiful bay windows incorporating elements of Gothic architecture, including a rosette, and at no. 27, a door and balcony in Art Nouveau style. At no. 29 the **Casa Ferrer** was built in 1908 by Vicente Ferrer Pérez in an Art Deco style. It features stylised rose motifs and ceramic disk-like elements on a chequerboard background raised above a triglyph.

▷ Continue along C. de Cirilo Amorós.

Mercado Colón★

Calle Cirilo Amorós, on the left, between Calle Jorge Juan and Calle Conde Salvatierra de Alava.

The beautiful brick, metal and glass-building from 1913 is the work of Francisco Mora y Belenguer. The main façade features a rich decor that is rooted in Valencia's artistic traditions including aged stone, colourful mosaics depicting harvest scenes, shiny ceramics and stained glass. It houses an upmarket selection of shops, bars and trendy restaurants.

▷ Turn left on C. Conde Salvatierra de Älava then left into C. de Sorni.

Casa de los Dragónes

At the corner of C/ de Sorni and C/Jorge Juan, the Casa del Dragón owes its name to the sculptures that adorn the façade. Built in 1901 by Jose Manuel Cortina, it incorporates Gothic-inspired elements.

▷ Cross C. Colon and continue to C. Don Juan de Austria.

Banco de Valencia

At the intersection of Calle Pintor Sorolla, this building features a pretty neo-Baroque style in hues of pink and yellow, with curved balconies, ornate, framed windows and a host of mouldings and decorative details.

▷ From C. Poeta Querol turn right at the Teatro Reial. Continue on C. Marqués de Dos Aguas and then turn left into C. de la Paz.

THE AMERICA'S CUP

Like Barcelona, Valencia latched upon an international event as a catalyst for change. Ironically Valencia won the bid to host the 32nd America's Cup – the world's most prestigious sailing event – against Barcelona, and as with Barcelona's triumphal 1992 Olympics, the shoreline was a major beneficiary. British architect David Chipperfield created an arresting headquarters for the event and a number of chic bars, restaurants and hotels were opened at the port. Transport to the port area also improved, and it is now served by metro, tram and wide avenues with bike lanes. Progress came at a price however and as gentrification continues even today, some mourn that the traditional charm of El Cabayal – Valencia's old maritime neighbourhood – has been lost forever.

Calle de la Paz

This street has lots of buildings of historic interest.

At the far end, in the Plaza de la Reina, La Isla de Cuba, a former retail complex, was designed by the architect Lucas García Cardona in 1896. He successfully blended classicism with new techniques (note the use of cast iron columns). The decoration is heaviest on the upper frieze, where you can see ceramic panels of ancient Greek dancers in blue and pink.

AVANT GARDE VALENCIA
Ciudad de las Artes y las Ciencias★★★

⊛ Buy your tickets online in advance to save waiting in line, particularly in peak periods, and also for possible discounts. The individual attraction prices given below are on the door only; buying online can save 10 per cent. Combination tickets offers access to two venues (see website for prices) or to all three venues, valid for three days: €37.90, child £28.80.

Car parking €2.30 per hour. All sites: ℘961 97 46 86. www.cac.es.

The City of Arts and Sciences is a 350 000sq m/ 420 000sq yd cultural and leisure complex consisting of a series of spectacular avant-garde, blinding white buildings that are reflected in pools of water. These were mostly designed by the world-renowned Valencian-born architect Santiago Calatrava.

🐾 L'Oceanogràfic★★

Open daily year-round. Mid-Jul–Aug 10am–midnight. Rest of year 10am–6pm/8pm. See website for details. €29.10, child €21.85.

The largest aquarium in Europe is set around a lake and joined by gardens and tunnels. The exhibits focus on marine life in the Mediterranean, the Arctic and the Antarctic (with plenty of penguins) and the oceans, the highlight here being a 30m/100ft aquarium-tunnel with sharks and rays. The dolphin enclosure hosts performances all day.

L'Umbracle★ – White parabolic arches shelter this pleasant palm garden on a terrace facing the Museu de las Ciencias.

Museu de las Ciencias ★★

Open daily year-round; Jul–first week Sept 10am–9pm; rest of year 10am–6pm/7pm. See website for details. €8, child €6.20.

The largest interactive Science Museum in Europe is set in a spectacular building that resembles the skeleton of a giant sea creature. Inside is a hands-on encounter with the human genome, space travel, astronomy and more.

L'Hemisfèric★

Open daily year-round. Shows usually 11am–6pm (Fri–Sun 8pm) See website for programme. €8.80, child €6.85.

The unusual Calatrava design symbolises a human eye, open to the world; appropriately it houses a planetarium and IMAX cinema projecting onto a giant concave screen of 900 sq m.

Palau de les Arts Reina Sofía (℘961 97 58 00; www.lesarts.com) – The four halls here host classical and modern opera, music, theatre and dance.

ADDITIONAL SIGHTS
Museo de Bellas Artes★
San Pío V 9. Open Tue–Sun 10am–8pm. Closed 1 Jan, Good Friday, 25 Dec. No charge. ℘963 87 03 00, http://museobellasartesvalencia.gva.es.
This fine arts museum is in an 18C–19C collegiate church and seminary, and a contemporary extension, near the Jardines del Real (Royal Gardens).
The collection is notable for its **Valencian Primitives★★** with outstanding altarpieces, while the Renaissance period is represented by Macip and Juan de Juanes. Other outstanding works include *St Bartholomew* by Luca Giordanom, *St John the Baptist* by El Greco, an impressive *St Sebastian* by Ribera and a self-portrait by Velázquez. Goya's mastery of portraits is shown in his paintings of Francisco Bayeu and Joaquina Candado.

Jardines del Real
(Royal Gardens)
San Pío V. Open daily 7.30am–sunset
The city's biggest park is close to the pleasant **Jardín de Monforte**. The **Puente del Real** (Royal Bridge) across the **Jardín del Turia** is 16C.

Instituto Valenciano de Arte Moderno (IVAM)
Guillem de Castro 118. Open Tue–Sun 11am–7.30pm (Fri until 9pm). €6, no charge Fri 7.30-9pm. ℘963 17 66 00. www.ivam.es.
This modern building houses more than 7 000 works of contemporary art on rotating display. It also owns the largest collection of the works of sculptor **Julio González** (1876–1942).

Jardín Botánico de la Universidad
(Botanical Garden)
Calle Quart, 80. Open year-round daily subject to weather, 10am–sunset (see website for hours). €2.50. ℘963 15 68 00. www.jardibotanic.org.
In 1802 Valencia was one of the first Spanish cities to embrace the trend for public gardens.

Convento de Santo Domingo
Pl. de Tetuán 22. Group visits only. www.visitvalencia.com.
Highlights of this building include a beautiful courtyard, the Capilla de los Reyes chapel and a front gate personally designed by King Philipe II.

Museo Valenciano de la Ilustración y la Modernidad MUVIM (Museum of Illustration and Modernity)
Calle Guillen de Castro, 8. Open Tue–Sat 10am–2pm, 4–8pm, Sun and hols 10am–8pm. €2, no charge Sat & Sun. ℘963 883 730. www.muvim.es.
The beautiful contemporary building by the architect Guillermo Vázquez Consuegra provides the backdrop for numerous fascinating art exhibitions. The permanent "Adventure of Thought" exhibition traces five centuries of social and intellectual history in Europe.

Museo de la Historia★
Valencia 42. Open Tue–Sat 10am–7pm, Sun & hols 10am–2pm. €2; no charge Sun and public holidays. ℘963 70 11 05. www.mhv.valencia.es.
Located in a beautifully restored 19C water works, this museum tells the story of Valencia from its beginnings to the end of the 20C with evocative dramatised audiovisual presentations.

ADDRESSES

🏠 STAY
Hostal Antigua Morellana – En Bou 2. ℘963 91 57 73. www.hostalam.com. 18 rooms. Close to the Lonja and main market, this family-run hotel offers comfortable and bright rooms with excellent views of the picturesque Carmen district.

Hotel Alkazar – Mosén Fernandes 1. ℘963 51 55 51. www.hotelalkazar.es. 17 rooms. ⌷€3.10. Smart, modern, recently refurbished rooms offer good value in the heart of town.

Hostal Venecia – Pl. Ayuntamiento (enter through Llop 5). ℘963 52 42 67. www.hotelvenecia.com.

66 rooms. €6.90. The building is outstanding, with balconies facing the plaza del Ayuntamiento. Rooms are attractively furnished in contemporary style.

Hotel Vincci Palace – La Paz 42. 962 062 377. www.vinccihoteles.com. 76 rooms. €13.20. Stylish boutique hotel five minutes from the cathedral. The bar is a popular meeting place for cocktails.

EAT

Tasca Ángel – Púrísima 1 (adjacent to Plaza Ibáñez). 963 91 78 35. Closed Sun. This legendary place (est 1946) serves simply seasoned, grilled sardines.

Kuzina – Salvador 5. 960 01 35 54. www.kuzinavlc.com. Greek cuisine meets Spanish tapas in this tiny central restaurant, popular with a young crowd. Reservations a must.

Montes – Pl. Obispo Amigó 5. 963 85 50 25. Open Tue– Sun for lunch, Wed–Sat for dinner. Good value Mediterranean market cuisine and good service.

Sagardi – San Vicente Mártir 6. 963 91 06 68. www.sagardi.com. This top-class Basque restaurant and tapas bar attracts local gourmands.

TAPAS

Bar La Pilareta – Moro Zeit 13. 963 91 04 97. www.barlapilareta.es. Open daily noon–midnight. Founded in 1917, Pilareta is one of the best tapas bars in the city. Try the *clochinas* (tiny mussels).

Las Cuevas – Conde de Almodóvar 8. Tapas the Valencian way, from mussels to stuffed red peppers, and sardines.

CAFÉS

Santa Catalina – Pl. Santa Catalina 6. 963 91 23 79. More than 100 years old, this beautiful tiled cafe is a chocolate maker, ice-cream producer and horchatería.

NIGHTLIFE

Calle Caballeros – This is the hub of Valencia's nightlife, especially between the Pl de la Virgen and Pl Tossal.

Café de las Horas – Conde de Almodóvar 1. 963 91 73 36. www. cafedelashoras.com. Sumptuous overblown café with decadent 19C decor.

Café del Negrito – Pl. Negrito 1. 665 13 05 28. Open from 4pm. This artists' café, on a small square in the old town, is a popular meeting-place for cocktails.

Cava Siglos – Cavallers 12. 963 91 62 71. www.cavasiglos.com. Smart wine bar serving Valencian vino.

SHOPPING

Lladró Boutique – Poeta Querol 9. 963 51 16 25. www.lladro.com. Open Mon–Sat 10am–8pm. The Valencia branch of this world-famous porcelain manufacturer, which is based just north of the city centre at Tavernes Blanques. See website for details of visiting the factory and museum.

Mercadillo de la Plaza Redonda – Open Mon–Sat 10am–8pm, Sun 8am–2pm. The Sunday open-air flea market is the best time to visit.

Turrones Ramos – Sombrerería 11 (next to pl. Redonda). 963 92 33 98. www. turronesramos.com. This shop has sold hand-made turrón since 1890.

FESTIVALS

Aside from **Las Fallas** (*see sidebar p42*), the end of Moorish rule on 9 Oct 1238 is also celebrated as a national day for the region. The solemn **Corpus Christi** procession and the festival of the **Virgen de los Desamparados**, (second Sun May; www.basilicadesamparados.org) are well worth seeing.

Las Fallas

© Lucas Vallecillos/age fotostock

Costa del Azahar

Sheltered by the mountains, the sunny Orange Blossom Coast is one of Spain's major tourist centres, marked by high-rise blocks and hotels along sandy beaches and orange groves. A number of small towns and villages preserve old quarters redolent of history.

🚗 DRIVING TOUR

FROM VINARÒS TO CASTELLÓN
72km/45mi.

▶ Follow either the N 340 or the AP 7 toll motorway.

The northern coast of the province of Castellón is separated from the interior by the Maestrazgo mountains, recalling knights from the Templar and Montesa orders who controlled this area during the Middle Ages. Large resorts include Peñíscola and Benicàssim.

Vinaròs
🚆Vinaròs.
Vinaròs has the 16C **Iglesia de Nuestra Señora de la Asunción** (pl. Parroquial; ℘964 45 19 33), and a pleasant promenade close to the fishing port.

Peñíscola★★
🚆Nearest station: Benicarló-Peñíscola (5km).
The **old quarter★**, surrounded by walls, sits on a small rocky peninsula in the shadow of an imposing fortress, while its sandy beaches extend to either side. A small **fishing port** is still active.

Castillo Peñíscola★
Castillo. Open daily Holy Week–15 Oct 9.30am–9.30pm; 16 Oct–Holy Week 10.30am–5.30pm. Closed 1 & 6 Jan, 7 & 9 Sept, 9 Oct, 25 Dec. €5. ℘964 48 00 21. www.dipcas.es/es/castillo-peniscola.
Built by Templars in the early 14C, the castle was subsequently modified by

🔖 **Michelin Map:** 577 K 31, L 30, M 29, N 28–29, O 28–29.

ℹ️ **Info:** Castellón de la Plana: Plaza de la Hierba; ℘964 35 86 88. Gandía: Paseo Marítimo Neptuno, s/n; ℘962 84 24 07. Peñíscola: Paseo Marítimo, s/n; ℘964 48 02 08. www.castellon-costaazahar.com.

◉ **Location:** Costa del Azahar stretches along the Mediterranean coast in eastern Spain, from Valencia. The AP 7 Autopista connects the beaches.

👪 **Kids:** Beaches and Cuevas de San José.

Pope Luna, whose coat of arms, featuring a crescent moon in allusion to his name, can be seen on a gate. Grouped around the parade ground are the vast church, with pointed vaulting and a free-standing tower. The castle featured in the famous 1961 Hollywood movie, *El Cid*.
The terrace offers a **panorama★** of the village and coastline. The castle is the setting for events such as the Festival of Baroque and Ancient Music, in the first fortnight of August. The coastal road passes through an arid landscape. The resort of Alcossebre, popular with Spanish families, stands between Peñíscola and Benicàssim.

Benicàssim
🚆Benicàssim.
This is the other major tourist centre in the province of Castellón, separated from the interior by the **Desierto de las Palmas** (Palm Desert), which has suffered badly from fire in the past few years. Benicàssim has excellent beaches, lined by villas and apartments. It hosts an internationally renowned music festival every July (www.fiberfib.com). The quieter town of Oropesa is located to the north.

A Legendary Siege

Sagunto has a heroic place in Spain's bloody ancient history. In 218 BC the Carthaginian general **Hannibal** besieged Sagunto, then a small seaport allied to Rome, for a period of eight months. Seeing only one alternative to surrender, the local inhabitants lit a huge fire and women, children, the sick and the old then proceeded to throw themselves into the furnace while soldiers and menfolk made a suicidal sortie against the enemy. The event marked the beginning of the Second Punic War. Five years later, Scipio Africanus Major rebuilt the city, which became an important Roman town.

Castelló/Castellón de la Plana

Pintor Oliet 2.
Just a couple of miles separate Benicàssim from the port of Castellón, whose origins date back to the 13C. The capital of the province is situated in La Plana, an extensive fertile area irrigated by the River Mijares. On the main square is the **Catedral de Santa María** (Arcipreste Balaguer 1; open Mon–Sat 8–12.45am, 5–8.45pm; Sun 8.30–1.45am, 6–8.45pm; no charge; ℘964 22 34 63, www.concatedral.com), rebuilt after the Spanish Civil War; the octagonal bell tower is late 16C.
The town hall *(ayuntamiento)* is from the late 17C. Other sights include paintings attributed to Zurbarán in the Convento de las Madres Capuchinas, and the Museo Provincial de Bellas Artes (av. Hermanos Bou 28; open Tue–Sat 10am–2pm, 4–8pm, Sun and public holidays 10am–2pm; no charge; ℘964 72 75 00; www.culturalcas.com/va/museu/bellas-artes), featuring prehistoric objects, canvases and ceramics.

FROM CASTELLÓN TO VALENCIA

69km/43mi. 22km/14mi NW on the CV 10 and CV 160.

Vilafamés★★

Nearest station:
Castellón de la Plana (27km).
Vilafamés is an attractive town of Moorish origin with whitewashed houses and artists' workshops extending below the ruins of a castle.

Museo Popular de Arte Contemporáneo de Vilafamés★

Diputación 20. Open Tue–Sun10am–2pm, 4–6.30pm; €3. ℘964 32 91 52. http://macvac.vilafames.es.
Works by Miró, Barjola, Serrano, Genovés, Chillida and Grupo Crónica are on display in a 15C palace.

▷ Return to Castellón; continue along the A 7 for 25km/15mi to Vall d'Uxo.

👥 Cuevas/las Grutas de San José

In Vall d'Uxo, follow signs to the caves (grutas; guided tours (45min) daily 10am–1pm, 3.30–5.30pm; Nov-Fev 10am-2pm. Closed 1 & 6 Jan, 25 Dec; €10, child €5; ℘964 69 05 76; www.covesdesantjosep.e). An underground river hollowed out these caves at the foot of the Parque Natural de la Sierra de Espadán. Tours by boat cover a distance of around 1.2km/0.75mi.

▷ Continue for 20km/12.4mi along the CV 230, then follow the N 234.

Segorb/Segorbe

Explanada Estación 2.
Visit the **cathedral museum** (pl. de San Cristóbal; open Tue–Sun 11am–1.30pm, except during mass; closed 1 Jan, Good Friday, 25 Dec; no charge; ℘964 71 10 14, www.catedraldesegorbe.es), which contains a large **collection of altarpieces** painted by the **Valencia School**★. There are several paintings by **Vicente Macip** (d. 1545), who was influenced by the Italian Renaissance style. Other works include a 15C marble *Madonna* by Donatello.

◐ Continue along the N 234, towards the coast.

Sagunt/Sagunto★
🚍Vía Férrea.
Historic Sagunto sits at the foot of a hill occupied by the ruins of a castle and Roman theatre.

Castillo and Roman Teatro de Sagunto
Calle del Castillo, access via the old Jewish quarter. Open Apr–Oct Tue–Sat 10am–8pm, Sun and public holidays 10am–2pm; Nov–Mar Tue–Sat 10am–6pm, Sun and public holidays 10am–2pm. Closed 1 Jan, Good Friday, 25 Dec. No charge. ℘962 65 58 59. www.turismo.sagunto.es.
The 1C theatre, restored and still in use, with fine acoustics, was built into the hillside by the Romans. The **Acropolis** consists of the ruins and remains of ramparts, temples and houses built by Iberians, Phoenicians, Carthaginians, Romans, Visigoths and Moors. Buildings to the west date from the War of Independence, when the French general Suchet besieged the town. The **view**★ encompasses the town, countryside and sea.

Valencia ◐See VALENCIA

VALENCIA TO JÁTIVA/XÀTIVA
122km/76mi.

◐ Leave Valencia along the coast road S.

Parque Natural de La Albufera
Centro de Interpretación del Racó de l'Olla. Ctra. El Palmar. Open daily 9am–2pm. Closed 1 & 6 Jan, 19 Mar, 24–25 & 31 Dec. ℘963 86 80 50. www.albufera.com.
This vast body of water (*albufera*, "small sea" in Arabic) south of Valencia is the largest freshwater lagoon in Spain, separated from the sea by an offshore bar, the Dehesa, that has been planted with rice since the 13C. Its eels appear on typical menus in restaurants in El

Palmar (to the south) which also serve Valencia's signature dish, **paella**.

◐ Continue along the CV 500.

Cullera
www.culleraturismo.com.
This resort lies at the mouth of the River Júcar; its bay is demarcated to the north by a lighthouse, the Faro de Cullera. In the town are remains of á 13C castle.

◐ Head 27km/17mi S along the N 332.

Gandia
🚍Parc de L'estació.
Gandia is at the centre of a *huerta* which produces large quantities of oranges. A resort has developed near the harbour along a 3km/1.8mi-long sandy **beach**.

Palacio Ducal
Duc Alfons El Vell 1. Open Mon–Sat 10am–1.30pm, 3–6.30pm (Apr–Sept 4–7.30pm). Sun & hols 10am–1.30pm. €6. ℘962 87/ 14 65. www.palauducal.com.
The mansion in which St Francis Borja was born, now a Jesuit college, underwent considerable modification between the 16C and 18C. Only the patio remains Gothic in appearance and is typical of those along this coast. **The Colegiata de Santa María** (6–8pm; no charge; ℘962 87 19 51), a collegiate church in nearby Plaza Mayor, was built in the 14C–15C and expanded in the 16C. It is one of the finest Gothic structures in Valencia province.

◐ Head inland along the CV 60. Before Palomar, bear right on the A 7.

Xàtiva/Játiva
🚍Xàtiva/Játiva.
Known as "the town of the thousand fountains", Xàtiva stands in a plain covered with a Mediterranean landscape of vineyards, orchards and cypress trees. The town was the birthplace of two members of the Borja family who became popes, Calixtus III (1455–58) and Alexander VI, and, in 1591, of the painter **José Ribera**. The 16C **colegiata** (collegiate church; pl. Calixto III; open

Tue–Sun 10.30am–1pm; ℘ 962 28 14 81; www.xativa.es), modified in the 18C, faces the former **Hospital Royal**, which has an ornate Gothic-Plateresque façade.

Museo de l'Almodí

Corretgeria 46. Open 16 Sept–14 Jun Tue–Fri 10am–2pm, 4–6pm, Sat–Sun 10am–2pm; 15 Jun–15 Sept Tue–Fri 9.30am–2.30pm, Sat–Sun 10am–2.30pm €2.40; free Sun. ℘962 27 65 97. www.xativa.es.

The Almudín, a Renaissance-style granary with a Gothic façade, houses fine Moorish-era artefacts, along with gold and silverwork and paintings. An 11C **Moorish fountain** (pila) of pink marble is exceptional for its depiction of human figures, extremely rare in Islamic art.

Ermita de Sant Feliu

◗ On the castle road. Open Nov–Mar Mon–Sat 10am–1pm, 3–6pm, Sun and public holidays 10am–1pm; Apr–Oct Mon–Sat 10am–1pm, 4–7pm, Sun and public holidays 10am–1pm. ℘962 27 33 46. www.xativa.es.

Built on the flank of the hill, this chapel contains a group of 15C–16C Valencian primitives. At the entrance, note the white marble **stoup★**.

Castillo

Subida al Castillo. Open Tue–Sun Apr–Sept 10am–7pm; Oct–Mar 10am–6pm. Closed 1 Jan, 25 Dec. €2.40. ℘962 27 42 74. www.xativa.es.

With 30 towers and four fortified gates, this enormous castle is a mix of an Iberian-Roman fortress and a later Arab castle. Cascading down from the castle are the walls, which until the 10C enclosed the Roman city. A second wall was added later, which took in what today is the historic quarter.

ADDRESSES

🛏 STAY

🍴🍴🍴 **Hotel Mare Nostrum** – Molino 4, Peñíscola. ℘964 48 16 26. www.hotelmarenostrum.net. 24 rooms. At the foot of the citadel near the beach, this small hotel has rooms with magnificent views. Breakfast is served on the rooftop terrace, facing the old city.

🍴🍴🍴 **Albatros** – Clot de la Mota 11 (near beach), Gandia. ℘982 84 56 00. www.hotel-albatros.com. 46 rooms. ⊒€8. Set 300 m from the beach, this hotel offers fairly basic rooms and a small pool.

🍴🍴🍴 **Hostería del Mar** – Av. Papa Luna 18, Peñíscola. ℘902 48 06 00. www.hosteriadelmar.net. 86 rooms. This smart modern hotel maintains a traditional Castillan atmosphere. The restaurant specialises in fish and rice dishes as well as grilled meats.

🍴🍴🍴 **Hotel Mont Sant** – Ctra de Castillo, Xàtiva. ℘962 27 50 81. www.mont-sant.com. 15 rooms. Restaurant 🍴🍴🍴. Set amidst a lush garden, this lovely boutique hotel has rooms decorated with antiques and a more contemporary vibe in a chalet-style annexe. The pool is sheltered by orange trees and the old Arab city wall.

🍴🍴🍴 **El Jardin Vertical** – Nou 15, Vilafamés. ℘964 32 99 38. www.eljardinvertical.com. 9 rooms. Perched high up in the village, this casa rural occupies a 17C mansion built over five levels. Rooms are nice and cosy and some feature a fireplace. Breakfast is served on a terrace with views to the horizon.

🍴 EAT

🍴🍴 **Casa La Abuela** – Reina 17, Xàtiva. ℘962 27 05 25. www.casalaabuela xativa.es. Closed Tue eve and Sun eve. This acclaimed restaurant has been specialising in rice dishes for 65 years.

🍴🍴 **RH Bayren** – Paseo de Neptuno, Playa de Gandia. ℘962 84 03 00. The restaurant in this four-star seafront hotel offers an excellent-value buffet lunch on a terrace with wonderful views.

🍴🍴🍴 **El Peñón** – Santos Mártires 22, Peñíscola. by the Ermita de la Virgen. ℘964 48 07 16. www.elpenyon.es. Set in the narrow streets of the old town, the Peñón is a friendly restaurant with attractive decor and a pleasant small terrace, where you can enjoy excellent fish dishes.

Morella

Morella has an amazing site★: 14C ramparts, punctuated by towers, form a mile-long girdle round a 1 004m/3 294ft hill which the town ascends in tiers to castle ruins.

▶ **Population:** 2 575
◔ **Michelin Map:** 577 K 29.
▤ **Info:** Pl. de San Miguel, s/n. ☎964 17 30 32. www.morellaturistica.com.
◗ **Location:** In the Maestrazgo of Valenciana, linked to the coast by the N 232 to Peñiscola (78km/49mi) and Castellón de la Plana (98km/61mi). ▭Nearest station: Benicarló-Peñiscola (73km).

SIGHTS

A stroll around Morella's concentric streets reveals many interesting mansions and religious buildings. The Iglesia de San Miguel, houses a small Temps de Dinosaures **museum** (Tue–Sun 11am–2pm, 4–6pm/7pm Apr–Oct; €2; ☎964 17 31 17).

Iglesia de Santa María la Mayor★

Placeta de la Iglesia. Open daily Jul–Aug 11am–2pm, 4–7pm; Sept–Jun Tue–Sat 11–2pm, 4–6pm. No charge. Museum €1.50. ☎964 16 07 93.

One of the most interesting Gothic churches in the Levante has two fine portals and a raised Renaissance *coro* which has a spiral staircase carved with biblical scenes. The small **museum** has a beautiful Valencian *Descent from the Cross* and a 14C Madonna by Sassoferrato.

Castillo

Pl. San Francisco. Open daily May–Oct 11am–7pm, Nov–Apr 11am–5pm. €3.50. ☎964 17 30 32.

On the way up are superb **views**★ of the town, the ruins of the Convento de San Francisco with its Gothic cloisters, the 14C–15C aqueduct and the mountains.

EXCURSIONS

Santuario de la Balma

◗ 25km/15.5mi NW along the CV 14. Open 10am–5pm (Sun until 7pm). ☎964 17 70 95. www.zoritadelmaestrazgo.es.

This unusual Marian sanctuary is where the Virgin supposedly appeared.

Mirambel

◗ 30km/19mi W on the CS 840. Bear left after 11km/7mi.

This small, well-preserved mountain village retains its medieval character.

Vallivana

◗ 24km/15mi SE via the N 232.

On the road down to Vinaròs, Morella and the Costa del Azahar, a few houses and a chapel make up this small village. The shrine houses a statue of the Virgin who, according to legend, is the one who stopped the plague in Morella in 1672.

Sant Mateu★

◗ 40km/25mi SE on the N 232 then right on the CV 132i.

In the historic capital of the Maestrazgo region, the **Iglesia de Sant Mateu/Arciprestal ★** (open by guided tour only Tue–Sun, see website for times; €1.50; ☎964 41 66 58, www.santmateu.com) is one of the most remarkable Gothic sanctuaries in Valencia. It is reached by a 13C Romanesque portal though the rest of the building dates from the 14C. Only the **chapel of San Clemente** was rebuilt in the 18C.

ADDRESSES

⌂ STAY

⊜⊜⊜ **El Hotel del Pastor** – San Julián 12, Morella. ☎964 16 10 16. www.hoteldelpastor.com. 12 rooms. Restaurant ⊜⊜⊜. Small, family-run establishment, with a lovely stone façade and traditional, very smart and well maintained rooms. The restaurant serves local cuisine.

Alicante/ Alacant★

The Greeks called Alicante *Akra Leuka* (white citadel), the Romans named it *Lucentum* (city of light). Today it buzzes as the gateway to the Costa Blanca.

 WALKING TOUR

OLD TOWN

▷ Follow the route on the map.

Explanada de España★

The most pleasant promenade in the region, running past the marina, is shaded by magnificent palms. Sunday concerts are held on the bandstand.

Catedral de San Nicolás

Pl. Abad Penalva. Open Mon–Fri 7.30am–1.30, 5.30–8pm, Sat–Sun from 8.30am. No charge. ✆965 21 26 62. http://concatedralalicante.com.
The 17C building on the site of a mosque – the city was only reconquered in 1296 – has a well-proportioned cupola, 45m/148ft high, over a Herreran nave. On calle Labradores, with its terraces, are the 18C Palacio Maisonnave, no. 9 (now the Municipal Archives; open Mon–Fri Sept–Jun 9am–2pm; Jul–Aug 9am–1.30pm); and an 18C mansion, no. 14, now a cultural centre.

Ayuntamiento (Town Hall)

Pl. del Ayuntamiento 1. Open Mon–Fri 9am–2pm. ✆965 14 91 00.
www.alicante-ayto.es.
Visit the Rococo chapel of this imposing golden stone balconied 18C palace, with *azulejos* from Manises, and reception rooms with blue silk hangings.

Museo de Bellas Artes Gravina★

Gravina, 13. Open Tue–Sat 10am–8pm Sun 10am–2pm. Jul–Aug Tue–Sat 11am–9pm, Sun 11am–3pm. No charge. ✆965 14 67 80. www.mubag.org.
The permanent collection occupies the first level of two 17C and 18C mansions.

▷ **Population:** 328 648
🗲 **Michelin Map:** 577 Q 28 (town plan) – map 123 COSTA BLANCA.
🗎 **Info:** Rambla Méndez Núñez, 41, ✆965 20 00 00. www.alicanteturismo.com.
▷ **Location:** Alicante is the mid-point of Spain's Mediterranean coast, 110km/69mi from Cartagena. 🚆Alicante; bus service from Alicante airport).
☺ **Don't Miss:** A stroll along the Explanada by the harbour.
🕐 **Timing:** Start with a view from the Castillo de Santa Bárbara.
👪 **Kids:** Castillo de Santa Bárbara.

Decorative art objects of note include three intricate sideboards from the 16–17C. In the paintings section, notice the beautiful *Calvary* by Rodrigo de Osona (late 15C), and *Saint John, Saint Joseph and Child* by **Cristobal Llorens** (16C). A view of Alicante by Vincente Suarez Ordoñez shows what the city was like in the early 19C.

Iglesia de Santa María

Pl. de Santa María. Open noon–1pm, 6–7.30pm. No charge. ✆965 21 60 26.
Formerly a mosque, the church was altered in the 17C when Churrigueresque decoration was added. Its 8C Baroque façade★ has wreathed columns, pillars and breaks in its cornices. Note the graceful Renaissance marble fonts and a painting of John the Baptist and John the Apostle by Rodrigo de Osuna the Younger.

Museo de Arte Contemporáneo de Alicante★

Pl. de Santa María 3. Open Tue–Sat 10am–8pm, Sun & hols 10am–2pm. No charge. ✆965 21 31 56. www.maca-alicante.es.
Opened in 2011, the new MACA has taken on the collection of the old fine

arts museum, previously on this site, which included 20C painting and sculpture donated by the sculptor Eugenio Sempere, and has added contemporary collections. Famous artists' works represented here include Miró, Picasso, Gargallo, Tàpies and Dalí, and Vasarely, Braque, Chagall and Kandinsky.

👥 Castillo de Santa Bárbara

Frente Playa Postiguet.
♿ Ascend by lift and walk down, either all the way (good views) or to the halfway stop. Guided tours Mon–Sat. Open 10am–8pm (Apr–Sept 10pm). Guided tour €2.70, child €1.50. ℘965 14 71 60. www.castillodesantabarbara.com.
This fortress atop Benacantil hill dates from the 9C in Muslim times, though outbuildings were raised in the 16C. The Revellín del Bon Repòs rampart was built in the 18C. The Philip II hall is a worthy highlight. The Plaza de la Torreta is surrounded by the oldest buildings. A platform commands a fine **view**★ of the harbour and town. The 16C section is at the halfway stop on the lift; the 17C perimeter is lower down. A footpath leads to the medieval streets and tiny squares of working-class Santa Cruz.

SIGHT

MARQ (Museo Arqueológico Provincial de Alicante)★★

Pl. Doctor Gómez Ulla. Open Tue–Sat 10am–7pm (Sat until 8.30pm), Sun and public holidays 10am–2pm. Jul & Aug 10am–2pm, 6-10pm. €3. ℘965 14 90 00. www.marqalicante.com.
MARQ opens archaeology to all, with a magnificent presentation focused on the ancients of this area. The museum is organised into large halls (Prehistory, Iberian, Roman, Middle Ages and Modern) around a space devoted to archaeology itself. Here you can get right into excavations in a cave, a church and an underwater site.

EXCURSIONS
ELCHE/ELX★

⏵ 24km/15ml SW. 🚩 Pl. del Parc 3.
℘966 65 81 96. www.turismedelx.com.
🚆Elche Parque.

El Palmeral, Elche/Elx
©Turespaña

Elche (Elx) lies along the Vinalopó river. The **Dama de Elche** (4C BC), a masterpiece of Iberian art now in the Museo Arqueológico de Madrid, was discovered in **La Alcudia** (2km/1.2mi S). **El Misteri** d'Elx is a medieval verse drama (with an all-male cast). It recounts the Dormition, Assumption and Coronation of the Virgin. It is on UNESCO's Oral and Intangible Heritage of Humanity list (played in the Basílica de Santa María; Aug, Oct and Nov; www.misteridelx.com). **El Palmeral (Palm Grove)** ★★ (Porta de la Morera 49; open daily 10am–sunset) – The groves, planted by the Phoenicians and expanded by the Arabs, are the largest in Europe with more than 200 000 trees, and are a UNESCO World Heritage Site. The palms flourish with the aid of a remarkable irrigation system. Female trees produce dates, and the fronds from the male trees are used in Palm Sunday processions and handicrafts. **Huerto del Cura**★★ (open daily from 10am; see website for closing times; €5; ℘966 61 00 11; http://jardin.huertodel cura.com) – This delightful garden of Mediterranean and subtropical plants lies under magnificent palm trees; one, with seven trunks, is said to be 160 years old. **Parque Municipal**★ (pas. de l'Estació) – A well-tended garden with palm trees. **Museo Arqueológico y de Historia de Elche (MAHE)** (Diagonal del Palau; open Mon–Sat 10am–6pm, Sun & hols 10am–3pm; €3; ℘966 65 82 03, www. visitelche.com) – The museum is in the Moorish Palacio de Altamira. The archaeological section traces Elche from its origins to the Visigoth era. Notable are sculpture and ceramics from the Iberian period and the *Venus of Illicis*, a delicately carved white marble Roman sculpture.

Basílica de Santa María (pl. del Congreso Eucarístico; open daily 7am– 1pm, 5.30–9pm; tower €2; ℘965 45 15 40, www.visitelche.com) – This monumental 17C–18C Baroque basilica with a beautiful portal by Nicolás de Bussi is the setting for the annual mystery play. View the palm groves from the tower. Nearby are the 17C–18C Almohad tower, **La Calahorra** (Uberna 14), and the Baños árabes.

Baños árabes (pas. de Santa Llucía 13; access by a side door of the Convento de la Merced; open Tue–Sat 10am– 2pm, 3–6pm, Sun and public holidays 10am–2pm; €1; ℘965 45 28 87, www. visitelche.com) – A well-prepared exhibition details the culture of the Arabic baths in the 12C.

La Alcudia: archaeological site and museum (ctra Dolores; 2km/1.2mi S; open Tue–Sat 10am–6pm; €5; ℘966 61 15 06, www.laalcudia.ua.es) – The remains and a museum reveal the story of this city from the Neolithic period to its decline in Visigoth times.

🚗 DRIVING TOUR

INLAND THROUGH ALICANTE
176km/110mi N.

▶ Take the N 340 in San Juan, then the Alcoi road and then turn right.

Cuevas de Canalobre
Guided tours (45min) Holy Week & Jul–Aug 10.30am–7.30pm, Sept–Jun Mon–Fri 10.30am–4.50pm, Sat–Sun until 5.50pm. Closed 1 Jan, Mon after Easter Monday, 25 Dec. €7. ℘965 69 92 50. www.turismobusot.com.

These caves are at 700m/2 296.5ft up Mount Cabezón de Oro, and take their name from their spectacular candelabra *(canalobre)*-like formations.

▶ Return to the N 340. Cross dry country of figs and carobs.

Jijona/Xixona
The speciality of this town is *turrón*, a nougat confection, typically made of honey, sugar, and egg white, with toasted almonds or other nuts.
You can visit the **Turrón Museum** and factory (El Lobo; ctra Jijona-Busot; open: museum, Jan–mid-Jul Mon–Sat 10am–1pm, 4–5.30pm; mid Jul–Sept Mon–Sat 10am–1pm, 3.30–6.30pm; factory usually operates mid-Jun–mid Dec, see operations from a viewing gallery in the museum; €1.50 low season; €3 high season; ℘965 61 07 12; www. museodelturron.com).
Beyond Jijona (Xixona) the road twists up through almond terraces to the **Puerto de la Carrasqueta★** (1,024m/3,360ft), a pass with a view towards Alicante.

Alcoy/Alcoi
🚃Plaza Estación.
Alcoy is an industrial town in a mountain setting. Every year, between 22 and 24 April, **Moors and Christians★** (Moros y Cristianos) **festival** (www.alcoi.org) celebrates a vital Christian victory in 1276. It is the biggest, most colourful and noisiest of Spain's many Moors and Christians events.

▶ Take the CV 795 to Barxell, then follow the CV 794.

Bocairent
🚃Camino de la Estación, Ontiyent 10km/7mi N.
The church in this hilltop market village has an interesting **Museo Parroquial** (Parish Museum; Abadía 36; guided tours (45min) by appointment only; €1.50; ℘962 90 50 62) with works by **Juan de Juanes** (1523–79) – who died here – and his school, and a 14C Last Supper by Marcial de Sax.

▶ Take the CV 81.

Villena

🚃 Ronda de la Estación.

The spectacularly located **Castillo de la Atalaya** (guided tours every hour Tue–Sun 11am–1pm, Tue–Sat and public holidays also 4–5pm; €3; ℘965 80 38 04, www.turismovillena.com), of Arabic origin, dominates its former feudal domain. Among its owners have been famed men of letters: **Don Juan Manuel** in the 14C and the poet prince, **Henry of Aragon (Marqués de Villena,** 1384–1434). The original castle keep survives, with circular towers in the corners, and large 15C Homenaje (homage) towers There are fine views from the walls.

Iglesia Arcedianal de Santiago (pl. de Santiago; visit by guided tours only, from the tourist office every half hour Tue–Sat 11am–2pm/Fri 1–2pm; Sun and public holidays 11.30am–1pm; €1; ℘965 81 39 19, www.turismovillena.com) – This Gothic-Renaissance church (14C–17C) with notable bell tower stands near the town hall. Note the unusual **spiral pillars★** supporting Gothic vaults, and a Renaissance-style baptismal font.

Museo Arqueológico (Archaeological Museum) – (pl. de Santiago 1; open Tue–Fri 10am–2pm, Sat–Sun and public holidays 11am–2pm; closed 1 Jan, 25 Dec; €2; ℘965 80 11 50; www.museovillena.com) – Housed in the town hall (Palacio Municipal) with a fine Renaissance façade and patio, this museum displays solid gold from the Bronze Age (1500–1000 BC). The outstanding **Villena Treasure★★** includes jewellery and gourds decorated with sea urchin shell patterns.

ADDRESSES

🛏 STAY

🛏🛏 **La Milagrosa Bed & Breakfast** – Villavieja 8, Alicante. ℘965 21 69 18. www.lamilagrosa.eu. 20 rooms. This basic pensión has bright rooms with

some overlooking the Plaza de Santa María. Garden-terrace upstairs.

🛏🛏 **Hostal Les Monges Palace** – San Agustín 4, Alicante. ℘965 21 50 46. www.lesmonges.es. 28 rooms. 🍴€6. An excellent location in the heart of old Alicante, with bright high quality rooms blending old and new. Features of this charming 18C building include a marble staircase and large mirrors and windows.

🛏🛏🛏 **Mediterránea Plaza** – Pl. de Ayuntamiento 6, Alicante. ℘965 21 0188. www.eurostarshotels.com. 49 rooms. 🍴€7.50. Located in the historical centre the ample facilities of this international class hotel make this a good base.

🍴 EAT

🛏🛏🛏 **La Taberna del Gourmet** – San Fernando 10, Alicante. ℘965 20 42 33. www.latabernadelgourmet.com. An always-bustling restaurant serving up sophisticated dishes at dinner and more relaxed tapas-style food for lunch. You can buy your favourite ingredients from the on-site delicatessen.

🛏🛏🛏🛏 **Nou Manolín** – Villegas 3. Alicante. ℘965 20 03 68. www.noumanolin.com. An Alicante classic, modern with a rustic feel, serving superb seafood cuisine.

🛏🛏🛏🛏 **La Ereta** – Parque de a Ereta. ℘965 14 32 50. www.laereta.es. Reservations essential. Situated on a hillside between the castle and city, this restaurant has large windows that afford exceptional views of Alicante. It serves exceptional gourmet cuisine and fine tasting menus.

TAPAS

El Canto – Alemania 26. ℘965 92 56 50. Beautiful authentic tapas bar.

Cervecería Sento Rambla – Ministra Federica Montseny 1. ℘646 93 22 13. Hearty breakfasts and great cured ham.

NIGHTLIFE

Barrio del Carmen – After 11pm Alicante's old quarter is transformed into one huge disco.

Puerto de Alicante – a very lively area on summer nights.

Costa Blanca★

The White Coast stretches south from Valencia to Murcia. It is mosly flat and sandy, with occasional highlands where the sierras drop to the sea. A hot climate, low rainfall, dazzling light, long beaches and turquoise waters attract vast numbers of tourists.

🚗 DRIVING TOUR

DENIA TO GUADALEST
115km/71mi. Allow 2 days.

Denia (Dénia)
🚂Denia.

The former Greek colony became Roman *Dianium*. Denia today is a fishing harbour, toy manufacturing centre and seaside resort. In the fortress (€3, including museum; 🖋 966 42 06 56, http://en.denia.net) above town is an archaeological museum. The coast south of here is steep, rocky and forested.

Cap de Sant Antoni★

Near the lighthouse on this headland, a last foothill of the Sierra del Mongó, is a good **view**★ towards Xàbia and the Cabo de la Nao headland.

Xàbia/Jávea★

The attractive old quarter is on the hill around a fortified 14C Gothic church. The modern part is set around the harbour, the excellent beach, and Parador.

Cap de la Nau/Cabo de la Nao★

The climb affords views over Jávea at the foot of the Sierra del Mongó; then enter thick pinewoods where villas stand in clearings. Cabo de la Nao is an eastern extension of the Sierras Béticas (Baetic Cordillera) that continues under the sea to reappear as the island of Ibiza. There is a beautiful **view**★ south from the point down the coast to the Penyal d'Ifac. Sea caves (approached by boat) and charming creeks such as **La Granadella** (south) and **Cala Blanca** (north) are excellent for diving.

⏱ **Michelin Map:** 577 P 29–30, Q 29–30 – Communidad Valenciana (Alicante/Alacant), Murcia.

ℹ **Info:** Altea: Plaza José María Planelles, 🖋965 84 41 14. Benidorm: Plaza de Canalejos 1, 🖋96 585 13 11. Denia: Dr. Manuel Lattur 1, 🖋966 42 23 67. www.costablanca.org.

▶ **Location:** Costa Blanca towns are linked by the N 332 and the AP 7 toll motorway.

🔍 **Don't Miss:** Guadalest.

👥 **Kids:** Tierra Mítica amusement park.

Calp/Calpe

The **Penyal d'Ifac**★, a rocky outcrop 332m/1 089ft high, is the setting of Calp. A path leads to the top of the Penyal (🔲about 1hr walk) with views along the coast of Calp and its salt pans, of the dark mountain chains, and northwards of the coast as far as Cabo de la Nao. The Sierra de Bernia road twists and turns before crossing the spectacular Barranco de Mascarat (Mascarat Ravine) in the hinterland to Cabo de la Nao.

Altea

Altea's white walls, rose-coloured roofs and glazed blue tile domes rise in tiers up a hillside overlooking the sea – a symphony of colour and reflected light below the Sierra de Bernia. A walk through the alleys to the church and then the view from the square over the village and beyond to the Penyal d'Ifac will reveal the attraction of so many painters towards Altea.

Benidorm
🚂Benidorm.

The excellent climate, cheap packaged holidays from Britain and Germany, and two immense beaches (the Levante and the Poniente), curving away on either side of a small rock promontory, are the elements of Benidorm's incredible growth from a modest fishing village in the 1950s to a Mediterranean Manhattan. From the Balcón del Mediterraneo lookout, there are fine **views★** of the beaches and sea. The often overlooked old quarter stands behind the point, close to the blue-domed church.

👫 Terra Mítica

3km/2mi from Benidorm. Exit 65 A of the AP 7. Open second week Apr–Oct 10.30am–8pm/midnight, see website for schedule. €39, child €28, inc. second (consecutive) day free. ℘902 02 02 20. www.terramiticapark.com.

This large excellent theme park is based upon ancient Egypt, Greece, Rome and Iberia. Terra Mítica has attractions and shows for visitors of all ages and tastes. **Main attractions** – In Ancient Egypt, enter the Pyramid of Terror, or descend the Cataracts of the Nile on an exciting white-water roller-coaster ride. In Greece, emulate Theseus in the Labyrinth of the Minotaur, or experience the sensation of falling down a waterfall in the Fury of Triton. The Magnus Colossus in Rome is a spectacular wooden roller coaster. In the Flight of the Phoenix, enjoy the excitement of a free fall from 54m/177ft, or battle against currents and whirlpools in the Rapids of Argos.

▶ Take the CV 70 to Callosa d'En Sarrià then head along the CV 755 to Alcoi.

On the drive inland, you pass through small valleys cloaked in all sorts of fruit trees, including citrus and medlars. The village of **Polop** stretches up a hillside in a picturesque mountain setting. Beyond, the landscape becomes more arid but the views more extensive, the mountains more magnificent.

Guadalest★

Guadalest rises above the terraced valleys of olive and almond trees and perches on a limestone escarpment of the Sierra de Aitana. The **site★** is breathtaking. The village, forced halfway up a ridge of rock, is a stronghold accessible only through an archway cut into stone. Walk round the **Castillo de San José**; Iglesia 2; open daily 10am–8pm; closed 1 Jan, 25 Dec; €4; ℘965 88 52 98) where ruins remain of fortifications wrecked by an earthquake in 1744. The splendid view takes in the Guadalest reservoir with its reflections of surrounding mountain crests, the amazing site of the old village, and, in the distance, the sea.

ADDRESSES

🏠 STAY

⊜🛏 **Hostal L'Ánfora** – Expl. Cervantes 8, Denia. ℘966 43 01 01. www.hostal lanfora.com. 20 rooms. This small building with its distinctive terracotta façade is located at the fishing port in Denia. Although small and basic, the rooms here are bright and clean with views of the local fishing fleet.

⊜🛏🛏 **Hostal Triskel** – Sor María Gallart 3. Jávea. ℘966 46 21 91. www. hostal-triskel.com. 5 rooms. ⊠€5. In the heart of the historic district in a beautiful building, each room is unique, boasting antiques, terracotta floor tiles, porcelain switches and retro phones.

🍴 EAT

⊜🛏🛏 **Oustau de Altea** – Mayor 5, Altea. ℘965 842 078. www.oustau.es. In a brightly decorated quaint house in the old town, this restaurant specialises in French-Mediterranean cuisine. Nice terrace.

⊜🛏🛏🛏 **Villa Venecia** – Plaza Sant Jaumé, Benidorm. ℘965 855 466. www.hotelvillavenecia.com. Gourmet Mediterranean cuisine is served in the waterside dining room or on the terrace of this five-star hotel.

TAPAS

La Cava Aragonesa – Pl. de la Constitución (also entry on Callejón Santo Domingo), Benidorm Old Town. ℘966 80 12 06. www.lacavaaragonesa.es. This typically Spanish restaurant and tapas bar, with its cured hams hanging from the ceiling, is an oasis in this gastronomically challenged resort.

Murcia★

Murcia, an historic but also booming university town, lies along the Segura in a fertile market-gardening area *(huerta)* known for its plethora of golf courses.

A BIT OF HISTORY

Murcia, founded in the reign of Abd ar-Rahman II in 825 as Madina Mursiya, was reconquered by the Spanish in 1266. Up to the 18C, Murcia prospered from agriculture and silk weaving.

SIGHTS

Catedral★

Pl. Cardenal Belluga. Open Sep-Jun Mon-Sat 7am-1pm, 5-8pm, Sun 7am-1pm, 6.30-8pm, Jul-Aug Mon-Fri 7am-1pm, 6.30-8pm, Sat & Sun 7am-1.15pm, 6.30-9pm. No charge. ℘968 21 63 44.

The original 14C cathedral is camouflaged beneath Renaissance and Baroque additions. The façade★, with an arrangement of columns and curves,

Star vaulting, Capilla de los Vélez, Catedral

© F. Monheim/B. Opitz/age fotostock

▶ **Population:** 439 889
◔ **Michelin Map:** 123. Costa Blanca.
▯ **Info:** Plaza Cardenal Belluga. ℘968 35 87 49. www.turismodemurcia.es.
◖ **Location:** 50km/31mi from the coast. ▭Murcia del Carmen.

is a brilliant example of Baroque. The impressive belfry, 95m/311ft in height, was completed by Ventura Rodríguez in the 18C. The interior, beyond the entry cupola, is preponderantly Gothic, apart from the 16C **Capilla de los Junterones** (fourth south chapel), which has rich Renaissance decoration.

The **Capilla de los Vélez★** (off the ambulatory) is sumptuous Late Gothic with splendid star vaulting, and wall decoration with Renaissance and Mudéjar motifs. The sacristy, approached through two successive Plateresque doors (beautiful panels on the first), is covered by an unusual radiating dome. The walls are richly panelled with Plateresque carving below and Baroque above.

Museo Salzillo★

Pl. San Agustín 3. Open mid-Jun–mid-Sept Mon–Fri 10am–2pm. Rest of year Mon–Sat 10am–5pm, Sun and public holidays 11am–2pm. Closed 1, 6 Jan, Holy Week, 1 May, 9 Jun, 6, 25 Dec. €5. ℘968 29 18 93. www.museosalzillo.es.

The museum possesses Salzillo's masterpieces including the eight polychrome wood sculptures of **pasos** carried in the Good Friday procession during Holy Week, kept in side chapels off the nave of the Church of Jesus. The deep emotion on the faces is impressive. The museum also contains vivid terracotta pieces used to create scenes from the life of Jesus.

Palacio Episcopal★

Plaza del Cardenal Belluga.
Built between 1748 and 1768, this palace shows a clear influence of Ital-

ian Baroque. The two-level patio has medallions embossed with figures of bishops in the pediments of the windows and the courtyard is decorated with many carved coats of arms. This leads to the grand staircase which is topped with a cupola. Don't miss the circular chapel.

Museo de Bellas Artes – MuBAM★

Calle Obispo Frutos 8–12. Open Sept–Jun Tue–Sat 10am (Sat 11am)–2pm, 5–8pm, Sun & hols 11am–2pm. Jul–Aug Tue–Fri 10am–2pm, Sat–Sun 11am–2pm. No charge. ☎968 23 93 46. www.museosdemurcia.com.

This museum contains some fine exhibits. On the ground floor is an altarpiece by Juan de Vitoria (16C) representing Calvary and the Martyrdom of Santiago. On the first floor, which is devoted to the Golden Age, is *St Jerome* (1613), attributed to José de Ribera. In the same room is a beautiful Crucifixion by Murillo (1670) and by the same artist, a moving Ecce Homo★.

Museo Santa Clara★★

Paseo Alfonso X El Sabio 1. Open Tue–Sat 10am–1pm, 4–6.30pm, Sun and holidays 10am–1pm; Jul–Aug Tue–Sun 10am–1pm. No charge. ☎968 27 23 98. www.murciaturistica.es.

This monastery was founded in the 14C on the site of an Almohad palace which had not been completely destroyed. The Gothic cloister was built around the central basin of the Arabian palace. The beds have been replanted with plant species in accordance with the original flora. Behind the magnificent arcades of the cloister stands a portico★ with three richly decorated arches, which gave access to one of the main halls of the palace.

Excavations have unearthed the oldest remains, including traces of a courtyard belonging to a 12C Almoravid palace. In the centre stand the remains of a colonnaded pavilion, in which is preserved a fragment of 12C painting representing a flutist★. The museum★ maintains a collection held by the community

of the convent of Santa Clara. Note a Christ on the Cross★★ (1770), by Francisco Salzillo. Carved life-size, the piece shows exceptional balance and features a serene face.

EXCURSIONS
Orihuela★

◆ 24km/15mi NE on the A 7.
🚌 Orihuela Intermodal.

This peaceful town, with its many churches, lies along the Segura, which provides water for market gardens *(huertas)* and for the local palm grove. For centuries, Orihuela was a university town. The house of the early 20C poet and dramatist Miguel Hernández is now a museum (Miguel Hernández 73; open Jun–Sept Tue–Sat 10am–2pm, 5–8pm; Oct–May Tue–Sat 10am–2pm, 4–7pm; Sun and public holidays 10am–2pm year-round; closed 1, 6 Jan, 25 Dec; no charge; ☎965 30 63 27; www.miguel-hernandezvirtual.es).

Catedral del Salvador★

Mayor. Open Tue–Fri 10.30am–2pm, 4–6.30pm, Sat 10.30am–2pm. €1. ☎966 74 36 27.

Constructed in the 14C–16C, the cathedral has a Renaissance north doorway. The interior has three cruciform Gothic naves, ambulatory, and unusual vaulting with spiral ribs.

The stalls of the choir are carved in Baroque style. There are notable Renaissance grilles around the choir and presbytery. The Museo de la Catedral houses a *Temptation of St Thomas Aquinas* by Velázquez, a *Christ* by Morales and a *Mary Magdalene* by Ribera.

The Palacio del Obispo on calle Ramón y Cajal behind the cathedral has a magnificent 18C patio.

Colegio de Santo Domingo

Adolfo Clavarana (north of the city). Open Tue–Sat 10am–2pm, 5–9pm, winter 9.30am–1.30pm, 4–7pm Sun & hols year-round 10am–2pm. Closed 1, 6 Jan, 17 Jul, 25 Dec. €2. ☎965 30 02 40. www.cdsantodomingo.com.

This monumental building (16C–18C), formerly the university, started out in

Renaissance style and transformed into Baroque. The long college façade conceals two sober cloisters (17C–18C). The 18C church★ is covered with murals and exuberant stucco mouldings.

Museo de la Muralla

Río. Open Tue–Sat 10am–2pm, 4–7pm (5–8pm in summer), Sun and public holidays 10am–2pm. No charge. ℘965 30 46 98. www.orihuelaturistica.es.
Descend below street level to the remains of the city wall, dwellings and baths from the Moorish era, and a Gothic palace and a Baroque building. The Iglesia de Santiago (pl. de Santiago 2; open Tue–Fri 10am–2pm, 4–6.30pm, Sat 10am–2pm; ℘965 30 46 45. www. orihuelaturistica.es), near the town hall, is Gothic in style, with Renaissance transept and apse. It was founded by the Catholic Monarchs whose yoke and arrow emblems, together with a statue of St James, are on the Gothic portal; the doorway on the right is Baroque. Inside, note statues attributed to Salzillo in the side chapels.

Santuario de la Fuensanta (La Fuensanta Shrine)

◐ 7km/4.3mi S. Follow the signs from Puente Viejo.
From the shrine of the Virgen de la Fuensanta, patron saint of Murcia, enjoy fine views of the town and the *huerta*.

Cartagena

◐ 62km/39mi SE along the N 301.
▭Cartagena.
In 223 BC this bay settlement was captured by the Carthaginians; it was subsequently colonised by the Romans, as *Cartago Nova*. Philip II fortified the surrounding hilltops, and Charles III built the Arsenal. The city is known for its dramatic Holy Week processions.
Near plaza del Ayuntamiento is an early submarine invented by native son Isaac Peral, in 1888. From the top of the Castillo de la Concepción (C/Gisbert), there is a good view of the harbour and the ruins of the former Romanesque cathedral of Santa María la Vieja.

Museo Teatro Romano★★

Plaza del Ayuntamiento. Open May–Sept Tue–Sat 10am–8pm (Oct–Apr until 6pm). Sun 10am–2pm. €6. ℘968 504 802. www.teatroromanocartagena.org.
As well as the remains of this restored Roman theatre, visitors can travel through a 'Corridor of History' from the city's origins to the present day.

Castillo de la Concepción★

Open Jul–mid-Sept daily 10am–8pm, Apr–Jun and mid-Sept–Oct Tue–Sun until 7pm, Nov–Mar Tue–Sun until 5.30pm. €3.75. ℘968 500 093.
This hilltop-castle not only gives great viwes over the city but also has a display on Cartagena's history. There is a lift for those who don't fancy the walk.

Museo Arqueológico Municipal★

Ramón y Cajal 45. Open May–Sept Tue–Fri 10am–2pm, 5–8pm; Sun 11am–2pm. No charge. ℘968 128 968. www.mueoarqueologicocartagena.es.
Built on a Roman burial ground (which you can see), this museum gives a good introduction to the history of the city. Highlights include a Roman tiled floor and a sculpture of a child's head dating from 1AD.

ARQUA - Museo Nacional de Arqueología Subacuática★★

Pas. del Muelle Alfonso XII 22. Open Tue–Sat 10am–8pm (mid-Apr–mid-Oct 9pm). Sun and public holidays 10am–3pm. €3; no charge Sat (from 2pm), Sun. ℘968 12 11 66. http://museoarqua.mcu.es.
This museum displays underwater finds, notably Phoenician, Punic and Roman amphorae. Maps and models of vessels (galleys, biremes and triremes) illustrate seafaring in times past.

Museo Naval★

Muelle de Alfonso XII. Open mid-Jun–Sept Tue–Fri 9am–2pm, rest of year Tue–Sat 10am–1.30pm, 4.30–7.30pm; Sun 10am–2pm. €3; ℘968 12 71 38.
Housed in an 18th-century arsenal, this museum gives an overview of Cartagena's role as an important naval port. Highlights include an exhibition

on Isaac Peral, the man who invented the submarine.

Mar Menor

◉ At La Manga: 81km/51mi SE via the N 301 and MU 312 and 33km/21mi from Cartagena.

The Mar Menor, or Little Sea, is a lagoon separated from the open Mediterranean by **La Manga**, a sand bar 500m/1 640ft wide which extends from the eastern end of the Cabo de Palos headland. Gilt-head, mullet and king prawns are fished from its shallow salt water.

La Manga del Mar Menor is a large, elongated sports-oriented seaside resort with futuristic tower blocks stretching for miles.

In **Santiago de la Ribera**, where there is no natural beach, pontoons with changing cabins line the seafront.

Alcantarilla

◉ 9km/5.6mi W on the N 340.

The **Museo Etnológico de la Huerta** (av. Príncipe; open Tue–Fri 9am–7pm/8pm in summer; Sat 10am–2pm, 4–7.30pm; Sun 10am–2pm; closed Aug; no charge; ℘968 893 866, www.alcantarilla.es) is dedicated to local **agriculture and irrigation**. Among the orange trees are white rustic dwellings (barracas) and a **noria**, a giant waterwheel devised for irrigation by the Moors.

Lorca★

◉ 67km/42mi SW along the N 340-E 12. 🚌Alameda de Menchirón.

Lorca lies in an irrigated valley at the foot of a hill crowned by a **castle**, the **Fortaleza del Sol** 👪 (open daily 10.30am until dusk; €5, child €4; ℘902 40 00 47; http://lorcatallerdeltiempo.es), where visitors can step back to the Middle Ages.

The main sights are the **Plaza de España**, surrounded by the Baroque façades of the **ayuntamiento** (town hall), the **Juzgado** (Law Courts), embellished with a corner sculpture, and the **Colegiata de San Patricio** (℘968 46 99 66), a collegiate church built in the 16C and 18C, and the **Palacio de Guevara★★** (open Tue–Sat 10am–1pm, 5.30–7.30pm, Sun

10.30am–2pm; no charge; ℘902 40 00 47; http://lorcatallerdeltiempo.es). Its late 17C doorway, although in poor condition, is a fine example of Baroque.

Caravaca de la Cruz★

◉ 70km/44mi W along the C 415. 🛈 Las Monjas, 17. ℘968 70 24 24. www.turismocaravaca.org.

This attractive town is topped by its castle of Muslim origin, which was extended in the 15C by the Knights Templars. Within the compound the **Santuario de la Santa Cruz** is an impressive Baroque monument. Below, the town also retains many fine examples of superb Renaissance architecture, the jewel in the crown being the **Iglesia de San Salvador**.

ADDRESSES

🛏 STAY

⊜⊜ **Hotel Arco de San Juan** – Plaza Ceballos 10, Murcia. ℘968 21 04 55. www.arcossanjuan.com. 97 rooms. Restaurant ⊜⊜⊜. Stylish, contemporary rooms lie behind the neoclassical façade of this three-star hotel near the cathedral. The restaraurant, Los Churrascos, serves regional cuisine with a modern touch.

⊜⊜ **NH Cartagena** – Real 2, Cartagena. ℘968 12 09 08. www.nh-hotels.com. 100 rooms. Next to the sea and a short walk from the port, this modern hotel has chic rooms, some with balconies, and a gastrobar serving tapas and cocktails.

♈/EAT

⊜ **Restaurante Casa Corro** – Avda, Dr. García Rogel 23, Orihuela. ℘965 30 29 63. www.restaurantecasacorro.com. Hearty regional cuisine is on the menu at this century-old restaurant. House specialities include cocido (stew) and roast goat. They also have eight simple rooms (⊜).

⊜⊜⊜ **Mare Nostrum** – Paseo de Alfonso XII, Cartagena. ℘968 52 92 15. By the port, this popular and well-established restaurant specialises, unsurprisingly, in seafood. The rice dishes are particularly good.

Balearic Islands

The Balearics evoke summer sunshine and frenetic nightlife, yet their history and beauty are as impressive as those of any island in the Mediterranean. Although the archipelago is now one of the most popular destinations in the world, over 40 per cent of its verdant landscapes are protected by law.

Highlights

1 A leisurely morning spent wandering **Palma's Historic Centre** (p445)

2 Exploring the coves and caves of Mallorca's **Costa Rocosa** (p451)

3 The traditional architecture of **tranquil Menorca** (p454)

4 Sunset or sunrise gazing on **Ibiza** (p458)

5 Laid-back and low-key **Formentera** (p461)

The **Balearic archipelago** lies off Spain's Levante, in the Mediterranean, and covers 5 000sq km/1 900sq mi. It includes three large islands – **Mallorca, Menorca and Ibiza** – each with a distinctive character, two smaller inhabited isles – Formentera and Cabrera – and many uninhabited islets. All three larger islands have airports and inter-island ferries link them together.

Caló des Mort beach near Migjorn, Formentera

© LUNAMARINA/iStockphoto.com

Palma, capital of Mallorca, and the only real city in the archipelago, is also administrative capital of the Comunidad Autónoma Balear (Balearic Autonomous Community). The language, Balearic, is derived from Catalan and runs alongside Castilian.

The Balearics took off as **holiday islands** in the 1950s and Mallorca in particular was in the vanguard of mass tourism. Initially a fashionable "jet-set" destination, **Majorca** (as it was then known in English) had by the 1980s become synonymous with the worst excesses of holiday commercialisation and badly behaved tourists. In order to reverse this trend, during the late 1990s the island was rebranded by the local authorities both from a marketing perspective and also physically, as the island infrastructure was moved upmarket. Old hotels were demolished with great ceremony, and new policies to encourage visitors to discover inland **Mallorca** were put in place. Today, mass tourism is still very much alive but the island also now attracts fashionable visitors and consequently a whole new range of designer-chic hotels, rural retreats, and restaurants, bars and nightclubs have sprung up to grace the island, particularly in and around the capital of Palma which has become virtually a city break destination in its own right.

The situation is similar in **Ibiza**. It, too, has long suffered from charmless mass-market tourist centres, like San António, but these contrast with its charming hippy-chic **Eivissa** (Ibiza Town) and, away from the noisy centres, much of the island is undisturbed and surprisingly rural. The music scene remains of prime importance and ensures an annual "pilgrimage" of young tourists from all over the world.

Menorca meanwhile is the quietest of the developed islands, relying on its beautiful sandy beaches, prehistoric sites and natural attractions to bring a constant stream of UK and German visitors to its low-key family-orientated resorts.

Costa Rocosa viewed from the Mirador des Colomer

© Bildagentur/Tips/Photoshot

Mallorca★★★

Mallorca, the largest and by far the most popular of the Balearic Islands, is a holiday paradise for north Europeans, particularly popular with British and German visitors. The dramatic, steep cliff landscapes of the north coast, indented with coves, contrast with the beaches of the gentle south coast with their crystalline turquoise waters. Concrete seaside developments are offset by Mallorca's picturesque inland towns and villages.

LANDSCAPE AND TRADITION

The **Serra de Tramuntana** in the northwest rises in limestone crests – the highest is **Puig Major** (1 445m/4 740ft) – parallel to the coast.
Spectacular cliffs plunging into the sea are high enough to block winds from the mainland. Pines, junipers and holm oaks cover the slopes, interspersed with Mallorca's famous olive trees. Terraces of vegetables and fruit trees surround hillside villages. The central plain, **Es Pla**, is divided by low walls into fields and fig and almond orchards; market towns, with outlying windmills to pump water, retain the regular medieval fortress plan. The **Serra de Levant** to the east is hollowed out into wonderful caves. The rocky coast is indented with sheltered, sand-carpeted coves.

A BIT OF HISTORY
A Short-lived kingdom (1262–1349)
– James I (Jaume I) of Aragón recaptured Mallorca from the Muslims in

▶ **Population:** 875 277
⚅ **Michelin Map:**
   579 –Baleares.
🛈 **Info:** Palma: Plaza de la
   Reina. ☏ 902 40 47 04
   www.illesbalears.es
   Airport: ☏ 971 78 95 56
👪 **Kids:** Marineland;
   Palma Aquarium.

1229. Thirty years later James united Mallorca-Baleares, Roussillon and Montpellier in a kingdom which he presented to his son, James II. He and his successor, Sancho, founded new Catalan towns. Pedro IV seized the archipelago in 1343 to reunite it with Aragón. A merchant navy was established which brought prosperity, and a school of cartography rapidly became famous.
The Mallorcan Primitives (14C–15C)
– Gothic Mallorcan painting, characterised by a gentleness of expression, was open to external influences: the so-called **Master of Privileges** (Maestro de los Privilegios) showed a Sien-

GETTING THERE
BY AIR – From the mainland, the Balearic Islands are served by Iberia (www.iberia.com), Vueling (www.vueling.com) and Air Europa (www.air-europa.com).
BY SEA – Trasmediterranea (www.trasmediterranea.es) and Baleària (www.balearia.com) run regular ferries from the mainland and between the islands.

ese preference for miniaturisation and warm colours; later, **Joan Daurer** and the **Maestro de Obispo Galiana** were inspired by Catalan painting.

Artists of the 15C included **Gabriel Moger**, **Miguel de Alcanyis** and **Martí Torner**, who had studied in Valencia. The **Maestro de Predelas** is distinguishable by his attention to detail, **Rafael Moger** by his realism. **Pedro (Pere) Nisart** and **Alonso de Sedano** introduced the Flemish style (€ see Museo de Mallorca, p455).

Famous Mallorcans and visitors – **Ramón Llull** (1232–1315) personified the cosmopolitan 13C outlook of Mallorca. He learned languages and studied philosophy, theology and alchemy, and was beatified. **Fray Junípero Serra** (1713–84) founded missions in California. He was beatified in 1988. Among the foreign artists to visit in the 19C were **Frédéric Chopin** and **George Sand**. **Robert Graves** (1895–1985), the English poet and author, lived here from 1929. The Austrian archduke **Ludwig Salvator** (1847–1915) compiled the most detailed study of the archipelago and was patron to the French speleologist E A Martel.

ADDRESSES

🛏 STAY

😐🛏 **Hostal Ritzi** – Apuntadores 6, Palma. 🖉971 71 46 10. 18 rooms. This lovely guesthouse offers traditional white-washed rooms and a warm welcome.

😐🛏 **Hotel Born** – Sant Jaume 3, Palma. 🖉971 71 29 42. www.hotelborn.com. 36 rooms. This hotel occupies a former 16C palace with a delightful Ibizan-style patio. The rooms are quiet with tasteful decor.

😐🛏 **Ca Sa Padrina** – Teresa 3, Palma. 🖉971 42 53 00. www.hotelcasapadrina. com. 6 rooms. No breakfast. This 19C mansion has been beautifully transformed into a comfortable hotel where furniture and decor evoke the era of the building.

😐🛏🛏🛏 **Santa Clara Urban Hotel & Spa** – Sant Alonso 16, Palma. 🖉971 72

92 31. www.santaclarahotel.es. 20 rooms. 🍽€15. This nobleman's townhouse has been converted to a boutique hotel and spa with very stylish rooms. The rooftop terrace has a superb view.

😐🛏🛏🛏 **Hotel San Lorenzo** – San Lorenzo 14, Palma. 🖉971 72 82 00. www.hotelsanlorenzo.com. 9 rooms. An attractive 17C stately mansion with an inviting atmosphere. Beautifully decorated modern minimalist rooms, pool and garden.

🍴/EAT

😐🛏 **Bar Bosch** – Pl. del Rei Joan Carles I, 6, Palma. 🖉971 72 22 28. http://barbosch.es/en. One of the most famous bars in Palma (est 1936). with a wide range of tapas, a buzzing atmosphere and a terrace overlooking the Passeig del Born.

😐🛏 **Cafè Es Pes de Sa Palla** –Pl. of Pes de sa Palla, Palma. 🖉971 72 25 05. http://cafesbotiga.amadipesment.org. Closed Sun. Managed by a local association for people with learning difficulties, this modern café is outside the touristy old city. Mediterranean cuisine at moderate prices served on a charming terrace overlooking the square. The perfect lunch spot.

😐🛏🛏 **La Bodeguilla** – Sant Jaume 1, Palma. 🖉971 71 82 74. www. la-bodeguilla.com. A smart restaurant spread over two floors with an adjoining wine shop. Large barrels are used as dining tables to enjoy dinner or tapas.

😐🛏🛏 **Forn de San Joan** – S. Joan 4, Palma. 🖉971 72 84 22. www. forndesantjoan.com. Stylish celeb-spotting bar-restuarant serving tapas, cocktails, contemporary Mediterranean cuisine and good-value.

😐🛏🛏 **Patrón Lunares** – Fábrica 30, Palma. 🖉971 577 154. www.patron lunares.com. Closed Mon. With the appearance of a 'fisherman's cantine', this hip restaurant in Santa Catalina serves excellent seafood. There is also brunch on Sundays.

😐🛏🛏🛏 **Marc Fosh** – Missió 7-A, Palma. 🖉971 720 114. www.marcfosh.com. Closed Sun. Michelin-star dining in contemporary surroundings in the old town. Creative use of local ingredients.

Palma de Mallorca★★

Palma spreads along a wide bay. Residential quarters with hotels stretch on either side of the historic centre, and along avinguda Gabriel Roca, shaded by palms. The old harbour, bordered by passeig Sagrera, serves passenger and merchant ships; the new harbour at the southern tip of El Terreno accommodates the largest liners. Bahía de Palma – the bay, protected from north and west winds by the highest peak on Mallorca – Puig Major – has a mild climate all year. To the west, hotels stand along the indented Bendinat coastline where there is little sand, except at Palmanova and Magaluf. The coast to the east is less sheltered, but has mile upon mile of fine sand with a series of resorts – Can Pastilla, Ses Meravelles and S'Arenal.

- ▶ **Population:** 400 578.
- ⚅ **Michelin Map:** pp450–451.
- 🛈 **Info:** Airport: ✆971 78 95 56. Plaza de la Reina: ✆971 173 990. Parc de la Mar: ✆902 102 365. www.palmademallorca.es. 🚋Palma de Mallorca. Narrow gauge & local service.
- ◖ **Location:** Palma is located on the southwest coast of of the island of Mallorca.
- ♟ **Kids:** The Spanish Village (Poble Espanyol).
- ◔ **Timing:** Allow a good half day to see the main sites of the city.

A BIT OF HISTORY

The "Ciutat de Mallorca" – Palma was known by this name after its liberation on 31 December 1229. Trade links were forged with the mainland, Africa and northern Europe; Jews and Genoese established themselves. James II (Jaume II) and his successors endowed the city with beautiful Gothic buildings. Aragonese expansion to Naples and Sicily enabled Palma to extend her commerce.

Palma's old mansions – In the 15C and 16C, the great families of Palma favoured the Italian style. They built elegant residences with stone façades, relieved by windows with Renaissance decoration. In the 18C a characteristic Mallorcan *casa* (house) appeared, with an inner court of massive marble columns, wide shallow arches and a high and graceful loggia.

Modern Palma – Palma is home to a large proportion of the population of the island and is one of the most popular cities in Spain to visit. Tourists congregate in and around **El Terreno**

– especially in plaza Gomila – and **Cala Major** quarters in the west of town. The native heart of the city remains the **passeig des Born**. Shops sell pearls, glassware and leather in the old town east of El Born, in pedestrian streets around Plaça Major and in avinguda Jaume III.

BARRIO DE LA CATEDRAL★
HISTORIC CENTRE
Catedral★★

Pl. Almoina. Open Apr–May and Oct Mon–Fri 10am–5.15pm, Sat 10am–2.15pm; Jun–Sept Mon–Fri 10am–6.15pm, Sat 10am–2.15pm; rest of the year Mon–Fri 10am–3.15pm, Sat 10am–2.15pm. €6, including museum. ✆902 02 24 45. www.catedraldemallorca.info.

The bold yet elegant Cathedral, its buttresses surmounted by pinnacles, rises above the sea. The Santanyí limestone of its walls changes colour according to the time of day: ochre, golden or pink. Begun in the early 14C, it is one of the great late-Gothic constructions. The west face was rebuilt in neo-Gothic style in the 19C after an earthquake; its 16C Renaissance portal remains intact. The south door, the **Portada del Mirador** (Viewpoint Doorway), overlooks the sea, the delicate Gothic decoration dating from the 15C. Statues of St

Catedral viewed from the port

© Bertrand Gardel/hemis.fr

Peter and St Paul on either side prove that Sagrera, architect of the Llotja (Exchange), was a talented sculptor. The **interior** is large and light, measuring 121m x 55m (397ft x 180ft) and 44m/144ft to the top of the vaulting. Slender octagonal pillars divide the nave from the aisles. The Capilla Mayor or Real (Royal Chapel) contains an enormous wrought-iron baldaquin by Gaudí (1912) with Renaissance choir stalls on either side. Tombs of the kings of Mallorca, James II and Jaume III, lie in the Capilla de la Trinidad (Trinity Chapel).

Museo de la Seu

Almoina house, next to the cathedral bell tower. Open same hours as cathedral. ℰ902 02 24 45. www.catedraldemallorca.info.
In the Gothic chapter house is the Santa Eulàlia altarpiece by the Maestro de los Privilegios (1335). In the oval Baroque chapter house are reliquaries including one of the True Cross.

Palacio Real de La Almudaina

Open year-round Tue–Sun 10am–6pm (Apr–Sept 8pm). €7, no charge Wed & Thu 3–6pm Oct–Mar and 5–8pm Apr–Sept for EU citizens, 18 May, 12 Oct. ℰ914 54 87 00.
www.patrimonionacional.es.
This fortress of the Córdoba caliphate was converted in the 14C and 15C into a royal palace. Today, as a residence of the King of Spain, several rooms have been restored and furnished with Flem-

ish tapestries and paintings. In the courtyard, note the carved eaves and the doorway of the Iglesia de Santa Ana (St Anne's Church), a rare Romanesque structure in the Balearics.

Ayuntamiento

Pl. Cort 1.
Carved wooden eaves overhang the 17C façade of the town hall.

Iglesia de Santa Eulàlia

Pl. Santa Eulàlia 2. Open Mon–Sat 9am–10.30am, 5–8pm. No charge. ℰ971 71 46 25.
The tall nave of this 13C–15C church is unusually bare for the Gothic period. In the first chapel off the south aisle is a 15C altarpiece. Between Santa Eulàlia and Sant Francesc, at no. 2 Carrer Savellà, is the 18C **Can Vivot**, its beautiful patio decorated with marble columns.

Basilica de Sant Francesc

Pl. Sant Francesc 7. Open Mon–Sat 10am–2.30pm, 3–6pm. €3. ℰ971 71 26 95.
The façade of this 13–14C church, rebuilt in the late 17C, has an immense Plateresque rose window and a Baroque portal with a beautifully carved tympanum by Francisco Herrera. The first apsidal chapel on the left contains the tomb of Ramón Llull. The **cloisters★** (claustro), begun in 1286, are elegant.

Baños Árabes

Casa Marqués del Palmer
Sol 7.
In Carrer del Sol stands Casa Marqués del Palmer (Can Catlar), a mansion built in 1556 in stone now blackened by age. Renaissance decoration around the upper-floor windows mellows the austerity of Gothic walls. The upper gallery, under deep eaves, is a replica of that on the Llotja. The old Jewish quarter, **La Portella**, lies close against the town wall.

Museo de Mallorca
Portella 5. Open Tue–Fri 10am–6pm, Sat 11am–2pm. €2.40. ℘971 17 78 38. http://museudemallorca.caib.es.
The ground floor displays Muslim capitals, *artesonado* ceilings and ceramics. The **Fine Arts★** section displays Mallorcan Gothic paintings. Works from the early 14C show clear Italian influence. Catalan works begin to appear after 1349 when Mallorca was annexed by Aragón: the *Crucifixion* by Ramón Destorrents, interesting for its composition and expression, was to influence other paintings. Francesch Comes, one of the most prestigious of the early 15C painters, is represented here by his **St George★** (room 3), remarkable for the depth and detail of the landscape.

Baños Árabes
Can Serra 7. Open year-round daily 9am–7pm. €2. ℘637 046 534. http://palmavirtual.palmademallorca.es.
These Moorish baths, the only relic from the caliphate, feature small circular windows and a classical dome on 12 columns with rudimentary capitals.

Museo Diocesano (Diocesan Museum)
Mirador 5. Open year-round daily 10am–2pm. €3. ℘971 72 38 60. www.illesbalears.es.
Among the many Gothic works is Pere Nisart's outstanding **St George★** (1568) which shows the saint slaying the dragon against a backdrop of 16C Palma.

WEST OF EL BORN
Museu Fundación Juan March★
Sant Miguel 11. Open Mon–Fri 10am–6.30 pm, Sat 10.30am–2pm. Closed 25 Dec, 1 Jan. No charge. ℘971 71 35 15. www.march.es/arte/palma.
This 18C mansion has a **permanent collection★** of contemporary Spanish art.

Fundació Palma Espai d'Art - Casal Solleric
Pg. des Born 27. Open Tue–Sat 11am–2pm, 3.30–8.30pm, Sun and public holidays 11am–2.30pm. No charge. ℘971 72 20 92. https://casalsolleric.palma.cat.
The 18C Palau Solleric, overlooking the Born, is completed by an elegant loggia. A narrow covered way leads to the most perfect **patio★** in Palma, along with a double staircase with delicate ironwork. The building now stages a dynamic programme of temporary exhibitions of contemporary art.

Casa Berga

Pl. Mercat 12.
This 1712 mansion is the Palacio de Justicia (Law Courts). The façade is encumbered with stone balconies but the vast inner courtyard is typically Mallorcan.

Sa Llotja (La Lonja)★

Pas. Sagrera. Open during exhibitions only: Tue–Sat 11am–2pm, 5–9pm, Sun 11am–2pm. ℘971 71 17 05.
Guillermo Sagrera designed this 15C commodities exchange. The Llotja's military features are only for appearances, to distract the eye from the buttresses and austerity of the walls. The interior, with pointed arches on spiral fluted columns, is very elegant.

Antiguo Consulado del Mar (Former Maritime Consulate)

Pas. Sagrera. ℘971 71 60 92.
The early 17C building with a Renaissance balcony was the meeting-place of the Tribunal de Comercio Marítimo (Merchant Shipping Tribunal). Today it houses the regional administration.

Es Baluard Museu d'Art Modern i Contemporani de Palma (Museum of Modern and Contemporary Art of Palma)

Pl. Porta Santa Catalina 10. Open Tue–Sat 10am–8pm, Sun 10am–3pm. Closed 1 Jan, 25 Dec. €6, exhibition only €4, Fri by donation (minimum €0.10). ℘971 90 82 00. www.esbaluard.org.
Occupying part of a medieval fortress Mallorca's newest major gallery occupies a stunning angular white concrete-and-glass building. The permanent collection includes: Mediterranean landscapes by the likes of Joaquín Sorolla, Santiago Rusiñol and Joan Miró; ceramics by Picasso; drawings by Chagall, Toulouse-Lautrec, and Barceló; a Miró gallery. High-quality temporary exhibitions feature international artists.

OUTSIDE THE CENTRE

Castell de Bellver★

Camilo José Cela 17. Open Tue-Sat 10am-7pm (Oct-Mar until 6pm), Sun 10am-3pm. €4.

No charge Sun. ℘971 73 50 65. http://castelldebellver.palmademallorca.es.
The castle, built by the Mallorcan kings of the 14C as a summer residence, served as a prison until 1915. The round buildings and circular perimeter and court are highly original; a free-standing keep dominates all. On display are Roman statues and finds from excavations in Pollença. Enjoy the **panorama**★★ of the bay from the terrace.

Fundació Pilar i Joan Miró (Pilar and Joan Miró Foundation).

Joan de Saridakis 29. Open year-round Tue–Sat 10am–6pm (mid-May–mid-Sept 7pm), Sun & hols 10am–3pm. Closed 1 Sept & 25 Dec. €7.50. No charge Sat. ℘971 70 14 20. http://miro.palmademallorca.es.
This museum is the legacy of Joan Miró, who worked here from 1956 until his death in 1983. The museum and exhibition spaces are set around his studio.

EXCURSIONS

▲▲ Palma Aquarium

Manuela De Los Herreros i Sora 21. Open daily Apr–Oct 9.30am–6.30pm. Nov–Mar Mon–Fri 10am–3.30pm, Sat–Sun & hols 10am–5.30pm. Ticket office closes 1hr 30min before park. €22; child (4–12 yrs) €14. ℘902 70 29 02. www.palmaaquarium.com.
Located near the airport, but in lovely grounds, this spectacular aquarium is one of the finest in Europe. It comprises over 50 different viewing areas with 8,000 specimens from 700 species – from seahorses to sharks – plucked from the Mediterranean and more exotic waters.

▲▲ Marineland

Calle Garcilaso de la Vega 9, Costa d'en Blanes. Open Apr–Oct daily 9.30am–6pm (ticket office closes 4.30pm). Online prices €24; child €15. ℘971 67 51 25. www.marineland.es.
This huge dolphinarium is rated among the best in Europe and also includes Californian Sea Lions. There are many other attractions on site including an exotic

birds show, an aquarium with penguins and sharks, a tropical bird house and aviary, and a children's water park.

🚗 DRIVING TOUR

3 SOUTH SIDE OF THE TRAMUNTANA RANGE

75km/46.5 mi. Allow 3hr.

◗ Leave Palma on the Ma 13 heading NE towards Alcúdia. **⬥ See map pp458–459.**

Inca

31km/19mi from Palma. 🚃 Inca.

This sizeable market town prospered during the wine making boom, but was virtually abandoned during the phylloxera vine epidemic of the late 19C – hence the number of *bodegas* (cellars), that have been converted into cafés and restaurants. The present prosperity of Inca is due to the leather industry in general and footwear in particular, and many famous Spanish brands are based here. Every Thursday the biggest market on the island takes place at Inca, featuring lots of authentic (and plenty of fake) leather items.

As you stroll around town seek out the Església de Santa Maria la Major and the Església de Sant Domingo – both Baroque buildings.

Coves de Campanet

15km/9mi along the Ma 13 and 4km/2mi along a secondary, signposted road. Guided tours (45min) daily 10am–6.30pm. €15. ☎971 51 61 30. www.covesdecampanet.com.

About half of these caves along the 1.3km/0.8mi-long path have ceased formation. In the waterlogged area, the most common features are straight and delicate stalactites.

◗ The road crosses countryside bristling with windmills.

Muro

The **Museu Etnologic de Mallorca** (Ethnological Museum; Major 15; open Tue–Sat 10am–3pm, Thu also 5–8pm; closed Aug; no charge; ☎971 86 06 47), set in a large 17C noble residence, displays exhibits on traditional furniture, dress, farming and many island trades.

◗ Return to the Ma 13 and follow it to Alcúdia.

Alcúdia

Alcúdia, encircled by 14C ramparts, guards the promontory which divides the bays of Pollença and Alcúdia. Two gates (**Puerta del Muelle** to the harbour, and the **Puerta de San Sebastián** across town) from early walls were incorporated into 14C ramparts. The streets in the shadow of the walls have a distinctive medieval air.

About 2km/1.2mi south is the site of Roman **Pollentia** founded in the 2C BC. Only the theatre ruins remain.

Museo Monográfico de Pollentia

Sant Jaume 30, Alcúdia. Open Tue–Fri 10am-3.30pm, Sat & Sun 10.30am-1.30pm. Closed holidays. €3, inc admission to Roman City remains. ☎971 54 70 04. www.alcudia.net/pollentia.

A chapel in Alcúdia's old quarter houses statues, oil lamps, bronzes and jewellery from the ancient city of Pollentia.

Port d'Alcúdia

2km/1.2mi E.

The port of Alcúdia overlooks a vast bay that has become a fully fledged resort built up with hotels. A beach stretches to the south as far as Can Picafort.

The marsh of S'Albufera (open daily year-round 9am–5pm/Apr–Sept 6pm); pick up a permit from the Visitor Centre before 4pm; no charge; www.mallorcaweb.net/salbufera; ☎971 89 22 50) is a nature reserve.

Tramuntana★★★

The western rocky coast of Mallorca is one of the island's highlights. Here, mountains drop steeply into deep turquoise waters. This sharp contrast is tempered by the presence of abundant Mediterranean vegetation in some places and acres of orchards in others. The beaches are a delight, especially north of Pollensa and Alcúdia and east of the beautiful Cap de Formentor, known locally as the "meeting point of the winds".

- **Michelin Map:** 579 I-M 4-6.
- **Info:** Pas. Pere Ventayol, Alcúdia. ℘971 54 90 22. www.alcudiamallorca.com.
- **Location:** The Tramuntana stretches west of the island from Palma and Alcúdia, along the coast 157km/ 98mi (55km/34mi inland).
- **Kids:** Discovering the coast's many *calas* (coves) and beaches.
- **Timing:** At least two days to explore the coast.

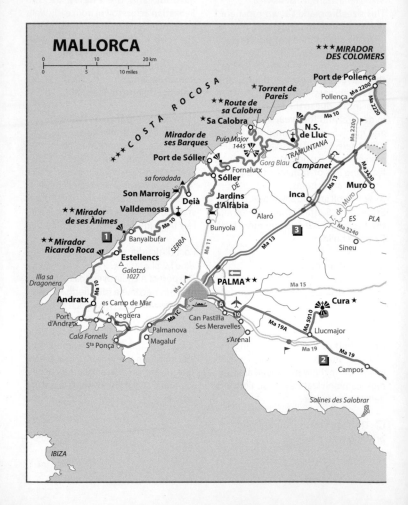

🚗 DRIVING TOUR

1 COSTA ROCOSA

264km/165mi. Allow 2 days. Leave Palma along passeig Sagrera. Palma to Alcúdia.

Mallorca's west coast is dominated by the limestone Serra de Tramuntana, rising to 1 445m/4 740ft at Puig Major. In the south, around Estellencs and Banyalbufar, slopes are terraced into *marjades* of olives, almonds and vines.

Port d'Andratx★

32km/18.6mi W of Palma.
The small fishing port is now also used by pleasure craft. The clifftop C 710 from Andratx to Sóller is scenic★★★.

Mirador Ricardo Roca★★

18km/11.2mi NE of Port d'Andratx.
The view from this lookout drops sheer to tiny coves lapped by the limpid sea.

▶ Follow the M 10.

Estellencs

This pretty little village is surrounded by stone terraces covered with almond and apricot trees.

▶ Continue along the M 10.

Mirador de Ses Ànimes★★

The panorama from the watchtower stretches south from the Isla de Dragonera and north to Port de Sóller.

Real Cartuja de Valldemossa (Valldemossa Royal Carthusian Monastery) & Palacio Rey Sancho

Pl. de la Cartuja, Valldemossa.
45km/28mi NE of Port d'Andratx.
Open Mon–Sat from 9.30am. Monastery closes Dec–Jan 3pm, Feb & Nov 5pm, Mar & Oct 5.30pm, rest of year 6.30pm. Sun 10am–1pm. Palace closes 10–15 mins later. Closed Sun Dec & Jan, 1 Jan, 25 Dec. €9.50 plus €4 Chopin cell. Buy online to visit the Chopin cell for free. 𝒫971 612 986. www.cartujadevalldemossa.com. www.celdadechopin.es.

The monastery was made famous by the visit George Sand and Chopin paid in the winter of 1838–39. The cell (celda) in which Chopin stayed is open to visitors (extra charge) and Chopin piano recitals (15min) occur at regular intervals during the day. Sand made his stay famous by invoking the countryside in *A Winter in Majorca*. Adjacent to the monastery is the royal palace built by King Jaume (Sancho) II in the early 14C for his asthmatic son.

Valldemossa is one of the prettiest villages on Mallorca but time your visit early or late in the day to avoid the coach parties.

Cap de Formentor ★

Cabo de Formentor Road ★★
Platja de Formentor

Alcúdia ★
Pollentia
Port d'Alcúdia

Parque Natural de s'Albufera
Can Picafort

Cala Agulla
Capdepera
Ma 12
Ma 3410
Arta   Ma 15
Cala Ratjada
Ses Païses
Ma 4040
ARTÀ ★★★
T. de S'Arvalls
San Llorenç des Cardassar
Son Servera
Petra
Ma 3370
Ma 15
Ma 4023
Ma 4020
2
Manacor
Hams   Porto Cristo
DRACH ★★★
Ma 14
LLEVANT
Felatnix
Ma 4010
Ma 4014
★ Sant Salvador
SERRA DE
Ma 14
LA COSTA DE LAS CALAS
Ma 19
Cala d'Or ★
Santanyí
Parque Natural de Mondargó
★Cala Santanyí   Cala Figuera★
Cap de ses Salines
N

Son Marroig

Ctra de Valldemossa-Deià. 7km/4.3mi N of Valldemossa. Open Mon–Sat 10am–6pm (Apr–Sept 9.30am-6.30pm). €4. ☏971 63 91 58. www.sonmarroig.com. The former residence of Archduke Ludwig Salvator includes an exhibition of archaeological finds and Mallorcan furniture.

Deià

4km/2.5mi E of Son Marroig.
Another charming honeypot Mallorcan village, enjoying a beautiful setting in the Tramuntana hills, Deià has maintained its character despite the hordes of visitors it receives. Writer and poet Robert Graves lived here from 1929, on and off, until his death in 1985, and is buried in Deià Cemetery. His house is open to visitors (open Apr–Oct Mon–Fri 10am–5pm, Sat until 3pm; Nov–Mar Mon–Fri 9am–4pm, Sat 9am–2pm; €7; ☏971 636 185; www.lacasaderobertgraves.org).

Sóller

11km/6.8mi NE of Deià. 🚋Sóller.
The delightful 19C houses of Sóller spread out in a quiet valley. The charming vintage narrow-gauge **Tren de Sóller** (€25 return to Palma; ☏971 75 20 51; www.trendesoller.com) has been running the 27km/17 miles from Palma direct to Sóller since 1913. Worth seeing here is the **Can Prunera Museu Modernista** (Lluna 86–90; open Mar–Oct daily 10.30am–6.30pm, Nov–Feb Tue–Sun until 6pm; €5, no charge second Sun in May, 18 May, 24 Aug; ☏971 638 973; www.canprunera.com), a restored Modernist house.

Port de Sóller

5km/3mi N of Sóller.
Port de Sóller, on an almost circular bay which shelters pleasure boats, is the major seaside resort of the west coast.

▶ C 711 from Sóller to Alfàbia.

Jardines de Alfàbia

Open Nov & mid-Feb–Mar Mon–Fri 9.30am–5.30pm, Sat 9.30am–1.30pm, rest of year Mon–Sat 9.30am–6.30pm. €7.50, winter €5.50 (10 per cent discount coupon on website). ☏971 61 31 23. www.jardinesdealfabia.com.
Only the *artesonado* ceiling over the porch remains from a 14C Moorish residence. Follow the path through the gardens to the **library** for a taste of a traditional seigniorial residence.

▶ Return to Sóller. Take the narrow mountain road via the picturesque villages of Biniaraix and Fornalutx, then follow the C 710.

Mirador de Ses Barques

From this viewpoint there is a **panorama** of Port de Sóller. The road heads through a long tunnel before following the upper valley of the Pareis.

▶ After skirting the Gorg Blau reservoir, take the Sa Calobra road.

Sa Calobra road★★★

This road plunges 900m/2 953ft in 14km/8.7mi through steep rocks.

Sa Calobra★

Near the village is the mouth of the **Pareis river★**, its clear water pouring over round white shingle.

▶ Return to the C 710.

About 1km/0.6mi north of the Sa Calobra fork, a small **mirador★** (lookout, alt 664m/2 178ft) gives a good view over the cleft hollowed out by the Pareis.

Monasterio de Nuestra Sra de Lluc

Open (museum) Sun–Fri 10am–2pm. €4. ☏971 87 15 25. www.lluc.net.
The monastery dates from the 13C when a young shepherd found a statue of the Virgin. *La Moreneta*, the dark stone statue, is patron of Mallorca.

Port de Pollença

This large resort has a perfect **setting★** in a vast sheltered bay between the Cabo Formentor headland to the north and Cabo del Pinar to the south.

Cabo de Formentor road★
The road commands spectacular views as it twists upward. The **Mirador des Colomer viewpoint★★★** (access along a stepped path) overlooks great rock promontories. The **Platja de Formentor** is a sheltered beach. The grand Hotel Formentor was once famous for its casino and millionaire guests.
The road continues through a tunnel and a steep and arid landscape. **Cabo de Formentor★** has a lighthouse.

La Costa de las Calas★★

The east coast of Mallorca is renowned for its string of *calas* – (coves), and also caves (*cuevas*). Formed through thousands of years of erosion and of varying sizes, they provide sheltered swimming spots and fascinating natural formations.

🚗 DRIVING TOUR

② EAST COAST COVES AND CAVES★★

From Artà to Palma
165km/102.5mi. Allow 1 day.
ℹ See map pp458–459.

Artà
The high rock site is crowned by the Iglesia de Sant Salvador and the ruins of an ancient fortress.

▶ Continue along the C 715.

Capdepera
Access to the fortress: by car, along narrow streets; on foot, up steps.
The remains of a 14C fortress give Capdepera an angular silhouette of crenellated walls and square towers.

Cala Rajada
3km/1.8mi NE of Capdepera.
Cala Rajada, once a delightful fishing village and pleasure boat harbour.

▶ Return to Capdepera and follow the signs to the Coves d'Artà.

ℹ **Michelin Map:** 579.
O5-8 and pp458–459.
🛈 **Info:** Plaza del Convent 3, Manacor. ℘662 350 891.

👥 Coves d'Artà★★★
Open daily Apr–Oct 10am–6pm (Jul Sept 7pm); rest of the year 10am–5pm.
€14, child (7–12yrs) €7. ℘971 84 12 93.
www.cuevasdearta.com.
Largely hollowed out by the sea, inside these caves are the Dantesque **Reina de las Columnas** (Queen of Columns), the **Sala del Infierno** (Chamber of Hell) and a fantastical **Sala de las Banderas**.

▶ Return to the PM 404; bear left. At Portocristo, take the Manacor road; turn shortly for the Coves dels Hams.

👥 Coves dels Hams
Guided tours (45min) year-round daily 10am–5pm (Nov–Mar until 4pm). €21, child €10.50. ℘971 82 09 88.
www.cuevas-hams.com.
As the caves meet the sea the water level in several pools rises and falls with the Mediterranean tide.

▶ Return to Portocristo, bear right.

👥 Coves del Drach★★★
Guided tours (1hr on the hour) daily mid-Mar–Oct 10am–5pm; rest of the year 10.45am, noon, 2pm, 3.30pm.
€15, child (3–12yrs) €8. ℘971 82 07 53.
www.cuevasdeldrach.com.
Four chambers succeed one another over a distance of 2km/1.2mi. The cave **roofs**, are amazing, glittering with countless sharply pointed icicles. Within the caves is Lake Martel is one of the largest subterranean lakes in the world, (177m by 30m). A boat takes you on the

lake and there are daily performances of classical music.

▷ Continue along the road towards Santanyí then right onto the PM 401.

Monasterio de Sant Salvador★
Open daily 8am–9pm. No charge. ℘971 51 52 60. www.santsalvadorhotel.com.
The monastery, on a rise 500m/1 640ft above the plain (🚗 tight hairpin bends), commands a wide **panorama★★**.
It was founded in the 14C. In the church, behind the Baroque high altar, is a venerated **Virgin and Child**, in the south chapels are three **Nativities** set in dioramas and a multicoloured 14C stone **altarpiece** carved with the Passion. Part of it has now been converted into a hotel and restaurant.

▷ Return to the Santanyí road.

Secondary roads lead to resorts built up in the creeks along the coast, namely **Cala d'Or**, **Cala Figuera★**, which is still a delightful little fishing village, and, in a lovely narrow bay, **Cala Santanyí★**.

▷ From Santanyí follow the C 717 towards Palma. In Llucmajor, bear right onto the PM 501.

Santuario de Cura★
Open 10am–5pm, summer 10am-6pm. ℘971 12 02 60. www.santuaridecura.com.
The road climbs to the monastery. The buildings have been restored and modernised by the Franciscans and include the 17C **church**, Sala de Gramática (Grammar Room), a small **museum** and bar/restaurant. From the terrace on the west side there is a **panorama★★**.

▷ Continue W on C 717 to Palma.

Menorca★★

Menorca, with an area of 669sq km/258sq mi, has managed to avoid the rampant development that has blighted its neighbours, and its coastline is dotted with sandy coves of crystal-clear water, excellent for diving. The island is also famous for its prehistoric monuments.

LANDSCAPE AND TRADITION
Menorca's highest point, Monte Toro, 358m/1 175ft, is in the north of the island, known as the Tramuntana, where there are outcrops of dark slate rock. Along the coast, these ancient, eroded cliffs have been cut into a saw's edge of *rías* (inlets) and deep coves. South of the Maó-Ciutadella line, the Migjorn limestone platform forms cliffs along the coast. Vegetation is typically Mediterranean: pinewoods, gnarled and twisted wild olives, heather and aromatic herbs such as rosemary, camomile and thyme. Drystone walls divide fields, punctuated by gates of twisted olive branches.

▶ **Population:** 93 313
🚴 **Michelin Map:** 579.
🅱 **Info:** Mahón: Plaça Constitució. ℘971 36 37 90. Cuitadella: Plaça des Born. ℘971 484 155. Menorca Call Center: ℘902 92 90 15/50. www.menorca.es.
◖ **Location:** Menorca is the furthest Balearic island from the mainland.

Megalithic monuments – In the second millennium BC, the cavernous nature of the Menorcan countryside offered shelter for both the living and the dead; some of the caves, such as **Calascoves**, are even decorated. At the same time, **talayots** began to appear (over 200 have been identified), great cones of stones, possibly covering a funeral chamber and forming the base for a wooden house. Other monuments of the civilisation include **taulas**, consisting of two huge stone blocks placed one on top of the other in the shape of a T, possibly serving as altars, and **navetas**, which take the form of upturned boats and contain funeral chambers.

🖂 A locally available map shows the monument sites: Mapa Arqueológico de Menorca, by J Mascaró Pasarius.

Architecture – The walls and even the roofs of Menorcan houses are brightly whitewashed; low dividing walls have a white band along the top. Tiles are used for roofing, chimneys and guttering.

Houses face south, their fronts characterised by wide, open bays. Northern walls, exposed to fierce *tramontana* winds, have small windows. English influence on architecture is evident. Many houses in towns have sash windows and some mansions are in the Palladian style of 18C Britain.

The fields around Ciutadella are scattered with *barracas*, curious stone constructions with false ceilings, which served as shelters for shepherds.

A BIT OF HISTORY

Prehistoric peoples have left monuments throughout the island. Menorca was colonised by the Romans, conquered by Vandals in 427, and came under Muslim control in 903. In the 13C, Alfonso III of Aragón invaded, made Ciutadella capital and encouraged settlers from Catalunya and Aragón.

In the 16C, Barbary pirates left Maó and Ciutadella in virtual ruin.

In 1713, Menorca, which had begun to prosper through trade in the late 17C, was ceded to the English crown by the Treaty of Utrecht. Maó became England's stronghold in the Mediterranean. Apart from a short period of French rule from 1756 to 1763, the island remained throughout the 18C under the British. The first road, between Maó and Ciutadella, still exists (north of the C 721), known as camino Kane for a British governor. At the beginning of the 19C, Menorca was restored to Spain.

The island's economy has gradually been orientated towards the leather industry and jewellery-making while cattle raising provides the island with its well-known cheeses.

SIGHTS
CIUTADELLA/CIUDADELA★

In the Middle Ages, Ciutadella, citadel and capital of Menorca, was ringed with walls. The fortified aspect of the city becomes evident when viewed from the harbour. Sacked by Turkish pirates in the 16C, Ciutadella was partly rebuilt in the late 17C and 18C.

The **Midsummer's Day festivities**, or **Fiestas de San Juan** (24 Jun), are celebrated in traditional fashion. On the preceding Sunday, a man representing John the Baptist, dressed in skins and carrying a lamb, runs to the sound of *fabiols* (flutes) and *tambourins*. On 24 and 25 June, over 100 horsemen take part in jousting tournaments and processions.

Barrio Antiguo (Old Quarter)

Plaza del Born, the ex-parade ground, is flanked by the eclectic 19C **ayuntamiento** (town hall) and the early 19C **Palacio de Torre-Saura**, a palace with side loggias. An obelisk commemorates resistance against the Turks in the 16C.

Castell de Sant Nicolau

Pl of Almirall Farragut. Open summer 10am–1pm, 5–9pm. Winter: call for times. No charge. 🖉 971 38 10 50.

This castle was built in the late 17C, before the British occupation, to defend the port. Its entrance is adorned with the emblem of the Crown of Aragón and the ground floor was used for storing food, weapons and ammunition.

A spiral staircase near the front door provides access to the upper floor and the top of the tower.

Catedral

Plaça de la Catedral. Open May–Oct Mon–Sat 10am–4pm, Nov–Apr 8am–1pm, 5–9pm. €3. 🖉971 38 03 43. www.bisbatdemenorca.com.

The late-14C fortified church retains a minaret from Islamic days. The single aisle is ogival and the apse pentagonal. View the Baroque doorway from calle del Rosario. At the end of the street, turn left into calle del Santísimo. **Palacio Saura** has a Baroque façade with a cornice. **Palacio Martorell** across

A British base

Menorca was ceded to Britain by the Treaty of Utrecht in 1713 and the British subsequently made Maó (Mahon) their Mediterranean economic base for the next 70 years. The city is built on a cliff at the edge of a deep harbour. This combination facilitated the protection of both harbour and city for centuries from the greed of European powers. Situated at the crossroads of maritime routes between Southern Europe and North Africa, Menorca held a strategic position.
Several companies offer a tour of the harbour with possible stops at various points along the way. Departures generally leave between 10am and 3.30pm and head south towards the Costa de Ses Voltes.

the street is more sober. Take calle del Obispo Vila, passing the Claustro de Socorro (Socorro Cloisters) and the Iglesia de Santo Cristo (Church of the Holy Christ) to the main street which leads to **plaza de España** and the arcaded **carrer de Ses Voltes**.

Puerto (Harbour)

The ramp approach to the harbour, which serves pleasure craft, is along a former counterscarp. Quayside cafés and restaurants bustle with life. The esplanade, plaça de Sant Joan, the centre for Midsummer's Day festivities, is bordered by boat shelters hollowed out of rock. The area comes alive at night.

EXCURSIONS

Lithica/Pedreres de s'Hostal

⊙ 1km/0.8mi from Ciutadella on the Me 1. Camí Vell 1. Open May–Sept Mon–Sat 9.30am–2.30pm, 4.30pm–sunset. Sun 9.30am–2.30pm. Rest of the year daily 9.30am–2.30pm. €5, no charge Nov–Apr. ✆971 48 15 78, www.lithica.es.
This unusual attraction is situated in sandstone quarries that are being reclaimed by nature. Plants, greenery and sculptures have been artfully

placed between the labyrinthine formations of the mined sandstone. In the summer, music, dance, cinema, arts and environmentally-focused events are staged here.

Nau or Naveta des Tudons

⊙ 5km/3mi E of Ciutadella.
This funerary monument, shaped like an upturned ship, is notable for the vast stones in the walls and lining the floor.

Cala Santandria

⊙ 3km/1.8mi S of Citadella.
This is a small sheltered beach in a creek, a local resort popular with locals.

Arenal de Son Saura, Cala en Turqueta, Cala Macarella

⊙ SE of Ciutadella. **Son Saura:** 12km/7.4mi via Torre Saura; **Turqueta:** 12km/7.4mi via Sant Joanet; **Macarella:** 14km/8.7mi via Sant Joan Gran.
The three beaches are set in small, beautifully unspoilt creeks fringed by pines. Arrive early, or late, in summer.

Maó/Mahón★★

⊙ 45km/28mi E of Ciutadella on Me 1.
Maó's **site★** is most striking when approached from the sea, atop a cliff in the curve of a deep, 5km/3mi-long natural harbour. Maó was endowed with Palladian-style mansions during English occupation. On the north side of the harbour is the Finca de San Antonio – the Golden Farm – where Admiral Nelson put the finishing touches to his book, *Sketches of My Life* (October 1799).
Most of Maó's shops are between **plaza del Ejército**, a large, lively square lined with cafés and restaurants, and the quieter **plaza de España** with its two churches: **Santa María**, with a beautiful Baroque organ, and **Carmen**, the Carmelite church, whose cloisters now hold the municipal market. Mahón also gave its name to mayonnaise!

Museo de Menorca

Av. de Guardia. Open Jun–Sep Tue–Sat 10am–2pm, 6–8.30pm, Sun 10am–2pm; Oct–May Mon–Fri 10am–6pm, Sat–Sun 10am–2pm. ✆971 35 09 55.

www.museudemenorca.com.

The museum is in a former Franciscan monastery. Rooms around a sober 18C cloister display prehistoric and other objects relating to Menorcan history. A room is dedicated to *talayot* culture.

Puerto (Harbour)

Walk down the steep ramp from carrer de Ses Voltes, cut by a majestic flight of steps, and follow the quay to the north side. From here is the classic view of the town lining the top of the cliff.

La Rada★ (Roadstead)

On the south side are coves and villages, among them Cala Figuera with its fishing harbour and restaurants. **Es Castell** was an English garrison named Georgetown. It has a grid plan, with a parade ground at its centre.

The islands in the harbour include Lazareto and Cuarentena, which was a quarantine hospital for sailors. A road follows the northern shore to the lighthouse affording views of Maó.

Talayot de Trepucó

▷ 1km/0.6mi S of Maó.

This megalithic site is famous for its 4.80m/16ft *taula*.

Sant Lluís

▷ 4km/2.5mi S.

This town with narrow streets was founded by the French. Small resorts have grown up nearby at **Alcaufar** and **Binibèquer Vell**, a new village that has been ingeniously made to look like a traditional old fishing hamlet – very popular with island visitors.

Es Grau

▷ 8km/5mi N.

Beside the attractive white village with its long beach is a vast lagoon, **Albufera de es Grau**, 2km/1.2mi long and 400m/437yd wide. An ideal spot to watch migrant birds.

Cala en Porter

▷ 12km/7.4mi W.

Promontories protect a narrow estuary, lined by a sandy beach. Houses perch upon the left cliff. Ancient troglodyte dwellings, the **Coves d'en Xoroi** (www.covadenxoroi.com), have been converted into a beautiful and very fashionable chill-out bar cum-nightspot overlooking the sea.

Mercadal

▷ 19km/11.8mi NW of Cala en Porter.

Mercadal, a village of brilliantly white-washed houses halfway between Maó and Ciutadella, is where roads to the coast meet on the north–south axis.

Monte Toro

▷ 3.5km/2mi along a narrow road.

On a clear day, the **view★★** from the church-crowned summit (358m/1 175ft) is of the entire island.

Fornells

▷ 8.5km/5.3mi N on the C 723.

Fornells, a fishing village of white-washed houses with green shutters, lies at the mouth of a deep inlet, surrounded by moors.

Cap de Cavalleria

▷ 12km/7.4mi N along the PM 722.

The drive to the cape, northernmost point on the island, is through wind-swept moorland, battered by the *tramontana*, with large, elegant country houses, like that at Finca Santa Teresa. The **view** from the lighthouse is of a rocky, indented coast, more Atlantic than Mediterranean.

Cala (Santa) Galdana

▷ 16km/10mi SW via Ferreries.

This lovely sandy cove set in a limpid bay flanked by tall cliffs has been marred by large hotels.

🚶 It is possible to walk to the cove from **the Algendar ravine** (on leaving Ferreries, take the track left towards Ciutadella; 3hr there and back).

Within walking distance of Cala Galdana are the idyllic Caribbean-like **white-sand coves** of Cala Mitjana, Cala Turqueta, Cala Macarella and Cala Trébaluger. They get very busy in peak season. Small boats service these beaches from Cala Galdana and Cala n'Bosch.

Ibiza★

Ibiza, covering 572sq km/221sq mi, is renowned for nightlife and its visiting hedonists, yet parts of the island remain a natural paradise. There are stunning beaches, hidden coves and delightful villages with narrow streets lined by whitewashed houses, all of which forge a personality that is unique in the Balearics.

▶ **Population:** 140 271
ⓖ **Michelin Map:** 579.
🗋 **Info:** Eivissa: Plaça de la Catedral. ✆971 397 600. www.ibiza.travel.
◖ **Location:** Ibiza is the closest island to the Spanish mainland (83km/52mi).

LANDSCAPE & TRADITION

Ibiza, the **Isla Blanca** (White Island), 72.4km/45mi southwest of Mallorca, is 41km/25mi in length. Dazzling white-washed walls, flat roof terraces, tortu-ous alleys and an atmosphere similar to that of a Greek island, all give Ibiza its unique character. It is mountain-ous, with little space for cultivation. Among pines and junipers on the hill-sides stand the cube-shaped houses of many small villages. The shore appears wild and indented; promon-tories are marked by rocks out to sea, some as high as the limestone nee-dle known as **Vedrá★** (almost 400m/ 1 300ft).

Traditional architecture – The typi-cal Ibizan cottage, or **casament**, now largely found inland, is made up of several white cubes with few windows. Arcaded porches provide shade and a sheltered area for storing crops.

Country churches are equally plain with gleaming white exteriors and dark interiors. Façades are square, sur-mounted by narrow bell gables, pierced by wide porches. Fortified churches once provided shelter from pirates in Sant Carles, Sant Joan, Sant Jordi and Sant Miquel.

Folklore and traditional costume – Ibiza's uncomplicated folklore lives on. Women still wear the traditional long gathered skirt and dark shawl. At fes-tivals the costume is brightened with fine gold filigree necklaces or **empren-dades**. Dances are performed to the accompaniment of flute, tambourine and castanets.

A BIT OF HISTORY

In the 10C BC, Phoenicians made the island a staging-post for ships loaded with Spanish ores; in the 7C BC, Carthage founded a colony; under the Romans the capital grew in size and prosperity.

EIVISSA (IBIZA TOWN)★

Eivissa's colourful beauty and impres-sive **site★★** are best appreciated from the sea; alternatively, take the **Tala-manca** road and look back (3km/1.8mi NE). The town, built on a hill, consists of an old quarter ringed by walls, the lively Marina district near the harbour, and, further out, residential and shopping areas. Along the shore are large hotels.

UPPER TOWN★ (DALT VILA)

Allow 1hr30min.

The Dalt Vila, enclosed by the 16C walls built under Emperor Charles V, is the heart of the old city and retains a rustic, medieval character. There remain many noble houses worth looking at particu-larly for their vast patios and Gothic windows. Enter the quarter through the **Porta de Taules**, a gateway surmounted by Philip II's crest. Continue by car up a steep slope to the Cathedral square or stroll the quiet meandering streets with their shops and art galleries.

Catedral

Pl. de la Catedral. Open year-round daily Tue–Sun 10am–2pm, 5–8pm (Jul–Aug 6–9pm). No charge. ✆971 31 27 73. www.ibiza.travel.

The Cathedral's massive 13C belfry, which resembles a keep, dominates the town. The nave was rebuilt in the 17C.

An ancient bastion behind the east end affords a **panoramic view★**.

Museo Arqueológico de Ibiza y Formentera★

Pl. de la Catedral 3. Currently closed for renovation. ✆971 30 17 71. www.maef.es.

The most impressive exhibits are its Punic art, which developed around the Mediterranean from the 7C BC to the AD 3C. Particularly impressive are the ex-votos discovered on Ibiza and Formentera, predominantly from excavations at Illa Plana and the Es Cuiram cave. The cave is believed to have been a temple to the goddess **Tanit**, who was venerated from the 5C BC to the 2C BC. Also worthy of note are the polychrome moulded glass and Punic, Roman and Moorish ceramics.

Museo Puget

Carrer Mayor 18. Open Apr–Sept Tue–Fri 10am–2pm, 5–8pm, Sat–Sun 10am–2pm; Oct–Mar Tue–Fri 10am–4.30pm, Sat–Sun 10am–2pm. No charge. ✆971 39 21 37.

Situated in Can Comasema, a nobleman's house, this museum exhibits 130 watercolours, drawings and paintings by **Narcís Puget Viñas** (1874–1960) and his son, Narcís Puget Riquer (1916–83). They are an interesting testimony to the customs and habits of Ibizans in the last century and the landscapes of the island.

LOWER TOWN
Necrópolis Puig des Molins★

Vía Romana 31. Open Apr–Sept Tue–Sat 10am–2pm, 6.30–9pm, Sun 10am–2pm; Oct–Mar Tue–Sat 9.30am–3pm, Sun 10am–2pm. Closed public holidays. €2.40. ✆971 30 17 71. www.maef.es.

The Puig des Molins hillside necropolis was a burial ground for the Phoenicians from the 7C BC and for the Romans until the AD 1C. There is a model of the site; some of the hypogea, or funerary chambers, of which over 3 000 have been discovered, may be visited. The objects displayed were found in the tombs and include everyday and ritual articles. The outstanding, partly coloured, 5C BC **bust of the goddess Tanit★**, a Punic version of the Phoenician Astarte, exemplifies Greek beauty. A second bust is more Carthaginian.

La Marina

The Marina district near the market and harbour, with its restaurants, bars and shops, stands in lively contrast to the quieter Dalt Vila.

Sa Penya★

This former fishermen's quarter, now the centre of Ibiza's nightlife, is built on a narrow rock promontory at the harbour mouth. White cubic houses overlap in picturesque chaos, completely blocking streets and forcing bypasses via steps cut out of the rock.

SANT ANTONI DE PORTMANY/ SAN ANTONIO ABA

Sant Antoni with its vast, curved bay has been extensively developed. The old quarter, hidden behind modern apartment blocks, centres on a fortified 14C church rebuilt in the 16C. There is a large pleasure boat harbour. Several coves and creeks are within easy reach.

EXCURSIONS
Cala Gració
▶ 2km/1.2mi N.
A lovely, accessible, sheltered creek.

Cala Salada
▶ 5km/3mi N.
The road descends through pines to a sheltered beach in a cove.

Port des Torrent & Cala Bassa
▶ 5km/3mi SW.
Port des Torrent is all rocks; Cala Bassa a long, pine-fringed beach. Rocks are smooth and separate and just above or just below the water line, providing perfect underwater swimming conditions.

Cala Vedella
▶ 15km/9.3mi S.
A road skirts the shoreline through pine trees between the beaches of

Cala Tarida (rather built-up), Es Molí (unspoiled) and Cala Vedella in its enclosed creek. You can return to Sant Antoni along a mountain road cut into the cliffs as far as Sant Josep.

Santa Eulària Des Riu/ Santa Eulàlia Del Río

Santa Eulària des Riu, in a fertile plain watered by Ibiza's only river, is a large seaside resort. Nearby beaches such as **Es Canar** have also been developed.

Puig de Missa★

◖ Bear right off the Eivissa/Ibiza road 50m/55yd after the petrol station (on the left).

This minute, fortified town crowning the hilltop provides a remarkable over-view of the island's traditional peasant architecture; in times of danger, the church (16C) served as a refuge.

Portinatx★

◗ 27km/17mi N on the PM 810, PM 811 and C 733.

The road passes through **Sant Carles**, which has a fine church and is a depar-ture point for quiet local beaches. It descends to the vast **Sant Vicent** creek *(cala)* with its sandy beach and oppo-site, the Isla de Togomago, then crosses a landscape covered in pines. The last section threads between holm oaks and almond trees looking down on **Cala Xar-raca**. Creeks sheltered by cliffs and pine-fringed beaches make **Cala de Portinatx** one of the island's most attractive areas.

ADDRESSES

🖙 STAY

⊜⊜⊜ **Hostal Las Nieves** – Joan d'Austria 18, Eivissa. ☎971 19 03 19. www.hostalibiza.com.com. 20 rooms. Near the harbour, about ten minutes' walk from the old town, this modern hostal has attractive white-washed rooms. There is also a roof terrace.

⊜⊜⊜⊜ **Hotel Finca La Colina** – Sangha Colina, ctra Ibiza a Santa Eulària. 5.5km/3.5mi SW of Santa Eulària des Ríu. ☎971 33 27 67. www.lacolina-ibiza.com.

Closed Nov–Jan. 12 rooms. This traditional, Ibizan-style country house stands on the side of a small hill. Now a quiet, family-run hotel, it is increasingly popular with foreign visitors. Pleasant outdoor areas, including a heated pool.

⊜⊜⊜⊜ **Hotel Rural Es Cucons** – Santa Agnès de Corona. 1km/0.6mi along Corona, Camí des Plà de Corona. ☎971 80 55 01. www.escucons.com. 15 rooms. Restaurant ⊜⊜⊜⊜. Closed Nov–Mar. The family who own this hotel have succeeded in converting a former Ibizan farm into an architectural jewel which has been decorated in rustic-chic style keeping with its origins. A perfect combination of luxury and simplicity with a lovely swimming pool set in a garden.

⊜⊜⊜⊜ **Vara de Rey** – Paseo Vara de Rey 7, Eivissa. ☎971 30 13 76. www. hibiza.com. 11 rooms. In the old town, this attractive high-ceilinged mansion offers comfortable accommodation in shabby-chic rooms, which either have a balcony or a terrace.

♈/EAT

Typical Ibizan desserts include flaó, a tart made of sheep or goat's cheese with mint and (sometimes) anise and greixonera, a sort of pudding made from leftover ensaimadas (a Balearic pastry) to which milk, eggs and cinnamon are added.

⊜ **Croissant Show** – Plaza de la Constitució 2, Eivissa. ☎971 31 76 65. An ideal place to enjoy coffee and good croissants and cakes before embarking on the climb to the old city.

⊜ **Peixet** – Plaza de Sa Tertúlia 4. ☎971 31 10 25, Eivissa. This bar with designer decor is located in the Sa Penya district. Greixonera is a speciality.

⊜⊜⊜⊜ **Ca n'Alfredo** – Vara de Rey 16, Eivissa. ☎971 311 274. www. canalfredo.com. Closed Mon. Smart, well-established restaurant on the northern edge of the old town serving traditional local food. The rice dishes are worth trying.

Formentera

Formentera, the Roman Island of Wheat (from *frumentum*), smallest in the archipelago (area 84sq km/32sq mi), is ideal for those in search of peace and quiet, impressive scenery and beautiful beaches lapped by crystal-clear water.

▶ **Population:** 11 545
◉ **Michelin Map:** 579.
▯ **Info:** Sant Francesc: Plaza de la Constitución. La Savina: Calpe ℘971 32 20 57 (both). www.formentera.es.
◐ **Location:** Formentera lies 7km/4.3mi south of Ibiza at its nearest point.

LANDSCAPE & TRADITION

Formentera is two islets and a sandy isthmus, 14km/8.7mi long. The capital, Sant Francesc de Formentera, the passenger port, Cala Savina, the salt pans, Cabo de Barbaria and the dry open expanse where cereals, figs, almonds and a few vines grow, are on the western islet; the island's 192m/630ft mountain rises from the **Mola** promontory on the eastern islet. Rock cliffs and sand dunes alternate along the shore. Access to the island is exclusively by sea, and the best way of exploring Formentera is by bicycle.

A BIT OF HISTORY

Formentera's inhabitants arrived comparatively recently, the island having been abandoned in the Middle Ages in the face of marauding Barbary pirates and only repopulated at the end of the 17C. Most of the present population consists of fishermen and farmers, shipping figs and fish to Ibiza and salt to Barcelona.

SIGHTS

The Beaches

White sandy beaches with clear water are the island's main attraction. Long beaches stretch along either side of the isthmus, the rocky Tramuntana to the north and the sheltered, sandy Migjorn to the south. Smaller beaches include Es Pujòls (the most developed), Illetes and Cala Saona.

Cala Savina/La Savina

Your landing point is in the main harbour: a few white houses stand between two big lagoons, salt marshes glisten in the distance on the left.

Sant Francesc
(San Francisco Javier)

◐ 3km/1.8mi SE of Savina.

Chief town on the island. Its houses are clustered around the 18C church-fortress.

El Pilar de la Mola

◐ 14km/8.7mi SE of Sant Francesc.

The hamlet at the centre of the Mola promontory has this geometrically designed church which is similar to those on Ibiza, only smaller.

Far de la Mola

◐ 2km/1.2mi SE of Pilar de la Mola.

The lighthouse overlooks an impressive cliff. There is a monument to Jules Verne who mentioned this spot in *Off on a Comet* (1877).

Island of the Sargantana

The symbol of Formentera is the Sargantana – a kind of lizard that is found almost exclusively on the "Pine Islands" (Ibiza, Formentera their islets). Larger than their reptilian cousins on the peninsula, they eat insects and pollen. Divided into thirty sub-species, their skins are shaded in whites, blues and greens of varying intensity.

Andalucía and the Canary Islands

Mijas, Costa del Sol
© Sebastian Wasek/age fotostock

N

PORTUGAL

MÉRIDA

EXTREMADURA

Embalse de
Garcia de Sola

Embalse
de Cijara

Embalse de
la Serena

Río

CORDOBA

*Parque Natural
de la Sierra de Aracena
y Picos de Aroche*

*Parque Natural de
la Sierra Norte de
Sevilla*

**GRUTA DE LAS
MARAVILLAS**

Medina Azahara

Minas de Riotinto

Almodóvar del Río

CÓRDOBA

HUELVA

Guadalquivir

Río

La Campiña

Itálica

Huelva

Moguer

**Palos de la
Frontera**

El Rocío

*Parque Natural de las
Marismas del Odiel*

Ayamonte

La Rábida

GOLFO DE CÁDIZ

Costa de la Luz

SEVILLA

Río

Carmona

Écija

Osuna

Estepa

Genil

**PARQUE NACIONAL
DE DOÑANA**

**Sanlúcar de
Barrameda**

Rota

El Puerto de Sta Maria

La Cartuja

CÁDIZ

San Fernando

Costa Cádiz

OCÉANO
ATLÁNTICO

**Jerez de
la Frontera**

**Arcos
de la F.**

**Zahara de
la Sierra**

Olvera

Antequera

**Desfiladero
de los Gaitanes**

Grazalema

Ronda

El Torcal

Alora

Ubrique

*Cueva de
la Pileta*

MALAGA

*Parque Natural de
los Alcornocales*

**Puerto
Banús**

Mijas

CÁDIZ

**Medina
Sidonia**

**Jimena de
la Frontera**

Marbella

Estepona

Costa

**Vejer de
la Frontera**

Cabo de Trafalgar

Gibraltar

Tarifa

ESTRECHO DE GIBRALTAR

MAROC

Ceuta

SEVILLA	★★★	Highly recommended
Baeza	★★	Recommended
Huelva	★	Interesting
Mojácar		Other sight described in this guide

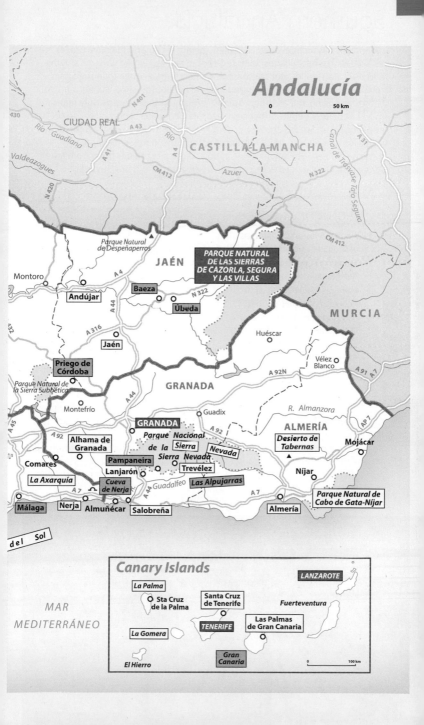

Andalucía

0   50 km

CIUDAD REAL

CASTILLA-LA-MANCHA

Río Guadiana

Valdeazogues

Río Azuer

Canal de Trasvase Tajo Segura

Parque Natural de Despeñaperros

JAÉN

PARQUE NATURAL DE LAS SIERRAS DE CAZORLA, SEGURA Y LAS VILLAS

MURCIA

Montoro

Andújar

Baeza

Úbeda

Jaén

Huéscar

Vélez Blanco

Priego de Córdoba

Parque Natural de la Sierra Subbética

GRANADA

Montefrío

Guadix

R. Almanzora

ALMERÍA

GRANADA

Parque Nacional de la Sierra Nevada

Desierto de Tabernas

Mojácar

Alhama de Granada

Pampaneira

Nevada

Comares

Lanjarón

Trevélez

Níjar

La Axarquía

Cueva de Nerja

Guadalfeo

Las Alpujarras

Parque Natural de Cabo de Gata-Níjar

Málaga

Nerja

Almuñécar

Salobreña

Almería

del Sol

Canary Islands

MAR MEDITERRÁNEO

La Palma

Sta Cruz de la Palma

Santa Cruz de Tenerife

LANZAROTE

Fuerteventura

La Gomera

TENERIFE

Las Palmas de Gran Canaria

El Hierro

Gran Canaria

0   100 km

Southern Andalucía

Andalucía is picture-postcard Spain. Inland, set among the olive groves are dazzling white villages, their red-roofed houses decked with geraniums and black iron-grilles. But southern Andalucía is much more than the Spain romanticized by Washington Irving, natural habitat for flamenco, fighting bulls, sherry, gazpacho and all things quintessentially Spanish: surprisingly maritime, five of Andalucía's eight provinces – each named for its capital city– are coastal and four are on Spain's southern coast, popular with holidaymakers since the 1950s for sun, sea, sand and tanning. This is both quintessential Spain and a pastiche of itself. Holidaymakers can do and see most things here, from an African wildlife safari to skiing the snowy slopes of the Sierra Nevada.

Highlights

1. A stroll in the shady gardens of Granada's **Generalife** (p480)
2. Stunning scenery of the **Alpujarras** (p484)
3. **Málaga**'s unexpected cultural riches in its museums (p489)
4. Extraordinary rock formations in the **Sierra del Torcal** (p493)
5. Contemplating *Death in the Afternoon* in the Bullring of **Ronda** (p494)

Southern Andalucía

The recently revitalised and thoroughly Spanish city of Málaga is the gateway to Málaga Province and the Costa del Sol, Spain's frenetic holiday playground. A few miles inland lie some of Spain's prettiest pueblos blancos (white villages) and quintessentially Andalucían towns, such as Antequera and Ronda, the home of bullfighting.

Southeast Andalucía

Granada is the glistening focus of this region with a fabulous natural setting and, in the Alhambra, one of the greatest Moorish palaces ever built. Despite its apeal to tourism the city has an earthy atmosphere and more than its share of attractions. Literally just beyond (actually above) the city is the snow-capped Sierra Nevada range. It is quite possible to ski here in the morning and sunbathe on the beach in the afternoon, perhaps on the sands of the Almería coastline, the latest of Spain's costas to be fashionably developed for sun-starved north Europeans. Although this is the driest part of Spain, it grows huge amounts of fruit and vegetables, mostly under giant swathes of plastic sheeting, which deface the landscape.

La Malagueta beach, Málaga

Granada★★★

Granada enjoys a glorious setting★★★ on a fertile plain overlooked by three hills and the majestic peaks of the Sierra Nevada. Watching over the modern Christian city stands the breathtaking Alhambra, one of the most magnificent monuments ever created by man and, for many, the highlight of Spain.

THE CITY TODAY

Granada has an undoubtedly glorious past and a bright present too. The vast majority of visitors take in more than just the Alhambra and the picturesque cobbled labyrinth that is the Albaicín district. The city beyond is young and vibrant, from the earthy Gypsy clubs of Sacromonte to its crammed tapas bars and hip nightclubs driven by a high student population.

A BIT OF HISTORY

Granada gained importance in the 11C as Córdoba declined. It became capital of the Almoravids, who were ousted a century later by the Almohads. In the 13C, Muslims from Córdoba, fleeing the Christians in 1236, sought refuge, enriching the city. In 1238, the new **Nasrid** ruler, Mohammed ibn Nasr, submitted to the authority of Ferdinand III, thus ensuring peace, and the kingdom flourished.

The fall of Granada – In the 15C, the Catholic Monarchs turned their attention to Granada. By 2 January 1492, after a six-month siege, the city fell. Boabdil, the last Nasrid king, delivered the keys of the city and went into exile. As he looked back, his mother is said to have scolded him: "You weep like a woman for what you could not hold as a man." Granada flourished again in the Renaissance, but its fortunes suffered during the ruthless suppression of the Las Alpujarras revolt in 1570.

Modern Granada – The old quarters east of **plaza Nueva**, havens of peace and greenery on the Alhambra and Albaicín hills, contrast with the noisy, bustling lower town and the pedestrian quarter around the Cathedral between the **Gran Vía de Colón** and **Calle de los Reyes Católicos**.

- ▶ **Population:** 235 800
- ⏱ **Michelin Map:** 578 U 19 (town plan) map 124 Costa del Sol.
- 🛈 **Info:** Central Tourist Office: Pl. del Carmen. ℘ 958 24 82 80. Info points: Alhambra; Carrera del Darro 16. www.granadatur.com.
- ◖ **Location:** Granada is in southern Andalucía, separated from the sea by the Sierra Nevada. The A 44 and other highways link with major cities in the region. 🚄Granada (AVE under construction).
- 🅿 **Parking:** Space is limited in the Albaicín; there is visitor parking at the Alhambra.
- ⊚ **Don't Miss:** The Alhambra.
- 👥 **Kids:** Parque de las Ciencias or a flamenco performance in the caves of Sacromonte.

THE ALHAMBRA AND THE GENERALIFE★★★

Real de la Alhambra. Open daily Apr–mid-Oct 8.30am–8pm; mid-Oct–Mar 8.30am–6pm. Night-time visits Apr–mid-Oct Tue–Sat 10–11.30pm; mid-Oct–Mar Fri–Sat 8–9.30pm. Closed 1 Jan, 25 Dec. General admission €14; advance purchase from la Caixa banks, using ATMs. One ticket covers the entire Alhambra and Generalife gardens and specifies entry time to the Nasrid Palace. €7 for gardens only. Night visit €8, visit to Generalife or Nasrid Palaces (combined with daytime visit over 2 days €14). Combined ticket with Fundación Rodríguez-Acosta (⏱see below) €17. ℘958 02 79 71. www.alhambra-patronato.es. www.alhambra-tickets.es.

Alhambra

©Turespaña

Nasrid architecture was the last desperate expression of a civilisation in decline. Nasrid princes built for the moment: beneath fabulous decoration lie ill-assorted bricks and rubble, so it is surprising how little time has diminished this masterpiece.

Decoration was the main concern. Walls and ceilings everywhere reveal an art without equal. Stuccowork is worked in patterns in a low relief of flat planes to catch the light; another type of decoration was made by cutting away layers of plaster to form stalactites (mocárabes). This type of ornament, painted and even gilded, covered capitals, cornice mouldings, arches, pendentives and entire cupolas.

Ceramic tiles provided geometric decoration for walls: alicatados formed a colourful marquetry, with lines of arabesque motifs making star designs; azulejos gave colour, different hues separated by a thin raised fillet or a black line (cuerda seca). Calligraphy employed elegant Andalucían cursive; the more decorative Cufic was reserved for religious aphorisms in scrollwork.

The Alhambra★★★

See map p479.

The Calat Alhambra (Red Castle) must be one of the most remarkable fortresses ever built. It commands views of the town, the Sacromonte heights, hillsides and the gardens of the Albaicín. Enter through the Puerta de Las Granadas (Pomegranate Gateway) built by Emperor Charles V; a paved footpath then leads through to the shrubbery★.

Palacios Nazaríes★★★ (Nasrid Palace)

The 14C Nasrid Palace was built around the Patio de los Arrayanes and Patio de los Leones. Its richness and the originality of its decoration defy description. In the Mexuar, used for government and judicial administration, a frieze of azulejos and an epigraphic border cover the walls.

An oratory stands at one end. Cross the Patio del Cuarto Dorado. The south wall, protected by a remarkable carved wood cornice, exemplifies Granada art: windows are surrounded by panels covered with every variety of stucco and tile decoration. The Cuarto Dorado (Golden Room) has tiled panelling, fine stuccowork and a beautiful wooden ceiling. The delightful view★ extends over the Albaicín.

Adjoining is the beautiful oblong Patio de los Arrayanes (Myrtle Courtyard). A pool banked by myrtles reflects the Torre de Comares (Comares Tower), which contrasts with slender porticoes that give onto the Sala de la Barca (from barakha, benediction) and the Salón de Embajadores (Hall of Ambassadors), an audience chamber with a magnificent domed cedar ceiling.

At the heart of a second palace stands the Patio de los Leones (Lion Courtyard) built by Mohammed V. Twelve rough stone lions support a low fountain. Arcades of slender columns lead to the main state apartments. The Sala de los Abencerrajes (named for the family massacred here) has a splendid starshaped mocárabe cupola.

GRANADA – La Alhambra (14C)

Mocárabes: decorative motifs of Muslim architecture formed by assembled prisms ending in concave surfaces. Used to adorn vaults, arches and cornices

A panel of **azulejos** with epigraphic and geometric decoration

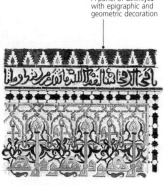

H. Choimet/MICHELIN

The vaulting of alcoves at the end of the **Sala de los Reyes** (Kings' Chamber) is atypically painted to illustrate pastimes of Moorish and Christian princes – possibly done after the Reconquest.

The **Sala de las Dos Hermanas** (Hall of the Two Sisters), named for two marble slabs in the pavement, is renowned for honeycomb cupola vaulting.

Beyond are the resplendent **Sala de los Ajimeces** and the **Mirador de Lindaraja**. Past a room once occupied by Washington Irving is a gallery with views of the Albaicín. Descend to the Patio de la Reja.

◗ Cross the Patio de Lindaraja to the Partal Gardens.

Gardens and perimeter towers★★

The terraced Jardines del Partal descend to the 14C porticoed **Torre de las Damas** (Ladies' Tower). The Torre de Mihrab (right) is a former oratory. The Torre de la Cautiva and Torre de las Infantas (Captive's and Infantas' towers) are sumptuously decorated inside.

◗ Enter the Palacio de Carlos V.

Palacio de Carlos V★★ (Emperor Charles V's Palace)

In 1526, Pedro Machuca was commissioned to design a palace to be financed by a tax on the Moors. The 1568 uprising delayed construction. It is one of the most successful Renaissance creations in Spain. Although in comparison with the Nasrid Palaces the building may at first appear lacking, its grandeur becomes apparent, in its perfect lines, its dignity, and its simple plan of a circle within a square.

Museo de la Alhambra★

Palacio de Carlos V. Open Apr–mid-Oct Wed–Sat 8.30am–8pm (until 6pm mid-Oct–Mar), Sun & Tue 8.30am–2.30pm. Closed 1 Jan, 25 Dec. ℘958 02 79 00. www.alhambra-patronato.es.
This museum is devoted to Hispano-Moorish art: ceramics, woodcarvings, panels and more. Outstanding are the famous 14C **blue** (or **gazelle**) **amphora**★ and the Pila de Almanzor, decorated with lions and deer.

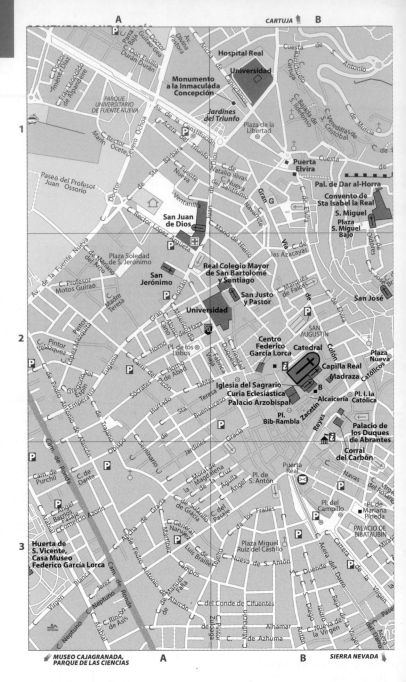

Museo de Bellas Artes (Fine Arts Museum)

Palacio de Carlos V. Open mid-Oct-Mar Tue-Sat 9am-6pm (Apr-Jun & Sep until 8pm, Jul-Sep until 3.30pm), Sun 9am-3pm. €1.50. ☏ 958 56 35 08. www. alhambra.org.

Religious sculpture and paintings of the 16C to the 18C predominate: works by Diego de Siloé, Pedro de Mena, Vicente Carducho and Alonso Cano, and a magnificent still life, **Thistle and Carrots★★**, by Brother Juan Sánchez Cotán.

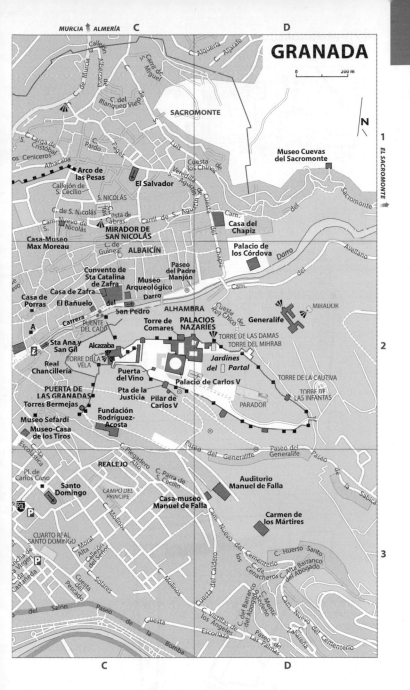

GRANADA

0   200 m

N

EL SACROMONTE

SACROMONTE

Museo Cuevas
del Sacromonte

Callejón
de Murcia
C. de Murcia
Calleja de la Albercada
Carril de
S. Miguel

C. del
Blanqueo Viejo

S. Larga de
Cristóbal
los Ceniceros

Arco de
las Pesas

El Salvador

Alhacaba

C.
Pardo
Pagés

Luis

Cuesta
los Chinos

Veredilla de Agustín

C. de S. Nicolás

S. NICOLÁS

Callejón de
S. Cecilio

Cam. Nuevo de
S. Nicolás

Cuesta de
Cabras

MIRADOR DE
SAN NICOLÁS

Carril de S. Agustín

Casa del
Chapiz

Cam.
del
Chapiz

Casa-Museo
Max Moreau

C. de
Guineú

ALBAICÍN

Palacio de
los Córdova

Darro

Avellano

Convento de
Sta Catalina
de Zafra

Museo
Arqueológico

Paseo
del Padre
Manjón

del
Darro

Casa de
Porras

Casa de Zafra

El Bañuelo

del

Carrera

San Pedro

ALHAMBRA

Cam.

Cuesta
Rey Chico

Casa de
Porras

A

Sta Ana y
San Gil

PUENTE
DEL CADÍ

Alcazaba

Torre de
Comares

PALACIOS
NAZARÍES

Generalife

MIRADOR

TORRE DE LAS DAMAS
TORRE DEL MIHRAB

Real
Chancillería

TORRE DE LA
VELA

Puerta
del Vino

Jardines
del Partal

TORRE DE LA CAUTIVA

PUERTA DE
LAS GRANADAS

Pta de la
Justicia

Pilar de
Carlos V

Palacio de Carlos V

TORRE DE
LAS INFANTAS

Torres Bermejas

Fundación
Rodríguez-
Acosta

PARADOR

Museo Sefardí

Museo-Casa
de los Tiros

C. Plegadero

REALEJO

C. Parra de
S. Cecilio

Paseo del
Generalife

Paseo del
Generalife

Paseo

de
la
Sabica

Sta
Escolástica

Pl. de
Carlos Cano

Santo
Domingo

Plegadero
Alto

CAMPO DEL
PRÍNCIPE

Casa-museo
Manuel de Falla

Auditorio
Manuel de Falla

POL

P

Molinos

Cam. Nuevo del Cementerio

Carmen de
los Mártires

CUARTO REAL
SANTO DOMINGO

Moral
Alta

Callejón
del Señor

C.

Molinos

C. Huerto Santo

C. Alta Barranco
del Abogado

Ancha de
la Virgen

P

Cuesta de
Solares

Cuesta del Caidero

C. de
Cenacheros

C. Meñe
Centeno

Cam. Nuevo del Cementerio

Cuesta de
Castañeda

Cuesta
del Pescado

Cuesta

C. Vistillas de
los Ángeles

C. del Barranco
del Abogado

del Salón

Paseo

de la

Paseo de
las Palmas

Zafareña

Bomba

Escoriaza

1

2

3

C   D

Alcazaba★

The two towers of this austere fortress
on the Plaza de los Aljibes (Cistern
Court) date to the 13C. The Torre de la
Vela (Watchtower) commands a fine
panorama★★ of the palace, gardens,
Sacromonte and the Sierra Nevada.

Puerta de la Justicia★

The massive Justice Gateway is built
into a tower in the outer walls. On the
façade, a strip of delightful 16C azulejos
bears an image of the Virgin and Child.

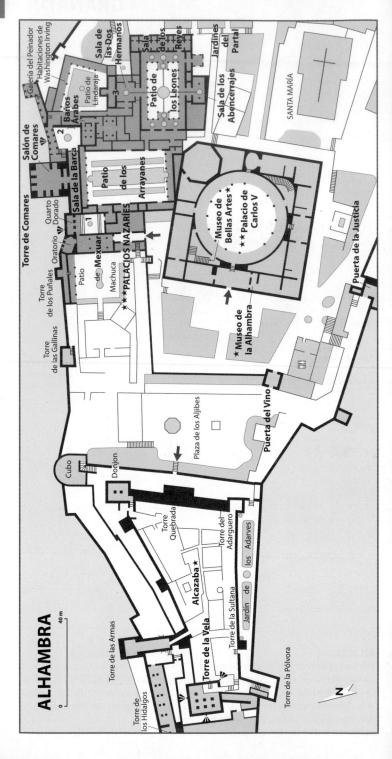

ALHAMBRA

0   40 m

Galería del Peinador
Habitaciones de
Washington Irving

Sala de las Dos Hermanos

Sala de los Reyes

Jardines del Partal

SANTA MARÍA

Patio de Lindaraja

Patio de los Leones

3

Baños Árabes

Salón de Comares

2

Sala de los Abencerrajes

Torre de Comares

Sala de la Barca

Patio de los Arrayanes

Quarto Dorado

Oratorio

1

Museo de Bellas Artes ★
★★ Palacio de Carlos V

C

★★★ PALACIOS NAZARÍES

Torre de los Puñales

Machuca

Patio de Mexuar

★ Museo de la Alhambra

Torre de las Gallinas

Puerta de la Justicia

Puerta del Vino

Plaza de los Aljibes

Cubo

Donjon

Torre Quebrada

Torre del Adarguero

Jardín de los Adarves

Alcazaba ★

Torre de la Sultana

Torre de las Armas

Torre de la Vela

Torre de la Pólvora

Torre de los Hidalgos

N

The Generalife★★

The **water gardens** are one of the most enjoyable parts of the 14C Generalife, the summer palace. The Patio de los Cipreses (Cypress Alley) and Patio de las Adelfas (Oleander) lead in. The nucleus is the **Patio de la Acequia** (Canal Court), a pool with fountains, a pavilion at either end, and a mirador in the middle. The pavilion to the rear contains the Sala Regia, with fine stuccowork.

The upper gardens contain the famous **escalera del agua**, or water staircase.

CATHEDRAL QUARTER

Capilla Real★★ (Chapel Royal)

Oficios 3. Open Mon–Sat 10.15am–6.30pm, Sun 11am–6.30pm. Closed 1 Jan, Good Friday, 25 Dec. €5. Free Sun. ℘958 22 78 48. www.capillarealgranada.com.

The **Catholic Monarchs** commissioned this Isabelline Gothic chapel by Enrique Egas. To enter (by the south door), cross the courtyard of the old **Lonja** (Exchange), also by Egas. The south front has an elegant Renaissance façade of superimposed arcades with turned columns. Every conceivable decoration of the Isabelline style is seen inside: ribbed vaulting, coats of arms, the yoke and fasces (revived in 1934 by the Falange), monograms, and the eagle of St John. In the chancel, closed by a gilded **screen★★★** by Master Bartolomé, are the **mausoleums★★★** of the Catholic Monarchs on the right, and of Philip the Handsome and Juana the Mad, the parents of Charles V, on the left. The first was carved by Fancelli in Genoa in 1517, the second, magnificent in scale and workmanship, by Bartolomé Ordóñez (the sarcophagi are in the crypt). The high altar **retable★** (1520) by Felipe Vigarny shows great movement and expression.

The lower register of the predella depicts the siege of Granada and the baptism of the Moriscos.

Sacristía-Museo

Among objects on display are **Queen Isabel's sceptre and crown, King Ferdinand's sword**, and outstanding **paintings★★** by Flemish (Rogier Van der Weyden), Italian (Perugino, Botticelli) and Spanish (Bartolomé Bermejo, Pedro Berruguete) artists.

The central section of the Triptych of the Passion was painted by the Fleming Dirk Bouts. Two sculptures of the Catholic Monarchs at prayer are by Felipe Vigarny. Opposite are the 18C Baroque-style former **town hall (ayuntamiento)**. Just below is the **Centro de Arte José Guerrero**, dedicated to modern art and especially the work of Granada's José Guerrero (1914–91) (Oficios 8; open Tue–Sat 10.30am–2pm, 4.30–9pm, Sun and public holidays 10.30am–2pm; closed 1 Jan, 25 Dec; no charge; ℘958 22 01 09; www.centroguerrero.org).

Catedral★

Gran Vía de Colón 5. Open Mon–Sat 10am–6.30pm, Sun 3–6pm. €5, free Sun. ℘958 22 29 59. www.catedraldegranada.com.

Construction started in 1518. Diego de Siloé introduced the Renaissance style to the design of Enrique Egas. The façade (1667) is by Alonso Cano. The **Capilla Mayor★** is surprising. Siloé designed a rotunda circled by an ambulatory, cleverly linked to the basilica. The rotunda combines superimposed orders, the uppermost with paintings by Alonso Cano of the Life of the Virgin and beautiful 16C stained glass. Marking the rotunda entrance are figures of the Catholic Monarchs by Pedro de Mena and, in a medallion by Alonso Cano, Adam and Eve.

The **organ★** from about 1750 is by Leonardo of Ávila. The finely carved Isabelline doorway in the south transept is the original **north portal★** of the older Capilla Real.

Alcaicería

This area, with craft and souvenir shops, was the silk market in Moorish times.

Corral del Carbón

Mariana Pineda. Open daily 9am–7pm. No charge.

This 14C former Moorish storehouse has an arched doorway with *alfiz* surround and panels of *sebka* decoration.

ALBAICÍN★★

This quarter covers a slope facing the Alhambra. It was here that the Moors lived after the Reconquest.

Alleys are lined by white-walled houses. Walls enclose luxuriant gardens of cármenes (town houses). Go to the **Iglesia de San Nicólas** (Plaza de San Nicolás) at sunset, for a truly memorable **view★★★** of the Alhambra and the Generalife. The Sierra Nevada beyond is spectacular under snow in winter.

Baños Árabes★ (El Bañuelo)

Car. del Darro 31. Open mid Sep-Apr daily 10am-5pm, May-mid Sep 9.30am-2.30pm, 5-8.30pm. Closed public holidays. No charge. ✆958 02 79 71.

These 11C baths with star-pierced vaulting are the best preserved in Spain. These were the first Arab baths in Europe to be reopened following their closure in the sixteenth century.

Monasterio de San Jerónimo★

Rector López Argüeta. Open daily 10am-1.30pm, 4-7pm. €4. ✆958 27 93 37.

This 16C monastery was principally designed by Diego de Siloé. Plateresque and Renaissance doorways lead to harmonious cloisters. The **church★★**, with the tomb of Gonzalo Fernández de Córdoba, the Gran Capitán, has a rich Renaissance apse, and superb coffers and vaulting adorned with saints, angels and animals. The **retable★★** is a jewel of the Granadine School. The paintings are from the 18C.

Basílica de San Juan de Dios★

San Juan de Dios 19. Open Mon–Sat 10am–1pm, 4–7pm; Sun 4–7pm. €4. ✆958 27 57 00. www.sjdgranada.es.

The Baroque Church of St John of God is noted for its richness and stylistic uniformity. Behind a massive Churrigueresque altarpiece of gilded wood is a lavish *camarín* with the funerary urn of **San Juan de Dios**, founder of the Order of Knights Hospitallers.

Monasterio de la Cartuja★

Pas. de la Cartuja. Open daily Apr–Oct 10am–1pm, 4–8pm; Nov–Mar 10am–1pm, 3–6pm. €5. ✆958 16 19 32.

Go in through the cloisters. The church is exuberantly decorated with Baroque stucco. At the back of the apse is the early 18C Sancta Sanctorum, a camarín decorated with multi-hued marble; beneath the cupola, painted in false relief, a marble Sagrario contains the Tabernacle.

The outstanding Late Baroque **sacristy★★** (1727–64) is called the Christian Alhambra for its intricate stuccowork. The door and cedarwood furnishings, inlaid with tortoiseshell, mother-of-pearl and silver, are by a Carthusian monk, José Manuel Vásquez.

♙♙ Parque de las Ciencias★

Av. de la Ciencia. Open Tue–Sat 10am–7pm; Sun and public holidays 10am–3pm.Closed 1 Jan, 1 May, 25 Dec. €7 (child €6), €2.50 planetarium (child €2). ✆958 13 19 00.

www.parqueciencias.com.

This spectacular new science park includes an interactive museum, planetarium, observatory, tropical butterfly collection, and much more.

Sacromonte

The hillside opposite the Generalife is the Gypsy quarter where flamenco performances are given in caves. At the end of Camino del Sacromonte is the 17C–18C abbey for which the hill is named. Here too is the Museo Cuevas (Cave Museum) del Sacromonte interpretation centre and ethnographic museum (Barranco de los Negros; open daily, mid-Mar–mid-Oct 10am–8pm/6pm winter; €5; ✆958 21 51 20; www.sacromontegranada.com), detailing local gypsy life past and present.

Hospital Real

Cuesta del Hospicio.

The royal hospital, now the university rectorate, was founded by the Catholic Monarchs. The plan, similar to those in Toledo and Santiago de Compostela,

is of a cross within a square. Four Plateresque windows adorn the façade.

Fundación Rodríguez-Acosta★

Callejón Niños del Rollo, 8. Open daily
mid-Mar–mid-Oct 10am–6.30pm
(until 4.30pm rest of the year). €5–6.
Combined ticket with Alhambra €17.
℘958 227 497. www.fundacion
rodriguezacosta.com.

Located just below the Alhambra, this
extraordinary modernist complex,
cascading down the hillside, was built
between 1914 and 1928 and is now
a National Monument. It comprises
the studio and library of acclaimed
painter José María Rodríguez-Acosta
(1886–1941) and the collection of
archaeologist Manuel Gómez-Moreno
(1870–1970).

Gómez-Moreno's personal collection
includes Romanesque and Gothic
pieces, and canvases by Zurbarán, Ribera, Alonso Cano and others, as well as
Aztec and Chinese items.

A guided 50-min tour also takes in the
splendid terraced gardens offering panoramic views, caves and underground
galleries.

Carmen de los Mártires

Pas. de los Mártires. Open Mon–Fri
10am–2pm, 6–8pm (4–6pm mid-
Oct–Mar), Sat–Sun and public holidays
10am–8pm (until 6pm mid-Oct–Mar).
No charge. ℘958 22 79 53.
www.granada.org.

The romantic terraced **gardens★** of this
Carmelite monastery on the Alhambra
hill are embellished with fountains and
sculptures.

OTHER SIGHTS
Museo Sefardí★

Placeta Berrocal 5. Open Mar-Oct Tue-Sat
9.30am-7.30pm, Nov-Feb 9.30am-6pm,
Sun 10am-3pm.. €3. ℘925 22 36 65.
www.museosefardidegranada.es.

This charming little house in the Realejo
area, formerly Granata al-Yahud, tells
the fascinating story of the city's influential Jewish population until its expulsion in 1492.

Huerta de San Vicente

Virgen Blanca. Open Tue–Fri 9am–5pm,
Sat-Sun 9.30am-5pm (Jun-Sep Tue-
Sun 9am-3pm. Guided vists every
45min from 10am. €3, no charge
Wed exc hols. ℘958 258 466. www.
huertadesanvicente.com.

On the south-west outskirts of Granada is the house where Lorca (✆see
Fuente Vaqueros) wrote many of his
best-known works. It is surrounded by
a public park with a children's play area
and outdoor cafés.

EXCURSIONS
Fuente Vaqueros

Federico García Lorca, poet and dramatist, was born 20km/12.4mi from Granada, in this village in 1898.

The Museo Casa Natal (birthplace
museum) (Poeta Federico García
Lorca, nº 4; open by guided tour only
on the hour Tue–Sun Oct–Mar 10am–
1pm, 4pm & 5pm; Apr–Jun 10am–1pm,
5pm & 6pm; Jul–Sept 10am–2pm;
closed Sun pm; €1.80; ℘958 51 64 53;
www.patronatogarcialorca.org) offers
admirers an insight into his life.

SIERRA NEVADA★★

The Sierra Nevada between the Costa
del Sol and Granada is massive, beautiful, and often snow-capped. There is
🎿 skiing at **Solynieve**❄❄, with over
60km/37mi of slopes, 45 runs and 20
ski lifts. Lodging is at **Pradollano**.

Vehicular access to the **national park**
is restricted; the best way to tour is on
foot. The most interesting routes are
the ascents to the Laguna de la Yeguas,
Mulhacén (3 482m/11 424ft) and **Veleta**
(3 394m/11 132ft). Contact **El Dornajo
Visitor Centre** (Ctra de Granada a Sierra
Nevada/A-395, km. 23; open Wed–Sun
(daily mid-Apr–Jun) 9.30am-2.30pm,
4.30-7.30pm; ℘958 34 06 25).

Alhama de Granada★

▶ 60km/37mi SW on the A 92 and A 335.
Alhama de Granada is a village of whitewashed houses and narrow streets
above a deep gorge, dominated by the
Iglesia de la Encarnación★, a well-proportioned church built of golden stone.

The Alpujarran Uprising

In 1499 the Arabs who did not wish to leave Spain were forced to renounce their religion and to convert to Christianity. They were known as Moriscos. In 1566 Philip II forbade them their language and traditional dress, which sparked off a serious uprising, especially in Las Alpujarras where the Moriscos proclaimed as king Fernando de Córdoba under the name Abén Humeya. In 1571 Philip II sent in the army under Don Juan of Austria, who crushed the rebellion. However, a tense feeling of unrest remained, and in 1609 Philip III ordered the expulsion of all the Moriscos (who numbered about 275 000) from Spain.

The stunning **view★** from the belvedere behind the Iglesia del Carmen encompasses the canyon of the Alhama River. Baths on the outskirts date from the Roman period. A Moorish **cistern★** survives.

🚗 DRIVING TOUR

THE ALPUJARRAS★★
90km/56mi. Allow one day.
This isolated region stretches across the southern slopes of the Sierra Nevada.

From Lanjarón to Valor
The High Alpujarras encompass the valley of the Guadalfeo river. Houses typically have a flat roof terrace, a terrao.

Lanjarón
This resort is famous for its medicinal mineral water and spa. The 16C castle affords fine valley views.

▷ 9km/5.6mi from Lanjarón, before Órgiva, take the GR 421, a narrow mountain road.

Pampaneira★★
Of all the villages in the **Poqueira Valley★★** Pampaneira best preserves its traditional architecture, including the 17C Iglesia de Santa Cruz.
Bubión, a centre of Morisco resistance in 1569, is 5km/3mi further along. In **Capileira** is the **Museo de Artes y Costumbres Populares**, a museum recreating 19C Alpujarran life through its popular arts and customs (℘958 76 30 51, www.capileira.es).

▷ Return to the GR 421. The road enters the **Trevélez Valley★**.

Trevélez★
Trevélez, the highest municipality in Spain (1 600m/5,248ft), is famous for its cured hams and dried sausages. Behind the village rises the **Mulhacén**, Spain's highest peak (3 482m/11 424ft). Beyond Trevélez, the valley opens and the verdant landscape gives way to drier terrain planted with the occasional vineyard. **Yegen** owes it fame to the Englishman Gerald Brenan, the author of **South from Granada**.
Abén Humeya (🕯️see The Alpujarran Uprising above) was born and lived in Válor, the next village after Yegen. Its 16C church, like many in the region, is built in Mudéjar style.

ADDRESSES

🛏️ STAY

🍽️ **Hotel Los Tilos** – Pl. Bib Rambla 4. ℘958 26 67 12. www.hotellostilos.com. 30 rooms. ⊑€7. This charming small stylish hotel fronts onto a pretty square filled with flower stalls, adjacent to the cathedral. Book a room with a view over the plaza. Excellent value.

🍽️🍽️ **Hotel Maciá Plaza** – Pl. Nueva 5. ℘958 22 75 36. www.maciaplaza.com. 44 rooms. ⊑€7. Attractive façade on a central square at the foot of the Alhambra. Standard international business-quality rooms.

🍽️🍽️🍽️ **Hotel América** – Real de la Alhambra 53. ℘958 22 74 71. www. hotelamericagranada.com. 16 rooms.

⌂€4–8.50. Restaurant ⊜⊜. Closed Dec–Feb. Small, family-run hotel superbly located within the confines of the Alhambra. A warm welcome and friendly service are the trademarks of the América which also has a pleasant patio.

🍽 EAT

⊜⊜⊜ **El Mercader** – Imprenta 2. 📞633 79 04 40. Reservations recommended. Small and cosy restuarant fast becoming a Granada institution. The husband and wife team who run El Mercader create quirky twists on Spanish classics.

⊜⊜⊜ **Chikito** – Pl. Campillo 9. 📞958 22 33 64. www.restaurantechikito.com. Reservations recommended. A hugely popular restaurant and bar with locals and visitors alike, and renowned for serving local specialities and superb cured hams. It was here that artists and intellectuals such as García Lorca used to meet in the 1930s.

⊜⊜⊜⊜ **Mirador de Morayma** – Pianista García Carrillo 2. 📞958 22 48 12. www.miradordemorayma.com. Closed Sun July–Aug, Sun eve rest of year. This Hotel Rural restaurant in the Albaicín district has one of the best settings of any in the city, featuring rustic décor, a plant-filled terrace and magnificent views of the Alhambra. Private-label wines; occasional flamenco shows.

TAPAS

Bodegas Castañeda – Almireceros 1. 📞958 21 54 64. Highly popular typical bodega, with hundreds of bottles on display, serving delicious hot and cold regional specialities.

Casa Enrique – Acera del Darro 8. 📞958 25 50 08. Closed Sun and fortnight in Aug. This small, beautifully decorated tavern dates from 1870 and has become a symbol of the city.

Los Diamantes – Navas 28. 📞958 22 70 70. www.barlosdiamantes.com. Closed Aug. One of the most popular seafood tapas bars in town.

La Trastienda – Pl. Cuchilleros 11. 📞958 22 69 65. Closed Aug. Founded in 1836. Once through the small entrance door, head down some steps to the former grocery store, which has retained its original counter, where you can enjoy excellent chorizo and tapas, either at the bar or in the small room to the rear.

BARS / CAFÉS

Teterías – Calderería Nueva. Calle Calderería Nueva, between the city centre and the Albaicín, is a typical example of a street found in the Moorish quarter of any city. The small and cosy *teterías* are typical cafés which give a welcoming feel to this particular street. Two are worth mentioning: the quiet and pleasant **Pervane** (no 24), with its huge selection of teas, coffees, milkshakes and cakes; and **Kasbah** (no 4), decorated in true Moorish style.

NIGHTLIFE

El Camborio – Camino de Sacromonte 47. 📞692 80 24 24. www.granadainfo. com/camborio/english.htm. Open Thu–Sat. One of Granada's oldest and most established night spots, El Camborio has been open for the past 30 years. Take a taxi as it is located in one of the city's least salubrious districts. The venue itself is four interconnected caves and with good dance music.

La Fontana – Carrera del Darro 19. 📞958 22 77 59. Housed in an old residence at the foot of the Alhambra and Albaicín hills, this inviting antique adorned café is an ideal place for a quiet drink in an atmosphere dominated by lively conversation.

Paripe – Calle Moras 1 📞629 42 38 55. This relaxed cocktail bar attracts the post-work crowd and the party continues with lively music playing until 2am.

Taller de Arte Vimaambi – Cuesta de San Gregorio 30. 📞958 22 73 34. www.vimaambi.com. Open Thu–Sat. This arts centre in the Albaicín hosts regular flamenco performances by up-and-coming artists.

FIESTAS

The city's religious festivals are lively, colourful events, especially those held in Holy Week and at Corpus Christi. The city also holds an annual **music and dance festival** (www.granadafestival. org) in June and July in the delightful surroundings of the Generalife gardens.

Almería

Almería is a swathe of white between the Mediterranean and a fortress-crowned hill. Its hot dry climate – hills shelter it from winds – has helped make it a tourist hotspot. Life bustles in the city centre on the tree-lined Paseo de Almería. Another oasis, the parque de Nicolás Salmerón, stretches along the harbour. Houses in La Chanca, the fishermen's quarter, are built into rock.

▶ **Population:** 194 203
⚅ **Michelin Map:** 124 Costa del Sol.
▤ **Info:** Plaza de la Constitución. ℘950 21 05 38. www.turismoalmeria.com.
▶ **Location:** Almería lies on the southern coast on the Mediterranean. 🚃Almería.
🔎 **Don't Miss:** The Alcazaba of Almería, the Moorish castle that overlooks the city.
🕐 **Timing:** Take a half day.
👫 **Kids:** Visit the Wild West at Oasys theme park.

A BIT OF HISTORY

The city was founded by Emir and Caliph of Córdoba Abd ar-Rahman III in 955, and played an important role in the 11C when it was the capital of a taifa kingdom. It was captured by Alfonso VII in 1147; however, upon his death ten years later, it fell into Moorish hands once more. Almería formed part of the Nasrid kingdom of Granada until 1489, when it was reconquered.

In the last third of the 20C, the development of advanced agricultural techniques and the opening-up of modern infrastructures placed this provincial capital at the forefront of Span's year-round fruit and vegetable cultivation.

SIGHTS

Alcazaba★

Open mid-Sept–Mar Tue–Sat 9am– 6pm. Apr–mid-Jun Tue–Sat 9am–8pm. Jun–mid-Sept Tue–Sun 9am–3pm. €1.50, no charge for EU citizens. ℘950 80 10 08. www.andalucia.org.

Abd ar-Rahman III ordered this fortress built in the 10C. Almotacín built a splendid palace, enlarged by the Catholic Monarchs. Its crenellated ochre walls dominate Almería. A section of old ramparts links the fort to San Cristóbal hill, once crowned by a castle. Attractive **gardens** are laid out in the first walled enclosure where rivulets spring from fountains. The bell in the Muro de la Vela, a wall separating the enclosures, once warned of pirates. In the third enclosure, the keep (torre del homenaje), with incredibly thick walls, looks down on the Christian *alcázar*. The **view★** from the battlements takes in the town, surrounding hills and sea.

Catedral★

Pl. de la Catedral. Guided tours Mon–Fri 10am–8.30pm; Sat 10am–7pm. Closed festive holidays. €5 (inc museum). ℘950 23 48 48. www.andalucia.org.

The cathedral was built in 1524, fortified against raids by Barbary pirates. It has two well-designed **portals★** and, at the east end, a **delicately carved sunburst★**. The high altar and pulpits of inlaid marble and jasper are 18C, the choir stalls are from 1560 and the *jasper trascoro* with three alabaster statues is 18C. A chapel in the ambulatory houses a statue of the Cristo de la Escucha.

Aljibes de Jayrán

Tenor Iribarne. Open Tue–Sun 10am –2pm and Fri–Sat Jun–Sept 6–9pm, Oct–May 5–8pm. No charge. ℘950 27 30 39. http://www.unique-almeria.com.

Take a peek inside the Moorish water cisterns that once supplied the city.

Museo de Almería

Ctra de Ronda 91. Open mid-Jun–mid-Sept Tue–Sun 9am–3.30pm, mid-Sept–mid-Jun Tue–Sat 9am–8.30pm, Sun 9am–3.30pm. No charge. ℘950 10 04 09. www.museosdeandalucia.es.

Museum exhibits cover prehistory through the Islamic era, with pieces from sites in the province, notably the El Argar and Los Millares cultures.

🚗 DRIVING TOUR

THE EAST COAST★
Approx. 240km/150mi. Take the airport road and turn right after 14.5km/9mi.

Parque Natural de Cabo de Gata-Níjar★★
📞950 38 02 99. Oficina de Turismo de San José. Avd. San José 27. Níjar. www.cabodegata-nijar.com.
South of the volcanic Cabo de Gata mountains, past the Acosta salt flats, this park is a haven of wild, unspoiled beaches. The lighthouse faces Mermaid Reef, popular for underwater fishing. On the other side of the mountain is the small summer resort of San José with two beautiful beaches; los **Genoveses★** and the nudist beach of **Monsul★** (about 2km/1.2mi from the centre of the town). Ask locally for directions to Cala Rajá and Cala de Entremedio, two quieter beaches.

▶ Take the AL 12; turn at Venta del Probe.

Agua Amarga
Agua Amarga is a pleasant seaside village with an attractive beach and a good café at Bar La Plaza.

▶ Follow the coast road to Mojácar (32km/20mi). The road twists upwards, offering views of the coast, a 17C fortified tower and a 13–14C Moorish watchtower.

Mojácar★
The village stands on a splendid **site★** on an outcrop with **views** of the coast (2km/1.2mi away) and a plain broken by odd rock formations. The steep, narrow village streets are clearly Moorish.

▶ Follow the AL 12 back towards Almería, turning off at Níjar.

Níjar
This one-time Arab village carries on the craft of weaving jarapas (blankets), using strips of material (trapos).

Tabernas
55km/34mi along the N 370.
The dunes stretching from Benahadux to Tabernas have been used countless times as film locations, from *El Cid, Lawrence of Arabia* and Sergio Leone's Spaghetti Westerns right up to an episode of *Dr Who* with Matt Smith. **Oasys/Mini Hollywood**, is a desert theme park, (Ctra nacional 340, km. 464, Tabernas open Holy Week–Oct 10am–sundown, winter: weekends only 10am–6/7pm, see website for days and events schedule; €22.50, child €12.50; 📞902 533 532; www.oasysparquetematico.com), which demonstrates some of the movie magic with Wild West shows in a mock-up town complete with saloon and Can-Can dancers. Less congruous is the park zoo, which includes a cactus garden and parrot shows as well as an African Savannah with giraffes, lions, white rhinos, ostriches, gazelles, warthogs, and hyenas. Pack your swimming costume for a dip in the park's pool.
Beyond Tabernas, the land is red and barren, and pottery making is the main occupation. **Sorbas** has a singular and vertiginous **setting★**. Its houses cling to a cliff, circled below by a river loop.

ADDRESSES

🛏 STAY

🍽 **Hotel Costasol** – Pas. de Almería 58. 📞950 23 40 11. www.hotelcostasol.com. 55 rooms. ⏛€6.90. The Costasol is set on Almería's busiest shopping street. Rrooms are bright, modern large and comfy, some with a balcony.

🍽 **Las Salinas de Cabo de Gata** – Las Salinas, 04150 El Cabo de Gata. 📞950 37 01 03. www.hoteldelassalinas.amhotel.com. 20 rooms. Restaurant 🍽. The hotel's tranquil location in Parque Natural de Cabo de Gata makes this an ideal base from which to enjoy a number of excursions.

Málaga★

Founded by Phoenicians, Málaga became a Roman colony and later, the main port of Moorish Granada. Today, it is the capital of the Costa del Sol, but it retains characteristic old houses and gardens that reflect its importance as a 19C port. Beaches stretch eastwards from La Malagueta, at one end of the Paseo Marítimo, to El Palo (5km/3mi E), a former fishermen's quarter.

▶ **Population:** 569 130
⌖ **Michelin Map:** 578 and 124.
🗊 **Info:** Granada 70. ℰ951 92 92 50. www.malaga turismo.com.
◖ **Location:** Málaga is 59km/ 37mi E of Marbella and 124km/77mi SW of Granada, set at the mouth of the Guadalmedina and on the Mediterranean. 🚃 Malaga (AVE).
🅿 **Parking:** Not in old quarter.
☺ **Don't Miss:** Museo Picasso; Alcazaba; Museo Carmen Thyssen Málaga; Centre Pompidou Málaga; Colección del Museo Ruso, San Petersburgo.

THE CITY TODAY

Málaga may be the gateway to the Costa del Sol but, unlike its resort neighbours, it has retained its authentic Spanish character and is well worth a full-day (or two) visit before hitting the beaches. Revitalised over the last decade by a slew of world-class art galleries, and major seaport and airport infrastructure, Málaga has finally taken its place as one of Andalucía's most vibrant cities. Plaza de la Merced is the city hub, while in spring and summer the action shifts to the beaches, particularly to Pedregalejo, on the edge of town.

SIGHTS

Museo Picasso Málaga★★

San Agustín 8. Open daily Jul–Aug 10am–8pm, Mar–Jun and Sept–Oct until 7pm, Nov–Feb until 6pm. Closed 1 & 6 Jan, 25 Dec. €7; no charge last two hours of Sun. ℰ952 12 76 00. www.museopicassomalaga.org. The 16C Palacio de Buenavista houses oils, sketches, engravings, sculptures and ceramics by Picasso, drawn from the collections of Christine and Bernard Ruiz-Picasso, the artist's daughter-in-law and grandson.
Among paintings are Bust of Woman with Arms Crossed Behind Head (1939), Woman in an Armchair (1946) and Jacqueline Seated (1954). There is also a library and archive. Temporary exhibitions (additional charge) of other artists' work are held.

Alcazaba★

Alcazabilla 2. Take the lift from C/ Guillén Sotelo, behind the Town Hall. Open daily, Apr–Oct Mon 9am–8pm, Nov–Mar Mon 9am–6pm. €2.20, €3.55 combined ticket with Castillo de Gibralfaro. ℰ952 93 29 87. www.malagaturismo.com. The ruins of a **Roman theatre** line the approach to this 11C Moorish fortress. Inside the final gateway are Moorish gardens. There is a **view★** of the harbour and city from the ramparts. The former Nasrid palace is within. Higher up is the **Castillo de Gibralfaro★** (same opening times as the Alcazaba) which houses a museum and the city's parador.

Catedral★

Molina Lario. Open Mon–Fri 10am–6pm, Sat 10am–5pm (Sun and pub hols mass only). €5 (inc. museum) ℰ952 22 03 45. Construction spanned three centuries (16C–18C); the south tower still lacks its full elevation. **Oven vaulting★** covers the aisles. Classically ordered Corinthian columns, entablatures and cornices add a monumental appearance. **Choir stalls★** bear figures by Pedro de Mena. There is an impressive early 15C carved and painted **Gothic retable★** in the ambulatory. The 18C **Palacio Episcopal**

(Episcopal Palace) on the square, in Baroque style, has a lovely marble façade. **El Sagrario**, an unusual 16C rectangular church in the cathedral gardens, features a fine **north portal★** in Isabelline Gothic style. The 18C interior is Baroque, with a beautiful **Mannerist altarpiece★★**.

Fundación Picasso/Museo-Casa Natal Pablo Picasso

Pl. de la Merced 15. Open daily 9.30am–8pm. Closed 1 Jan, 25 Dec and Tue Nov–Mar. €3, €4 to include exhibition hall next door; no charge Sun after 4pm. ℘951 92 66 60. http://fundacionpicasso.malaga.eu.

This mid-15C building on the **Plaza de la Merced** shows a number of Picasso's drawings as well as photos and ceramics.

Museo de Artes y Costumbres Populares★ (Museum of Popular Arts and Customs)

Pasillo de Santa Isabel 10. Open Mon–Fri 10am–5pm, Sat 10am–3pm. Closed public holidays. €4. ℘952 21 71 37. www.museoartespopulares.com.

This charming rustic folk museum, housed in what was a 17C inn, displays numerous interesting objects from the 18C and 19C, once used in the home, or for work on the land or at sea, as well as costumes.

Santuario de la Virgen de la Victoria★

Pl. del Santuario. Guided tours (45min) Tue–Fri, Sun 10am–noon, 4.30–7pm, Sat 10am–noon. ℘951 92 66 20.

The sanctuary was founded by the Catholic Monarchs. The church is dominated by a large 17C altarpiece at the centre of which stands the **camarín★★**, a Baroque masterpiece covered by stuccowork and presided over by a fine 15C German Virgin and Child.

Centro de Arte Contemporáneo de Málaga

Alemania s/n. Open Tue–Sun 10am–8pm; late Jun–second week Sept 10am–2pm, 5–9pm. Closed 1 Jan, 25 Dec. No charge. ℘952 12 00 55. www.cacmalaga.org.

The old wholesale market, a Rationalist building by Luis Gutiérrez Soto (1939), houses a modern art centre with rotating exhibitions.

Museo Carmen Thyssen Málaga

Compañía 10. Tue–Sun 10am–8pm. Closed 1 Jan, 25 Dec. €6 (inc temporary shows), no charge Sun after 5pm. ℘902 303 131. www.carmenthyssenmalaga.org.

The stately 16C Palacio de Villalón is the setting for 230 works of art from the collection of Baroness Carmen von Thyssen-Bornemisza. The paintings concentrate on 19C Spanish artists with works by Julio Romero de Torres, Joaquim Sorolla and Ignacio Zuloaga among the most famous.

Centre Pompidou Málaga★★

Puerto de Málaga, Pasaje Dr. Carnillo Casaux. Open Wed–Mon mid-Jun–mid-Sept 11am–10pm, mid-Sept mid-Jun 9.30am–8pm. Closed 1 Jan and 25 Dec. €9 for combined permanent and temporary exhibitions, no charge Sun after 4pm. ℘951 92 62 00. http://centrepompidou-malaga.eu.

Opened in 2015, this outpost of the Centre Pompidou in Paris is housed in 'El Cubo', a pop-up white 'cube', in the city's revitalised port area.There are works by Picasso, Magritte and Kahlo in the permanent exhibition and three temporary contemporary art exhibitions will be held each year.

Colección del Museo Ruso, San Petersburgo Málaga★★

Avda. Sor Teresa Prat. Open Tue–Sun 9.30am–8pm. Closed 1 Jan, 25 Dec. €8 for combined permanent and temporary exhibitions, no charge Sun after 4pm. ℘951 926 150. www.coleccionmuseoruso.es.

Housed in a grand 1920s tobacco factory, this branch of the Russian Museum in St Petersburg which opened in 2015, has a permanent collection of 100 pieces of Russian art dating from the 15th to 20th century. Kandinsky and Chagall are names that will be familiar to many visitors. There will also be two temporary exhibitions each year.

Mercado de Atarazanas

Atarazanas 10. Open Mon–Sat
8am–2pm. Closed 1 Jan, 25 Dec.
No charge. ℘951 92 60 10.
The recently restored and refurbished central food market, one street in from the Alameda Principal, is a colourful place for all the senses.

Beaches

Málaga's favourite strand is the Pedregalejo beach northeast of the city, where nightlife rages and the famous Malagueño sardine barbecues are an attraction at any time of the year. *Espetas de sardinas* are sardines cooked on stakes inclined over coals so the juice runs down into the sand instead of dripping into the fire and creating a conflagration. The beaches west of Málaga proceed from La Malagueta through San Andrés, La Misericordia, Guadalmar, Los Álamos, Playamar and La Carihuela to Torremolinos, each with lifeguards, rentable lounge chairs and blue flag ratings.

EXCURSION

Jardín Botánico Histórico Finca de la Concepción★

◖ Ctra de las Pedrizas, 7km/4.3mi N.
Open Tue–Sat Oct–Easter 9.30am–4.30pm. Easter–Sept 9.30am–7.30pm.
€5.20. ℘951 92 61 80.
http://laconcepcion.malaga.eu.
Visitors will enjoy strolling through this delightful jungle, planted with more than 300 tropical and subtropical species and dotted with streams, ponds, waterfalls and Roman ruins.

🚗 DRIVING TOURS

AXARQUÍA★

This pocket-sized and little-known region is filled with hillsides covered with almond and olive trees with waves of grain spreading out at their feet. Bordered on the west side by the Sierra de

Málaga and on the east by the Sierras de Tejeda and Almijara, the Axarquía falls south to the Costa del Sol. Pretty Mudéjar bell towers rise over narrow alleyways as most of the villages are marked by the nearly 800-year Moorish sojourn here, while others were built by villagers attempting to escape the attacks of the Barbary pirates along the coast. The Axarquía was also the base for the Moorish uprising that followed the 1492 completion of the Christian Reconquest.

Comares

About 40km/25mi from Rincón de la Victoria toward Benagalbón (approx. 45min).
Comares, accessible via a serpentine but scenic road, is know as "the balcony of the Axarquía". Perched on a hilltop, the town overlooks the entire region and has magical sunsets. A marked route has been set up to guide you through the tiny streets of this village of Moorish origins: just follow the ceramic tiles set into the pavement. (Several long-range hiking trails also originate in the main square). During the walk, you'll come across the Mudéjar **Iglesia de Nuestra Señora de la Encarnación**, built on the footprint of the former mosque. **Plaza de los Verdiales**, named for the typical regional dances of Málaga, leads into a street through two exposed-brick Moorish arches. From the ruins of the **Moorish castle**, the view over the rooftops and the mountains is memorable. Comares was a strategic military prize. Omar ibn Hafsun was based here during his revolt against the Ummayyads. Don't miss the **cemetery★** for a look at a typical burial technique: as the earth was too rocky, superimposed tombs were constructed into which caskets were introduced. The oldest tombs are at the entrance, to the right.

Northen Axarquía

Allow half a day.
The small roads leading to **Alfarnate** (via Riogordo) cross though fruit and olive orchards. More than the village itself, the countryside around Alfarnate is what

merits the detour: the rough terrain as a result of the proximity of the mountains and the vegetation of Mediterranean scrub and oak trees. Three marked GR circuits depart from the village.

The most spectacular leads to the summit of the **Pico de Vilo** (1 415m/4 600ft), from which a 360° view looks over the Sierra Nevada, the Maroma peak, Viñuela lake and the sea (moderately difficult 4hr round trip). After resting up at the Venta, you can descend to the south through olive-oil producing **Periana** and **Viñuela** (a large dammed lake). En route, to the east is the impressive **Ventas de Zafarraya**, a breach carved through the Sierra de Almijara back to Alhama de Granada.

The Nerja Road

South of Viñuela, the superb MA 4106 and MA 4105 connect several adorable villages.

Salares, built next to a roaring brook spanned by a Roman bridge, is filled with sleepy little streets with the sweet perfume of Al-Andalus. Don't miss the beautiful brick and tile bell tower-**minaret** from the Almohade era. On the far side of the bridge follow the marked path (an easy 3hr, 6km/4mi loop) that winds along the flank of the mountain, after having croossed an irrigated zone planted with orange, lemon, walnut and cherry trees. The bell tower-minaret of **Archez** is a gem of Mudéjar art, with motifs in brick *sekba* in its main body. The largest village of the Axarquía, Competa (23km/14mi from Nerja and 60km/37mi from Málaga) has a lovely old nucleus as well as real tourist infrastructure. The excellent **Málaga wine**, for sale everywhere, celebrates its popular fiesta on 15 August. Another perfect example of the many picture-postcard white villages perched above the coast is **Frigiliana**, beautifully restored but overrun by tourists. It boasts pretty streets, the ruins of a castle, and a sugar cane manufacturer installed in a former palace. Frigiliana is connected to Nerja (6km/4mi) by bus, which runs regularly during the day Mon–Sat.

ADDRESSES

STAY

Hotel Castilla y Guerrero – Córdoba 7. 952 21 86 35. www.hotelcastillaguerrero.com. 46 rooms. €4. Plain but comfortable and well located, with everything needed for a good rest, and adequate bathrooms. Go up the stairs to check in. Good value.

Hotel Don Curro – Sancha de Lara 7. 952 22 72 00. www.hoteldoncurro.com. 118 rooms Restaurant . This high-rise hotel is in the centre of town, with plain, modern rooms and a games room that's always full.

EAT

El Chinitas – Moreno Monroy 4–6. 952 21 09 72. www.elchinitas.com. Ceramic murals, photos and pictures of popular personalities and artists make this one of the most characterful restaurants in Málaga. The terrace on a pedestrianised street is pleasant, and there are dining areas on three floors.

Restaurante-Museo La Casa del Ángel – Madre de Dios 29 (facing Teatro Cervantes). 952 60 87 50. Closed Mon. Ángel Garó appeals to all the senses by conjuring up the best of Andalucían gastronomy in a unique artistic setting. Enjoy delicious cuisine while surrounded by paintings by Picasso, Dalí, Miró, Sebastiano del Piombo and Julio Romero de Torres.

TAPAS

Bar La Mesonera – Gómez Pallete 11. 609 93 36 45. This small bar fills up with stars and the rich and famous before and after performances at the Teatro Cervantes opposite. Delicious tapas and a colourful, typically Andalucían atmosphere.

Bar Lo Güeno – Marín García 9. 952 22 30 48. www.logueno.es. Over 75 choices from wild mushrooms to venison stew to quail and partridge fill the tapas menu in this classic Malagueño favourite.

Antigua Casa de Guardia – Alameda 18. 952 21 46 80. www.antiguacasadeguardia.net. Málaga's oldest bar, dating from 1840, brims with olde-worlde character.

CAFÉS

Café Central – Pl. de la Constitución 11. ℘952 22 49 72. www.cafecentral malaga.com. One of Málaga's most typical and long-standing coffee houses. Although the terrace on the square is particularly pleasant, the large tea room stands out as the café's most impressive feature.

Casa Aránda – Herrería del Rey 3. ℘952 22 28 12. www.casa-aranda.net This lively, atmospheric café (est 1932) is the perfect place for meeting friends over *chocolate con churros*.

NIGHTLIFE

El Pimpi – Granada 62. ℘952 22 89 90. www.elpimpi.com. One of Málaga's most traditional bodegas, in the old town, perfect for enjoying wine and tapas. World-famous luminaries have signed its casks and the walls display old bullfighting posters.

Puerta Oscura – Molina Lario 5. ℘952 22 19 00. www.puertaoscura malaga.com. The perfect place to relax with a coffee or a cocktail, while you listen to chamber music. The setting is classically elegant, intimate and distinguished.

Kelipe, Centro de Arte Flamenco – Alamos 7. ℘692 82 98 85. www.kelipe.net. Thu–Sat show starts 9pm. Reservations essential (English spoken). An intimate 19C palace is the setting for easily the best and most authentic flamenco show in town. Highly recommended.

Antequera★

Set against the backdrop of the Sierra del Torcal, an extraordinary range of eroded rock formations, whitewashed Antequera overlooks a fertile plain with the silhouette of the Peña de los Enamorados ("the lovers' cliff") in the distance. According to local legend, an Arab princess and a young Christian threw themselves off here, rather than be captured by the soldiers sent by the girl's father. The town's cobblestone alleys, grilled windows, churches and the fine brick Mudéjar belfry of the parish church are quintessential Andalucía.

- ▶ **Population:** 41 141
- ◔ **Michelin Map:** 578 U 16.
- ▯ **Info:** Plaza de San Sebastián 7. ℘952 70 25 05 http://turismo.antequera.es.
- ▶ **Location:** Antequera lies in southern Andalucía, inland from the Costa del Sol. ▭Antequera. AVE - Antequera-Santa Ana (18km).
- ⊛ **Don't Miss:** Ancient dolmens (burial chambers).
- ▲▲ **Kids:** Unusual rock formations in the Parque Natural de El Torcal.

A BIT OF HISTORY

The geographical centre of Andalucía, Antequera, the Roman Antikaria ("old city"), has always been prized as a natural crossroads between Málaga, Córdoba, Granada and Sevilla, much fought over by Castilian and Nasrid troops. The same strategic position after the Reconquest by Ferdinand of Castile in 1410, brought important artistic and religious treasures and many monuments.

SIGHTS

Alcazaba★

Open daily 10am–6pm, closed 1 & 6 Jan, 25 Dec. ℘952 70 07 37.

This was the first fortress taken by the Christians during the reconquest of the kingdom of Granada (1410), but it was soon lost again. Today, its walls shelter a pleasant garden and its towers offer a fine **view★** over Antequera.

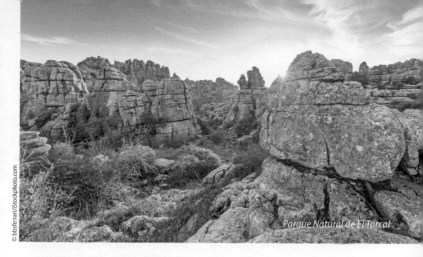
Parque Natural de El Torcal

© bbsferrari/iStockphoto.com

Real Colegiata de Santa María★

Pl. de Santa María. Open Mon-Sat 10am-7pm; mid-Sep-Mar Mon-Sat 10.30am-5.30pm, Sun 10.30am-3pm year round. €3. ℘952 70 07 37.

Access to this church, at the foot of the castle gardens, is by the 16C **Arco de los Gigantes** (Arch of Giants). Built in 1514, it has one of the earliest Renaissance façades in Andalucía. The adjacent observation point looks out on 1C Roman baths.

Iglesia del Carmen★

Pl. del Carmen. Open Tue–Fri 11.30am–1.30pm, 4.30–5.45pm, Sat–Sun and pub hols 11.30am–2pm €1.50.

The central nave of the church boasts a Mudéjar *artesonado* ceiling and a magnificent Churrigueresque altarpiece.

Museo de la Ciudad de Antequera

Palacio de Nájera, Pl. del Coso Viejo. Open Tue–Fri 9.30am–2pm, 4.30–6.30pm, Sat 9.30am–2pm, 4–7pm, Sun 10am–2pm. Mid-Jun–mid-Sept same morning hours, afternoons Tue–Fri 7–9pm, Sat 6–9pm. Closed public holidays. €3, no charge Sun for EU citizens. ℘952 70 83 00.

The town's main museum, set in a 17C palace, exhibits archaeological pieces. The most outstanding item is the **Ephebus of Antequera★**, a 1C bronze Roman sculpture.

EXCURSION
Parque Natural de El Torcal★

◑ 14km/8.7mi SE. Take the C 3310 towards Villanueva de la Concepción; Centro de Recepción/Visitantes "El Torcal" (signposted) open daily Apr–Sept 10am–7pm (5pm rest of year). ℘952 24 33 24.
http://torcaldeantequera.com.

The park, spread over 12ha/30 acres, has some of Spain's most unusual eroded karst scenery. Learn all about its natural history in the Interpretation Centre, have a coffee on the cafe terrace overlooking the rocky landscape, then strike out along one of the two signposted paths (1hr or 3hr).

Stargazers may also like to note that the centre also includes an observatory.

🚗 DRIVING TOURS

DÓLMENES DE MENGA Y VIERA★

Ctra de Málaga 5. To the left of the Antequera exit on the A 354, towards Granada. Open Jun–mid-Sept Tue–Sun 9am–3pm; Apr–May Tue–Sat 9am–7.30pm, Sun until 3pm; mid-Sept–Mar Tue–Sat 9am–5.30pm, Sun until 3.30pm. No charge. ℘952 71 22 06. www.museosdeandalucia.es.

Dating from 2 500 to 2 200 BC, these dolmens are enormous funerary chambers beneath great stone slabs, and are Spain's newest UNESCO site. Menga, the older and larger, is oblong, divided by pillars supporting stone slabs.

▷ Continue along the A 354 and turn left onto the N 331.

Dolmen de El Romeral★

Cerro Romeral. Antigua CN 232 towards Córdoba. Open same times as Menga y Viera.
This is the most recent chamber (1800 BC), consisting of small flat stones laid to create a trapezoidal section.

TOUR TO THE DESFILADERO DE LOS GAITANES★★

50km/31mi SW.
This protected area in the Subbética mountain range includes the spectacular Gaitaines Gorge through which the River Guadalhorce flows. Golden eagles nest in the peaks.

▷ Take the A 343 to Álora.

After the Abdajalís Valley, the road zigzags through superb mountain scenery up to **Álora★**, an attractive village of twisting alleyways overlooking the Guadalhorce river.

▷ Take the MA 444 from Álora. Leave your car at the El Chorro campsite. Continue on foot along a tarmac track (30min there and back) up to a metal bridge with canyon views.

FROM ANTEQUERA TO MÁLAGA★

62km/39mi S by the A 45, C 356, C 345.
These pleasant roads, within sight of majestic hills, afford splendid **views★★** beyond the Puerto del León (Lion Pass, 960m/3 150ft) to Málaga and the sea.

Ronda★★

Ronda stands in a spectacular natural site above a deep ravine. Its isolation and legends of local highwaymen made it a place of pilgrimage for writers and poets during the 19C Romantic period and afterwards. Erich Maria Remarque and Ernest Hemingway were 20C Ronda regulars, each seduced by the cobbled streets, whitewashed houses and impressive mansions that still combine to make the town an enchanted mountain getaway.

SIGHTS

Museo Municipal★★

Pl. Mondragón. Open spring & summer Mon–Fri 10am–7pm, Sat–Sun & hols 10am–3pm. Fall & winter Mon–Fri 10am–6pm. Closed 1 & 6 Jan, Good Friday, 25 Dec. €3.50. ℘952 87 08 18. www.museoderonda.es.

▶ **Population:** 35 676
ⓒ **Michelin Map:** 578 V 14.
🅱 **Info:** Paseo de Blas Infante. ℘952 18 71 19. www.turismoderonda.es.
▷ **Location:** 60km/37mi inland and over the mountains from Marbella. 🚃Ronda.

The museum's charming **Mudéjar patio★★** has the remains of azulejos and stucco work between its arches. The collection includes the natural habitats of the Serranía de Ronda, and historical and ethnographic sections.

Plaza de Toros: Museo Taurino★

Virgen de la Paz. Open daily from 10am; 6–8pm seasonally. €7, bullring and museum. ℘952 87 41 32. www.rmcr.org.

Puente Nuevo over the El Tajo ravine

Dating from 1785 and with a capacity for 6 000, this is one of Spain's oldest and most beautiful bullrings (ⓒ see Box, below). Enter through an elegant gateway. Traditional Corridas Goyescas, fights in period costumes, are held annually. The museum contains sumptuous costumes and mementoes of Ronda matadors.

Casa del Rey Moro

Cuesta de Santo Domingo. Closed for renovations. ℘952 18 71 19.
Inside are impressive Moorish steps, known as **La Mina**, which descend to the river. The **gardens★** were laid out in 1912 by French landscapist **Jean-Claude Forestier**, who also designed María Luisa Park in Sevilla.

Museo del Bandolero

Armiñán 65. Open daily: winter and Fall 11am–7pm; spring & summer 11am–8.30pm. €3.75. ℘952 87 77 85. www.museobandolero.com.
The Serranía de Ronda range was once frequented by bandits, brigands and outlaws. This museum provides insight into these legendary figures.

👣 WALKING TOUR

The River Guadalevín divides Ronda into two parts, connected by the 18C Puente Nuevo, offering a **view★** of the El Tajo ravine: to the south, the **Ciudad**, the old quarter; and, to the north, the **Merca-** dillo, the old market area. The Camino de los Molinos road provides views★ of the cliffs and the ravine.

LA CIUDAD★★

Guided tours (2hr) from Puente Nuevo.
The old walled town, a vestige of Moorish occupation until 1485, is a picturesque quarter of alleys and whitewashed houses with wrought-iron balconies.

▷ Cross the bridge and follow Santo Domingo, passing the 18C neo-Mudéjar Casa del Rey Moro.

Palacio del Marqués de Salvatierra

This small mansion is graced with an exceptional Renaissance **portal★★** and a wrought-iron balcony decorated with pre-Columbian-inspired statues.

▷ From the Arco de Felipe V, by the Puente Viejo, a stone path leads to the Baños Árabes.

Baños Árabes★

Molino. Open Mon–Fri 10am–6pm (until 7pm in spring & summer), Sat–Sun 10am–3pm. Closed 1 & 6 Jan, 24 Dec. €3. ℘952 18 71 19.
www.juntadeandalucia.es.
Built at the end of the 13C in the artisans' and tanners' district, the Moorish baths comprise three rooms topped with barrel vaults and illuminated by star-shaped skylights or *lunettes*.

Cradle of Bullfighting

Ronda is indelibly linked with the world of bullfighting. Francisco Romero, who was born here in 1700, laid down the rules of bullfighting, which until then had been only a display of audacity and agility. He became the father of modern bullfighting by his introduction of the artistic work with the small cape, or *muleta*. His son Juan introduced the *cuadrilla*, or supporting cast, and his grandson, Pedro Romero (1754–1839), became one of Spain's greatest bullfighters. He founded the Ronda School, known for artistic classicism, strict observance of the rules, and for the *estocada recibiendo*, in which the matador holds his ground and allows the charging bull to impale himself on the sword, considered the most dangerous and beautiful kill.

◐ Follow a stone staircase parallel to the walls, then pass through a 13C gateway, the Puerta de la Acijara.

Minarete de San Sebastián★

This graceful minaret is the only one remaining from a 14C Nasrid mosque. A horseshoe arch frames the door.

Iglesia de Santa María la Mayor★

Pl. de la Duquesa de Parcent. Open Mon–Sat 10am–8pm; Sun 10am–12.30pm, 2–8pm. €4.50. ℘952 87 22 46. www.turismoderonda.es.
The Collegiate Church of St Mary was built over the town's main mosque. Today, only a 13C horseshoe arch, decorated with *atauriques* and calligraphic motifs, and a minaret remain from the original building. The interior is divided into three distinct architectural styles: Gothic (aisles), Plateresque (high altar); and Baroque (choir stalls).

◐ Continue along Manuel Montero.

Palacio de Mondragón

Two Mudéjar towers crown the Renaissance façade of the palace, now the **Museo de la Ciudad** (◐see p493).

EXCURSIONS

Iglesia Rupestre de la Virgen de la Cabeza★

◐ 2.7km/1.7mi on the A 369 Algeciras. Open Mon–Sat 10.30am–2pm. €3. www.turismoderonda.es.
This 9C Mozarabic monastery was excavated out of rock. The frescoes in the church were painted in the 18C. The **views★★** of Ronda are impressive.

Ruinas de Acinipo

◐ 19km/11.8mi along the A 376 towards Sevilla. Open Tue–Sat 10am–5pm, Sun 9–2.30pm. Call to confirm. No charge. ℘952 187 119. www.turismoderonda.es.
Known as Ronda la Vieja, the ruins of Acinipo retain a 1C AD theatre, with part of the stage and terraces.

Cueva de la Pileta★

◐ 20km/12.4mi SW. Take the A 376 towards Sevilla, then the MA 555 towards Benaoján. Bear onto the MA 561. Guided tours (1hr) daily 10am–1pm, 4–5pm (6pm Apr–Sept). €8. ℘687 13 33 38. www.cuevadelapileta.org.
The cave has over 2km/1.2mi of galleries. Red and black wall paintings predate those of Altamira (◐see page 517), with figurative motifs from the Palaeolithic era (20 000 BC) and symbolic art and Neolithic animal drawings (goats, panthers, etc) of 4 000 BC.

Ronda to San Pedro de Alcántara★★

◐ 49km/30mi SE on the C 339.
About 1hr.
For 20km/12.4mi the road crosses a bare mountain landscape; it then climbs steeply into a **corniche★★** above the Guadalmedina valley. The route is deserted; there's not a single village.

🚗 DRIVING TOURS

RONDA TO ALGECIRAS★

118km/71mi SW on the C 341, C 3331 and A 7. About 3hr.

The road climbs to overlook the Genal Valley, then winds around the foot of **Jimena de la Frontera** (🚌 Juan de Dios 17) perched on a hill, and crosses the **Parque Natural de los Alcornocales★**, one of the largest forests of cork oaks in Spain.

After 22km/13mi, a narrow road leads (right) to **Castellar de la Frontera★**, a village of flower-filled alleyways huddled within the castle grounds.

Pueblos Blancos★★

To the west of Ronda, in often curiously shaped mountains, are the remains of the pinsapos forest of pines dating from the beginning of the Quaternary era. The beauty of the countryside is set off by delightful white towns (pueblos blancos), characteristically perched on rocky crags or stretched along escarpments, their whitewashed houses dominated by a ruined castle or a church.

FROM RONDA TO ARCOS DE LA FRONTERA

By the northern route; 130km/81mi. About 4hr.

▷ Take the MA 428 towards Arriate, then continue on the CA 4211.

Setenil de las Bodegas★

In this unique village, in the gorge of the Guadalporcún river, are a number of troglodyte dwellings built into the rock. Also of interest are the **tourist office** (Villa 2; ✆659 54 66 26; www.setenil.com), in an impressive building with a handsome 16C **artesonado ceiling**, the keep (torre del homenaje), and the Iglesia de la Encarnación.

▷ Travel 16km/10mi NW.

Olvera

Olvera enjoys an impressive hillside **site★★** amid olive groves, crowned by the keep of its triangular-shaped **castle** and the Iglesia de la Encarnación (Pl. de la Iglesia; open Tue–Sun 11am–1pm; €2 with museum; ✆956 12 08 16, www.turismolvera.es). Olvera is renowned for its superb olive oil.

▷ Take the A 384 for Algodonales; turn off to the right onto the CA 531.

Zahara de la Sierra★

The village enjoys an extraordinary hilltop **setting★★**. Zahara was a defensive enclave for the Nasrids, and later for Christians. The outlines of the 12C **castle** and the 18C Baroque **Iglesia de Santa María de Mesa** stand out.

▷ Return to the A 382 and continue towards Villamartín.

Villamartín

The **Alberite dolmen** (✆956 733 396), dating from around 4 000 BC, can be visited 4km/2.4mi to the south. A 20m/65ft gallery is formed by large stone slabs.

Bornos

The Plaza del Ayuntamiento is fronted by the **Castillo-Palacio de los Ribera★** (Pl. Alcalde José González; ✆956 72 82 64), now home to the tourist office. Inside are a Renaissance-style **patio** and a 16C garden. Also on the square is the **Iglesia de Santo Domingo**, a Gothic church built in the late 15C.

Espera

10km/6.2mi NW of Bornos via CA 402 This village on a small outcrop is dominated by the ruins of a Moorish castle, the **Castillo de Fatetar** (no charge; ✆956 72 00 11).

Arcos de la Frontera★★

Arcos has a remarkable **site★★** atop a crag enclosed by a loop in the Guadalete river. The old town huddles against formidable crenellated castle walls and those of the two churches.

The Adoration of Orson and Papa

Ronda's romantic landscape and link to bullfighting inspired both Ernest "Papa" Hemingway and Orson Welles, who now have paseos named in their honour. In *Death in the Afternoon* (1932), Hemingway states that Ronda "is where you should go if you ever go to Spain on a honeymoon". The ashes of Orson Welles are interred in the nearby farm of El Recreo (on the estate of Antonio Ordóñez, whom Hemingway wrote about in *The Dangerous Summer*). In Welles' own words "A man is not from where he is born, but where he chooses to die".

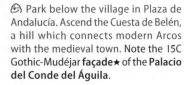

Park below the village in Plaza de Andalucía. Ascend the Cuesta de Belén, a hill which connects modern Arcos with the medieval town. Note the 15C Gothic-Mudéjar **façade★** of the **Palacio del Conde del Águila**.

Continue to the right along Calle Nueva to Plaza del Cabildo.

Plaza del Cabildo

Overhanging the precipice, one side of the plaza boasts a **view★** that extends to a meander of the Guadalete. On the plaza are the town hall (ayuntamiento), the parador (a former palace), and the castle (closed to visitors).

Basilica de Santa María★

Pl. del Cabildo. Open Mon-Sat 10am-8pm, Sun 10am-12.30pm, 2-8pm. Closed 1, 6 Jan, 25 Dec. €4.50. ℘952 87 22 46.

This church was built around 1530. The **west façade★** is Plateresque. Don't miss the 17C **altarpiece** of the Ascension of the Virgin. A charming maze of alleys leads to the other side of the cliff, where the Capilla de la Misericordia, the Palacio del Mayorazgo and the **Iglesia de San Pedro** can be seen.

Iglesia de San Pedro

San Pedro. Open Mon-Sat 10am-1pm, 4-7pm, Sun 10am-1.30pm.

This church dates from the early 15C and boasts a façade crowned by an impressive Neoclassical bell tower.

ARCOS DE LA FRONTERA TO RONDA

102km/61mi – about 3hr. 🚂 Nearest station: Jerez de la Frontera (36km).

Leave Arcos along the A 372 towards **El Bosque**. The Parque Natural Sierra de Grazalema visitor centre is here (Av. de la Diputación; ℘956 72 70 29; www.andalucia.com).

Leave El Bosque on the A 373.

Ubrique

The **road★** enters the heart of the Sierra de Grazalema. Beyond the **Plaza del Ayuntamiento**, is the 18C parish church of **Nuestra Señora de la O**.

From Ubrique, continue 10km/6.2mi E along the A 374.

Villaluenga del Rosario

This village is the highest in Cádiz province. Its irregularly shaped **bullring** (Plaza de toros; Calle Real 19; ℘956 46 00 01) is built on top of a rock.

Head 15km/9.3mi NE on the A 374.

Grazalema★★

Grazalema, one of Andalucía's most charming villages, is the wettest place in Spain. It retains its Moorish layout, as well as the tower of the **Iglesia de San Juan** (José M Jiménez; ℘956 13 20 10). The 18C **Iglesia de la Aurora** (Pl. de España 8) is adorned with an unusual fountain. Grazalema is famous for its white and brown woollen blankets.

Return to Ronda on the A 372.

Costa del Sol★

Sheltered by the Sierra Nevada, Spain's Sun Coast enjoys mild winters and hot summers. Millions of visitors are attracted by sandy beaches, whitewashed towns and villages and a variety of leisure activities. In summer, the beaches are packed, and the nightlife continues until dawn.

🚗 DRIVING TOURS

TOUR OF THE WESTERN COASTLINE★★

From Estepona to Málaga
139km/86mi. Allow one day.

Estepona★
🚃 Nearest station: Fuengirola 40km east or San Roque-La Linea 40km west. The **old quarter★** retains its Andalucían charm. Its attractions are the **Plaza de las Flores**, the ruins of the castle and the 18C **Iglesia de los Remedios** (Pl. San Francisco).

In the hills above Estepona is **Selwo Aventura Park** 👪 (open third week Feb–Jan 6, daily 10am–6/7pm (8pm Jul–Aug) see www.selwo.es/en/calendar; large discounts for booking seven days in advance online (from €16.90 adult, €14.90 child) or on the day €24.90 adults, €17 kids, car park €3; ✆952 577 773; www.selwo.es), a safari park with rhinos, giraffes, zebras, lions and tigers roaming freely in large enclosures.

Casares★, 24km/15mi inland along the A 377 and MA 539, is a charming much photographed whitewashed town of Moorish origin with a maze of narrow streets, clinging to a rock in the Sierra de Crestenilla.

San Pedro de Alcántara
22km/14mi E of Estepona, off E 15. Archaeological sites close to the beach include **Las Bóvedas** (thermal baths dating from the 3C AD) and the pal-aeo-Christian basilica of Vega del Mar (guided tours (1hr45min); no charge; it is advisable to reserve a day ahead; ✆ 952 82 50 35; for a description of the road from Ronda, 🖝see RONDA, p494).

Puerto Banús★★
4km/2.5mi E of San Pedro along A 7. This magnificent marina attracts some of the world's most luxurious sailing craft. Its many restaurants, bars and boutiques are hugely popular on summer evenings.

Marbella★★
8km/5mi E of Puerto Banús along N 340. 🚃 Nearest station: Fuengirola 30km. The long-established capital of the Costa del Sol is still an international jet-set destination. Whitewashed old buildings stand beside shops, bars and restaurants along a maze of streets and lanes in the **old quarter★**. The enchanting **Plaza de los Naranjos★**, named for its orange trees, is lined by the 16C town hall, the 17C Casa del Corregidor, and a small 15C chapel, the Ermita de Nuestro Señor Santiago. Other sights in the old quarter are the 17C Iglesia de Santa María de la Encarnación and the **Museo del Grabado**

Right column info box:

🧭 **Michelin Map:** 578 V16-22, W 14-15-16.

ℹ️ **Info:** Estepona: Plaza de Flores; ✆952 80 20 02. Marbella: Glorieta de la Fontanilla; ✆952 768 760. Nerja: Carmen 1; ✆952 52 15 31. Salobreña: Plaza de Goya; ✆958 61 03 14. www.visitcostadelsol.com.

🔵 **Location:** The Costa del Sol stretches along from the Straits of Gibraltar to east of Almería.

🅿️ **Parking:** You'll have to search in beach towns, so get there early.

👪 **Kids:** Selwo Aventura Park, Selwo Marina Dolphinarium.

Español Contemporáneo★ (Open Mon and Sat 10am-2pm, Tue-Fri 10am-2pm, 5-8.30pm; €3; &952 76 57 41; www.mgec.es) devoted to contemporary prints, set in a 16C former hospital. Marbella also has a marina, luxury accommodations, excellent beaches, a long promenade, designer boutiques, health spas and golf courses.

Fuengirola

35km/22mi E of Marbella off E 15.
The Castillo de Sohail, a castle of Moorish origin, dominates this large resort. The remains of some Roman baths and villas are in the Santa Fe district.

▶ Head N for 9km/5.6mi to Mijas.

Mijas★

🚃 Nearest station: Fuengirola 8km
Views★ from this picturesque white-washed town in the sierra encompass much of the coast. It is well worth strolling narrow, winding streets dotted with tiny squares and charming nooks and crannies. Highlights are sections of the old Moorish wall, and the 16C Iglesia de la Inmaculada Concepción, crowned by a Mudéjar tower. Shops display Andalucían arts and crafts (pottery, basketwork and textiles). Mijas also has an unusual miniatures museum, known as the **Carromato de Max** (Avenida del Compás; open daily 10am–8pm (10pm in summer, 6pm Nov-Easter); €3; Tourist Office; &952 58 90 34, www.mijas.es).

Benalmádena

8km/5mi E of Mijas along A 7.
🚃Benalmadena-Arroyo de la Miel.
Benalmádena stands several kilometres inland from the resort of Benalmádena Costa. Its main historical sights include several 16C watchtowers and the **Museo de Arte Precolombino Felipe Orlando** (Museum of Pre-Columbian Art; Avda. Juan Luis Peralta 43; open Tue–Sat 9.30am–1.30pm, 5–7pm (6–8pm in summer); Sun & hols 10am–2pm; closed 1 & 6 Jan, Good Fri, 1 May, 24–25 & 31 Dec; no charge; &952 44 85 93), one of the most important collections of its kind in Spain.

The village is also now famous for its **teléferico**★ (cable cars; open, see website for schedule; €14.50 return; www.telefericobenalmadena.com), which fly up to the summit of the Sierra Calamorro, offering unrivalled views of the Costa del Sol, the Sierra Nevada and even Gibraltar and the African Coast.
Owned by the same people behind Selvo Aventura Park is the recently opened **Selwo Marina Dolphinarium** 👥 (open third week Feb–Jan 6, daily 10am–late, see website; large discounts for booking seven days in advance online (from €15.90 adults, €13.50 kids) or on the day €19.90 adults, €15.00 kids, car park €3; &952 57 77 73; www.selwomarina.es). In addition to spectacular dolphin shows it also features birds of prey, snake handling shows, sea lions and exotic bird shows, penguins, squirrel monkeys and Aldabra giant tortoises.

Torremolinos

12km/7.4mi NE of Benalmádena, off E 15.
www.torremolinos.es.
The promenade and the long beach are the main attractions of this one-time fishing village, now a huge resort.

Málaga★ 🚗See MÁLAGA

17km/10.5mi NE from Torremolinos off A 7. 🚃Málaga.

TOUR OF THE EASTERN COASTLINE★

From Málaga to Almería

204km/127mi. Allow one day.
This beautiful coast is punctuated by the ruins of torres de vigía, fortified watchtowers built after the Reconquest against attacks by Barbary pirates.

Nerja★

53km/33mi E of Málaga along E 15.
🚃 Nearest station: Malaga 67km.
Nerja, a medium-sized resort, overlooks the Mediterranean from the top of a promontory. The **Balcón de Europa**★ is a magnificent mirador offering views of this dramatic coastline and occasional glimpses of North Africa.

♣♣ Cueva de Nerja★★

4.5km/2.7mi E along the Motril road. Open Sept–Jun 9am–3pm; Jul–Aug 9am–5.30pm Closed 1 Jan, 15 May. €10. ☎952 52 95 20. www.thenerjacaves.com. Paintings, weapons, jewels and bones were found in this huge cave, indicating Palaeolithic habitation. Its size and its stalactites and stalagmites are impressive and include the world's largest stalagmite, standing 105ft (32m) tall. An annual festival of music and dance is held in the Sala de la Cascada (Cascade Chamber) in July.

THE ROAD FROM NERJA TO LA HERRADURA★

The scenic road snakes along a mountainside with delightful views★★.

Almuñécar

23km/14mi E of Nerja along N 340. Bananas, medlars, pomegranates and mangoes are grown on the small alluvial plain (hoya) behind this resort.
The **Cueva de los Siete Palacios** houses an archaeological museum (open Tue–Sat 10am–1.30pm, 4–6.30pm, Sun 10am–1pm; €2.35; ☎958 838 623, www.turismoalmunecar.es). Visit the ruined **Castillo de San Miguel** with the same ticket (same times and contact details).

Salobreña★

13km/8mi E of Almuñécar along E 15. Salobreña, perhaps the the prettiest town on this coast, spreads across a hill, a white blanket punctuated by purple splashes of bougainvillea. The Castillo de Salobreña (open daily 10am–2pm, afternoon times vary; €4, free Mon afternoon; ☎958 61 03 14, www.ayto-salobrena.es), an imposing Moorish **fortress** converted into a palatial residence by Nasrid kings in the 14C, stands at the top of the town.

THE ROAD FROM CALAHONDA TO CASTELL DE FERRO★

The road hugs the rocky coast, offering mountain and sea views. After Balanegra the N 340 turns inland through an immense sweep of greenhouses around El Ejido, where flowers, vegetables and tropical fruit are grown.

Almería ♿See ALMERÍA

ADDRESSES

🏠 STAY

ALMUÑÉCAR

⊝🍴🍴 **Hotel Casablanca** – Pl.San Cristóbal 4. ☎958 63 55 75. www.hotel casablancaalmunecar.com. 35 rooms. ⬜€4. Restaurant ⊝🍴. Set in front of the two main beaches and decorated in Moorish style.

BENALMÁDENA

⊝🍴🍴 **Hotel La Fonda** – Santo Domingo 7. ☎952 56 90 47. www. lafondabenalmadena.com 28 rooms. ⬜12 Restaurant ⊝🍴🍴🍴. Located in the newer part of town but with a backdrop of the Sierra de Castillejos and overlooking the sea. Spacious rooms, indoor pool, flower-filled patios and terraces with views of the hills and sea.

ESTEPONA

⊝🍴 **Hotel Boutique Al-Ana** – Tamesis 16. ☎952 92 85 75. www. al-anamarbella.com. 9 rooms. The sea is a 10-minute stroll from this pretty egg yolk-yellow hotel. Rooms have private patios and the communal gardens and pool are charming.

MARBELLA

⊝🍴🍴🍴 **Hotel La Morada Más Hermosa** – Montenebros 16. ☎952 92 44 67. www.lamoradamashermosa.com. 8 rooms. ⬜€9. You'll find this hotel on a plant-bedecked alley right in the old part of town. Charming rooms in a colonial Andalucían style.

⊝🍴🍴🍴 **Marbella Club** – Bulevar Príncipe Alfonso von Hohenlohe. ☎952 82 22 11. www.marbellaclub.com. 121 rooms. ⬜€36. Three restaurants ⊝🍴🍴🍴. One of the best hotels along the coast, built in the middle of a superb garden planted with palm trees. The bungalow accommodation here frequently hosts the rich and famous. The Marbella Club is the perfect place to unwind.

NERJA

⊜⊜ **Hostal San Miguel** – San Miguel 36. ✆952 52 18 86. 13 rooms. ⌂€3. This hostal is in a recently restored town house near the centre, with modest but comfortable rooms. There's a bar-coffee shop, and a top-floor terrace with pool and sea and mountain views.

⊜⊜⊜ **Hostal Marissal** – Pas. Balcón de Europa 3. ✆952 52 01 99. www. hostalmarissal.com. 22 rooms. Restaurant⊜⊜. Modern hotel with traditional styling in a superb location, next to the Balcón de Europa lookout point, with fine views from some rooms. Coffee shop and restaurant.

OJÉN

⊜⊜⊜ **Refugio de Juanar** – Sierra Blanca s/n. ✆952 88 10 00. www. juanar.com. 26 rooms. ⌂€8.80. This charming hotel located in the middle of a game preserve is a peaceful getaway from the beaches. Rooms are spacious, with country-style furnishings.

♀/EAT

MARBELLA

⊜⊜ **El Balcón de la Virgen** – Remedios 2. ✆952 77 60 92. www. elbalcondelavirgen.com. Closed Jan, 1–15 Feb. In an attractive street lined by a succession of restaurant terraces. The restaurant serves Andalucían cuisine.

⊜⊜⊜ **Casa de la Era** – 1km/0.6mi N. ✆952 77 06 25. www.casadelaera.com. See website or call for opening times. In a typical chalet house, this restaurant affords mountain views and Andalucían and Moroccan cuisine.

MIJAS

⊜⊜⊜ **La Alcazaba de Mijas** – Pl. de la Constitución. ✆952 59 02 53. www.restaurantelaalcazabamijas.com. Closed Sat and Feb. Reservations recommended. Perched on the Arab walls of Mijas with fine vistas and careful decoration, La Alcazaba's best feature is its Mozarabic dining room.

⊜⊜⊜ **El Olivar** – Av. Virgen de la Peña, edificio El Rosario. ✆952 48 61 96. www.restaurantemesonelolivar.com. Closed Feb, Sat. This country restaurant offers fine sierra views through its large windows and finer views from its terrace.

NERJA

⊜⊜⊜ **Pepe Rico** – Almirante Ferrándiz 28. ✆952 52 02 47. www.peperico.info. Closed 3 weeks in Jan, Sun. On a pedestrianised street, this cosy, Swedish-run eatery serves Spanish-international dishes. Holiday flats are available around a patio (⊜⊜⊜).

OJÉN

⊜⊜ **Mesón Lorente** – Junquillo 32. ✆952 88 11 74. Closed 2nd half of Jan and Jul, Thu. Reservations recommended. Many Andalucíans and tourists looking for a breather from the coast head for this restaurant, which is well known for its home cooking. The conservatory looks onto a lively street.

TAPAS

The pedestrianised district of **La Carihuela**, alongside the beach, is the original and most attractive part of Torremolinos, with dozens of bars, restaurants, hotels and shops. Two of the best restaurants are **Restaurante Juan** (pas. Marítimo 28; ✆952 38 56 56, www.restaurantejuan.es), which has been specialising in seafood for more than 30 years, and **La Jábega** (Mar 17; ✆952 38 47 65; www.chiringuito lajabega.com), overlooking the promenade.

SHOPPING

Marbella is one of the best places for shopping on the Costa del Sol with all the top names in international fashion represented here. Most of these stores are concentrated in Puerto Banús where there is an impressive nucleus of designer boutiques, and in the centre of Marbella, particularly along **Avenida Ricardo Soriano** and **Calle Ramón y Cajal**. The best indoor shopping centre on the Costa del Sol is also here.

Markets are an important feature of life on the Costa del Sol. The one in Marbella takes place on **Saturday mornings** next to the Nueva Andalucía bullring (Pl. de Toros) near Puerto Banús.

Northern Andalucía

N orthern Andalucía begins south of the spectacular Despeñaperros Pass, the natural barrier separating the *meseta* or tableland of Castilla and the Guadalquivir Valley. The Guadalquivir river is the thread that connects much of Andalucía, from its headwaters in the Sierra de Cazorla to the estuary at Sanlúcar de Barrameda. The river that launched ships to the New World in the late 15C passes through the olive groves of Jaén and Úbeda and then the urban hubs of Córdoba and Sevilla, two of the "three sisters" (including Granada) that developed into the most important cities in southern Spain.

Córdoba

Córdoba was the Manhattan of the 9C, the city where the three cultures that defined the Iberian Peninsula – Christian, Muslim and Jewish – lived in harmony for a brief but fruitful interlude during the reign of King Abderraman III. Seneca, Averroës, Lucan and Maimónides all called Córdoba home at one time or another and the city still celebrates their thinking with monuments and museums such as the Torre de Calahorra where a facsimile of Alfonso X El Sabio – the great Christian warrior, king, musician and poet – debates the Muslim and Judaic philosophies of Maimónides and Averroës. The painter Julio Romero de Torres is modern Córdoba's favourite son, a multi-talented artist known for his dashing figure and his flamenco *cante hondo* performances as well as for his sensual and symbolic canvases.

Northern Andalucía today

Jaén province is the most overlooked part of Andalucía which is possibly a bonus for independent travellers as its majestic scenery, magnificent castles and historic paradors make it perfect unspoiled touring country, with little in the way of tourist fripperies. Baeza and Úbeda are two of Andalucía's architectural treasures and either make a good touring base. Jaén is famous for its cathedral and Moorish Baths. way from the monumental buildings, a driving excursion and walk in the hills of the Sierras de Cazorla, Spain's largest nature reserve, is highly recommended.

Highlights

1 Walking between the 856 columns of the Mezquita in **Córdoba** (p495)

2 Baroque and Moorish jewels in **Priego de Córdoba** (p503)

3 Exploring Rennaissance **Baeza**, capital of olive oil (p504)

4 Driving through the dramatic **Parque Natural de las Sierras de Cazorla, Segura y Las Villas** (p508)

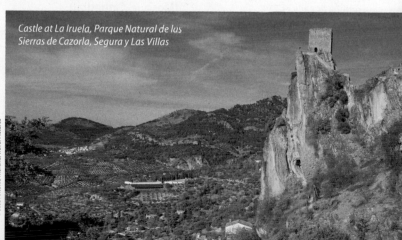

Castle at La Iruela, Parque Natural de las Sierras de Cazorla, Segura y Las Villas

Córdoba★★★

Córdoba owes its fame to the brilliance of the Roman, Moorish, Jewish and Christian civilisations that have endowed its rich and varied history. The Mezquita, the city's most precious jewel, dominates the old section whose narrow, whitewashed streets and charming small squares are embellished with wrought-iron grilles and flower-filled patios.

▶ **Population:** 327 362
◔ **Michelin Map:** 578 S 15.
▯ Info: Calle Rey Heredia, 22. ✆957 20 17 74. www.turismodecordoba.org.
◖ **Location:** Córdoba lies along the Guadalquivir river in Andalucía, between ranchland and olive country. The A4 highway runs to Écija (52km/32mi SW) and Sevilla (143km/89mi SW). ▰Córdoba (AVE).
℗ **Parking:** Park outside the old city and walk Córdoba's lanes and alleys.
◉ **Don't Miss:** The Mezquita.
◕ **Timing:** See the Mezquita, followed by the Jewish quarter.

THE CITY TODAY

The city is on the same well-trodden "Moorish Treasures" sightseeing trail as Seville and Granada, though due to its distance from the coast it receives fewer visitors. However, Córdoba is not just a preserved tourist theme park: beyond the medieval core lies a lively modern sophisticated centre with buzzing bars and nightlife.

A BIT OF HISTORY

The Roman city – Córdoba was the birthplace of **Seneca the Rhetorician** (55 BC–AD 39), and his son **Seneca the Philosopher** (4 BC–AD 65). A noted early bishop was **Hossius** (257–359), counsellor to Emperor Constantine. Of Roman Córdoba only the mausoleum in the Jardines de la Victoria, a ruined 1C temple, and the bridge linking the old section with the Torre de la Calahorra remain.
The Córdoba Caliphate – Emirs from Damascus established themselves in Córdoba as early as 719.
In 756 **Abd ar-Rahman I**, sole survivor of the **Umayyads**, founded the dynasty which was to rule Muslim Spain for three centuries. In 929 **Abd ar-Rahman III** proclaimed himself Caliph of Córdoba. In the 10C a university was founded. Christians, Jews and Muslims lived side by side and enriched each other intellectually and culturally. On the accession, in 976, of the feeble **Hisham II**, power fell into the hands of the ruthless **Al-Mansur** (the Victorious). Al-Andalus fragmented into warring kingdoms, the **reinos de taifas**. Córdoba became part of the Kingdom of Sevilla in 1070. However, intellectual life flourished. **Averroës**, physicist, astrologer, mathematician and doctor, brought the learning of Aristotle to the West. The Jew **Maimónides** (1135–1204) was famed in medicine, theology and philosophy, but fled persecution. Reconquered in 1236, Córdoba declined until the 16C and 17C, when its tooled leatherwork became fashionable.

SIGHTS
THE MEZQUITA AND THE JUDERÍA★★★
Mezquita-Catedral★★★ (Mosque-Cathedral)
Torrijos. ⚭Open Visita Diurna (day visits) Mon–Sat 10am–6pm (Mar–Oct until 7pm), Sun and public holidays 8.30–11.30am, 3–6pm (Mar–Oct until 7pm). €10. No charge Mon–Sat (excl hols) 8.30–9.30am for individual silent visits. For Visita Nocturna (night visits) see website to confirm dates and times. €18. ✆957 47 05 12. www.catedraldecordoba.es.

The Mezquita
The traditional Muslim crenellated square encloses the Patio de los Naranjos (Orange Tree Court) with a **Basin of**

Mezquita

Al-Mansur (1) for ritual ablution, a hall for prayer and a minaret.

The first Muslims in Córdoba shared the Visigothic church of St Vincent with the Christians. Soon Abd ar-Rahman I (731–788) purchased part of the site. He razed the church and around the year 780 began the construction of a splendid mosque with 11 aisles each opening onto the Patio de los Naranjos. Marble pillars and Roman and Visigothic stone were re-used. The mosque became famous for an innovation: the superimposition of two tiers of arches to add height and spaciousness. After the reconquest, Christians built chapels in the west nave, including the 17C **Capilla de la Purísima Concepción (2)**, completely covered with marble.

In 848 Abd ar-Rahman II had the mosque extended to the present-day Capilla de Villaviciosa (Villaviciosa Chapel). In 961 El Hakam II built the mihrab, and in 987, Al-Mansur added eight aisles (with red-brick floors).

Interior

Enter by the Puerta de las Palmas. The interior is a forest of columns (about 850) and the horseshoe-shaped arches.

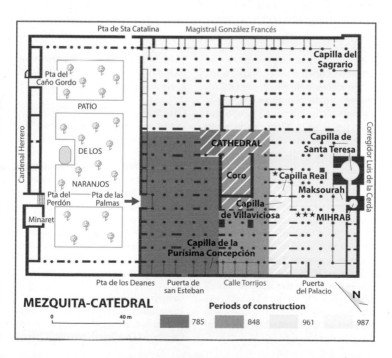

MEZQUITA-CATEDRAL

Pta de Sta Catalina — Magistral González Francés

Capilla del Sagrario

Pta del Caño Gordo

PATIO

Cardenal Herrero

DE LOS

NARANJOS

Pta del Perdón — Pta de las Palmas

Minaret

CATHEDRAL

Coro

Capilla de Villaviciosa

Capilla de la Purísima Concepción

Capilla de Santa Teresa

★ Capilla Real

Maksourah

★★★ MIHRAB

Corregidor Luis de la Cerda

Pta de los Deanes — Puerta de san Esteban — Calle Torrijos — Puerta del Palacio

N

Periods of construction

0 — 40 m

| 785 | 848 | 961 | 987 |

The Sephardic Jews

No history of Spain is complete without a mention of the **Sefardíes** whose presence may still be felt in **juderías** (old Jewish quarters) and synagogues. The main Jewish towns in the past were Córdoba, Toledo and Granada.

The Sephardic Jews (**Sepharad** is the Hebrew word for Spain) came to the Iberian Peninsula in Antiquity at the same time as the Greeks and Phoenicians. In the 8C, during the Arab occupation, they welcomed the Muslims, who regarded them as sympathetic allies. The Muslims put them in charge of negotiating with the Christian community. As merchants, bankers, craftsmen, doctors and scholars, Jews played an important economic role and influenced the domains of culture and science. Some became famous, like the Torah scholar Maimónides of Córdoba (1135–1204). The Jews were particularly prosperous under the Caliphate of Córdoba (929–1031). However, at the end of the 11C, Jews from Andalucía moved to Toledo and Catalunya, especially Girona, as a result of intolerance and persecution under the Almohads. They were often persecuted by Christians during the Reconquest: a royal decree forced them to wear a piece of red or yellow cloth.

Maimónides

The Alhambra Decree expelling all non-Catholics from Spain was proclaimed in 1492 by the Catholic Monarchs. Some chose to convert, others (known as **Marranos**), though having publicly converted, continued practising their Jewish faith in hiding. The Inquisition was established In 1478 for the purpose of identifying and punishing so-called crypto-Jews. Most of Spain's Jewish community emigrated to other parts of the Mediterranean.Today, Sephardic Jews account for up to 16 per cent of the total Jewish population in the world. Most of them have kept their language, Ladino, derived from 15C Castilian.

The wide main aisle off the doorway has a beautiful *artesonado* ceiling. It leads to the **kiblah** wall, where the faithful prayed, and the **mihrab★★★**, normally a simple niche, but here a sumptuous room preceded by a triple **maksourah (3)** (enclosure) reserved for the caliph. Its three ribbed domes rest on unusual apparently interweaving multifoil arches. Alabaster plaques and ornate stucco arabesques and palm-leaf motifs sometimes framed by Cufic script enhance the architecture.

In the 13C, Christians walled off the aisles from the court. A few columns were removed and pointed arches substituted for Moorish ones when the first **cathedral (4)** was built. Alfonso X was responsible for the chancel in the **Capilla de Villaviciosa** or **Lucernario (5)**, and built the **Capilla Real★ (6)** decorated in the 13C with Mudéjar stucco.

Chapels were built in the western nave, including the fine marble-faced 17C **Purísima Concepción (2)**.

Catedral

In the 16C the canons cut away the centre of the mosque to erect loftier vaulting. Emperor Charles V was far from pleased: "You have destroyed something unique," he said, "to build something commonplace." The roof is a mix of 16C and 17C styles (Hispano-Flemish, Renaissance and Baroque). Additional enrichments are the Baroque **choir stalls★★ (8)** by Pedro Duque Cornejo (c. 1750) and two **pulpits★★ (7)** of marble, jasper and mahogany.

Tesoro

The treasury, built by the Baroque architect Francisco Hurtado Izquierdo, in the **Capilla del Cardenal** (Cardinal's Chapel)

(9), includes a large 16C monstrance★ by E Arfe and an exceptional Baroque figure of Christ in ivory.

Exterior features include the minaret, enveloped by a 17C Baroque tower. Giving onto the street is the 14C Mudéjar Puerta del Perdón (Pardon Doorway) faced with bronze. Further on is the small chapel of the Virgen de los Faroles (Virgin of the Lanterns) (10).

Judería★★
(Old Jewish Quarter)

NW of the Mezquita. Narrow streets, flower-draped walls, cool patios, and lively nightlife characterise the quarter from which Jews were expelled.

Sinagoga

Judíos. & Open mid Sep-mid Jun Tue–Sat 9am–8.30pm, Sun until 3.30pm, mid Jun-mid Sep 9am–3pm. €0.30; free for EU citizens. ℘957 20 29 28.

Built in the early 14C, this synagogue is a small square room with a balcony for the women. The upper walls are covered in Mudéjar stucco.

Casa de Sefarad★

Judíos. Open Mon–Sat 11am–6pm, Sun 11am–2pm. €4. ℘957 421 404. www.casadesefarad.es.

This modern cultural centre has become a key venue devoted to Spain's Sephardic Jews. Five rooms spread around a central patio show the daily life of the medieval Jewish community; other rooms evoke the history of the Cordoban Jewish quarter, the Hebrew fiestas and traditions, and Sephardic music. Concerts are held in the patio. Nearby is the Zoco Municipal (souk; open daily 10am–8pm; no charge) where craftsmen work around a large patio, a setting for flamenco dancing in summer. In the 16C Casa de las Bulas is the Museo Taurino (open Tue–Sat 8.30am–3pm, Winter Tue–Fri 8.30am–8.45pm, Sat 8.30am–4.30pm; Sun & hols year-round 8.30am–2.30pm. €4; ℘957 201 056, www.museotaurinodecordoba.es) with a collection of costumes, posters, documents engravings and tributes to the most famous Cordoban matadors

such as El Cordobés, Machaquito and Lagartijo. On the first floor a room is dedicated to Manolete, an iconic bullfighter who died in the bullring in 1947. One of the cases contains the ears and tail of the bull that killed him.

Palacio de Viana★★

Pl. de Don Gome 2. Guided tours (1hr) Sept–Jun Tue–Sat 10am–7pm, Sun & hols 10am–3pm. Jul–Aug Tue–Sun 9am–3pm. €8 (€5 patios only, no tour). ℘957 49 67 41. www.palaciodeviana.com.

This fine example of 14C–19C Córdoban civil architecture has 12 patios and an attractive garden, outstanding in a city famous for its beautiful patios.

On the ground floor are collections of porcelain, 17C–19C side-arms and tapestries. The staircase to the first floor has a beautiful Mudéjar *artesonado* ceiling of cedar. The most interesting areas are the Córdoban leather room; tapestries made in the royal workshops from cartoons by Goya; the library; and the main room with a rich artesonado ceiling and tapestries illustrating the Trojan War and Spanish tales.

Museo Arqueológico★★

Pl. Jerónimo Páez. Open mid Jun–mid-Sept Tue–Sun 9am–3pm; mid-Sept–mid-Jun Tue–Sat 9am–8pm, Sun 9am–3pm. €1.50; no charge for EU citizens. ℘957 35 55 17. www.museosdeandalucia.es.

The archaeological museum is in the 16C Palacio de los Páez, a palace designed by Hernán Ruiz. Displayed here are prehistoric Iberian objects, Visigothic remains and, in particular, the Roman collection★ (reliefs, capitals, sarcophagi and mosaics). There are also Muslim ceramics, capitals, and the outstanding 10C stag★ (*cervatillo*) from Medina Azahara (see Excursions).

Alcázar de los Reyes Cristianos★

Caballerizas Reales. Open Tue–Sat 8.30am–8pm (mid Jun-mid Sep 8.30am–3pm), Sun 8.30am–2.30pm. €4.50, €7 to include evening light show, see website for details. No charge Tue–

Thu (excl hols) 8.30–9.30am. ℘957 20 17 16. www.alcazardelosreyescristianos. cordoba.es.

This 14C complex, later expanded, retains attractive Moorish patios with ornamental basins and pools, baths, rooms with Roman **mosaics★** and a fine 3C **sarcophagus★**. The towers afford garden and city **views**. The **gardens★**, in Arabic style, are terraced and refreshed with pools and fountains. In the evenings the grounds, fountains and buildings are transformed into a spectacular show by ingenious, lighting projection and sound techniques.

Posada del Potro - Centro Flamenco Fosforito

Plaza del Potro. Open Tue–Sat 8.30am –7.30pm, Sun 9.30am-2.30pm. €2. ℘957 47 68 29. www.centroflamenco fosforito.cordoba.es.com.

Housed in an inn dating from the 15th century which was mentioned in Cervantes' *Don Quixote*, this cultural centre specialises in the study and interpretation of Andalucían flamenco. A museum traces the history of the art from its origins to the present day. They regularly hold lunchtime musical performances.

Museo de Bellas Artes (Fine Art Museum)

Plaza del Potro. Open mid-Jun–mid-Sept Tue–Sun 9am–3pm; mid–Sept–mid-Jun Tue–Sat 9am–8pm, Sun and hols 9am–3pm. €1.50, no charge for EU citizens. ℘957 103 659. www.museosdeandalucia.es.

This museum in a former hospital specialises in art from the Córdoba area from the Middle Ages to the 20th century.

Iglesias Fernandinas★

The beauty of the 14 parish churches built soon after the reconquest by Ferdinand in 1236 can still be seen today, particularly in **Santa Marina** (Pl. del Conde de Priego), **San Miguel** (Pl. de San Miguel) and **San Lorenzo** (Pl. de San Lorenzo). Built in a primitive Gothic style, they show a sober beauty in purely structural elements. The single trumpet-shaped doorways are the only lighter aspect of the architecture.

Palacio de la Merced★

Pl. de Colón.

The provincial Parliament building is the former Convento de la Merced, built in the 18C. The façade is graced by a white marble Baroque doorway. Inside are a patio, staircase and church.

Museo Torre de la Calahorra

Puente Romano. Open daily Oct–Apr 10am–6pm, May–Sept 10am–2pm, 4.30–8.30pm €4.50. ℘957 29 39 29. www.torrecalahorra.com.

In the 14C Moorish fortress a museum traces the caliphate using audio headphones and a Multivision video (55 min, extra €1.20). There is also a fine **model★** of the mosque as it was in the 13C.

El Cristo de los Faroles

The Calvary surrounded by lanterns (*faroles*) in **Plaza de Capuchinos★** is known throughout Spain.

EXCURSIONS

Medina Azahara★★

❯ Leave Córdoba on the A 431 (W of plan). After 8km/5mi bear right. Open Tue–Sat: mid-Sept–Mar 9am–6.30pm; Apr–mid-Jun 9am–8.30pm; mid-Jun– mid-Sept 9am–3.30pm. Sun and public holidays year-round 9am–3.30pm. €1.50, no charge for EU citizens. ℘957 35 28 74. www.museosdeandalucia.es.

This sumptuous city, built by Abd ar-Rahman III from 936, rose in three tiers – mosque below, gardens and public areas, and an *alcázar* above. It was intended to be the capital of a new province of the Caliphate of Cordoba, but was sacked by Berbers in 1013, and today only ruins remain. The archaeological complex includes the visitor centre and Musuem of Madinat Al-Zahra. The **Abd ar-Rahman III room** features magnificent carved stone work.

Castillo de Almodóvar del Río★★

❯ 25km/15mi W along the A 431. Open Mon–Fri 11am–2.30pm, 4–7/8pm.

Sat–Sun 11am–7/8pm. Jul–Aug Mon–Fri 10am–3pm (Thu 7pm–midnight), Sat 10am–midnight, Sun & hols 10am–6pm. Closed 25 Dec, 1 Jan. €6.50. ℘957 63 40 55. www.castillodealmodovar.com. This imposing 14C eight-towered Gothic **castle** dominates town and countryside. Stroll the path behind the parapet, parade ground and towers.

Andújar★

◯ 76km/47mi E along the A 4.
Andújar retains many 15–16C houses and churches. On the last Sunday of April, a popular *romería* (pilgrimage) is held to the **Santuario de la Virgen de la Cabeza** (32km/20mi N on the J 5010), set in the **Parque Natural de la Sierra de Andújar★**, with pasture and ravines.

Iglesia de Santa María

Pl. Santa María. ℘953 50 01 39.
The 15C–17C Church of St Mary holds El Greco's *Christ in the Garden of Olives★★*, set in a chapel enclosed by a fine **grille★** by Master Bartolomé.
An *Assumption of the Virgin* by Pacheco is in the north apsidal chapel.

ADDRESSES

STAY

◉ **Hostal La Milagrosa** – Rey Heredia 12. ℘957 47 33 17. www.lamilagrosahostal.es. 8 rooms. Good central location near the Mezquita. Attractive features are the typically plant lined Córdoban patio and well-kept large, cool guest rooms with full bathrooms.

◉◉ **Hostel Séneca** – Conde y Luque 7. ℘957 49 15 44. www.senecahostel.com. 12 rooms. The Seneca is a quiet hostel near the Mezquita with typical Andalucían décor and a flower-filled patio. Despite the rooms being fairly basic (some without a bathroom), the hotel is often full, so advance booking is recommended.

◉◉◉ **Hostal El Triunfo** – Corregidor Luis de la Cerda 79. ℘957 49 84 84. www.hostaltriunfo.com. 58 rooms. ⊑€5. Restaurant◉. Most of the rooms look onto the Mezquita, just across a narrow street. Stay on the top floor if you can to make use of the huge terrace.

◉◉◉ **Hotel Casa de los Azulejos** – Fernando Colón 5. ℘957 47 00 00. www.casadelosazulejos.com. 8 rooms. This charming hotel is a traditional Andalucían house with a colonial flavour. Outstanding features include a lovely interior garden with plants, and magnificent large rooms with period furnishings, iron headboards, original floors and colourful designer baths.

◉◉◉ **Hotel González** – Manríquez 3. ℘957 47 98 19. www.hotel-gonzalez.com. 16 rooms. ⊑€5. Restaurant◉◉◉. The rooms in this 16C palace, close by the Mezquita, the Judería and the Alcázar, are spacious and well appointed. The Moorish-inspired patio is used as a cafe area.

◉◉◉◉ **Hotel Hacienda Posada de Vallina** – C. del Corregidor Luis de la Cerda 83. ℘957 49 87 50. www.hhposadadevallina.es. 24 rooms. ⊑€5. Expect elegance and comfort at this small hotel in a tastefully restored Córdoban house; windows look out onto the Mezquita. Pleasant cafe area.

EAT

Córdoba does full justice to Andalucía's great tapas tradition with a wide range of bars offering a huge selection of local specialities such as *salmorejo* (a type of local gazpacho), *rabo de toro* (braised oxtail), *embutidos* (sausage).

◉◉ **El Rincón de Carmen** – Romero 4. ℘957 29 10 55. Closed Mon in low season and Sun in high season. The patio provides an escape from the frenzied tourist activity in the Judería. Plenty of choice and an interesting wine list.

◉◉◉ **Almudaina** – Pl. Campo Santo de los Mártires 1. ℘957 47 43 42. www.restaurantealmudaina.com. Closed Sun eve. A beautiful restaurant near the Alcázar with painstakingly detailed regional décor, and dining on two levels around a lovely covered patio. Superb Córdoban cuisine.

◉◉◉ **Casa Palacio Bandolero** – Torrijos 6. ℘957 47 64 91. Set in a beautiful building opposite the Mezquita, this is a popular place with

Córdoban patio

©Turespaña

locals as well as tourists. Home-made local cuisine and tapas are served at the bar, in the medieval-style dining room or on the flower-decked patio. Long wine list.

TAPAS

Taberna/Bodega Guzman – Calle de los Judíos 7. Local Moriles-Montilla sherries and vermouths served straight from the barrel. Bullfighting memorabilia decorates the bar.

Casa Pepe de la Judería –Romero 1. 957 20 07 44. Reservations recommended. This taberna opened in 1928 and boasts original fittings alongside stylish modern furnishings. Several rooms around an attractive patio offer tapas.

Taberna Salinas – Tundidores 3. 957 48 01 35. www.tabernasalinas.com. Closed Aug, Sun. Open for over a century, this welcoming bar consists of a counter, a small patio, two rooms decorated with *azulejos* and photos of celebrities.

Taberna San Miguel-Casa El Pisto – Pl. San Miguel 1. 957 47 01 66. www.casaelpisto.com. Closed Sun and Aug. Founded in 1886, the Taberna San Miguel is a popular choice for tapas. The beautiful traditional décor includes bullfighting posters and old photos.

BARS / CAFÉS

Café Málaga – Málaga 3. 957 47 41 07. Open from 4pm. A quiet café with classical décor and comfy sofas and armchairs near Plaza de las Tendillas in the city centre.

NIGHTLIFE

Tablao Cardenal – Calle Torrijos 10. 691 217 922. www.tablaocardenal.es. Popular flamenco club with great reviews, set in a lovely 16C courtyard.

SHOPPING

The city's traditional craftwork includes embossed leather and cordovans (horse-hide shoes), plus gold and silver filigree. Another good buy are the local Jerez-style wines and brandies from **Montilla-Moriles**, just south of town.

FESTIVALS

Festival of the Crosses (Cruces de Mayo) (www.turismodecordoba.org). At the beginning of **May**, the central squares of the city (San Basilio, Santa Marina and San Augustín) are adorned with over 80 large crosses made of flowers with a prize for the best.

Also in early May Córdoba is famous for its glorious **patios**, with many of these opened up to the public for a close look. As with the Crosses, many compete in the Concurso de Patios Córdobes for the title of town's best patio.

Ask at the *turismo* for a map, or simply browse the Old Town, particularly on and around Calle San Basilio, looking out for Patio signs. The ever-popular **Feria** is held at the end of the month with the usual Andalucían equestrian events, fireworks, flamenco and revelries.

Jaén

Jaén is known for its imposing castle, and is famous for the oil produced from its olive trees. Its name derives from *geen* (meaning on the caravan route). Its heritage includes Moorish remains and Renaissance buildings, many designed by Andrés de Vandelvira.

▶ **Population:** 115 395

Michelin Map: 578 S 18.

Info: Calle Maestra 8. ℘953 19 04 55. www.turjaen.org.

▶ **Location:** Jaen is at the base of the Sierra de Jabalcuz. The A 44 heads south to Granada (94km/59mi S) past the Parque Natural de la Sierra Mágina. 🚃Jaén (AVE).

Timing: 1 or 2 days .

SIGHTS

Catedral★★

Pl. Santa María. Open Mon–Fri 10am –2pm, 5–8pm (Sat 7pm). Sun 10am– noon. €5, inc sacristry and museum. ℘953 23 42 33. www.catedraldejaen.org.

The Cathedral looms over the historical quarter. It was built in the 16C and 17C by **Andrés de Vandelvira**, master of Andalucían Baroque. The façade with statues, balconies and pilasters resembles that of a palace.

The triple-nave **interior★★** is crowned by fine ribbed vaulting and an imposing cupola above the transept. Behind the Renaissance altarpiece with its Gothic image of the **Virgen de la Antigua★**, a chapel holds the **Reliquía del Santo Rostro★** – believed to be the cloth used by St Veronica to wipe Christ's face. The **choir stalls★★** are carved in the Berruguete style. The sacristy, also by Vandelvira, houses a **museum**, which includes two canvases by Ribera, a Flemish Virgin and Child, a large bronze candelabra by Master Bartolomé, and miniature choir books.

Baños Árabes★★

Pl. de Santa Luisa de Marillac. Open Tue– Sat & hols 9am–10pm, Sun 9am–3pm. Closed 1 & 6 Jan, 24–25 & 31 Dec. ℘953 24 80 68. No charge. www.bañosarabesjaen.es.

These Moorish baths are the largest in Spain (470sq m/5 059sq ft). They lie beneath the 16C **Palacio de Villardompardo**, which now contains a cultural centre as well as museums of naive art and local arts and traditions, and have been restored to their 11C appearance.

Castillo de Santa Catalina★

Ctra del Neveral 5. Open Tue–Sat 10am–2pm also mid-May–mid-Oct 5–9pm and mid-Oct–mid May 3.30– 7.30pm. €3.50. ℘902 54 79 79. www.parador.es.

On a ridge to the west of Jaén stands the Castillo de Santa Catalina (Castillo de Jaén), built during a period of Arab rule in the early 13C. It was captured in 1246 by Ferdinand III and extended to hold out against the repeated attacks by the Moors over the next two hundred years. The castle was rebuilt and extended to form the Parador, which opened in 1968, though you can visit the castle quite separately. There is a magnificent 360° panorama from here.

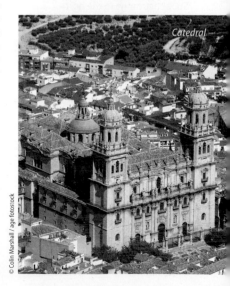

Catedral

© Colin Marshall / age fotostock

Priego de Córdoba★★

This capital of Córdoban Baroque flourished with the silk industry in the 18C. Its fountains, churches and delightful old Moorish quarter come as a pleasant surprise in this isolated part of Andalucía.

▶ **Population:** 22 936
ⓒ **Michelin Map:** 578 T 17.
🈁 **Info:** Pl. de la Constitución.
   📞957 70 06 25.
   www.turismodepriego.com
◖ **Location:** Priego is on a plain in the Subbética Cordobesa range, away from major road and rail links. 🚆Nearest station: Jaén (67km).

SIGHTS

Fuentes del Rey y de la Salud★★ (Fountains of the King and of Health)

At the end of calle del Río.
The older fountain, the **Fuente de la Salud**, is a 16C Mannerist master piece. The lavish **Fuente del Rey** was completed at the beginning of the 19C. Its dimensions and rich design evoke Baroque palace gardens; 139 jets spout water from masks. The central display represents Neptune's chariot.

Barrio de la Villa★★

This charming quarter, dating back to Moorish times, has narrow, winding streets and flower-decked houses.

El Adarve★

This delightful viewpoint looks onto the Subbética range to the north.

Parroquia de la Asunción★ (Parish Church of the Assumption)

Abad Palomino. Open for Mass Mon–Tue and Thu–Sat 7.15–8pm, Sun 11.15am–noon. This 16C church was remodelled in Baroque style in the 18C. The presbytery is dominated by a carved and painted 16C Mannerist **altarpiece**.

El Sagrario★★

Open Tue–Sun 11.30am–2pm. €2.
📞957 70 06 25.
The chapel, which opens on to the Nave del Evangelio, is a masterpiece of Andalucían Baroque. An antechamber leads into an octagonal space. Light plays on the scene; intensified by white walls and ceiling, it shimmers over the

Fuentes del Rey y de la Salud

extensive and lavish **yeserías★★★** (plasterwork decoration), creating a magical atmosphere. In spite of excessive adornment, the effect is one of delicacy.
From the paseo del Abad Palomino view the remains of a Moorish **fortress** (open Mon–Fri 10am–2pm, 4–7pm, Sat 11.30am–1.30pm, 5–7pm, Sun 11.30am–1.30pm; €1.05), modified in the 13C and 14C. Priego has numerous churches: the charming Rococo-style **Iglesia de las Angustias**; the **Aurora**, with a fine portal; and **San Pedro**, adorned with interesting statues. Also noteworthy amid this Baroque splendour is the 16C **royal abattoir★** (Carnicerías Reales, San Luis; open mid Sep-May Tue–Sat 11.30am–1.30pm, 4.30–6.30pm, Sun 11.30am-1.30pm, Jun-mid Sep Tue-Sun 11.30am-1.30pm, 7-10pm; €1.50), now an exhibition centre.

Baeza★★

This Renaissance gem with golden stonework overlooking the fertile valleys of the Guadalquivir and its tributary, the Guadalimar, stands over an undulating landscape. Along with Úbeda, 9km/5mi away, Baeza is an exceptional urban architectural complex, declared a UNESCO World Heritage Site. It lies at the heart of a region in which olive oil, elevated nearly to the status of a religion, occupies centre stage of social and economic life. The peaceful historical centre is perfect for a leisurely stroll.

- ▶ **Population:** 16 163
- **Michelin Map:** 578 S 19.
- **Info:** Plaza del Pópulo. ℘953 77 99 82. http://turismo.baeza.net.
- ▶ **Location:** With nearby Úbeda, Baeza is in the green centre of Jaén province, near the Parque Natural de Cazorla (to the east). 🚃Nearest station: Linares Baeza (16km)
- **Don't Miss:** The heritage plazas.
- **Timing:** Take half a day for the old quarter.

SIGHTS
MONUMENTAL CENTRE★★★
Plaza del Pópulo★

In the small, irregular square is the **Fuente de los Leones** (Lion Fountain), built with fragments from Cástulo. The Renaissance building to the left, bearing the coat of arms of Charles V, was, surprisingly, the **carnicería** (abattoir). The **Casa del Pópulo** (now the tourist office), at the end of the square, has Plateresque windows and medallions. Six doors once opened on six notaries' offices; court hearings were held upstairs. A balcony projects onto the **Puerta de Jaén**, which, along with the Villalar arch, honoured Charles V. The Jaén gate marked the emperor's visit on his way to Sevilla to marry Isabel of Portugal in 1526.

The **Arco de Villalar** was erected in submission to the king after his victory, in 1521, over the Comuneros, whom the town had supported.

Plaza de Santa María★

The walls of the 17C **Seminario de San Felipe Neri** bear inscriptions – traditionally done in bull's blood upon graduation. Behind the **Fuente de Santa María**, an arch adorned with atlantes, is the Gothic façade of the **Casas Consistoriales Altas**, with the coats of arms of Juana the Mad and Philip the Fair.

Also in the plaza is the **Iglesia de San Andrés**, notable for the **Gothic paintings★** in the sacristy.

Catedral★

Pl. de Santa María. Museum open Mon–Fri 10.30am–2pm, 4–7pm. Sat 10.30am–7pm, Sun 10.30am–6pm. €4. ℘953 74 41 57. http://turismo.baeza.net.

The **interior★★** was remodelled by Vandelvira and his followers in the 16C. The outstanding Capilla Dorada (Gold Chapel) bears Italianate relief; St James' chapel has a fine Antique setting and St Joseph's is flanked by caryatids. The sacristy door has scrollwork and angels' heads. A monumental iron grille by Bartolomé closes the first bay in the nave; a pulpit of painted metal (1580) is in the transept. In the **Capilla del Sagrario**, to one end on the right, is a Baroque silver monstrance carried in procession on the feast of Corpus Christi.

In the cloisters are four Mudéjar chapels with *atauriques*, inscribed in Arabic.

Palacio de Jabalquinto★

Pl. de Santa Cruz. Open Mon–Fri 9am–2pm. Closed public holidays. ℘953 74 27 75.

The palace **façade★★**, in perfect Flamboyant-Gothic style, is best seen in the morning when the sun accentuates the decoration of windows and pinna-

Capital of Olive Oil

"An olive grove opens and closes like a fan," wrote Federico García Lorca. Olive plantations stretch as far as the eye can see across the undulating expanse around Jaén, Spain's leading producer of olives with 60 000 trees and an annual harvest of 370 000 tonnes (about 45% of national production).
The principal olive varietal cultivated is the slightly acidic **picual** The province of Jaén has three **Denominación de Origen** zones: Sierras de Segura, de Cazorla and Mágina.

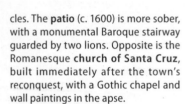

cles. The **patio** (c. 1600) is more sober, with a monumental Baroque stairway guarded by two lions. Opposite is the Romanesque **church of Santa Cruz**, built immediately after the town's reconquest, with a Gothic chapel and wall paintings in the apse.

Antigua Universidad

Conde de Romanones.
Now a secondary school, the seat of the university was built between 1568 and 1593 and functioned until the 19C. Past the plain façade is an elegant Renaissance patio (open Tue–Sun 10am–2pm, 4–7pm; no charge).

Plaza del Mercado Viejo (Plaza de la Constitución)

This busy square is lined by bars and cafés. Fronting it are the **Antigua Alhóndiga** (former grain and cereals market), with porticoed façade (1554), and the **Casas Consistoriales Bajas** (1703) whose gallery is used by officials to view celebrations.

Ayuntamiento★ (Town Hall)

Pj Cardenal Benavides.
The old law courts and prison has a Plateresque façade and ornate balconies.

Ruinas de San Francisco

San Francisco.
Only the vast transept, apse and majestic stone altarpieces remain of the beautiful 16C church that once stood here. It is now an auditorium.

Palacio de Los Salcedo (Palace of the Counts of Garcíez)

San Pedro 18.
Beautiful Gothic windows and a Plateresque patio adorn this early-16C palace, now a hotel. Along the street is the **Iglesia de San Pablo**, with its Renaissance façade.

EXCURSION

Museo de la Cultura del Olivio★

❍ On the Jaén road 9km/5.5mi SW of Baeza, turn right toward Complejo la Laguna (1km/.06mi). Puente del Obispo. Open daily 10.30am–1.30pm, spring 4.30-7pm, summer 5.30-8pm, autumn 4.30-7pm, winter 4-6.30pm. €3.60. Guided tours in English. ✆953 76 51 42. www.museodelaculturadelolivo.com.
This excellent museum on olive culture occupies the premises of a former olive manufacturer. From the botanical garden, which displays different kinds of olives, to the magnificent bodega, where deep barrels stand in rows under vaulted ceilings, to the powerful wooden olive presses, the secrets of Jaén's green gold are revealed. Some 2.5km/1.5mi away, **Laguna Grande** is a protected natural area reached by crossing several beautiful olive groves.

ADDRESSES

🛏 STAY

⊟⊟⊟ **Puerta de la Luna** – Canónigo Melgares Raya 7. ✆953 74 70 19. www.hotelpuertadelaluna.com. 44 rooms. ⊡€14.50. Restaurant ⊟⊟⊟. This beautifully restored 16C palace by the cathedral perfectly blends all mod cons with old-world tranquillity. Outside is a very nice pool.

Úbeda★★

Set amid olive groves, Úbeda is one of Andalucía's architectural treasures. It flourished in the 16C, when palaces, churches and fine squares were built.

BARRIO ANTIGUO★★ (OLD QUARTER)

Allow one day.

Plaza Vázquez de Molina★★

The square is lined with historic buildings, such as the Palacio del Deán Ortega, which now serves as a Parador.

Palacio de las Cadenas★ (Palace of Chains)

Pl. Vázquez de Molina. Open Mon–Fri 8am–2.30pm. No charge. ℘953 75 04 40.
Now the ayuntamiento (town hall) and historical archive, this mansion is named for the chains round the forecourt.
It was designed in 1562 by Vandelvira, also responsible for the Jaén Cathedral. The majestic façade★★, relieved by bays and pilasters, is decorated with caryatids and atlantes.
The Renaissance patio is delightful. On the upper floor is the Archivo Histórico Municipal, with views of the square.

Basílica de Santa María de los Reales Alcázares★

Pl. Vázquez de Molina. Open May–Aug Mon–Sat 10am–2pm, 5–8pm; Sun 11am–2pm, 5–8pm; see website for rest of year. €4. ℘953 756 583. www.santamariadeubeda.es.
The church was built in the 13C on the site of a mosque and damaged in the Civil War. Note the harmonious façade; the main door; the late 16C Puerta de la Consolada (left side); and the 16C Renaissance cloisters. Several delightful chapels★, are adorned with sculptures and profuse decoration and enclosed by impressive grilles★, most the work of Master Bartolomé.

▶ **Population:** 34 930
⚙ **Michelin Map:** 578 R 19.
🅱 **Info:** Calle Baja del Marqués 4 (Palacio Marqués de Contadero). ℘953 77 92 04. www.turismoubeda.com.
◖ **Location:** Úbeda is south of Madrid, between the Guadalquivir and Guadalimar rivers. 🚋Nearest station: Linares Baeza (27km).
◉ **Don't Miss:** The music and dance festival in May and June.

Capilla de El Salvador★★

Pl. Vázquez de Molina. Open year-round Mon–Sat 9.30am–2pm, Sun 11.30am–2pm (until 3pm Oct–Mar). Afternoons: Apr–May 4.30pm–6.30pm (Sun 7.30pm), Jun–Sept 5–7pm (Sun 8pm), Oct–Mar 4–6pm (Sun 7pm). €5. ℘609 27 99 05. http://en.fundacion medinaceli.org/monumentos/capilla.
Diego de Siloé designed this sumptuous church in 1536. Its façade is ornamented with Renaissance motifs.

Interior, Capilla de El Salvador

© Quadriga Images/Look/Photononstop

The **interior★★** is almost theatrical: the single nave, closed by a monumental grille, has vaulting outlined in blue and gold. The Capilla Mayor (chancel) forms a kind of rotunda. A huge 16C altarpiece includes a baldaquin with a sculpture by Berruguete of the Transfiguration. The **sacristy★★**, by Vandelvira, is ornamented with coffered decoration, caryatids and atlantes with all the splendour of the Italian Renaissance style.

Casa de los Salvajes (House of the Savages)

Ventaja. On the façade, two savages in animal skins support a bishop's crest.

Iglesia de San Pablo★

Pl. Primero de Mayo. Open for Mass Mon–Sat 7.30–8.30pm, Sun and public holidays 11.30am–1pm. No charge.
The church mixes a Gothic west door and the Isabelline style, in the **south door** (1511). The Capilla de las Calaveras (Skull Chapel) was designed by Vandelvira. The Isabelline Capilla de las Mercedes is enclosed by an extraordinary **grille★★** – note the highly imaginative depiction of Adam and Eve.

Palacio del Torrente

Pl. Primero de Mayo.
This early Renaissance palace has a monumental gate flanked by twisted columns.

Casa Mudéjar/Museo Arqueológico

Cervantes 6. Open mid-Jun–mid-Sept Tue–Sun 9am–3.30pm; mid-Sept–mid-Jun Tue–Sat 9am–8.30pm, Sun & hols 9am–3.30pm. Closed 1 & 6 Jan, 1 May, 24–25 & 31 Dec. €1.50, no charge for EU citizens. ℰ953 10 86 23. www.museosdeandalucia.es.
In this restored 14C Mudéjar house is the **Museo Arqueológico**, displaying local finds.

Palacio del Conde de Guadiana

Real. The early 17C Palace of the Count of Guadiana is crowned by a fine **tower★**.

Palacio de la Vela de los Cobos

Juan Montilla. ℰ953 75 00 34.
The palace's façade is late 18C. A Renaissance appearance bears witness to the long survival of this style in Úbeda.

Palacio del Marqués del Contadero (Palace of the Marquis of Contadero)

Baja del Marqués 4. Open Mon–Fri 9am–3.30pm, Sat–Sun 9.30am–3pm. No charge. ℰ953 77 92 04. www.andalucia.org
The late 18C façade, crowned by a gallery, is also Renaissance in style.

Antiguo Hospital de Santiago

Av. Cristo Rey. Open daily 7am–2.30pm, 5–10pm. Closed Sun in Jul and Sat–Sun in Aug.
This "Andalusian Escorial"is probably Vandelvira's most accomplished work. Its sober façade provides a marked contrast to its interior. Don't miss its chapel.

ADDRESSES

STAY

Hotel Postigo – Postigo 5. ℰ953 75 00 00. http://elpostigo. zenithoteles.com. 26 rooms. €6. Stylish, modern three-star hotel in the old town. Small pool and terrace.

Palacio de la Rambla – Pl. del Marqués 1. ℰ953 75 01 96. www.palaciodelarambla.com. 8 rooms. Closed mid-Jul–early Aug. This fine 16C palace with magnificent Renaissance patio boasts beautiful rooms and treats you like a family guest.

EAT

Mesón Gabino – Fuente Seca. ℰ953 75 75 53. Closed Mon eve. Set in the fortress walls, this very atmospheric restaurant specialises in grilled meats and regional dishes. Degustación menus also available.

Asador de Santiago – av Cristo Rey 4. ℰ953 75 04 63. www.asadordesantiago.com. A lively tapas bar and two dining rooms. One is contemporary in style, the other has a more traditional decor.

Parque Natural de las Sierras de Cazorla, Segura y Las Villas★★★

Spain's largest nature reserve extends over 214 300ha/529 535 acres at an altitude of between 600m/1 968ft and 2 017m/6 616ft. Steep cliffs, deep gorges and a complex of rivers and streams, including the source of the Guadalquivir, make up this park. The dense montane vegetation is similar to that found in Mediterranean regions. Deer, mountain goats, wild boar, golden eagles, griffon vultures and osprey abound.

- ⓒ **Michelin Map:** 578 S 20-21-22 R 20-21-22 Q 21-22.
- 🗐 **Info:** Ctra del Tranco, Km48.3, Torre del Vinagre. Coto-Rios ✆953 71 30 17. www.sierrasde cazorlaseguraylasvillas.es
- ⓒ **Location:** The park lies in southeastern Spain, east of Úbeda. 🚉Nearest station: Linares Baeza (113km).
- ⓒ **Timing:** Allow a full day at least for the park.

🚗DRIVING TOURS

ⓢ Before exploring the park, visit one of the **information offices** at Torre del Vinagre, Cazorla, Segura de la Sierra, or Siles (ⓒsee website, above, for details). Mountain-bikers, horse-riders and hikers can follow the extensive network of forest tracks and marked footpaths.

FROM TÍSCAR TO THE EMBALSE DEL TRANCO DE BEAS
92km/57mi. Allow one day.

Tíscar★
The **Santuario de Tíscar** (open for worship daily Oct–May 11.30am–12.30pm; Jun–Sept 11am–2pm, 6–8pm) enjoys a superb site enclosed by rocks. Below this place of pilgrimage is the impressive **Cueva del Agua★**, a cave formation, that you can walk through, where a torrent of water emerges from between the rocks.

ⓒ Follow the C 323 as far as Quesada.

Quesada
Quesada sits on the Cerro de la Magdalena hill, amid olive groves. A **museum** is dedicated to painter Rafael Zabaleta (1907–60) (Pl. Cesáreo Rodríguez Aguilera; open Wed–Sat Mar–Oct 10am–2pm, 5–8pm; Nov–Apr 10am–2pm, 4–7pm; Sun & pub hols year-round 10am–2.30pm; closed 1 Jan, 25 Dec; €6; ✆953 73 42 60 ; www.museozabaleta.org).

The Cañada de las Fuentes, a ravine on the outskirts, is the **source of the Guadalquivir river** (access via a track off the A 315, to the N of Quesada). Wall paintings from the Palaeolithic era can be viewed in Cerro Vitar and in the Cueva del Encajero, a short distance from the town.

ⓒ Take the A 315 towards Peal de Becerro; bear right on the A 319.

Cazorla★
Cazorla occupies an outstanding **site★** below the Peña de los Halcones, dominated by the **Castillo de la Yedra** (Camino del Castillo; open mid-Jun–mid-Sept Tue–Sun 9am–3pm, mid-Sept–mid-Jun Tue–Sat 9am–8.30pm; Sun 10am–3pm. €1.50, no charge for citizens of EU; ✆953 10 14 02), its whitewashed houses adorned with balconies. At the centre of the plaza de Santa María stands a Renaissance fountain; the ruins of the Iglesia de Santa María (Pl. Santa María), by Vandelvira, are now used as an auditorium.

ⓒ Head 1.5km/1mi NE along the A 319; turn right at a signposted junction.

La Iruela
The remains of a Templar castle offer superb **views★★** (Camino del Castillo;

no charge) of the Guadalquivir Valley. The Iglesia (church) de Santo Domingo was designed by Vandelvira.

THE ROAD FROM LA IRUELA TO THE TRANCO RESERVOIR★

The first 17km/10.5mi stretch provides **spectacular views★★**. The Parador de **El Adelantado** is 8km/5mi along a branch road up through pine forests.

◐ Follow the A 319 along the river.

Torre del Vinagre
Carretera del Tranco, A 319. Open daily 10am–2pm, 4–7pm (Jul–Aug 5–8pm). Closed 25 Dec. ℘953 71 30 17.
This is the park's main information centre, including a hunting museum as well as a botanical garden with species native to the park. Several routes start here. A game reserve, **Parque Cinegético de Collado del Almendral**, 15km/9.3mi along the A 319, has lookouts for viewing deer, mouflons and mountain goats.

Embalse del Tranco de Beas
⚠ Several camping areas and hotels are close to this reservoir. Water sports are available. Islands in the reservoir are Isla de Cabeza la Viña; and **Isla de Bujaraiza**, with the ruins of a Moorish castle. Both are seen from the **Mirador Rodríguez de la Fuente** viewpoint.

SANTIAGO-PONTONES TO SILES
80km/50mi. Allow half a day.

Santiago-Pontones
This municipality includes scattered mountain villages, the 9 000 year-old, **Cueva del Nacimiento**, and the **Cuevas de Engalbo**, with impressive wall art.

◐ From Pontones, go NW on the A 317.

Hornos
Fortress remains rise above a steep cliff from where there are some spectacular **views★** of the reservoir and the Guadalquivir Valley.

◐ Take the A 317, then bear right to Segura de la Sierra at a junction.

Segura de la Sierra★
This picturesque village, birthplace of the 15C poet Jorge Manrique, is at an altitude of 1 240m/4 067ft in the shelter of its superb Mudéjar **castle** (open Wed–Sun 10.30am–2pm, 4–7pm; €4; ℘953 48 21 73; www.sierradesegura.com) with its sweeping **panorama★★** of the Sierra de Segura. Also worth a look is the **town hall**, which boasts a Plateresque doorway; the **parish church** (for its delicate, polychrome statue of the Virgin Mary, and a recumbent Christ attributed to Gregorio Hernández) and the **Moorish baths** (baños árabes).

◐ Follow the JV 7020 to Orcera.

Orcera
The Iglesia de Nuestra Señora de la Asunción, with its sober Renaissance portal, and the Fuente de los Chorros, a 15C fountain, can be seen in the main square. Vestiges of the former Moorish fortress are on the outskirts of Orcera.

◐ Continue along the JV 7020 beyond Benatae, then take the JV 7021.

Siles
The village retains part of its old walls. Nearby is Las Acebeas nature reserve.

ADDRESSES

🏠 STAY
🍽🍽🍽 **Molino La Fárraga** – Cam. de la Hoz. ℘953 72 12 49. www.molinola farraga.com. 8 rooms. Closed 15 Dec–15 Feb. This 18C olive oil mill offers simple rooms, a garden with a small stream and a swimming pool with views of the castle and mountains.

🍴 EAT
CAZORLA
🍽🍽🍽 **Mesón Don Chema** – Escaleras del Mercado 2. ℘953 71 05 29. Venison, wild boar and other game are speciality at this old-fashioned restaurant.

Western Andalucía

Cádiz and its province are acclaimed as the birthplace of that most famous Spanish culinary institution, tapas, while Huelva's uplands are famous for the dehesa oak park and the Ibérico pig. Each province attracts Spanish holidaymakers, with most north European tourists found among the surfers who have colonised the windy beaches of the Costa de la Luz. Cádiz is a very characterful, very Spanish city which hosts relatively few visitors.

Jerez de la Frontera, by contrast, is the home of sherry bodegas and Andalucían horsemanship, both of which attract coachloads of holidaymakers. Aracena's Cave of Marvels is a popular day trip, though only the most determined make it as far inland as the Aracena Mountains; their reward is stunning scenery and quiet picturesque villages.

Cádiz: Birthplace of Tapas

The eternal debate about who invented tapas and whose are best can be settled quickly with a tour through Cádiz and its province. Sanlúcar de Barrameda, Puerto de Santa María, and Jerez de la Frontera, along with the city of Cádiz itself, offer such a bewildering variety of top quality miniature cuisine that the mere sight of a northern Spanish tapas counter laden with puddings and pastes on bread pales by comparison. Cádiz's privileged location at the confluence of the Atlantic, the Mediterranean and the Guadalquivir river estuary creates such an abundance of seafood that tapas tend to be pure product, fresh and raw or quickly cooked.

Spain's caviar

La dehesa ("the pasture") is the southwestern Spanish oak park, an ecosystem maintained primarily by and for the free-range Ibérico pig, a direct descendant of the *sus mediterraneus* boar that roamed the Mediterranean oak forests of antiquity. These strictly regulated black pigs eat only acorns for the final three months of their lives, giving their marbled meat an exceptionally nutty, grassy taste and aroma.

Highlights

1. Dazzling white sands on the **Costa de la Luz** (p533)
2. Spotting flamingos in the **Parque Nacional de Doñana** (p535)
3. Enjoying a tipple in a sherry bodega in **Jerez** (p537)
4. **Cádiz** at carnival time, the most famous and lively in Spain (p541)
5. Cheeky Barbary apes on a tour of the Rock of **Gibraltar** (p547)

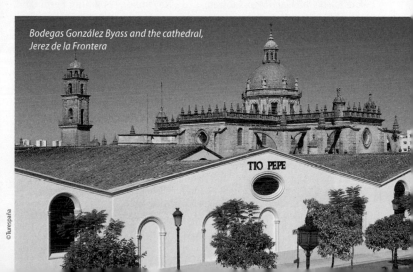

Bodegas González Byass and the cathedral, Jerez de la Frontera

TIO PEPE

Sevilla★★★

Sevilla, set in the plain of the Guadalquivir, is capital of Andalucía and Spain's fourth largest city. To appreciate its many moods, take time to stroll the narrow streets of old quarters like Santa Cruz, or ride slowly through peaceful parks and gardens in a horse-drawn carriage. Sevilla is the centre of flamenco, famous for its bullfights, its 18C Maestranza bullring, and for its cafés and tapas bars.

THE CITY TODAY

If Spain had a beauty contest for its cities, or a contest for the most Spanish city in Spain, Sevilla would probably win both. It boasts more monumental set pieces and more pretty, unspoiled corners than any other Andalucían city. It also claims the best tapas, the best nightlife and the best *ferias*, and is a stronghold for bullfighting and flamenco. Come here in spring when the orange blossom is in full fragrance, but avoid the heat of high summer.

A BIT OF HISTORY

Sevilla is summed up on the Puerta de Jerez (Jerez Gate): "Hercules built me; Caesar surrounded me with walls and towers; the King Saint reconquered me." Sevilla was chief city of Roman Baetica and capital of the Visigothic kingdom before Toledo. In 712 the Moors arrived;

▶ **Population:** 693 878
♿ **Michelin Map:** 578 T 11-12 (town plan).
Info: Plaza del Triunfo, ☎954 21 00 05. www.visitasevilla.es.
◐ **Location:** Sevilla, in southwestern Spain, is lined by motorways and dual carriageways to Huelva (92km/57mi W), Jerez de la Frontera (90km/56mi SW), Cádiz (123km/77mi SW) and Córdoba (143km/89mi NE). 🚂Sevilla Santa Justa (AVE).
P Parking: Find a space in the centre, leave your car, and stroll the streets.
☞ **Don't Miss:** The Giralda and the Alcázar.
⏱ **Timing:** Take at least a day for the marvels of central Sevilla, then enjoy quarters such as Santa Cruz, Triana and La Macarena and sites nearby.
👪 Kids: Isla Mágica beckons for at least a day.

in the 11C, it became capital of a kingdom which prospered under the Almohads. In 1195 **Sultan Yacoub al-Mansur** (1184–99), builder of the Giralda, defeated the Christians at Alarcos. On 19 November 1248, **King Ferdinand**

A Tradition of Fiestas

The great festivals, when vast crowds flock to the city from all over Spain and overseas, reveal the provincial capital in many guises. During **Semana Santa**, or **Holy Week**, **pasos** processions are organised nightly in each city quarter by rival brotherhoods. **Pasos** are great litters sumptuously bejewelled and garlanded with flowers on which are mounted religious, polychrome wood statues; these constructions are borne through the crowd on the shoulders of between 25 and 60 men. Accompanying the statues are penitents, hidden beneath tall pointed hoods; from time to time a voice is raised in a **saeta**, an improvised religious lament. During the **April Fair or Feria**, which began life in the middle of the 19C as an animal fair, the city becomes a fairground with horse and carriage parades. The women in ruffled dresses and the men in full Andalucían costume ride up to specially erected canvas pavilions to dance **sevillanas**.

Sevilla skyline viewed from Metropol Parasol, La Giralda and the cathedral in the background

III of Castilla, the Saint, delivered the city from the Moors. The discoveries brought new prosperity. By 1503, Isabel the Catholic created the **Casa de contratación** or Exchange to control trade with America. This monopoly lasted until 1717.

Art and architecture in Sevilla – The northern ramparts, the Alcázar walls, the **Torre del Oro** (Golden Tower) and the Giralda were all built by the Moors. The **Mudéjar style**, a mix of Moorish and Christian, is testimony to the lasting influence of Arab design in the Alcázar and other monuments after the city's reconquest.

Golden Age painters of the **Seville School** corresponded to three reigns: under Philip III (1598–1621) **Roelas** and **Pacheco**; under Philip IV (1621–65) **Herrera the Elder** and **Zurbarán** (1598–1664), who portrayed figures with spiritual intensity. Finally, under Charles II (1665–1700) **Murillo** (1617–82) created radiant Immaculate Conceptions and brilliant everyday scenes. The best work of **Valdés Leal** (1622–90) can be seen in the Hospital de la Caridad. **Diego Velázquez** (1599–1660) was born in Sevilla. Many statues are the work of 17C sculptor **Martínez Montañés**. Well known are the **Cristo del Gran Poder** (Christ of Great Power) by **Juan de Mesa** and the **Cachorro** by Francisco Antonio Gijón in the **Capilla del Patrocinio** (calle Castilla). The **Macarena Virgin** is the most popular figure in Sevilla.

THE GIRALDA AND CATHEDRAL★★★

Allow 1hr 30min. Open Sept–Jun: Mon 11am–3.30pm (afternoon session 4.30–6pm, must be booked in advance, inc free audio tour); Tue–Sat 11am–5pm. Jul–Aug: Mon 9.30am–2.30pm (afternoon session 3.30–5pm, must be booked in advance, inc free audio tour); Tue–Sat 9.30am–4pm. Year-round Sun 2.30–6pm. Closed 1, 6 Jan, 20, 22 Mar, 26, 30 May, 15 Aug, 8, 25 Dec. Restricted opening times during Holy Week. €9 including both sites. ℘902 099 692. www.catedraldesevilla.es.

La Giralda★★★

Alemanes.

When this bell tower was built in the 12C, its 98m/322ft minaret resembled the Koutoubia in Marrakesh. The top storey and Renaissance lantern were added in the 16C. Typically Almohad, it creates grandeur in harmony with the ideal of simplicity. A gently sloping ramp (accessible from inside the cathedral) leads to the top (70m/230ft) for excellent views★★★.

Cathedral★★★

Av. de la Constitución.

Sevilla's cathedral is the third largest in Europe after St Peter's in Rome and St Paul's in London. When its construction began in 1401, members of the cathedral chapter are said to have declared "Let us build a cathedral so immense

GETTING THERE

Airport – Aeropuerto de San Pablo, 8km/5mi towards Madrid on the N IV motorway, (📞954 44 90 00; www.aena.es). A bus service operates from the airport to the railway station and city centre.

Trains – Estación de Santa Justa. The high-speed AVE (Tren de Alta Velocidad) departs from this station, taking just 45min to Córdoba and 2hr 15min to Madrid. For information and bookings, call 📞912 320 320 or visit www.renfe.com.

Inter-city buses – Sevilla has two bus stations: **Estación Plaza de Armas** 📞954 90 80 40; and **Estación del Prado de San Sebastián**. 📞955 479 290.

Taxis – Radio Taxi. 📞954 57 11 11. www.radiotaxidesevilla.es.

SIGHTSEEING

Publications – Two free bilingual publications (Spanish-English) are published for tourists every month;

Welcome Olé and **The Tourist**, can be obtained from major hotels and sights around the city. Sevilla City Hall's Department of Culture **(NODO)** also publishes a monthly brochure listing all the city's cultural events. A monthly publication covering the whole of Andalucía, **El Giraldillo**, contains information on the region's fairs, exhibitions and theatres, as well as details on cinemas, restaurants and shops. www.elgiraldillo.es.

Horse-drawn carriages – It is well worth taking a trip in one of the numerous horse-drawn carriages operating in the city. They can normally be hired by the Cathedral, in front of the Torre del Oro and in the María Luisa park.

Boat trips on the Guadalquivir– Boat trips lasting 1hr during the day and 1hr 30min at night depart every half-hour from the Torre del Oro. Ask at the tourist office for details.

---

that everyone, on beholding it, will take us for madmen".

The late Gothic cathedral shows Renaissance influence. The main portals are modern. However, the Puerta de la Natividad (Nativity Doorway) and the Puerta del Bautismo (Baptism Doorway), right and left of the west door, include beautiful sculptures by Mercadente de Bretaña (c. 1460). Miguel Perrin (1520) made full use of Renaissance perspective in the tympana of the Puerta de los Palos and Puerta de las Campanillas (east end doorways).

▷ Enter by the Puerta de San Cristóbal.

The **interior** is striking. Massive columns appear slender because they are so tall. Flamboyant Gothic vaulting rises massively 56m/184ft above the transept crossing. A **mirror** on the floor affords a striking view.

Capilla Mayor (Chancel)

Splendid Plateresque **grilles★★** (1518–33) precede an immense Flemish **altarpiece★★★**, profusely carved with scenes from the life of Christ and gleaming with gold leaf (1482–1525).

Tesoro (Treasury)

The **Sacristía de los Cálices** (Chalice Sacristy) contains canvases by Goya (*Santa Justa* and *Santa Rufina*), Valdés Leal, Murillo and Zurbarán, and a triptych by Alejo Fernández.

In the 16C **Sacristía Mayor** are a Renaissance **monstrance** by Juan de Arfe, 3.9m/13ft in height and weighing 475kg/1 045lb, and paintings by Zurbarán and Lucas Jordán.

Capilla Real★★ (Chapel Royal)

An elegant Renaissance dome is decorated with carved busts. On either side are the tombs of Alfonso X of Castilla (d. 1284) and his mother, Beatrice of

Swabia. On the high altar is the robed **Virgen de los Reyes**, patron of Sevilla, given by St Louis of France to St Ferdinand of Spain, who is buried in a silver gilt shrine below.

Patio de los Naranjos (Orange Tree Court) – This patio served as the ablutions area in the mosque.

Exit by the **Puerta del Perdón**, an Almohad arch decorated with stucco and two statues by Miguel Perrin.

AROUND THE CATHEDRAL
Real Alcázar★★★

Patio de Banderas. Open Oct–Mar daily 9.30am–5pm. Apr–Sept daily 9.30am–7pm. See website for details of Night Visits. Closed 1 & 6 Jan, Good Fri, 25 Dec, and for official ceremonies. €9.50, Cuarto Real Alto additional €4.50 Night visits, from €13. ℘954 50 23 24. www.alcazarsevilla.org.

All that remains of the 12C Almohad Alcázar are the **Patio de Yeso** and a courtyard wall. In the 13C, Alfonso X, the Wise, built a palace, known today as **Charles V's rooms**. Peter the Cruel (1350–69) erected the nucleus of the present building, known as **Peter the Cruel's Palace**, in 1362, using masons from Granada. It is one of the purest examples of the Mudéjar style.

Cuarto Real Alto

An optional 30-min guided tour enables visitors to view the King and Queen of Spain's official residence in Sevilla. The various rooms, with their fine *artesonado* ceilings, contain an impressive display of 19C furniture and clocks, 18C tapestries and French lamps. Of particular note are the **Capilla de los Reyes Católicos** (Chapel of the Catholic Monarchs) – an exquisite oratory with a ceramic font, by Nicola Pisano – and the Mudéjar **Sala de Audiencias**.

Cuarto del Almirante
(Admiral's Apartments)

Right side, the Patio de la Montería. In the Sala de Audiencias (Audience Chamber) the **Virgin of the Navigators★** altarpiece (1531–36) is by Alejo Fernández.

Salón de Embajadores, Palacio de Pedro el Cruel

Palacio de Pedro el Cruel★★★
(Palace of Peter the Cruel)

A passage leads to the **Patio de las Doncellas** (Court of the Maidens), a Moorish arched patio; the upper storey was added in the 16C. An elevated round arch leads to the **Dormitorio de los Reyes Moros** (Bedroom of the Moorish Kings), two rooms decorated with blue-toned stucco and a magnificent *artesonado* ceiling. Through a small room is the **Patio de las Muñecas** (Dolls' Court) with Granada-type decoration. The gallery on the upper floor dates from the 19C. The Catholic Monarchs' bedroom leads to the **Salón de Felipe II** (Philip II Salon), the **Arco de los Pavones** (Peacock Arch) and the **Salón de Embajadores** (Ambassadors Hall), the most sumptuous room, with a remarkable 15C half-orange cedarwood **cupola★★★**. The **Sala del Techo de Carlos V** (Charles V Room), the former chapel, has a magnificent ceiling.

WEST OF THE CATHEDRAL
Museo de Bellas Artes★★★
(Fine Arts Museum)

Pl. del Museo 9. Open mid-June–mid-Sept Tue–Sun and public holidays 9am–3pm. Mid-Sept–mid-Jun Tue–Sat 9am–8.30pm, Sun and public holidays 9am–3pm. Closed 1 & 6 Jan, 1 May, 24–25 & 31 Dec. €1.50;

no charge for EU citizens. Advance booking recommended. ☎955 54 29 42. www.museodebellasartesdesevilla.es.

The Convento de la Merced (Merced Friary) was built in the 17C by Juan de Oviedo around three beautiful patios. **Sala I** of the museum inside contains medieval art. **Room II** is dedicated to Renaissance art, in particular a fine sculpture of *St Jerome* by Pietro Torrigiani, a contemporary of Michelangelo. Two magnificent portraits of *A Lady and a Gentleman* by Pedro Pacheco are the highlight in **Room III**.

In **Room V★★★** walls decorated with paintings by the 18C artist Domingo Martínez are a stunning backdrop to outstanding work by Murillo and a Zurbarán masterpiece, *The Apotheosis of St Thomas Aquinas* (in the nave), with its skilful play of light and shade. **Murillo**'s monumental *Immaculate Conception,* with its energetic movement, is in the transept. On the right-hand side of the transept is a benevolent *Virgen de la Servilleta* (note the effect of the Child approaching).

Upper Floor: Room VI displays a fine collection of saints. **Room VIII** is devoted to Baroque artist Valdés Leal. European Baroque is represented in **Room IX**. **Room X★★** includes works of **Zurbarán**. In *Christ on the Cross*, the body of Christ appears as if sculpted. His *St Hugh and Carthusian Monks at Table* displays errors in perspective.

The ceiling of the inner room should not be missed. In **Room XI** is **Goya**'s *Portrait of Canon José Duato.*

Metropol Parasol★

Pl de la Encarnación. Rooftop open 10.30am–10.30pm (Fri–Sat 11pm). €3. ☎955 47 15 80. www.setasdesevilla.com.

This stunning new 100-ft (30-m) high city icon was unveiled in 2011. Its name comes from the shade it offers in this famously hot city, though its shape and appearance has been more frequently likened to a wooden cloud, waffle or a giant mushroom; in fact it is known locally as Las Setas, the mushrooms. Covering some 18,000 square meters it is said to be the world's largest wooden

structure and in its shade sits an archeological site, farmers market, multiple bars and restaurants. On the roof there is a restaurant, viewing gallery, and a winding, undulating walkway.

Iglesia de San Luis de los Franceses★

San Luis 37. Due to reopen in 2016.

This church, by Leonardo de Figueroa, is one of the best examples of the Sevillan Baroque. The exuberant **interior★★** is a mix of outstanding murals, sumptuous *retables* and fine *azulejos*.

Monasterio de Santa Paula★

Santa Paula 11. Shop open Tue–Sun 10am–1pm, 5–6.30pm. Museum Tue–Sun 10am–1pm. Buildings closed for certain religious ceremonies. €3. ☎954 53 63 30. www.santapaula.es.

This is still a functioning convent and the nuns living here sell their homemade sweets to visitors. The church's breathtaking **portal★** (1504) is adorned with ceramics. Despite its mix of styles, the overall effect is harmonious. **Inside★**, the nave is covered by a 17C roof and the chancel by a Gothic vault with attractive frescoes.

The **museum★** (entrance through no. 11 on the plaza) has works by Ribera, Pedro de Mena, Alonso de Cana and others. The gilded **Capilla de San José★** gleams at night.

Palacio de la Condesa de Lebrija★

Cuna 8. Open Sept–Jun Mon–Fri 10.30am–7.30pm. Sat 10am–2pm, 4–6pm. Sun 10am–2pm. Jul–Aug Mon–Fri 9am–3pm, Sat 10am–2pm. €8, €5 ground floor only. ☎954 22 78 02. www.palaciodelebrija.com.

This noble home is decorated with **Roman mosaics★** from Itálica, Mudéjar *artesonado* ceilings, 16C–17C *azulejos*, and a sumptuous **stairway★**.

Iglesia del Salvador★

Pl. del Salvador. Open Mon–Sat and public holidays 11am (9.30 hols)–5.30pm, 7.30–9pm. Sun noon–1.30pm, 3–7pm, 7.30–9pm. €3 donation. ☎954 59 54 05.

This 17C–18C church has some of the city's most impressive 18C **Baroque retables★★**.

Ayuntamiento
(Town Hall)

Pl. Nueva 1. Open for guided visits Mon–Thu 7pm and 8pm, Sat 10am. Reserve in advance. €4. ℘902 55 93 86. The attractive **east façade★** (1527–34) is Renaissance in style and adorned with delicate scrollwork decoration.

Basílica de la Macarena★

Bécquer 1–3. Open Mon–Sun 9.30am–2pm, 6pm-8pm (5–9pm Oct–mid-Apr). Closed 1, 6 Jan, 1 May, 24, 25, 31 Dec. €5 museum, no charge for Basílica. ℘954 90 18 00.
Home to Sevilla's most beloved icon, La Virgen de la Esperanza Macarena, the basilica is also the hub of a vibrant working-class neighbourhood.
Built in 1949 by Aurelio Gómez Millán, the neo-Baroque Basílica de la Macarena contains the most universally admired Marian image in Sevilla. Sculpted in the 17C by Luisa Roldán, La Macarena is named for the Puerta de la Macarena, an entrance through the city walls built by Roman centurion Macarius Ena in the 2C AD. Her face, glistening with glass tears, is acclaimed as the most beautiful of all. A favourite of gypsies and bullfighters, La Macarena's Easter Week procession through the streets is one of the celebration's most emotional moments.

Iglesia de la Magdalena★

Calle San Pablo 10. Open Mon–Sat 7.45am–1.30pm, 6.30–9pm, Sun 8.45am–2pm, 6.30–9pm. Closed 1 & 6 Jan, 1 May, 24–25 & 31 Dec. No charge. ℘954 22 96 03.
This immense monolith between Plaza Nueva and the Museo de Bellas Artes contains important artistic treasures. From the Mudéjar **Capilla de la Quinta Angustia** (Chapel of the fifth anguish) to the 1709 Baroque section by architect Leonardo de Figueroa, this rambling jumble of cupolas and domes is filled with art. Zurbarán's *Santo Domingo de Soria* and the Lucas Valdés frescoes *Alegoría del triunfo de la fé (Allegory of the Triumph of Faith)* are the works to look out for.

▶ Cross the Patio de la Montería and go down a vaulted passage (right).

Palacio Gótico or Salones de Carlos V (Gothic Palace or Charles V's Rooms)

The palace, which was built in the reign of Alfonso X, houses magnificent **tapestries★★** from the Real Fábrica de Tapices illustrating Charles V's conquest of Tunis in 1535.

Jardines★

Continue to the Mercurio pool and 17C **Galería del Grutesco★** to view the magnificent Moorish gardens. The most enchanting parts are **Charles V's pavilion**, the maze and the English garden. The silhouette of the Giralda rises above the **Patio de Banderas** (Flag Court), bordered by elegant façades.

Hospital de la Caridad★
(Hospital of Charity)

Temprado 3. Open Mon–Sun 10am-7.30pm, Sun 1-2.30pm. €5. ℘954 22 32 32. www.santa-caridad.es.
The hospital was founded in 1625. Great Sevillan artists decorated the **church★★**. Valdés Leal illustrated Death with a striking sense of the macabre. Murillo showed Charity in *The Miracle of the Loaves and Fishes*, *Moses Smiting Water from the Rock*, *St John of God* and *St Isabel of Hungary Caring for the Sick*. Pedro Roldan's **Entombment★★** adorns the high altar.

Archivo General de Indias
(Archives of the Indies)

Av. de la Constitución 3. Open Mon–Sat 9.30am-5pm, Sun 10am-2pm. No charge. ℘954 50 05 28. www.mcu.es/archivos/MC/AGI.
The building (1572), designed as an exchange *(lonja)* by Juan de Herrera, houses priceless documents on the Americas at the time of the Conquest, including maps and charts.

Plaza de la Alianza, Barrio de Santa Cruz

EAST OF THE CATHEDRAL
Parque de María Luisa★★

The vast **plaza de España**★ of this 19C park remains from the 1929 Ibero-American Exhibition. Each ceramic bench represents a province of Spain.

Museo Arqueológico★

Pl. de América. Open mid-June–mid-Sept Tue–Sun and public holidays 9am–3.30pm, mid-Sept–mid-Jun Tue–Sat 9am–8pm, Sun and public holidays 9am–3pm. Closed 1 & 6 Jan, 1 May, 24–25 & 31 Dec. €1.50; no charge for EU citizens. 955 12 06 32. www.museosdeandalucia.es.

The archaeological museum is in a palace on plaza de América. The 7C–6C BC **Carambolo Treasure**★ includes a statue with a Phoenician inscription. In the **Roman section**★ are statues and mosaics from Itálica (see Excursions).

BARRIO DE SANTA CRUZ★★★
(SANTA CRUZ QUARTER)

The former Jewish quarter is replete with alleys, wrought-iron grilles and flower-filled patios. It is delightful in the evenings when cafés and restaurants overflow into the squares.

Casa de Pilatos★★
(Pilate's House)

Pl. de Pilatos 1. Open daily Apr–Oct 9am–7pm; Nov–Mar 9am–6pm. €10, €8 ground floor only. 954 22 52 98.

www.fundacionmedinaceli.org/monumentos/pilatos.

The large Mudéjar patio of this 15C–16C palace displays fine stuccowork and magnificent lustre **azulejos**★★. *Artesonado* ceilings, the chapel with Gothic vaulting and *azulejo* and stucco decoration, and a remarkable wood **dome**★ over the grand **staircase**★★ illustrate the vitality of the Mudéjar style during the Renaissance. The gardens are open to the public.

Hospital de los Venerables★

Pl. de los Venerables 8. Open daily 10am–2pm, 4–8pm. Closed 1 Jan, 25 Mar, 25 Dec. €5.50; free Sun afternoon. 954 56 26 96. www.focus.abengoa.es.

This building, in lively plaza de los Venerables, is one of the best examples of 17C Sevillan Baroque. Its fine **church**★ is covered with frescoes by Valdés Leal and his son Lucas Valdés.

Museo del Baile Flamenco

Manuel Rojas Marcos 3. Open daily 10am–7pm (flamenco performance 7–8pm or 8.45–9.45pm in summer). Closed 1 & 6 Jan, 1 May, 24, 25, 31 Dec. €10, performance only €20, combined €24. 954 34 03 11. www.museodelbaileflamenco.com.

Everything you ever wanted to know about the world of flamenco. **Cristina Hoyos**, one of the great *bailaoras* in the history of Andalucía's most important art form, founded and promoted this museum as an introduction for tourists and flamenco beginners as well as a repository of flamenco history for aficionados and professionals.

Iglesia de Santa María la Blanca★

Santa María la Blanca 5. No charge. ℘954 21 50 40.

In the **interior**★ of this former synagogue, exuberant Baroque ceilings are balanced by pink marble columns.

ISLA DE LA CARTUJA
Isla Mágica★

Open Holy Week– first weekend Nov, see website for dates and times. €29 day & evening; €11 evening only; child (4–12) €21/€11. ℘902 16 17 16. www.islamagica.es.

This major theme park takes visitors around Seville, Spain, the New World, Eldorado, Amazonia and the Mayan civilization. Anyone familiar with US theme parks will know pretty much what to expect, and it's all done well. Rides vary from gentle carousels to the latest white-knuckle roller coasters and water rides, 3-D films and simulators, and there are live shows in most areas. The fun doesn't stop after dark, so allow yourself a full day and night here, culminating in a fireworks-and-laser extravaganza on the lake.

Visitors to Spain's hottest city can also now cool off while having fun with a new waterpark in the complex, **Aqua Mágica** (open only to Isla Mágica ticket holders, same season, see website for dates and times; €7).

Centro Andaluz de Arte Contemporáneo

Av. de Américo Vespucio 2. Open Tue –Sat 11am–9pm, Sun 11am–3.30pm. Closed 1 & 6 Jan, 3 Apr, 1 May, 12 Oct, 2 Nov, 7, 24, 25 & 31 Dec. €3.01; no charge Tue–Fri 5–9pm, Sat all day. ℘955 03 70 70. www.caac.es.

This contemporary art museum is in the former La Cartuja monastery; some **convent buildings**★ remain. The collection includes art from 1957 onwards.

ADDITIONAL SIGHTS
Barrio de Triana★

Triana is Sevilla's classic Bohemian neighbourhood (think sailors, gypsys, bullfighters and flamenco dancers) on the western bank of the Guadalquivir river. Even though most gypsies and bullfighters have moved out to the edge of town, Triana remains a colourful Bohemian quarter with a flamenco vibe. The Santa Ana church, the food produce market, and the **Capilla de los Marineros** are important sights, along with the Capilla de la Estrella and the Iglesia de San Jacinto. Calle Alfarería is the ceramics centre of Sevilla, while Calle Betis along the edge of the Guaqalquivir is lined with taverns and restaurants. Casa Anselma on Calle Pagés del Corro is a popular flamenco jam session that starts up around midnight.

Also here on the waterfront is the **Pabellón de la Navegación** (open May–Oct Tue–Sat 10am–8.30pm, Sun until 3pm; Nov–Apr Tue–Sat 10am–7.30pm, Sun until 3pm; €4.90; ℘954 04 31 11), a museum dedicated to Spanish sailing and discovery. The entry ticket allows you to take a lift to the top of the 65m **Torre Schindler** for panormanic views.

EXCURSIONS
Ruinas de Itálica★

▶ Av. de Extremadura 2, Santiponce. 9km/6mi NW on the N 630. Open mid-Jun–mid-Sept Tue–Sun 9am–3pm. Apr–mid-Jun Tue–Sat 9am–8m, Sun 9am–3pm. Mid-Sept–Mar Tue–Sat 9am–6pm, Sun 9am–3pm. €1.50; no charge for EU citizens. ℘600 14 17 67. www.museosdeandalucia.es.

This **Roman town** was the birthplace of emperors Hadrian and Trajan. Mosaics of birds and Neptune are in their original sites. The **Anfiteatro** (amphitheatre), seating 25 000, was one of the largest in the empire.

Carmona★★

▶ 40km/25mi W along the A 4. Carmona, with its heritage buildings, overlooks the River Corbones. ⓟ Park in the lower part of town.

The Legendary *Jamón*

The free-range, Ibérico black pig stores monounsaturated fats from acorns in marbled layers in its muscle tissue. Not only are these acorn-based oleic acids relatively healthy, but their flavours and aromas, after two years of ageing, are so complex, nutty, buttery, earthy and floral that Japanese enthusiasts have declared Ibérico ham "umami". The fat in *Jamón ibérico de bellota* (Ibérico pig fed exclusively on acorns – up to 10kg/22lb a day) liquefies at room temperature, so it literally melts in your mouth. It can cost twice as much as normal *ibérico* ham.

Old Town★

Note the **Baroque tower**★ of the **Iglesia de San Pedro**★ *(Arco de la Carne)*, a church with a sumptuous sacrarium chapel (Capilla del Sagrario), and, further along, the **Convento de la Concepción** with its fine cloisters and Mudéjar church.

Through the **Puerta de Sevilla**★ is the 17C–18C **Iglesia de San Bartolomé** (Prim 29). The capilla mayor in the Mudéjar church of **San Felipe**★ (San Felipe) is covered with 16C ceramics.

The Baroque **town hall** *(ayuntamiento)*, facing **Plaza de San Fernando** (entrance on calle de El Salvador), has a Roman mosaic. Next door, the 17C–19C **Iglesia del Salvador** is adorned with a magnificent Churrigueresque altarpiece (open Mon, Thu, Fri 11am–2pm, 4–6pm, Sat–Sun 11am–2pm; €4; ℘954 14 12 70). The 15C Gothic **Iglesia de Santa María la Mayor**★ is nearby. A monumental **Plateresque altarpiece**★ illustrates the Passion. The **Convento de las Descalzas**★ is a stunning example of 18C Sevillan Baroque. The Mudéjar church of the **Convento de Santa Clara** contains paintings by Valdés Leal.

The **Alcázar de Arriba** (Upper Fortress), a Roman structure, offers superb **views**★. It is now a Parador.

Necrópolis Romana★

Av. de Jorge Bonsor 9, Carmona.
♿Access to the Roman necropolis is indicated along the road to Sevilla. Open mid-Jun–mid-Sept Tue–Sun 9am–3pm. Apr–mid-Jun Tue–Sat 9am–8pm, Sun until 3pm. Mid-Sept–Mar Tue–Sat 9am–6pm, Sun & pub hols 9am–3pm. €1.50, no charge for EU citizens. ℘600 14 36 32. www.museosdeandalucia.es.

Of more than 300 1C tombs, mausoleums and crematoria, the most interesting are the large **Tumba del Elefante** and the huge **Tumba de Servilia**.

Aracena★

Aracena rises in tiers up a hillside, crowned by the remains of a Templars castle, its whitewashed houses adorned with ornate grilles. No trip to Aracena is complete without trying the exquisite **pata negra** cured ham.

👥 Gruta de las Maravillas (Cave of Wonders) ★★★

Pozo de la Nieve. Guided tours (45min) daily 10am–1.30pm, 3–6pm. Closed 24, 25, 31 Dec & 6 Jan. €14 child €13. Advance booking recommended. ℘663 93 78 76. www.aracena.es.

Rivers below the castle formed vast caves with limpid pools. Formations include draperies and pipes coloured by iron and copper oxide or brilliant white calcite crystal as in the **Salón de la Cristalería de Dios**★★ (God's Crystal Chamber). Here also is the **Museo del Jamón** (open daily 10.45am–2.30pm, 3.45–7pm; €3.50), a museum dedicated to Iberian pigs and their delicious ham.

Castillo e Iglesia del Mayor Dolor

Open daily Sept–Jun 10am–5.30pm; Jul–Aug 10am–7pm. No charge.

The castle was built in the 9C over an Almohad fortress. Note the decoration on the north side of the tower next to the church, similar to that of the Giralda in Sevilla.

Parque Natural de la Sierra de Aracena y Picos de Aroche★★

www.marcaparquenatural.com.
The cool forests of this park are punctuated by slender peaks and picturesque unspoiled villages such as whitewashed Alájar★, and Almonaster la Real★, concealed amid chestnut, eucalyptus, cork and holm oak, which has a rare intact mosque★ (open Sat–Sun and public holidays 11am–7pm). Nearby, Jabugo is justifiably famous for its delicious cured hams.

👤👤 Parque Minero de Riotinto★★

🚃 Nearest station La Palma del Condado 55km (Seville 86km). See website for schedule. €19, child €15, inc train rides and museum. 🖉959 59 00 25. www.parqueminroderiotinto.es.
The mining tradition of this area dates back to Antiquity. This fascinating park will not only explain its long history but also take you on a ride along a 19C line, built by the Río Tinto Company, through the spectacular open-cast Peña de Hierro mines of Corta Atalaya★★★ and Cerro Colorado★★. and to the source of the Río Tinto (the Red River) which gives this area its name. The refurbished House no 21, dating from 1895, gives you an idea of what daily life would have been like for the workers and managers (many of whom were British), at the mine.

ADDRESSES

🏨 STAY

Sevilla has a huge range of accommodation for visitors, but beware that during Holy Week and the Feria, prices are likely to double or even triple. If you're planning to stay in the city for these events, book well in advance and check the room rate carefully.

🛏🛏 Hotel Londres – San Pedro Mártir 1. 🖉954 212 896. www.hotel-londres-sevilla.com. 22 rooms. ⚏€12. This centrally located hotel has basic but tastefully furnished rooms, some with balconies overlooking the street.

🛏🛏 Reyes Catolicos –Gravina 57. 🖉954 21 12 00. www.hotelreyes catolicos.info. 29 rooms. ⚏€/. Restaurant 🛏🛏. Centrally located close to the Plaza de Armas and the Isla Mágica theme park. Well-equipped (somewhat characterless) rooms.

🛏🛏🛏🛏 Hotel Amadeus Sevilla & La Musica – Farnesio 6. 🖉954 50 14 43. www.hotelamadeussevilla.com. 30 rooms. ⚏€9. A family of musicians converted two typically Sevillan houses with courtyards in the heart of the Santa Cruz district into a delightful hotel, in which the décor enhances the buildings' original architectural features. There is a lovely roof terrace, a piano for guests and the hotel hosts concerts.

🛏🛏🛏🛏 Hotel Las Casas de la Judería – Callejón Dos Hermanas 7, Pl. de Santa María La Blanca. 🖉954 41 51 50. www. lascasasdelajuderiasevilla.com. 116 rooms. ⚏€15. Restaurant🛏🛏🛏🛏. Set in the city's old Jewish quarter, this elegant, traditional charming hotel is made up of 27 former houses, now dotted with Roman statues and pedestals, vases, jugs, antique and original furniture. Courtyards, gardens and a pool are its other delights.

🛏🛏🛏🛏 La Casa del Maestro – Niño Ricardo 5. 🖉954 50 00 07. www.lacasa delmaestro.com. 12 rooms. A delightful hotel, the Maestro is located in the birthplace of the famous flamenco guitarist Niño Ricardo (1904–72). A pleasant patio area and rooms decorated in yellow and earth red.

🛏🛏🛏🛏 Hotel Alfonso XIII – San Fernando 2. 🖉954 91 70 00. www. starwoodhotels.com. 151 rooms. ⚏€25. Built in 1928 in neo-Mudéjar style, the Alfonso XIII is Sevilla's most luxurious and famous hotel. An excellent location opposite the gardens of the Alcázar.

ARACENA

🛏🛏 Hotel Los Castaños – Av. de Huelva 5. 🖉959 12 63 00. www.los castanoshotel.com. 30 rooms. ⚏€4. This modern, three-storey Andalucían-style building is in the centre of town. Accommodation is functional, comfortable and well maintained. Some rooms face a large inner patio. The hotel also has a fine restaurant.

⌂/EAT

◒◒🍷 **Corral del Agua** – Callejón del Agua 6. 𝄞954 22 48 41. www.corraldel agua.es. Closed Sun. A pleasant, refreshing surprise awaits in this quiet, atmospheric alley. The terrace, with its abundant vegetation, is delightful in the heat of summer. Classic Andalucían cuisine.

◒◒🍷 **Az-Zait** – Plaza de San Lorenzo 1. 𝄞954 90 64 75. www.az-zait.es. Creative twists on Andalucian cuisine and an amazingly pocket-friendly tasting menu make Az-Zait a favourite with foodies in the city.

◒◒🍷🍷 **Taberna del Alabardero** – Zaragoza 20. 𝄞954 50 27 21. www. tabernadelalabardero.es. Closed Aug. This 19C mansion houses one of the best restaurants in Sevilla, a high-class hotel with a dozen or so rooms, a very pleasant tea room and the city's school of hotel management.

ARACENA

◒◒🍷 **José Vicente** – Av. Andalucía 53. 𝄞959 12 84 55. Call to check opening times. One of the best restaurants in the province where only fresh produce is served. The menu in this tastefully decorated restaurant includes local cep mushrooms and a range of cured ham and pork dishes.

TAPAS

Bar Europa – Siete Revueltas 35 (Pl. del Pan) 𝄞954 21 79 08. www.bareuropa. info. A traditional pub-like bar that has retained its Belle-Epoque feel. Popular with a young crowd early evening.

Bodeguita Romero – Harinas 10. 𝄞954 22 95 56. http://bodeguita-romero.com. Closed Sun pm, Mon and fortnight in Aug. This traditional family-run bar overflows with top quality tapas.

Bodega San José – Adriano 10. 𝄞954 22 41 05. Close to the Maestranza bullring, it's not surprising that this typical bodega with sawdust-covered floor is popular with aficionados of bullfighting and good fino sherry.

La Giralda – Mateos Gago 1. 𝄞954 22 82 50. Built into what was once a Moorish bath, this little bar near the cathedral serves unusual tapas.

El Rinconcillo – Gerona 40 y Alhóndiga 2. 𝄞954 22 31 83. www. elrinconcillo.es. Closed 3 weeks Jul–Aug. One of the oldest and most attractive bars in Sevilla; it dates back to 1670, the décor is mostly from the 19C.

CAFÉS

Confitería La Campana – Sierpes 1. 𝄞954 22 35 70. www.confiteriala campana.com. One of Sevilla's classic cafeterias. The Modernist décor creates a pleasant atmosphere in which to enjoy La Campana's famous pastries.

Horno San Buenaventura – Av. de la Constitución 16. 𝄞954 22 18 19. http://hornosanbuenaventura.com. Particularly popular because of its proximity to the Cathedral and its spacious lounge on the top floor. Its cakes are justifiably famous.

NIGHTLIFE

Casa Anselma – Pagos del Corro 49. 𝄞606 16 25 02. There's a bit of a secret, underground vibe to Casa Anselma, where live flamenco music raises the roof until the small hours. Arrive early if you want to bag a seat.

La Carbonería – Levíes 18 (Pl. de las Mercaderías). 𝄞954 56 37 49. www. levies18.com. One of Sevilla's institutions and key to the culture of the city's alternative crowd. Housed in a former coal warehouse, La Carbonería is split up into a number of different areas, where you can listen to a musical recital or to authentic flamenco. There are also art and photography exhibitions.

Paseo de las Delicias – This avenue is home to three buzzing music bars with terraces: Chile (http://barchile.es), Líbano (www.kioscolibano.com) and Bilindo (www.terrazabilindo.com).

ENTERTAINMENT

Casa Anselma – Pagés del Corro 49. 𝄞954 21 28 89. Spontaneous flamenco 11.30pm–4am. Anselma herself is the hostess, MC and occasional performer in this rollicking late-night tablao.

El Patio Sevillano – Pas. de Cristóbal Colón 11 A. 𝄞954 21 41 20. www. elpatiosevillano.com. A long-running flamenco club catering to aficionados of the art.

Tablao El Arenal – Rodó 7 (Arenal). ℘954 21 64 92. www.tablaoelarenal.com. Flamenco in its pure form.

SHOPPING

Antique lovers should wander the historic centre of the city, particularly the Santa Cruz district. The **Jueves** (Thursday) is a weekly small market held along Calle Feria. Sevilla has a rich arts and crafts tradition. Potters can still be found in the Santa Cruz and **Triana** districts (in the latter on calle Alfarería). The La Cartuja factory is heir to this tradition, which dates back to Roman times and the period of Moorish occupation of the city. Other products from Sevilla include inlaid woodwork, shawls, fans, wrought iron, harnesses, guitars and castanets.

Osuna★★

This elegant town in the Sevillan countryside retains a beautiful monumental centre★ from its past as a ducal seat of the house of Osuna, one of the most powerful on the Iberian Peninsula.

▶ **Population:** 17 801
⚲ **Michelin Map:** 578 U 14.
🇮 **Info:** Sevilla 37. ℘954 81 57 32. www.osuna.es.
◖ **Location:** Osuna rises to the south of the Guadalquivir Basin, near the A 92 highway linking Granada (160km/100mi E) with Sevilla. ▆▆Osuna.
◉ **Don't Miss:** Heritage buildings untouched by time.

TOWN CENTRE

Mainly around Pl. del Duque and Pl. España.

Osuna's streets are lined by numerous Baroque **mansion houses and palaces ★★**, whose massive wooden doors, darkly shining and copper nailed, reveal fine wrought-iron grilles and cool green patios. Of particular note are the **calle San Pedro★** (Cilla del Cabildo, Palacio de los Marqueses de la Gomera), the Antigua Audencia (former Law Courts), the Palacio de los Cepeda, the former Palacio de Puente Hermoso, several fine churches (Santo Domingo, la Compañía) and the **belfry of the Iglesia de la Merced★**, built by the same architect as the **Cilla del Cabildo.**

SIGHTS

Zona Monumental★
Follow signs to Centro Ciudad (town centre) and Zona Monumental.

Colegiata
(Museo de Arte Sacro)★
Pl. de la Encarnación. Open Tue–Sun 10am–1.30pm, 3.30–6.30pm (4–7pm May–Sept, closed Sun afternoon Jul & Aug). €3. ℘954 81 04 44. www.osuna.es.

This 16C Renaissance-style collegiate church houses five **paintings★★** by **José (Jusepe) de Ribera "El Españoleto"** (1591–1652), including *The Expiration of Christ*, in the side chapel off the Nave del Evangelio. The remainder are exhibited in the sacristy.

Panteón Ducal★★
(Ducal Pantheon)
The pantheon was built in Plateresque style in 1545 for the Dukes of Osuna. It is approached by a delightful patio. The chapel (1545) stands below the Colegiata's main altar and is crowned by a blue-and-gold polychrome coffered ceiling, now blackened by candle smoke. Another crypt, built in 1901, holds the tombs of the most important dukes. Nearby stand the 16C **former university** (Antigua Universidad) and the 17C **Monasterio de la Encarnación★** (cuesta de San Antón 15; open same hours as Colegiata; €2.50; ℘954 81 11 21, in which the highlight

Osuna with the Colegiata

© Stuart Black/age fotostock

is the magnificent **dado★** of 17C Sevillan *azulejos* in the patio. The nuns here produce and sell several types of delicious biscuits and pastries.

On the descent into the town centre, note the 12C–13C Torre del Agua, a former defensive tower now a small **archaeological museum** (Pl. de la Duquesa; open same hours as Colegiata; €2.50; ☏954 81 12 07).

EXCURSIONS

Écija★

▶ 34km/21mi N along the A 351.

The town lies in the Guadalquivir depression and is renowned for its lofty Baroque belfries decorated with ceramic tiles, such as the 18C **Torre de San Juan★** (Pl. de San Juan; park car in plaza de España; open Tue–Sat 10am–1pm, 4.30–5.30pm, Sun 10am–1pm; €2; www.turismoecija.com).

The **Ayuntamiento** (town hall) has two **Roman mosaic floors★** and a *camara obscura* that offers lovely and surprising perspectives of the city (Pl. de España 1; open daily 10am–1.30pm; €3; ☏955 90 02 40).

Écija has several delightful small squares, and houses adorned with decorative columns, coats of arms and charming patios. Along the streets adjoining avenida Miguel de Cervantes are several old palaces with fine **façades★**.

The 18C Baroque **Palacio de Benamejí** houses the tourist office and the Museo Histórico Municipal (Cánovas del Castillo; open Oct–May Tue–Fri 10am–1.30pm, 4.30–6.30pm, Sat 10am–2pm, 5.30–8pm, Sun and public holidays 10am–3pm; Jun–Sept Tue–Fri 10am–2.30pm, Sat 10am–2pm, 8–10pm, Sun and public holidays 10am–3pm; no charge; ☏954 83 04 31, http://museo.ecija.es). Note too the concave, fresco-adorned **Palacio de Peñaflor** (Emilio Castelar 26), its portal built on columns; and the Plateresque-style **Palacio de Valdehermoso** (Emilio Castelar 37).

Several churches are noteworthy. **Los Descalzos is** renowned for the exuberant decoration of its **interior★**.

Santa María (Pl. de Santa María; open Mon–Sat 9.30am–1.30pm, 5.30–8.30pm, Sun 9.30am–1.30pm; no charge; ☏954 83 04 30, www.iglesia-desantamaria.org), boasts an impressive tower.

The Convento de los Santísima Trinidad y Purísima Concepción, better known as "Las Marroquíes", also has a lofty **bell tower★**; its delicious *marroquíes* biscuits are produced and sold by the nuns.

The **Iglesia de Santiago★** retains the Mudéjar windows of an earlier building and a Gothic **retable★** at the high altar illustrating the Passion and the Resurrection.

The Iglesia de Santa Cruz houses the **Museo de Arte Sacro** (sacred art museum) with 16C-19C works. (Pl. Virgen del Valle; open Mon–Fri 9am–1pm, 4-7.30pm (Sat 5-7.30pm), Sun 10am–1pm 6–8pm; €4; ☏954 83 06 13; www.turismoecija.com).

Estepa★

◐ 25km/15mi E of Osuna. ▦Nearest station Huelva (52km).

The town gained unwanted fame as a result of the collective suicide of its inhabitants, in 206 BC, rather than be captured by the Roman army. In the 19C Washington Irving chronicled the *bandoleros*, both Spanish and Moorish, who plagued Estepa. Today it is a peaceful labyrinth of narrow streets and elegant mansions. The **Iglesia de Nuestra Señora del Carmen** is Estepa's best architectural site, while the Iglesia de San Sebastián and Palacio de los Marqueses de Cerverales are also examples of Andalucían rural architecture.

Cerro de San Cristóbal offers memorable panoramas of Estepa's towers, such as the **Torre de la Victoria★** rising from the plaza of the same name, and rolling countryside, *la campiña*, beyond.

Costa de la Luz★

The southwestern coast in the provinces of Huelva and Cádiz is edged with beaches interrupted by the mouths of major rivers – the Guadiana, Tinto and Guadalquivir. Several resorts are being developed beside the dazzling white sand and translucent skies that make this the Coast of Light.

◔ **Michelin Map:** 578 U 7-8-9-10, V 10, W 10-11, X 11-12-13 – Andalucía (Huelva, Cádiz)

▤ **Info:** El Puerto de Santa Maria: Palacio de Aranibar, Plaza del Castillo; ℘956 483 715. Huelva: Fernando El Católico, 14; ℘959 25 74 67. Sanlúcar de Barrameda: Calzada Duquesa Isabel; ℘956 36 61 10. Tarifa: Paseo de la Alameda; ℘956 68 09 93. www.andalucia.org.

◔ **Location:** From Ayamonte, at the mouth of the Guadiana,

🚗 DRIVING TOURS

THE HUELVA COAST★

Ayamonte to the Parque Nacional de Doñana – 135km/84mi. A low one day.

Ayamonte★

This fishing port at the mouth of the Guadiana is a lively border town of cobbled streets and whitewashed and brightly coloured houses. In the old quarter are the 16C colonial-style Iglesia de las Angustias, the Convento de San Francisco, with its elegant bell tower and magnificent *artesonado* work, and the 13C Iglesia del Salvador.

Boat service is available to Vila Real de Santo António in Portugal. Coastal resorts between Ayamonte and Huelva include **Isla Canela, Isla Cristina** (www. islacristina.org), **La Antilla** (www.lepe. es) and **Punta Umbría** (www.ayto-puntaumbria.es). This area also includes the marshland of the **Marismas del Río Piedras y Flecha de El Rompido★**, the Portil lagoon, and the Enebrales de Punta Umbría, a landscape dominated by juniper trees.

Huelva★

▦Huelva.

In the 15C and 16C, the estuary formed by the Tinto and Odiel rivers saw the departure of numerous expeditions to the New World, notably those led by Columbus. A large monument to these explorers, the **Monumento a Colón** (1929), stands near the harbour at Punta del Sebo.

In Huelva, see the unusual **Barrio Reina Victoria★**, an English-style district named after Queen Victoria; the **Cat-**

edral de La Merced (Pl. de la Merced; 959 24 30 36), with its Renaissance façade and sculpture of the Virgen de la Cinta, the town's patron saint, by Martínez Montañés; and paintings by Zurbarán in the Iglesia de la Concepción (Concepción) and the Museo de Huelva (Alameda Sundheim 13; open mid-Jun–mid-Sept Tue–Sun 9am–3pm; mid-Sept–mid-Jun Tue–Sat 9am–8pm, Sun 9am–3pm; €1.50, no charge EU citizens; 959 65 04 24, www.museos deandalucia.es).

Paraje Natural de las Marismas del Odiel★★
2km/1.2mi SE. Exit Huelva along Avenida Tomás Domínguez. Anastasio Senra Visitor Centre, Carretera del Dique Juan Carlos I. Book activities. 959 52 43 34/35.
www.juntadeandalucia.es.
This marshland (marisma) of outstanding beauty, at the mouth of the Tinto and Odiel rivers is a World Biosphere Reserve. It provides a habitat for over 200 bird species and can only be visited by boat.

La Rábida★
10km/6.2mi SE of Huelva off N 442.
Nearest station Huelva (10km).
In 1484, the Prior of the Monasterio de Santa María (Camino del Monasterio; open Nov–Mar Tue–Sat 10am–1pm, 4–6.15pm, Apr-Oct Tue-Sat 10am-1pm, 4-7pm. €3.50; 959 35 04 11, www. monasteriodelarabida.com), Juan Pérez, believed in Columbus and his claim that the world was round and acted as an intermediary to obtain the support of the Catholic Monarchs.

The church★ preserves old frescoes, wooden artesonado work and the delicate 14C alabaster statue of the Virgen de los Milagros★ (Virgin of Miracles), in front of which Columbus is said to have prayed prior to setting sail. A small room displays a mapamundi★, by Juan de la Cosa, which outlined the coast of America for the first time.

Full-scale replicas of Columbus' three caravels are moored at the Muelle de las Carabelas★ (open mid-Sept–mid-

Jun Tue–Sun 9.30am–7.30pm, mid-Jun–mid-Sept Tue–Sun 10am–9pm; €3.60; 959 53 05 97, www.andalucia.org), a modern dock and museum on the Tinto Estuary.

Palos de la Frontera★
13km/8mi SE of Huelva by A 5026.
Nearest station Huelva 13 km
This picturesque town on the left bank of the Río Tinto was the birthplace of the Pinzón brothers, who sailed with Columbus. The Casa-Museo de Martín Alonso Pinzón (open Mon–Fri 10am–2pm; €1; 959 10 00 41, www. andalucia.org) and the azulejos dotted around the town provide a reminder of the first voyage. The 15C Iglesia de San Jorge is fronted by an interesting Gothic-Mudéjar doorway.

Moguer★
20km/12.4mi NE of Huelva off A 494.
Expeditions left this tranquil town with its elegant houses for points unknown. The verses of Juan Ramón Jiménez (1881–1958), Moguer's most illustrious son and winner of the Nobel Prize for Literature in 1956, adorn azulejo panelling dotted around the town centre. His home is a museum, the Casa-Museo Juan Ramón Jiménez★ (Juán Ramón Jimenez 10; open by guided tour every hour, Tue–Sun 10am-2pm, also Tue–Sat 5–8pm; €3.50; 959 37 21 48, www. fundacion-jrj.es).

The town hall (ayuntamiento) has a fine Renaissance façade★. Head along the pedestrianised Calle Andalucía★, lined by interesting buildings, including the Archivo Histórico Municipal and Biblioteca Iberoamericana; and the 15C Convento de San Francisco, with its Mannerist cloisters, Baroque altarpiece and lofty belfry. The tower★ of the Iglesia de Nuestra Señora de la Granada recalls the Giralda in Sevilla.

Convento de Santa Clara★
Guided tours (40min) each hour Tue–Sat 10.30am–12.30pm and 5.30–6.30pm. Sun 10.30am, 11.30am. Closed public holidays. €3.50. 959 37 01 07.
www.monasteriodesantaclara.com.

The church of this Gothic-Mudéjar monastery houses the Renaissance-style marble **tombs of the Portocarrero family★**, noteworthy **tombs★** at the high altar, and some quite exceptional 14C **Nasrid-Mudéjar choir stalls★★**.

▶ Return to the C 442, which follows the coast.

Parque Nacional de Doñana★

🚉 Nearest station Huelva 64 km. El Acebuche visitor centre. Pl. Acebuchal, 22 El Rocío, Carretera A-483, km. 37,5; ✆959 43 96 27. www.magrama.gob.es/es/red-parques-nacionales/nuestros-parques/donana; www.donanavisitas.es.

At the crossroads of continents and of the Atlantic and the Mediterranean, the Doñana – Spain's largest wildlife reserve with a protected area of 73 000ha/180 387 acres – acts as a rest stop for African and European migratory birds. The **salt marshes** are the larger part of the park and are the ideal habitat for birds which migrate to Europe over the winter. **Sand dunes** are grouped in formation parallel to the Atlantic and advance inland at a rate of 6m/19.6ft per year. The stabilised sands or **cotos** are dry, undulating areas covered with heather, rockrose, rosemary and thyme, and trees such as cork oak and pine. The Doñana is home to lynx, wild boar, deer and a wide variety of birds, including Spanish imperial eagles, flamingos, herons, wild ducks and coots.

Because of the park's fragile ecology, entry to the **Doñana** is rigorously controlled. The El Acebuche visitor centre coordinates all park activities (book jeep tours in advance with Marismas del Rocío tours; two visits per day Tue–Sun at 8.30am and 3pm/5pm May–mid-Sept; €30,✆959 430 432). Itineraries vary according to the time of year.

Walking tours depart from the El Acebuche and other information centres, where details on the level of difficulty and duration are available. Excursions may also be available by horseback or horse-drawn carriage.

El Rocío

65km/40.4mi E of Huelva, along A 483.
This small village is famous as the site of the **Santuario de Nuestra Señora del Rocío** (Sanctuary of the Virgin of the Dew; ✆959 44 24 25), to which Spain's most popular religious pilgrimage *(romería)* is made during Whitsun weekend every year.

CÁDIZ COAST★

From Sanlúcar de Barrameda to Tarifa 160km/99.4mi. Allow one day.

Sanlúcar de Barrameda★

🚉 Nearest station El Puerto de Santa María 24km
The fishing port of Sanlúcar, at the mouth of the Guadalquivir, is the home town of *manzanilla*, a sherry matured like *fino* but which has a special salty flavour thanks to the sea air. The bodegas (wine cellars) are in the old quarter on the hill around the massive **Castillo de Santiago** (Cava de Castillo).
The **Iglesia de Nuestra Señora de la O** (Pl. de la Paz) close by has a fine Mudéjar **doorway★★** and a 16C **Mudéjar artesonado ceiling★**. The **Palacio de Orleans y Borbón** (Cuesta de Belén), a 19C palace built in neo-Moorish style, is now Sanlúcar's town hall, and home to the tourist office. Note its **covachas★**, a mysterious series of five ogee arches decorated with Gothic tracery. The lower town has two main churches: the **Iglesia de la Trinidad** (Pl. de San Roque), with its magnificent 15C Mudéjar **artesonado★★**; and the **Iglesia de Santo Domingo**, with the noble proportions of a Renaissance building.
The **Centro de Visitantes Fábrica de Hielo** (open daily 9am–7pm/later in summer; ✆956 38 65 77, www.juntade-andalucia.es), a visitor centre in an old ice factory, at Bajo de Guía, near the mouth of the Guadalquivir, provides information on the Parque Nacional de Doñana across the river. Park excursions also depart from here.

Rota

23km/14mi S of Sanlúcar off A 491.
The **old town★** inside the ramparts is laid out around the **Castillo de la Luna** (Avenida Mancomunidad Bajo Guadalquivir 3; ℘ 956 84 63 45) and the **Iglesia de Nuestra Señora de la O★** (Luis Vázquez 2; ℘956 81 00 84). Rota is known for beaches such as the **Playa de la Costilla★**. A large naval base is on the outskirts of the town.

El Puerto de Santa María★

℗See p544.
24km/15mi SE of Sanlúcar, off A 491.
El Puerto de Santa María.
This harbour town, in the bay of Cádiz, played a prominent role in early trade with the New World. Today, fishing, sherry exports and tourism drive the town's economy.

Cádiz★★ ℗See CÁDIZ, p541.

52km/32mi S of Sanlúcar.
South of Cádiz, there are good beaches at **La Barrosa★★**, Chiclana de la Frontera and **Conil de la Frontera** (**Playa de la Fontanilla** and **Playa de los Bateles**).

Vejer de la Frontera★

57km/35mi SE of Cádiz along E 5.
Nearest station Cadiz (57km).
Vejer, perched on a crag, is one of the prettiest white villages of Andalucía. The best approach is along the hillside road from the south.
The **Iglesia del Divino Salvador,** a mix of Romanesque and Gothic, has a three-aisle **interior★**. The road on to Tarifa runs through the Baetic foothills. The **Parque Natural La Breña y Marismas de Barbate★** (Barbate, Puerto Pesquero; ℘956 45 97 80, www.juntade-andalucia.es), has spectacular cliffs and picturesque coves, such as the **Cala de los Caños de Meca★★**, some 10km/6mi from Vejer.

Ruinas Romanas de Baelo Claudia★

Open Tue–Sun from 9am–6pm (Apr–mid-Jun until 8pm, mid-Jun–mid-Sept until 3pm). €1.50; no charge for EU citizens. ℘956 10 67 97.
www.andalucia.org.

The remains of the Roman city of Baelo Claudia date back to the 2C BC, when a salting factory specialising in the production of *garum* (a pungent sauce made from fermented fish) was established here. Vestiges of the basilica, forum and theatre are still visble.

Tarifa

105km/65mi S of Cádiz, along E 5.
Nearest station: Algeciras (23km).
Spain's breezy southernmost point is a major centre for windsurfing and kitesurfing.
The **Castillo de Guzmán el Bueno,** dominates the town. It was taken by the Christians in 1292, and commanded by Guzmán el Bueno who famously chose to accept the execution of his own sons, captured by the Moors, rather than surrender the town back to them.

ADDRESSES

STAY

 Hotel Convento de San Francisco – La Plazuela, Vejer de la Frontera. ℘956 45 10 01. www.tugasa.com. 25 rooms. Restaurant . This former convent dating from the 17C is situated in Vejer's old quarter. Although soberly decorated, the rooms are pleasant, with high ceilings and exposed beams. The hotel also has a good restaurant.

 Hotel Copacabana Tarifa Beach – Playa de Valdevaqueros Los Porro, 12 ℘956 681 709 www.copacabanatarifa.com. 26 rooms. Set on Valdevaqueros Beach, the hotel offers great views of the Moroccan coast and the dunes of Punta Paloma Beach. There is free Wi-Fi and all the brightly decorated rooms are air-conditioned and have flat-screen TV.

 Hotel Toruño – Pl. del Acebuchal 22, El Rocío. ℘959 44 23 23. www.toruno.es. 31 rooms. At the edge of Parque Nacional de Doñana, this traditional great house blends perfectly into the village of El Rocío. Some rooms have lovely marsh views and the hotel offers several Doñana exploration package. Beware, prices soar during the pilgrimage of El Rocio.

⊖⊖⊖⊖ **Posada de Palacio** – Caballeros 11 (Barrio Alto), Sanlúcar de Barrameda. ☏956 36 48 40. www.posadapalacio.com. 34 rooms. ⊇€6. This family-run hotel is in a lovely 18C mansion opposite the town hall in the upper section of Sanlúcar. The rooms, laid out around an attractive patio, are simply yet tastefully decorated.

⯊/ EAT

⊖⊖⊖ **Casa Bigote** – Bajo de Guía 10, Sanlúcar de Barrameda. ☏956 36 26 96. www.restaurantecasabigote.com. Closed Sun. This old tavern in the river district of Bajo Guía has become a gastronomic landmark. Run by the same family for the past 50 years. Pride of place on the extensive menu is given to local fish and prawns.

⊖⊖⊖ **Trafalgar** – Pl. de España 31, Vejer de la Frontera. ☏956 44 76 38. www.restaurantetrafalgar.com. Dishes and flavours of Andalucía are on the menu in this attractive contemporary-rustic restaurant.

⊖⊖⊖ **La Casona** – Pedro Cortes 6, Tarifa. ☏956 68 25 23. La Casona has an easy-going, family-friendly appeal but still serves up excellent Moroccan-Mediterranean raciones and tapas. If you have space, the house desserts are imaginative and fun.

Jerez de la Frontera★★

Jerez looks out at fertile countryside. A provincial capital, it springs into life at fiesta time, sharing its traditions of wine, horsemanship and flamenco.

THE CITY TODAY

Modern Jerez was built around 150 years ago on its Anglo-Spanish sherry wealth and retains its elegant, aristocratic, rather staid air. Relatively few visitors stay overnight but those that do can enjoy authentic flamenco (the town has a large *gitano* population) and may also like to seek out the lively bars just north of the Alcázar.

A BIT OF HISTORY

Jerez was one of the first towns to be founded by the Moors on the Iberian Peninsula. A number of vestiges remain from the Moorish "Sahrish", including sections of the old walls, the fortress *(alcazaba)* and a mosque. In 1264, Jerez was conquered by the troops of Alfonso X, and developed into a settlement of

- ▶ **Population:** 212 876
- ⚹ **Michelin Map:** 578 V 11.
- ⓘ **Info:** Pl. del Arenal, Edificio Los Arcos. ☏956 34 17 11. www.turismojerez.com.
- ⊙ **Location:** Jerez is in the Andalucían countryside, just 35km/22mi from the provincial capital Cádiz and 90km/56mi from Sevilla. ⇉Jerez de la Frontera. Train to city from Jerez airport 9mins
- ⊛ **Don't Miss:** A bodega tour.
- ◔ **Timing:** Take several hours to stroll around the town's historic quarters, stopping off at at least one bodega.

strategic importance as well as a leading commercial centre. The economic resurgence experienced by the province of Cádiz in the 18C left its mark on Jerez, with the construction of fine Baroque buildings and its famous wine cellars, some of which can still be seen today.

SIGHTS
Bodegas Domecq
Madre de Dios. Guided tours by arrangement. Reservation necessary. €6. ℘670 09 99 90. www.migueldomecq.com.
A visit to the oldest Jerez bodega includes storehouses where a host of celebrities have signed their names.

Bodegas González Byass (Tio Pepe)
Manuel María González 12. Guided tours in English Jun–Oct Mon–Sat noon, 1pm, 2pm, 5.15pm (Nov–May last visit at 5pm); Sun noon, 1pm and 2pm. Reserve online. From €15 (inc two wine tastings) . ℘902 44 00 77. www.bodegastiopepe.com.
The most famous storehouse is the spectacular La Concha bodega, designed by Gustave Eiffel in 1862.

Palacio del Tiempo★★
Cervantes 3. Open by guided tour, Mon–Fri 9.30am–1.15pm. Closed 24–25, 31 Dec. €6. ℘956 18 21 00. www.museosdelaatalaya.com.
This clock museum, housed in the 19C Palacete de la Atalaya, exhibits over 280 18–19C timepieces in perfect working order.

Real Escuela Andaluza del Arte Ecuestre★
Av. Duque de Abrantes. Guided tour (30min) including facilities and training sessions. See website for times of tours and shows. Closed public holidays. €11 for tours; show €21 or €27 (two front rows). ℘956 31 96 35. www.realescuela.org.
This foundation, set in a 19C mansion by Charles Garnier, is dedicated to

Santa María de Gracia	B
Palacio del Marqués de Bertemati	C
Museo Arqueológico	E
Palacio de Riquelme	F

JEREZ DE LA FRONTERA

equestrian arts, with two museums and includes the training of horses. A **show★★** in the arena is the highlight.

Museo Arqueológico de Jerez

Pl. del Mercado. Open mid-Sept–mid-Jun Tue–Fri 10am–2pm, 4–7pm, Sat–Sun and public holidays 10am–2pm; mid-Jun– mid-Sept Tue–Fri 9am–2.30pm. Sat Sun 10am–2.30pm €5, no charge first Sun of month. www.jerez.es.

The outstanding exhibit in the archaeological museum is a **Greek helmet★**.

✦✦ WALKING TOUR

THE OLD TOWN

Plaza del Mercado

The medieval market is now a tranquil square bordered by the **Palacio Riquelme**, with imposing Renaissance façade, the 15C **Iglesia de San Mateo**, and the **Museo Arqueológico**.

◗ Take Cabezas to the **Iglesia de San Lucas**, then Ánimas de Lucas, Plaza de Orbaneja and San Juan.

Iglesia de San Juan de los Caballeros★

Pl. de San Juan.

This medieval church has a magnificent 14C **polygonal apse★**, topped by a ribbed cupola with jagged decoration.

◗ Take Francos, then Canto to Plaza de Ponce de León.

Note the fine **Plateresque window★★** on one of the corners.

◗ Go along Juana de Dios Lacoste, cross Francos, then follow Compañía.

Iglesia de San Marcos

Pl. de San Marcos.

This late 15C church has a beautiful 16C **star vault**. The apse is hidden by a 16C polygonal **altarpiece★** showing strong Flemish influence.

◗ From the square, Tonería leads to Plaza de Plateros.

Plaza de Plateros

The **Torre de Atalaya**, a 15C tower, is adorned with Gothic windows.

◗ Head down José Luis Díez.

Plaza de la Asunción★

The Renaissance façade of the **Casa del Cabildo★★** (1575) is adorned with grotesque figures. The Gothic **Iglesia de San Dionisio** (℘956 34 29 40) shows Mudéjar influence.

◗ Continue along José Luis Díez.

Plaza del Arroyo

The **Palacio del Marqués de Bertemati★** has fine Baroque balconies.

◗ Continue on José Luis Díez and on to Plaza del Arroyo, turn left at del Encarnación, then right at Manuel María González.

Catedral★★

Pl. de la Encarnación. Open Mon–Sat 10am–6.30pm. €5. ℘956 16 90 59. www.catedraldejerez.es.

This monumental cathedral, with five aisles, combines Renaissance and Baroque features. The cupola bears basreliefs of the Evangelists. The annual wine harvest festival is held in front of the Cathedral.

◗ Return to Manuel María González and head NE. Turn right at Plaza Monti, left at Armas and right at Plaza del Arenal.

Alcázar★

Alameda Vieja. Open Jul–Sept Mon–Fri 10am–5.30pm, Sat–Sun 9.30am–2.30pm; Rest of year Mon–Sat 9.30am–2.30pm. Closed 1, 6 Jan, 25 Dec. €7 (inc camera obscura). ℘956 14 99 55. www.jerez.es. From this 12C Almohad fortress, enjoy an excellent **view★★** of the cathedral. Enter by the **Puerta de la Ciudad** (City Gateway). The prayer room in the

mosque★★, located within the walls of the Alcázar, is covered by a delightful **octagonal cupola**. A **camera obscura** in the **Palacio de Villavicencio** provides a unique view of Jerez via its mirrors and lenses.

◖ Head NE along Plaza del Arenal towards Caballeros, turn right at San Miguel and bear left towards the church.

Iglesia de San Miguel★★
Pl. de San Miguel.
Construction began in Gothic style in the late 16C; the Baroque tower dates from two centuries later.
The older San José façade is a fine example of the Hispano-Flemish style. The Renaissance **altarpiece★** is by Martínez Montañés.

EXCURSIONS
La Cartuja★
◖ Carrera de Jerez a Algeciras, 6km/3.5mi SE. Gardens and patio are open Tue–Sat 7am–7am. Closed public holidays. No charge. ☎956 15 64 65. www.turismojerez.com.
This Carthusian monastery, founded in 1477, has a Greco-Roman portal attributed to Andrés de Ribera. The Flamboyant Gothic church has a richly decorated Baroque **façade★★★**.

⚍⚍ La Cartuja Stud Farm★ (Yeguada de la Cartuja)
◖ At the Finca Fuente del Suero, 6.5km/4mi from Jerez on the Medina Sidonia road. Guided tours. Sat show (11am–1.30pm inc visit) €16– €22 adults, €10-16 kids. See website for dates, times and other prices. ☎956 16 28 09. www.yeguadacartuja.com.
In the 16C, the local Carthusian monastery crossed Andalucían, Neapolitan and German breeds, thereby creating the famous **Cartujana** breed. Visitors to this stud farm get a close look at their famous descendant.

ADDRESSES

🏠 STAY

⊝⊜⊜ **Serit** – Higueras 7. ☎956 34 07 00. www.hotelserit.com. 35 rooms. ⊑€7. A central family-run hotel, functional and up-to-date. Best rooms, in the annex, have wood floors and wrought-iron furniture.

⊝⊜⊜⊜ **Hotel Doña Blanca** – Bodegas 11. ☎956 34 87 61. www. hoteldonablanca.com. 30 rooms. ⊑€7. This unpretentious hotel in an attractive Andalucían-style building has a perfect central location. Bedrooms are spacious with all the usual comforts.

♀/EAT

⊝⊜ **Atuvera** – Ramon de Cala 13. ☎675 54 85 84. www. atuvera. apartamentosjerez.com. Just off Plaza Arenal, Atuvera is a calm haven in the centre of the city. In summer tables spill out into the street and groan with beautifully plated tapas and local craft beers.

⊝⊜⊜ **La Taberna Flamenca** – Angostillo de Santiago 3. ☎956 32 36 93. www.latabernaflamenca.com. Reservations advised. This restaurant in an ex-wine storehouse offers meals with a tablao flamenco performance.

TAPAS
Juanito – Pescadería Vieja 8–10. ☎956 33 48 38. www.bar-juanito.com. Closed during Jerez fair. This Jerez classic in a pedestrianised street lined with outdoor terraces, has been serving its huge choice of tapas for over 50 years. The décor could not be more Andalucían, with its ceramic tiles and bullfighting-inspired pictures.

NIGHTLIFE
Bereber – Cabezas 10. ☎605 94 75 77. Reservations recommended. Bereber, in a Moorish palace, is the obligatory night-time stopping-point. Its spaces (café, bar, patios, dance floors in wine cellars and restaurant with flamenco) are variously decorated in impeccable Arabian and Andalucían style.

ENTERTAINMENT

The **Teatro Villamarta** (Pl. Romero Martínez; ✆956 14 96 85; www.jerez.es) offers opera, music, dance and theatre, including flamenco. The city's best-known flamenco clubs (peñas flamencas) are the **Peña Tío José de Paula** (Merced 11; ✆956 32 01 96), and the popular **Peña el Garbanzo** (Santa Clara 9; ✆956 33 76 67).

LEISURE

Baños Árabes Hammam Andalusí – Salvador 6. ✆956 34 90 66. www.hammamandalusi.com. Baths 10am–10pm in 2hr sessions (reservation essential). From €24. These re-created Moorish baths transport visitors to other times. The terrace and tea house look out to the Cathedral.

FIESTAS

Horses are as important as sherry in Jerez. In **early May** there are racing, dressage and carriage competitions at the **Feria del Caballo** (Horse Fair). www.jerez.es/especiales/feria.

In **September** the **Fiesta de la Vendimia** (Wine Harvest Festival) showcases a cavalcade and a flamenco festival;

Cante Jondo (literally deep song, actually a flamenco gypsy style of singing) is alive and kicking in Jerez, a town which is home to such famous singers as **Antonio Chacón** (1869–1929) and **Manuel Torres (1878–1933)**.

Cádiz★★

Surrounded by water on three sides, Cádiz has attracted mariners for over 3 000 years. It is also one of Andalucía's most delightful provincial capitals, with charming squares, narrow alleyways and a quiet air, broken only by the exuberant Carnival, the best on the Iberian Peninsula.

THE CITY TODAY

Despite its location and the fine beaches on either side of the town, Cádiz has never embraced costa-style tourism. In summer Spanish holidaymakers and, to a lesser degree, cruise ship day trippers make up most of its visitors. At other times of year its fishing and shipbuilding ports make it a hive of activity with all nationalities passing through, adding a dash of colour to the cobbled streets, and custom to the many excellent fish restaurants of its old town.

A BIT OF HISTORY

Oldest city in Europe – Cádiz was founded by the Phoenicians in 1100 BC. It was conquered by the Romans

- ▶ **Population:** 120 468
- ⚲ **Michelin Map:** 578 W 11.
- ▤ **Info:** Paseo de Canalejas. ✆956 241 001. www.cadizturismo.com.
- ◖ **Location:** This coastal city is positioned with the Atlantic to the south and west, the Bahía de Cádiz to the north and east. ▭Cádiz (AVE).
- ▣ **Parking:** It's difficult in the old quarter.
- ☺ **Don't Miss:** A wander within the walls.

in 206 BC, and in turn by the Visigoths and Moors. Alfonso X reconquered the city in 1262. During the 16C, Cádiz was attacked by English corsairs, and partially destroyed by the Earl of Essex in 1596.

In the 18C, Cádiz became a great port. **Constitution of Cádiz** – During the French siege of 1812, patriots convened the Cortes which promulgated Spain's first liberal constitution.

Watchtowers – Between the 16C and 18C, merchants in Cádiz built over 160 towers to watch over the arrival and departure of their ships.

SIGHTS

Iglesia de Santa Cruz (Catedral Vieja)★

Pl. Fray Féliz. Open Tue–Fri 9.45am–12.45pm, 5.30–7pm (5.30–6.30pm Sat); Sun 10am–12.30pm, 5.30–6.30pm. No charge. 𝒫956 28 77 04. www.turismo.cadiz.es.

The old cathedral was rebuilt following the sacking by the Earl of Essex in 1596. Robust Tuscan columns define spaces. The church museum (**Museo Catedralicio**) is alongside in the (&see Sights).

Museo y Archivos Catedralicio★

Pl. Fray Félix. Open daily 10am–4pm. €5, includes entry to Catedral Nueva. 𝒫956 28 66 20. www.catedraldecadiz.com.

Alongside the old cathedral, in the Casa de la Contaduría, with a fine 16C **Mudéjar patio★** , this museum holds liturgical objects and art, including the 16C **Custodia del Cogollo★**, a gold-plated monstrance attributed to Enrique Arfe, and the 18C **Custodia del Millón**.

Catedral Nueva★★

Pl. de la Catedral. Open Mon–Sat 10am–7pm, Sun 2-7pm. €5, includes entry to Museo Catedralico and Torre de Reloj. 𝒫956 28 61 54. www.catedraldecadiz.com.

Work on the new cathedral began in 1722 and lasted over a century. The result is Baroque in character with the occasional Neoclassical feature. The **façade★** is flanked by two lofty towers. The triple-aisle interior is surprisingly light and spacious. The crypt holds the remains of the composer **Manuel de Falla** (1876–1946). You can also ascend the cathedral Torre de Poniente tower.

Oratorio de la Santa Cueva★

Rosario. Open Tue–Sat 10.30am–2pm and Tue–Fri Jul-Aug 5.30–8.30pm Sept–Jun 4.30–8pm; Sun 10am–1pm year round. €3. 𝒫956 22 22 62.

www.turismo.cadiz.es.
Three **canvases★★** in this elliptical oratory were painted by Goya in 1795.

Museo de Cádiz★

Pl. de Mina. Open mid-Jun–mid-Sept Tue–Sun 9am–3pm, mid-Sept–mid-Jun Tue–Sat 9am–8pm, Sun 9am–3pm. Closed 1 & 6 Jan, 1 May, 24–25 & 31 Dec. €1.50, no charge for EU citizens. 𝒫856 105 023. www.museosdeandalucia.es.

The city's museum is in a small mid-19C Neoclassical palace. The collection includes vases, oil lamps and jewellery, including two 5C BC Greek **anthropoidal sarcophagi★★** based on Egyptian models. Paintings include nine **panels★** by Zurbarán from the Carthusian monastery in Jerez.

Torre Tavira★

Marqués del Real Tesoro 10. Open daily May–Sept 10am–8pm, Oct–Apr until 6pm. €6. 𝒫956 21 29 10. www.torretavira.com.

This 18C watchtower houses the very first **camera obscura** in Spain.

Oratorio de San Felipe Neri

Santa Inés. Open: Oratorio: Tue–Sat 10am–2pm, Tue–Fri 4.30–8pm, Sun 10am–1pm. Interpretation Centre: Tue–Sun 11am–1.45pm. €3 for oratorio. 𝒫956 807 018. www.turismo.cadiz.es.

In this elliptical Baroque church the Cortes proclaimed the liberal Constitution of Cádiz in 1812. The **Immaculate Conception** was painted by Murillo in 1680 shortly before his death.

Museo de las Cortes de Cádiz

Open Tue–Fri 9am–6pm, Sat–Sun 9am–2pm. Closed public holidays. No charge. 𝒫956 22 17 88. www.turismo.cadiz.es.

The museum's main exhibit is a **model★** of Cádiz in the reign of Charles III.

Playa de la Caleta★

Could this charming beach facing the ocean have been the site of the first Phoenician landing in the 11C BC? In any case, this was Cádiz's natural port for many years. The location is very

Cádiz viewed from Catedral Nueva

pleasant, with a small spa protected from Atlantic by the long breakwater leading out to the **Castillo de San Sebastián**. The other extremity of the beach ends in the **Castillo de Santa Catalina** where, in season, there are musical performances (Paseo Antonio Burgos s/n; open daily Mar–Oct 11am–8.30pm, Nov–Feb until 7pm; no charge; ℘956 226 333; www.turismo.cadiz.es).

WALKING TOUR

AROUND SANTA MARÍA AND THE PÓPULO DISTRICT

Plaza de San Juan de Dios
This 16C square is the most popular in the city. On one side stands the Neoclassical façade of the 1799 **town hall** (ayuntamiento), by Torcuato Benjumeda, beside the Baroque tower of the Iglesia de San Juan de Dios. The tourist office is in an attractive Neoclassical building.

▶ Take Sopranis, to the left of the Iglesia de San Juan de Dios.

Calle Sopranis
The street contains some of the best Baroque civil architecture in Cádiz, particularly the houses at nos. 9, 10 and 17. At the end of the street note the 19C iron-and-brick former **tobacco**

factory, and the **Convento de Santo Domingo** (open daily 10am–1pm, 6.30–9.30pm; no charge; www.turismo.cadiz.es).

▶ Continue along Plocia as far as Concepción Arenal.

Cárcel Real★
Concepción Arenal.
The 1792 royal jail, by Torcuato Benjumeda, is one of the most important Baroque civil buildings in Andalucía. The façade with triumphal-arch entry bears the escutcheon of the monarchy. It houses the city's law courts.

The Battle of Trafalgar

On 21 October 1805, Admiral de Villeneuve sailed out of Cádiz harbour with his Franco-Spanish fleet to confront the English under Nelson off the Cabo de Trafalgar headland. The ships were ill equipped and poorly manned; after some heroic combat Villeneuve's fleet was destroyed and he was taken prisoner. Nelson had been mortally wounded during the course of the battle but England's supremacy at sea was established.

The Order of Alcántara

The Knights of San Juan de Pereiro became the Order of Alcántara when entrusted with the defence of the town in 1218. Like the other great orders of chivalry in Spain its aim was to free the country from the Moors. Each order, founded as a military unit under the command of a master, lived in a community under Cistercian rule. These religious militias, always prepared for combat and capable of withstanding long sieges, played a major role in the Reconquest.

Iglesia de Santa María
Santa María.
The spire on the belfry of this 17C Mannerist church is adorned with *azulejos*.

◖ Continue along Santa María, past the 18C Casa Lasquetty to the left; cross Félix Soto towards the 13C Arco de los Blancos.

Casa del Almirante
Pl. de San Martín. Closed to the public.
The outstanding feature of this 17C Baroque palace is the double-section Italian marble **doorway★★**.

Iglesia de Santa Cruz (Catedral Vieja)★ and Catedral★★ (◖see above)

FROM PLAZA SAN JUAN DE DIOS TO THE CATHEDRAL

◖ Follow Nueva to Pl. San Juan de Dios. Turn left into Cristóbal Colón.

Casa de las Cadenas
This Baroque mansion has a Genoese marble **doorway★**.

◖ Continue along calles Cristóbal Colón and Cobos to Pl. de la Candelaria; return to Nueva. Past Pl. de San Agustín, take Rosario, to the Oratorio de la Santa Cueva (◖see Sights).

Plaza de San Francisco
This charming plaza, under the Baroque tower of the Iglesia de San Francisco, is lined by lively bars and cafés.

Plaza de Mina★★
Once the kitchen garden of the Convento de San Francisco, this verdant square is imbued with a colonial feel. Fine examples of Isabelline buildings around the square include the **Museo de Cádiz** (◖see Sights).

◖ Head down de San José to the Oratorio de San Felipe Neri. The oratory stands alongside the Museo de las Cortes de Cádiz (◖see Sights).

Hospital de Mujeres★
Hospital de Mujeres. Open only Fri 9am–1.30pm due to restoration. No charge. ✆956 22 36 47. www.turismo.cadiz.es.
This Baroque building is planned around two patios linked by an extraordinary Imperial-style **stairway★★**. The Vía Crucis in the patio is created from 18C Triana *azulejos*.

◖ Continue to the Torre Tavira (◖see Sights) on Sacramento.

Plaza de las Flores
Flower and plant stalls, cafés and shops contribute to the delightful atmosphere in one of the city's liveliest squares.

◖ Return to Pl. de la Catedral.

EXCURSIONS
El Puerto de Santa María
🚃El Puerto de Santa María.
On the northern shore of the bay facing Cádiz (23km/14mi), El Puerto de Santa María is heavily frequented by tourists but pleasant in the off-season. Christopher Columbus set sail twice from the docks of El Puerto de Santa

María, and the town subsequently prospered with the commerce from the American colonies. One of Jerez's sherry capitals, it is also known for its bullfights. The old part of town is on the west bank of the Guadalete river, known as **La Ribera del Marisco** (seafood coast). Avenida de la Bejamar runs along the river and borders the old quarter.

Fiestas and Festivals

The *corridas* (bullfights) held here are among the most important in Andalucía, staged in an arena dating from 1880 with a capacity for up to 15 000 spectators (on the southwest edge of town). *Corridas* are usually held on Sundays, in summer, and during the spring festival in April ($\wp$ 902 15 78 70; €25–60).

Plaza de las Galeras Reales

At the edge of the Guadalete on the spot where royal galleys used to dock, stands this bustling square. Restaurant seating spills out around the square, and Calle Luna, the main shopping street, leads to the Tourist Office and Plaza de España.

Iglesia Mayor Prioral

Plaza de España. Open Mon–Fri 10am–12.30pm, 5–7.30pm, Sat 10am–12pm, 6–7.30pm, Sun 8.30am–1.45pm, 6.30–9pm. €1. $\wp$ 956 85 17 16. www.iglesiamayorialelpuerto.com.
Consecrated in 1493, completed a few years later and rebuilt many times since then, this church stands next to Plaza de España. The **Portada del Sol** (17C), with both Plateresque and Baroque elements is the church's main treasure.

Fundación Rafael Alberti

Calle Santo Domingo, 25. Open mid Sep–Jun Tue-Fri 10am-2pm, Sat-Sun 11am-2pm, Jul-mid Sep open Tue-Fri see website for opening hours, Sat-Sun 11am-2pm. €4. $\wp$ 956 85 07 11. www.rafaelalberti.es.
Painter, poet and communist, Rafael Alberti (1902–99) was born in this house. He was part of the literary "generation of 1927", a movement that included, among others, Federico García Lorca and the Machado brothers, Antonio and Miguel. Alberti's alphabet work, unifying poetry and calligraphy, is on display here, demonstrating his commitment to the cause of social justice throughout Spain's turbulent 20C.

Castillo de San Marcos★

This castle was built by Alfonso X on the site of a mosque, of which the *mihrab* is still visible. The conquering Christians enlarged the building, converting it to a fortified church. The castle attained its full size in the 15C.

Las Bodegas

The *bodegas* (wineries) are almost all open to the public by guided tour (usually Mon–Sat), with prior booking. All finish with a tasting. For more information on visiting, call the bodega directly or enquire at the tourist office.
Bodega Barbadillo (Luis de Eguilaz 11; Open daily 10am-3pm; $\wp$ 956 38 55 11, www.barbadillo.com) is the perfect place to try a glass of the delicious local manzanilla sherry.
Bodega Osborne (Bodega de Mora, Calle Los Moros; call for schedule and prices; $\wp$ 956 86 91 00, www.bodegas-osborne.com) is famous for its black bull silhouette found along highways all over Spain. Originally created in order to elude a ban on roadside billboards these iconic figures have become so cherished they have been classified, and protected, as national monuments.

San Fernando

◗ 9km/5.5mi SE along the CA 33. $\wp$ 956 94 42 26.
This town has been a naval base since the 18C. The main monuments – the town hall, Iglesia del Carmen and Museo Histórico Municipal – all have Royal *(Real)* grants. The main civil building is the Neoclassical **Real Instituto y Observatorio de la Armada** (Cecilio Pujazón; guided tours (1hr); $\wp$ 956 545 099; from 1753.

Medina Sidonia★

▶ 44km/27mi E on CA 33, A 48 and
A 390. Calle San Juan. ☎956 41 24 04.
www.medinasidonia.es.

The **Iglesia Mayor Santa María la Cor-
onada★** (Pl. de la Iglesia Mayor); a 15C
Gothic church, holds an exquisite Plateresque **altarpiece★** by Juan Bautista
Vázquez el Viejo. The **Torre de Doña
Blanca**, a tower next to the church, provides access to the remains of the alcázar
and the old quarter, with its 16C houses.
The descent to the modern town passes
under the Arco de la Pastora, to reach
the **Conjunto Arqueológico Romano**,
a Roman complex with 30m/98ft of
underground galleries from the 1C AD.
(Espíritu Santo 3; Open 10.30am–2pm,
5.30–7.30pm (Apr–Jun 8pm; Jul–Oct
5–9.30pm); €4; ☎956 41 24 04). The
cardo maximus was the main street in
Roman days. On the Plaza de España lies
the 18C Neoclassical **town hall**.

ADDRESSES

🏠 STAY

🛏🍽🛁 **Hostal Fantoni** – Flamenco 5.
☎956 28 27 04. www.hostalfantoni.es 12
rooms. Closed Dec–mid-Feb. No breakfast.
Pleasant hostal in the centre of town.
Request a room with a (smart ensuite)
bathroom facing the pedestrianised lane.

🛏🍽🛁 **Hospedería Las Cortes de Cádiz**
– San Francisco 9. ☎956 22 04 89. www.
hotellascortes.com. 36 rooms. ⌑8.25.
Rooms in this 19C home in the old
quarter are well equipped, set around
a covered patio individually decorated,
and dedicated to a local event or
personality. Attractive outside areas.

🛏🍽🛁🛁 **Hotel de Francia y París** –
Pl. de San Francisco 6. ☎956 21 23 19.
www.hotelfrancia.com. 57 rooms. ⌑€6.
An early 20C hotel with pleasant rooms
fronting an attractive small square in the
centre of the city.

🍴 EAT

🛏🍽🛁 **El Faro** – San Félix 15. ☎902 21
10 68. www.elfarodecadiz.com. This fine
50-year old family-run restaurant-tapas
bar offers a cosy traditional interior and
a menu that emphasises local fare.

TAPAS

Aurelio – Zorrilla 1. ☎956 04 64 46.
Closed Mon in Aug–Jun. This popular
seafood bar is one of *the* places for
tapas in Cádiz. Get there early; it is small
so soon fills up. A good central location.
Casa Manteca – Corralón de los
Carros 66. ☎956 21 36 03. Closed Mon.
Possibly the most rustic Andalucían
tavern in the city, serving Ibérico ham or
sausage on wax paper where your tally
is chalked up on low wooden counters.
Ultramar&Nos – Enrique de Las Marinas
2. ☎856 07 69 46. www.ultramarynos.
com. A fish lover's heaven, as the
name suggests. Classic tapas and
contemporary dishes such as ceviche.

BARS / CAFÉS

Café de Levante – Rosario 35. ☎956 22
02 27. www.cafedelevantecadiz.com. A
quiet café with tasteful modern décor
on one of the old quarter's most typical
streets. Its relaxed atmosphere attracts
an eclectic, arty crowd.
La Cava – Antonio López 16. ☎956
21 18 66. www.flamencolacava.com.
Closed Jan–Feb. Show and drink €22
(shows Apr–Nov Tue, Thu & Sat 9.30pm).
Cosy tavern offers authentic flamenco
interpreted by young artists.

FESTIVALS

Carnaval de Cádiz – www.carnavalde
cadiz.com. Early Feb. This Carnival on
the week before Ash Wednesday, is
without doubt the most famous and
lively in Spain. It is famed for uniformed
chirigotas (comedy groups), and poet-
dramatic *comparsas*.

NIGHTLIFE

Gran Teatro Falla – Pl. Falla. ☎956
22 08 34. Named after the composer
Manuel de Falla (1876–1946), this theatre
organises events throughout the year.
The city's **cultural centres** – El Palillero
(Pl. Palillero; ☎956 22 65 16), **El Bidón**
(Alcalde Juan de Dios Molina 23; ☎956
26 15 02), and **Sala Central La Lechera**
(Pl. Argüelles 2; ☎956 22 06 28) host a
wide range of exhibitions, workshops
etc, as well as flamenco concerts at the
Baluarte de la Candelaria (Alameda
Marqués de Comillas; ☎956 808 472).

Upper Rock of Gibraltar

Gibraltar★

One of the last outposts of the British Empire and a self-governing British Overseas Territory, the towering bulk of Gibraltar is impressive and distinctive, visible for miles. For many visitors, the first contact with Gibraltar is likely to be the unusual experience of driving across an aircraft landing strip, to cross into the territory!

▸ **Population:** 29 436
◔ **Michelin Map:** 578 X 13.
▯ **Info:** 13 John Mackintosh Square. ☎+350 200 45000; www.visitgibraltar.gi.
◖ **Location:** The SW tip of Spain, 24km/15mi from North Africa. ▭ Nearest station San Roque-La Linea 15km.
⊛ **Don't Miss:** Top of the Rock.
▲▲ **Kids:** The Apes' Den; dolphin spotting.

A BIT OF GEOGRAPHY

The **Rock of Gibraltar★** is a gigantic monolith of Jurassic limestone which forms a craggy promontory connected with mainland Spain to the north and stretching south into the Strait. It covers an area of about 6.5km/2.5sq mi (4.5km/3mi long and 1.4km/0.9mi at its widest), rising to 423m/1 388ft at its highest point, Mount Misery.
The east face of the Rock drops sheer into the sea, while the less steep west face has been partially reclaimed at the water's edge and forms the site of the town.

A BIT OF HISTORY

Archaeological discoveries on Gibraltar testify to 100 000 years of human occupation, by Carthaginians, Phoenicians and even Neanderthal Man.

The Rock of Gibraltar, considered by the Ancient Greeks to be one of the **Pillars of Hercules**, was transformed into an Islamic citadel after the Moors invaded under **Tarik-ibn-Zeyad** in AD 711. Jebel Tarik (Tarik's Mountain, hence Gibraltar) was the site of a castle, now in ruins but still known as the Moorish Castle.
Gibraltar was recaptured by Spain on 20 August 1462. During the War of Spanish Succession, Anglo-Dutch naval forces, under **Admiral Rooke**, captured the Rock in 1704. Gibraltar was ceded to Britain in the Treaty of Utrecht in 1713. The citadel guarding the Strait of Gibraltar has remained in British hands ever since. In the **Great Siege of 1779–83**, the garrison heroically resisted Spanish

and French efforts to starve or bomb them into submission. The old city of Gibraltar was destroyed, but the Rock lived up to its reputation of being impregnable. Gibraltar became a British Crown Colony in 1830.

In 1967, Gibraltar's inhabitants voted resoundingly to retain their connection with Britain, by 12 138 votes to 44, in a referendum. In 1969, Spain closed the border and maintained a blockade until 1985. Even today it is still not unusual for Spanish customs to delay vehicles. With its people descended from a variety of races, religions and cultures, their identity shaped by years of resisting sieges, Gibraltar is an excellent example of a harmonious, multicultural society. The territory is a free port and trade is based on transit and refuelling; the economy is based on financial services and tourism.

The naval and commercial ports, as well as the town with its mixture of English- and Spanish-style houses, pubs and shops, lie against the west face of the Rock. Numerous examples of Moorish architecture are still to be found, notably in the cathedral which has the ground plan of a mosque.

SIGHTS
Tour of the Rock★

Open daily 9.30am–5.45pm. Cable car daily 9.30am–7.15pm (Nov–Mar 5.15pm). Tickets include return trip and Nature Reserve (includes Apes' Den, Great Siege Tunnels, St Michael's Cave and Moorish Castle) €22 adult (€13.50 child). ✆350 200 12700. www.gibraltarinfo.gi. www.gibraltartaxiassociation.com (official Rock Tour by taxi).

The Top of the Rock can be reached on foot, by cable car and in official tour vehicles (✆ private cars are not allowed on the Upper Rock). Go down Queensway and follow the signs to Upper Rock, a **nature reserve** and home to a number of Gibraltar's most interesting historical sites. The road leads first to **St Michael's Cave★**, (www.gibraltarinfo.gi) once inhabited by Neolithic man, which features beautifully illuminated stalactites and stalagmites. From here, it is possible to walk to the Top of the Rock (1hr there and back), from where there are excellent **views★★** of both sides of the rock and of the Spanish and North African coasts.

The road continues to the **Apes' Den** 👥, home of the famous Barbary Apes. Don't miss the fascinating story of the **Great Siege Tunnels★**, excavated in 1779 to mount guns on the north face of the Rock, creating a defence system still impressive for its ingenuity. A military heritage centre is housed in Princess Caroline's Battery. Finally there are the ancient ruins of the **Moorish Castle** and the northern defences dominating the hillside.

Barbary Apes

The origin of the apes, one of Gibraltar's best-known attractions, is unknown. Legend has it that British rule will last as long as the apes remain in residence on the Rock. When it looked as if they might become extinct in 1942, Churchill sent a signal ordering reinforcements. The ape colony has since flourished – there are currently some 300 of them. They are renowned for their charm and highly inquisitive natures. The apes, in reality tailless monkeys, are the mascots of the Gibraltar Regiment.

©David Stanley/iStockphoto.com

PRACTICALITIES

Customs and other formalities:
Gibraltar is a British Crown Colony.
The border is open 24hr a day.
Visitors must be in possession of
a valid passport. Holders of UK
passports and citizens of other EU
countries do not need a visa. Other
nationalities should check visa
requirements with a British consulate,
high commission, or embassy.
Gibraltar is a VAT-free shopping area.

Travel and accommodation:
There are daily scheduled flights
from London Heathrow, Gatwick,
Luton and Manchester, and a daily
ferry service to Tangier, Morocco
(www.directferries.co.uk). Regular
flights also operate to and from
Málaga and Jerez. There are many
hotels but no campsites.

Money matters: The currency is the
Gibraltar pound, on a par with sterling.

The Euro and credit cards are widely
accepted.

Language: The official language
spoken on the Rock is English, but
most people speak some Spanish.

Time: Gibraltar is on European time
(one hour ahead of GMT).

Motoring: Driving is on the right.
Drivers must have a current licence,
vehicle registration documents,
evidence of insurance and
nationality plates.

Telephoning: The international code
for Gibraltar is 350 (from Spain, omit
this and dial 9567 before the five-digit
local number).

Tourist information: Tourist
information in the UK is available
from: Gibraltar Government Office,
150 Strand, London WC2R 1JA. ✆0207
836 0777. www.visitgibraltar.gi.

Gibraltar Museum

18/20 Bomb House Lane. Open Mon–Fri
10am–6pm, Sat 10am–2pm (last entry
30min before closing). £5. ✆350 200
74289. www.gibmuseum.gi.

This museum contains extensive collections on local military and natural history. It also houses the well-preserved
Moorish Baths.

The **Alameda Gardens** display interesting and exotic plants, including Canary
Islands dragon trees, cacti, succulents
and Mediterranean vegetation. Gibraltar is home to some 600 species of
flowering plant, which flourish in the
subtropical climate, including a few
unique to the Rock, such as its national
flower, the Gibraltar Candytuft.

If you are interested in seeing more
examples of Gibraltar's plant and bird
life, take the **Mediterranean Steps**,
leading from Jew's Gate (good view of
the other Pillar of Hercules and Jebel
Musa in Morocco) round the south of
the Rock and up the east face of the
Rock to the summit, which make a
rewarding walk (⬥3hr from Jew's Gate,
steep in parts; wear good boots).

STRAITS OF GIBRALTAR

Michelin map 578 X 1, Gibraltar: British
Overseas Territory. The A 7 motorway
links the southernmost part of Spain to
the Costa del Sol.

The Straits, the gateway to the Mediterranean and a mere 14km/9mi wide,
have always played a strategic role in
the region. The Bay of Algeciras is surrounded by Algeciras and La Línea de
la Concepción, and the British outpost
of Gibraltar.

TOURING THE STRAITS

Fourteen species of cetaceans – whales,
dolphins and porpoises – are to be
found in the Straits so **whale- and
dolphin-watching cruises** 👥 are
consequently very popular, sailing from
Gibraltar, Algeciras, La Línea and Tarifa.
Reputable operators include Dolphin
Safari (✆350 200 71914, http://dol-
phinsafari.gi), Turmares Tarifa (✆956
68 07 41; www.turmares.com) and
Whale Watch (✆670 79 66 50; www.
whalewatchtarifa.net). The probability
of seeing these beautiful creatures is
90–95 per cent and some operators will

Mountains in Morocco across the Straits of Gibraltar viewed from near Tarifa

refund your money in the unlikely event of a "no-show".

While boats for larger groups may provide underwater viewing areas, small fast boats provide more thrills as they race along with the dolphins swimming in their wake and criss-crossing the bows. The 21km/13mi of road linking Tarifa to Algeciras provides stunning views★★★ of the North African coast. The best viewpoint is at the Mirador del Estrecho, 8km/5mi from Tarifa.

Tarifa
See COSTA DE LA LUZ

Algeciras
Arabs arrived in al-Yazirat-al-jadra (Green Island, now joined to the mainland) in 711 and remained until 1344.

Neanderthal Man or Gibraltar Woman?

Eight years before the discovery in 1856 of a 60 000-year-old skeleton in the Neander Tal (Valley), east of Düsseldorf, Germany, a skull of the same age, thought to be that of a woman, was discovered on Gibraltar. However, delays in publicising the Gibraltar findings meant that Gibraltar Woman didn't gain the fame of Neanderthal Man.

The Bahía de Algeciras is a safe anchorage and strategic vantage point overlooking the Straits.

Algeciras is Spain's busiest passenger port with crossings to Tangier and **Ceuta** several times a day. The main sights of interest are the plaza Alta, the hub of the town, fronted by two churches: the 18C **Iglesia de Nuestra Señora de la Palma**, and the Baroque Iglesia de Nuestra Señora de la Aurora, and the **Museo Municipal** (Ortega y Gasset; open late Oct–Mar Mon–Fri 9am–2pm, 5–7pm; Sat 10am–2pm; Apr–late Oct Mon–Fri 9am–2pm; closed public holidays; no charge; ℘956 57 06 72; www.andalucia.org), displaying interesting exhibits on the **Siege of Algeciras** (1342–44).

ACROSS THE STRAITS
Ceuta
Michelin map 742 folds 5 and 10 – North Africa. Population 84 263.
Trasmediterránea operates services between Algeciras and Ceuta (also Algeciras and Tangier). Journey time: 40min. ℘902 45 46 45. www.trasmediterranea.es.

Ceuta occupies a strategic position, dominating the Straits of Gibraltar. With its European architecture, it is situated on a narrow isthmus on the coast of North Africa. The closest African port to Europe, Ceuta was conquered by the Portuguese in 1415, and passed to Spain in 1580.

Museo del Revellín

Pas. de Revellín 30. Open Tue–Sat
11am 2pm, 5–9pm. Public holidays
11am–2pm. No charge. ℘956 511 770.
www.ceuta.es/museos.
This museum houses a white marble
Roman sarcophagus, Punic and Roman
amphorae, a collection of coins and old
weapons and ceramic ware.

Parque Marítimo del Mediterráneo

Compañía del Mar. Open daily
11am–8.30pm except Thu Sept–May.
€2–6, price varies by day and time.
℘956 51 74 91. www.ceutasi.com.
Palm trees, exotic plants, swimming
pools, lakes, waterfalls and sculptures
have all been perfectly integrated by
the great Lanzarote landscape artist,
César Manrique, to create this spectacular leisure park on 56ha/138 acres
facing the sea. Several restaurants, a
nightclub and a casino operate inside
the fort which dominates the park.
A cinema complex is in the Poblado
Marinero.
Other places of interest are the Iglesia
de Nuestra Señora de África (Church
of Our Lady of Africa; Pl. de África;
℘956 51 17 23), housing the statue
of the town's patron saint, the 18C
Catedral (Pl. de África; open Tue–Sun
9am–1.30pm, 6.15–7.15pm; ℘956 51 77
71) and Foso de San Felipe (open daily
11am–7pm; ℘956 51 17 70), a Portuguese fort where San Juan de Dios, the
founder of the Order of the Hospitallers
of St John, worked in 1530.

Monte Hacho★

Best visited in the morning.
Calle Independencia and Calle Recin-
tor Sur, parallel to the seafront, lead to
the foot of Monte Hacho, which has a
citadel at its summit. The corniche road
encircling the peninsula offers beautiful
views of the Western Rif coastline to
the south and the Spanish coast and the
Rock of Gibraltar to the north.

▶ Before reaching the lighthouse
(no entry), bear left.

Ermita de San Antonio

♿ Leave your car in the car park.
The wide flight of steps leads to a
charming square fronted by the 16C
Capilla de San Antonio (Chapel of St
Anthony). The imposing Fortaleza
de Hacho (ctra. de circunvalación del
Monte Hacho; guided tours available
by booking beforehand; ℘956 51 16
21) stands atop a hill nearby.
From here there is a magnificent
view★★ of the town, port and coastline.

ADDRESSES

🛏 STAY

⊖ **Emile Youth Hostel** – 25 Line
Wall Road. ℘350 200 51106. www.
emilehostel.net. In the heart of Gibraltar
100m/110yd from Casemates Square,
this 42-bed hostel is arranged in single,
double and triple rooms. Great value.

⊖⊖ **Cannon Hotel** – 9 Cannon Lane.
℘350 200 51711 www.cannonhotel.gi.
18 rooms. This intimate hotel is a central
location is a cosy hideaway. Price inc.
full English breakfast.

⊖⊖⊖⊖ **Hotel Bristol** – 8 Cathedral
Square. ℘350 200 76800. www.bristol
hotel.gi. 60 rooms. ⊑£6. With a pool
and a subtropical garden, the Bristol is a
breath of fresh air in this busy enclave.

🍴 EAT

⊖ **The Venture Inn** – 2 Lynch's Lane,
Gibraltar. ℘350 200 75776. Irish pub
and sports bar serving traditional British
and Irish food such as fish and chips.

⊖⊖⊖ **Cafe Rojo** – 54 Irish Town.
℘+350 200 51738. Stylish restaurant
serving modern Mediterranean cuisine.
Try the chicken stuffed with goats'
cheese and spinach with tomato sauce.

⊖⊖⊖⊖ **Parador de Ceuta** –
Pl. Nuestra Señora de África 15, Ceuta
℘956 51 49 40. www.parador.es. A
good place to pause during your visit,
an attractive dining area with lush
tropical plants and exposed beams.
The cooking is Andaucían with Arab
influences.

The Canary Islands

The Canary Islands – seven in total with six smaller isles – lie between 100km/62mi and 300km/186.4mi off the northwest coast of North Africa. Ferries and inter-island flights connect the islands, though (unlike in Greece) there is no "island-hopping" culture. They provide visitors with many contrasts: from exuberant vegetation to desert landscapes; steep cliffs to endless beaches; picturesque villages to over-commercialised resorts. All this, coupled with a fantastic climate, has turned the Canaries into one of the world's leading holiday destinations, particularly during the European winter.

Highlights

1 Exploring the **Parque Nacional del Teide** on Tenerife (p553)
2 An evening stroll along the Paseo Cornisa, **Las Palmas** (p561)
3 The early morning sun on the **Playa de las Canteras** (p564)
4 Getting lost in the sand dunes of **Maspalomas beach** (p567)
5 Hiking the **Valle de Hermigua** on the island of La Gomera (p574)

Volcanic creation

The islands were thrust up from the Atlantic seabed by volcanic eruptions. La Gomera and Gran Canaria have a conic silhouette and most of the islands are hilly and end in steep cliffs. Crowning Tenerife, Pico del Teide at 3 718m/ 12 195ft is the highest point in Spain. La Palma rises to 2 426m/7 959ft and because of its relatively small area is said to be the steepest island in the world. It features the world's largest *caldera* (volcanic crater) too. Here, as elsewhere in the archipelago, lava, slag fields and cinder cones form what is known as *malpaís*, most extensive and most spectacular on Lanzarote where huge areas resemble a moonscape. The Spanish Conquistadores found a native Stone Age population known as the **Guanches**, who lived in caves, practised trepanning and mummified their dead. The Guanches had little answer to the invaders and were decimated, not least as a result of common illnesses introduced inadvertently by the Spaniards, to which they had no natural resistance. By the end of the century the islands were taken and most Guanches were either dead or had assimilated into the new order.

The Fortunate Islands

Ancient mariners nicknamed the archipelago The Fortunate Islands on account of their year-round mild climate and the coastal temperature rarely drops below 18°C/65°F. The climate varies, however, between the north and south of the larger islands, most notably on Tenerife and Gran Canaria. This has encouraged sun-and-fun resorts (such as Playa de las Américas and Playa del Inglés) to develop in the south, which remains sun-kissed almost all year round. By contrast, the northern coasts of Tenerife and Gran Canaria respectively can be (relatively) chilly and wet in winter and as a result have been less commercialised for the holiday trade.

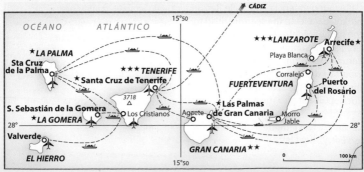

Tenerife★★★

The snow-capped silhouette of El Teide, the highest peak in Spain, is the symbol of this beautiful island; Tenerife meant "snow-covered mountain" in Guanche. At its foot, the spectacular Las Cañadas crater is witness to Tenerife's violent volcanic past. Year-round sun draws package tourists and youngsters to the man-made resorts of the parched south, while natural beauty attracts other visitors north.

▶ **Population:** 889 936

Info: Santa Cruz de Tenerife: Plaza de España. ☎922 892 903; Puerto de la Cruz: Puerto Viejo. ☎922 38 60 00. www.webtenerife.co.uk.

◐ **Location:** Tenerife is the largest of the Canary Islands, with an area of 2 036sq km/786sq mi.

Kids: Loro Parque, Lago Martiánez, Siam Park, Parque Ecológico de las Aguilas del Teide, Aqualand.

PICO DEL TEIDE★★★

Clouds often enshroud Mount Teide and the superb panoramas from its viewpoints.

☺ Wear comfortable footwear and a warm jacket. Weather can change dramatically in a short time.

La Esperanza Approach★

The road climbs to the crest which divides the island.

Pinar de la Esperanza★

The road runs for several miles through this extensive pinewood. In a clearing at **Las Raíces**, an obelisk commemorates the rebellion in July 1936 against the Republican government by Francisco Franco, who was stationed here.

Miradores★★

When the cloud disperses, admire the stark contrast between the lush north coast and the aridity of the Güimar Valley from the roadside belvederes. After La Crucita, the road enters a high-mountain landscape. The Astronomical Observatory at Izaña is visible (left).

El Portillo

Alt 2 030m/6 660ft. This pass is the gateway to the extraordinary geological world of the Las Cañadas crater.

Parque Nacional del Teide★★★

There are two visitor centres (both open daily 9am–4pm; ☎922 35 60 00;

GETTING TO THE CANARY ISLANDS

BY PLANE – Each island has an airport (Tenerife has two), offering easy, rapid access to the Spanish mainland and the rest of Europe. Several inter-island routes operate throughout the year. The hub airports are on **Tenerife** and **Gran Canaria.** www.aena-aero puertos.es. **Iberia** (☎901 111 500, www.iberia.com); **easyJet** (www.easyjet.com); **Air Europa** (☎971 57 55 27, www.air-europa.com) and **Vueling** (☎807 300 745, www.vueling.com)

fly to the islands from the mainland; **Binter Canarias** operate inter-island flights (☎902 39 13 92, www.binter canarias.com).

BY FERRY – From mainland Spain, a two-day boat trip leaves from Cádiz and travels to Santa Cruz de Tenerife and Las Palmas de Gran Canaria. Ferry, jet-foil and hydrofoil services also travel between the islands, though distances, cost and timetables do not encourage "island-hopping". **Trasmediterránea** ☎902 45 46 45, www.trasmediterranea.es.

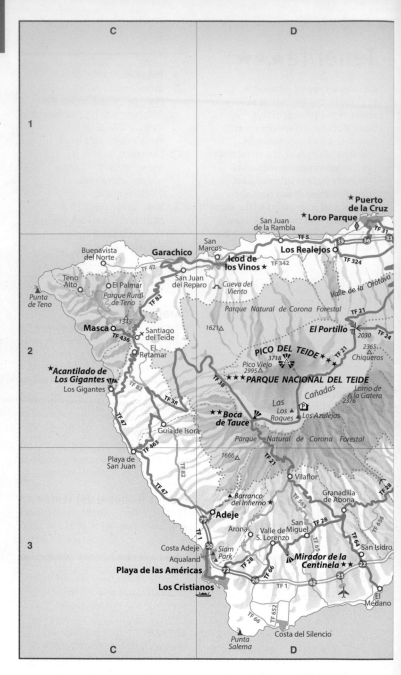

www.webtenerife.com); the El Portillo Centre has exhibits on volcanism,
and trail information, the geology of
the park and its flora and fauna; the
Cañada Blanca Visitor Centre (next to
the Parador, currently under renovation)
features a recreation of a volcanic tube

and explains the formation of the park
with interactive exhibits.
About 350m/1 150ft below the summit
lies Las Cañadas plateau, a spectacular crater, over 2 000m/6 560ft across,
which imploded before El Teide was created. The peak rises from its northern

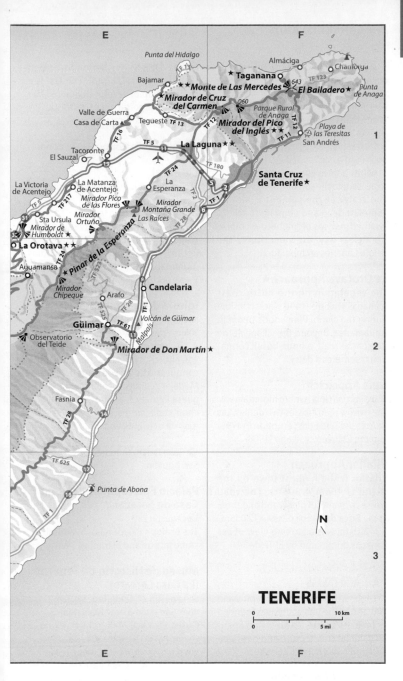

TENERIFE

Scale:
0 — 10 km
0 — 5 mi

side. In the centre of the park, opposite the parador, are **Los Roques**, a spectacular outcrop of lava boulders, laid bare by erosion. Another geological feature is **Los Azulejos**, spectacularly flecked boulders covered with copper oxide, which glint blue-green in the sun.

Pico del Teide★★★

⛰ Ascent by **cable car** from La Rambleta (2 356m/7 728ft); not suitable for those with respiratory or heart problems (the cable car climbs 1 199m/3 932ft in 10min). Operates daily 9am–4pm, weather permitting. Closed

1 Jan, 25 Dec. €27 round-trip (bought online). ☎922 01 04 45. www.volcanoteide.com.

⚡ If you intend to walk to the very top (along the Telesfero Bravo path) you need to apply for a permit (no charge) at www.reservasparquesnacionales.es. Book in advance. From the top (3 555m/ 11 660ft), a steep 30min walk across scree leads to the summit).

The crater at the summit is almost 25m/82ft deep and 50m/164ft across, swathed in wisps of sulphurous smoke. On a clear day, the view covers the whole Canaries archipelago.

La Orotava Approach★

The vegetation on the north coast (bananas, fruit trees and vines) is visible during the climb. Pinewoods begin in **Aguamansa**. Beyond the village at the side of the road, a huge basalt formation resembles a daisy.

Guía Approach

The climb via Guía is more mountainous. The narrow road crosses two defiles, Las Narices del Teide (last eruption in 1798) and the Chinyero volcano (1909).

Vilaflor Approach

Vilaflor is the highest town on the island (1 466m/4 806ft). The road crosses a beautiful pinewood and then, at the **Boca de Tauce pass★★** (2 055m/ 6 742ft), reveals a striking view of Las Cañadas dominated by El Teide.

(SAN CRISTÓBAL DE) LA LAGUNA★

La Laguna, the former island capital and now seat of the university, was founded in 1496. Its centre features fine Spanish colonial architecture and has been declared a World Heritage site.

Plaza del Adelantado

Fronting this pleasant, tree-lined square are the old **Convent of Santa Catalina**, which retains its original upper gallery, a feature rarely seen nowadays; the 17C **Palacio de Nava** with stone façade, reminiscent of the Bishop's Palace, and the **ayuntamiento**, with its Neoclassical

façade (Obispo Rey Redondo 1; open Mon–Fri 10am–1.30pm). The last is a combination of several buildings. The 16C and 18C portals on calle Obispo Rey Redondo are impressive.

▷ Follow calle Obispo Rey Redondo.

Catedral

Pl. Fray Albino. Closed for restoration. ☎902 00 31 21.

The elegant Neoclassical façade was erected in 1819; the nave and four aisles were rebuilt in neo-Gothic style in 1905. In the Capilla de los Remedios (right transept), note the retable, a 16C Virgin and 17C Flemish panels.

Iglesia de la Concepción★

Pl. Doctor Olivera. Open daily 10am–5pm. €3. ☎922 25 91 30.

A 17C grey stone tower rises over this 16C church, typical of the time of the conquest. The interior retains several Mudéjar ceilings, a ceiling with Portuguese influence, a Baroque pulpit and choir stalls, and a beaten silver altar (Capilla del Santísimo).

▷ Take Belén, then head down San Agustín.

Palacio Episcopal or Antigua Casa de Salazar

San Agustín 28.

The Bishop's Palace has a beautiful 17C stone façade and attractive patio.

Museo de Historia de Tenerife (La Casa Lercaro)

San Agustín 22. Open Tue–Sat 9am– 8pm. Sun–Mon & hols 10am–5pm. Closed 1 & 6 Jan, 24–25, 31 Dec. €5; no charge Fri–Sat 4–8pm. ☎922 82 59 49. www.museosdetenerife.org.

In the late-16C **Casa Lercaro**, with its fine patio, exhibits provide an overview of the island's history from the 15C.

SANTA CRUZ DE TENERIFE★

The capital began as a port serving La Laguna. An oil refinery, tobacco factory and other industries operate here. From the harbour breakwater there is

© W. G. Allgoewer/Blickwinkel/age fotostock

Las Cañadas and the Pico del Teide

a **view**★ of the stepped semicircle of high-rise buildings against the backdrop of the Pico del Teide.

The Guimera Theatre – the oldest theatre in the Canaries inaugurated in 1851 – and the stunning, space-age Auditorio de Tenerife, designed by Santiago Calatrava, witness the city's strong cultural tradition.

Santa Cruz is also famous for its **Carnival** (last week in Feb), arguably the most colourful and certainly the largest in all Spain.

Iglesia de la Concepción

Tomás Pérez. Open daily 9am–1pm, 4.30–8pm. No charge. ✆922 33 01 87.
A few houses with balconies around this 16C–18C church (fine Baroque retables) are all that remains of the old city.

Museo de la Naturaleza y el Hombre★ (Museum of Nature and Man)

Fuente Morales. Open Tue–Sat 9am–8pm. Sun–Mon & hols 10am–5pm. Closed 1 & 6 Jan, Carnival Tue, 24–25, 31 Dec. €5; no charge Fri–Sat 4–8pm. ✆922 53 58 16. www.museosdetenerife.org.
The old Hospital Civil, a large Neoclassical building, now houses archaeology and natural science collections.

Palacio de Carta

Pl. de la Candelaria.
This 18C palace on Plaza de la Candelaria, now a bank, retains its delightful wooden arches, galleries and patio.

Iglesia de San Francisco

San Francisco 13. Open for Mass. ✆922 24 45 62.
This 17C–18C church is typical of Canarian churches from this era: naves with wooden roofs and cylindrical pillars.

Parque Municipal García Sanabria★

This alluring tropical and Mediterranean garden is a respite from the often busy city centre.

Centro de Interpretación Castillo de San Cristóbal

Pl. de España. Open Mon–Sat 10am–6pm. No charge. ✆922 28 56 05. www.museosdetenerife.org.
Nelson lost both the battle and his right arm when attacking this castle on 24 July 1797. The star exhibit is the cannon ("El Tigre") that repulsed him.

👥 Parque Marítimo César Manrique★

Avenida Constitución 5. Open daily 10am–6pm. €2.50 adults, €1.50 kids. ✆922 22 93 68.
www.maritimosantacruz.com.
This superb lido, designed by the late great Lanzarote artist, César Manrique, combines water, volcanic rock and island vegetation to great effect.

PUERTO DE LA CRUZ★

Puerto de la Cruz is the principal resort on the north coast, boasting black beaches and first-class visitor attractions. It attracts an older clientele than the south but is still lively, particularly at Carnival time. The old town, between the Plaza de la Iglesia and Plaza del Charco, features many attractive 17C and 18C balconied houses and, unlike the other resorts on the island, has a genuine Canarian atmosphere. Just east of town the **Mirador de Humboldt★★★** offers a magnificent view of the town and the verdant sweep of the **Orotava Valley** running down to the sea from the slopes of mighty Mount Teide.

▲▲ Costa Martiánez★

Av. de Colon. Open daily 10am–5pm. Closed fortnight in May. €3.50, child €1.20. ℘922 37 05 72. www.ociocostamartianez.com.
This beautifully designed landmark lido (also known as the Lido or Lago Martiánez), famous for its fountains, is another example of the work of César Manrique, using vernacular architectures and local natural features to maximum visual effect. The **Casino Taoro** is located within the Costa Martiánez complex.

Playa Jardín★

This black-sand beach is surrounded by gardens designed by César Manrique. The **Castillo de San Felipe** (℘922 38 36 63), a watchtower now used for cultural functions, can be seen at its eastern end.

▲▲ Loro Parque (Parrot Park)★

Avda Loro Parque. Open year-round daily 8.30am–6.45pm; last admission at 4pm. €35; child (6-11yrs) €24; combined ticket with Siam Park €58/€39.50. ℘922 37 38 41. www.loroparque.com.
Originally just a bird park, this is now one of the finest animal and marine theme parks in the world outside Florida, and is the island's most popular destination after Mount Teide. It features a world-class dolphinarium, a killer whale show, sea lions, a penguinarium, a large aquarium, tigers, gorillas, chimps and one of the world's finest collections of birds, all set in beautiful grounds. Kinderlandia is a mini-African theme park for little ones.

LA OROTAVA★★

This ancient town is arranged in terraces at the foot of Mount Teide. It boasts elegant balconied mansions and is famous for its Corpus Christi festival.

Plaza de la Constitución

The square is fronted by the 17C Baroque church of San Agustín and the Liceo Taoro cultural centre.

Iglesia de la Concepción

Tomás Pérez. Open daily 9am–1pm, 4.30–8pm. No charge. ℘922 33 01 87.
The 18C church has a graceful Baroque façade. Visit the treasury.

Calle de San Francisco★

This street is adorned with some of the most beautiful balconied houses on the island.

La Casa de los Balcones y del Turista

San Francisco 3 & 4. *Casa de los Balcones (no. 3):* open daily 8.30am–6.30pm; *Casa del Turista (no. 4):* open daily 9am–6.30pm. €2 (museum). ℘922 33 06 29. www.casa-balcones.com.
These two adjacent 17C houses feature delightful patios, a handicraft shop and a small museum which shows the inside of a local bourgeois house

Museo de Artesanía Iberoamericana

Tomás Zerolo 34. Open Mon–Fri 10am–3pm, 5–7pm, Sat 9am–1pm . €2. ℘922 334 013. www.artenerife.com.
Set in the ex-Convento de San Benito Abad (17C) this displays Spanish and Latin-American handicrafts.

Jardín de Aclimatación de la Orotava★★

Retama 2. Open daily Apr–Sept 9am–7pm; Oct–Mar 9am–6pm. Closed 1 Jan, Good Fri, 24 & 25 Dec. €3. ℘922 922 981. www.icia.es.
This 2ha/5-acre botanical garden, created in the 18C, contains trees and flowers from the Canary Islands and elsewhere, some of which are over 200 years old.

EXCURSIONS
MONTE DE LAS MERCEDES★★

⊙ Round trip of 49km/30mi from La Laguna. Allow 3hr.

The Anaga headland traps clouds from the north; tree laurel, giant heather and *fayas*, a local species, flourish.

Mirador de Cruz del Carmen★

See the La Laguna Valley from this viewpoint in the Parque Rural de Anaga (Cruz del Carmen visitor centre open daily 9.30am–3pm (4pm winter); ℘922 63 35 76).

Mirador del Pico del Inglés★★

A marvellous panorama spreads from the 1 024m/3 360ft peak of the Anaga headland to distant Pico del Teide.

El Bailadero★

The road crossing this pass commands good views in both directions.

Taganana★

On the way down to this coastal village are magnificent **views★★**. Visit the **Iglesia parroquial de Nuestra Señora de Las Nieves** for its Hispano-Flemish altarpiece (Pl. de la Virgen de las Nieves; open 10am–7pm; no visits during religious services; ℘922 59 01 86).

Icod de los Vinos

⊙ On the north coast of the island, 60km/37mi W of Santa Cruz de Tenerife via the TF 5.

The heart and hub of Tenerife's wine district, the peaceful town of Icod de los Vinos, 26km/16mi west of Puerto de la Cruz, is a patchwork of charming squares surrounded by elegant colonial houses with their characteristic Canarian pine balconies. The Casa Museo del Vino (Plaza de la Pila 4) offers Canary Island wines and cheese tasting.

The most famous feature of the village is its 3 000-year-old **Dragon Tree**, towering 17m/57ft over the shore. The *Dracaeno draco* or dragon tree is the official symbol of the Canary Islands; the Guanche civilization worshipped these trees as sources of wisdom and fertility, using the sap, which turns red on contact with the air, in healing ceremonies.

🚗 DRIVING TOUR

TOUR OF THE ISLAND
310km/194mi.
⟳See pp554–555 for map.

Garachico

Set on a picturesque stretch of rocky coast with natural pools, Garachico was the finest harbour on the north coast until in 1706 when the lava slick, clearly visible today, destroyed the old town. Its elegant 16C Castillo de San Miguel (Avenida de Tomé Cano; open for temporary exhibitions; €1; ℘922 83 00 00) was the most notable survivor and is now home to a museum. The Iglesia de San Francisco also dates from the 16C, while the 17C Convento de Santo Domingo houses a museum of contemporary art.

Masca

This remote hamlet is well worth the detour, set in lovely **countryside★** where the houses are set on narrow ridges which plunge down into a verdant valley of dramatic rock formations.

Los Gigantes★

The Teno mountain range ends in black cliffs called Los Gigantes, "the giants", for their 400m/1 300ft vertical drop.

Adeje

Close to the village lies the **Barranco del Infierno (Hell Canyon)★** which is justifiably popular with walkers.

Playa de las Américas

This large sprawling man-made resort is the most popular destination on the island. It features beaches of black sand, several family attractions on its outskirts, and a raucous nightlife. Neighbouring **Los Cristianos** is a busy port (ferries depart to La Gomera; www.fredolsen.es), which has been subsumed into the tourist sprawl.

▶ Follow the TF 28 in the Valle de San Lorenzo.

Mirador de la Centinela★
Like a sentinel, the viewpoint on a rocky projection commands a vast area.

▶ Return to the inland road.

Mirador de Don Martín★
The belvedere provides a view of the Güimar rift valley and its plantations.

Güimar
A major town near the east coast.

Candelaria
This coastal town is a well-known place of pilgrimage. Its **basílica** (Pl. de la Basílica; ☎922 50 01 00) houses a statue of the Virgin to which islanders make a pilgrimage on 14 and 15 August.

ADDRESSES

🛏 STAY

Hotel Monopol – Quintana 15, Puerto de la Cruz. ☎922 38 46 11. www.monopoltf.com. 92 rooms. Restaurant. This attractive four-storey whitewashed building adorned with wooden balconies stands in a pedestrianised street in a lively shopping district near the seafront. Comfortable rooms, arranged around a Canarian-style patio.

Finca Salamanca – Ctra. Puertito, Sureste 1.5km/1mi Güimar. ☎922 51 45 30. www.hotel-finca salamanca.com. 20 rooms. Restaurant. Set among the avocado trees of a former plantation estate, this Hotel Rural offers comfortable lodging in various buildings and in different kinds of room.

Hotel Aguere – Obispo Rey Redondo (Calle Carrera) 55, La Laguna. ☎922 31 40 36. www.hotelaguere.es. 23 rooms. One of the few hotels on the island to retain its seigniorial charm. The wooden door provides access to a large, patio-style open hall area around which are all the rooms. The wooden floors, antique furniture and somewhat antiquated bathrooms provide further old-world charm. Highly recommended.

Hotel Rural Victoria – Hermano Apolinar 8, La Orotava. ☎922 33 16 83. www.hotelruralvictoria.com. 14 rooms. Restaurant. A traditional balconied Canarian country house with country cooking to match.

Senderos de Abona – La Iglesia 5, Granadilla de Abona. ☎922 77 02 00. 17 rooms. Restaurant. This Hotel Rural has a country-living atmosphere, with serene patios, gardens and swimming pool. Friendly polite staff.

Hotel San Roque – Esteban de Ponte 32, Garachico. ☎922 13 34 35. www.hotelsanroque.com. 32 rooms. Restaurant. This luxury desgner-boutique hotel is tucked away in a quiet street in the centre of Garachico. It combines traditional Canarian design with contemporary style, fittings and all mod cons.

🍽 EAT

Totem – Av. Jose Antonio Tavio 4. ☎922 78 58 49. A cosy, if slightly kitsch, interior. Big, hearty portions of crowd-pleasers including fresh pizzas, pastas and jugs of sangria. Perfect for families.

Régulo – San Felipe 16, Puerto de la Cruz. ☎922 38 45 06. www.restauranteregulo.com. Closed Sun, Mon lunch, fortnights in Jun and Jul. This traditional island house retains all its charm, with a lovely patio and dining areas on two floor. Antiques and plants are prominent in the décor.

Solana – Pérez de Rozas 15, Santa Cruz de Tenerife. ☎922 24 37 80. www.solanarestaurante.es. Closed Sun, Mon, Aug 7–31. Minimalist décor and contemporary cooking using top-quality local products.

Los Limoneros – Los Naranjeros, Crtra General del Norte 447, Tacoronte. ☎922 63 66 37. Closed Sun dinner. One of the area's established favourites offers Spanish dishes made with local produce.

Gran Canaria★★

Gran Canaria is often described as a continent in miniature on account of its many diverse landscapes. Almost half of its area is a UNESCO Biosphere Reserve. From the Pozo de las Nieves (1 949m/6 393ft) at its centre, ravines fan out in all directions. The mountain barrier divides the wetter landscapes of the north and west from extensive semi-desert-like areas in the south. The north and west coast are steep and rocky; on the accessible south coast are long golden sand beaches and throbbing man-made resorts.

▶ **Population:** 851 157
▤ **Info:** Las Palmas: Parque de Santa Catalina. ℘928 44 68 24; Playa del Inglés: Avenida España (CC Yumbo). ℘928 77 15 50. www.grancanaria.com.
◖ **Location:** Gran Canaria, the third-largest Canary Island (area: 560sq km/602sq mi), is wedged between Tenerife and Fuerteventura.

LAS PALMAS DE GRAN CANARIA★

Las Palmas de Gran Canaria, founded in a palm grove in 1478, is nowadays the biggest city in the Canaries and also one of Spain's major ports. It was the most fashionable resort on the island for many decades but over the past 20 years or so it has lost its position to the burgeoning resorts of the sunnier south. Nonetheless, it is still easily the most interesting place to stay on Gran Canaria. The old city, **Vegueta**, dates from the Conquest and with Triana form the historic centre of Las Palmas; **Puerto de la Luz** and **Las Palmas** compose the tourist district, flanked by the harbour and Alcaravaneras beach in the east and Canteras beach in the west.

Vegueta–Triana★
Allow 2hr.

Plaza de Santa Ana

The palm-bordered square is over-looked by the town hall (1842) on one side, and the Cathedral on the other. To the side are the Bishop's Palace (Palacio Episcopal, 17C), with an *alfiz*-decorated portal showing clear Mudéjar influence, the Renaissance-style Casa del Regente and the Archivo Histórico Provincial (archives). During the Corpus Christi procession, the square is carpeted with flowers, and coloured sawdust and salt in beautiful patterns.

Catedral – Pl. de Santa Ana. Open Mon–Fri 10am–4.30pm, Sat 10am–1.30pm. No charge. ℘928 33 14 30.

The Cathedral, begun in the early 16C, was not completed until the 19C. It has three elegant aisles.

Museo Diocesano de Arte Sacro

Entrance in Pl. Espíritu Santo.
See cathedral for opening times and price. ℘928 31 49 89.

The museum of sacred art, in buildings around the 16C Patio de los Naranjos, contains 16C–19C engravings and gold and silverwork. In the chapterhouse is a mosaic from Manises (Valencia).

Casa de Colón★

Colón 1. Open Mon–Sat 10am–6pm, Sun & hols 10am–3pm. Closed 1 Jan, 24–25 & 31 Dec. €4, no charge first weekend of month. ℘928 31 23 73. www.casadecolon.com.

The palace of the island's first governors, where Columbus stayed in 1502, houses a museum. Maps and instruments evoke Columbus' expeditions. Note the fine *artesonado* ceilings. On the upper floor are 16C–19C paintings. The **Iglesia de San Antonio Abad** (Pl. San Antonio Abad 4), on the site where Columbus attended Mass, has a fine Baroque interior.

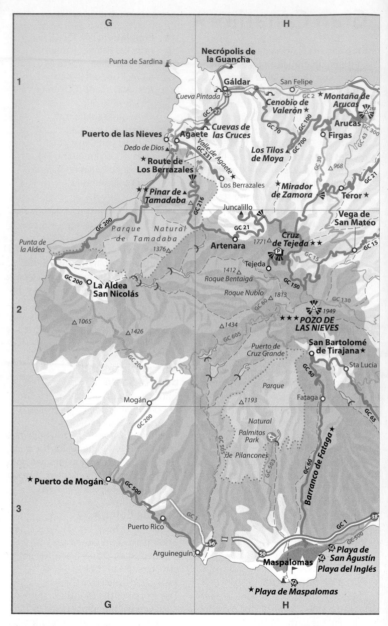

Centro Atlántico de Arte Moderno

Balcones 9–11. Open Tue–Sat 10am–9pm, Sun 10am–2pm. Closed public holidays. €5, no charge Wed 6–9pm, ℘902 31 18 00. www.caam.net.
Along **Calle de los Balcones** in one of several 18C buildings with fine door-

ways this modern gallery displays works by 20C artists from the Canary Islands, the Spanish mainland and abroad.

Museo Canario★

Doctor Verneau 2. Open Mon–Fri 10am–8pm, Sat–Sun and public holidays 10am–2pm. Closed 1 Jan, 25 Dec. €4, no

Gran Canaria (whose purpose remains a mystery) a re-creation of Gáldar's Cueva Pintada (👁 see p565).

Adjacent are the picturesque plazas of **Espíritu Santo** and **Santo Domingo**.

Casa-Museo Pérez Galdós

Cano 2 and 6. Open Tue–Sun & pub hols 10am–6pm (7pm Jul–Sept). Closed 1 Jan, 24–25 & 31 Dec. €3, free first Sat–Sun month. ✆928 36 69 76. www.casamuseoperezgaldos.com. Manuscripts, photographs and objects belonging to Pérez Galdós (1843–1920), the leading literary figure in 19C Spain, are displayed in the house where he was born.

Parque de San Telmo

Calle Mayor de Triana, leading from this park, is the main street in the old town. The small **Iglesia de San Bernardo** is full of character with its Baroque altars and paintings. An unusual Modernist kiosk stands in a corner of the park.

MODERN TOWN

Allow 2hr.

▷ Drive along avenida Marítima del Norte, skirting the town.

Parque Doramas

In this park are the Santa Catalina Hotel with its casino, and the **Pueblo Canario**, an idyllicised part re-creation of a Canary Island village co-founded by the Las Palmas-born Modernist painter Néstor de la Torre (1887–1938; open Tue–Sat 10am–8pm, Sun 10.30am–2.30pm; closed 1 Jan, Holy Thu, Good Fri, 25 Dec; €3; ✆928 24 51 35). Regular folklore shows and festivals are held here, there are craft shops, a bodega and the **Museo Néstor** (open Tue–Sat 10am–7pm, Sun and public holidays 10.30am–2.30pm; €3; ✆928 24 51 35).

Parque Santa Catalina

Down by the port, in **Puerto de la Luz**, the Parque Santa Catalina is home to the Museo Elder de la Ciencia y Tecnología (Science and Technology Museum; open Tue–Sun 10am–8pm;

GRAN CANARIA

0 _____ 10 km
0 _____ 5 mi

charge Mon & Wed 5–8pm. ✆928 33 68 00. www.elmuseocanario.com. This fascinating collection of artefacts from pre-Hispanic culture, includes mummies, idols and skins. **Don't miss** the collection of Guanche skulls some of which have been trepanned, the terracotta seals *(pintaderas)* found only on

Christopher Columbus

It is often said that but for the Canary Islands, Christoper Columbus (1451–1506) would never have reached America. His persistence in trying to convince the sovereigns of Portugal, England, France and Castile of the existence of a westerly passage to Asia is well known. Eventually Ferdinand and Isabella of Castile provided three ships – the **Niña**, the **Pinta** and the **Santa María** – for an expedition to the Indies. Colombus (known as Colón in Spanish) set sail westward from Palos in August 1492 but was forced to put into Las Palmas and La Gomera for repairs to the **Pinta**. On 12 October 1492 he spied land and set foot for the first time on the American continent – on the Caribbean Island of San Salvador. On each of his three subsequent voyages he landed at Las Palmas de Gran Canaria or on La Gomera before going on to discover the rest of the Antilles (1493), the Orinoco delta (1498) and the shores of Honduras (1502).

with its many interactive stations, 3-D Cinema, Science Show and Planetarium); €6, call to check; ☏828 011 828 www.museoelder.org).

The bustling surrounding streets are lined with restaurants and bars while cheap shops and Asian-owned bazaars sell electronics at duty-reduced prices.

Playa de las Canteras★

This superb 3.5km/2mi beach is sheltered by a line of rocks offshore and backed by a pleasant promenade with restaurants and cafés. At its southeastern end, the landmark **Auditorio Alfredo Kraus** (www.auditorioteatrolaspalmasgc.es), built in 1997, hosts an opera season. It is the site of the Canaries Music Festival (www.festivaldecanarias.com) held annually Jan–Feb.

Castillo de la Luz

Juan Rejón. Open Mon–Sat 10am–7pm, Sun until 2pm. €4. ☏928 463 162. This 16C fort is home to the foundation of local sculptor Martin Chirino.

🚗 DRIVING TOURS

THE NORTH COAST

LAS PALMAS TO LA ALDEA DE SAN NICOLÁS

128km/79mi. Allow 1 day. ♿See map pp562–563.

▶ Leave Las Palmas on the GC 2, heading W. Take exit 8.

Arucas

Arucas is the third-largest town on the island. A narrow road leads up **Montaña de Arucas**, shaped like a sugar loaf, offering a **panorama★** to Las Palmas de Gran Canaria. The black-rock church below stands out against white houses.

▶ Take the C 813. At Buenlugar, 6km/3.7mi beyond Arucas, turn left.

Firgas

This is the source of the archipelago's most popular sparkling mineral water. The village's Paseo de Gran Canaria pays a picturesque homage to the island's communities dedicating to each a series of azulejo tile plaques and small azulejo-covered benches.

▶ Return to the main road.

Los Tilos de Moya

Los Tilos is a protected area with a wood of wild laurel trees.

▶ At Guía, turn right to join the C 810. Head towards Las Palmas, then turn off to Cenobio de Valerón.

Cenobio de Valerón★

Cuesta de Silva, Santa María de Guía. Open Tue–Sun: Oct–Mar 10am–5pm, Apr–Sept 10am–6pm. Closed 1, 5 & 6

Jan, 1 May, 24–25 & 31 Dec. €3. ℘618 60 78 96. www.cenobiodevaleron.com.

Cenobio means convent and tradition has it that here daughters of the nobility dwelt until they were wed, watched over by protective priests and priestesses. In fact this honeycomb of caves hollowed out of tufa was merely an ancient granary. Today visitors can enter the caves. Above, Guanche chiefs met in council *(tagoror)*.

▶ Return to the C 810 and head towards Gáldar.

Gáldar
At the foot of Mount Gáldar the Guanche king held his court *(guanarteme)*.
The **Museo y Parque Arqueológico Cueva Pintada** (Audiencia 2; open mid-Jun–mid-Sept Tue–Sat 10.30am–7.30pm, Sun & hols 11am–7pm; mid-Sept–mid-Jun Tue–Sat 10am–6pm, Sun and hols 11am–6pm; last tour 1hr 30 min before closing, booking required; closed 1, 5 & 6 Jan, 1 May, 24–25 & 31 Dec; €6, no charge first weekend each month; ℘928 89 54 89; www.cuevap-intada.com), is devoted to the island's most important ancient discovery, the "Painted Cave", of **Guanche origin★**. Guanche objects excavated nearby are also displayed and the cave is viewed behind glass in order to protect it from visitors' body heat and humidity.

Necrópolis de la Guancha
2km/1.2mi N of Gáldar on coast.
Excavations have brought to light the knee-high remains of a Guanche settlement and a necropolis of circular constructions of great blocks of lava and a large burial mound.

▶ Return to Gáldar; take the C 810 S.

Cuevas de las Cruces
Halfway between Gáldar and Agaete.
These are attractive caves in the tufa.

Agaete
In this charming white-walled village is an important burial site, currently being prepared for interpretation to visitors.

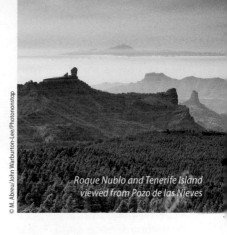

Roque Nublo and Tenerife Island viewed from Pozo de las Nieves

© M. Abreu/John Warburton-Lee/Photononstop

On 4 August the village celebrates the **Fiesta de la Rama**, one of the island's most popular festivals.

Los Berrazales Road★
SE of Agaete.
The road parallels the verdant **Agaete Valley★** sheltered by mountains.

Puerto de las Nieves
1.3km/0.8mi W of Agaete.
This little fishing harbour once shipped bananas. From the quay there is a good view of what remains of the **Finger of God** *(Dedo de Dios)*, a heavily eroded pointed rock. The village hermitage **(ermita)** contains an interesting 15C Flemish triptych by Joos van Clave (visits by prior arrangement; ℘928 55 43 82).

La Aldea de San Nicolás
A spectacular road follows cliffs and crosses several ravines to La Aldea de San Nicolás, a village in a fertile basin growing sugar cane and tomatoes.

THE CENTRE OF THE ISLAND
156km/97mi. Allow 1 day.
⚑See map pp562–563.

▶ Leave Las Palmas on the GC 110, heading S.

Tafira
A holiday resort favoured by islanders, the town is the site of a university.

Jardín Canario★
Camino del Palmeral. Open daily 9am–6pm. ℘928 21 95 80. No charge.

www.jardincanario.org.
The largest botanical garden in Spain (27ha/67 acres) is devoted to Canarian flora, with more than 500 species.

▶ In Monte Lentiscal turn left.

Mirador de Bandama★★
A road leads to the summit of Bandama (569m/1 867ft) and a superb view of the enormous Caldera de la Bandama, a crater with its eruption formations intact. The **panorama** takes in Tafira, the Montaña de Arucas and Las Palmas to the north, the crater, and the Real Club de Golf (the oldest in Spain) and Telde to the south. In the caldera are old incised drawings.

▶ Return to the C 811.

Santa Brígida
This village sits close to a ravine planted with palms. A plant and flower market is held weekends. The Casa del Vino de Gran Canaria sells wines (Calvo Sotelo 26; open Mon–Fri 10am–2pm; ℘928 64 42 45; www.museosdelvino.es).

Vega de San Mateo
A large fruit and vegetable market is held here Saturdays and Sundays. The **Casa-Museo Cho Zacarías** (currently closed to the pubiic), explores the island's ethnography in a series of traditional houses with displays of pottery, furniture, textiles and tools...

▶ Continue along the C 811 for 6km/3.7mi, then bear left.

Pozo de las Nieves★★★
From the summit (1 949m/6 394ft), which is sometimes snow-capped, there is a spectacular **panorama★★★** of the island. On a clear day, Mount Teide (Tenerife) stands on the horizon.

Cruz de Tejeda★★
NW of Pozo de las Nieves.
Near the Parador at the top of the pass (1 450m/4 757ft) lies the village of **Tejeda** in a huge volcanic basin. Out of the chaotic landscape rise the peaks of

Roque Bentaiga and Roque Nublo, both venerated by the indigenous people.

▶ Bear W to Artenara along the GC 110.

The drive includes **views★** of the troglodyte village of **Juncalillo**.

Artenara
This village is the highest on the island (1 230m/4 035ft). In the enchanting **Ermita de la Cuevita**, a hermitage dug into the rock, is a statue of the Virgin with Child. The **panorama★** is impressive. From the edge of the village, there is a superb **view★** of Roque Bentayga.

Pinar de Tamadaba★★
The road passes through Canary pines extending to the edge of a cliff which drops sheer to the sea.

▶ Continue to the end of a tarred road, to the Zona de Acampada, then park and walk 200m/220yd.

On a clear day, the **view★★** of Agaete, Gáldar and the coast, with the Pico del Teide on the horizon, is superb.

▶ Return by the same road and turn left onto the GC 110 to Valleseco.

Mirador de Zamora★
Just north of Valleseco there is an attractive **view★** of Teror.

Teror
Teror has fine mansions with wooden balconies. The 18C **Basílica de Nuestra Señora del Pino** houses a statue of Our Lady of the Pine Tree, the island's patron, who is said to have appeared here on 8 September in 1481 (Pl. Nuestra Señora del Pino; open Mon 1-8.30pm, Tue-Fri 9am-1pm, 3-8.30pm, Sat 9am-8.30pm, Sun 7.30am-7.30pm; ℘928 63 01 18). Thousands gather each anniversary to present their gifts and join in worship. On Sunday morning a lively market is held, at which you'll find nuns selling hand-made sweets.

THE SOUTH COAST

LAS PALMAS TO MASPALOMAS
59km/37mi. Allow about 2hr.
See map pp562–563.

Leave Las Palmas along the GC 1, and then take exit 8 (Telde).

Telde
This was a Guanche kingdom. In the lower town is the 15C **Iglesia de San Juan Bautista** (Párroco Morales 2; 922 76 81 25), a church rebuilt in the 17C and 18C, which contains a 16C Flemish retable.

Take Calle Inés Chimida. Follow C 813 towards Ingenio. Beyond the junction with the C 816 turn left after some cottages into a rough track; the last 250m/270yd is on foot.

Yacimiento Arqueológico de Cuatro Puertas★
6km/3.7mi S of Telde. No formal visiting hours. 928 13 90 50.
The cave, which has four openings *(cuatro puertas)*, is where the indigenous council *(tagoror)* used to meet. The east face of the mountain is riddled with caves where the Guanche embalmed their dead.

Maspalomas/Playa del Inglés/ Playa de San Agustín
This is one of Spain's largest resort areas, a sprawl of apartments *urbanizaciones* and *centros commerciales*, spread along the sandy coastline. Maspalomas has developed around its spectacular dunes and **beach★** and part of a 400ha/990-acre protected zone, including a palm grove and lighthouse. Playa del Inglés and Maspalomas are favourite haunts of the island's large contingent of gay holidaymakers.

Puerto de Mogán★
38km/24mi NW.
This is a picturesque man-made resort in typical Canarian style, built around an attractive marina.

San Bartolomé de Tirajana★
48km/30mi N on the GC 520.
The way up passes through the **Barranco de Fataga★★**, a beautiful ravine. San Bartolomé is set in a magnificent green mountain cirque.

ADDRESSES

STAY

Aloe Canteras – Sagasta 98, Las Palmas de Gran Canaria. 928 46 49 07. 42 rooms. €8. Just a step from the beach with comfortable rooms and updated, well-equipped bathrooms.

Hotel Escuela Santa Brígida – Real de Coello 2. 928 47 84 00. www.hecansa.com. 40 rooms. Set in a lovely century-old building, an intimate tropical garden with pool, traditional rooms and a good restaurant.

Casa de Los Camellos – Progreso 12, Agüimes. 928 78 50 03. www.hecansa.com. 12 rooms. Restaurant This small Hotel Rural, in the old part of Agüimes, has been beautifully restored in a welcoming, rustic style, with wooden floors and furniture, and very attractive bedrooms. Good restaurant.

Hotel Rural El Refugio – Cruz de Tejeda. 928 66 65 13. www.hotel ruralelrefugio.com. 10 rooms. €8. Restaurant. Extraordinary setting in an area of lush vegetation deep in the interior. Cosy bedrooms with wooden floors, attractive furniture.

EAT

El Arrosar – Salvador Cuyás 10, Las Palmas de Gran Canaria. 928 27 26 45. Galician cooking at manageable prices in intimate dining rooms.

Casa Osmunda – Subida Mirador de La Concepcion 2, Las Palmas de Gran Canaria. 922 41 26 35. A pretty cellar restaurant with friendly staff, fresh healthy fare and an extensive wine list to suit all budgets.

Deliciosa Marta – Pérez Galdós 23, Las Palmas de Gran Canaria. 928 37 08 82. Creative modern cuisine and minimalist décor set the tone at this very popular spot. Book ahead.

Lanzarote★★★

Lanzarote, designated a Biosphere Reserve, is by far the most unusual and intriguing of the Canary Islands. With an area of 846sq km/326sq mi, its lava-black landscape is dotted with oases of bright green vegetation and crops and dazzling white houses. Unlike many parts of Gran Canaria and Tenerife it has retained a vernacular style and identity; there are no high-rise hotels, advertising boards nor pylons, nor many of the other familiar accretions of modern life and mass-market tourism. This is mostly a result of the conservation work of island champion César Manrique (1919–92), ecologist, modern artist and landscaper extraordinaire. Wherever you go on Lanzarote you will meet his works and philosophy, and any visitor attraction that bears his mark is worth a visit.

LANDSCAPE & TRADITION

In 1730, a massive series of eruptions occurred in the area now known as the **Montañas del Fuego** (Mountains of Fire). These lasted six years with 26 volcanoes covering one third of the island in lava. In 1824 a new volcano, Tinguatón, engulfed fields and houses. Lava fields *(malpaís)* and thick black ash and pebbles are pitted with over 100 craters. In **La Geria**, where volcanic pebbles *(lapilli)* are plentiful, vines are protected by low semicircular walls. The grapes produce an excellent light white wine – Malvasía – with a distinctive bouquet. Throughout the island the fields are covered with a deep layer of the *lapilli* to retain moisture from the evening and morning dew, on an island where it rarely rains.

A BIT OF HISTORY

From the 14C to the present – The island owes its name to Lanceloto Malocello from Genoa, who landed in the 14C. In 1401 the Normans **Gadifer de**

▶ **Population:** 141 940

Info: Arrecife: Parque José Ramírez Cerdá. ☎620 26 47 03. Puerto del Carmen: Avda de Las Playas, ☎928 51 33 51. www.turismolanzarote.com.

◐ **Location:** 100km/62mi from North Africa.

la Salle and **Jean de Bethencourt** captured the island for the King of Castile. Lanzarote was a base for expeditions against the other islands and became prey to marauding slavers.

SIGHTS
Arrecife

This important port, and modern-day island capital, was originally defended by the **Castillo de San Gabriel** (open only for occasional exhibitions, see notice at entrance), built in the 16C on an islet, linked to the town by bridges. Recently given a makeover by the island authorities to entice more visitors to come here for a day trip, Arrecife has good shopping, a pleasant beach and promenade; on it picturesque lagoon, Charco de San Ginés, local fisherman shelter their small boats.

The 18C **Castillo de San José,** restored by César Manrique, houses the **Museo Internacional de Arte Contemporáneo** (MIAC, Carretera de Naos; open daily 10am–8pm; €4; ☎901 20 03 00, www.centrosturisticos.com).

West of Arrecife via the LZ-2, the former house of Portuguese Nobel Laureate, José Saramago, has been converted into a museum (Calle Los Topes 2; open Mon–Sat 10am–2.30pm, last admission 1.30pm; €8; ☎928 83 30 53; http://acasajosesaramago.com).

🚗 DRIVING TOURS

Each tour departs from Arrecife.

THE CENTRE OF THE ISLAND
62km/39mi through the centre.

Fundación César Manrique★

Taro de Tahíche, Villa de Teguise. Open year-round daily 10am–6pm. Closed 1 Jan. €10 or €15 combined with Casa-Museo Manrique in Haría (🕐see p571). 📞928 84 31 38. www.fcmanrique.org.

The foundation devoted to the greatest modern Lanzaroteño is in a remarkable and quite probably unique house that sits atop five volcanic bubbles. César Manrique chose this location to live – his extraordinary home is open to the public – and to demonstrate the bond between architecture and nature.

Monumento al Campesino

This monument near **Mozaga**, by César Manrique, marks the centre of the island, and pays homage to the peasant farmers of Lanzarote.

Next to it is the **Casa-Museo del Campesino** (open daily 10am–6pm; no charge; 📞928 52 01 36, www.centros-turisticos.com), a characteristic peasant house, with an excellent restaurant (lunchtime only).

Museo Agrícola El Patio▲

Echeyde 18, Tiagua. Open Mon–Fri 10am–5pm, Sat 10am–2pm. €5. 📞928 52 91 34.

Exhibits of rural life on the island and Malvasía wine tastings.

La Geria★★

La Geria lies between Yaiza and Mozaga in a black-lava desert pockmarked with craters where vines grow a bright green. The village is a wine centre.

Museo del Vino El Grifo

El Islote 121, San Bartolomé. Open daily 10.30am–6pm. Guided tours Mon–Fri 11am & 3pm, Sat–Sun 11am. Museum €3, tour including wine tasting €9. 📞928 52 49 51. www.elgrifo.com.

This 18C bodega is the oldest in the Canaries and hosts a museum of traditional winemaking.

THE SOUTH OF THE ISLAND
Round-trip of 124km/77mi from Arrecife.

Parque Nacional de Timanfaya★★★
Guided tours of the parque (Ruta de los Volcanes) are by coach only (cars only allowed into the parque as far as the car park area) 9am–5pm, last tour (6pm Jul–Sept). ♿ To avoid crowds Jul–Sept we recommend visiting 9am–10.30 or 3–5pm. €9. ☎928 118 042 (Visitor Centre, Mancha Blanca, Tinajo). www.parquesnacionalesdecanarias.com.
This range of volcanic cones, which emerged in the 1730–36 eruptions, stands out sometimes red, sometimes black, above cinder and slag. It is the major attraction on the island. The **Montañas de Fuego** form the centre of this massif.
Dromedaries, once common beasts of burden on Lanzarote, wait by the roadside (at the **Echadero dos Camellos**) 5km/3mi north of Yaiza to provide a swaying and jolting ride up the mountainside, from where there is a good view of the next crater. Although the volcanoes have not erupted since 1736, their fires burn and bubble still. To demonstrate the point, at the visitor centre, twigs are dropped into a shallow hole (by the park ranger) and instantly catch fire; water poured into a pipe set into the lava steams immediately because of the subsoil temperature (140°C/284°F at 10cm/4in, over 400°C/752°F at 6m/19.6ft), and in the El Diablo restaurant, food is cooked using the heat of the earth as a giant barbecue. There are fine views from the restaurant. Buses from here follow the 14km/8.7mi **Ruta de los Volcanes**. A lookout affords a view over an immense lava field stretching to the sea.

Los Hervideros
In the caverns at the end of the tongue of lava, the sea boils (*hervir*: to boil) in an endlessly fascinating spectacle. It is at its best on a windy day.

El Golfo★★
A lagoon is filled with vivid emerald-green water; a steep cliff of pitted black rock forms an impressive backdrop.

Salinas de Janubio★
Deep blue seawater entering a crater is harvested to leave gleaming white pyramids of salt in square salinas (salt pans).

Playa Blanca
This pleasant resort, although now very built up, retains some of its old character, with a promenade between old fishermen's houses and the main beach.

Punta del Papagayo★
This (Rubicón) region is where Bethencourt settled. The only trace is the Castillo de las Coloradas, a tower on the cliff edge. Dusty roads lead from Playa Blanca to the protected **Reserva Natural de los Ajaches** (open daily 9am–7pm; €4 vehicle fee; ☎928 17 34 52), which leads to the isolated, largely uncommercialised white-sand Papagayo beaches, the finest on the island. From here there are fine **views★** of Playa Blanca and Fuerteventura.

THE NORTH OF THE ISLAND
Round trip of 77km/47mi from Arrecife. About half a day.

Jardín de Cactus★
Ctra General del Norte, Guatiza. Open daily 10am (9am Jul–Sept)–5.45pm. €5. ☎928 52 93 97. www.centrosturisticos.com.
This beautiful cactus garden, landscaped by César Manrique, artfully displays over 1 000 species from the Canary Islands, America and Madagascar, on terraces in an old quarry.

Cueva de los Verdes★★★
Haría. Guided tours (1hr) daily 10am–6pm (7pm Jul–Sept), last admission 1hr before closing. €9.50. ☎901 20 03 00. www.centrosturisticos.com.
At the foot of the Corona Volcano are volcanic galleries where the Guanches took refuge from marauding pirates. There are 2km/1mi of illuminated passages at different levels; the tour ends with an amazing trompe l'oeil.

Jameos del Agua★★

Carretera de Orzola, Haría.
Open daily 10am–6.30pm; also Tue,
Fri–Sat 7.30pm–2am. €9.50 (Tue,
Fri & Sat evenings extra charge for
entertainment). ☎901 20 03 00.
www.centrosturisticos.com.

A jameo is a cavity formed when the top
of a volcanic tube collapses. César Manrique has turned two jameos into an
extraordinary fantasy grotto, regarded
by most people as his tour de force on
Lanzarote. Quite separately, a lagoon in
the cave is the habitat of a minute, blind
albino millenary crab, only found here.
The **Casa de los Volcanes** on the upper
level is an excellent exhibition and
important international study centre
on vulcanism. On Tuesay and Saturday
nights the Jameos del Agua becomes an
intimate stylish leisure complex with a
restaurant, bar, DJs and concerts.

Mirador del Río★★

Carretera del norte, Ye. Open daily 10am
–5.45pm (6.45pm Jul–Sept). €4.50. ☎928
52 65 48. www.centrosturisticos.com.

At the north end of the island stands
a steep isolated headland, **Riscos de
Famara**. The belvedere commands
a stunning **panorama★★** across the
azure waters of the **El Río** strait to La
Graciosa and its neighbouring islands;
immediately below are salt pans. A **passenger ferry** (⛴Orzola to La Graciosa,
25min: see website for schedule; €20
round-trip; ☎ 928 596 107; www.lineas
romero.com) operates between Orzola
and La Graciosa.

Haría

From afar Haría resembles a typical
North African village, set in a lush valley replete with palm trees. The best
view is from the **Mirador de Haría★**,
some 5km/3mi south. Also here is the
Casa-Museo César Manrique (open
daily 10.30am–2.30pm; €10 or €15
combined with Fundación Manrique
(ⓒ see p569); ☎928 84 31 38; www.
fcmanrique.org), the house, in the middle of a palm forest, where the painter
lived and worked during his final years.

Teguise★★

Teguise, the former capital, is a beautifully restored and very atmospheric
town with some of the finest colonial
buildings in the archipelago. Several of
these have been tastefully converted to
restaurants, bars and shops.

However Teguise is most famous nowadays for its **Sunday Market** (open 9am–
2pm), which draws coaches from all
over the island.

Overlooking town, and commanding
a wonderful view is the **Castillo de
Santa Bárbara,** built in the 16C on the
Guanapay volcano. It is is now home
to the **Museo del Pirateria** (open daily
10am–4pm; €3; ☎928 84 50 01, www.
museodelapirateria.com), which tells
the story of piracy in the Canaries.

ADDRESSES

🛏 STAY

⬡⬡⬡ **Hotel Miramar** – Coll 2, Arrecife.
☎928 81 26 00. www.hmiramar.com.
85 rooms. ⬜€8. Restaurant ⬡⬡. On
the seafront, opposite the Castillo de
San Gabriel, balconies offer good sea
views, rooms are on the basic side.

⬡⬡⬡⬡ **Hotel The Volcan** – Castillo
del Aguila, Playa Blanca. ☎928 51 91 85.
www.hotelvolcanlanzarote.com. 255
rooms. Characterful five-star resort set
in 20 traditional houses with communal
gardens and pools. The five restaurants
include Japanese and Italian. (⬡⬡⬡⬡).
There is also a spa.

🍽 EAT

⬡⬡⬡ **Amura** – Pas. Marítimo,
Puerto Calero. ☎928 51 31 81. www.
restauranteamura.com. This restaurant
in an attractive colonial-style building
has a spectacular terrace. Its location
opposite the marina, surrounded by
palms, is outstanding.

⬡⬡⬡ **La Cañada** – César Manrique 3,
Puerto del Carmen. ☎928 51 04 15. This
restaurant is located on a small hill. It
has a lovely terrace and dining room,
and a kitchen that takes pride in the
quality of its ingredients.

Fuerteventura

Fuerteventura has a captivating elemental beauty thanks to its bare landscape and beaches of white sand with turquoise water all around. Strong winds and a calm sea on the east coast make this island ideal for sailing, diving, fishing and, in particular, kitesurfing and windsurfing.

▶ **Population:** 106 930

Info: Corralejo: Avenida Marítima 2. ✆928 86 62 35. www.fuerteventura turismo.com.

▶ **Location:** 100km/62mi NW of the coast of Africa. Immediately N is Lanzarote.

▲▲ **Kids:** Oasis Park.

LANDSCAPE AND CLIMATE

Arid Fuerteventura is dotted with bare crests and extinct volcanoes. It was described as a "skeletal island" by its most famous native, the poet and writer **Miguel de Unamuno**, exiled here in 1924. The harsh terrain is only suitable for grazing goats, which far outnumber humans. Villages are marked by palm trees and windmills.

Fuerteventura shares the climate of nearby Africa; sand, blown across the sea, formed the southern isthmus, El Jable, now famous for its beaches.

🚗 DRIVING TOUR

NORTH TO SOUTH

Corralejo★

This likeable one-time fishing village, now the island's main tourist resort, is at the northern tip of the island beyond the *malpaís*. Crystal-clear water laps at the immense beautiful white dune **beaches** of the Parque Natural Dunas de Corralejo and the Isla de Lobos, a Robinson Crusoe island, accessible by ferry. Lanzarote is visible north.

▶ Leave Corralejo along the FV 101.

La Oliva

The **Centro de Arte Canario** (open Mon–Fri 10am–5pm, Sat 10am–2pm; admission charges vary; ✆928 86 82 33, www.centrodeartecanario.com) is the island's best art gallery, devoted to Canarian art. Opposite stands the landmark **Casa de Coroneles**, a grand 18C house; once the residence of the governor of the island, it is now an arts and cultural centre (open Tue–Sat 10am–6pm; €3, no charge 18 & 30 May; ✆928 868 280; www.lacasadeloscoroneles.org).

▶ Continue on the FV 10 passing the Guanche's sacred Mount Tindaya on your right. Just before you turn right onto the FV 207 look for the large hillside statue of Miguel de Unamuno. Pass through Tefia.

Ecomuseo de la Alcogida

La Alcogida, Tefia. Open Tue–Sat 10am–5.30pm. €5. ✆928 17 54 34. www.artesaniaymuseosdefuerte ventura.org.

This is the island's most engaging museum, depicting rural country life around 50 to 100 years ago, scattered among seven houses and farms.

Betancuria★

This pretty valley settlement, no bigger than a small village, was once the island capital, founded in 1404 by island conqueror Jean de Bethencourt.

Betancuria retains a ruined Franciscan monastery and an ancient **cathedral**, with white walls and a picturesque wooden balcony, now called the **Iglesia de Santa María la Antigua**. The baptistery contains an interesting crucifix; the sacristy has a fine panelled ceiling. On the south side, a small **Museo Arqueológico** displays Guanche artefacts (Roberto Roldán; open Tue–Sat 10am–6pm; closed public holidays; €2; ✆928 878 241).

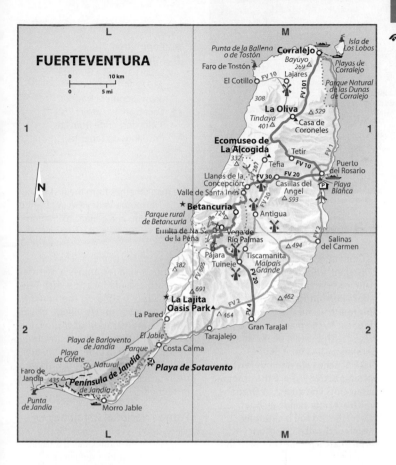

The road south provides an attractive contrast between the wide horizon of bare rose-tinted peaks and the village of **Vega de Río Palmas** nestling in its green valley-oasis.

◗ Head SW along the FV 617, turn left onto the FV2 coast road, then NE for a short distance.

♨♨ La Lajita Oasis Park★

Ctra General de Jandia, La Lajita. Open daily 9am–6pm. €33 (€12 camel ride); child €19.50 (€8 camel ride). ℘928 161 102. www.fuerteventuraoasispark.com. Located at the gateway to the Jandía Peninsula, Oasis Park is indeed an oasis of beautiful botanical gardens and exotic animals amid the parched southern landscape. This zoo park includes

over 200 species of birds and hundreds of small animals, and is famous for its camel rides (common on the island until mid-20C). There are also shows featuring sea lions, birds of prey and crocodiles, and a large African area.

◗ Head back SW on the FV2.

Península de Jandía

The leeward (southern) side of this protected southernmost part of the island is famous for magnificent beaches★★. These are largely uncommercialised though a number of low-key resorts popular with German visitors have grown up over the last three decades. This is the main centre for windsurfing and kitesurfing; world championships are staged here.

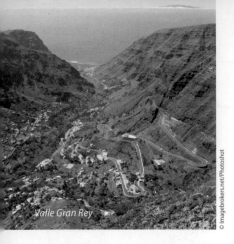
Valle Gran Rey

La Gomera★

La Gomera, with an area of 378sq km/146sq mi, is ideal for visitors seeking peace, contact with nature and outdoor activities. This round island rises from coastal cliffs, cut by deep ravines, to a *meseta* with a single peak, Mount Garajonay (1 487m/4 880ft). Black beaches are reminders of volcanic activity as are the dramatic basalt cliffs known as Los Órganos, which are only visible by boat. The fertile red soil is carefully husbanded and picturesque terraces are a feature of the island.

SIGHTS
San Sebastián de la Gomera
Christopher Columbus stayed here during his first voyage. His route can be traced down the main street from the corner house where he took on water (ask to see the well, el pozo, in the patio), past the **Iglesia de la Asunción** (Medio; ☎922 87 03 03), where he heard Mass, to the **Casa de la Aguada**, a small house located before the post office, where he is said to have slept.

🚗 DRIVING TOUR

15km/9.3mi.

▶ Leave San Sebastián de la Gomera on the TF 711.

▶ **Population:** 20 721
ℹ **Info:** Calle Real 32, San Sebastián de La Gomera. ☎922 14 15 12. www.lagomera.travel.
▶ **Location:** La Gomera is a 35min ferry ride from Los Cristianos on Tenerife.

The road emerges from the first tunnel in the **Hermigua Valley**★★ amid white houses, palms and banana plantations.

Agulo★
19km/11.8m NW from San Sebastián.
This small villages enjoys a picture-postcard seaside location with Tenerife clearly visible on the horizon. In the adjacent pretty village of **Las Rosas** demonstration of *El Silbo*, the unique whistling language invented by the islanders in order to communicate with each other across Gomera's many ravines, are given at the Las Rosas restaurant.

Parque Nacional Garajonay★★
Juego de Bolas visitor centre. Open daily 9.30am–4.30pm. Guided walking tours on Sat by prior arrangement. ☎922 80 09 93. www.parquesnacional esdecanarias.com.
This national park is covered by laurels, traces of the Tertiary era, and giant heathers, punctuated by rocks. Mist caused by trade winds lends an air of mystery.

Valle Gran Rey★★
55km/34mi from San Sebastián de la Gomera on the TF 713.
The road ascends the slopes to the south; the climb to the central *meseta* in the park is less steep. There are a handful of small roadside villages, including **Chipude**, famous for its pottery. Drive through **Arure** and after the bridge there is a fine **panorama**★ of Taguluche. **The highlight is the Barranco del Valle Gran Rey**★★ the most spectacular ravine on the island.

© Imagebrokers.net/Photoshot

El Hierro

This small remote windblown island, just 278sq km/107sq mi, sees very few visitors. Those who come witness fertile farmland, spectacular cliffs plunging into the sea, volcanic cones, fields of lava carpeted in laurel, and an underwater world popular with divers.

▶ **Population:** 10 675

Info: Calle Dr Quintero 4, Valverde. ☎922 55 03 02. www.elhierro.travel.

◖ **Location:** El Hierro is in the far southwest of the archipelago. Ferries run to neighbouring islands (☎902 100 107; www.fredolsen.es).

SIGHTS

Tamaduste

◖ 8km/5mi NE.

A large sandbank by the small seaside resort forms a lagoon.

El Golfo★★

◖ 8km/5mi W.

There is a fine view★★ of El Golfo from the **Mirador de La Peña**. The rim of a crater is covered with laurels and giant heather; the level floor is cultivated. La Fuga de Gorreta, near the Salmor rocks (NE), is the habitat of a primeval lizard.

TOUR THROUGH LA DEHESA

◖ 105km/65mi. Head S from Valverde along the TF 912. The excursions below depart from Valverde, the capital of the island, at an altitude of 571m/1 873ft.

Tiñor – Pyramid-shaped formations of ash among fertile fields denote this area. Until 1610, when it was blown down, a Garoé tree was venerated by natives.

Sabinosa – A spa-hotel treats skin and digestive diseases.

La Dehesa – A track 3 km/1.8mi further on crosses the arid La Dehesa region and provides extensive views★ of the south coast where the fiery red earth, pitted with craters, slopes to the sea.

Punta de Orchilla – Orchilla Point was the zero meridian before Greenwich. Beyond the lighthouse are sabine trees, conifers with twisted trunks found only on El Hierro.

Ermita de Nuestra Señora de los Reyes – In this hermitage is a statue of the Virgen de Los Reyes, patron saint of the island. Every four years since 1741, it is carried in procession to Valverde (Bajada Virgen de los Reyes). It will next take place on the first Saturday of July in 2013.

El Pinar – An aromatic **pine forest★** extends all over this central region of the island. A shaded picnic area at **Hoya del Morcillo** offers a respite from the bright Canary Island sunlight. With barbecue pits, picnic tables, toilets, a football field and a playground for children, camping is permitted in this convenient base camp for hikes through the mountainous wooded wilderness at the heart of the El Hierro. Camping permits must be obtained in advance in Valverde (☎922 55 00 17).

ADDRESSES

🛏 STAY

⊖⊖⊜⊜ **Parador de El Hierro** – Las Playas. ☎922 55 80 36. www.parador.es. 45 rooms. ⚏€18. Restaurant ⊖⊖⊜⊜. In the Las Playas beach district 20km/12.5mi SW of Valverde, this restful parador built on a ledge of volcanic rock has panoramic views, handsome colonial furnishings, and a restaurant specialising in island dishes such as local fish with periwinkles (or with limpet sauce), and Hierro cheese broth.

ⵏ/EAT

⊖⊖ **La Higuera de Abuela** ⵖ – Valverde 38900. ☎922 55 10 26. A family establishment in Echedo 5km/3mi north east of Valverde, this friendly and rustic spot serves local specialities.

La Palma★

With a surface of just 706sq km/272sq mi and its highest peak rising to 2 426m/7 962ft, La Palma has the highest average altitude of any island in the world. Rain is more abundant than in the rest of the Canaries, resulting in numerous streams and springs. It is called, justifiably on both counts, the "Beautiful Island" and the "Green Island" because of its woods of laurel and pine and numerous banana plantations. La Palma has distanced itself from major tourist development and appeals to nature-lovers, walkers, and those seeking peace and quiet.

A BIT OF HISTORY

The Caldera de Taburiente, a huge mountain arch curiously shaped like a crater, spreads over 10km/6.2mi. A chain of peaks, Las Cumbres, extends south; ravines produce an indented coastline. In the mountains, rainwater is collected to irrigate the lower terraces.

SIGHTS
SANTA CRUZ DE LA PALMA

The administrative centre was founded in 1493 by the conquistador Alonso Fernández de Lugo. In the 16C, with rising sugar exports and the expansion of the naval yards, Santa Cruz was one of the Spanish Empire's major ports (third only to Sevilla and Antwerp) and prey to pirates; now it is a peaceful city where elegant façades line the seafront. Its most famous native is Manolo Blahnik. At Playa de Los Cancajos (5km/3mi S) the beach and rocks are black.

Plaza de España

Several buildings date from the Renaissance. The 16C **Iglesia de El Salvador** has beautiful ceilings with **artesonado ornament★**; the sacristy has Gothic vaulting. Opposite stand the 16C town hall and houses in colonial style. Walk uphill to the delightful **Plaza de Santo Domingo**.

▶ **Population:** 83 456
🛈 **Info:** Plaza de la Constitución, Santa Cruz de la Palma. ☎922 41 21 06. www.visitlapalma.es.
◖ **Location:** La Palma is located in the far northwest of the archipelago.

Next to a college stands the **chapel** of a former monastery with beautiful Baroque altars. 🔑 To visit the chapel, ask for the keys at the Iglesia de El Salvador, ☎922 41 32 50.

🚗 DRIVING TOURS

The two tours suggested below both depart from Santa Cruz de la Palma.

THE NORTH OF THE ISLAND

Observatorio Roque de los Muchachos★★★

36km/22.3mi NW of Santa Cruz de la Palma. Allow 1hr45min for the ascent.
Laurel bushes and pine trees line the winding road which offers extensive views as it climbs to the **astrophysical observatory**, at 2 432m/7 981ft, including the William Herschel Telescope, one of the largest in the world with a 4.2m/ 13.7ft mirror (guided tours at 9.30am & 11.30am by prior arrangement, see website for schedule and application form; €9; ☎922 405 500; www.iac.es). From the Roque de los Muchachos a fantastic **panorama★★★** encompasses the Caldera, Los Llanos de Aridane, the islands of El Hierro and La Gomera, and Mount Teide on Tenerife.

Punta Cumplida

36km/22.3mi N.
There are fine views of the coast from the cliff road which crosses deep ravines *(barrancos)* in the Los Tilos Biosphere Reserve. Note the impressive number of craters.

Observatorio Roque de los Muchachos

La Galga

(15km/9.3mi N off LP 1) – North of the village, after the tunnel, the road crosses a steep and well-wooded ravine★.

San Andrés

(22km/13.6mi N off LP 1) – In the church is a beautiful Mudéjar ceiling in the chancel.

Charco Azul – Natural seawater pools.
Puerto Espíndola – A fishing village where boats are drawn up onto a shingle beach in a breach in the cliff face.
Punta Cumplida – Walk round the lighthouse to see waves breaking on basalt rock piles. The attractive Fajana swimming pools are north of here.

Los Sauces

(2km/1.2mi W of San Andrés) – The main agricultural centre in the north of the island.

Los Tiles★

Detour up Agua Ravine to the lime tree forest. **Los Tiles Interpretation and Investigation Centre** (open Mon-Sun 9am-5pm; ☎922 45 12 46) interprets the flora in the reserve.

THE CENTRE AND SOUTH OF THE ISLAND

Via Los Llanos and Fuencaliente

190km/118mi. Head N out of Santa Cruz. After the ravine, take the first left.

On the seafront of Santa Cruz, stands the **Castillo de Santa Catalina**, built to fend off pirate raiders in the 17C.
In the **Barco de la Virgen** *(the Virgin's Boat)*, a curious cement reproduction of Columbus' Santa María, is a small **naval museum** (Pérez Galdós 18; ☎922 41 17 87). The road passes the **Fuerte de la Virgen**, a 16C fortress.

Las Nieves

At the foot of Pico de las Nieves, shaded by laurel trees, the **Real Santuario de Nuestra Señora de las Nieves** houses the statue of the island's patron saint. Every five years (the next will be in 2015) it is the centrepiece of a grand parade.

La Concepción★

The summit of the Caldereta commands a wonderful **bird's-eye view★** of Santa Cruz de la Palma, the harbour and the mountains.

▷ Take the TF 812 westwards.

Parque Nacional de la Caldera de Taburiente★★★

4km/2.5mi W of the tunnel on the right is the **Centro de Visitantes** (Ctra. General de Padrón, no. 47, El Paso; ☎922 922 280), info on marked footpaths.

▷ Ahead, turn right for La Cumbrecita.

Parque Nacional de la Caldera de Taburiente

© Flavio Vallenari/Getty Images

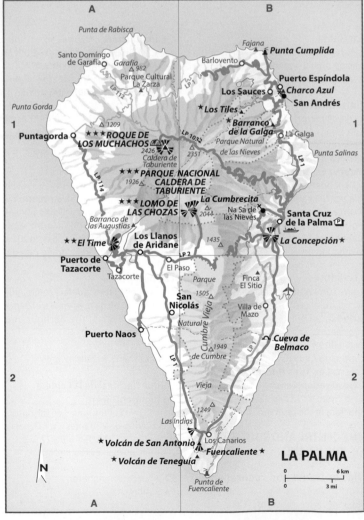

Punta de Rabisca

Santo Domingo
de Garafía ○
Garafía
△ 982
Parque Cultural
La Zarza
LP 112

Punta Gorda

Puntagorda ●

△ 1209

★★★ ROQUE DE
LOS MUCHACHOS
2426 △
Caldera de
Taburiente

★★★ PARQUE NACIONAL
CALDERA DE
TABURIENTE
△ 1926

★★★ LOMO DE
LAS CHOZAS
2044 △

Barranco de
las Augustias

★★ El Time

Los Llanos
de Aridane ○
LP 2

Puerto de
Tazacorte ●
Tazacorte ○

El Paso ○

Parque

△ 1505

San
Nicolás ●

Natural

Puerto Naos ●

Cumbre Vieja

△ 1949
de Cumbre

Vieja

LP 2

△ 1249

Las Indias

★ Volcán de San Antonio
★ Volcán de Teneguía
▲

Fajana

★ Punta Cumplida

Barlovento ○

Los Sauces ●
Puerto Espíndola
★ Charco Azul
San Andrés ★

★ Los Tiles

★ Barranco
de la Galga
La Galga ○

LP 1032

Parque Natural
de las Nieves
△ 2351

LP 1

Punta Salinas

La Cumbrecita ★
Na Sa de
las Nieves ●

Santa Cruz
de la Palma ℗

★ La Concepción ★

△ 1435

Finca
El Sitio

Villa de
Mazo ○

★ Cueva de
Belmaco

Los Canarios ○
★ Fuencaliente ★

LA PALMA

Punta de
Fuencaliente

0 ————— 6 km
0 ————— 3 mi

A   B

1   1

2   2

A   B

N

The **Cumbrecita Pass** (1 833m/6 014ft) and the **Lomo de las Chozas Pass** (1km/0.6mi further on) provide a splendid **panorama★★★** of the Caldera de Taburiente, dotted with Canary pines and crowned by rose-tinted peaks.

Los Llanos de Aridane
The island's second largest town is in a plain of bananas and avocado trees.

El Time★★
The top of El Time cliff affords a remarkable **panorama★★** of the Aridane plain, a sea of banana palms, and of the Barranco de las Angustias, a rock fissure which is the only outlet for the Caldera de Taburiente.

Puntagorda
This fine landscape is particularly beautiful in spring, when the almond trees are in blossom.

▶ Return to El Time.

Puerto de Tazacorte
Alonso Fernández de Lugo landed in this small harbour in 1492. In 1585, Francis Drake raided this town on his way to the Caribbean. Nicknamed "París chiquito" (little Paris), the small beach is popular on Sundays.

Puerto Naos
Descend through lava fields from the 1949 eruption and then through thhe lush avocado and banana plantations irrigated by La Caldera de Taburiente, to the Puerto with its large beach of black volcanic sand.

San Nicolás
The lava stream from the Nambroque volcano cut the village in two in 1949.

Fuencaliente de la Palma★
Before reaching Fuencaliente, look back from the Mirador de las Indias for a **glimpse★** of the coast through the pines. A hot water spring disappeared during the eruption of **San Antonio volcano★** in 1677. Circle the volcano to see the craters of **Teneguía volcano★**, which appeared in October 1971, and the lava stream which separated the lighthouse from the village.

Cueva de Belmaco
5km/3mi from the airport fork.
The cave of Guanche King Belamaco. At the back of the cave are rocks with inscriptions.

ADDRESSES

🛏 STAY

🛏 **Pensíon La Cubana** – Calle O'Daly 24. ☎922 41 13 54. 6 rooms. www.cubana-pension.com This tiny pension in a traditional townhouse ten minutes from the beach offers excellent value for budget lodging.

🛏🛏🛏 **Parador de la Palma** – Crtra. El Zumacal. ☎922 43 58 28. www.parador.es. 78 rooms. ⊑€18. Restaurant 🍴🍴🍴. The views from this promontory on the San Antonio to Breña Alta road 6km/4 mi SE of town are extraordinary. Public spaces are open and ample, and guest rooms are spacious.

🍴 EAT

🍴🍴🍴 **La Placeta** – Placeta de Borrero 1, Santa Cruz de La Palma. ☎922 41 52 73. www.restaurante laplaceta.com. Closed Sun, Aug. Set in an 18C mansion in a picturesque part of town with views of the typical balconies, this bistro-restaurant serves full meals and snacks.

🍴🍴🍴 **Parrilla Las Nieves** – Plaza de las Nieves 2, Santa Cruz de La Palma. ☎922 41 66 00. Closed Thu. Cooking over coals is the speciality at this highly rated comfortable and rustic dining spot. Roast rabbit and goat are favourites.

INDEX

A

INDEX

INDEX

INDEX

INDEX

🛏️ STAY

🍷 EAT

Thematic Maps

Maps and Plans

	Sight	Seaside resort	Winter sports resort	Spa
Highly recommended	★★★	≘≘≘	✲✲✲	‡‡‡
Recommended	★★	≘≘	✲✲	‡‡
Interesting	★	≘	✲	‡

Selected monuments and sights

◉ ⊏⊐	Tour - Departure point
⌂ ⸸	Catholic church
⌂ ⸸	Protestant church, other temple
▨ ▭ ⬚	Synagogue - Mosque
▬	Building
■	Statue, small building
⸸	Calvary, wayside cross
◎	Fountain
●━●━■▸	Rampart - Tower - Gate
✕	Château, castle, historic house
∴	Ruins
◡	Dam
✿	Factory, power plant
☆	Fort
∩	Cave
▭	Troglodyte dwelling
⊓	Prehistoric site
▼	Viewing table
Ⱨ	Viewpoint
▲	Other place of interest

Sports and recreation

⛷	Racecourse
⛸	Skating rink
⩴ ▨	Outdoor, indoor swimming pool
⛺	Multiplex Cinema
⛵	Marina, sailing centre
⬙	Trail refuge hut
▭━■━■━▭	Cable cars, gondolas
▭━┼┼┼┼━▭	Funicular, rack railway
▭━⬛	Tourist train
◆	Recreation area, park
⛹	Theme, amusement park
⚕	Wildlife park, zoo
⊕	Gardens, park, arboretum
⊕	Bird sanctuary, aviary
🚶	Walking tour, footpath
◉	Of special interest to children

Abbreviations

G, POL	Police (Federale Politie)	**P**	Local government offices (Gouvernement provincial)
H	Town hall (Hôtel de ville ou maison communale)	ℙ	Provincial capital (Chef-lieu de provincial)
J	Law courts (Palais de justice)	**T**	Theatre (Théâtre)
M	Museum (Musée)	**U**	University (Université)

Additional symbols

🛈	Tourist information	✉	Post office
═ ═	Motorway or other primary route	☎	Telephone
❶ ❶	Junction: complete, limited	▭	Covered market
▭ ═	Pedestrian street	•✕•	Barracks
ᴵ═════ᴵ	Unsuitable for traffic, street subject to restrictions	△	Drawbridge
▭▭▭ ----	Steps – Footpath	⛏	Quarry
🚆 🚉	Train station – Auto-train station	✕	Mine
🚌 🚌	Coach (bus) station	Ⓑ Ⓕ	Car ferry (river or lake)
•━━•	Tram	⛴	Ferry service: cars and passengers
◉	Metro, underground	⛵	Foot passengers only
ℙ	Park-and-Ride	③	Access route number common to Michelin maps and town plans
♿	Access for the disabled	Bert (R.)...	Main shopping street
		AZ B	Map co-ordinates

Useful Words and Phrases

The following phrases denote translations between English and **Castilian**, the official language of Spain and better known as Spanish in the wider world. Yet there are also four other languages officially recognised in various regions of Spain: **Catalan** (Catalonia, Valencia and the Balearics); **Basque** (Basque Country); **Galician** (Galicia); and **Aranès** (northwest Catalonia). These languages are widespread in these areas and many inhabitants see Castilian as their second language.

COMMON WORDS

	Translation
Agreed	De acuerdo
Excuse me	Perdone
Good morning	Buenos días
Good afternoon	Buenas tardes
Goodbye	Hasta luego, Adiós
How are You?	¿Qué tal?
I don't understand	No entiendo
Madam, Mrs	Señora
Miss	Señorita
OK	Vale
Please	Por favor
Sir, Mr; You	Señor; Usted
Thank you (very much)	(Muchas) Gracias
Yes, No	Sí, No

CORRESPONDENCE

	Translation
Letter	Carta
Postbox	Buzón
Postcard	(Tarjeta) Postal
Post Office	Correos
Stamp	Sello
Telephone	Teléfono
Telephone Call	Llamada
Tobacco Shop	Estanco, Tabaquería

FOOD AND DRINK

	Translation
Apple	Manzana
Anchovies	Boquerones
Banana	Plátano
Beef	Vaca/buey
Beer	Cerveza
(Black) pepper	Pimienta (Negra)
Bread	Pan
Butter	Mantequilla
Café solo	Black coffee
Cheese	Queso
Coffee with hot milk	Café con leche
Cream	Crema
Dessert	Postre
Egg	Huevo
Fish	Pescados

Garlic	Ajo
Ham	Jamón
Ice cream	Helado
I'm allergic to...	Tengo alergia a...
Lactose	Lactosa
Lemon	Limón
Meat	Carne
Meatballs	Albóndigas
Mejillones	Mussels
Milk	Leche
Mushrooms	Setas/hongos
Nut(s)	Nuez (Nueces)
Oil, Olives	Aceite, Aceitunas
Omelette	Tortilla
Onion	Cebolla
Orange	Naranja
Potatoes	Patatas
Pork	Cerdo
Prawns	Gambas
Red wine	Vino tinto
Rice	Arroz
Salad	Ensalada
Salad of diced vegetables in mayonaise	Ensalada Rusa
Salt	Sal
Sausages	Salchichas
Seafood, shellfish	Mariscos
Sparkling/still water	Agua con/sin gas
Soup	Potaje
Soya	Soja
Sugar	Azúcar
Vegetables	Legumbres
Vegetarian	Vegetariano/a
Wheat	Trigo
White/rosé wine	Vino blanco/ rosado

NUMBERS

	Translation
0	cero
1	uno/una
2	dos
3	tres
4	cuatro
5	cinco
6	seis
7	siete
8	ocho
9	nueve
10	diez
20	veinte
50	cincuenta
100	cien
1 000	mil

ON THE ROAD, IN TOWN

	Translation
After, Beyond	Después de
Beware, Take care	Cuidado
Car	Coche, Auto
Danger, Dangerous	Peligro, Peligroso
On the right	A la derecha
On the left	A la izquierda
Petrol, Gasoline	Gasolina
Roadworks	Obras

OUT AND ABOUT

Also See architectural terms in the Introduction.

	Translation
Artificial Lake	Pantano
Audience, Court	Audiencia

Avenue, Promenade	Paseo	Island, Isle	Isla
Beautiful	Hermoso/a	Keep	Torreón
Belfry	Campanario	Lake	Lago
Belvedere, Viewpoint, Lookout Point	Mirador	Light	Luz
		Main Road	Carretera
Bridge	Puente	Main Square	Plaza Mayor
Bullring	Plaza de Toros	Main street	Calle Mayor
Cape, Headland	Cabo	May one visit...?	¿Se puede visitar...?
Carved Wood	Talla	Monastery	Monasterio
Castle	Castillo	Moorish architectural style under Christian rule	Mudéjar
Cave, Grotto	Cueva, Gruta, Cava		
Cavern, Grotto	Gruta	Mosque	Mezquita
Chapel	Capilla	Mount, Mountain	Monte
Ceiling	Techo	Muslim Palace	Alcázar
Century	Siglo	Museum	Museo
Church	Iglesia	No Entry, Not allowed	Prohibido el paso
Church	Santuario	Open, Closed	Abierto, Cerrado
College, Colegiata Church	Colegio, Collegiate	Outskirts	Alrededores
Cloisters	Claustro	Pass, High Pass	Collado
Convent	Convento	Pass, Harbour, Port	Puerto
Cross	Cruz	Picture	Cuadro
Dam	Presa	Portal, Porch	Pórtico
Defile, Cleft	Desfiladero	Porter, Caretaker	Guarda, Conserje
Door, Gate, Entrance	Puerta	Property, Domain	Finca
Entrance, Exit	Entrada, Salida	Quarter	Barrio
Estuary	Ría	Religious Statue/	Sculpture Imágen
Excavations	Excavaciones	Reservoir, Dam	Embalse
Exuberant early baroque style named for the Churriguera brothers	Churrigueresco	River, Stream	Río
		Road, Track	Camino
		(Royal) Palace	Palacio (Real)
		Source, Birthplace	Nacimiento
Fountain	Fuente	Spa	Balneario
Gorges	Gargantas	Square	Plaza
Guide	Guía	Stained-glass window	Vidriera
Gully, Ravine	Barranco	Station	Estación
Hermitage, Chapel	Ermita	Storey, Stairs, Steps	Piso, Escalera
High Pass, Pass	Collado/Alto	Street	Calle
House	Casa		

GETTING BY IN SPAIN'S OTHER LANGUAGES

English	Aranès	Basque	Catalan	Galician
good morning/hello	bon dia/ola/adiu	egun on/kaixo	bon dia	boas días/ola
good evening	bona tarde	gabon	bona nit	boas noites
please	se vos platz	mesedez	per favor	por favor
thank you	gràcies/mercès	eskerrik asko	gràcies	grazas
today	auè	gaur	avui	hoxe
left	ara esquèra	ezker	esquerre(a)	esquerda
right	ara dreta	eskuin	dret(a)	dereita
open	obert	ireki	obert(a)	aberto
closed	tancat	hertsi	tancat	pechado
toilet	comuns	komuna	servies	servizos

Tapestries	Tapices
Tower, Belfry	Torre
Town, City	Ciudad
Town Hall	Ayuntamiento
Town Hall	Casa Consistorial
Treasury, Treasure	Tesoro
Vegetable/Market Garden	Huerto, Huerta
Vaulting	Boveda
Village, Market Town	Pueblo
Vineyard	Viña
View, Panorama	Vista
Wait!	Espere
Where is...?	¿Dónde está...?
Wine Cellar/store	Bodega

SHOPPING

	Translation
How much?	¿Cuánto (vale)?
(Too) Expensive	(Demasiado) Caro
A Lot, Little	Mucho, Poco
More, Less	Más, Menos
Big, Small	Grande, Pequeño
Credit Card	Tarjeta de Crédito
Receipt	Recibo

TIME

	Translation
Today	Hoy
Tomorrow	Mañana
What time?	¿A qué hora?
When?	¿Cuándo?
Yesterday	Ayer

MICHELIN IS CONTINUALLY INNOVATING FOR SAFER, CLEANER, MORE ECONOMICAL, MORE CONNECTED... BETTER ALL-ROUND MOBILITY.

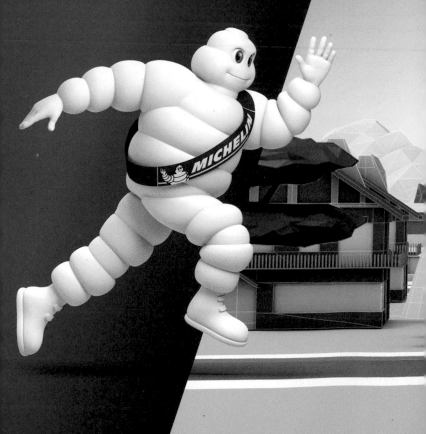

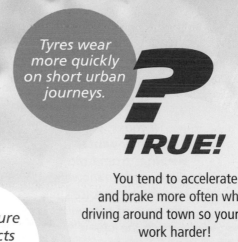

Tyres wear more quickly on short urban journeys.

?

TRUE!

You tend to accelerate and brake more often when driving around town so your tyres work harder!
If you are stuck in traffic, keep calm and drive slowly.

Tyre pressure only affects your car's safety.

?

FALSE!

Driving with underinflated tyres (0.5 bar below recommended pressure) doesn't just impact handling and fuel consumption, it will shave 8,000 km off tyre lifespan.
Make sure you check tyre pressure about once a month and before you go on holiday or a long journey.

Fitting **2 winter tyres** on my car guarantees maximum safety.

FALSE!

In the winter, especially when temperatures drop below 7°C, to ensure better road holding, all four tyres should be identical and fitted at the same time.

2 WINTER TYRES ONLY = risk of compromised road holding.

4 WINTER TYRES = **safer handling** when cornering, driving downhill and braking.

If you regularly encounter rain, snow or black ice, choose a **MICHELIN Alpin tyre**. This range offers you sharp handling plus a comfortable ride to safely face the challenge of winter driving.

MICHELIN IS COMMITTED

▶ MICHELIN IS **GLOBAL LEADER IN FUEL-EFFICIENT TYRES** FOR LIGHT VEHICLES.

▶ **EDUCATING OF YOUNGSTERS IN ROAD SAFETY,** NOT FORGETTING TWO-WHEELERS. LOCAL ROAD SAFETY CAMPAIGNS WERE RUN IN **16 COUNTRIES** IN 2015.

QUIZ

1. TYRES ARE BLACK SO WHY IS THE MICHELIN MAN WHITE?

Back in 1898 when the Michelin Man was first created from a stack of tyres, they were made of natural rubber, cotton and sulphur and were therefore light-coloured. The composition of tyres did not change until after the First World War when carbon black was introduced. But the Michelin Man kept his colour!

2. FOR HOW LONG HAS MICHELIN BEEN GUIDING TRAVELLERS?

Since 1900. When the MICHELIN guide was published at the turn of the century, it was claimed that it would last for a hundred years. It's still around today and remains a reference with new editions and online restaurant listings in a number of countries.

3. WHEN WAS THE "BIB GOURMAND" INTRODUCED IN THE MICHELIN GUIDE?

The symbol was created in 1997 but as early as 1954 the MICHELIN guide was recommending "exceptional good food at moderate prices". Today, it features on the MICHELIN Restaurants website and app.

If you want to enjoy a fun day out and find out more about Michelin, why not visit the l'Aventure Michelin museum and shop in Clermont-Ferrand, France:

www.laventuremichelin.com

A better way forward

THEGREENGUIDE **SPAIN**

Editorial Director	Cynthia Clayton Ochterbeck
Editor	Sophie Friedman
Edited & Produced by	Victoria Trott
Principal Writer	Paul Murphy
Production Manager	Natasha George
Cartography	Peter Wrenn
Picture Editor	Yoshimi Kanazawa
Interior Design	Natasha George, Jonathan P. Gilbert
Cover Design	Chris Bell, Christelle Le Déan
Layout	Natasha George

Contact Us

Michelin Travel and Lifestyle North America
One Parkway South
Greenville, SC 29615
USA
travel.lifestyle@us.michelin.com

Michelin Travel Partner
Hannay House
39 Clarendon Road
Watford, Herts WD17 1JA
UK
☏ 01923 205240
travelpubsales@uk.michelin.com
www.viamichelin.co.uk

Special Sales

For information regarding bulk sales,
customized editions and premium sales,
please contact us at:
travel.lifestyle@us.michelin.com

Michelin Travel Partner

Société par actions simplifiées au capital de 11 288 880 EUR
27 cours de l'Ile Seguin - 92100 Boulogne Billancourt (France)
R.C.S. Nanterre 433 677 721

© Michelin Travel Partner
ISBN 978-2-067229-57-0
Printed: February 2018
Printed and bound in France : Imprimerie CHIRAT, 42540 Saint-Just-la-Pendue - N° 201802.0214

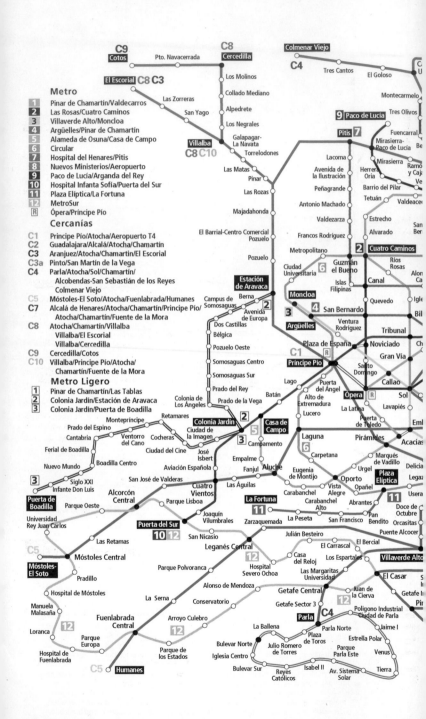

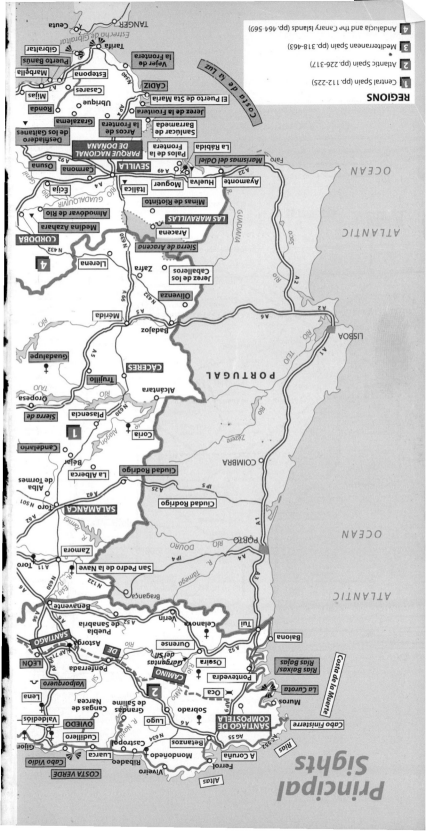

Principal Sights

REGIONS

1. Central Spain (pp. 112-225)
2. Atlantic Spain (pp. 226-317)
3. Mediterranean Spain (pp. 318-463)
4. Andalucía and the Canary Islands (pp. 464-569)

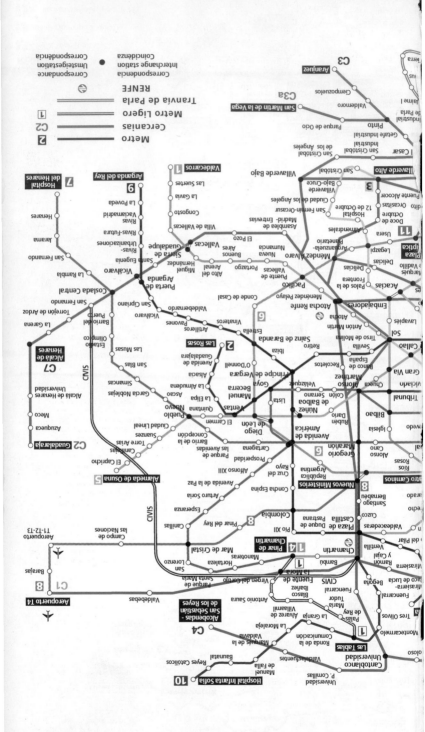